# Honda
## Civic & CR-V
## Automotive
## Repair
## Manual

**by Jeff Killingsworth
and John H Haynes**
Member of the Guild of Motoring Writers

**Models covered:**

**Honda Civic** - 2012 through 2015
**Honda CR-V** - 2012 through 2016

*Does not include information specific to CNG or hybrid models*

**Haynes Group Limited**
Sparkford Nr Yeovil
Somerset BA22 7JJ England

**Haynes North America, Inc.**
2801 Townsgate Road, Suite 340
Thousand Oaks, CA 91361 USA

**www.haynes.com**

(42027-6W1)

ABCDE
FGHIJ
KLMN

## Acknowledgements

Technical writers who contributed to this project include Demian Hurst, Trip Aiken and Scott "Gonzo" Weaver.

© Haynes North America, Inc. 2016

With permission from Haynes Group Limited

A book in the Haynes Automotive Repair Manual Series

Printed in India

ISBN-13: 978-1-62092-255-2
ISBN-10: 1-62092-255-X

Library of Congress Control Number: 2016959206

While every attempt is made to ensure that the information in this manual is correct, no liability can be accepted by the authors or publishers for loss, damage or injury caused by any errors in, or omissions from, the information given.

# Contents

**Haynes mechanic and photographer with a 2014 Honda Civic**

# About this manual

## Its purpose

The purpose of this manual is to help you get the best value from your vehicle. It can do so in several ways. It can help you decide what work must be done, even if you choose to have it done by a dealer service department or a repair shop; it provides information and procedures for routine maintenance and servicing; and it offers diagnostic and repair procedures to follow when trouble occurs.

We hope you use the manual to tackle the work yourself. For many simpler jobs, doing it yourself may be quicker than arranging an appointment to get the vehicle into a shop and making the trips to leave it and pick it up. More importantly, a lot of money can be saved by avoiding the expense the shop must pass on to you to cover its labor and overhead costs. An added benefit is the sense of satisfaction and accomplishment that you feel after doing the job yourself.

## Using the manual

The manual is divided into Chapters. Each Chapter is divided into numbered Sections, which are headed in bold type between horizontal lines. Each Section consists of consecutively numbered paragraphs.

The reference numbers used in illustration captions pinpoint the pertinent Section and the Step within that Section. That is, illustration 3.2 means the illustration refers to Section 3 and Step (or paragraph) 2 within that Section.

Procedures, once described in the text, are not normally repeated. When it's necessary to refer to another Chapter, the reference will be given as Chapter and Section number. Cross references given without use of the word "Chapter" apply to Sections and/or paragraphs in the same Chapter. For example, "see Section 8" means in the same Chapter.

References to the left or right side of the vehicle assume you are sitting in the driver's seat, facing forward.

Even though we have prepared this manual with extreme care, neither the publisher nor the author can accept responsibility for any errors in, or omissions from, the information given.

## NOTE

A **Note** provides information necessary to properly complete a procedure or information which will make the procedure easier to understand.

## CAUTION

A **Caution** provides a special procedure or special steps which must be taken while completing the procedure where the Caution is found. Not heeding a Caution can result in damage to the assembly being worked on.

## WARNING

A **Warning** provides a special procedure or special steps which must be taken while completing the procedure where the Warning is found. Not heeding a Warning can result in personal injury.

# Introduction

Civic models are available in two-door coupe and four-door sedan body styles. CR-V models are available in a four-door SUV body style only.

The transversely mounted inline four-cylinder engine used in these models is equipped with sequential electronic fuel injection or, on 2015 and later CR-V models, sequential direct fuel injection.

The engine drives the front wheels through either a five-speed manual transaxle, six-speed manual transaxle, five-speed automatic transaxle or a Continuously Variable Transaxle (CVT) via independent driveaxles.

On AWD CR-V models, power is transmitted to the rear wheels (automatically) through a transfer case, driveshaft, differential and independent driveaxles, when the front wheels begin to lose traction.

The suspension is independent at all four corners, featuring front coil sping/shock absorber units, and either rear coil spring/shock absorber units or shock absorbers with independently mounted rear coil springs.

The power-assisted rack-and-pinion steering unit is mounted behind the engine.

The brakes are disc at the front and either discs or drums at the rear, with power assist standard. An Anti-lock Braking System (ABS) is standard equipment on all models.

Most models have a power assisted disc-type front and rear brake system with an Anti-lock Brake System (ABS) as standard equipment.

# Vehicle identification numbers

Modifications are a continuing and unpublicized process in vehicle manufacturing. Since spare parts manuals and lists are compiled on a numerical basis, the individual vehicle numbers are essential to correctly identify the component required.

## Vehicle Identification Number (VIN)

This very important identification number is stamped on a plate attached to the dashboard inside the windshield on the driver's side of the vehicle (see illustration). It can also be found on the certification label located on the driver's side door post. The VIN also appears on the Vehicle Certificate of Title and Registration. It contains information such as where and when the vehicle was manufactured, the model year and the body style.

On the models covered by this manual the model year codes* are:

C   2012
D   2013
E   2014
F   2015
G   2016

   * The model year code is the tenth character in the VIN.

## Engine identification numbers

On the models covered by this manual the engine identification numbers are:

**2015 and earlier Civic models, 2014 and earlier CR-V models**
   #R18Z1   1.8L SOHC i-VTEC
   #K24Z7   2.4L DOHC i-VTEC

**2015 and later CR-V models**
   #K24W9   2.4L DOHC i-VTEC Direct fuel-injection (produced in USA and Canada)
   #K24V1   2.4L DOHC i-VTEC Direct fuel-injected (produced in Mexico)

## Certification label

6   The certification label is attached to the driver's door post (see illustration). The plate contains the name of the manufacturer, the month and year of production, the Gross Vehicle Weight Rating (GVWR), the Gross Axle Weight Rating (GAWR) and the certification statement.

## Service parts identification or Regular Production Option (RPO) code label

This label is located in the glove box (see illustration). It lists the VIN, paint number, options and other information specific to the vehicle. You may sometimes need to refer to this label when you order parts.

The Vehicle Identification Number (VIN) is located on a plate on top of the dash (visible through the windshield)

The engine number is stamped on the front of the engine block, at the left (driver's) end, near the transaxle

The vehicle certification label is located on the driver's door jamb

# Recall information

Vehicle recalls are carried out by the manufacturer in the rare event of a possible safety-related defect. The vehicle's registered owner is contacted at the address on file at the Department of Motor Vehicles and given the details of the recall. Remedial work is carried out free of charge at a dealer service department.

If you are the new owner of a used vehicle which was subject to a recall and you want to be sure that the work has been carried out, it's best to contact a dealer service department and ask about your individual vehicle - you'll need to furnish them your Vehicle Identification Number (VIN).

The table below is based on information provided by the National Highway Traffic Safety Administration (NHTSA), the body which oversees vehicle recalls in the United States. The recall database is updated constantly. For the latest information on vehicle recalls, check the NHTSA website at www.nhtsa.gov, www.safercar.gov, or call the NHTSA hotline at 1-888-327-4236.

| Recall date | Recall campaign number | Model(s) affected | Concern |
|---|---|---|---|
| May 18, 2011 | 11V288000 | 2012 Civic | On certain models, an O-ring, which seals a connection in the fuel feed line, is misaligned. If the O-ring is misaligned, a small fuel leak may occur. Fuel leakage, in the presence of an ignition source, could result in a fire. |
| June 4, 2012 | 12V256000 | 2012 Civic | On certain models, duringassembly, the process required to seat the driver's side driveaxle and set theretaining clip was not completed. As a result, the driveaxle may separate. Ifthis occurs, the vehicle will have a loss of drive power and may roll away ifthe parking brake has not been set when the gear selector has been placed in the "park" position, increasing the risk of crash or pedestrian injury. |
| July 19, 2012 | 12V338000 | 2012 CR-V | On certain models, if the manual or power door lock is activated while an interior front door handle is being operated by an occupant, the cable connecting the interior door handle to the door latch mechanism may become loose and move out of position. There is a possibility that the cable can move far enough out of position to prevent the door from properly latching. If the door is not fully latched, the door may open while driving or in a crash, increasing the risk of personal injury to the vehicle occupants. |

| Recall date | Recall campaign number | Model(s) affected | Concern |
|---|---|---|---|
| Oct 16, 2012 | 12V501000 | 2012 CR-V | On some models, the incorrect values for Gross Vehicle Weight Rating, Gross Axle Weight Rating front and rear, tire size, and rim size were specified on the safety certification label. A misprinted label could lead to improper vehicle loading. Improper loading could result in a tire failure, increasing the risk of a crash. |
| Nov 21, 2012 | 12V548000 | 2012 Civic | Some models were assembled with the incorrect steering column assembly. The steering column may not have proper energy absorbing characteristics, which could increase the risk of injury during a vehicle crash. |
| Apr 15, 2013 | 13V143000 | 2013 Civic, CR-V | On some models, during sub-freezing temperatures, the brake-shift interlock mechanism may become slow and allow the gear selector to be moved from the Park position without pressing the brake pedal. If the gear selector is moved from the park position without pressing the brake pedal it can allow the vehicle to roll away, increasing the risk of a crash. |
| March 10, 2014 | 14V109000 | 2014 Civic | Certain models, during mounting of the tires, the tire bead may have gotten pinched between the assembly equipment and the steel wheel rims, resulting in damage to the tire. The tire damage could cause the tire to lose air, increasing the risk of a crash. |
| March 2, 2015 | 15V121000 | 2015 CR-V | Honda is recalling certain models that may have been assembled with improperly torqued connecting rod bolts, which can cause the engine to lose power or leak oil. Loss of engine power may result in a vehicle stall, increasing the risk of a crash. If the engine leaks oil in the proximity of hot engine or exhaust components, there is an increased risk of a fire. |
| Oct 29, 2015 | 15V714000 | 2016 CR-V | On some models, the metal housing surrounding the driver's air bag inflator may have been manufactured incorrectly. In the event of a crash necessitating deployment of the driver's frontal air bag, the inflator could rupture with metal fragments striking the driver or other occupants resulting in serious injury or death. |
| Sept 15, 2015 | 15V574000 | 2014, 2015 Civic | On some models, the software settings that control the transmission operation may result in damage to the transmission drive pulley shaft. If the transmission drive pulley shaft is damaged, it may break, and the vehicle may lose acceleration or the front wheels may lock up while driving, increasing the risk of a crash. |

# Buying parts

Replacement parts are available from many sources, which generally fall into one of two categories - authorized dealer parts departments and independent retail auto parts stores. Our advice concerning these parts is as follows:

*Retail auto parts stores:* Good auto parts stores will stock frequently needed components which wear out relatively fast, such as clutch components, exhaust systems, brake parts, tune-up parts, etc. These stores often supply new or reconditioned parts on an exchange basis, which can save a considerable amount of money. Discount auto parts stores are often very good places to buy materials and parts needed for general vehicle maintenance such as oil, grease, filters, spark plugs, belts, touch-up paint, bulbs, etc. They also usually sell tools and general accessories, have convenient hours, charge lower prices and can often be found not far from home.

*Authorized dealer parts department:* This is the best source for parts which are unique to the vehicle and not generally available elsewhere (such as major engine parts, transmission parts, trim pieces, etc.).

*Warranty information:* If the vehicle is still covered under warranty, be sure that any replacement parts purchased - regardless of the source - do not invalidate the warranty!

To be sure of obtaining the correct parts, have engine and chassis numbers available and, if possible, take the old parts along for positive identification.

# Maintenance techniques, tools and working facilities

## Maintenance techniques

There are a number of techniques involved in maintenance and repair that will be referred to throughout this manual. Application of these techniques will enable the home mechanic to be more efficient, better organized and capable of performing the various tasks properly, which will ensure that the repair job is thorough and complete.

## Fasteners

Fasteners are nuts, bolts, studs and screws used to hold two or more parts together. There are a few things to keep in mind when working with fasteners. Almost all of them use a locking device of some type, either a lockwasher, locknut, locking tab or thread adhesive. All threaded fasteners should be clean and straight, with undamaged threads and undamaged corners on the hex head where the wrench fits. Develop the habit of replacing all damaged nuts and bolts with new ones. Special locknuts with nylon or fiber inserts can only be used once. If they are removed, they lose their locking ability and must be replaced with new ones.

Rusted nuts and bolts should be treated with a penetrating fluid to ease removal and prevent breakage. Some mechanics use turpentine in a spout-type oil can, which works quite well. After applying the rust penetrant, let it work for a few minutes before trying to loosen the nut or bolt. Badly rusted fasteners may have to be chiseled or sawed off or removed with a special nut breaker, available at tool stores.

If a bolt or stud breaks off in an assembly, it can be drilled and removed with a special tool commonly available for this purpose. Most automotive machine shops can perform this task, as well as other repair procedures, such as the repair of threaded holes that have been stripped out.

Flat washers and lockwashers, when removed from an assembly, should always be replaced exactly as removed. Replace any damaged washers with new ones. Never use a lockwasher on any soft metal surface (such as aluminum), thin sheet metal or plastic.

## Fastener sizes

For a number of reasons, automobile manufacturers are making wider and wider use of metric fasteners. Therefore, it is important to be able to tell the difference between standard (sometimes called U.S. or SAE) and metric hardware, since they cannot be interchanged.

All bolts, whether standard or metric, are sized according to diameter, thread pitch and length. For example, a standard 1/2 - 13 x 1 bolt is 1/2 inch in diameter, has 13 threads per inch and is 1 inch long. An M12 - 1.75 x 25 metric bolt is 12 mm in diameter, has a thread pitch of 1.75 mm (the distance between threads) and is 25 mm long. The two bolts are nearly identical, and easily confused, but they are not interchangeable.

In addition to the differences in diameter, thread pitch and length, metric and standard bolts can also be distinguished by examining the bolt heads. To begin with, the distance across the flats on a standard bolt head is measured in inches, while the same dimension on a metric bolt is sized in millimeters (the same is true for nuts). As a result, a standard wrench should not be used on a metric bolt and a metric wrench should not be used on a standard bolt. Also, most standard bolts have slashes radiating out from the center of the head to denote the grade or strength of the bolt, which is an indication of the amount of torque that can be applied to it. The greater the number of slashes, the greater the strength of the bolt. Grades 0 through 5 are commonly used on automobiles. Metric bolts have a property class (grade) number, rather than a slash, molded into their heads to indicate bolt strength. In this case, the higher the number, the stronger the bolt. Property class numbers 8.8, 9.8 and 10.9 are commonly used on automobiles.

Strength markings can also be used to distinguish standard hex nuts from metric hex nuts. Many standard nuts have dots stamped into one side, while metric nuts are marked with a number. The greater the number of

dots, or the higher the number, the greater the strength of the nut.

Metric studs are also marked on their ends according to property class (grade). Larger studs are numbered (the same as metric bolts), while smaller studs carry a geometric code to denote grade.

It should be noted that many fasteners, especially Grades 0 through 2, have no distinguishing marks on them. When such is the case, the only way to determine whether it is standard or metric is to measure the thread pitch or compare it to a known fastener of the same size.

Standard fasteners are often referred to as SAE, as opposed to metric. However, it should be noted that SAE technically refers to a non-metric fine thread fastener only. Coarse thread non-metric fasteners are referred to as USS sizes.

Since fasteners of the same size (both standard and metric) may have different

strength ratings, be sure to reinstall any bolts, studs or nuts removed from your vehicle in their original locations. Also, when replacing a fastener with a new one, make sure that the new one has a strength rating equal to or greater than the original.

### Tightening sequences and procedures

Most threaded fasteners should be tightened to a specific torque value (torque is the twisting force applied to a threaded component such as a nut or bolt). Overtightening the fastener can weaken it and cause it to break, while undertightening can cause it to eventually come loose. Bolts, screws and studs, depending on the material they are made of and their thread diameters, have specific torque values, many of which are noted in the Specifications at the beginning of each Chapter. Be sure to follow the torque recommen-

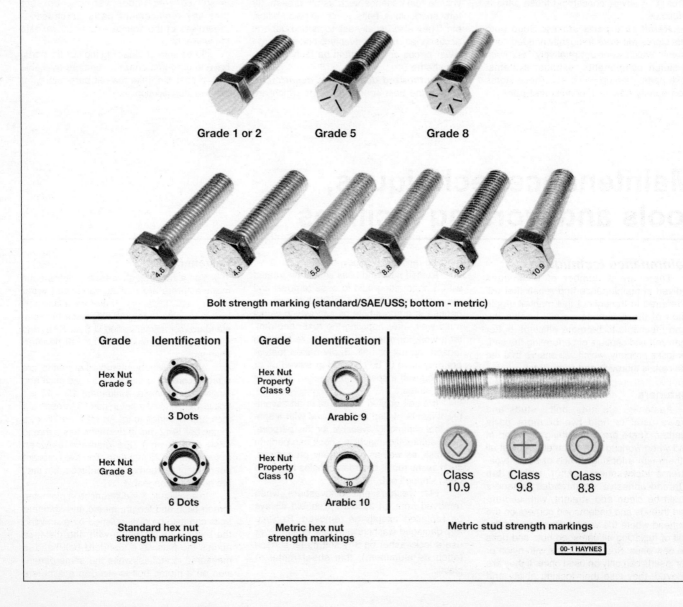

Grade 1 or 2          Grade 5          Grade 8

Bolt strength marking (standard/SAE/USS; bottom - metric)

| Grade | Identification |
|---|---|
| Hex Nut Grade 5 | 3 Dots |
| Hex Nut Grade 8 | 6 Dots |

**Standard hex nut strength markings**

| Grade | Identification |
|---|---|
| Hex Nut Property Class 9 | Arabic 9 |
| Hex Nut Property Class 10 | Arabic 10 |

**Metric hex nut strength markings**

Class 10.9          Class 9.8          Class 8.8

**Metric stud strength markings**

dations closely. For fasteners not assigned a specific torque, a general torque value chart is presented here as a guide. These torque values are for dry (unlubricated) fasteners threaded into steel or cast iron (not aluminum). As was previously mentioned, the size and grade of a fastener determine the amount of torque that can safely be applied to it. The figures listed here are approximate for Grade 2 and Grade 3 fasteners. Higher grades can tolerate higher torque values.

Fasteners laid out in a pattern, such as cylinder head bolts, oil pan bolts, differential cover bolts, etc., must be loosened or tightened in sequence to avoid warping the component. This sequence will normally be shown in the appropriate Chapter. If a specific pattern is not given, the following procedures can be used to prevent warping.

Initially, the bolts or nuts should be assembled finger-tight only. Next, they should be tightened one full turn each, in a crisscross or diagonal pattern. After each one has been tightened one full turn, return to the first one and tighten them all one-half turn, following the same pattern. Finally, tighten each of them one-quarter turn at a time until each fastener has been tightened to the proper torque. To loosen and remove the fasteners, the procedure would be reversed.

## Metric thread sizes

| | Ft-lbs | Nm |
|---|---|---|
| M-6 | 6 to 9 | 9 to 12 |
| M-8 | 14 to 21 | 19 to 28 |
| M-10 | 28 to 40 | 38 to 54 |
| M-12 | 50 to 71 | 68 to 96 |
| M-14 | 80 to 140 | 109 to 154 |

## Pipe thread sizes

| | | |
|---|---|---|
| 1/8 | 5 to 8 | 7 to 10 |
| 1/4 | 12 to 18 | 17 to 24 |
| 3/8 | 22 to 33 | 30 to 44 |
| 1/2 | 25 to 35 | 34 to 47 |

## U.S. thread sizes

| | | |
|---|---|---|
| 1/4 - 20 | 6 to 9 | 9 to 12 |
| 5/16 - 18 | 12 to 18 | 17 to 24 |
| 5/16 - 24 | 14 to 20 | 19 to 27 |
| 3/8 - 16 | 22 to 32 | 30 to 43 |
| 3/8 - 24 | 27 to 38 | 37 to 51 |
| 7/16 - 14 | 40 to 55 | 55 to 74 |
| 7/16 - 20 | 40 to 60 | 55 to 81 |
| 1/2 - 13 | 55 to 80 | 75 to 108 |

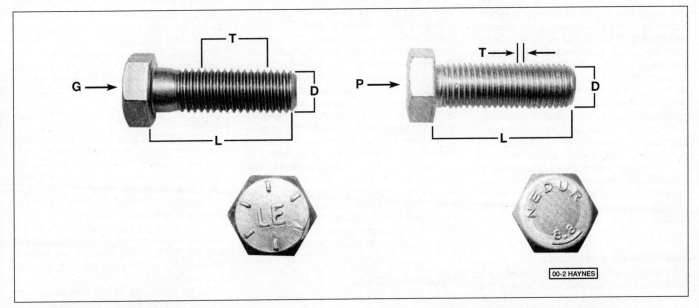

**Standard (SAE and USS) bolt dimensions/grade marks**

G   Grade marks (bolt strength)
L   Length (in inches)
T   Thread pitch (number of threads per inch)
D   Nominal diameter (in inches)

**Metric bolt dimensions/grade marks**

P   Property class (bolt strength)
L   Length (in millimeters)
T   Thread pitch (distance between threads in millimeters)
D   Diameter

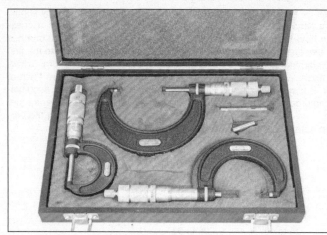

Micrometer set

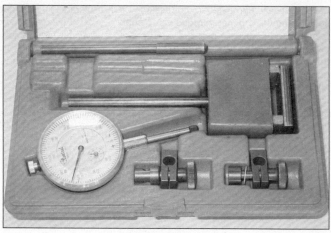

Dial indicator set

## Component disassembly

Component disassembly should be done with care and purpose to help ensure that the parts go back together properly. Always keep track of the sequence in which parts are removed. Make note of special characteristics or marks on parts that can be installed more than one way, such as a grooved thrust washer on a shaft. It is a good idea to lay the disassembled parts out on a clean surface in the order that they were removed. It may also be helpful to make sketches or take instant photos of components before removal.

When removing fasteners from a component, keep track of their locations. Sometimes threading a bolt back in a part, or putting the washers and nut back on a stud, can prevent mix-ups later. If nuts and bolts cannot be returned to their original locations, they should be kept in a compartmented box or a series of small boxes. A cupcake or muffin tin is ideal for this purpose, since each cavity can hold the bolts and nuts from a particular area (i.e. oil pan bolts, valve cover bolts, engine mount bolts, etc.). A pan of this type is especially helpful when working on assemblies with very small parts, such as the carburetor, alternator, valve train or interior dash and trim pieces. The cavities can be marked with paint or tape to identify the contents.

Whenever wiring looms, harnesses or connectors are separated, it is a good idea to identify the two halves with numbered pieces of masking tape so they can be easily reconnected.

## Gasket sealing surfaces

Throughout any vehicle, gaskets are used to seal the mating surfaces between two parts and keep lubricants, fluids, vacuum or pressure contained in an assembly.

Many times these gaskets are coated with a liquid or paste-type gasket sealing compound before assembly. Age, heat and pressure can sometimes cause the two parts to stick together so tightly that they are very difficult to separate. Often, the assembly can

be loosened by striking it with a soft-face hammer near the mating surfaces. A regular hammer can be used if a block of wood is placed between the hammer and the part. Do not hammer on cast parts or parts that could be easily damaged. With any particularly stubborn part, always recheck to make sure that every fastener has been removed.

Avoid using a screwdriver or bar to pry apart an assembly, as they can easily mar the gasket sealing surfaces of the parts, which must remain smooth. If prying is absolutely necessary, use an old broom handle, but keep in mind that extra clean up will be necessary if the wood splinters.

After the parts are separated, the old gasket must be carefully scraped off and the gasket surfaces cleaned. Stubborn gasket material can be soaked with rust penetrant or treated with a special chemical to soften it so it can be easily scraped off. **Caution:** *Never use gasket removal solutions or caustic chemicals on plastic or other composite components.* A scraper can be fashioned from a piece of copper tubing by flattening and sharpening one end. Copper is recommended because it is usually softer than the surfaces to be scraped, which reduces the chance of gouging the part. Some gaskets can be removed with a wire brush, but regardless of the method used, the mating surfaces must be left clean and smooth. If for some reason the gasket surface is gouged, then a gasket sealer thick enough to fill scratches will have to be used during reassembly of the components. For most applications, a non-drying (or semi-drying) gasket sealer should be used.

## Hose removal tips

**Warning:** *If the vehicle is equipped with air conditioning, do not disconnect any of the A/C hoses without first having the system depressurized by a dealer service department or a service station.*

Hose removal precautions closely parallel gasket removal precautions. Avoid scratching or gouging the surface that the

hose mates against or the connection may leak. This is especially true for radiator hoses. Because of various chemical reactions, the rubber in hoses can bond itself to the metal spigot that the hose fits over. To remove a hose, first loosen the hose clamps that secure it to the spigot. Then, with slip-joint pliers, grab the hose at the clamp and rotate it around the spigot. Work it back and forth until it is completely free, then pull it off. Silicone or other lubricants will ease removal if they can be applied between the hose and the outside of the spigot. Apply the same lubricant to the inside of the hose and the outside of the spigot to simplify installation.

As a last resort (and if the hose is to be replaced with a new one anyway), the rubber can be slit with a knife and the hose peeled from the spigot. If this must be done, be careful that the metal connection is not damaged.

If a hose clamp is broken or damaged, do not reuse it. Wire-type clamps usually weaken with age, so it is a good idea to replace them with screw-type clamps whenever a hose is removed.

## Tools

A selection of good tools is a basic requirement for anyone who plans to maintain and repair his or her own vehicle. For the owner who has few tools, the initial investment might seem high, but when compared to the spiraling costs of professional auto maintenance and repair, it is a wise one.

To help the owner decide which tools are needed to perform the tasks detailed in this manual, the following tool lists are offered: *Maintenance and minor repair, Repair/overhaul* and *Special*.

The newcomer to practical mechanics should start off with the *maintenance and minor repair* tool kit, which is adequate for the simpler jobs performed on a vehicle. Then, as confidence and experience grow, the owner can tackle more difficult tasks, buying additional tools as they are needed. Eventually the basic kit will be expanded into the *repair and overhaul* tool set. Over a period of time, the

Dial caliper

Hand-operated vacuum pump

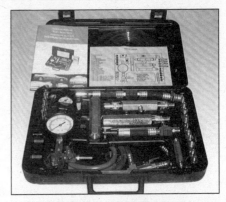
Fuel pressure gauge set

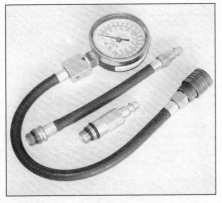
Compression gauge with spark plug hole adapter

Damper/steering wheel puller

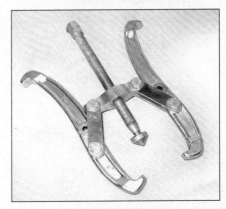
General purpose puller

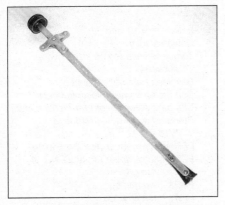
Hydraulic lifter removal tool

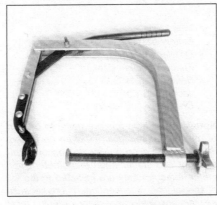
Valve spring compressor

Valve spring compressor

Ridge reamer

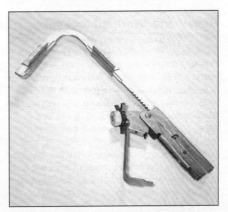
Piston ring groove cleaning tool

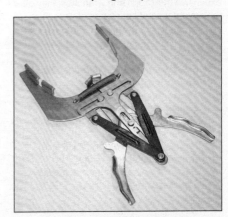
Ring removal/installation tool

Ring compressor

Cylinder hone

Brake hold-down spring tool

Torque angle gauge

Clutch plate alignment tool

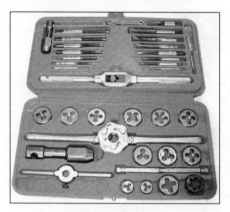
Tap and die set

experienced do-it-yourselfer will assemble a tool set complete enough for most repair and overhaul procedures and will add tools from the special category when it is felt that the expense is justified by the frequency of use.

## Maintenance and minor repair tool kit

The tools in this list should be considered the minimum required for performance of routine maintenance, servicing and minor repair work. We recommend the purchase of combination wrenches (box-end and open-end combined in one wrench). While more expensive than open end wrenches, they offer the advantages of both types of wrench.

> *Combination wrench set (1/4-inch to*
> *   1 inch or 6 mm to 19 mm)*
> *Adjustable wrench, 8 inch*
> *Spark plug wrench with rubber insert*
> *Spark plug gap adjusting tool*
> *Feeler gauge set*
> *Brake bleeder wrench*
> *Standard screwdriver (5/16-inch x*
> *   6 inch)*
> *Phillips screwdriver (No. 2 x 6 inch)*
> *Combination pliers - 6 inch*
> *Hacksaw and assortment of blades*
> *Tire pressure gauge*
> *Grease gun*
> *Oil can*
> *Fine emery cloth*

> *Wire brush*
> *Battery post and cable cleaning tool*
> *Oil filter wrench*
> *Funnel (medium size)*
> *Safety goggles*
> *Jackstands (2)*
> *Drain pan*

**Note:** *If basic tune-ups are going to be part of routine maintenance, it will be necessary to purchase a good quality stroboscopic timing light and combination tachometer/dwell meter. Although they are included in the list of special tools, it is mentioned here because they are absolutely necessary for tuning most vehicles properly.*

## Repair and overhaul tool set

These tools are essential for anyone who plans to perform major repairs and are in addition to those in the maintenance and minor repair tool kit. Included is a comprehensive set of sockets which, though expensive, are invaluable because of their versatility, especially when various extensions and drives are available. We recommend the 1/2-inch drive over the 3/8-inch drive. Although the larger drive is bulky and more expensive, it has the capacity of accepting a very wide range of large sockets. Ideally, however, the mechanic should have a 3/8-inch drive set and a 1/2-inch drive set.

> *Socket set(s)*
> *Reversible ratchet*

> *Extension - 10 inch*
> *Universal joint*
> *Torque wrench (same size drive as*
> *   sockets)*
> *Ball peen hammer - 8 ounce*
> *Soft-face hammer (plastic/rubber)*
> *Standard screwdriver (1/4-inch x 6 inch)*
> *Standard screwdriver (stubby -*
> *   5/16-inch)*
> *Phillips screwdriver (No. 3 x 8 inch)*
> *Phillips screwdriver (stubby - No. 2)*
> *Pliers - vise grip*
> *Pliers - lineman's*
> *Pliers - needle nose*
> *Pliers - snap-ring (internal and external)*
> *Cold chisel - 1/2-inch*
> *Scribe*
> *Scraper (made from flattened copper*
> *   tubing)*
> *Centerpunch*
> *Pin punches (1/16, 1/8, 3/16-inch)*
> *Steel rule/straightedge - 12 inch*
> *Allen wrench set (1/8 to 3/8-inch or*
> *   4 mm to 10 mm)*
> *A selection of files*
> *Wire brush (large)*
> *Jackstands (second set)*
> *Jack (scissor or hydraulic type)*

**Note:** *Another tool which is often useful is an electric drill with a chuck capacity of 3/8-inch and a set of good quality drill bits.*

## Special tools

The tools in this list include those which are not used regularly, are expensive to buy, or which need to be used in accordance with their manufacturer's instructions. Unless these tools will be used frequently, it is not very economical to purchase many of them. A consideration would be to split the cost and use between yourself and a friend or friends. In addition, most of these tools can be obtained from a tool rental shop on a temporary basis.

This list primarily contains only those tools and instruments widely available to the public, and not those special tools produced by the vehicle manufacturer for distribution to dealer service departments. Occasionally, references to the manufacturer's special tools are included in the text of this manual. Generally, an alternative method of doing the job without the special tool is offered. However, sometimes there is no alternative to their use. Where this is the case, and the tool cannot be purchased or borrowed, the work should be turned over to the dealer service department or an automotive repair shop.

*Valve spring compressor*
*Piston ring groove cleaning tool*
*Piston ring compressor*
*Piston ring installation tool*
*Cylinder compression gauge*
*Cylinder ridge reamer*
*Cylinder surfacing hone*
*Cylinder bore gauge*
*Micrometers and/or dial calipers*
*Hydraulic lifter removal tool*
*Balljoint separator*
*Universal-type puller*
*Impact screwdriver*
*Dial indicator set*
*Stroboscopic timing light (inductive pick-up)*
*Hand operated vacuum/pressure pump*
*Tachometer/dwell meter*
*Universal electrical multimeter*
*Cable hoist*
*Brake spring removal and installation tools*
*Floor jack*

## Buying tools

For the do-it-yourselfer who is just starting to get involved in vehicle maintenance and repair, there are a number of options available when purchasing tools. If maintenance and minor repair is the extent of the work to be done, the purchase of individual tools is satisfactory. If, on the other hand, extensive work is planned, it would be a good idea to purchase a modest tool set from one of the large retail chain stores. A set can usually be bought at a substantial savings over the individual tool prices, and they often come with a tool box. As additional tools are needed, add-on sets, individual tools and a larger tool box can be purchased to expand the tool selection. Building a tool set gradually allows the cost of the tools to be spread over a longer period of time and gives the mechanic the freedom to choose only those tools that will actually be used.

Tool stores will often be the only source of some of the special tools that are needed, but regardless of where tools are bought, try to avoid cheap ones, especially when buying screwdrivers and sockets, because they won't last very long. The expense involved in replacing cheap tools will eventually be greater than the initial cost of quality tools.

## Care and maintenance of tools

Good tools are expensive, so it makes sense to treat them with respect. Keep them clean and in usable condition and store them properly when not in use. Always wipe off any dirt, grease or metal chips before putting them away. Never leave tools lying around in the work area. Upon completion of a job, always check closely under the hood for tools that may have been left there so they won't get lost during a test drive.

Some tools, such as screwdrivers, pliers, wrenches and sockets, can be hung on a panel mounted on the garage or workshop wall, while others should be kept in a tool box or tray. Measuring instruments, gauges, meters, etc. must be carefully stored where they cannot be damaged by weather or impact from other tools.

When tools are used with care and stored properly, they will last a very long time. Even with the best of care, though, tools will wear out if used frequently. When a tool is damaged or worn out, replace it. Subsequent jobs will be safer and more enjoyable if you do.

## How to repair damaged threads

Sometimes, the internal threads of a nut or bolt hole can become stripped, usually from overtightening. Stripping threads is an all-too-common occurrence, especially when working with aluminum parts, because aluminum is so soft that it easily strips out.

Usually, external or internal threads are only partially stripped. After they've been cleaned up with a tap or die, they'll still work. Sometimes, however, threads are badly damaged. When this happens, you've got three choices:

1) *Drill and tap the hole to the next suitable oversize and install a larger diameter bolt, screw or stud.*
2) *Drill and tap the hole to accept a threaded plug, then drill and tap the plug to the original screw size. You can also buy a plug already threaded to the original size. Then you simply drill a hole to the specified size, then run the threaded plug into the hole with a bolt and jam nut. Once the plug is fully seated, remove the jam nut and bolt.*
3) *The third method uses a patented thread repair kit like Heli-Coil or Slimsert. These easy-to-use kits are designed to repair damaged threads in straight-through holes and blind holes. Both are available as kits which can handle a variety of sizes and thread patterns. Drill the hole, then tap it with the special included tap. Install the Heli-Coil and the hole is back to its original diameter and thread pitch.*

Regardless of which method you use, be sure to proceed calmly and carefully. A little impatience or carelessness during one of these relatively simple procedures can ruin your whole day's work and cost you a bundle if you wreck an expensive part.

## Working facilities

Not to be overlooked when discussing tools is the workshop. If anything more than routine maintenance is to be carried out, some sort of suitable work area is essential.

It is understood, and appreciated, that many home mechanics do not have a good workshop or garage available, and end up removing an engine or doing major repairs outside. It is recommended, however, that the overhaul or repair be completed under the cover of a roof.

A clean, flat workbench or table of comfortable working height is an absolute necessity. The workbench should be equipped with a vise that has a jaw opening of at least four inches.

As mentioned previously, some clean, dry storage space is also required for tools, as well as the lubricants, fluids, cleaning solvents, etc. which soon become necessary.

Sometimes waste oil and fluids, drained from the engine or cooling system during normal maintenance or repairs, present a disposal problem. To avoid pouring them on the ground or into a sewage system, pour the used fluids into large containers, seal them with caps and take them to an authorized disposal site or recycling center. Plastic jugs, such as old antifreeze containers, are ideal for this purpose.

Always keep a supply of old newspapers and clean rags available. Old towels are excellent for mopping up spills. Many mechanics use rolls of paper towels for most work because they are readily available and disposable. To help keep the area under the vehicle clean, a large cardboard box can be cut open and flattened to protect the garage or shop floor.

Whenever working over a painted surface, such as when leaning over a fender to service something under the hood, always cover it with an old blanket or bedspread to protect the finish. Vinyl covered pads, made especially for this purpose, are available at auto parts stores.

# Booster battery (jump) starting

Observe the following precautions when using a booster battery to start a vehicle:

a) *Before connecting the booster battery, make sure the ignition switch is in the Off position.*
b) *Turn off the lights, heater and other electrical loads.*
c) *Your eyes should be shielded. Safety goggles are a good idea.*
d) *Make sure the booster battery is the same voltage as the dead one in the vehicle.*
e) *The two vehicles MUST NOT TOUCH each other.*
f) *Make sure the transmission is in Park.*
g) *If the booster battery is not a maintenance-free type, remove the vent caps and lay a cloth over the vent holes.*

Connect the red jumper cable to the positive (+) terminals of each battery.

Connect one end of the black cable to the negative (-) terminal of the booster battery. The other end of this cable should be connected to a good ground on the engine block (see illustration) . Make sure the cable will not come into contact with the fan, drivebelts or other moving parts of the engine.

Start the engine using the booster battery, then, with the engine running at idle speed, disconnect the jumper cables in the reverse order of connection.

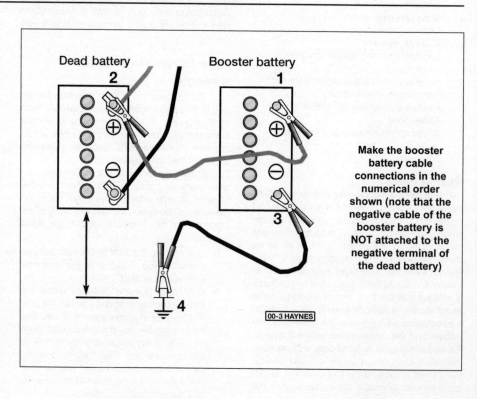

Make the booster battery cable connections in the numerical order shown (note that the negative cable of the booster battery is NOT attached to the negative terminal of the dead battery)

# Jacking and towing

## Jacking

1    The jack supplied with the vehicle should only be used for raising the vehicle for changing a tire or placing jackstands under the frame.

**Warning:** *Never crawl under the vehicle or start the engine when the jack is being used as the only means of support.*

2    All vehicles are supplied with a scissors-type jack. When jacking the vehicle, it should be engaged with the notch in the rocker panel flange (see illustration).

3    The vehicle should be on level ground with the wheels blocked and the transmission in Park. Pry off the hub cap (if equipped) using the tapered end of the lug wrench. Loosen the lug nuts one-half turn and leave them in place until the wheel is raised off the ground.

4    Place the jack under the side of the vehicle in the indicated position. Use the supplied wrench to turn the jackscrew clockwise until the wheel is raised off the ground. Remove the lug nuts, pull off the wheel and install the spare.

5    With the beveled side in, install the lug nuts and tighten them until snug. Lower the vehicle by turning the jackscrew counterclockwise. Remove the jack and tighten the nuts in a diagonal pattern to the torque listed in the Chapter 1 Specifications 0 . If a torque wrench is not available, have the torque checked by a service station as soon as possible. Install the hubcap by placing it in position and using the heel of your hand or a rubber mallet to seat it.

## Towing

### All Civic models and 2015 and later CR-V models

6    These models must be towed with the drive wheels off the ground (the best method is to have the vehicle placed on a flat-bed tow truck, and the only method for AWD models). If they can't be raised, place them on a dolly. The ignition key must be in the Off position, since the steering lock mechanism isn't strong enough to hold the front wheels straight while towing.

### 2012 through 2014 CR-V models

7    These models can be towed with all four wheels on the ground, provided that the proper towing equipment is used, towing speed does not exceed 65 miles per hour, and the ignition key is turned to the accessory position (with all accessories turned off so the battery doesn't go dead). Additionally, before towing, the following procedure must be performed, or the transaxle will be severely damaged:

a)  *Check the transaxle fluid level.*
b)  *Start the engine.*
c)  *Depress the brake pedal and move the shift lever through all of the gear ranges.*
d)  *Place the shifter in Drive (D) for five seconds, then to the Neutral (N) position.*
e)  *Allow the engine to run for three minutes, then shut it off by turning the key to the ACC position. Make sure all accessories are turned off to prevent the battery from draining.*

**The jack fits between the two dimples in the raised portion of the rocker panel flange (there are two jacking points on each side of the vehicle)**

# Automotive chemicals and lubricants

A number of automotive chemicals and lubricants are available for use during vehicle maintenance and repair. They include a wide variety of products ranging from cleaning solvents and degreasers to lubricants and protective sprays for rubber, plastic and vinyl.

## Cleaners

*Carburetor cleaner and choke cleaner* is a strong solvent for gum, varnish and carbon. Most carburetor cleaners leave a dry-type lubricant film which will not harden or gum up. Because of this film it is not recommended for use on electrical components.

*Brake system cleaner* is used to remove brake dust, grease and brake fluid from the brake system, where clean surfaces are absolutely necessary. It leaves no residue and often eliminates brake squeal caused by contaminants.

*Electrical cleaner* removes oxidation, corrosion and carbon deposits from electrical contacts, restoring full current flow. It can also be used to clean spark plugs, carburetor jets, voltage regulators and other parts where an oil-free surface is desired.

*Demoisturants* remove water and moisture from electrical components such as alternators, voltage regulators, electrical connectors and fuse blocks. They are non-conductive and non-corrosive.

*Degreasers* are heavy-duty solvents used to remove grease from the outside of the engine and from chassis components. They can be sprayed or brushed on and, depending on the type, are rinsed off either with water or solvent.

## Lubricants

*Motor oil* is the lubricant formulated for use in engines. It normally contains a wide variety of additives to prevent corrosion and reduce foaming and wear. Motor oil comes in various weights (viscosity ratings) from 0 to 50. The recommended weight of the oil depends on the season, temperature and the demands on the engine. Light oil is used in cold climates and under light load conditions. Heavy oil is used in hot climates and where high loads are encountered. Multi-viscosity oils are designed to have characteristics of both light and heavy oils and are available in a number of weights from 0W-20 to 20W-50.

*Gear oil* is designed to be used in differentials, manual transmissions and other areas where high-temperature lubrication is required.

*Chassis and wheel bearing grease* is a heavy grease used where increased loads and friction are encountered, such as for wheel bearings, balljoints, tie-rod ends and universal joints.

*High-temperature wheel bearing grease* is designed to withstand the extreme temperatures encountered by wheel bearings in disc brake equipped vehicles. It usually contains molybdenum disulfide (moly), which is a dry-type lubricant.

*White grease* is a heavy grease for metal-to-metal applications where water is a problem. White grease stays soft under both low and high temperatures (usually from -100 to +190-degrees F), and will not wash off or dilute in the presence of water.

*Assembly lube* is a special extreme pressure lubricant, usually containing moly, used to lubricate high-load parts (such as main and rod bearings and cam lobes) for initial start-up of a new engine. The assembly lube lubricates the parts without being squeezed out or washed away until the engine oiling system begins to function.

*Silicone lubricants* are used to protect rubber, plastic, vinyl and nylon parts.

*Graphite lubricants* are used where oils cannot be used due to contamination problems, such as in locks. The dry graphite will lubricate metal parts while remaining uncontaminated by dirt, water, oil or acids. It is electrically conductive and will not foul electrical contacts in locks such as the ignition switch.

*Moly penetrants* loosen and lubricate frozen, rusted and corroded fasteners and prevent future rusting or freezing.

*Heat-sink grease* is a special electrically non-conductive grease that is used for mounting electronic ignition modules where it is essential that heat is transferred away from the module.

## Sealants

*RTV sealant* is one of the most widely used gasket compounds. Made from silicone, RTV is air curing, it seals, bonds, waterproofs, fills surface irregularities, remains flexible, doesn't shrink, is relatively easy to remove, and is used as a supplementary sealer with almost all low and medium temperature gaskets.

*Anaerobic sealant* is much like RTV in that it can be used either to seal gaskets or to form gaskets by itself. It remains flexible, is solvent resistant and fills surface imperfections. The difference between an anaerobic sealant and an RTV-type sealant is in the curing. RTV cures when exposed to air, while an anaerobic sealant cures only in the absence of air. This means that an anaerobic sealant cures only after the assembly of parts, sealing them together.

*Thread and pipe sealant* is used for sealing hydraulic and pneumatic fittings and vacuum lines. It is usually made from a Teflon compound, and comes in a spray, a paint-on liquid and as a wrap-around tape.

## Chemicals

*Anti-seize compound* prevents seizing, galling, cold welding, rust and corrosion in fasteners. High-temperature anti-seize, usually made with copper and graphite lubricants, is used for exhaust system and exhaust manifold bolts.

*Anaerobic locking compounds* are used to keep fasteners from vibrating or working loose and cure only after installation, in the absence of air. Medium strength locking compound is used for small nuts, bolts and screws that may be removed later. High-strength locking compound is for large nuts, bolts and studs which aren't removed on a regular basis.

*Oil additives* range from viscosity index improvers to chemical treatments that claim to reduce internal engine friction. It should be noted that most oil manufacturers caution against using additives with their oils.

*Gas additives* perform several functions, depending on their chemical makeup. They usually contain solvents that help dissolve gum and varnish that build up on carburetor, fuel injection and intake parts. They also serve to break down carbon deposits that form on the inside surfaces of the combustion chambers. Some additives contain upper cylinder lubricants for valves and piston rings, and others contain chemicals to remove condensation from the gas tank.

## Miscellaneous

*Brake fluid* is specially formulated hydraulic fluid that can withstand the heat and pressure encountered in brake systems. Care must be taken so this fluid does not come in contact with painted surfaces or plastics. An opened container should always be resealed to prevent contamination by water or dirt.

*Weatherstrip adhesive* is used to bond weatherstripping around doors, windows and trunk lids. It is sometimes used to attach trim pieces.

*Undercoating* is a petroleum-based, tar-like substance that is designed to protect metal surfaces on the underside of the vehicle from corrosion. It also acts as a sound-deadening agent by insulating the bottom of the vehicle.

*Waxes and polishes* are used to help protect painted and plated surfaces from the weather. Different types of paint may require the use of different types of wax and polish. Some polishes utilize a chemical or abrasive cleaner to help remove the top layer of oxidized (dull) paint on older vehicles. In recent years many non-wax polishes that contain a wide variety of chemicals such as polymers and silicones have been introduced. These non-wax polishes are usually easier to apply and last longer than conventional waxes and polishes.

# Conversion factors

## Length (distance)
| | | | | | |
|---|---|---|---|---|---|
| Inches (in) | X | 25.4 | = Millimeters (mm) | X 0.0394 | = Inches (in) |
| Feet (ft) | X | 0.305 | = Meters (m) | X 3.281 | = Feet (ft) |
| Miles | X | 1.609 | = Kilometers (km) | X 0.621 | = Miles |

## Volume (capacity)
| | | | | | |
|---|---|---|---|---|---|
| Cubic inches (cu in; in³) | X | 16.387 | = Cubic centimeters (cc; cm³) | X 0.061 | = Cubic inches (cu in; in³) |
| Imperial pints (Imp pt) | X | 0.568 | = Liters (l) | X 1.76 | = Imperial pints (Imp pt) |
| Imperial quarts (Imp qt) | X | 1.137 | = Liters (l) | X 0.88 | = Imperial quarts (Imp qt) |
| Imperial quarts (Imp qt) | X | 1.201 | = US quarts (US qt) | X 0.833 | = Imperial quarts (Imp qt) |
| US quarts (US qt) | X | 0.946 | = Liters (l) | X 1.057 | = US quarts (US qt) |
| Imperial gallons (Imp gal) | X | 4.546 | = Liters (l) | X 0.22 | = Imperial gallons (Imp gal) |
| Imperial gallons (Imp gal) | X | 1.201 | = US gallons (US gal) | X 0.833 | = Imperial gallons (Imp gal) |
| US gallons (US gal) | X | 3.785 | = Liters (l) | X 0.264 | = US gallons (US gal) |

## Mass (weight)
| | | | | | |
|---|---|---|---|---|---|
| Ounces (oz) | X | 28.35 | = Grams (g) | X 0.035 | = Ounces (oz) |
| Pounds (lb) | X | 0.454 | = Kilograms (kg) | X 2.205 | = Pounds (lb) |

## Force
| | | | | | |
|---|---|---|---|---|---|
| Ounces-force (ozf; oz) | X | 0.278 | = Newtons (N) | X 3.6 | = Ounces-force (ozf; oz) |
| Pounds-force (lbf; lb) | X | 4.448 | = Newtons (N) | X 0.225 | = Pounds-force (lbf; lb) |
| Newtons (N) | X | 0.1 | = Kilograms-force (kgf; kg) | X 9.81 | = Newtons (N) |

## Pressure
| | | | | | |
|---|---|---|---|---|---|
| Pounds-force per square inch (psi; lbf/in²; lb/in²) | X | 0.070 | = Kilograms-force per square centimeter (kgf/cm²; kg/cm²) | X 14.223 | = Pounds-force per square inch (psi; lbf/in²; lb/in²) |
| Pounds-force per square inch (psi; lbf/in²; lb/in²) | X | 0.068 | = Atmospheres (atm) | X 14.696 | = Pounds-force per square inch (psi; lbf/in²; lb/in²) |
| Pounds-force per square inch (psi; lbf/in²; lb/in²) | X | 0.069 | = Bars | X 14.5 | = Pounds-force per square inch (psi; lbf/in²; lb/in²) |
| Pounds-force per square inch (psi; lbf/in²; lb/in²) | X | 6.895 | = Kilopascals (kPa) | X 0.145 | = Pounds-force per square inch (psi; lbf/in²; lb/in²) |
| Kilopascals (kPa) | X | 0.01 | = Kilograms-force per square centimeter (kgf/cm²; kg/cm²) | X 98.1 | = Kilopascals (kPa) |

## Torque (moment of force)
| | | | | | |
|---|---|---|---|---|---|
| Pounds-force inches (lbf in; lb in) | X | 1.152 | = Kilograms-force centimeter (kgf cm; kg cm) | X 0.868 | = Pounds-force inches (lbf in; lb in) |
| Pounds-force inches (lbf in; lb in) | X | 0.113 | = Newton meters (Nm) | X 8.85 | = Pounds-force inches (lbf in; lb in) |
| Pounds-force inches (lbf in; lb in) | X | 0.083 | = Pounds-force feet (lbf ft; lb ft) | X 12 | = Pounds-force inches (lbf in; lb in) |
| Pounds-force feet (lbf ft; lb ft) | X | 0.138 | = Kilograms-force meters (kgf m; kg m) | X 7.233 | = Pounds-force feet (lbf ft; lb ft) |
| Pounds-force feet (lbf ft; lb ft) | X | 1.356 | = Newton meters (Nm) | X 0.738 | = Pounds-force feet (lbf ft; lb ft) |
| Newton meters (Nm) | X | 0.102 | = Kilograms-force meters (kgf m; kg m) | X 9.804 | = Newton meters (Nm) |

## Vacuum
| | | | | | |
|---|---|---|---|---|---|
| Inches mercury (in. Hg) | X | 3.377 | = Kilopascals (kPa) | X 0.2961 | = Inches mercury |
| Inches mercury (in. Hg) | X | 25.4 | = Millimeters mercury (mm Hg) | X 0.0394 | = Inches mercury |

## Power
| | | | | | |
|---|---|---|---|---|---|
| Horsepower (hp) | X | 745.7 | = Watts (W) | X 0.0013 | = Horsepower (hp) |

## Velocity (speed)
| | | | | | |
|---|---|---|---|---|---|
| Miles per hour (miles/hr; mph) | X | 1.609 | = Kilometers per hour (km/hr; kph) | X 0.621 | = Miles per hour (miles/hr; mph) |

## Fuel consumption*
| | | | | | |
|---|---|---|---|---|---|
| Miles per gallon, Imperial (mpg) | X | 0.354 | = Kilometers per liter (km/l) | X 2.825 | = Miles per gallon, Imperial (mpg) |
| Miles per gallon, US (mpg) | X | 0.425 | = Kilometers per liter (km/l) | X 2.352 | = Miles per gallon, US (mpg) |

## Temperature
Degrees Fahrenheit = (°C x 1.8) + 32    Degrees Celsius (Degrees Centigrade; °C) = (°F - 32) x 0.56

*It is common practice to convert from miles per gallon (mpg) to liters/100 kilometers (l/100km), where mpg (Imperial) x l/100 km = 282 and mpg (US) x l/100 km = 235

## DECIMALS to MILLIMETERS

| Decimal | mm | Decimal | mm |
|---|---|---|---|
| 0.001 | 0.0254 | 0.500 | 12.7000 |
| 0.002 | 0.0508 | 0.510 | 12.9540 |
| 0.003 | 0.0762 | 0.520 | 13.2080 |
| 0.004 | 0.1016 | 0.530 | 13.4620 |
| 0.005 | 0.1270 | 0.540 | 13.7160 |
| 0.006 | 0.1524 | 0.550 | 13.9700 |
| 0.007 | 0.1778 | 0.560 | 14.2240 |
| 0.008 | 0.2032 | 0.570 | 14.4780 |
| 0.009 | 0.2286 | 0.580 | 14.7320 |
| | | 0.590 | 14.9860 |
| 0.010 | 0.2540 | | |
| 0.020 | 0.5080 | | |
| 0.030 | 0.7620 | | |
| 0.040 | 1.0160 | 0.600 | 15.2400 |
| 0.050 | 1.2700 | 0.610 | 15.4940 |
| 0.060 | 1.5240 | 0.620 | 15.7480 |
| 0.070 | 1.7780 | 0.630 | 16.0020 |
| 0.080 | 2.0320 | 0.640 | 16.2560 |
| 0.090 | 2.2860 | 0.650 | 16.5100 |
| | | 0.660 | 16.7640 |
| 0.100 | 2.5400 | 0.670 | 17.0180 |
| 0.110 | 2.7940 | 0.680 | 17.2720 |
| 0.120 | 3.0480 | 0.690 | 17.5260 |
| 0.130 | 3.3020 | | |
| 0.140 | 3.5560 | | |
| 0.150 | 3.8100 | | |
| 0.160 | 4.0640 | 0.700 | 17.7800 |
| 0.170 | 4.3180 | 0.710 | 18.0340 |
| 0.180 | 4.5720 | 0.720 | 18.2880 |
| 0.190 | 4.8260 | 0.730 | 18.5420 |
| | | 0.740 | 18.7960 |
| 0.200 | 5.0800 | 0.750 | 19.0500 |
| 0.210 | 5.3340 | 0.760 | 19.3040 |
| 0.220 | 5.5880 | 0.770 | 19.5580 |
| 0.230 | 5.8420 | 0.780 | 19.8120 |
| 0.240 | 6.0960 | 0.790 | 20.0660 |
| 0.250 | 6.3500 | | |
| 0.260 | 6.6040 | | |
| 0.270 | 6.8580 | 0.800 | 20.3200 |
| 0.280 | 7.1120 | 0.810 | 20.5740 |
| 0.290 | 7.3660 | 0.820 | 21.8280 |
| | | 0.830 | 21.0820 |
| 0.300 | 7.6200 | 0.840 | 21.3360 |
| 0.310 | 7.8740 | 0.850 | 21.5900 |
| 0.320 | 8.1280 | 0.860 | 21.8440 |
| 0.330 | 8.3820 | 0.870 | 22.0980 |
| 0.340 | 8.6360 | 0.880 | 22.3520 |
| 0.350 | 8.8900 | 0.890 | 22.6060 |
| 0.360 | 9.1440 | | |
| 0.370 | 9.3980 | | |
| 0.380 | 9.6520 | | |
| 0.390 | 9.9060 | 0.900 | 22.8600 |
| 0.400 | 10.1600 | 0.910 | 23.1140 |
| 0.410 | 10.4140 | 0.920 | 23.3680 |
| 0.420 | 10.6680 | 0.930 | 23.6220 |
| 0.430 | 10.9220 | 0.940 | 23.8760 |
| 0.440 | 11.1760 | 0.950 | 24.1300 |
| 0.450 | 11.4300 | 0.960 | 24.3840 |
| 0.460 | 11.6840 | 0.970 | 24.6380 |
| 0.470 | 11.9380 | 0.980 | 24.8920 |
| 0.480 | 12.1920 | 0.990 | 25.1460 |
| 0.490 | 12.4460 | 1.000 | 25.4000 |

## FRACTIONS to DECIMALS to MILLIMETERS

| Fraction | Decimal | mm | Fraction | Decimal | mm |
|---|---|---|---|---|---|
| 1/64 | 0.0156 | 0.3969 | 33/64 | 0.5156 | 13.0969 |
| 1/32 | 0.0312 | 0.7938 | 17/32 | 0.5312 | 13.4938 |
| 3/64 | 0.0469 | 1.1906 | 35/64 | 0.5469 | 13.8906 |
| 1/16 | 0.0625 | 1.5875 | 9/16 | 0.5625 | 14.2875 |
| 5/64 | 0.0781 | 1.9844 | 37/64 | 0.5781 | 14.6844 |
| 3/32 | 0.0938 | 2.3812 | 19/32 | 0.5938 | 15.0812 |
| 7/64 | 0.1094 | 2.7781 | 39/64 | 0.6094 | 15.4781 |
| 1/8 | 0.1250 | 3.1750 | 5/8 | 0.6250 | 15.8750 |
| 9/64 | 0.1406 | 3.5719 | 41/64 | 0.6406 | 16.2719 |
| 5/32 | 0.1562 | 3.9688 | 21/32 | 0.6562 | 16.6688 |
| 11/64 | 0.1719 | 4.3656 | 43/64 | 0.6719 | 17.0656 |
| 3/16 | 0.1875 | 4.7625 | 11/16 | 0.6875 | 17.4625 |
| 13/64 | 0.2031 | 5.1594 | 45/64 | 0.7031 | 17.8594 |
| 7/32 | 0.2188 | 5.5562 | 23/32 | 0.7188 | 18.2562 |
| 15/64 | 0.2344 | 5.9531 | 47/64 | 0.7344 | 18.6531 |
| 1/4 | 0.2500 | 6.3500 | 3/4 | 0.7500 | 19.0500 |
| 17/64 | 0.2656 | 6.7469 | 49/64 | 0.7656 | 19.4469 |
| 9/32 | 0.2812 | 7.1438 | 25/32 | 0.7812 | 19.8438 |
| 19/64 | 0.2969 | 7.5406 | 51/64 | 0.7969 | 20.2406 |
| 5/16 | 0.3125 | 7.9375 | 13/16 | 0.8125 | 20.6375 |
| 21/64 | 0.3281 | 8.3344 | 53/64 | 0.8281 | 21.0344 |
| 11/32 | 0.3438 | 8.7312 | 27/32 | 0.8438 | 21.4312 |
| 23/64 | 0.3594 | 9.1281 | 55/64 | 0.8594 | 21.8281 |
| 3/8 | 0.3750 | 9.5250 | 7/8 | 0.8750 | 22.2250 |
| 25/64 | 0.3906 | 9.9219 | 57/64 | 0.8906 | 22.6219 |
| 13/32 | 0.4062 | 10.3188 | 29/32 | 0.9062 | 23.0188 |
| 27/64 | 0.4219 | 10.7156 | 59/64 | 0.9219 | 23.4156 |
| 7/16 | 0.4375 | 11.1125 | 15/16 | 0.9375 | 23.8125 |
| 29/64 | 0.4531 | 11.5094 | 61/64 | 0.9531 | 24.2094 |
| 15/32 | 0.4688 | 11.9062 | 31/32 | 0.9688 | 24.6062 |
| 31/64 | 0.4844 | 12.3031 | 63/64 | 0.9844 | 25.0031 |
| 1/2 | 0.5000 | 12.7000 | 1 | 1.0000 | 25.4000 |

# Safety first!

Regardless of how enthusiastic you may be about getting on with the job at hand, take the time to ensure that your safety is not jeopardized. A moment's lack of attention can result in an accident, as can failure to observe certain simple safety precautions. The possibility of an accident will always exist, and the following points should not be considered a comprehensive list of all dangers. Rather, they are intended to make you aware of the risks and to encourage a safety conscious approach to all work you carry out on your vehicle.

## Essential DOs and DON'Ts

**DON'T** rely on a jack when working under the vehicle. Always use approved jackstands to support the weight of the vehicle and place them under the recommended lift or support points.

**DON'T** attempt to loosen extremely tight fasteners (i.e. wheel lug nuts) while the vehicle is on a jack - it may fall.

**DON'T** start the engine without first making sure that the transmission is in Neutral (or Park where applicable) and the parking brake is set.

**DON'T** remove the radiator cap from a hot cooling system - let it cool or cover it with a cloth and release the pressure gradually.

**DON'T** attempt to drain the engine oil until you are sure it has cooled to the point that it will not burn you.

**DON'T** touch any part of the engine or exhaust system until it has cooled sufficiently to avoid burns.

**DON'T** siphon toxic liquids such as gasoline, antifreeze and brake fluid by mouth, or allow them to remain on your skin.

**DON'T** inhale brake lining dust - it is potentially hazardous (see *Asbestos* below).

**DON'T** allow spilled oil or grease to remain on the floor - wipe it up before someone slips on it.

**DON'T** use loose fitting wrenches or other tools which may slip and cause injury.

**DON'T** push on wrenches when loosening or tightening nuts or bolts. Always try to pull the wrench toward you. If the situation calls for pushing the wrench away, push with an open hand to avoid scraped knuckles if the wrench should slip.

**DON'T** attempt to lift a heavy component alone - get someone to help you.

**DON'T** rush or take unsafe shortcuts to finish a job.

**DON'T** allow children or animals in or around the vehicle while you are working on it.

**DO** wear eye protection when using power tools such as a drill, sander, bench grinder, etc. and when working under a vehicle.

**DO** keep loose clothing and long hair well out of the way of moving parts.

**DO** make sure that any hoist used has a safe working load rating adequate for the job.

**DO** get someone to check on you periodically when working alone on a vehicle.

**DO** carry out work in a logical sequence and make sure that everything is correctly assembled and tightened.

**DO** keep chemicals and fluids tightly capped and out of the reach of children and pets.

**DO** remember that your vehicle's safety affects that of yourself and others. If in doubt on any point, get professional advice.

## Steering, suspension and brakes

These systems are essential to driving safety, so make sure you have a qualified shop or individual check your work. Also, compressed suspension springs can cause injury if released suddenly - be sure to use a spring compressor.

## Airbags

Airbags are explosive devices that can **CAUSE** injury if they deploy while you're working on the vehicle. Follow the manufacturer's instructions to disable the airbag whenever you're working in the vicinity of airbag components.

## Asbestos

Certain friction, insulating, sealing, and other products - such as brake linings, brake bands, clutch linings, torque converters, gaskets, etc. - may contain asbestos or other hazardous friction material. Extreme care must be taken to avoid inhalation of dust from such products, since it is hazardous to health. If in doubt, assume that they do contain asbestos.

## Fire

Remember at all times that gasoline is highly flammable. Never smoke or have any kind of open flame around when working on a vehicle. But the risk does not end there. A spark caused by an electrical short circuit, by two metal surfaces contacting each other, or even by static electricity built up in your body under certain conditions, can ignite gasoline vapors, which in a confined space are highly explosive. Do not, under any circumstances, use gasoline for cleaning parts. Use an approved safety solvent.

Always disconnect the battery ground (-) cable at the battery before working on any part of the fuel system or electrical system. Never risk spilling fuel on a hot engine or exhaust component. It is strongly recommended that a fire extinguisher suitable for use on fuel and electrical fires be kept handy in the garage or workshop at all times. Never try to extinguish a fuel or electrical fire with water.

## Fumes

Certain fumes are highly toxic and can quickly cause unconsciousness and even death if inhaled to any extent. Gasoline vapor falls into this category, as do the vapors from some cleaning solvents. Any draining or pouring of such volatile fluids should be done in a well ventilated area.

When using cleaning fluids and solvents, read the instructions on the container carefully. Never use materials from unmarked containers.

Never run the engine in an enclosed space, such as a garage. Exhaust fumes contain carbon monoxide, which is extremely poisonous. If you need to run the engine, always do so in the open air, or at least have the rear of the vehicle outside the work area.

## The battery

Never create a spark or allow a bare light bulb near a battery. They normally give off a certain amount of hydrogen gas, which is highly explosive.

Always disconnect the battery ground (-) cable at the battery before working on the fuel or electrical systems.

If possible, loosen the filler caps or cover when charging the battery from an external source (this does not apply to sealed or maintenance-free batteries). Do not charge at an excessive rate or the battery may burst.

Take care when adding water to a non maintenance-free battery and when carrying a battery. The electrolyte, even when diluted, is very corrosive and should not be allowed to contact clothing or skin.

Always wear eye protection when cleaning the battery to prevent the caustic deposits from entering your eyes.

## Household current

When using an electric power tool, inspection light, etc., which operates on household current, always make sure that the tool is correctly connected to its plug and that, where necessary, it is properly grounded. Do not use such items in damp conditions and, again, do not create a spark or apply excessive heat in the vicinity of fuel or fuel vapor.

## Secondary ignition system voltage

A severe electric shock can result from touching certain parts of the ignition system (such as the spark plug wires) when the engine is running or being cranked, particularly if components are damp or the insulation is defective. In the case of an electronic ignition system, the secondary system voltage is much higher and could prove fatal.

## Hydrofluoric acid

This extremely corrosive acid is formed when certain types of synthetic rubber, found in some O-rings, oil seals, fuel hoses, etc. are exposed to temperatures above 750-degrees F (400-degrees C). The rubber changes into a charred or sticky substance containing the acid. *Once formed, the acid remains dangerous for years. If it gets onto the skin, it may be necessary to amputate the limb concerned.*

When dealing with a vehicle which has suffered a fire, or with components salvaged from such a vehicle, wear protective gloves and discard them after use.

# Troubleshooting

## Contents

This section provides an easy reference guide to the more common problems which may occur during the operation of your vehicle. These problems and their possible causes are grouped under headings denoting various components or systems, such as Engine, Cooling system, etc. They also refer you to the chapter and/or section which deals with the problem.

Remember that successful troubleshooting is not a mysterious black art practiced only by professional mechanics. It is simply the result of the right knowledge combined with an intelligent, systematic approach to the problem. Always work by a process of elimination, starting with the simplest solution and working through to the most complex - and never overlook the obvious. Anyone can run the gas tank dry or leave the lights on overnight, so don't assume that you are exempt from such oversights.

Finally, always establish a clear idea of why a problem has occurred and take steps to ensure that it doesn't happen again. If the electrical system fails because of a poor connection, check the other connections in the system to make sure that they don't fail as well. If a particular fuse continues to blow, find out why - don't just replace one fuse after another. Remember, failure of a small component can often be indicative of potential failure or incorrect functioning of a more important component or system.

## Engine

### 1 Engine will not rotate when attempting to start

1 Battery terminal connections loose or corroded (Chapter 1).
2 Battery discharged or faulty (Chapter 1).
3 Automatic transaxle/Continuously Variable Transaxle (CVT) not completely engaged in Park (Chapter 7A) or clutch not completely depressed (Chapter 8).
4 Broken, loose or disconnected wiring in the starting circuit (Chapters 5 and 12).
5 Starter motor pinion jammed in flywheel ring gear (Chapter 5).
6 Starter solenoid faulty (Chapter 5).
7 Starter motor faulty (Chapter 5).
8 Ignition switch faulty (Chapter 12).
9 Starter pinion or flywheel teeth worn or broken (Chapter 5).

### 2 Engine rotates but will not start

1 Fuel tank empty.
2 Battery discharged (engine rotates slowly) (Chapter 5).
3 Battery terminal connections loose or corroded (Chapter 1).
4 Leaking fuel injector(s), faulty fuel pump, pressure regulator, etc. (Chapter 4).
5 Fuel not reaching fuel rail (Chapter 4).
6 Ignition components damp or damaged (Chapter 5).
7 Worn, faulty or incorrectly gapped spark plugs (Chapter 1).
8 Broken, loose or disconnected wires at the ignition coil or faulty coil (Chapter 5).

### 3 Engine hard to start when cold

1 Battery discharged or low (Chapter 1).
2 Fault in the fuel injection or engine control system (Chapters 4 and 6).
3 Injector(s) leaking (Chapter 4).

### 4 Engine hard to start when hot

1 Air filter clogged (Chapter 1).
2 Fuel not reaching the fuel injection system (Chapter 4).
3 Corroded battery connections (Chapter 1).

### 5 Starter motor noisy or excessively rough in engagement

1 Pinion or flywheel gear teeth worn or broken (Chapter 5).
2 Starter motor mounting bolts loose or missing (Chapter 5).

### 6 Engine starts but stops immediately

1 Loose or faulty electrical connections at coil or alternator (Chapter 5).
2 Insufficient fuel reaching the fuel injector(s) (Chapter 4).
3 Vacuum leak at the gasket between the intake manifold and throttle body (Chapter 4).

### 7 Oil puddle under engine

1 Oil pan gasket and/or oil pan drain bolt washer leaking (Chapter 2A).
2 Oil pressure sending unit leaking (Chapter 2A).
3 Valve cover leaking (Chapter 2A).
4 Engine oil seals leaking (Chapter 2A).

### 8 Engine lopes while idling or idles erratically

1 Vacuum leakage (Chapters 2A, 2B, 2C and 4).
2 Air filter clogged (Chapter 1).
3 Fuel pump not delivering sufficient fuel to the fuel injection system (Chapter 4).
4 Leaking head gasket (Chapter 2A).

5 Timing belt worn (Chapter 2A).
6 Camshaft lobes worn (Chapter 2A).

### 9 Engine misses at idle speed

1 Spark plugs worn or not gapped properly (Chapter 1).
2 Vacuum leaks (Chapter 1).
3 Uneven or low compression (Chapter 2A).
4 Fault in the fuel injection or engine control system (Chapters 4 and 6).

### 10 Engine misses throughout driving speed range

1 Fuel filter clogged and/or impurities in the fuel system (Chapter 1).
2 Low fuel pressure (Chapter 4).
3 Faulty or incorrectly gapped spark plugs (Chapter 1).
4 Faulty emission system components (Chapter 6).
5 Low or uneven cylinder compression pressures (Chapter 2A).
6 Weak or faulty ignition system (Chapter 5).
7 Vacuum leak in fuel injection system, intake manifold, air control valve or vacuum hoses (Chapter 4).

### 11 Engine stumbles on acceleration

1 Spark plugs fouled (Chapter 1).
2 Fuel injection system faulty (Chapter 4).
3 Fuel filter clogged (Chapters 1 and 4).
4 Intake manifold air leak (Chapters 2A, 2B, 2C and 4).

### 12 Engine surges while holding accelerator steady

1 Intake air leak (Chapter 4).
2 Fuel pump faulty (Chapter 4).

3    Loose fuel injector wire harness connectors (Chapter 4).
4    Defective PCM or information sensor (Chapter 6).

## 13  Engine stalls

1    Fuel filter clogged and/or water and impurities in the fuel system (Chapters 1 and 4).
2    Faulty emissions system components (Chapter 6).
3    Faulty or incorrectly gapped spark plugs (Chapter 1).
4    Vacuum leak in the fuel injection system, intake manifold or vacuum hoses (Chapters 2A, 2B, 2C and 4).
5    Valve clearances incorrectly set (Chapter 1).

## 14  Engine lacks power

1    Faulty or incorrectly gapped spark plugs (Chapter 1).
2    Fault in the fuel injection or engine control system (Chapters 4 and 6).
3    Faulty coils (Chapter 5).
4    Brakes binding (Chapter 9).
5    Automatic transaxle/Continuously Variable Transaxle (CVT) fluid level incorrect (Chapter 1).
6    Clutch slipping (Chapter 8).
7    Fuel filter clogged and/or impurities in the fuel system (Chapters 1 and 4).
8    Emission control system not functioning properly (Chapter 6).
9    Catalytic converter plugged (Chapter 6).
10   Low or uneven cylinder compression pressures (Chapter 2A).
11   Obstructed exhaust system (Chapter 4).

## 15  Engine backfires

1    Emission control system not functioning properly (Chapter 6).
2    Faulty secondary ignition system (cracked spark plug insulator, faulty coil(s), (Chapters 1 and 5).
3    Fuel injection system malfunctioning (Chapter 4).
4    Vacuum leak at fuel injector(s), intake manifold, air control valve or vacuum hoses (Chapters 2A, 2B, 2C and 4).
5    Valve clearances incorrectly set and/or valves sticking (Chapter 1).

## 16  Pinging or knocking engine sounds during acceleration or uphill

1    Incorrect grade of fuel.
2    Fuel injection system faulty (Chapter 4).
3    Improper or damaged spark plugs (Chapter 1).

4    Vacuum leak (Chapters 2A, 2B, 2C and 4).
5    Knock sensor malfunctioning (Chapter 6).

## 17  Engine runs with oil pressure light on

1    Low oil level (Chapter 1).
2    Short in wiring circuit (Chapter 12).
3    Faulty oil pressure sender (Chapter 2A).
4    Worn engine bearings and/or oil pump (Chapter 2A).

## 18  Engine continues to run after switching off

1    Idle speed too high (Chapter 6)
2    Excessive engine operating temperature (Chapter 3).

## Engine electrical system

## 19  Battery will not hold a charge

1    Alternator drivebelt defective or not adjusted properly (Chapter 1).
2    Battery electrolyte level low (Chapter 1).
3    Battery terminals loose or corroded (Chapter 1).
4    Alternator not charging properly (Chapter 5).
5    Loose, broken or faulty wiring in the charging circuit (Chapter 5).
6    Internally defective battery (Chapters 1 and 5).

## 20  Alternator light fails to go out

1    Faulty alternator or charging circuit (Chapter 5).
2    Alternator drivebelt defective or out of adjustment (Chapter 1).
3    Alternator voltage regulator inoperative (Chapter 5).

## 21  Alternator light fails to come on when key is turned on

1    Warning light bulb defective (Chapter 12).
2    Fault in the printed circuit, dash wiring or bulb holder (Chapter 12).

## Fuel system

## 22  Excessive fuel consumption

1    Dirty or clogged air filter element (Chapter 1).

2    Emissions system not functioning properly (Chapter 6).
3    Faulty fuel injection system (Chapter 4) .
4    Low tire pressure or incorrect tire size (Chapter 1).

## 23  Fuel leakage and/or fuel odor

1    Leaking fuel line (Chapters 1and 4).
2    Tank overfilled.
3    Evaporative canister defective (Chapters 1 and 6).
4    Faulty fuel injection system (Chapter 4).

## Cooling system

## 24  Overheating

1    Insufficient coolant in system (Chapter 1).
2    Radiator core blocked or grille restricted (Chapter 3).
3    Thermostat faulty (Chapter 3).
4    Cooling fan switch faulty (Chapter 3).
5    Electric coolant fan blades broken or cracked (Chapter 3).
6    Radiator cap not maintaining proper pressure (Chapter 3).

## 25  Overcooling

1    Faulty thermostat (Chapter 3).
2    Inaccurate temperature gauge sending unit (Chapter 3)

## 26  External coolant leakage

1    Deteriorated/damaged hoses; loose clamps (Chapters 1 and 3).
2    Water pump defective (Chapter 3).
3    Leakage from radiator core or coolant reservoir bottle (Chapter 3).
4    Engine drain or water jacket core plugs leaking (Chapter 2A).

## 27  Internal coolant leakage

1    Leaking cylinder head gasket (Chapter 2A).
2    Cracked cylinder bore or cylinder head (Chapter 2A).

## 28  Coolant loss

1    Too much coolant in system (Chapter 1).
2    Coolant boiling away because of overheating (Chapter 3).
3    Internal or external leakage (Chapter 3).
4    Faulty radiator cap (Chapter 3).

## 29 Poor coolant circulation

1 Inoperative water pump (Chapter 3).
2 Restriction in cooling system (Chapters 1 and 3).
3 Thermostat sticking (Chapter 3).

## Clutch

## 30 Pedal travels to floor - no pressure or very little resistance

1 No fluid in reservoir (Chapter 1)
2 Faulty clutch master cylinder, release cylinder or hydraulic line (Chapter 8).
3 Broken release bearing or fork (Chapter 8).

## 31 Unable to select gears

1 Faulty transaxle (Chapter 7A).
2 Faulty clutch disc (Chapter 8).
3 Release lever and bearing not assembled properly (Chapter 8).
4 Faulty pressure plate (Chapter 8).
5 Pressure plate-to-flywheel bolts loose (Chapter 8).

## 32 Clutch slips (engine speed increases with no increase in vehicle speed)

1 Clutch plate worn (Chapter 8).
2 Clutch plate is oil soaked by leaking rear main seal (Chapter 8).
3 Clutch plate not seated. It may take 30 or 40 normal starts for a new one to seat.
4 Warped pressure plate or flywheel (Chapter 8).
5 Weak diaphragm spring (Chapter 8).
6 Clutch plate overheated. Allow to cool.

## 33 Grabbing (chattering) as clutch is engaged

1 Oil on clutch plate lining, burned or glazed facings (Chapter 8).
2 Worn or loose engine or transaxle mounts (Chapters 2A, 2B, 7A and 7B).
3 Worn splines on clutch plate hub (Chapter 8).
4 Warped pressure plate or flywheel (Chapter 8).
5 Burned or smeared resin on flywheel or pressure plate (Chapter 8).

## 34 Transaxle rattling (clicking)

1 Release lever loose (Chapter 8).

2 Clutch plate damper spring failure (Chapter 8).
3 Low engine idle speed (Chapter 1).

## 35 Noise in clutch area

1 Fork shaft improperly installed (Chapter 8).
2 Faulty bearing (Chapter 8).

## 36 Clutch pedal stays on floor

1 Faulty clutch master or release cylinder (Chapter 8).
2 Broken release bearing or fork (Chapter 8).

## 37 High pedal effort

1 Piston binding in bore of clutch master or release cylinder (Chapter 8).
2 Pressure plate faulty (Chapter 8).

## Manual transaxle

## 38 Knocking noise at low speeds

1 Worn driveaxle constant velocity (CV) joints (Chapter 8).
2 Worn driveaxle bore in differential case (Chapter 7A).*

## 39 Noise most pronounced when turning

Differential gear noise (Chapter 7A).*

## 40 Clunk on acceleration or deceleration

1 Loose engine or transaxle mounts (Chapters 2A, 2B, 7A and 7B).
2 Worn differential pinion shaft in case.*
3 Worn driveaxle bore in differential case (Chapter 7A).*
4 Worn or damaged driveaxle inboard CV joints (Chapter 8).

## 41 Clicking noise in turns

Worn or damaged outboard CV joint (Chapter 8).

## 42 Vibration

1 Rough wheel bearing (Chapters 1 and 10).

2 Damaged driveaxle (Chapter 8).
3 Out of round tires (Chapter 1).
4 Tire out of balance (Chapters 1 and 10).
5 Worn CV joint (Chapter 8).

## 43 Noisy in neutral with engine running

1 Damaged input gear bearing (Chapter 7A).*
2 Damaged clutch release bearing (Chapter 8).

## 44 Noisy in one particular gear

1 Damaged or worn constant mesh gears (Chapter 7A).*
2 Damaged or worn synchronizers (Chapter 7A).*
3 Bent reverse fork (Chapter 7A).*
4 Damaged fourth speed gear or output gear (Chapter 7A).*
5 Worn or damaged reverse idler gear or idler bushing (Chapter 7A).*

## 45 Noisy in all gears

1 Insufficient lubricant (Chapter 7A).
2 Damaged or worn bearings (Chapter 7A).*
3 Worn or damaged input gear shaft and/or output gear shaft (Chapter 7A).*

## 46 Slips out of gear

1 Worn or improperly adjusted linkage (Chapter 7A).
2 Transaxle loose on engine (Chapter 7A).
3 Shift linkage does not work freely, binds (Chapter 7A).
4 Input gear bearing retainer broken or loose (Chapter 7A).*
5 Worn shift fork (Chapter 7A).*

## 47 Leaks lubricant

1 Driveaxle oil seals worn (Chapter 7A).
2 Excessive amount of lubricant in transaxle (Chapters 1 and A).
3 Loose or broken input gear shaft bearing retainer (Chapter 7A).*
4 Input gear bearing retainer O-ring and/or lip seal damaged (Chapter 7A).*

*Although the corrective action necessary to remedy the symptoms described is beyond the scope of the home mechanic, the above information should be helpful in isolating the cause of the condition so that the owner can communicate clearly with a professional mechanic.*

## 48 Locked in gear

1 Lock pin or interlock pin missing (Chapter 7A).*

*Although the corrective action necessary to remedy the symptoms described is beyond the scope of the home mechanic, the above information should be helpful in isolating the cause of the condition so that the owner can communicate clearly with a professional mechanic.*

## Automatic transaxle/Continuously Variable Transaxle (CVT)

### 49 Fluid leakage

1 Automatic transmission fluid is a deep red color. Fluid leaks should not be confused with engine oil, which can easily be blown onto the transaxle by air flow.
2 To pinpoint a leak, first remove all built-up dirt and grime from the transaxle housing with degreasing agents and/or steam cleaning. Then drive the vehicle at low speeds so air flow will not blow the leak far from its source. Raise the vehicle and determine where the leak is coming from. Common areas of leakage are:

a) *Pan (Chapters 1 and 7B)*
b) *Dipstick tube (Chapters 1 and 7B)*
c) *Transaxle oil lines (Chapter 7A or 7B)*
d) *Speed sensor (Chapter 7A or 7B)*

### 50 Transaxle fluid brown or has a burned smell

Transaxle fluid burned (Chapter 1).

### 51 General shift mechanism problems

1 Chapter 7A deals with checking and adjusting the shift linkage on automatic transaxles. Common problems which may be attributed to poorly adjusted linkage are:

a) *Engine starting in gears other than Park or Neutral.*
b) *Indicator on shifter pointing to a gear other than the one actually being used.*
c) *Vehicle moves when in Park.*

2 Refer to Chapter 7B for the shift linkage adjustment procedure.

### 52 Engine will start in gears other than Park or Neutral

Transmission range switch malfunctioning (Chapter 6).

### 53 Transaxle slips, shifts roughly, is noisy or has no drive in forward or reverse gears

There are many probable causes for the above problems, but the home mechanic should be concerned with only one possibility - fluid level. Before taking the vehicle to a repair shop, check the level and condition of the fluid as described in Chapter 1. Correct the fluid level as necessary or change the fluid and filter if needed. If the problem persists, have a professional diagnose the cause.

## Driveaxles

### 54 Knock or clunk when accelerating after coasting

Worn or damaged CV joint. Check for cut or damaged boots (Chapter 1). Repair as necessary (Chapter 8).

### 55 Clicking noise in turns

Worn or damaged outer CV joint. Check for cut or damaged boots (Chapter 1).

### 56 Shudder or vibration during acceleration

1 Worn or damaged CV joints (Chapter 8).
2 Sticking inboard CV joint assembly (Chapter 8).

### 57 Vibration at highway speeds

1 Out-of-balance front wheels and/or tires (Chapters 1 and 10).
2 Out-of-round front tires (Chapters 1 and 10).
3 Worn CV joint(s) (Chapter 8).

## Brakes

### 58 Vehicle pulls to one side during braking

1 Incorrect tire pressures (Chapter 1).
2 Front end out of alignment (have the front end aligned).
3 Front, or rear, tires not matched to one another.
4 Restricted brake lines or hoses (Chapter 9).
5 Malfunctioning drum brake or caliper assembly (Chapter 9).

6 Loose suspension parts (Chapter 10).
7 Excessive wear of brake shoe or pad material or disc/drum on one side.

### 59 Noise (squeal or grinding when the brakes are applied)

1 Disc brake pads worn out. Replace pads with new ones immediately (Chapter 9).
2 Drum brake shoes worn out. Replace the shoes immediately (Chapter 9).

### 60 Brake roughness or chatter (pedal pulsates)

1 Excessive brake disc lateral runout or brake drum out-of-round (Chapter 9).
2 Parallelism of disc not within specifications (Chapter 9).
3 Defective brake disc (Chapter 9).

### 61 Excessive brake pedal effort required to stop vehicle

1 Malfunctioning power brake booster (Chapter 9).
2 Partial system failure (Chapter 9).
3 Excessively worn pads or shoes (Chapter 9).
4 Piston in caliper or wheel cylinder stuck or sluggish (Chapter 9).
5 Brake pads or shoes contaminated with oil or grease (Chapter 9).
6 New pads or shoes installed and not yet seated. It will take a while for the new material to seat against the disc or drum.

### 62 Excessive brake pedal travel

1 Partial brake system failure (Chapter 9).
2 Insufficient fluid in master cylinder (Chapters 1 and 9).
3 Air trapped in system (Chapters 1 and 10).

### 63 Dragging brakes

1 Incorrect adjustment of brake light switch (Chapter 9).
2 Master cylinder pistons not returning correctly (Chapter 9).
3 Restricted brakes lines or hoses (Chapters 1 and 9).
4 Incorrect parking brake adjustment (Chapter 9).

### 64 Grabbing or uneven braking action

1 Malfunction of proportioning valve (Chapter 9).

2    Malfunction of power brake booster unit (Chapter 9).
3    Binding brake pedal mechanism (Chapter 9).

## 65    Brake pedal feels spongy when depressed

1    Air in hydraulic lines (Chapter 9).
2    Master cylinder mounting bolts loose (Chapter 9).
3    Master cylinder defective (Chapter 9).

## 66    Brake pedal travels to the floor with little resistance

1    Little or no fluid in the master cylinder reservoir caused by leaking caliper piston(s) (Chapter 9).
2    Loose, damaged or disconnected brake lines (Chapter 9).

## 67    Parking brake does not hold

Parking brake improperly adjusted (Chapter 9).

## Suspension and steering systems

## 68    Vehicle pulls to one side

1    Mismatched or uneven tires (Chapter 10).
2    Broken or sagging springs (Chapter 10).
3    Wheels out of alignment (Chapter 10).
4    Front brakes dragging (Chapter 9).

## 69    Abnormal or excessive tire wear

1    Wheels out of alignment (Chapter 10).
2    Sagging or broken springs (Chapter 10).
3    Tire out of balance (Chapter 10).
4    Worn shock absorber (Chapter 10).
5    Overloaded vehicle.
6    Tires not rotated regularly.

## 70    Wheel makes a thumping noise

1    Blister or bump on tire (Chapter 10).
2    Improper shock absorber/coil spring action (Chapter 10).

## 71    Shimmy, shake or vibration

1    Tire or wheel out-of-balance or out-of-round (Chapter 10).
2    Loose or worn wheel bearings (Chapter 10).
3    Worn tie-rod ends (Chapter 10).
4    Worn balljoints (Chapter 10).

5    Excessive wheel runout (Chapter 10).
6    Blister or bump on tire (Chapter 10).

## 72    Hard steering

1    Lack of lubrication at balljoints and tie-rod ends (Chapter 10).
2    Front wheels out of alignment (Chapter 10).
3    Low tire pressure(s) (Chapters 1 and 10 ).

## 73    Poor returnability of steering to center

1    Lack of lubrication at balljoints and tie-rod ends (Chapter 1).
2    Binding in balljoints (Chapter 10).
3    Binding in steering column (Chapter 10).
4    Front wheels out of alignment (Chapter 10).

## 74    Abnormal noise at the front end

1    Lack of lubrication at balljoints and tie-rod ends (Chapter 1).
2    Damaged shock absorber/coil spring mount (Chapter 10).
3    Worn control arm bushings or tie-rod ends (Chapter 10).
4    Loose stabilizer bar (Chapter 10).
5    Loose wheel nuts (Chapter 1).
6    Loose suspension bolts (Chapter 10)

## 75    Wander or poor steering stability

1    Mismatched or uneven tires (Chapter 10).
2    Lack of lubrication at balljoints and tie-rod ends (Chapter 1).
3    Worn shock absorber/coil spring assemblies (Chapter 10).
4    Loose stabilizer bar (Chapter 10).
5    Broken or sagging springs (Chapter 10).
6    Wheels out of alignment (Chapter 10).

## 76    Erratic steering when braking

1    Front hub bearings worn (Chapter 10).
2    Broken or sagging springs (Chapter 10).
3    Leaking wheel cylinder or caliper (Chapter 10).
4    Warped discs or drums (Chapter 10).

## 77    Excessive pitching and/or rolling around corners or during braking

1    Loose stabilizer bar (Chapter 10).
2    Worn shock absorbers or mounts (Chapter 10).
3    Broken or sagging springs (Chapter 10).
4    Overloaded vehicle.

## 78    Suspension bottoms

1    Overloaded vehicle.
2    Worn shock absorbers (Chapter 10).
3    Incorrect, broken or sagging springs (Chapter 10).

## 79    Cupped tires

1    Front wheel or rear wheel alignment (Chapter 10).
2    Worn shock absorbers (Chapter 10).
3    Wheel bearings worn (Chapter 10).
4    Excessive tire or wheel runout (Chapter 10).
5    Worn balljoints (Chapter 10).

## 80    Excessive tire wear on outside edge

1    Inflation pressures incorrect (Chapter 1).
2    Excessive speed in turns.
3    Front end alignment incorrect (excessive toe-in). Have professionally aligned.
4    Suspension arm bent or twisted (Chapter 10).

## 81    Excessive tire wear on inside edge

1    Inflation pressures incorrect (Chapter 1).
2    Front end alignment incorrect (toe-out). Have professionally aligned.
3    Loose or damaged steering or suspension components (Chapter 10).

## 82    Tire tread worn in one place

1    Tires out of balance.
2    Damaged or buckled wheel. Inspect and replace if necessary.
3    Defective tire (Chapter 1).

## 83    Excessive play or looseness in steering system

1    Front hub bearing(s) worn (Chapter 10).
2    Tie-rod end loose (Chapter 10).
3    Steering gear loose or worn (Chapter 10).
4    Worn or loose steering intermediate shaft (Chapter 10).

## 84    Rattling or clicking noise in steering gear

1    Steering gear loose (Chapter 10).
2    Steering gear defective (Chapter 10).

# Notes

# Chapter 1
# Tune-up and routine maintenance

## Contents

## Specifications

### Recommended lubricants and fluids

**Note:** *The fluids and lubricants listed here are those recommended by the manufacturer at the time this manual was written. Vehicle manufacturers occasionally upgrade their fluid and lubricant specifications, so check with your local auto parts store for the most current recommendations.*

| | |
|---|---|
| Engine oil | |
| Type | API "Certified for gasoline engines" |
| Viscosity | SAE 0W-20 |
| Automatic transaxle fluid | Honda ATF-DW1 |
| Automatic continuously variable transmission (CVT) fluid | HCF-2 fluid only |
| Manual transaxle fluid | Honda manual transmission fluid (MTF or equivalent) |
| Rear differential fluid (CR-V) | Honda Dual Pump System Fluid or equivalent |
| Brake fluid type | DOT 3 brake fluid |
| Clutch fluid type | DOT 3 brake fluid |
| Power steering system fluid | Honda power steering fluid |
| Fuel type | Unleaded gasoline, 86 octane or higher |
| Engine coolant | 50/50 mixture of Honda All Season Antifreeze/Coolant Type 2 or equivalent |

### Capacities*

| | |
|---|---|
| Engine oil (including oil filter) | |
| 1.8L engine | 3.9 quarts (3.7 liters) |
| 2.4L engine | 4.4 quarts (4.2 liters) |
| Automatic transaxle fluid (drain and refill)** | |
| Civic | 2.5 quarts (2.4 liters) |
| CR-V | |
| 2WD non-CVT | 2.3 quarts (2.2 liters) |
| AWD non-CVT models | 2.7 quarts (2.6 liters) |
| 2WD CVT | 3.9 quarts (3.7 liters) |
| AWD CVT models | 4.5 quarts (4.3 liters) |
| Manual transaxle (drain and refill) | |
| 1.8L models | 1.5 quarts (1.4 liters) |
| 2.4L models | 2.0 quarts (1.9 liters) |
| Rear differential (CR-V) | 1.3 quarts (1.2 liters) |
| Cooling system | |
| Civic | 5.8 quarts (5.5 liters) |
| CR-V | |
| 2014 and earlier models | 6.58 quarts (6.23 liters) |
| 2015 and later models | 6.65 quarts (6.3 liters) |

*All capacities approximate. Add as necessary to bring to appropriate level.*

** *If you want to flush the converter during a fluid change, purchase twice the amount of fluid listed here.*

## Valve clearances (cold engine)

1.8L SOHC models
  Intake valve ............................................................................. 0.007 to 0.008 inch (0.18 to 0.22 mm)
  Exhaust valve .......................................................................... 0.009 to 0.010 inch (0.23 to 0.27 mm)
2.4L DOHC models
  Intake valve ............................................................................. 0.008 to 0.010 inch (0.21 to 0.25 mm)
  Exhaust valve .......................................................................... 0.010 to 0.011 inch (0.25 to 0.29 mm)

## Ignition system

Spark plug type and gap
  Type
    1.8L engines ....................................................................... NGK: DILZKR7B11GS
    2014 and earlier 2.4L engines ........................................... NGK: ILZKR7B-11S
    2015 and later 2.4L engines .............................................. DENSO: DXE22HQR-D11S
  Gap ......................................................................................... 0.039 to 0.043 inch (1.0 to 1.1 mm)
Engine firing order ........................................................................ 1-3-4-2

## Cooling system

Thermostat rating
  Starts to open........................................................................... 169 to 176 degrees F (76 to 80 degrees C)
  Fully open................................................................................. 194 degrees F (90 degrees C)

## Brakes

Disc brake pad lining thickness (minimum) ............................. 1/8 inch (3 mm)
Drum brake shoe lining thickness (minimum)........................... 1/16 inch (1.5 mm)
Parking brake adjustment............................................................ See Chapter 9

## Torque specifications

| | Ft-lbs (unless otherwise indicated) | Nm |
|---|---|---|

**Note:** *One foot-pound (ft-lb) of torque is equivalent to 12 inch-pounds (in-lbs) of torque. Torque values below approximately 15 ft-lbs are expressed in inch-pounds, since most foot-pound torque wrenches are not accurate at these smaller values.*

| | Ft-lbs (unless otherwise indicated) | Nm |
|---|---|---|
| Engine oil drain plug | | |
|   1.8L and 2014 and earlier 2.4L engines | 29 | 39 |
|   2015 and later 2.4L engines | 30 | 40 |
| Automatic transaxle drain plug | 36 | 49 |
| Automatic Continuously Variable Transmission (CVT) | | |
|   Check/fill plug | 32 | 44 |
|   Drain plug | 36 | 49 |
| Cylinder block drain plug | 61 | 83 |
| Drivebelt tensioner mounting bolts | | |
|   1.8L engines | | |
|     8 mm bolt | 17 | 23 |
|     10 mm bolt | 40 | 54 |
|   2.4L engines | | |
|     2014 and earlier models | 16 | 22 |
|     2015 and later models | | |
|       8 mm bolt | 18 | 24 |
|     10 mm (reverse Allen) bolt | 41 | 55 |
| Drivebelt hydraulic damper to tensioner body mounting bolt | 24 | 32 |
| Idler pulley (2014 and earlier 2.4L engines) | 33 | 45 |
| Manual transaxle | | |
|   2015 and earlier models | | |
|     Check/fill plug | 32 | 44 |
|     Drain plug | 29 | 39 |
|   2016 models | | |
|     Check/fill plug | 108 in-lbs | 12 |
|     Drain plug | 32 | 44 |
| Rear differential fill and drain plugs (CR-V models) | 35 | 47 |
| Spark plugs | 156 in-lbs | 17.5 |
| Wheel lug nuts | 80 | 108 |

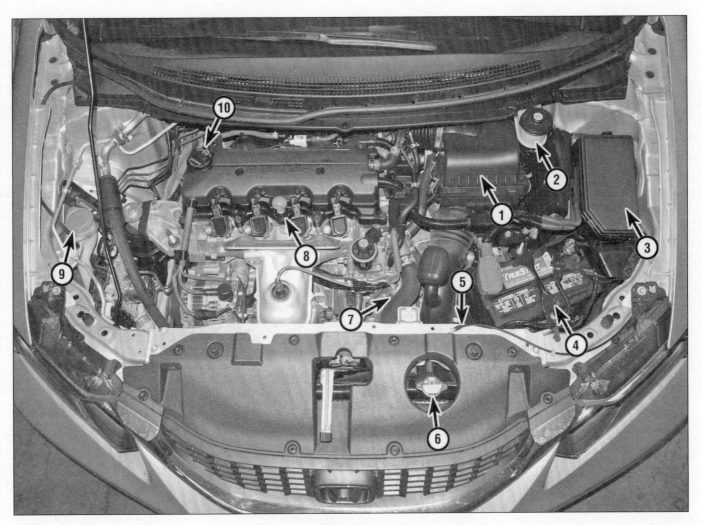

**1.8L SOHC engine compartment layout**

| | | | | |
|---|---|---|---|---|
| 1 | Air filter housing | 5 | Coolant reservoir | 8  Engine oil dipstick |
| 2 | Brake fluid reservoir | 6 | Radiator cap | 9  Windshield washer fluid reservoir |
| 3 | Underhood fuse/relay block | 7 | Upper radiator hose | 10  Engine oil filler cap |
| 4 | Battery | | | |

**Under-vehicle engine compartment layout - 1.8L SOHC shown, other models similar**

| | | | |
|---|---|---|---|
| 1 | Steering gear (electric assist) | 4 | Engine oil pan drain plug |
| 2 | Brake disc | 5 | Transaxle drain plug (CVT) |
| 3 | Inner driveaxle boot | | |

| | |
|---|---|
| 6 | Engine oil filter |
| 7 | Front brake caliper and brake pads |

**Typical rear underside components**

| | | | | |
|---|---|---|---|---|
| 1 | Muffler | 3 | Brake drum | 5  Fuel tank |
| 2 | Coil spring | 4 | Shock absorber | |

# 1 Maintenance schedule

The maintenance intervals in this manual are provided with the assumption that you, not the dealer, will be doing the work. These are the minimum maintenance intervals recommended by the factory for vehicles that are driven daily. If you wish to keep your vehicle in peak condition at all times, you may wish to perform some of these procedures even more often. Because frequent maintenance enhances the efficiency, performance and resale value of your car, we encourage you to do so. If you drive in dusty areas, tow a trailer, idle or drive at low speeds for extended periods or drive for short distances (less than four miles) in below freezing temperatures, shorter intervals are also recommended.

When your vehicle is new, follow the maintenance schedule to the letter, record the maintenance performed in your owner's manual and keep all receipts to protect the new vehicle warranty. In many cases, the initial maintenance check is done at no cost to the owner.

## Every 250 miles (400 km) or weekly, whichever comes first

Check the engine oil level (Section 4)
Check the engine coolant level (Section 4)
Check the windshield washer fluid level (Section 4)
Check the brake fluid level (Section 4)
Check the power steering fluid level (Section 4)
Check the automatic transaxle fluid level (Section 4)
Check the tires and tire pressures (Section 5)
Check the operation of all lights
Check the horn operation

## Every 3000 miles (4800 km) or 3 months, whichever comes first

*All items listed above plus:*
Change the engine oil and oil filter (Section 6)

## Every 7500 miles (12,000 km) or 6 months, whichever comes first

*All items listed above plus:*
Inspect (and replace, if necessary) the windshield wiper blades (Section 7)
Check and service the battery (Section 8)
Check the cooling system (Section 9)
Rotate the tires (Section 10)
Check the seat belts (Section 11)
Inspect the brake system (Section 12)

## Every 15,000 miles (24,000 km) or 12 months, whichever comes first

*All items listed above plus:*
Check the manual transaxle lubricant (Section 4)
Check the rear differential lubricant (4WD CR-V models) (Section 4)

Inspect the suspension, steering components and drive axle boots (Section 13)
Inspect and replace, if necessary, all underhood hoses (Section 14)
Replace the air filter (Section 15)*
Replace the interior ventilation filter (Section 16)
Inspect the fuel system (Section 17)
Check the exhaust system (Section 18)

## Every 30,000 (48,000 km) miles or 24 months, whichever comes first

*All items listed above plus:*
Check and adjust, if necessary, the engine drivebelts (Section 19)
Replace the brake fluid (Section 20)
Check (and replace, if necessary) the spark plugs (conventional, non-platinum or iridium type) (Section 24)

## Every 60,000 miles (96,000 km) or 36 months

Service the cooling system (drain, flush and refill) (Section 21)

## Every 90,000 miles (145,000 km) or 60 months

Change the rear differential lubricant (Section 22)

## Every 110,000 miles (177,000 km) or 36 months, whichever comes first

Valve clearance check and adjustment (only if noisy) (see Section 23)
Replace the spark plugs (platinum or iridium type) (Section 24)
Replace the timing belt, and inspect the auto tensioner and water pump (see Chapter 2A and Chapter 3)

## Every 120,000 miles (193,000 km) or 72 months, whichever comes first

Change the automatic transaxle fluid (Section 25)**
Change the manual transaxle lubricant (Section 27)***

* This item is affected by "severe" operating conditions as described below. If your vehicle is operated under "severe" conditions, perform all maintenance indicated with a * at 5000 mile/6 month intervals.

Severe conditions are indicated if you mainly operate your vehicle under one or more of the following conditions :

a) Operating in dusty areas

b) Towing a trailer
c) Idling for extended periods and/or low speed operation
d) Operating when outside temperatures remain below freezing and when most trips are less than five miles

** If operated under one or more of the following conditions, change the automatic transaxle fluid every 30,000 miles.
*** If operated under one or more of the following conditions, change the manual transaxle fluid every 60,000 miles.

a) In heavy city traffic where the outside temperature regularly reaches 90-degrees F (32-degrees C) or higher
b) In hilly or mountainous terrain

## 2  Introduction

1    This Chapter is designed to help the home mechanic maintain the Civic and CR-V with the goals of maximum performance, economy, safety and reliability in mind.
2    Included is a master maintenance schedule, followed by procedures dealing specifically with each item on the schedule. Visual checks, adjustments, component replacement and other helpful items are included. Refer to the accompanying illustrations of the engine compartment for the locations of various components.
3    Servicing the vehicle, in accordance with the mileage/time maintenance schedule and the step-by-step procedures, will result in a planned maintenance program that should produce a long and reliable service life. Keep in mind that it is a comprehensive plan, so maintaining some items but not others at the specified intervals will not produce the same results.
4    As you service the vehicle, you will discover that many of the procedures can - and should - be grouped together because of the nature of the particular procedure you're performing or because of the close proximity of two otherwise unrelated components to one another.
5    For example, if the vehicle is raised for chassis lubrication, you should inspect the exhaust, suspension, steering and fuel systems while you're under the vehicle. When you're rotating the tires, it makes good sense to check the brakes since the wheels are already removed. Finally, let's suppose you have to borrow or rent a torque wrench. Even if you only need it to tighten the spark plugs, you might as well check the torque of as many critical fasteners as time allows.
6    The first step in this maintenance program is to prepare yourself before the actual work begins. Read through all the procedures you're planning to do, then gather up all the parts and tools needed. If it looks like you might run into problems during a particular job, seek advice from a mechanic or an experienced do-it-yourselfer.

### Owner's Manual and VECI label information

7    Your vehicle owner's manual was written for your year and model and contains very specific information on component locations, specifications, fuse ratings, part numbers, etc. The owner's manual is an important resource for the do-it-yourselfer to have; if one was not supplied with your vehicle, it can generally be ordered from a dealer parts department.
8    Among other important information, the Vehicle Emissions Control Information (VECI) label contains specifications and procedures for applicable tune-up adjustments and, in some instances, spark plugs. The information on this label is the exact maintenance data recommended by the manufacturer. This data often varies by intended operating altitude, local emissions regulations, month of manufacture, etc.
9    This Chapter contains procedural details, safety information and more ambitious maintenance intervals than you might find in manufacturer's literature. However, you may also find procedures or specifications in your owner's manual or VECI label that differ with what's printed here. In these cases, the owner's manual or VECI label can be considered correct, since it is specific to your particular vehicle.

## 3  Tune-up general information

1    The term tune-up is used in this manual to represent a combination of individual operations rather than one specific procedure.
2    If, from the time the vehicle is new, the routine maintenance schedule is followed closely and frequent checks are made of fluid levels and high wear items, as suggested throughout this manual, the engine will be kept in relatively good running condition and the need for additional work will be minimized.
3    More likely than not, however, there will be times when the engine is running poorly due to lack of regular maintenance. This is even more likely if a used vehicle, which has not received regular and frequent maintenance checks, is purchased. In such cases, an engine tune-up will be needed outside of the regular routine maintenance intervals.
4    The first step in any tune-up or diagnostic procedure to help correct a poor running engine is a cylinder compression check. A compression check (see Chapter 2C) will help determine the condition of internal engine components and should be used as a guide for tune-up and repair procedures. If, for instance, a compression check indicates serious internal engine wear, a conventional tune-up will not improve the performance of the engine and would be a waste of time and money. Because of its importance, the compression check should be done by someone with the right equipment and the knowledge to use it properly.
5    The following procedures are those most often needed to bring a generally poor running engine back into a proper state of tune.

### Minor tune-up

Check all engine related fluids (Section 4)
Clean, inspect and test the battery (Section 8)
Check the cooling system (Section 9)
Check all underhood hoses (Section 14)
Check the air filter (Section 15)
Check and adjust the drivebelts (Section 19)

### Major tune-up

All items listed under minor tune-up, plus . . .
Replace the air filter (Section 15)
Check the fuel system (Section 17)
Replace the spark plugs (Section 24)

4.2a Engine oil dipstick location -
1.8L engine

4.2b Engine oil dipstick location -
2.4L engine

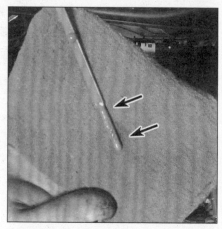

4.4a On 1.8L engines, the oil level should
be in the crosshatched range on the
dipstick (preferably near the top of
the range)

## 4   Fluid level checks (every 250 miles [400 km] or weekly)

1   Fluids are an essential part of the lubrication, cooling, brake, clutch and other systems. Because these fluids gradually become depleted and/or contaminated during normal operation of the vehicle, they must be periodically replenished. See *Recommended lubricants and fluids and Capacities* in this Chapter's Specifications before adding fluid to any of the following components.
**Note:** *The vehicle must be on level ground before fluid levels can be checked.*

### Engine oil

2   The engine oil level is checked with a dipstick located on top of the valve cover or a tube at the front side of the engine (see illustrations). The dipstick extends through the cyl-

inder head or through a metal tube from which it protrudes down into the engine oil pan.
3   The oil level should be checked before the vehicle has been driven, or about five minutes after the engine has been shut off. If the oil is checked immediately after driving the vehicle, some of the oil will remain in the upper engine components, producing an inaccurate reading on the dipstick.
4   Pull the dipstick from the valve cover or tube and wipe all the oil from the end with a clean rag or paper towel. Insert the clean dipstick all the way back into its metal tube and pull it all out again. Observe the oil at the end of the dipstick (see illustrations).
5   It takes about one quart of oil to raise the level from the lower mark to the upper mark on the dipstick. Do not allow the level to drop below the lower mark or oil starvation may occur and cause engine damage. Conversely, overfilling the engine (adding oil above the

upper mark) may cause oil fouled spark plugs, oil leaks, oil seal failures, or foaming of the oil (which will also result in inadequate lubrication and engine damage.
6   Remove the filler cap from the valve cover to add oil (see illustrations). Use a funnel to prevent spills. After adding the oil, install the filler cap hand tight. Start the engine and run it for about 30 seconds. Stop the engine and check the oil level again after it has had sufficient time to drain from the upper block and cylinder head galleys.
7   Checking the oil level is an important preventive maintenance step. A continually dropping oil level indicates oil leakage through damaged seals, from loose connections, or past worn rings or valve guides. If the oil looks milky in color or has water droplets in it, a cylinder head gasket may be blown or the oil cooler could be leaking. The engine should be checked immediately. The condition of the oil

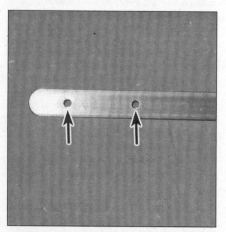

4.4b On 2.4L engines, the oil level should
be between the two holes (preferably near
the upper hole)

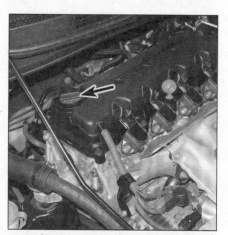

4.6a The oil filler cap is located on the
valve cover - always make sure the
area around the opening is clean before
unscrewing the cap to prevent dirt from
contaminating the engine (1.8L SOHC
engine shown)

4.6b 2.4L engine oil filler cap location

**4.9a On Civic models, the coolant reservoir is located behind the radiator on the left side (on CR-V models it's on the right side, behind the headlight)**

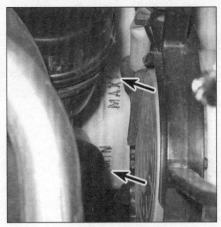

**4.9b Coolant reservoir MIN and MAX marks**

**4.14 Fluid for the windshield washer system is stored in this plastic reservoir (Civic model shown)**

should also be checked. Each time you check the oil level, slide your thumb and index finger up the dipstick before wiping off the oil. If you see small dirt or metal particles clinging to the dipstick, the oil should be changed (see Section 6).

### Engine coolant

**Warning:** *Do not allow antifreeze to come in contact with your skin or painted surfaces of the vehicle. Flush contaminated areas immediately with plenty of water. Don't store new coolant or leave old coolant lying around where it's accessible to children or pets - they're attracted by its sweet smell. Ingestion of even a small amount of coolant can be fatal! Wipe up garage floor and drip pan spills immediately. Keep antifreeze containers covered and repair cooling system leaks as soon as they're noticed.*

8    All vehicles covered by this manual are equipped with a pressurized coolant recovery system. A coolant reservoir is connected by a hose to the base of the radiator filler neck. If the coolant overheats, it can escape through the spring loaded filler cap, then through the connecting hose into the reservoir. As the engine cools, the coolant is automatically drawn back into the cooling system to maintain the correct level.

9    The coolant level in the reservoir should be checked regularly. It must be between the MAX and MIN lines on the tank. The level will vary with the temperature of the engine. When the engine is cold, the coolant level should be at or slightly above the MIN mark on the tank. Once the engine has warmed up, the level should be at or near the MAX mark. If it isn't, allow the fluid in the tank to cool, then remove the cap from the reservoir (see illustrations) and add coolant to bring the level up to the MAX line. Use only the recommended coolant and water in the mixture ratio listed in this Chapter's Specifications. Do not use supplemental inhibitors or additives. If only a small amount of coolant is required to bring the sys-

tem up to the proper level, water can be used. However, repeated additions of water will dilute the recommended antifreeze and water solution. In order to maintain the proper ratio of antifreeze and water, it is advisable to top up the coolant level with the correct mixture.

**Warning:** *Do not remove the radiator cap to check the coolant level when the engine is warm!*

10    If the coolant level drops within a short time after replenishment, there may be a leak in the system. Inspect the radiator, hoses, engine coolant filler cap, drain plugs and water pump. If no leak is evident, have the radiator cap pressure tested.

**Warning:** *Never remove the radiator cap or the coolant reservoir cap when the engine is running or has just been shut down, because the cooling system is hot. Escaping steam and scalding liquid could cause serious injury.*

11    If it is necessary to open the radiator cap, wait until the system has cooled completely, then wrap a thick cloth around the cap and turn it to the first stop. If any steam escapes, or you hear any hissing, wait until the system has cooled further, then remove the cap.

12    When checking the coolant level, always note its condition. It should be relatively clear. If it is brown or rust colored, the system should be drained, flushed and refilled. Even if the coolant appears to be normal, the corrosion inhibitors wear out with use, so it must be replaced at the specified intervals.

13    Do not allow antifreeze to come in contact with your skin or painted surfaces of the vehicle. Flush contacted areas immediately with plenty of water.

### Windshield washer fluid

14    Fluid for the windshield washer system is stored in a plastic reservoir which is located in various locations depending on model and year (see illustration). In milder climates, plain water can be used to top up the reservoir, but the reservoir should be kept no more than 2/3 full to allow for expansion should the water

**4.16 The brake fluid level should be kept at the MAX mark on the translucent plastic reservoir**

freeze. In colder climates, the use of a specially designed windshield washer fluid, available at your dealer and any auto parts store, will help lower the freezing point of the fluid. Mix the solution with water in accordance with the manufacturer's directions on the container. Do not use regular antifreeze. It will damage the vehicle's paint.

### Brake and clutch fluid

15    The brake master cylinder is located on the driver's side of the engine compartment firewall. The clutch master cylinder fluid reservoir is located right next to it on the firewall, behind the left shock tower. They both use the same type of fluid.

16    The level should be maintained between the MIN and MAX marks on the reservoir (see illustration).

17    If additional fluid is necessary to bring the level up, use a rag to clean all dirt off the top of the reservoir. If any foreign matter enters the master cylinder when the cap is removed, blockage in the brake or clutch release system lines can occur. Also, make sure all painted

**4.25a The automatic transaxle dipstick is located on the left side**

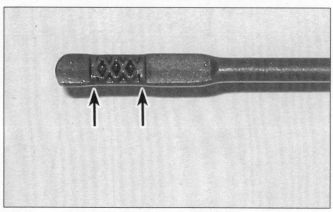

**4.25b The automatic transaxle fluid level should be in the cross-hatched area on the dipstick**

**4.31 Location of the CVT transaxle fluid check plug**

surfaces around the master cylinder are covered, since brake fluid will ruin paint. Carefully pour new, clean brake fluid into the master cylinder. Be careful not to spill the fluid on painted surfaces. Be sure the specified fluid is used; mixing different types of brake fluid can cause damage to the system. See Recommended lubricants and fluids at the beginning of this Chapter or your owner's manual.

18   At this time the fluid and the master cylinder can be inspected for contamination. If deposits, dirt particles or water droplets are seen in the fluid, the system should be drained and refilled with fresh fluid (see Section 20).

19   Reinstall the master cylinder cap.

20   The brake fluid in the master cylinder will drop slightly as the brake shoes or pads at each wheel wear down during normal operation. If the master cylinder requires repeated replenishing to keep the level up, it's an indication of leaks in the brake system, which should be corrected immediately. Check all brake lines and connections, along with the wheel cylinders, if equipped, and booster (see Chapter 9 for more information). As the clutch wears, the fluid level in the clutch master cylinder reservoir will rise. Unless there is a leak in either system, fluid additions shouldn't be necessary.

21   If you discover that the reservoir is empty or nearly empty, the brake (or clutch) system should be filled, bled (see Chapter 9) and checked for leaks.

## Automatic transaxle fluid

22   The level of the automatic transaxle fluid should be carefully maintained. Low fluid level can lead to slipping or loss of drive, while overfilling can cause foaming, loss of fluid and transaxle damage.

23   The transaxle fluid level should only be checked when the transaxle is hot (at its normal operating temperature). If the vehicle has just been driven over 10 miles (15 miles in a frigid climate), and the fluid temperature is 160 to 175-degrees F, the transaxle is hot.

**Caution:** *If the vehicle has just been driven for a long time at high speed or in city traffic in hot weather, or if it has been pulling a trailer, an accurate fluid level reading cannot be obtained. Allow the fluid to cool down for about 30 minutes.*

24   If the vehicle has not just been driven, park the vehicle on level ground, set the parking brake and start the engine. While the engine is idling, depress the brake pedal and move the selector lever through all the gear ranges, beginning and ending in Park.

## Automatic transaxle (non-CVT models)

25   With the engine still idling, remove the dipstick from its tube. Check the level of the fluid on the dipstick and note its condition (see illustrations).

26   Wipe the fluid from the dipstick with a clean rag and reinsert it back into the filler tube until the cap seats.

27   Pull the dipstick out again and note the fluid level. The fluid level should be in the operating temperature range (between the upper and lower mark). If the level is at the low side of either range, add the specified automatic transmission fluid through the dipstick tube with a funnel.

28   Add just enough of the recommended fluid to fill the transaxle to the proper level. It takes about one pint to raise the level from the low mark to the high mark when the fluid is hot, so add the fluid a little at a time and keep checking the level until it is correct.

29   The condition of the fluid should also be checked along with the level. If the fluid at the end of the dipstick is black or a dark reddish brown color, or if it emits a burned smell, the fluid should be changed (see Section 25). If you are in doubt about the condition of the fluid, purchase some new fluid and compare the two for color and smell.

## Automatic Continuously Variable Transmission (CVT) models

**Note:** *It isn't necessary to check this fluid weekly - every 15,000 miles (24,000 km) or 12 months will be adequate (unless a fluid leak is noticed).*

30   A dipstick is available on some 2.4L engine models. If the CVT is equipped with a dipstick, see Steps 25 through 29.

31   On other models, the CVT transaxle does not have a dipstick. To check the fluid level, raise the vehicle and support it securely on jackstands. On the front side of the transaxle housing, remove the fluid check plug (see illustration). If the fluid level is correct, it should just drip from the hole.

4.32a A hose and fluid pump can be used to add fluid through the check hole . . .

4.32b . . . or fluid can be added to the fill hole at the top of the transaxle case (battery removed for clarity)

**Note:** *Both ends of the vehicle should be raised and supported on jackstands for an accurate check.*

32  If the transaxle needs more fluid (if the fluid doesn't trickle out of the hole), you can either use a pump to add more through the check hole, or remove the fill plug at the top of the transaxle and add the fluid there (see illustrations). Stop filling the transaxle when the lubricant begins to run out the hole. Allow the fluid to flow from the hole until it just drips out.

33  Install the plug and tighten it to the torque listed in this Chapter's Specifications. Drive the vehicle a short distance, then check for leaks.

34  The condition of the fluid should also be checked along with the level. If the fluid is black or a dark reddish brown color, or if it emits a burned smell, the fluid should be changed (see Section 25). If you are in doubt about the condition of the fluid, purchase some new fluid and compare the two for color and smell.

### Manual transaxle lubricant

**Note:** *It isn't necessary to check this lubricant weekly; every 15,000 miles (24,000 km) or 12 months will be adequate.*

35  The manual transaxle does not have a dipstick. To check the fluid level, raise the vehicle and support it securely on jackstands. On the left end of the transaxle housing, remove the check/fill plug. If the lubricant level is correct, it should be up to the lower edge of the hole.

36  If the transaxle needs more lubricant (if the level is not up to the hole), use a syringe or a gear oil pump to add more through the hole. Stop filling the transaxle when the lubricant begins to run out the hole.

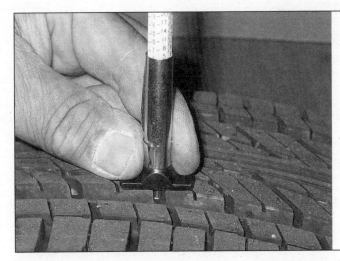

5.2 A tire tread depth indicator should be used to monitor tire wear - they are available at auto parts stores and service stations and cost very little

37  Install the plug and tighten it to the torque listed in this Chapter's Specifications. Drive the vehicle a short distance, then check for leaks.

### Rear differential lubricant (CR-V)

**Note:** *It isn't necessary to check this lubricant weekly; every 15,000 miles (24,000 km) or 12 months will be adequate.*

38  To check the fluid level, raise the vehicle and support it securely on jackstands. On the axle housing, remove the check/fill plug. If the lubricant level is correct, it should be up to the lower edge of the hole.

39  If the differential needs more lubricant (if the level is not up to the hole), use a syringe or a gear oil pump to add more. Stop filling the differential when the lubricant begins to run out the hole.

40  Install the plug and tighten it securely.

Drive the vehicle a short distance, then check for leaks.

### 5   Tire and tire pressure checks (every 250 miles [400 km] or weekly)

1    Periodic inspection of the tires may spare you from the inconvenience of being stranded with a flat tire. It can also provide you with vital information regarding possible problems in the steering and suspension systems before major damage occurs.

2    Tires are equipped with 1/2-inch wide bands that will appear when tread depth reaches 1/16-inch, at which point they can be considered worn out. Tread wear can be monitored with a simple, inexpensive device known as a tread depth indicator (see illustration).

**UNDERINFLATION**

**CUPPING**

Cupping may be caused by:

• Underinflation and/or mechanical irregularities such as out-of-balance condition of wheel and/or tire, and bent or damaged wheel.

• Loose or worn steering tie-rod or steering idler arm.

• Loose, damaged or worn front suspension parts.

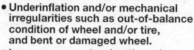

**OVERINFLATION**

**FEATHERING DUE TO MISALIGNMENT**

**INCORRECT TOE-IN OR EXTREME CAMBER**

**5.3 This chart will help you determine the condition of your tires, the probable cause(s) of abnormal wear and the corrective action necessary**

3    Note any abnormal tread wear (see illustration). Tread pattern irregularities such as cupping, flat spots and more wear on one side than the other are indications of front end alignment and/or balance problems. If any of these conditions are noted, take the vehicle to a tire shop or service station to correct the problem.

4    Look closely for cuts, punctures and embedded nails or tacks. Sometimes a tire will hold its air pressure for a short time or leak down very slowly even after a nail has embedded itself into the tread. If a slow leak persists, check the valve core to make sure it is tight (see illustration). Examine the tread for an object that may have embedded itself into

the tire or for a plug that may have begun to leak (radial tire punctures are repaired with a plug that is installed in a puncture). If a puncture is suspected, it can be easily verified by spraying a solution of soapy water onto the puncture area (see illustration). The soapy solution will bubble if there is a leak. Unless the puncture is inordinately large, a tire shop

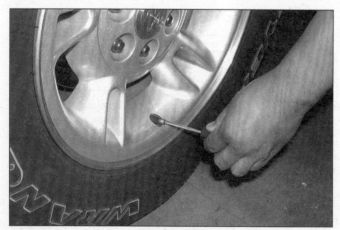

**5.4a If a tire loses air on a steady basis, check the valve core first to make sure it's snug (special inexpensive wrenches are commonly available at auto parts stores)**

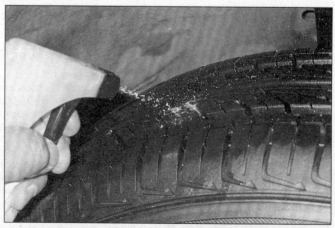

**5.4b If the valve core is tight, raise the corner of the vehicle with the low tire and spray a soapy water solution onto the tread as the tire is turned slowly - slow leaks will cause small bubbles to appear**

or gas station can usually repair the punctured tire.

5   Carefully inspect the inner side of each tire for evidence of brake fluid leakage. If you see any, inspect the brakes immediately.

6   Correct tire air pressure adds miles to the lifespan of the tires, improves mileage and enhances overall ride quality. Tire pressure cannot be accurately estimated by looking at a tire, particularly if it is a radial. A tire pressure gauge is therefore essential. Keep an accurate gauge in the glove box. The pressure gauges fitted to the nozzles of air hoses at gas stations are often inaccurate.

7   Always check tire pressure when the tires are cold. "Cold," in this case, means the vehicle has not been driven over a mile in the three hours preceding a tire pressure check. A pressure rise of four to eight pounds is not uncommon once the tires are warm.

8   Unscrew the valve cap protruding from the wheel or hubcap and push the gauge firmly onto the valve (see illustration). Note the reading on the gauge and compare this figure to the recommended tire pressure shown on the tire placard on the left door jamb or in your owner's manual. Be sure to reinstall the valve cap to keep dirt and moisture out of the valve stem mechanism. Check all four tires and, if necessary, add enough air to bring them up to the recommended pressure levels.

9   Don't forget to keep the spare tire inflated to the specified pressure (consult your owner's manual). Note that the air pressure specified for the compact spare is significantly higher than the pressure of the regular tires.

## 6   Engine oil and oil filter change (every 3000 miles [4800 km] or 3 months)

1   Frequent oil changes are the best preventive maintenance the home mechanic can give the engine, because aging oil becomes diluted and contaminated, which leads to premature engine wear.

2   Make sure you have all the necessary tools before you begin this procedure (see illustration). You should also have plenty of rags or newspapers handy for mopping up any spills.

3   Access to the underside of the vehicle is greatly improved if the vehicle can be lifted on a hoist, driven onto ramps or supported by jackstands.
**Warning:** *Do not work under a vehicle which is supported only by a hydraulic or scissors-type jack.*

4   If this is your first oil change, get under the vehicle and familiarize yourself with the locations of the oil drain plug and the oil filter. The engine and exhaust components will be warm during the actual work, so try to anticipate any potential problems before the engine and accessories are hot.

5   Park the vehicle on a level spot. Start the engine and allow it to reach its normal operating temperature. Warm oil and sludge will flow

**5.8 To extend the life of your tires, check the air pressure at least once a week with an accurate gauge (don't forget the spare!)**

out more easily. Turn off the engine when it's warmed up. Remove the filler cap from the valve cover.

6   Raise the vehicle and support it securely on jackstands.
**Warning:** *Never get beneath the vehicle when it is supported only by a jack. The jack provided with your vehicle is designed solely for raising the vehicle to remove and replace the wheels. Always use jackstands to support the vehicle when it becomes necessary to place your body underneath the vehicle.*

7   Remove center portion of the under-vehicle splash shield (see illustration).

8   Being careful not to touch the hot exhaust components, place the drain pan under the drain plug in the bottom of the pan and remove the plug (see illustration). You may want to wear gloves while unscrewing the plug the final few turns if the engine is hot.

9   Allow the old oil to drain into the pan. It may be necessary to move the pan farther under the engine as the oil flow slows to a trickle. Inspect the old oil for the presence of

**6.7 Splash shield fastener locations**

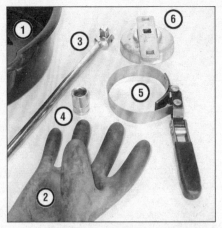

**6.2 These tools are required when changing the engine oil and filter**

*1   Drain pan* - *It should be fairly shallow in depth, but wide to prevent spills*
*2   Rubber gloves* - *When removing the drain plug and filter, you will get oil on your hands (the gloves will prevent burns)*
*3   Breaker bar* - *Sometimes the oil drain plug is tight, and a long breaker bar is needed to loosen it*
*4   Socket* – *To be used with the breaker bar or a ratchet (must be the correct size to fit the drain plug - six-point preferred)*
*5   Filter wrench* - *This is a metal band-type wrench, which requires clearance around the filter to be effective*
*6   Filter wrench* - *This type fits on the bottom of the filter and can be turned with a ratchet or breaker bar (different-size wrenches are available for different types of filters)*

metal shavings and chips.

10   After all the oil has drained, wipe off the drain plug with a clean rag. Even minute metal particles clinging to the plug would immediately contaminate the new oil.

11   Clean the area around the drain plug opening, reinstall the plug and tighten it to the

**6.8 Use the proper size box-end wrench or socket to remove the oil drain plug and avoid rounding it off**

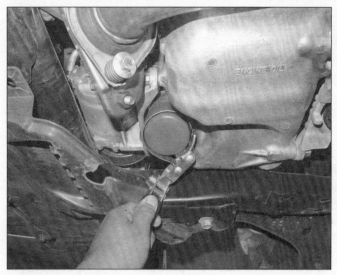

**6.13 Use an oil filter wrench to remove the filter (1.8L model shown, other models similar)**

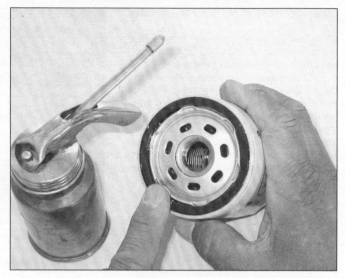

**6.15 Lubricate the oil filter gasket with clean engine oil before installing the filter on the engine**

torque listed in this Chapter's Specifications.

12   Move the drain pan into position under the oil filter.

13   Loosen the oil filter (see illustration) by turning it counterclockwise with an oil filter wrench. Once the filter is loose, use your hands to unscrew it from the block. Keep the open end pointing up to prevent the oil inside the filter from spilling out.

**Warning:** *The exhaust system may still be hot, so be careful.*

14   With a clean rag, wipe off the filter mounting surface. If a residue of old oil is allowed to remain, it will smoke when the engine is heated up. Also make sure that none of the old gasket remains stuck to the mounting surface. It can be removed with a scraper if necessary.

15   Compare the old filter with the new one to make sure they are the same type. Smear some clean engine oil on the rubber gasket of the new filter (see illustration).

16   Attach the new filter to the engine, following the tightening directions printed on the filter canister or packing box. Most filter manufacturers recommend against using a filter wrench due to the possibility of overtightening and damaging the seal.

17   Remove all tools, rags, etc., from under the vehicle, being careful not to spill the oil in the drain pan, then lower the vehicle.

18   Add new oil to the engine through the oil filler cap in the valve cover. Use a funnel, if necessary, to prevent oil from spilling onto the top of the engine. Pour three quarts of fresh oil into the engine. Wait a few minutes to allow the oil to drain into the pan, then check the level on the oil dipstick (see Section 4). If the oil level is at or near the upper hole on the dipstick, install the filler cap hand tight, start

the engine and allow the new oil to circulate.

19   Allow the engine to run for about a minute, then turn it off. Look under the vehicle and check for leaks at the oil pan drain plug and around the oil filter. If either is leaking, tighten the plug or filter.

20   Wait a few minutes to allow the oil to trickle down into the pan, then recheck the level on the dipstick and, if necessary, add enough oil to bring the level to the upper hole.

21   During the first few trips after an oil change, make it a point to check frequently for leaks and proper oil level.

22   The old oil drained from the engine cannot be reused in its present state and should be disposed of. Check with your local auto parts store, disposal facility or environmental agency to see if they will accept the oil for recycling. After the oil has cooled it can be drained into a container (capped plastic jugs, topped bottles, milk cartons, etc.) for transport to one of these disposal sites. Don't dispose of the oil by pouring it on the ground or down a drain!

### *Oil life indicator - resetting*
#### Civic models

23   Turn the ignition to the On position but do not start the vehicle.

24   Push the select/reset button repeatedly until the engine oil life indicator comes on.

25   Once the display is on, press and hold the select/reset button for 10 seconds. The display should go to the reset display mode (start blinking).

26   Press and hold the select/reset button again for more than five seconds. The display reset mode will disappear and the engine oil life display will reset to 100 percent.

#### CR-V models

27   Turn the ignition to the "ON" position but do not start the vehicle.

28   Push the select/reset knob repeatedly until the engine oil life appears on the screen.

29   Press and hold the select/reset knob for 10 seconds.

30   Turn the select/reset knob until "oil life" is displayed. When the display starts blinking, push the select/reset knob.

31   When the engine oil life and maintenance item code begins to blink, push the select/reset knob; the engine oil life should reset to "100" and the maintenance item code should disappear.

---

### 7   Windshield wiper blade inspection and replacement (every 7500 miles [12,000 km] or 6 months)

---

1   The windshield wiper and blade assembly should be inspected periodically for damage, loose components and cracked or worn blade elements.

2   Road film can build up on the wiper blades and affect their efficiency, so they should be washed regularly with a mild detergent solution.

3   The action of the wiping mechanism can loosen bolts, nuts and fasteners, so they should be checked and tightened, as necessary, at the same time the wiper blades are checked.

4   If the wiper blade elements are cracked, worn or warped, or no longer clean adequately, they should be replaced with new ones.

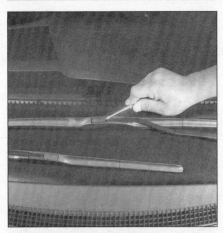

**7.5a To release the blade holder, pull up on the release tab . . .**

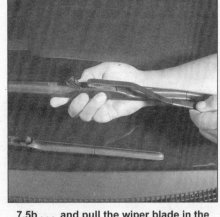

**7.5b . . . and pull the wiper blade in the direction of the windshield to separate it from the arm**

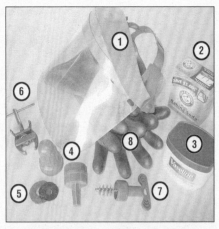

**8.1 Tools and materials required for battery maintenance**

*1    **Face shield/safety goggles** - When removing corrosion with a brush, the acidic particles can easily fly up into your eyes*

*2    **Baking soda** - A solution of baking soda and water can be used to neutralize corrosion*

*3    **Petroleum jelly** - A layer of this on the battery posts will help prevent corrosion*

*4    **Battery post/cable cleaner** - This wire brush cleaning tool will remove all traces of corrosion from the battery posts and cable clamps*

*5    **Treated felt washers** - Placing one of these on each post, directly under the cable clamps, will help prevent corrosion*

*6    **Puller** - Sometimes the cable clamps are very difficult to pull off the posts, even after the nut/bolt has been completely loosened. This tool pulls the clamp straight up and off the post without damage*

*7    **Battery post/cable cleaner** - Here is another cleaning tool which is a slightly different version of Number 4 above, but it does the same thing*

*8    **Rubber gloves** - Another safety item to consider when servicing the battery; remember that's acid inside the battery!*

5    Lift the arm assembly away from the glass for clearance, pull up on the release lever, then slide the wiper blade assembly out of the hook at the end of the arm (see illustrations).

6    Attach the new wiper to the arm. Connection can be confirmed by an audible click.

## 8    Battery check, maintenance and charging (every 7500 miles [12,000 km] or 6 months)

**Warning:** *Certain precautions must be followed when checking and servicing the battery. Hydrogen gas, which is highly flammable, is always present in the battery cells, so keep lighted tobacco and all other open flames and sparks away from the battery. The electrolyte inside the battery is actually diluted sulfuric acid, which will cause injury if splashed on your skin or in your eyes. It will also ruin clothes and painted surfaces. When removing the battery cables, always detach the negative cable first and hook it up last!*

1    A routine preventive maintenance program for the battery in your vehicle is the only way to ensure quick and reliable starts. But before performing any battery maintenance, make sure that you have the proper equipment necessary to work safely around the battery (see illustration).

2    There are also several precautions that should be taken whenever battery maintenance is performed. Before servicing the battery, always turn the engine and all accessories off and disconnect the cable from the negative terminal of the battery (see Chapter 5, Section 1).

3    The battery produces hydrogen gas, which is both flammable and explosive. Never create a spark, smoke or light a match around the battery. Always charge the battery in a ventilated area.

4    Electrolyte contains poisonous and corrosive sulfuric acid. Do not allow it to get in your eyes, on your skin on your clothes. Never ingest it. Wear protective safety glasses when working near the battery. Keep children away from the battery.

5    Note the external condition of the battery. If the positive terminal and cable clamp on your vehicle's battery is equipped with a rubber protector, make sure that it's not torn or damaged. It should completely cover the terminal. Look for any corroded or loose connections, cracks in the case or cover or loose hold-down clamps. Also check the entire length of each cable for cracks and frayed conductors.

6    If corrosion, which looks like white, fluffy deposits (see illustration) is evident, particularly around the terminals, the battery should be removed for cleaning. Loosen the cable clamp bolts with a wrench, being careful to remove the ground cable first, and slide them off the terminals (see illustration). Then disconnect the hold-down clamp bolt and nut, remove the clamp and lift the battery from the

**8.6a Battery terminal corrosion usually appears as light, fluffy powder**

**8.6b Removing a cable from the battery post with a wrench - sometimes a pair of special battery pliers are required for this procedure if corrosion has caused deterioration of the nut hex (always remove the ground (-) cable first and hook it up last!)**

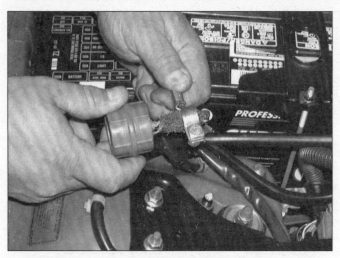

**8.7a When cleaning the cable clamps, all corrosion must be removed (the inside of the clamp is tapered to match the taper on the post, so don't remove too much material)**

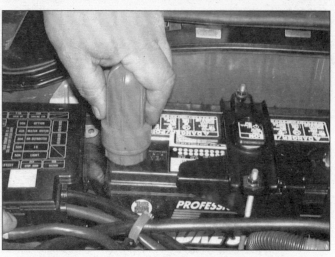

**8.7b Regardless of the type of tool used to clean the battery posts, a clean, shiny surface should be the result**

engine compartment.

7    Clean the cable clamps thoroughly with a battery brush or a terminal cleaner and a solution of warm water and baking soda (see illustration). Wash the terminals and the top of the battery case with the same solution but make sure that the solution doesn't get into the battery. When cleaning the cables, terminals and battery top, wear safety goggles and rubber gloves to prevent any solution from coming in contact with your eyes or hands. Wear old clothes too - even diluted, sulfuric acid splashed onto clothes will burn holes in them. If the terminals have been extensively corroded, clean them up with a terminal cleaner (see illustration). Thoroughly wash all cleaned areas with plain water.

8    Make sure that the battery tray is in good condition and the hold-down clamp fasteners are tight. If the battery is removed from the tray, make sure no parts remain in the bottom of the tray when the battery is reinstalled. When reinstalling the hold-down clamp bolts, do not overtighten them.

9    Information on removing and installing the battery can be found in Chapter 5. If you disconnected the cable(s) from the negative and/ or positive battery terminals, see Chapter 5, Section 1. Information on jump starting can be found at the front of this manual. For more detailed battery checking procedures, refer to the *Haynes Automotive Electrical Manual*.

10    Corrosion on the hold-down components, battery case and surrounding areas can be removed with a solution of water and baking soda. Thoroughly rinse all cleaned areas with plain water.

11    Any metal parts of the vehicle damaged by corrosion should be covered with a zinc-based primer, then painted.

## Charging

**Warning:** *When batteries are being charged, hydrogen gas, which is very explosive and*

*flammable, is produced. Do not smoke or allow open flames near a charging or a recently charged battery. Wear eye protection when near the battery during charging. Also, make sure the charger is unplugged before connecting or disconnecting the battery from the charger.*

12    Slow-rate charging is the best way to restore a battery that's discharged to the point where it will not start the engine. It's also a good way to maintain the battery charge in a vehicle that's only driven a few miles between starts. Maintaining the battery charge is particularly important in the winter when the battery must work harder to start the engine and electrical accessories that drain the battery are in greater use.

13    It's best to use a one- or two-amp battery charger (sometimes called a "trickle" charger). They are the safest and put the least strain on the battery. They are also the least expensive. For a faster charge, you can use a higher amperage charger, but don't use one rated more than 1/10th the amp/hour rating of the battery. Rapid boost charges that claim to restore the power of the battery in one to two hours are hardest on the battery and can damage batteries not in good condition. This type of charging should only be used in emergency situations.

14    The average time necessary to charge a battery should be listed in the instructions that come with the charger. As a general rule, a trickle charger will charge a battery in 12 to 16 hours.

## 9    Cooling system check (every 7500 miles [12,000 km] or 6 months)

**Warning:** *Wait until the engine is completely cool before beginning this procedure.*

1    Many major engine failures can be attributed to a faulty cooling system. The cooling system also cools the transaxle fluid and thus plays an important role in prolonging transaxle life.

2    The cooling system should be checked with the engine cold. Do this before the vehicle is driven for the day or after the engine has been shut off for at least three hours.

3    On 1.8L and 2.4L models, remove the radiator cap by turning it to the left until it reaches a stop. If you hear a hissing sound (indicating there is still pressure in the system), wait until it stops. Now press down on the cap with the palm of your hand and continue turning to the left until the cap can be removed.

4    Thoroughly clean the cap, inside and out, with clean water. Also clean the filler neck on the radiator.

5    All traces of corrosion should be removed. The coolant inside the radiator or expansion tank should be relatively transparent. If it's rust colored, the system should be drained and refilled (see Section 21). If the coolant level isn't up to the top, add additional antifreeze/coolant mixture (see Section 4).

6    Carefully check the large upper and lower radiator hoses along with the smaller diameter heater hoses which run from the engine to the firewall. Inspect each hose along its entire length, replacing any hose which is cracked, swollen or shows signs of deterioration. Cracks may become more apparent if the hose is squeezed (see illustration). Regardless of condition, it's a good idea to replace hoses with new ones every two years.

7    Make sure that all hose connections are tight. A leak in the cooling system will usually show up as white or rust colored deposits on the areas adjoining the leak. If wire-type clamps are used at the ends of the hoses, it may be a good idea to replace them with more secure screw-type clamps.

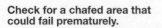

Check for a chafed area that
could fail prematurely.

Check for a soft area indicating
the hose has deteriorated inside.

Overtightening the clamp on a
hardened hose will damage the
hose and cause a leak.

Check each hose for swelling and
oil-soaked ends. Cracks and breaks
can be located by squeezing the hose.

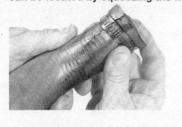

**9.6 Hoses, like drivebelts, have a habit
of failing at the worst possible time - to
prevent the inconvenience of a blown
radiator or heater hose, inspect them
carefully as shown here**

8    Use compressed air or a soft brush to
remove bugs, leaves, etc., from the front of
the radiator or air conditioning condenser. Be
careful not to damage the delicate cooling fins
or cut yourself on them.
9    Every other inspection, or at the first indication of cooling system problems, have the
cap and system pressure tested. If you don't
have a pressure tester, most gas stations and
repair shops will do this for a minimal charge.

## 10   Tire rotation (every 7500 miles [12,000 km] or 6 months)

1    The tires should be rotated at the specified intervals and whenever uneven wear is
noticed. Since the vehicle will be raised and
the tires removed anyway, check the brakes

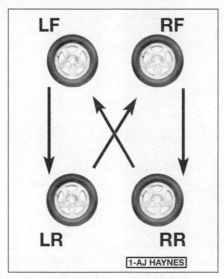

**10.2a The recommended rotation pattern
for non-directional radial tires**

(see Section 12) at this time.
2    Radial tires must be rotated in a specific
pattern (see illustrations). Most models are
equipped with non-directional tires, but some
models may have directional tires, which have
a different rotation pattern. When rotating
tires, examine the sidewalls. Directional tires
have arrows on the sidewall that indicate the
direction they must turn. The left and right side
tires must not be rotated to the other side.
3    Refer to the information in *Jacking and
towing* at the front of this manual for the
proper procedures to follow when raising the
vehicle and changing a tire. If the brakes are
to be checked, do not apply the parking brake
as stated. Make sure the tires are blocked to
prevent the vehicle from rolling.
4    Preferably, the entire vehicle should be
raised at the same time. This can be done
on a hoist or by jacking up each corner and
then lowering the vehicle onto jackstands
placed under the frame rails. Always use four
jackstands and make sure the vehicle is firmly
supported.
5    After rotation, check and adjust the tire
pressures as necessary and be sure to check
the lug nut tightness. Ideally, lug nuts should
be tightened to the torque listed in this Chapter's Specifications with a torque wrench, and
rechecked after 25 miles of driving.
6    For further information on the wheels
and tires, refer to Chapter 10.

## 11   Seat belt check (every 7500 miles [12,000 km] or 6 months)

1    Check seat belts, buckles, latch plates
and guide loops for obvious damage and
signs of wear.
2    See if the seat belt reminder light comes
on when the key is turned to the Run or Start
position. A chime should also sound. On

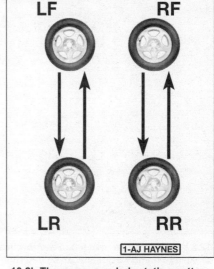

**10.2b The recommended rotation pattern
for directional radial tires**

passive restraint systems, the shoulder belt
should move into position in the A-pillar.
3    The seat belts are designed to lock up
during a sudden stop or impact, yet allow
free movement during normal driving. Make
sure the retractors return the belt against your
chest while driving and rewind the belt fully
when the buckle is unlatched.
4    If any of the above checks reveal problems with the seat belt system, replace parts
as necessary.

## 12   Brake system check (every 7500 miles [12,000 km] or 6 months)

**Warning:** *The dust created by the brake system is harmful to your health. Never blow it out
with compressed air and don't inhale any of
it. An approved filtering mask should be worn
when working on the brakes. Do not, under
any circumstances, use petroleum-based solvents to clean brake parts. Use brake system
cleaner only!*
**Note:** *For detailed photographs of the brake
system, refer to Chapter 9.*
1    In addition to the specified intervals, the
brakes should be inspected every time the
wheels are removed or whenever a defect is
suspected.
2    Any of the following symptoms could
indicate a potential brake system defect: The
vehicle pulls to one side when the brake pedal
is depressed; the brakes make squealing or
dragging noises when applied; brake pedal
travel is excessive; the pedal pulsates; or
brake fluid leaks, usually onto the inside of the
tire or wheel.

### Disc brakes

3    Disc brakes can be visually checked
without removing any parts except the
wheels. Remove the hub caps (if applicable)

**12.6 You will find an inspection window in each caliper - the inner brake pad lining thickness can be determined by looking through this window**

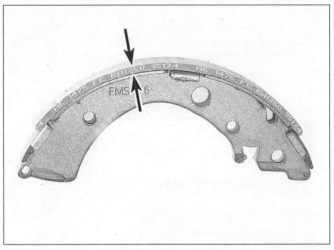

**12.14 If the lining is bonded to the brake shoe, measure the lining thickness from the outer surface to the metal shoe; if the lining is riveted to the shoe, measure from the lining outer surface to the rivet head**

**12.16 Carefully peel back the wheel cylinder boot and check for leaking fluid, indicating that the cylinder must be replaced**

and loosen the wheel lug nuts a quarter turn each.

4   Raise the vehicle and place it securely on jackstands. **Warning:** *Never work under a vehicle that is supported only by a jack!*

5   Remove the wheels. Now visible is the disc brake caliper which contains the pads. There is an outer brake pad and an inner pad. Both must be checked for wear.

6   Measure the thickness of the outer pad at each end of the caliper and the inner pad through the inspection hole in the caliper body (see illustration). Compare the measurement with the limit given in this Chapter's Specifications; if any brake pad thickness is less than specified, then all brake pads must be replaced (see Chapter 9).

7   If you're in doubt as to the exact pad thickness or quality, remove them for measurement and further inspection (see Chapter 9).

8   Check the disc for score marks, wear and burned spots. If any of these conditions exist, the disc should be removed for servicing or replacement (see Chapter 9).

9   Before installing the wheels, check all the brake lines and hoses for damage, wear, deformation, cracks, corrosion, leakage, bends and twists, particularly in the vicinity of the rubber hoses and calipers.

10   Install the wheels, lower the vehicle and tighten the wheel lug nuts to the torque given in this Chapter's Specifications.

### Drum brakes

11   Loosen the rear wheel lug nuts, then raise the vehicle and support it securely on jackstands. Make sure the parking brake is off, then tap on the outside of the drum with a rubber mallet to loosen it.

12   Remove the brake drums. If the drum still won't come off, refer to Chapter 9

13   With the drums removed, carefully clean the brake assembly with brake system cleaner.

**Warning:** *Don't blow the dust out with compressed air and don't inhale any of it (it is harmful to your health).*

14   Note the thickness of the lining material on both front and rear brake shoes (see illustration). Compare the measurement with the limit given in this Chapter's Specifications; if any lining thickness is less than specified, then all of the brake shoes must be replaced (see Chapter 9). The shoes should also be replaced if they're cracked, glazed (shiny areas), or covered with brake fluid.

15   Make sure all the brake assembly springs are connected and in good condition.

16   Check the brake components for signs of fluid leakage. With your finger or a small screwdriver, carefully pry back the rubber cups on the wheel cylinder located at the top of the brake shoes (see illustration). Any leakage here is an indication that the wheel cyl-

inders should be replaced immediately (see Chapter 9). Also, check all hoses and connections for signs of leakage.

17   Wipe the inside of the drum with a clean rag and denatured alcohol or brake cleaner. Again, be careful not to breathe the dangerous brake dust.

18   Check the inside of the drum for cracks, score marks, deep scratches and hard spots which will appear as small discolored areas. If imperfections cannot be removed with fine emery cloth, the drum must be taken to an automotive machine shop for resurfacing.

19   Repeat the procedure for the remaining wheel. If the inspection reveals that all parts are in good condition, reinstall the brake drums, install the wheels and lower the vehicle to the ground.

### Brake booster check

20   Sit in the driver's seat and perform the following sequence of tests.

21   With the brake fully depressed, start the engine - the pedal should move down a little when the engine starts.

22   With the engine running, depress the brake pedal several times - the travel distance should not change.

23   Depress the brake, stop the engine and hold the pedal in for about 30 seconds - the pedal should neither sink nor rise.

24   Restart the engine, run it for about a minute and turn it off. Then firmly depress the brake several times - the pedal travel should decrease with each application.

25   If your brakes do not operate as described, the brake booster has failed. Refer to Chapter 9 for the replacement procedure.

### Parking brake

26   Slowly pull up on the parking brake and count the number of clicks you hear until the handle is up as far as it will go. The adjustment is correct if you hear the specified number of

**13.4 Check the shocks for leakage at the indicated area**

**13.10 To check the balljoint for wear, try to pry the control arm up and down to make sure there is no play in the balljoint (if there is, replace it)**

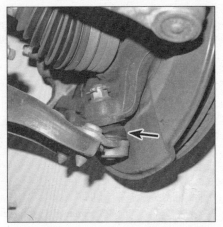

**13.11 Check the balljoint boot for damage**

clicks (see this Chapter's Specifications). If you hear more or fewer clicks, it's time to adjust the parking brake (see Chapter 9).

27    An alternative method of checking the parking brake is to park the vehicle on a steep hill with the parking brake set and the transmission in Neutral. If the parking brake cannot prevent the vehicle from rolling, it is in need of adjustment (see Chapter 9).

## 13   Steering, suspension and driveaxle boot check (every 15,000 miles [24,000 km] or 12 months)

**Note:** *For detailed illustrations of the steering and suspension components, refer to Chapter 10.*

### With the wheels on the ground

1    With the vehicle stopped and the front wheels pointed straight ahead, rock the steering wheel gently back and forth. If freeplay is excessive, a front wheel bearing, steering shaft universal joint or lower arm balljoint is worn or the steering gear is out of adjustment or broken. Refer to Chapter 10 for the appropriate repair procedure.

2    Other symptoms, such as excessive vehicle body movement over rough roads, swaying (leaning) around corners and binding as the steering wheel is turned, may indicate faulty steering and/or suspension components.

3    Check the shock absorbers by pushing down and releasing the vehicle several times at each corner. If the vehicle does not come back to a level position within one or two bounces, the shocks/struts are worn and must be replaced. When bouncing the vehicle up and down, listen for squeaks and noises from the suspension components.

4    Check the struts and shock absorbers for evidence of fluid leakage (see illustration). A light film of fluid is no cause for con-

cern. Make sure that any fluid noted is from the shocks and not from some other source. If leakage is noted, replace the shocks as a set.

5    Check the shocks to be sure they are securely mounted and undamaged. Check the upper mounts for damage and wear. If damage or wear is noted, replace the shocks as a set (front and rear).

6    If the shocks must be replaced, refer to Chapter 10 for the procedure.

### Under the vehicle

7    Raise the vehicle with a floor jack and support it securely on jackstands. See Jacking and towing at the front of this book for the proper jacking points.

8    Check the tires for irregular wear patterns and proper inflation. See Section 5 in this Chapter for information regarding tire wear and Chapter 10 for information on hub bearing replacement.

9    Inspect the universal joint between the steering shaft and the steering gear housing. Check the steering gear housing for lubricant leakage. Make sure that the dust seals and boots are not damaged and that the boot clamps are not loose. Check the steering linkage for looseness or damage. Check the tie-rod ends for excessive play. Look for loose bolts, broken or disconnected parts and deteriorated rubber bushings on all suspension and steering components. While an assistant turns the steering wheel from side to side, check the steering components for free movement, chafing and binding. If the steering components do not seem to be reacting with the movement of the steering wheel, try to determine where the slack is located.

10    Check the balljoints for wear by trying to move each control arm up and down with a pry bar (see illustration) to ensure that its balljoint has no play. If any balljoint does have play, replace it. See Chapter 10 for the balljoint replacement procedure.

11    Inspect the balljoint boots for damage and leaking grease (see illustration). Replace

**13.14 Flex the driveaxle boots by hand to check for cracks and/or leaking grease**

the balljoints with new ones if they are damaged (see Chapter 10).

12    At the rear of the vehicle, inspect the suspension arm bushings for deterioration. Additional information on suspension components can be found in Chapter 10.

### Driveaxle boot check

**Note:** *For detailed illustrations of the driveaxles, refer to Chapter 8.*

13    The driveaxle boots are very important because they prevent dirt, water and foreign material from entering and damaging the constant velocity (CV) joints. Oil and grease can cause the boot material to deteriorate prematurely, so it's a good idea to wash the boots with soap and water. Because it constantly pivots back and forth following the steering action of the front hub, the outer CV boot wears out sooner and should be inspected regularly.

14    Inspect the boots for tears and cracks as well as loose clamps (see illustration). If there is any evidence of cracks or leaking lubricant, they must be replaced as described in Chapter 8.

15.1a Flip open the spring clips . . .

15.1b . . . then lift the cover up and remove the filter element

## 14   Underhood hose check and replacement (every 15,000 miles [24,000 km] or 12 months)

**Warning:** *Replacement of air conditioning hoses must be left to a dealer service department or air conditioning shop that has the equipment to depressurize the system safely. Never remove air conditioning components or hoses until the system has been depressurized.*

### General

1    High temperatures under the hood can cause deterioration of the rubber and plastic hoses used for engine, accessory and emission systems operation. Periodic inspection should be made for cracks, loose clamps, material hardening and leaks.

2    Information specific to the cooling system hoses can be found in Section 9.

3    Most (but not all) hoses are secured to the fittings with clamps. Where clamps are used, check to be sure they haven't lost their tension, allowing the hose to leak. If clamps aren't used, make sure the hose has not expanded and/or hardened where it slips over the fitting, allowing it to leak.

### PCV system hose

4    To reduce hydrocarbon emissions, crankcase blow-by gas is vented through the PCV valve in the rocker arm cover to the intake manifold via a rubber hose on most models. The blow-by gases mix with incoming air in the intake manifold before being burned in the combustion chambers.

5    Check the PCV hose for cracks, leaks and other damage. Disconnect it from the valve cover and the intake manifold and check the inside for obstructions. If it's clogged, clean it out with solvent. See Chapter 6 for check and replacement.

### Vacuum hoses

6    It's quite common for vacuum hoses, especially those in the emissions system, to be color coded or identified by colored stripes molded into them. Various systems require hoses with different wall thickness, collapse resistance and temperature resistance. When replacing hoses, be sure the new ones are made of the same material.

7    Often the only effective way to check a hose is to remove it completely from the vehicle. If more than one hose is removed, be sure to label the hoses and fittings to ensure correct installation.

8    When checking vacuum hoses, be sure to include any plastic T-fittings in the check. Inspect the fittings for cracks and the hose where it fits over each fitting for distortion, which could cause leakage.

9    A small piece of vacuum hose (1/4-inch inside diameter) can be used as a stethoscope to detect vacuum leaks. Hold one end of the hose to your ear and probe around vacuum hoses and fittings, listening for the hissing sound characteristic of a vacuum leak.

**Warning:** *When probing with the vacuum hose stethoscope, be careful not to come into contact with moving engine components such as drivebelts, the cooling fan, etc.*

### Fuel hose

**Warning:** *Gasoline is flammable, so take extra precautions when you work on any part of the fuel system. Don't smoke or allow open flames or bare light bulbs near the work area, and don't work in a garage where a gas-type appliance (such as a water heater or clothes dryer) is present. Since fuel is carcinogenic, wear fuel-resistant gloves when there's a possibility of being exposed to fuel, and, if you spill any fuel on your skin, rinse it off immediately with soap and water. Mop up any spills immediately and do not store fuel-soaked rags where they could ignite. The fuel system is under constant pressure, so, if any fuel lines are to be disconnected, the fuel pressure in the system must be relieved first (see Chapter 4 for more information). When you perform any kind of work on the fuel system, wear safety glasses and have a Class B type fire extinguisher on hand.*

10    The fuel lines are usually under pressure, so if any fuel lines are to be disconnected be prepared to catch spilled fuel. Warning: Your vehicle is equipped with fuel injection and you must relieve the fuel system pressure before servicing the fuel lines. Refer to Chapter 4 for the fuel system pressure relief procedure.

11    Check all flexible fuel lines for deterioration and chafing. Check especially for cracks in areas where the hose bends and just before fittings, such as where a hose attaches to the fuel pump, fuel filter and fuel injection unit.

12    When replacing a hose, use only hose that is specifically designed for your fuel injection system.

13    Spring-type clamps are sometimes used on fuel return or vapor lines. These clamps often lose their tension over a period of time, and can be sprung during removal. Replace all spring-type clamps with screw clamps whenever a hose is replaced. Some fuel lines use spring-lock type couplings, which require a special tool to disconnect. See Chapter 4 for more information on this type of coupling.

### Metal lines

14    Sections of metal line are often used for fuel line between the fuel pump and the fuel injection unit. Check carefully to make sure the line isn't bent, crimped or cracked.

15    If a section of metal fuel line must be replaced, use seamless steel tubing only, since copper and aluminum tubing do not have the strength necessary to withstand vibration caused by the engine.

16    Check the metal brake lines where they enter the master cylinder and brake proportioning unit (if used) for cracks in the lines and loose fittings. Any sign of brake fluid leakage calls for an immediate thorough inspection of the brake system.

## 15   Air filter replacement (every 15,000 miles [24,000 km] or 12 months)

1    Release the spring clips, then lift the housing cover and remove the air filter element (see illustrations).

2    Inspect the outer surface of the filter element. If it is dirty, replace it. If it is only mod-

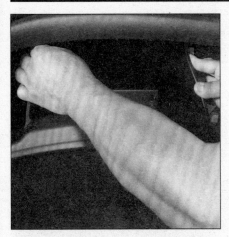

**16.2 Release the glove box stops by pushing the sides of the glove box inward, then lower the box**

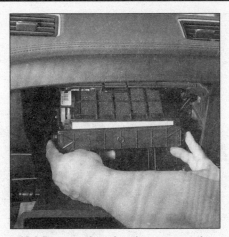

**16.3 Depress the tabs, then remove the filter door**

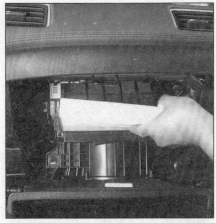

**16.4a Pull the filter from the housing . . .**

erately dusty, it can be reused by blowing it clean from the back to the front surface with compressed air. Because it is a pleated paper type filter, it cannot be washed or oiled. If it cannot be cleaned satisfactorily with compressed air, discard and replace it. While the cover is off, be careful not to drop anything down into the housing.

3    Wipe out the inside of the air filter housing.

4    Place the new filter into the air filter housing, making sure it seats properly.

5    Installation of the housing is the reverse of removal.

## 16    Interior ventilation filter replacement (every 15,000 miles [24,000 km] or 12 months)

1    These models are equipped with an air filtering element in the air conditioning system, located in a housing next to the evaporator, under the right side of the instrument panel.

2    Release the glove box stops, then lower the glove box and let it hang (see illustration).

3    Release the tabs and remove the filter door (see illustration).

4    Remove the filter element and install the new one (see illustration). Make sure the arrows on the filter element point in the same direction as the arrows on the housing (down) (see illustration).

5    Installation is the reverse of the removal procedure.

## 17    Fuel system check (every 15,000 miles [24,000 km] or 12 months)

**Warning:** *Gasoline is flammable, so take extra precautions when you work on any part of the fuel system. Don't smoke or allow open flames or bare light bulbs near the work area, and don't work in a garage where a gas-type*

appliance (such as a water heater or clothes dryer) is present. Since fuel is carcinogenic, wear fuel-resistant gloves when there's a possibility of being exposed to fuel, and, if you spill any fuel on your skin, rinse it off immediately with soap and water. Mop up any spills immediately and do not store fuel-soaked rags where they could ignite. When you perform any kind of work on the fuel system, wear safety glasses and have a Class B type fire extinguisher on hand. The fuel system is under constant pressure, so, before any lines are disconnected, the fuel system pressure must be relieved (see Chapter 4).

1    If you smell gasoline while driving or after the vehicle has been sitting in the sun, inspect the fuel system immediately.

2    Remove the fuel filler cap and inspect it for damage and corrosion. The gasket should have an unbroken sealing imprint. If the gasket is damaged or corroded, install a new cap.

3    Inspect the fuel feed line for cracks. Make sure that the connections between the fuel lines and the fuel injection system are secure and dry. **Warning:** *Your vehicle is fuel injected, so you must relieve the fuel system pressure before servicing fuel system components. The fuel system pressure relief procedure is outlined in Chapter 4.*

4    Since some components of the fuel system - the fuel tank and the fuel lines, for example - are underneath the vehicle, they can be inspected more easily with the vehicle raised on a hoist. If that's not possible, raise the vehicle and support it on jackstands.

5    With the vehicle raised and safely supported, inspect the gas tank and filler neck for punctures, cracks and other damage. The connection between the filler neck and the tank is particularly critical. Sometimes a rubber filler neck will leak because of loose clamps or deteriorated rubber. Inspect all fuel tank mounting brackets and straps to be sure that the tank is securely attached to the vehicle.

**16.4b . . . and install the new one with the AIRFLOW arrows pointing down**

**Warning:** *Do not, under any circumstances, try to repair a fuel tank (except rubber components); the fuel tanks in these vehicles are made of plastic and must be replaced if damaged.*

6    Carefully check all hoses and lines leading away from the fuel tank. Check for loose connections, deteriorated hoses, crimped lines and other damage. Repair or replace damaged sections as necessary (see Chapter 4).

## 18    Exhaust system check (every 15,000 miles [24,000 km] or 12 months)

1    With the engine cold (at least three hours after the vehicle has been driven), check the complete exhaust system from the engine to the end of the tailpipe. Ideally, the inspection should be done with the vehicle on a hoist to permit unrestricted access. If a hoist isn't

**18.2 Be sure to check each exhaust system rubber hanger for damage**

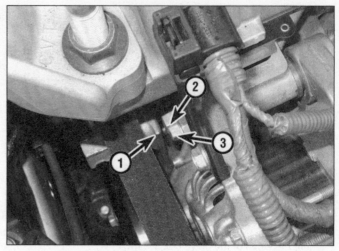

**19.1 Automatic drivebelt tensioner details (1.8L engine shown)**

| 1 | Tensioner arm mark | 3 | Worn belt |
|---|---|---|---|
| 2 | New belt | | |

ACCEPTABLE

Cracks Running Across
"V" Portions of Belt

1/2"

Missing Two or More Adjacent
Ribs 1/2" or longer

UNACCEPTABLE

**19.3 Here are some of the more common problems associated with drivebelts (check the belts very carefully to prevent an untimely breakdown)**

Cracks Running Parallel
to "V" Portions of Belt

available, raise the vehicle and support it securely on jackstands.

2    Check the exhaust pipes and connections for evidence of leaks, severe corrosion and damage. Make sure that all brackets and hangers are in good condition and tight (see illustration).

3    At the same time, inspect the underside of the body for holes, corrosion, open seams, etc., which may allow exhaust gases to enter the passenger compartment. Seal all body openings with silicone or body putty.

4    Rattles and other noises can often be traced to the exhaust system, especially the mounts and hangers. Try to move the pipes, muffler and catalytic converter. If the components can come in contact with the body or suspension parts, secure the exhaust system with new mounts.

5    Check the running condition of the engine by inspecting inside the end of the tailpipe. The exhaust deposits here are an indication of engine state-of-tune. If the pipe is black and sooty or coated with white deposits, the engine may need a tune-up, including a thorough fuel system inspection and adjustment.

---

**19    Drivebelt check, adjustment and replacement (every 30,000 miles [48,000 km] or 24 months)**

**Warning:** *The electric cooling fan(s) on these models can activate at any time the ignition switch is in the On position. Make sure the ignition is Off when working in the vicinity of the fan(s).*

### Check

1    The drivebelts are located at the front of the engine and play an important role in the operation of the vehicle and its components. Due to their function and material makeup, the belts are prone to failure after a period of time and should be inspected and adjusted periodically to prevent major damage. No adjustment is necessary because all models are equipped with an automatic drivebelt tensioner. Locate the tensioner pointer (see illustration) and start the vehicle. If the indicator moves or fluctuates excessively, the tensioner needs to be replaced.

2    A single drivebelt is used to turn the alternator, water pump, and air conditioning compressor.

**Note:** *All engines use a hydraulic type auto-tensioner. The wrench must be rotated slowly for at least three seconds to move the tensioner pulley.*

3    With the engine turned off, open the hood and locate the drivebelts at the front of the engine. Use a flashlight to carefully check each belt. Check for a severed core, separation of the adhesive rubber on both sides of the core and for core separation from the belt side. Inspect the ribs for separation from the adhesive rubber and for cracking or separation of the ribs, torn or worn ribs or cracks in the inner ridges of the ribs (see illustration). Also check for fraying and glazing, which gives the belt a shiny appearance. Inspect both sides of the belt by twisting the belt to check the underside. Use your fingers to feel the belt where you can't see it. If any of the above conditions are evident, replace the belt(s).

### Replacement

4    Apply the parking brake, loosen the right (passenger's side) front wheel lug nuts, raise the front of the vehicle and support it securely on jackstands. Remove the wheel, then remove the inner fender splash shield (see Chapter 11).

**19.5 Place a wrench or a socket on the tensioner pulley bolt and rotate it counterclockwise on 1.8L models and clockwise on 2.4L models**

**19.12 1.8L engine automatic tensioner mounting bolts**

A    10 mm mounting bolt              B    8 mm mounting bolt

**Note:** *On 1.8L Civic models it isn't absolutely necessary to remove the wheel and splash shield, but it does make the job easier.*
5    The automatic tensioner must be released to allow drivebelt replacement. Place a wrench or a socket on the hex casting on the tensioner arm and rotate it counterclockwise on 1.8L models and clockwise on 2.4L models, until the belt can be removed (see illustration). Remove the belt and slowly release the tensioner. Install the new belt, then rotate the tensioner to allow the belt to slip over it. Release the tensioner slowly until it contacts the drivebelt.
**Note:** *All engines use a hydraulic type auto-tensioner, the wrench must be rotated slowly for at least three seconds to move the tensioner pulley.*
6    When installing the belt, make sure the belt is centered on the pulleys.
7    Install the splash shield, wheel and lug nuts. Lower the vehicle and tighten the lug nuts to the torque listed in this Chapter's Specifications.

## Automatic tensioner replacement
8    Remove the drivebelt (see Steps 4 and 5).

### 1.8L engines
9    Remove the alternator (see Chapter 5).
10    Remove the water pump pulley mounting fasteners (see Chapter 3).
11    Remove the automatic tensioner fasteners and tensioner assembly.
12    Install the tensioner and fasteners (see illustration) and tighten to the torque listed in this Chapter's Specifications.
13    Place a wrench or a socket on the tensioner (see illustration 19.5). Slowly compress the tensioner downward, holding it for three seconds. Push the tensioner slowly upward and hold for three seconds.
14    Repeat this procedure three times to bleed the tensioner assembly.

15    The remaining installation is the reverse of removal.

### 2.4L engines
16    If you're working on a 2014 and earlier 2.4L engine, remove the idler pulley mounting bolts, then remove the pulley.
17    Unscrew the mounting bolts and remove the tensioner.
18    Installation is the reverse of removal.

## 20    Brake fluid change (every 30,000 miles [48,000 km] or 24 months)

**Warning:** *Brake fluid can harm your eyes and damage painted surfaces, so use extreme caution when handling or pouring it. Do not use brake fluid that has been standing open or is more than one year old. Brake fluid absorbs moisture from the air. Excess moisture can cause a dangerous loss of braking effectiveness.*
1    At the specified intervals, the brake fluid should be drained and replaced. Since the brake fluid may drip or splash when pouring it, place plenty of rags around the master cylinder to protect any surrounding painted surfaces.
2    Before beginning work, purchase the specified brake fluid (see *Recommended lubricants and fluids* in this Chapter's Specifications).
3    Remove the cap from the master cylinder reservoir.
4    Using a hand suction pump or similar device, withdraw the fluid from the master cylinder reservoir.
5    Add new fluid to the master cylinder until it rises to the base of the filler neck.
6    Bleed the brake system as described in Chapter 9 at all four brakes until new and uncontaminated fluid is expelled from the bleeder screw. Be sure to maintain the fluid level in the master cylinder as you perform the

bleeding process. If you allow the master cylinder to run dry, air will enter the system.
7    Refill the master cylinder with fluid and check the operation of the brakes. The pedal should feel solid when depressed, with no sponginess.
**Warning:** *Do not operate the vehicle if you are in doubt about the effectiveness of the brake system.*

## 21    Cooling system servicing (draining, flushing and refilling) (every 60,000 miles [96,000 km] or 36 months)

**Warning:** *Do not allow antifreeze to come in contact with your skin or painted surfaces of the vehicle. Rinse off spills immediately with plenty of water. Antifreeze is highly toxic if ingested. Never leave antifreeze lying around in an open container or in puddles on the floor; children and pets are attracted by its sweet smell and may drink it. Check with local authorities about disposing of used antifreeze. Many communities have collection centers which will see that antifreeze is disposed of safely. Never dump used antifreeze on the ground or pour it into drains.*
1    Periodically, the cooling system should be drained, flushed and refilled to replenish the antifreeze mixture and prevent formation of rust and corrosion, which can impair the performance of the cooling system and cause engine damage. When the cooling system is serviced, all hoses and the radiator cap should be checked and replaced if necessary.

## Draining
**Warning:** *If the vehicle has just been driven, wait several hours to allow the engine to cool down before beginning this procedure.*
2    Apply the parking brake and block the rear wheels, then raise the front of the vehicle

21.3 Location of the radiator drain fitting - before opening the valve, push a short length of rubber hose onto the plastic fitting to prevent the coolant from splashing

21.4 On SOHC engines, unscrew the engine block drain plug (located on the front side of the block, in front of cylinder no. 4)

23.5 When the engine is at TDC for cylinder number 1, the "UP" mark on the camshaft sprocket will be visible, and the two lines on the sprocket will be parallel with the machined surface of the cylinder head

and support it securely on jackstands. Turn the heater control to maximum heat.

3    Remove the center portion of the under-vehicle splash shield (see illustration 6.7). Move a large container under the radiator drain to catch the coolant, then open the drain fitting until coolant starts flowing from the drain hole (a pair of pliers may be required to turn it) (see illustration).

**Note:** *Not all radiators are equipped with a plastic fitting that will accommodate a hose.*

4    Remove the radiator cap and allow the radiator to drain, then move the container under the engine. If you're working on an SOHC engine, loosen the engine block drain plug and allow the coolant in the block to drain (see illustration).

5    While the coolant is draining, check the condition of the radiator hoses, heater hoses and clamps.

6    Replace any damaged clamps or hoses. Close the drain fitting and, if removed, install and tighten the block drain plug to the torque listed in this Chapter's Specifications.

## Flushing

7    Fill the cooling system with clean water, following the Refilling procedure (see Step 13).

8    Start the engine and allow it to reach normal operating temperature, then rev up the engine a few times.

9    Turn the engine off and allow it to cool completely, then drain the system as described earlier.

10   Repeat Steps 7 through 9 until the water being drained is free of contaminants.

11   In severe cases of contamination or clogging of the radiator, remove the radiator (see Chapter 3) and have a radiator repair facility clean and repair it if necessary.

12   Many deposits can be removed by the chemical action of a cleaner available at auto parts stores. Follow the procedure outlined in the manufacturer's instructions.

**Note:** *When the coolant is regularly drained and the system refilled with the correct anti-freeze/water mixture, there should be no need*

*to use chemical cleaners or descalers.*

## Refilling

13   Fill the cooling system with the proper type and mixture of antifreeze (see this Chapter's Specifications), up to the base of the radiator cap filler neck. Loosely install the radiator cap.

14   Start the engine and run it at approximately 1500 rpm until the radiator fan comes on two times. Feel the upper radiator hose - it should be warm, indicating the thermostat has opened.

15   Turn off the engine and let it cool down. Slowly remove the radiator cap and check the coolant level, adding as necessary.

**Warning:** *If you hear a hissing sound as you unscrew the cap, STOP. Let the engine cool down longer.Fill the coolant reservoir up to the MIN mark, if necessary.*

16   Start the engine, allow it to reach normal operating temperature once again and check for leaks.

## 22   Rear differential lubricant change (CR-V) (every 90,000 miles [145,000 km] or 60 months)

1    This procedure should be performed after the vehicle has been driven, so the lubricant will be warm and therefore will flow out of the differential more easily.

2    Raise the vehicle and support it securely on jackstands. You'll be draining the lubricant by removing the drain plug, so move a drain pan, rags, newspapers and wrench under the vehicle. Remove the check/fill plug.

3    Remove the fill plug and drain plug and allow the lubricant to drain into the pan, then clean and reinstall the drain plug. Tighten the plug securely.

4    Using a hand pump, syringe or squeeze bottle, fill the differential housing with the specified lubricant until it's level with the bottom of the fill plug hole.

5    Install the plug and tighten it securely. Drive the vehicle a short distance, then check

for leaks.

6    The old lubricant drained from the differential cannot be reused in its present state and should be disposed of. Check with your local auto parts store, disposal facility or environmental agency to see if they will accept the lubricant for recycling. After the lubricant has cooled it can be drained into a container (capped plastic jugs, topped bottles, milk cartons, etc.) for transport to one of these disposal sites. Don't dispose of the lubricant by pouring it on the ground or down a drain!

## 23   Valve clearance check and adjustment (every 110,000 miles [177,000 km] or 36 months)

## Check

1    Valve clearances generally do not need adjustment unless valvetrain components have been replaced, a valve job has been performed, or the valvetrain is noisy.

2    The simplest check for proper valve adjustment is to listen carefully to the engine running with the hood open. If the valvetrain is noisy, adjustment is necessary.

## Adjustment

3    The valve clearance must be checked and adjusted with the engine cold.

4    Remove the valve cover (see Chapter 2A or 2B).

### SOHC engines

5    Place the number one piston (closest to the drivebelt end of the engine) at Top Dead Center (TDC) on the compression stroke. This is accomplished by rotating the crankshaft in the normal direction of rotation (which is clockwise) until the white TDC mark on the crankshaft pulley aligns with the timing pointer on the timing chain cover and the UP mark on the camshaft sprocket is at the twelve o'clock position (see accompanying illustration and Chapter 2A).

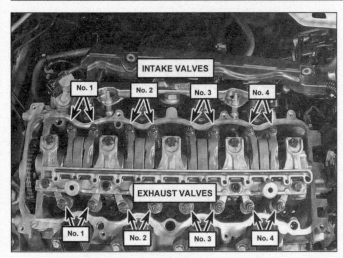

**23.6 Valve layout (1.8L SOHC engine)**

**23.7 When the adjustment is correct, you will feel a slight drag as you pull the feeler gauge**

**23.8 Hold the adjuster screw stationary with the screwdriver while you tighten the locknut**

**23.9 When the number 3 cylinder is at TDC, the "3" mark will appear at 12 o'clock and the machined line on the cam sprocket will be parallel with the cylinder head surface**

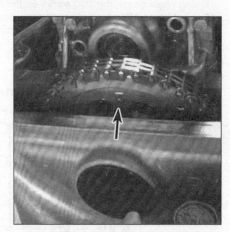

**23.10 When the number 4 cylinder is at TDC, the "4" mark will appear at 12 o'clock and the machined line on the cam sprocket will be parallel with the cylinder head surface**

6    With the engine in this position, the number one cylinder valve adjustment can be checked and adjusted (see illustration).

7    Start with the intake valve clearance. Insert a feeler gauge of the correct thickness (see this Chapter's Specifications) between the valve stem and the rocker arm (see illustration). Withdraw it; you should feel a slight drag. If there's no drag or a heavy drag, loosen the adjuster nut and back off the adjuster screw. Carefully tighten the adjuster screw until you can feel a slight drag on the feeler gauge as you withdraw it.

8    Hold the adjuster screw with a screwdriver (to keep it from turning) and tighten the locknut (see illustration). Recheck the clearance to make sure it hasn't changed. Repeat the procedure in this Step and the previous Step on the other intake valve, then on the two exhaust valves.

9    Rotate the crankshaft pulley 180-degrees clockwise (the camshaft pulley will turn 90-degrees) until the number three cylinder is at TDC (see illustration). Check and adjust the

number three cylinder valves.

10   Rotate the crankshaft pulley 180-degrees clockwise until the number four cylinder is at TDC (see illustration). Check and adjust the number four cylinder valves.

11   Rotate the crankshaft pulley 180-degrees clockwise to bring the number two cylinder to TDC (see illustration). Check and adjust the number two cylinder valves.

12   Install the valve cover (see Chapter 2A).

**23.11 When the number 2 cylinder is at TDC, the "2" mark will appear at 12 o'clock and the machined line on the cam sprocket will be parallel with the cylinder head surface**

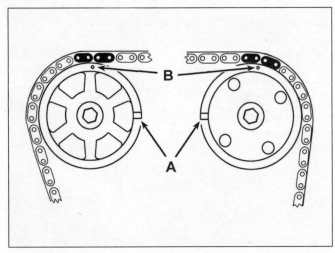

**23.13 When the engine is at TDC for cylinder no. 1, the mark on the crankshaft pulley must be aligned with the pointer on the timing chain cover, the TDC marks on the camshaft sprockets (A) must be pointing towards each other and the dimples on the sprockets (B) must be pointing UP**

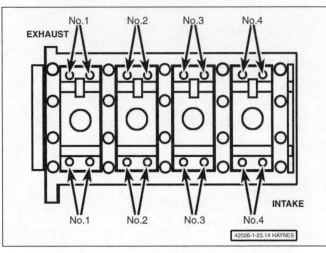

**23.14a 2014 and earlier 2.4L DOHC engine valve layout**

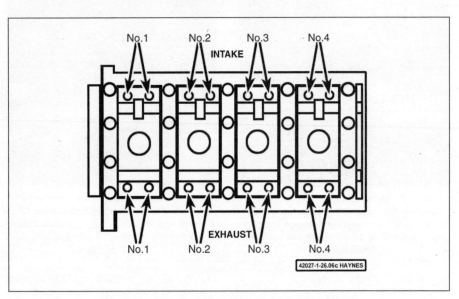

**23.14b 2015 and later 2.4L DOHC engine valve layout**

## DOHC engines

13   Place the number one piston (closest to the drivebelt end of the engine) at Top Dead Center (TDC) on the compression stroke. This is accomplished by rotating the crankshaft in the normal direction of rotation (which is clockwise) until the white TDC mark on the crankshaft pulley aligns with the timing pointer on the lower timing belt cover (see Chapter 2A Section 3). The punch marks on the camshaft sprockets should be at the twelve o'clock position and the TDC marks aligned on both sprockets (see illustration).

14   With the engine in this position, the number one cylinder valve adjustment can be checked and adjusted (see illustrations).

15   Start with the intake valve clearance. Insert a feeler gauge of the correct thickness (see this Chapter's Specifications) between an intake valve stem and the rocker arm. Withdraw it; you should feel a slight drag. If there's no drag or a heavy drag, loosen the adjuster nut and back off the adjuster screw. Carefully tighten the adjuster screw until you can feel a slight drag on the feeler gauge as you withdraw it (see illustration 23.7).

16   Hold the adjuster screw with a screwdriver (to keep it from turning) and tighten the locknut (see illustration 23.8). Recheck the clearance to make sure it hasn't changed. Repeat the procedure in this Step and the previous Step on the other intake valve, then on the two exhaust valves.

17   Rotate the crankshaft pulley 180-degrees clockwise (the camshaft pulley will turn 90-degrees) until the number three cylinder is at TDC. With the number three cylinder at TDC, the punch marks on the camshaft sprockets will be at the three o'clock position. Check and adjust the number three cylinder valves.

18   Rotate the crankshaft pulley 180-degrees clockwise until the number four cylinder is at TDC. With the number four cylinder at TDC, the punch marks on the camshaft sprockets will be pointed straight down. Check and adjust the number four cylinder valves.

19   Rotate the crankshaft pulley 180-degrees clockwise to bring the number two cylinder to TDC. The punch marks on the camshaft sprockets will be at the nine o'clock position. Check and adjust the number two cylinder valves.

20   Install the valve cover (see Chapter 2B).

## 24   Spark plug check and replacement (see Maintenance schedule for service intervals)

1   The spark plugs are located in the center of the cylinder head.

2   In most cases the tools necessary for spark plug replacement include a spark plug socket which fits onto a ratchet (this special socket is padded inside to protect the porcelain insulators on the new plugs and hold them in place), various extensions and a feeler gauge to check and adjust the spark plug gap (see illustration). Since these engines are equipped with an aluminum cylinder head, a torque wrench should be used when tightening the spark plugs.

3   The best approach when replacing the spark plugs is to purchase the new spark plugs beforehand, adjust them to the proper gap and then replace each plug one at a time. When buying the new spark plugs, be sure to obtain the correct plug for your specific

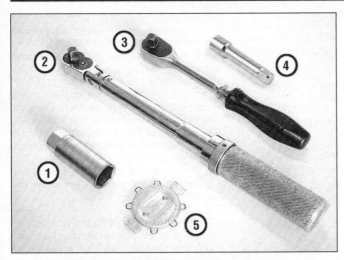

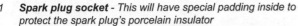

24.2 Tools required for changing spark plugs

24.5 If the wire does not slide between the electrodes with a slight drag, the spark plug should be replaced

1   **Spark plug socket** - *This will have special padding inside to protect the spark plug's porcelain insulator*
2   **Torque wrench** - *Although not mandatory, using this tool is the best way to ensure the plugs are tightened properly*
3   **Ratchet** - *Standard hand tool to fit the spark plug socket*
4   **Extension** - *Depending on model and accessories, you may need special extensions and universal joints to reach one or more of the plugs*
5   **Spark plug gap gauge** - *This gauge for checking the gap comes in a variety of styles. Make sure the gap for your engine is included*

engine. This information can be found in this Chapter's Specifications or in your owner's manual.

4    Allow the engine to cool completely before attempting to remove any of the plugs. During this cooling off time, each of the new spark plugs can be inspected for defects and the gaps can be checked.

5    The gap is checked by inserting the proper thickness gauge between the electrodes at the tip of the plug (see illustration). The gap between the electrodes should be as listed in this Chapter's Specifications or in your owner's manual. Also check for cracks in

the spark plug body (if any are found, the plug must not be used).
**Caution:** *The manufacturer recommends against adjusting the gap on platinum- or iridium-tipped spark plugs; if the gap is out of specification, replace the plug.*

6    Cover the fender to prevent damage to the paint. Fender covers are available from auto parts stores but an old blanket will work just fine.

7    Remove the ignition coils (see Chapter 5).

8    If compressed air is available, use it to blow any dirt or foreign material away from

the spark plug area. This will eliminate the possibility of material falling into the cylinder through the spark plug hole as the spark plug is removed.

**Warning:** *Wear eye protection!*

9    Place the spark plug socket over the plug and remove it from the engine by turning it in a counterclockwise direction (see illustration).

10    Compare the spark plug to those shown in the photos located on the inside back cover of this book to get an indication of the general running condition of the engine.

11    Apply a small amount of anti-seize compound to the spark plug threads (see illustration). Install one of the new plugs into the hole until you can no longer turn it with your fingers, then tighten it with a torque wrench (if available) or the ratchet. It is a good idea to slip a short length of rubber hose over the end of the plug to use as a tool to thread it into place (see illustration). The hose will grip the plug well enough to turn it, but will start to slip if the plug begins to cross-thread in the hole - this will prevent damaged threads and the accompanying repair costs.

24.9 Use a ratchet and extension to remove the spark plugs

24.11a Apply a thin coat of anti-seize compound to the spark plug threads

24.11b A length of snug-fitting rubber hose will save time and prevent damaged threads when installing the spark plugs

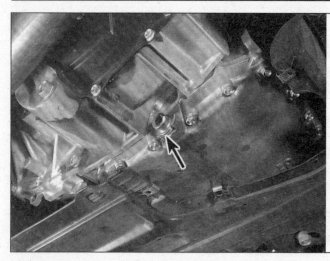

**25.6 Location of the automatic transaxle fluid drain plug**

12    Attach the coil to the new spark plug using a twisting motion until it is firmly seated on the end of the spark plug. Tighten the mounting bolt securely.
13    Repeat the procedure for the remaining spark plugs.

### 25    Automatic transaxle fluid change (every 120,000 miles [193,000 km] or 72 months)

1    The automatic transaxle fluid should be changed at the recommended intervals.
2    Before beginning work, purchase the specified transmission fluid (see *Recommended lubricants and fluids* in this Chapter's Specifications).
3    Other tools necessary for this job include jackstands to support the vehicle in a raised position, wrenches, a drain pan, newspapers and clean rags.
4    The fluid should be drained immediately after the vehicle has been driven. Hot fluid is more effective than cold fluid at removing built up sediment.
**Warning:** *Fluid temperature can exceed 350-degrees F in a hot transaxle. Wear protective gloves.*
5    After the vehicle has been driven to warm up the fluid, raise the front of the vehicle and support it securely on jackstands.
**Warning:** *Never work under a vehicle that is supported only by a jack!*
6    Place the drain pan under the drain plug in the transaxle pan and remove the drain plug (see illustration). Be sure the drain pan is in position, as fluid will come out with some force. Once the fluid is drained, reinstall the drain plug securely. Measure the amount of fluid drained and write down this figure for reference when refilling.
7    Lower the vehicle.
8    With the engine off, add new fluid to the transaxle through the dipstick tube (if equipped) or the fill plug (see illustration 4.32b) (see *Recommended lubricants and*

*fluids* for the recommended fluid type). Begin the refill procedure by initially adding 1/3 of the amount drained. On non-CVT models, with the engine running, add 1/2-pint at a time (cycling the shifter through each gear position between additions) until the level is correct on the dipstick. On CVT models, see Section 4 for the fluid level adjustment procedure.
9    If desired, repeat Steps 5 through 8 once to flush any contaminated fluid from the torque converter.
10    The old fluid drained from the transaxle cannot be reused in its present state and should be disposed of. Check with your local auto parts store, disposal facility or environmental agency to see if they will accept the fluid for recycling. After the fluid has cooled it can be drained into a container (capped plastic jugs, topped bottles, milk cartons, etc.) for transport to one of these disposal sites. Don't dispose of the fluid by pouring it on the ground or down a drain!

### 26    Automatic transaxle filter change (every 120,000 miles [193,000 km] or 72 months)

**Note:** *An inline filter is installed on all non-CVT automatic transaxles.*
1    The automatic transaxle filter should be changed at the same time as the fluid recommended intervals.
2    Before beginning work, purchase the specified transmission fluid (see *Recommended lubricants and fluids* in this Chapter's Specifications).
3    Other tools necessary for this job include jackstands to support the vehicle in a raised position, wrenches, drain pan capable of holding at least four quarts, newspapers and clean rags.
4    Remove the air filter housing (see Chapter 4).
5    Raise the front of the vehicle and support it securely on jackstands.
**Warning:** *Never work under a vehicle that is*

*supported only by a jack!*
6    Remove the lower splash shield fasteners and remove the complete shield.
**Note:** *The lower splash shield has separate sections that can be removed individually. Remove the entire shield as one assembly.*
7    Place the drain pan under the filter and disconnect the hose to the filter. Once the fluid is drained, remove the filter bracket and filter from the vehicle. Measure the amount of fluid drained and write down this figure for reference when refilling.
8    Install a new filter and the mounting bracket, then tighten the mounting bolt securely.
9    Lower the vehicle.
10    With the engine off, add new fluid to the transaxle through the dipstick tube (see Recommended lubricants and fluids for the recommended fluid type). Begin the refill procedure by initially adding 1/3 of the amount drained. Then, with the engine running, add small amounts until the level is correct on the dipstick.
11    The old oil drained from the transaxle cannot be reused in its present state and should be disposed of. Check with your local auto parts store, disposal facility or environmental agency to see if they will accept the oil for recycling. After the oil has cooled it can be drained into a container (capped plastic jugs, topped bottles, milk cartons, etc.) for transport to one of these disposal sites. Don't dispose of the oil by pouring it on the ground or down a drain!

### 27    Manual transaxle fluid change (every 120,000 miles [193,000 km] or 72 months)

1    Raise the vehicle and support it securely on jackstands in a level position.
**Warning:** *Never work under a vehicle that is supported only by a jack!*
2    Remove the splash shield fasteners and lower the splash shield (see illustration 6.7).
3    Place a drain pan under the transaxle. Remove the fill plug, followed by the drain plug and allow the fluid to drain.
4    After the fluid has completely drained, install the drain plug and tighten it to the torque given in this Chapter's Specifications.
5    Fill the transaxle with the recommended fluid (see *Recommended lubricants and fluids* in this Chapter's Specifications).
6    The old fluid drained from the transaxle cannot be reused in its present state and should be disposed of. Check with your local auto parts store, disposal facility or environmental agency to see if they will accept the fluid for recycling. After the fluid has cooled it can be drained into a container (capped plastic jugs, topped bottles, milk cartons, etc.) for transport to one of these disposal sites. Don't dispose of the fluid by pouring it on the ground or down a drain!

# Chapter 2 Part A
# 1.8L single overhead camshaft (SOHC) engine

## Contents

## Specifications

### General

| | |
|---|---|
| Firing order | 1-3-4-2 |
| Bore | 3.19 inches (81.0 mm) |
| Stroke | 3.44 inches (87.3 mm) |
| Engine designation | R18Z1 |
| Displacement | 110 cubic inches (1.8 liters) |
| Oil pressure | See Chapter 2C |
| Valve adjustment | See Chapter 1 |

**Front** → 

42026-1-specs HAYNES

**Cylinder locations**

### Camshaft

| | |
|---|---|
| Endplay | |
| Standard | 0.002 to 0.010 inch (0.05 to 0.25 mm) |
| Maximum | 0.016 inch (0.4 mm) |
| Lobe height | |
| Intake (primary) | 1.41204 inches (35.866 mm) |
| Intake (secondary A) | 1.21330 inches (30.818 mm) |
| Intake (secondary B) | 1.40508 inches (35.689 mm) |
| Exhaust | 1.41220 inches (35.870 mm) |
| Runout | |
| Standard | 0.001 inch (0.03 mm) |
| Service limit | 0.002 inch maximum (0.05 mm) |
| Journal oil clearance | |
| Standard | 0.0018 to 0.0033 inch (0.046 to 0.084 mm) |
| Service limit | 0.006 inch maximum (0.15 mm) |

### Oil pump

| | |
|---|---|
| Rotor-to-cover clearance | |
| Standard | 0.001 to 0.002 inch (0.02 to 0.07 mm) |
| Service limit | 0.005 inch maximum (0.13 mm) |
| Tooth tip clearance | |
| Standard | 0.001 to 0.006 inch (0.02 to 0.16 mm) |
| Service limit | 0.007 inch maximum (0.20 mm) |
| Outer rotor-to-pump body clearance | |
| Standard | 0.004 to 0.006 inch (0.100 to 0.175 mm) |
| Service limit | 0.007 inch maximum (0.20 mm) |

## Torque specifications

| | Ft-lbs (unless otherwise indicated) | Nm |
|---|---|---|

**Note:** *One foot-pound (ft-lb) of torque is equivalent to 12 inch-pounds (in-lbs) of torque. Torque values below approximately 15 ft-lbs are expressed in inch-pounds, since most foot-pound torque wrenches are not accurate at these smaller values.*

| | Ft-lbs (unless otherwise indicated) | Nm |
|---|---|---|
| Camshaft sprocket bolt | 42 | 57 |
| Camshaft thrust cover bolts | 88 in-lbs | 10 |
| Crankshaft pulley bolt | | |
|   Original bolt | | |
|     Step 1 | 51 | 69 |
|     Step 2 | Tighten an additional 90-degrees | |
|   New bolt | | |
|     Step 1 | 133 | 180 |
|     Step 2 | Loosen bolt 2 full turns | |
|     Step 3 | 37 | 50 |
|     Step 4 | Tighten an additional 82-degrees | |
| Cylinder head bolts* | | |
|   Step 1 | 30 | 40 |
|   Step 2 | Tighten an additional 90-degrees | |
|   Step 3 | Tighten an additional 90-degrees | |
|   Step 4 | Tighten an additional 60-degrees | |
| Driveplate-to-crankshaft bolts | 55 | 74 |
| Intake manifold bolts/nuts | 18 | 24 |
| Intake manifold bracket bolts | | |
|   Lower | 18 | 24 |
|   Upper (x2) | 86 in-lbs | 10 |
| Exhaust manifold-to-cylinder head nuts/bolts | 24 | 32 |
| Exhaust manifold heat shield upper bolts (manifold bolts) | 16 | 22 |
| Exhaust pipe-to-manifold bolts | 16 | 22 |
| Flywheel-to-crankshaft bolts | 76 | 103 |
| Mounts | | |
|   Mount bracket-to-engine bolts | 47 | 64 |
|   Mount-to-body bolts* | 69 | 93 |
|   Mount side bracket bolt/nut | 36 | 49 |
|   Transaxle bracket-to-body bolts | 62 | 84 |
|   Tranaxle bracket-to-transaxle bolt/nut | 55 | 74 |
|   Lower torque rod | | |
|     Torque rod-to-subframe through bolt | 69 | 93 |
|     Torque rod-to-engine bolts | | |
|       R18Z1 models | 55 | 74 |
|       R18A9 models | 47 | 64 |
| Oil baffle plate | 86 in-lbs | 9.5 |
| Oil pan drain plug | 29 | 39 |
| Oil pan-to-engine bolts | 156 in-lbs | 17.5 |
| Oil pump pick-up screen-to-main bearing cap fasteners | 108 in-lbs | 9 |
| Oil pump cover-to-housing screws | 53 in-lbs | 6 |
| Oil pump pressure relief valve plug | 29 | 39 |
| Lost motion holder bolts | | |
|   Step 1 two outer bolts (see illustration 8.15) | 48 in-lbs | 5 |
|   Step 2 all bolts in sequence (see illustration 8.16) | 132 in-lbs | 15 |
| Timing chain cover bolts | | |
|   8 mm bolts | 23 | 31 |
|   6 mm bolts | 86 in-lbs | 9.5 |
|   Dowel bolts | 104 in-lbs | 12 |
| Timing chain guide bolts | 104 in-lbs | 12 |
| Timing chain guide pivot bolt | 16 | 22 |
| Timing chain tensioner bolts | 86 in-lbs | 9.5 |
| Valve cover bolts | 84 in-lbs | 10 |

*Always replace with new bolt/nut*

## 1  General Information

1    This Part of Chapter 2A is devoted to in-vehicle repair procedures for the 1.8L four-cylinder engine. This engine utilizes a Single Overhead Camshaft (SOHC), with 4 valves per cylinder (16V). The 1.8L engine incorporates the VTEC (Variable valve Timing and lift Electronic Control) system, which electronically alters valve timing to enhance engine performance. For more information on the VTEC system, see Section 7 of this Chapter.

2    The SOHC engines are lightweight in design with an aluminum alloy block (with steel cylinder liners) and an aluminum alloy cylinder head. The crankshaft rides in a single carriage unit that houses the renewable insert-type main bearings, with separate thrust bearings at the number four position to control crankshaft endplay.

3    The pistons have two compression rings and one oil control ring. The semi-floating piston pins are press fitted into the small end of the connecting rod. The connecting rod big ends are also equipped with renewable insert-type plain bearings.

4    The engine is liquid-cooled, utilizing a centrifugal impeller-type pump (driven by the drivebelt) to circulate coolant around the cylinders and combustion chambers and through the intake manifold.

5    Lubrication is handled by a rotor-type oil pump mounted on the front of the engine (in the timing chain cover). It is driven directly by the crankshaft. The oil is filtered continuously by a cartridge-type filter mounted on the rear of the oil pan.

6    Information concerning engine removal and installation can be found in Part C of this Chapter.

7    The following repair procedures are based on the assumption that the engine is installed in the vehicle. If the engine has been removed from the vehicle and mounted on a stand, many of the steps outlined in this Part of Chapter 2A will not apply.

8    The Specifications included in this part of Chapter 2A apply only to the procedures contained in this Chapter. Chapter 2C contains the Specifications necessary for certain engine block assembly procedures.

## 2  Repair operations possible with the engine in the vehicle

1    Clean the engine compartment and the exterior of the engine with some type of degreaser before any work is done. It will make the job easier and help keep dirt out of the internal areas of the engine.

2    Depending on the components involved, it may be helpful to remove the hood to improve access to the engine as repairs are performed (refer to Chapter 11 if necessary).

**3.5 Align the white (TDC) mark on the crankshaft pulley with the pointer on the timing chain cover**

Cover the fenders to prevent damage to the paint. Special pads are available, but an old bedspread or blanket will also work.

3    If vacuum, exhaust, oil or coolant leaks develop, indicating a need for gasket or seal replacement, the repairs can generally be made with the engine in the vehicle. The intake and exhaust manifold gaskets, oil pan gasket, crankshaft oil seals and cylinder head gasket are all accessible with the engine in place.

4    Exterior engine components, such as the intake and exhaust manifolds, the oil pan, the water pump, the starter motor, the alternator, and the fuel system components can be removed for repair with the engine in place.

5    Since the cylinder head can be removed without pulling the engine, camshaft and valve component servicing can also be accomplished with the engine in the vehicle. Replacement of the timing chain, timing belt and sprockets is also possible with the engine in the vehicle.

6    In extreme cases caused by a lack of necessary equipment, repair or replacement of piston rings, pistons, connecting rods and rod bearings is possible with the engine in the vehicle. However, this practice is not recommended because of the cleaning and preparation work that must be done to the components involved.

## 3  Top Dead Center (TDC) for number one piston - locating

**Note:** *These engines are not equipped with a distributor. Piston position must be determined by feeling for compression at the number one spark plug hole, then aligning the ignition timing marks as described in Step 5.*

**Note:** *Positioning the piston(s) at TDC is an essential part of certain repair procedures discussed in this manual.*

1    Top Dead Center (TDC) is the highest point in the cylinder that each piston reaches as it travels up-and-down during crankshaft rotation. Each piston reaches TDC on the compression stroke and again on the exhaust stroke, but TDC generally refers to piston position on the compression stroke.

2    Before beginning this procedure, be sure to place the transmission in Neutral and apply the parking brake or block the rear wheels. Remove the spark plugs (see Chapter 1). Install a compression gauge in the spark plug hole for cylinder no. 1.

3    Disconnect the cable from the negative terminal of the battery (see Chapter 5).

4    In order to bring any piston to TDC, the crankshaft must be turned to line up the TDC mark. When looking at the front (timing belt or timing chain end) of the engine, normal crankshaft rotation is clockwise.

5    Turn the crankshaft with a socket and ratchet or breaker bar until compression registers on the gauge, then turn it slowly until the TDC notch is aligned with the pointer on the timing belt cover (see illustration). The number one piston is now at TDC on the compression stroke.

**Note:** *There are two marks on the pulley. The white mark is for TDC, the red mark is only for checking ignition timing with a timing light.*

6    After the number one piston has been positioned at TDC on the compression stroke, TDC for any of the remaining pistons can be located by turning the crankshaft in its normal direction of rotation, in 180-degree (1/2-turn) increments, and following the firing order. Divide the crankshaft pulley into two equal sections with chalk marks at each point, each indicating 180-degrees of crankshaft rotation. Rotating the engine past TDC no. 1 to the next mark will place the engine at TDC for cylinder no. 3.

4.2 Remove the engine cover fasteners and lift the cover off of the valve cover

4.3 Disconnect the electrical connectors from the ignition coils, then remove the wiring harness fasteners and position the harness out of the way

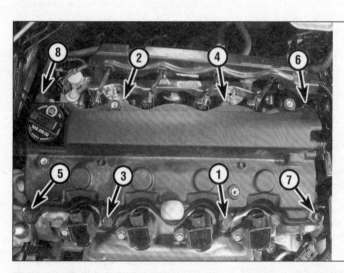

4.10 Valve cover bolt TIGHTENING sequence

## 4   Valve cover - removal and installation

### Removal

1   Disconnect the cable from the negative terminal of the battery (see Chapter 5).
2   Remove the engine cover (see illustration).
3   Mark and detach any hoses or wires from the throttle body, alternator or valve cover (see illustration) that will interfere with the removal of the valve cover.
4   Remove the engine oil dipstick.
5   Wipe off the valve cover thoroughly to prevent debris from falling onto the exposed cylinder head or camshaft/valve train assembly.
6   Remove the valve cover bolts, following the reverse of the tightening sequence (see illustration 4.10).
7   Carefully lift off the valve cover and gas-

ket. If the cover is stuck to the cylinder head, tap it with a rubber mallet to break the gasket seal. Do not pry between the cover and cylinder head or you'll damage the gasket mating surfaces.

### Installation

8   Remove the old gasket and clean the mating surfaces of the cylinder head and the valve cover. Clean the surfaces with a rag soaked in brake system cleaner.
9   Install a new molded rubber gasket into the groove around the valve cover perimeter. Apply beads of RTV sealant where the timing chain cover meets the cylinder head.
10   Place the cover into position and tighten the bolts in the recommended sequence (see illustration) to the torque listed in this Chapter's Specifications.
11   The remainder of installation is the reverse of removal.
12   Reconnect the battery (see Chapter 5).

## 5   Intake manifold - removal and installation

**Warning:** *Gasoline is extremely flammable, so take extra precautions when you work on any part of the fuel system. Don't smoke or allow open flames or bare light bulbs near the work area, and don't work in a garage where a gas-type appliance (such as a water heater or clothes dryer) is present. If you spill any fuel on your skin, rinse it off immediately with soap and water. When you perform any kind of work on the fuel system, wear safety glasses and have a Class B type fire extinguisher on hand.*
**Warning:** *Wait until the engine is completely cool before beginning this procedure.*

### Removal

1   Relieve the fuel system pressure (see Chapter 4), then disconnect the cable from the negative terminal of the battery (see Chapter 5).
2   Remove the intake air duct and air filter housing (see Chapter 4).
3   Clearly label and detach any vacuum lines and electrical connectors which will interfere with removal of the manifold.
4   Disconnect the electrical connectors from the throttle body.
5   Clamp off and disconnect the coolant hoses at the throttle body.
6   Disconnect the fuel feed line at the fuel rail (see Chapter 4).
7   Raise the vehicle and support it securely on jackstands.
8   Remove the lower splash shields (see illustrations 14.3a and 14.3b).
9   Working from underneath the engine compartment, remove the intake manifold (see illustration) support bracket.

5.9 Remove the intake manifold support bracket bolts

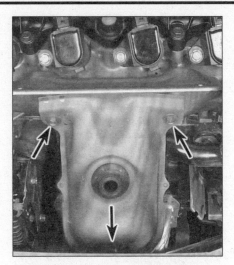

6.7 Heat shield mounting bolts

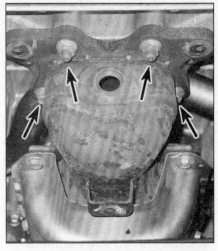

6.9 Location of the exhaust manifold mounting nuts and bolts

10   Disconnect the heater hoses from the intake manifold bracket.

11   Remove the intake manifold nuts and bolts and remove the manifold from the cylinder head.

12   Remove the intake manifold gaskets from the cylinder head.

## Installation

13   Check the mating surfaces of the manifold for flatness with a precision straightedge and feeler gauges.

14   Inspect the manifold for cracks and distortion. If the manifold is cracked or warped, replace it or see if it can be resurfaced at an automotive machine shop.

15   Check carefully for any stripped or broken intake manifold bolts/studs. Replace any defective fasteners with new parts.

16   Remove all traces of old gasket material from the cylinder head and manifold mating surfaces.

17   Install the intake manifold with new gaskets, then install the fasteners and tighten them to the torque listed in this Chapter's Specifications.

18   Reconnect the battery (see Chapter 5).

19   The remainder of installation is the reverse of removal. Refer to Chapter 1 and check the coolant level, adding as necessary.

## 6   Exhaust manifold - removal and installation

### Removal

1   Disconnect the cable from the negative terminal of the battery (see Chapter 5).

2   Raise the front of the vehicle and support it securely on jackstands.

3   Remove the lower splash shields (see illustrations 14.3a and 14.3b).

**Note:** *The exhaust manifold and the catalytic converter are one unit.*

4   Disconnect the oxygen sensor electrical connectors and remove the sensors (see Chapter 6).

5   Remove the EGR pipe mounting bolts and EGR pipe (see Chapter 6).

6   Detach the exhaust pipe from the catalytic converter/exhaust manifold. Apply penetrating oil to the fastener threads if they are difficult to remove.

7   Remove the heat shield mounting bolts and shield (see illustration). Be sure to soak the bolts and nuts with penetrating oil before attempting to remove them.

8   Remove the lower support bracket mounting bolts, if equipped.

9   Remove the exhaust manifold/catalytic converter nuts and bolts (see illustration) and detach the manifold/converter from the cylinder head.

### Installation

10   Discard the old gaskets and use a scraper to clean the gasket mating surfaces, then wipe the surfaces with a rag soaked in brake system cleaner.

11   Place the manifold/converter in position on the cylinder head and install the nuts and bolts. Tighten the nuts and bolts to the torque listed in this Chapter's Specifications.

12   Install the heat shield(s) and tighten the bolts securely.

13   Install the EGR tube using new gaskets and tighten the bolts securely, if equipped.

14   Connect the exhaust pipe to the converter, using new bolts. Tighten the bolts to the torque listed in this Chapter's Specifications.

15   The remainder of installation is the reverse of removal.

16   Reconnect the battery (see Chapter 5).

17   Start the engine and check for exhaust leaks at the cylinder head and the exhaust pipe.

## 7   VTEC system - description and component checks

### General description

1   The VTEC system has the capability of being able to continuously change the valve lift and timing - not just above a certain engine speed. The VTEC uses three different intake cam lobe profiles and two exhaust cam lobes for each cylinder. It is also equipped with a rocker arm oil control valve, and a rocker arm oil pressure switch that works with the ECM/PCM and EGR valve, which alters the phasing of the secondary rocker arms to yield maximum potential power output and proper emissions for any given engine speed. For more information on the VTEC system, see Chapter 6.

2   The differences between conventional engines and the VTEC-equipped engines are strictly in the components and operation of the valve train.

3   The engine management computer has the ability to physically change which camshaft intake lobes are being used to operate the intake valves. The computer turns the system ON or OFF, depending on sensor input.

4   The PGM-FI engine management system relies on information from the vehicle speed sensor (vehicle speed), CKP sensor (engine speed), throttle position sensor (throttle angle), coolant temperature sensor (coolant temperature) and the MAP sensor (engine load).

5   The camshaft has two different intake valve lobe profiles (lift and duration specifications).

6   At low speeds, the secondary intake valve operates on its own camshaft lobe, which has lift and duration profiles designed specifically for the low end torque and responsiveness. The opening (valve duration) is intended to be just enough to keep atomized

**7.8 Rocker arm oil control valve (A) and rocker arm oil pressure switch (B)**

fuel from puddling at the valve head. This limited valve operation is designed to provide good low end torque and responsiveness, by inducing swirl in the combustion chamber from the primary intake valve, which operates with a normal profile.

7    When performance is needed, the primary and secondary rocker arms are locked together through the use of an electrically controlled hydraulic system. Hydraulically operated synchronizing pistons lock two rocker arms together. When activated, the intake valves open to the higher lift and duration of the rocker arm, which has its own camshaft lobe designed with the higher lift profile.
**Note:** *Refer to this Chapter's Specifications for the camshaft lobe lift dimensions.*

## Component checks

**Note:** *The VTEC system requires specialized diagnostic equipment to access the on-board computer to test the electrical circuits, actuators and sensors. However, there are some mechanical tests of the VTEC system that the home mechanic can perform to check for obvious and simple problems within the system. Have the VTEC system diagnosed by a dealer service department or other qualified automotive repair facility. Also, some checks and inspections of the VTEC components require removal of the rocker arm assembly (see Section 8).*

### Rocker arm oil control valve

**Note:** *Most common problems in the VTEC system are associated with the rocker arm oil control valve and its filter. Regular engine oil and filter changes are necessary for trouble-free operation of the valve.*

8    The rocker arm oil control valve is located on the right end of the cylinder head, on the firewall side (see illustration). The rocker arm oil pressure switch is located just below the solenoid valve.
9    Remove the rocker arm oil control valve (see Chapter 6) and check the filter O-ring for clogging. Clean and reinstall with a new O-ring. A clogged filter screen is often the

cause of system problems.
**Note:** *The filter is part of the gasket.*

### Rocker arms

10    Position the number one piston at Top Dead Center (see Section 3). Remove the valve cover (see Section 4).
11    Press on the secondary intake rocker arm(s) for cylinder number 1 to see that it moves independently of the primary intake rocker arm. Check the rockers for the other cylinders at their own TDC positions.

### Synchronizing assembly

12    Once the rocker arm assemblies have been removed and disassembled (see Section 8), separate the rocker arms and synchronizing components.

### VTEC components:

a)  *Primary rocker arm*
b)  *Secondary rocker arms, one for each cylinder.*
c)  *Synchronizing pistons*

13    Inspect the timing spring, making sure it's not broken or collapsed. Replace it if necessary.
14    Inspect all other parts (rocker arms and rocker arm pistons) for wear, galling, scoring or signs of overheating (bluish in color) (see illustration 8.12). Use your finger to push on the rocker arm pistons to check for smooth movement. Replace any parts, if necessary.
15    Reassemble each cylinder's components and wrap a rubber band around the rocker arms before trying to assemble them on the rocker shaft (see Section 8).

---

## 8    Rocker arm assembly - removal, inspection and installation

---

### Removal

1    Remove the engine cover (see illustration 4.2).
2    Remove the valve cover (see Section 4).
3    Position the number one piston at Top Dead Center (see Section 3).
4    Loosen the rocker arm/lost motion holder bolts one turn at a time, in the correct order, until the spring pressure is relieved. Follow the reverse of the tightening sequence (see illustration 8.15).
5    Lift the lost motion holder and lost motion assemblies off of the rocker arm assembly.
6    Lift the rocker arms and shaft assembly from the cylinder head.

### Oil control orifice

7    Pull the orifice from the cylinder head (see illustration 8.12).
**Note:** *There is an O-ring on the lower section of the oil control orifice that must be replaced once it's removed.*

### Inspection

8    If you wish to disassemble and inspect the rocker arm assembly (a good idea as long

as you have them off), remove the retaining bolts and slip the rocker arms, springs, collars and bearing caps off the shafts. Mark the relationship of the shaft(s) to the bearing caps or rocker shaft holders and keep the components in order. They must be reassembled in the same positions they were removed from.
**Caution:** *The rocker arm pistons, located between the secondary intake rocker arms, are spring loaded and can come apart once they are removed from the rocker arm shaft.It is a good idea to bundle the rocker arms together with rubber bands.*
9    Thoroughly clean the components and inspect them for wear and damage. Check the rocker arm faces that contact the camshaft and the rocker arm tips. Check the surfaces of the shafts that the rocker arms ride on, as well as the bearing surfaces inside the rocker arms, for scoring and excessive wear. Replace any parts that are damaged or excessively worn. Note: If any one of the secondary rocker arms is damaged, it must be replaced as an assembly. Make sure the oil holes in the shafts are not plugged.
10    Clean the orifice so there are no obstructions and oil flows freely through the orifice.

### Installation

11    Lubricate all components with engine assembly lubricant or engine oil and reassemble rocker arms on to the shafts. When installing the rocker arms, shafts and springs, note the markings and the difference between the left and right side components (see illustration).
12    Replace the O-ring on the oil control orifice, then install the orifice in the cylinder head (see illustration).
13    Install the rocker arm assembly on the cylinder head.
14    Place the lost motion assemblies into the holder, then install the lost motion holder on the rocker assemblies and tighten the outer two motion holder bolts to the torque listed in this Chapter's Specifications.
15    Tighten all the rocker arm/lost motion holder mounting bolts a little at a time, in the proper sequence (see illustration) to the torque listed in this Chapter's Specifications.
16    The remainder of installation is the reverse of removal. Check and, if necessary, adjust the valve clearance (see Chapter 1).
17    Run the engine and check for oil leaks and proper operation.

---

## 9    Timing chain cover/oil pump housing - removal and installation

---

### Removal

1    Disconnect the cable from the negative battery terminal (see Chapter 5).
2    Loosen the right front wheel lug nuts.
3    Raise the front of the vehicle and support it securely on jackstands. Remove the right front wheel.

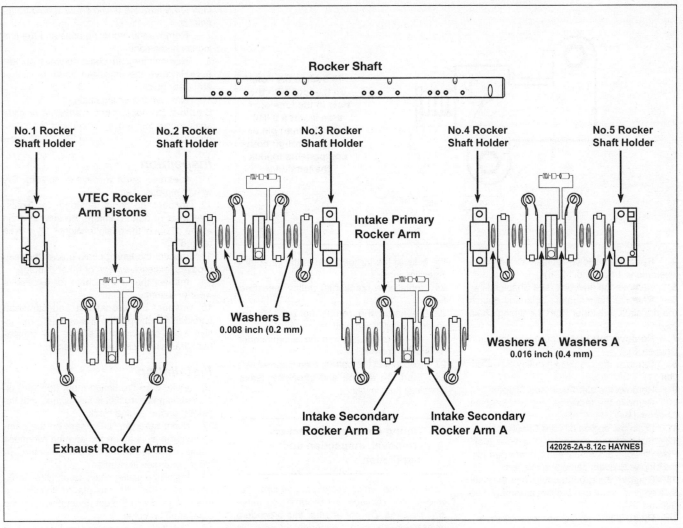

8.11 Exploded view of the rocker arms and shafts

8.12 The oil control orifice and O-ring is located at the right end of the cylinder head, under the No. 1 rocker shaft holder

8.15 Rocker arm and lost motion holder assembly bolt TIGHTENING sequence

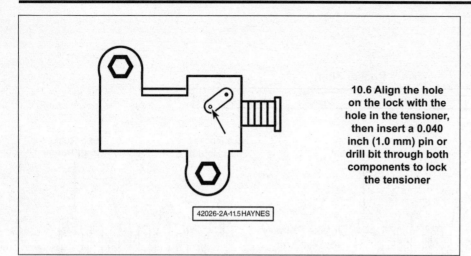

**10.6 Align the hole on the lock with the hole in the tensioner, then insert a 0.040 inch (1.0 mm) pin or drill bit through both components to lock the tensioner**

42026-2A-11.5 HAYNES

4    Remove the lower splash shields (see illustrations 14.3a and 14.3b).
5    Remove the drivebelt (see Chapter 1).
6    Remove the mounting bolts and detach the drivebelt tensioner from the timing chain cover.
7    Remove the water pump pulley (see Chapter 3).
8    Remove the crankshaft pulley (see Section 11).
9    Remove the alternator (see Chapter 5).
10   Remove the tensioner and bracket (see Chapter 1).
11   Drain the engine oil (see Chapter 1).
12   Support the engine with a floor jack. Place a wood block between the jack pad and the oil pan to avoid damaging the pan.
13   Remove the ground cable, and the right side engine mount and bracket assembly (see Section 18).
14   Remove the valve cover (see Section 4).
15   Remove the mounting bolts and the timing chain cover.
16   Remove the engine cover-to-block silicone gasket.

## Installation

17   Inspect and clean all sealing surfaces of the timing chain cover and the block.
**Caution:** *Be very careful when scraping on aluminum engine parts. Aluminum is soft and gouges easily. Severely gouged parts may require replacement.*
18   If necessary, replace the crankshaft seal in the timing chain cover (see Section 11).
19   Apply RTV sealant to the cylinder block mating surfaces on the timing chain cover, the upper surface contact areas and to the oil pan mating surfaces. Also, apply a small amount of RTV sealant to the inner thread holes.
20   Install a new timing chain cover O-ring.
21   Install the timing chain cover and fasteners. Make sure the fasteners are in their original locations. Tighten the fasteners by hand until the cover is contacting the block around its entire periphery.
22   Tighten the bolts, a little at a time, to the torque listed in this Chapter's Specifications.
23   Install the drivebelt tensioner, tightening

the bolts to the torque listed in the Chapter 1 Specifications.
24   Install the crankshaft pulley (see Section 11).
25   Reinstall the remaining parts in the reverse order of removal.
26   Fill the crankcase with the recommended oil (see Chapter 1).
27   Reconnect the battery (see Chapter 5).
28   Start the engine and check for leaks. Check all fluid levels.

## 10   Timing chain and sprockets - removal, inspection and installation

**Caution:** *The timing system is complex. Severe engine damage will occur if you make any mistakes. Do not attempt this procedure unless you are highly experienced with this type of repair. If you are at all unsure of your abilities, consult an expert. Double-check all your work and be sure everything is correct before you attempt to start the engine.*

## Removal

1    Disconnect the cable from the negative battery terminal (see Chapter 5).
2    Remove the lower splash shields (see illustrations 14.3a and 14.3b).
3    Set the engine to TDC number 1 (see Section 3).
4    Remove the valve cover (see Section 4).
5    Remove the timing chain cover (see Section 9).
6    Rotate the crankshaft counterclockwise slightly to compress the chain tensioner. Install a 0.040 inch (1.0 mm) pin into the alignment holes (see illustration), then rotate the crankshaft slightly clockwise to secure the pin. The timing mark (triangle) on the crankshaft sprocket must align with the pointer on the engine block.
**Note:** *Before removing the tensioner, measure the tensioner rod length between the tensioner body and flat surface on the tensioner rod at the bottom. If the length is more than 0.571*

inch (14.5 mm) the timing chain should be replaced.
7    Remove the mounting bolts and the timing chain tensioner.
8    Remove the cam chain (forward) guide.
9    Remove the camshaft chain tensioner arm (rear guide).
10   Remove the timing chain.
**Caution:** *Do not turn the crankshaft or camshaft once the timing chain has been removed.*

## Inspection

11   Clean all parts with clean solvent. Dry with compressed air.
12   Inspect the chain tensioner for excessive wear or other damage. Be sure to drain all the oil out of the chain tensioner if it is to be reused.
13   Inspect the timing chain guides for deep grooves, excessive wear, or other damage.
14   Inspect the timing chain for excessive wear or damage.
15   Inspect the crankshaft and camshaft sprocket for chipped or broken teeth, excessive wear, or damage. Replace any component that is in questionable condition.

## Installation

16   Make sure the timing mark (triangle) on the crankshaft sprocket is still aligned with the pointer on the engine block.
17   Make sure the "UP" mark on the camshaft sprocket is at the top and the two index marks are in line with the top edge of the cylinder head (see illustration).
18   Install the timing chain around the crankshaft sprocket with the plated link on the chain aligned with the dot (indentation) on the crankshaft sprocket.
19   Install the timing chain over the camshaft sprocket with the dot (circular indentations) aligned with the colored chain link.
20   Install the camshaft timing chain guide and the tensioner arm. Tighten the bolts to the torque listed in this Chapter's Specifications.
21   Install the timing chain tensioner. Tighten the bolts to the torque listed in this Chapter's Specifications.
22   Remove the pin from the timing chain tensioner and verify the marks are aligned (see illustration).
23   Slowly turn the crankshaft clockwise two revolutions and recheck the timing marks and camshaft sprocket index marks for proper alignment.
**Caution:** *If the crankshaft binds or seems to hit something, do not force it, as the valves may be hitting the pistons. If this happens, valve timing is incorrect. Remove the chain and repeat the installation procedure and verify that the installation is correct.*
24   Install the valve cover (see Section 4).
25   Install the timing chain cover (see Section 9).
26   The remainder of installation is the reverse of the removal steps.
27   Reconnect the battery (see Chapter 5).
28   Run the engine and check for leaks.

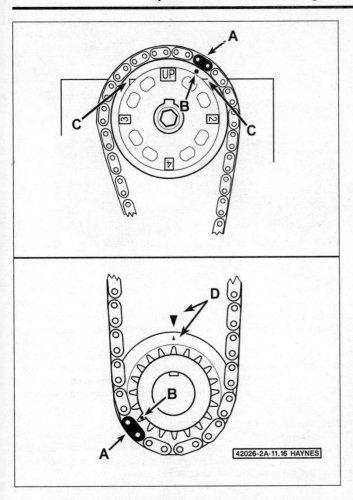

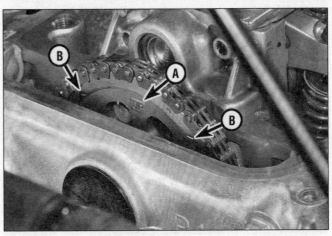

**10.22 Verify the sprocket "UP" mark is at the 12 o'clock position (A). The TDC lines (B) on the camshaft sprocket should line up with the top edge of the cylinder head**

**10.17 Timing chain installation details (engine at TDC compression for cylinder No. 1)**

A   *Plated links on the timing chain*
B   *Sprocket marks*
C   *TDC marks aligned with cylinder head upper surface*
D   *Crankshaft sprocket TDC marks*

**11.4 Carefully pry the oil seal out with a removal tool or a screwdriver - don't nick or scratch the crankshaft or oil pump housing or the new seal will leak**

## 11  Crankshaft pulley and front oil seal - replacement

1   Disconnect the cable from the negative battery terminal (see Chapter 5). Loosen the right front wheel lug nuts. Raise the vehicle and support it securely on jackstands. Remove the wheel and the splash shield from below the engine compartment.
2   Remove the drivebelt (see Chapter 1).
3   Unscrew the crankshaft pulley bolt. A special tool that engages with the recessed hex in the pulley opening is available to prevent the crankshaft from turning while unscrewing the bolt. If you can't obtain one of these tools, remove the flywheel/driveplate inspection cover and wedge a screwdriver into the starter ring gear teeth. Slip the pulley off the crankshaft.
**Note:** *The crankshaft pulley bolt can be incredibly tight; it may be necessary to use an*

*impact tool if the pulley holding tools are not used.*
4   Carefully pry the seal out of the housing with a seal removal tool or a screwdriver (see illustration). Don't scratch the seal bore or damage the crankshaft in the process (if the crankshaft is damaged, the new seal will end up leaking).
5   Clean the bore in the seal housing and coat the outer edge of the new seal with engine oil or multi-purpose grease. Using a seal driver or a socket with an outside diameter slightly smaller than the outside diameter of the seal, carefully drive the seal into place with a hammer until the inner edge of the seal is 7/32 to 15/64-inch (5.55 to 5.95 mm) deep. If a socket is not available, a short section of a large diameter pipe will work. Check the seal after installation to be sure the spring did not pop out.
6   Lubricate the lip of the seal with a thin film of engine oil or multi-purpose grease, then

lubricate the crankshaft bolt with oil between the head of the bolt and the washer and the first few threads of the oil ONLY and install the crankshaft pulley.
**Note:** *The crankshaft pulley has flats on the sleeve that must be aligned with the inner oil pump gear.*
7   The remainder of installation is the reverse of removal.
8   Run the engine and check for leaks.

## 12  Camshaft - removal, inspection and installation

### *Endplay and runout check*
1   To check camshaft endplay:
   a) *With the camshaft installed, reinstall the rocker arm assembly (with the rocker arms removed from it).*

**12.1 To check camshaft endplay, set a dial indicator like this, with the gauge plunger touching the nose of the camshaft - typical gauge setup shown**

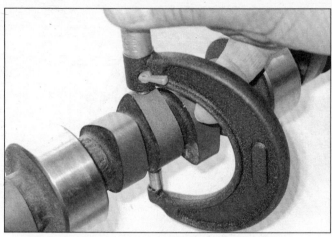

**12.10 Measure the camshaft lobe heights with a micrometer**

**12.14 Be sure to apply camshaft assembly lubricant to the lobes and bearing journals before installing the camshaft**

b) *Mount a dial indicator on the cylinder head with the pointer resting on the camshaft nose (see illustration). Using a large screwdriver as a lever at the opposite end, move the camshaft forward-and-backward and note the dial indicator reading.*

c) *Compare the reading with the endplay listed in this Chapter's Specifications.*

d) *If the indicated reading is excessive, replace the thrust cover with a new one and recheck the endplay. If it's still excessive, either the camshaft or the cylinder head is worn. Replace parts as necessary.*

2    To check camshaft runout:

a) *Support the camshaft with a pair of V-blocks and set up a dial indicator with the plunger resting against the center bearing journal on the camshaft.*

b) *Rotate the camshaft and note the indicated runout.*

c) *Compare the results to the camshaft runout listed in this Chapter's Specifications.*

d) *If the indicated runout exceeds the specified runout limit, replace the camshaft.*

### Removal

3    Remove the ignition coils (see Chapter 5).

4    Remove the valve cover (see Section 4).

5    Set the engine at TDC for cylinder number one (see Section 3) and remove the timing chain (see Section 10).

6    Remove the rocker arm assembly (see Section 8).

7    Hold the camshaft from turning by placing an open-end wrench on the hex at the end of the camshaft opposite that of the sprocket, then unscrew the sprocket bolt and separate the sprocket from the camshaft.

8    Remove the camshaft position sensor (see Chapter 6), then remove the camshaft thrust cover from the end of the cylinder head. Slide the camshaft out of the head.

### Inspection

9    Check the camshaft bearing journals and caps for scoring and signs of wear. If they are worn, replace the cylinder head with a new or rebuilt assembly.

10    Check the cam lobes for wear:

a) *Check the toe and ramp areas of each cam lobe for score marks and uneven wear. Also check for flaking and pitting.*

b) *If there's wear on the toe or the ramp, replace the camshaft, but first try to find the cause of the wear. Look for abrasive substances in the oil and inspect the oil pump and oil passages for blockage. Lobe wear is usually caused by inadequate lubrication or dirty oil.*

c) *Using a micrometer, measure the cam lobe height (see illustration). If lobe wear is indicated, replace the camshaft.*

11    Inspect the rocker arms for wear, galling and pitting of the contact surfaces (see Section 8).

12    If any of the conditions described above are noted, the cylinder head is probably getting insufficient lubrication or dirty oil. Make sure you track down the cause of this problem (low oil level, low oil pump capacity, clogged oil passage, etc.) before installing a new cylinder head, camshaft or rocker arm assembly.

### Installation

13    Thoroughly clean the camshaft, the bearing surfaces in the head and caps and the rocker arms. Wipe off all components with a clean, lint-free cloth.

14    Lubricate the camshaft bearing surfaces in the head and the bearing journals and lobes on the camshaft with camshaft assembly lubricant (see illustration).

**Caution:** *Failure to adequately lubricate the camshaft and related components can cause serious damage to bearing and friction surfaces during the first few seconds after engine start-up, when the oil pressure is low or non-existent.*

15    Install the camshaft.

16    Install the camshaft thrust cover and camshaft position sensor, then install the camshaft sprocket, tightening the bolt to the torque listed in this Chapter's Specifications.

17    Rotate the camshaft as necessary and position the camshaft sprocket with the "UP" mark stamped on the sprocket at the twelve o'clock position.

18    Make sure the camshaft and crankshaft marks are still set to TDC for cylinder number 1, then install the rocker arm assembly (see Section 8).

19    Install the timing chain and related components as described in Section 10.

20    Rotate the crankshaft clockwise, slowly by hand through two complete revolutions and recheck the alignment marks on the sprockets. The timing marks should still be aligned. If they're not, reset all the timing marks again.

**Caution:** *If you feel resistance while rotating the crankshaft, stop immediately!*

21    The remainder of installation is the reverse of removal.

### 13 Cylinder head - removal and installation

**Warning:** *Allow the engine to cool completely before beginning this procedure.*

## Removal

1 Relieve the fuel system pressure (see Chapter 4), then disconnect the cable from the negative terminal of the battery (see Chapter 5).
2 Position the number one piston at Top Dead Center (see Section 3).
3 Drain the cooling system and remove the spark plugs (see Chapter 1).
4 Disconnect the heater hoses, the upper and lower radiator hoses and the bypass hose (see Chapter 3).
5 Remove the air filter housing and intake resonator (see Chapter 4).
6 Remove the drivebelts (see Chapter 1). Unbolt the power steering pump and set it aside without disconnecting any hoses, then remove the power steering pump bracket (see Chapter 10).
7 Disconnect the accelerator cable and cruise control cable (if equipped) from the throttle body (see Chapter 4).
8 Disconnect the EVAP canister hose, the brake booster vacuum hose, the PCV hose and intake breather hose (Chapters 4 and 6).
9 Disconnect the injector harness, the ECT sensor, the TP sensor, the MAP sensor, oxygen sensor, EGR sensor, the CKP sensor, the CMP sensor, the VTEC solenoid (if equipped) and the IAC control valve connectors. Label each connector to prevent incorrect reassembly.
10 Remove the coolant connector hose from the coolant housing.
11 On models equipped with hydraulically assisted power steering, remove the power steering pump without disconnecting the hoses (see Chapter 10).
12 Remove the alternator (see Chapter 5).
13 Remove the power steering bracket (if appliable) and the alternator bracket from the cylinder head.
14 Support the engine with a floor jack. Place a wood block between the jack pad and the oil pan to avoid damaging the pan. Remove the right engine mount bracket (see Section 18).
15 Remove the intake manifold brace, the intake manifold (see Section 5) and the exhaust manifold (see Section 6).
16 Remove the valve cover (see Section 4).
17 Remove the timing chain (see Section 10) and the rocker arm assembly (see Section 8).
18 Loosen the cylinder head bolts in 1/4-turn increments until they can be removed by hand. Work in a pattern that's the reverse of the tightening sequence to avoid warping the cylinder head (see illustration 13.26).
**Caution:** *Discard the old bolts and obtain new ones (re-using the old bolts is not recommended, and, the final tightening stage assumes*

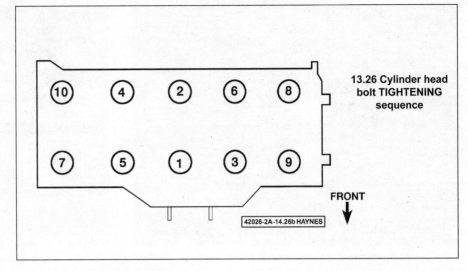

**13.26 Cylinder head bolt TIGHTENING sequence**

FRONT

42026-2A-14.26b HAYNES

*that new bolts are being installed).*
19 Lift the cylinder head off the engine. If resistance is felt, don't pry between the head and block gasket mating surfaces - damage to the mating surfaces will result. Instead, pry between a casting protrusion and the engine block. Set the head on blocks of wood to prevent damage to the gasket sealing surfaces.
20 Have an automotive machine shop check the cylinder head for warpage, and, if necessary, resurface it.

## Installation

21 The mating surfaces of the cylinder head and block must be perfectly clean when the head is installed.
22 Use a gasket scraper to remove all traces of carbon and old gasket material, then clean the mating surfaces with brake system cleaner. If there's oil on the mating surfaces when the cylinder head is installed, the gasket may not seal correctly and leaks may develop. When working on the engine block, stuff the cylinders with clean shop rags to keep out debris. Use a vacuum cleaner to remove material that falls into the cylinders. Since the cylinder head and engine block are made of aluminum, aggressive scraping can cause damage. Be extra careful not to nick or gouge the mating surfaces with the scraper.
23 Check the block and cylinder head mating surfaces for nicks, deep scratches and other damage. If damage is slight, it can be removed with a file; if it's excessive, machining may be the only alternative.
24 Use a tap of the correct size to chase the threads in the cylinder head bolt holes. Use a wire brush to remove corrosion and clean the bolt threads. Dirt, corrosion, sealant and damaged threads will affect torque readings.
25 Place a new gasket on the engine block.
**Note:** *Always install a new coolant separator (the timing chain end of the engine) into the block if the block was replaced or the separator was damaged before installing a new head gasket. Check to see if there are any markings (such as "TOP") on the gasket to indicate how it is to be installed. Those identification*

marks must face up. Set the cylinder head in position.
26 Lubricate the threads and the seats of the NEW cylinder head bolts with clean engine oil, then install them. Tighten the bolts in the recommended sequence, in stages, to the torque listed in this Chapter's Specifications (see illustration). Because of the critical function of cylinder head bolts, the manufacturer specifies the following conditions for tightening them:

a) *A beam-type or dial-type torque wrench is preferable to a pre-set (click-stop) torque wrench. If you use a pre-set torque wrench, tighten slowly and be careful not to overtighten the bolts.*
b) *If a bolt makes any sound while you're tightening it (squeaking, clicking, etc.), loosen it completely and tighten it again in the specified stages.*

27 Install the timing chain (see Section 10) and rocker arm assembly (see Section 8).
28 Rotate the crankshaft, clockwise, slowly by hand through two complete revolutions, then recheck the alignment marks on the sprockets.
**Caution:** *If you feel any resistance while turning the engine over, stop and re-check the camshaft timing. The valves might be hitting the pistons.*
29 Reinstall the remaining parts in the reverse order of removal.
30 Refill the cooling system and change the engine oil and filter (see Chapter 1).
31 Reconnect the battery (see Chapter 5).
32 Run the engine until normal operating temperature is reached. Check for leaks and proper operation.

### 14 Oil pan - removal and installation

## Removal

1 Drain the engine oil and replace the oil filter (see Chapter 1).
2 Disconnect the cable from the negative terminal of the battery (see Chapter 5).

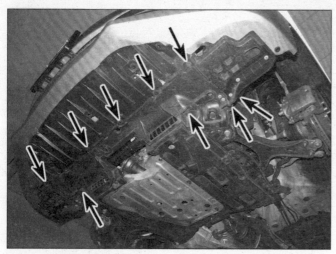

**14.3a Radiator splash shield fastener locations**

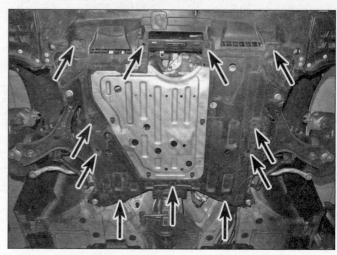

**14.3b Engine splash shield fastener locations**

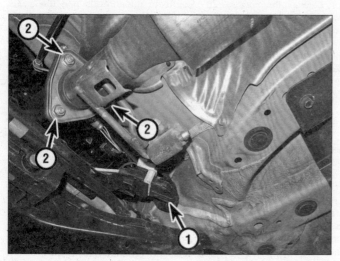

**14.4 Disconnect the CVT harness connector (1), then the exhaust pipe nuts (2)**

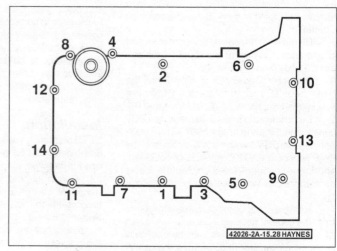

**14.19 Engine oil pan bolt tightening sequence**

3    Raise the vehicle and support it securely on jackstands. Remove the splash shields from under the engine (see illustrations).

4    On CVT models, disconnect the CVT harness electrical connector (see illustration).

5    Remove the front section of the exhaust pipe (see Chapter 4).

6    Remove the lower torque rod (see Section 18).

7    Remove the lower torque rod bracket bolts and bracket.

8    Remove the air conditioning compressor bracket (see Chapter 3).

9    On models equipped with an automatic transmission, remove the shift cable cover bolts, torque converter cover bolts and remove the covers.

10   On models equipped with a manual transmission, remove the clutch cover bolts and cover.

11   Remove the bottom two transmission mounting bolts.

12   Remove the bolts securing the oil pan to the engine block.

13   Tap on the pan with a soft-face hammer to break the gasket seal and detach the oil pan from the engine.

**Note:** *Pull the dowel pins out from the block once the pan has been removed.*

### Installation

14   Using a gasket scraper, remove all traces of old gasket and/or sealant from the engine block and the oil pan. Also make sure the threaded bolt holes in the block are clean.

15   Clean the oil pan with solvent and dry it thoroughly. Check the gasket flanges for distortion, particularly around the bolt holes. If necessary, place the pan on a wood block and use a hammer to flatten and restore the

gasket surface.

16   Clean the mating surfaces on the engine block and the oil pan with brake system cleaner to remove any oil residue which will prevent the new gasket from sealing properly.

17   Replace the O-rings and apply a 1/8-inch wide bead of RTV sealant to the perimeter of the oil pan, along the inboard side of the bolt holes.

18   Carefully place the oil pan in position and install the bolts finger-tight.

19   Tighten the oil pan bolts in the correct sequence (see illustration) and to the torque listed in this Chapter's Specifications.

20   The remainder of installation is the reverse of removal.

21   Reconnect the battery (see Chapter 5).

22   Wait at least one hour before adding oil (see Chapter 1), then run the engine and check for oil leaks.

**15.3a Use a feeler gauge and straight-edge to check the clearance between the rotors and the cover**

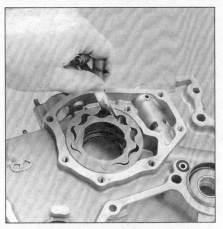

**15.3b Use a feeler gauge to check the tooth-tip clearance between the inner and outer rotors**

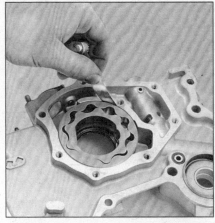

**15.3c Use a feeler gauge to check the outer rotor-to-pump body clearance**

## 15  Oil pump - removal, inspection and installation

### Removal

1    Remove the timing chain cover (see Section 9).

2    Remove the screws from the oil pump cover-to-timing chain cover and separate the oil pump cover from the timing chain cover and disassemble the oil pump. You may need to use an impact screwdriver to loosen the pump cover screws without stripping the heads.

### Inspection

3    Check the oil pump rotor-to-cover clearance, tooth tip clearance and rotor-to-body clearance (see illustrations). Compare your measurements to the values listed in this Chapter's Specifications. Replace the pump if any of the measurements exceed the specified limits.

4    Remove the pressure relief valve plug and extract the spring and pressure relief valve plunger from the pump housing or cover. Check the spring for distortion and the relief valve plunger for scoring. Replace parts as necessary.

5    Install the pump rotors. Pack the spaces between the rotors with petroleum jelly (this will prime the pump).

6    Apply thread-locking compound to the pump cover screws, install the cover and tighten the screws to the torque listed in this Chapter's Specifications. Install the oil pressure relief valve and spring assembly. Use a new sealing washer on the plug and tighten the plug securely.

### Installation

7    Apply a thin coat of anaerobic sealant to the timing chain cover-to-block sealing surface and new O-rings in the engine cover. Install the timing chain cover (see Section 9)

**16.3 Remove the flywheel/driveplate bolts from the crankshaft**

to the engine block and tighten the bolts to the torque listed in this Chapter's Specifications.

8    The remainder of installation is the reverse of removal. Add the specified type and quantity of oil and coolant (see Chapter 1); run the engine and check for leaks.

## 16  Flywheel/driveplate - removal and installation

### Removal

1    Raise the vehicle and support it securely on jackstands, then refer to Chapter 7A and remove the transaxle.

2    If the vehicle is equipped with a manual transaxle, remove the pressure plate and clutch disc (see Chapter 8). Now is a good time to check/replace the clutch components and pilot bearing.

3    Remove the bolts that secure the flywheel/driveplate to the crankshaft (see illustration). If the crankshaft turns, wedge a screwdriver in the ring gear teeth (manual transaxle

models), or insert a long punch through one of the holes in the driveplate and allow it to rest against a projection on the engine block (automatic transaxle models).

4    Remove the flywheel/driveplate from the crankshaft. Since the flywheel is fairly heavy, be sure to support it while removing the last bolt.

5    Clean the flywheel to remove grease and oil. Inspect the surface for cracks, rivet grooves, burned areas and score marks. Light scoring can be removed with emery cloth. Check for cracked and broken ring gear teeth. Lay the flywheel on a flat surface and use a straightedge to check for warpage.

6    Clean and inspect the mating surfaces of the flywheel/driveplate and the crankshaft. If the rear main oil seal is leaking, replace it before reinstalling the flywheel/driveplate (see Section 17).

### Installation

7    Position the flywheel/driveplate against the crankshaft. Note that some engines have an alignment dowel or staggered bolt holes to

**17.4 Carefully pry the oil seal out with a seal removal tool or a screwdriver (don't nick or scratch the crankshaft, or the new seal will be damaged and leaks will develop)**

is checked. Use a small ruler or caliper and record the distance. The new seal must not be driven in past this measurement.

4    The seal can be replaced without removing the oil pan or seal retainer (if equipped). Use a screwdriver to carefully pry the seal out (see illustration).

5    Apply a film of clean oil to the crankshaft seal journal and the lip of the new seal and carefully tap the seal into place. The lip is stiff, so carefully work it onto the seal journal of the crankshaft with a smooth object like the end of a socket extension (see illustration). Tap the seal into the retainer with a seal driver.

6    The remaining steps are the reverse of removal.

7    Run the engine and check for oil leaks.

**17.5 Lubricate the journal and the seal lip with multi-purpose grease and carefully work the seal over the journal with a smooth, blunt object**

ensure correct installation. Before installing the bolts, apply thread-locking compound to the threads.

8    Prevent the flywheel/driveplate from turning by using one of the methods described in Step 3. Using a criss-cross pattern, tighten the bolts to the torque listed in this Chapter's Specifications.

9    The remainder of installation is the reverse of the removal procedure.

## 17   Rear main oil seal - replacement

1    The transaxle must be removed from the vehicle for this procedure (see Chapter 7A).

2    Remove the flywheel/driveplate (see Section 16).

3    Before removing the seal, it is very important that the clearance between the seal and the outside edge of the retainer or block

## 18   Engine mounts - check and replacement

1    Engine mounts seldom require attention, but broken or deteriorated mounts should be replaced immediately or the added strain placed on the driveline components may cause damage or wear.

### Check

2    During the check, the engine must be raised slightly to remove the weight from the mounts.

3    Raise the vehicle and support it securely on jackstands, then position a jack under the engine oil pan. Place a large wood block between the jack head and the oil pan, then carefully raise the engine just enough to take the weight off the mounts.

**Warning:** *DO NOT place any part of your body under the engine when it's supported only by a jack!*

4    Check the mount insulators to see if the rubber is cracked, hardened or separated from the metal in the center of the mount.

5    Check for relative movement between the

mount plates and the engine or frame (use a large screwdriver or pry bar to attempt to move the mounts). If movement is noted, lower the engine and tighten the mount fasteners.

### Replacement

6    Disconnect the cable from the negative terminal of the battery (see Chapter 5). If the lower torque rod is being replaced, raise the vehicle and support it securely on jackstands (if not already done). Support the engine as described in Step 3.

#### Engine mounts

7    Remove the fasteners, raise the engine with the jack and detach the mount from the frame bracket and engine.

8    Install the new mount, making sure it is correctly positioned in its bracket (see illustrations). Install the fasteners and tighten them securely.

**18.8a Engine mount bracket fasteners**

1    *Mount bracket-to-engine bolts*
2    *Mount-to-body bolts*
3    *Mount through-bolt*
4    *Mount side bracket bolt/nut*

**18.8b Lower torque rod mounting bolt locations - R18Z1 model shown**

**18.11 Air filter housing bracket bolts**

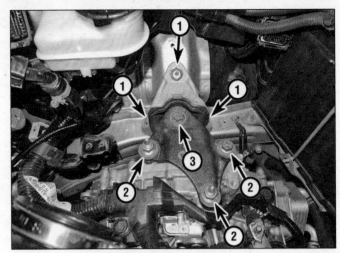

**18.13 Transaxle mount fastener locations - automatic transaxle shown, manual transaxle similar**

1    *Mount bracket-to-body bolts*
2    *Mount bracket-to-transaxle nuts/bolt*
3    *Mount through-bolt*

## Transaxle mount

9    Remove the air filter housing (see Chapter 4).
10    Remove the PCM (see Chapter 6).
11    Remove the PCM and air filter housing bracket mounting bolts (see illustration) and remove the bracket.
12    Support the transaxle with the jack.
13    Remove the transaxle mount fasteners (see illustration) and remove the mount.

14    Installation is the reverse of removal, tighten all the mount fasteners to the torque listed in this Chapter's Specifications.

# Notes

# Chapter 2 Part B
# 2.4L double overhead camshaft (DOHC) engines

## Contents

## Specifications

### General

| | |
|---|---|
| Firing order | 1-3-4-2 |
| Bore | 3.43 inches (87 mm) |
| Stroke | 3.90 inches (99 mm) |
| Displacement | 144 cubic inches (2.4 liters) |
| Oil pressure | See Chapter 2C |
| Valve adjustment | See Chapter 1 |

**①②③④**

**Front**

↓

42026-2B-specs HAYNES

**Cylinder locations**

### Camshafts

| | |
|---|---|
| Lobe height | |
| Intake | |
| Primary | 1.32850 inch (33.744 mm) |
| Mid | 1.3959 inches (35.456 mm) |
| Secondary | 1.32850 inches (33.744 mm) |
| Exhaust | 1.35004 inches (34.291 mm) |
| Endplay | 0.002 to 0.008 inch (0.050 to 0.20 mm) |
| Runout | 0.0012 inch (0.030 mm) |
| Journal-to-bearing (oil) clearance | |
| Journal number 1 | 0.00118 to 0.00272 inch (0.030 to 0.069 mm) |
| Journal number 2, 3, 4, 5 | 0.00236 to 0.00390 inch (0.060 to 0.099 mm) |

## Oil pump

Rotor-to-cover clearance
    Standard ................................................................................. 0.0014 to 0.0028 inch (0.035 to 0.070 mm)
    Service limit ............................................................................ 0.005 inch maximum (0.12 mm)
Tooth tip clearance
    Standard ................................................................................. 0.002 to 0.005 inch (0.05 to 0.15 mm)
    Service limit ............................................................................ 0.007 inch maximum (0.19 mm)
Outer rotor-to-pump body clearance
    Standard ................................................................................. 0.006 to 0.008 inch (0.15 to 0.20 mm)
    Service limit ............................................................................ 0.009 inch maximum (0.23 mm)
Balance shaft end play
    Standard ................................................................................. 0.0028 to 0.00425 inch (0.063 to 0.108 mm)
    Service limit ............................................................................ 0.0055 inch (0.14 mm)

## Torque specifications

**Note:** *One foot-pound (ft-lb) of torque is equivalent to 12 inch-pounds (in-lbs) of torque. Torque values below approximately 15 ft-lbs are expressed in inch-pounds, since most foot-pound torque wrenches are not accurate at these smaller values.*

|  | Ft-lbs (unless otherwise indicated) | Nm |
|---|---|---|
| Oil pump/balance shaft sprocket bolt | 33 | 45 |
| Balance shaft case bolt | | |
|     Short bolts | 108 in-lbs | 12 |
|     Long bolts | 20 | 27 |
| Balance shaft assembly-to-engine block bolts | | |
|     Short bolts (8 mm) | 16 | 22 |
|     Long bolts (10 mm) | 33 | 45 |
| Camshaft sprocket bolts | | |
|     Intake camshaft sprocket (VTC actuator) | 85 | 115 |
|     Exhaust camshaft sprocket | 54 | 73 |
| Camshaft holder bolts | | |
|     6 mm bolts | 108 in-lbs | 12 |
|     8 mm bolts | 16 | 22 |
| Crankshaft pulley bolt | | |
|     Old bolt and pulley | | |
|         Step 1 | 36 | 49 |
|         Step 2 | Tighten an additional 90-degrees | |
|     New bolt or pulley | | |
|         Step 1 | 131 | 177 |
|         Step 2 | Remove the bolt | |
|         Step 3 | 37 | 50 |
|         Step 4 | Tighten an additional 90-degrees | |
| Cylinder head bolts* | | |
|     Step 1 | 29 | 39 |
|     Step 2 | Tighten an additional 90-degrees | |
|     Step 3 | Tighten an additional 90-degrees | |
|     Step 4 | Tighten an additional 90-degrees | |
| Drivebelt tensioner bolts | 16 | 22 |
| Driveplate bolts | 54 | 73 |
| Flywheel bolts | 91 | 123 |
| Exhaust manifold bolts/nuts | 23 | 31 |
| Exhaust manifold heat shield bolts | | |
| Exhaust manifold heat shield bolts | 16 | 22 |
|     Civic, 2014 and earlier CR-V models | 89 in-lbs | 10 |
|     2015 and later CR-V models | 16 | 22 |
| Timing chain cover bolts | 108 in-lbs | 12 |
| Intake manifold bolts | | |
|     Civic, 2014 and earlier CR-V models | 16 | 22 |
|     2015 and later CR-V models | 18 | 24 |
| Oil cooler hose joint pipe mounting bolt | 104 in-lbs | 11.5 |
| Oil pump housing bolts | 108 in-lbs | 12 |
| Oil pump pressure relief valve plug | 29 | 39 |
| Oil pan bolts | 108 in-lbs | 12 |
| Timing chain tensioner bolts | 108 in-lbs | 11.5 |
| Timing chain guides | | |
|     Camshaft chain guide bolts | 108 in-lbs | 12 |
|     Tensioner arm bolt | 16 | 22 |
|     Upper timing chain guide bolts | 16 | 22 |
| Valve cover nuts/bolts | | |
|     Civic/2014 and earlier CR-V models | 104 in-lbs | 12 |
|     2015 and later CR-V models | 62.5 in-lbs | 7 |
| Engine cover bolts | 108 in-lbs | 12 |

**Note:** *\*Bolts must be replaced.*

## 1   General Information

1    This part of Chapter 2B is devoted to in-vehicle repair procedures for the 2.4L DOHC (Double Overhead Camshaft), engine as well as procedures such as timing chain and sprocket(s), balance shaft chain and balance shafts and oil pan removal. All information concerning engine removal and installation can be found in Part C of this Chapter.

2    Two different versions of this engine have been produced by Honda for the CR-V and Civic models, both of which are covered in this part of Chapter 2B. All versions of this engine utilize a Double Overhead Camshaft (DOHC), with 4 valves per cylinder (16V). This engine incorporates the i-VTEC (intelligent Variable Valve Timing and lift Electronic Control) system, which electronically alters valve timing to enhance engine performance. For more information on the i-VTEC system, see Section 10 of this Chapter.

3    Engine designations and application include:

a) *K24Z7- 2.4L 16 valve DOHC i-VTEC (Civic models)*

b) *K24Z7- 2.4L 16 valve DOHC i-VTEC, 2014 and earlier CR-V models*

c) *K24W9- 2.4L 16 valve DOHC i-VTEC engine, 2015 and later CR-V models (product of USA and Canada)*

d) *K24V1- 2.4L 16 valve DOHC i-VTEC engine, 2015 and later CR-V models (product of Mexico)*

4    The Specifications included in this Chapter apply only to the procedures contained in this part. Chapter 2C contains the Specifications necessary for certain procedures concerning engine rebuilding.

## 2   Repair operations possible with the engine in the vehicle

1    Many major repair operations can be accomplished without removing the engine from the vehicle.

2    Clean the engine compartment and the exterior of the engine with some type of degreaser before any work is done. It will make the job easier and help keep dirt out of the internal areas of the engine.

3    Depending on the components involved, it may be helpful to remove the hood to improve access to the engine as repairs are performed (refer to Chapter 11 if necessary). Cover the fenders to prevent damage to the paint. Special pads are available, but an old bedspread or blanket will also work.

4    If vacuum, exhaust, oil or coolant leaks develop, indicating a need for gasket or seal replacement, the repairs can generally be made with the engine in the vehicle. The intake and exhaust manifold gaskets, oil pan gasket, crankshaft oil seals and cylinder head gasket are all accessible with the engine in place.

5    Exterior engine components, such as the intake and exhaust manifolds, the oil pan, the oil pump, the water pump, the starter motor, the alternator and the fuel system components can be removed for repair with the engine in place.

6    Since the cylinder head can be removed without pulling the engine, camshaft and valve component servicing can also be accomplished with the engine in the vehicle. Replacement of the timing chain and sprockets is also possible with the engine in the vehicle.

7    In extreme cases caused by a lack of necessary equipment, repair or replacement of piston rings, pistons, connecting rods and rod bearings is possible with the engine in the vehicle. However, this practice is not recommended because of the cleaning and preparation work that must be done to the components involved.

## 3   Top Dead Center (TDC) for number one piston - locating

1    Remove the spark plugs (see Chapter 1) and install a compression gauge in the number one cylinder. Turn the crankshaft clockwise with a socket and breaker bar.

2    When the piston approaches TDC, compression will be noted on the compression gauge. Continue turning the crankshaft until the notch with the white mark in the crankshaft pulley is aligned with the TDC mark on the timing chain cover. At this point, number one cylinder is at TDC on the compression stroke.

3    After the number one piston has been positioned at TDC on the compression stroke, TDC for any of the remaining pistons can be located by turning the crankshaft clockwise, 180-degrees at a time, and following the firing order.

## 4   Valve cover - removal and installation

### *Removal*

1    Disconnect the cable from the negative battery terminal (see Chapter 5).

2    On Civic models, remove the cowl cover (see Chapter 11).

3    Remove the two engine cover screws, then pull the cover up and off of the ballstud to remove the cover.

4    Remove the ignition coils (see Chapter 5).

5    On 2015 and later CR-V models, disconnect the wiring to the alternator, then release the harness retainers and move the harness out of the way.

6    On CR-V models, remove the dipstick, disconnect the valve cover breather hose and PCV hose.

7    On 2015 and later CR-V models, remove the high-pressure fuel pump cover.

8    Remove the valve cover nuts or bolts (see illustrations 4.11). Lift the valve cover off. Tap gently with a soft-face hammer if necessary to break the gasket seal.

### *Installation*

9    Clean the gasket surfaces on the intake manifold, cylinder head and valve cover. Use a shop rag and brake system cleaner to wipe off all residue and gasket material from the sealing surfaces.

10   Insert a new valve cover gasket into the grooved recess in the valve cover. Make sure the gasket is positioned properly inside the valve cover groove.

11   Install new seals on the spark plug tubes.

12   Apply a slight amount of RTV sealant to

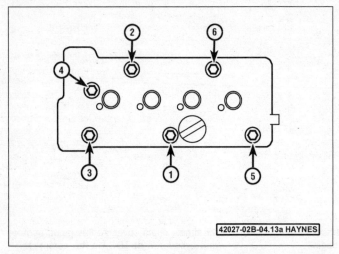

4.13a Valve cover nut tightening sequence - Civic, 2014 and earlier CR-V models

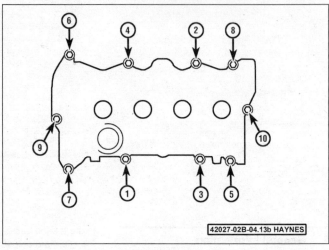

4.13b Valve cover bolt tightening sequence - 2015 and later CR-V models

the timing chain cover grooves and the high-pressure fuel pump base (if equipped), mating areas.

13  Tighten the valve cover nuts/bolts in the correct sequence to the torque listed in this Chapter's Specifications (see illustrations).

14  The remainder of installation is the reverse of removal.

15  Reconnect the battery (see Chapter 5).

## 5  Intake manifold - removal and installation

**Warning:** *Wait until the engine is completely cool before beginning this procedure.*

### Removal

1  If you're working on a 2015 or later CR-V model, relieve the fuel system pressure (see Chapter 4).

2  Disconnect the cable from the negative battery terminal (see Chapter 5).

3  Remove the engine cover bolts and pull the cover off of the ballstuds, then disconnect the breather hose from the valve cover and the intake manifold.

4  Remove the intake duct and the air filter housing (see Chapter 4).

5  Unbolt the throttle body from the intake manifold and position it aside (see Chapter 4).

**Note:** *Do not disconnect the coolant hoses from the throttle body.*

### Civic and 2014 and earlier CR-V models

6  Disconnect the vacuum hoses from the intake manifold. Mark each hose with tape to insure correct reassembly.

7  Disconnect the IAC valve, the TPS, the knock sensor and any other electrical connectors that may interfere with manifold removal.

8  Disconnect the purge solenoid vacuum hose and the EVAP purge solenoid (see Chapter 6).

9  Raise the front of the vehicle and support it securely on jackstands, then remove the under-vehicle splash shield (see illustrations 14.3a and 14.3b in Chapter 2A).

10  Remove the intake manifold bracket from below the intake manifold.

11  Remove the intake manifold mounting bolts/nuts and pull the manifold back to disconnect the PCV hose from the retainer and manifold.

12  Lift the intake manifold from the engine compartment.

### 2015 and later CR-V models

13  Disconnect the fuel line to the fuel rail (see Chapter 4).

14  Disconnect the brake booster vacuum hose and PCV hose from the intake manifold (see Chapter 1). Release the fuel line clips and remove the fuel line.

15  Raise the front of the vehicle and support it securely on jackstands, then remove the under-vehicle splash shield (see illustrations 14.3a and 14.3b in Chapter 2A).

16  Remove the intake manifold support bracket bolt/nuts and remove the bracket from under the manifold.

17  Remove the intake manifold mounting bolts and nuts.

18  Lift the intake manifold from the engine compartment.

### Installation

19  Clean away all traces of old gasket material. Remove oil and dirt.

20  Install a new gasket.

21  Install the manifold and mounting fasteners. Tighten the fasteners to the torque listed in this Chapter's Specifications, starting with the center bolts and working toward the ends.

22  The remainder of installation is the reverse of the removal steps.

23  Reconnect the battery (see Chapter 5).

24  Run the engine and check for oil, coolant and vacuum leaks.

## 6  Exhaust manifold - removal and installation

### Removal

**Note:** *The exhaust manifold and the warm-up catalytic converter are one unit.*

1  Disconnect the cable from the negative terminal of the battery (see Chapter 5).

2  Raise the front of the vehicle and support it securely on jackstands.

3  On Civic, 2014 and earlier CR-V models, remove the cowl panel (see Chapter 11).

4  Remove the lower splash shields (see illustrations 14.3a and 14.3b in Chapter 2A).

5  Disconnect the oxygen sensor electrical connectors and remove the sensors (see Chapter 6).

6  Detach the exhaust pipe from the catalytic converter/exhaust manifold. Apply penetrating oil to the fastener threads if they are difficult to remove.

7  Remove the heat shield mounting bolts and shields. Be sure to soak the bolts and nuts with penetrating oil before attempting to remove them from the manifold.

8  Remove the lower support bracket mounting bolts.

9  Remove the converter nuts and bolts and detach the converter from the cylinder head.

### Installation

10  Discard the old gaskets and use a scraper to clean the gasket mating surfaces on the exhaust manifold or catalytic converter and cylinder head, then clean the surfaces with a rag soaked in brake system cleaner.

11  Place the exhaust manifold/catalytic converter in position on the cylinder head and install the nuts and bolts. Tighten the nuts and bolts to the torque listed in this Chapter's Specifications.

12  Install the heat shield(s) and tighten the bolts securely.

13  Connect the exhaust pipe to the con-

verter, using new bolts. Tighten the bolts securely.

14 The remainder of installation is the reverse of removal.

15 Reconnect the battery (see Chapter 5).

16 Start the engine and check for exhaust leaks at the cylinder head and the exhaust pipe.

## 7   Timing chain cover - removal and installation

**Warning:** *Wait until the engine is completely cool before beginning this procedure.*

### Removal

1 Disconnect the cable from the negative battery terminal (see Chapter 5).

2 Remove the VTC oil control solenoid valve from the timing chain cover.

3 On Civic models, remove the cowl panel (see Chapter 11).

4 Loosen the right front wheel lug nuts. Raise the front of the vehicle and support it securely on jackstands. Remove the right front wheel.

5 Remove the splash shields from below the engine compartment (see Chapter 2A, illustrations 14.3a and 14.3b).

6 Drain the engine oil (see Chapter 1) and remove the drivebelt (see Chapter 1).

7 Remove the mounting bolts and detach the drivebelt tensioner from the timing chain cover.

8 Remove the crankshaft pulley (see Section 9).

9 Disconnect the crankshaft position sensor harness and other electrical connectors that may interfere with timing chain cover removal.

10 Drain the cooling system (see Chapter 1). Remove the oil cooler joint pipe mounting bolt from the water pump (if equipped). Pull the joint pipe back and out, then remove the O-ring.

11 Support the engine with a floor jack. Place a wood block between the jack head and the oil pan to avoid damaging the pan.

12 Remove the ground cable and the right-side engine mount and bracket assembly (see Section 18).

13 Remove the valve cover (see Section 4).

14 Remove the mounting bolts and the timing chain cover.

15 Remove the cover-to-block gasket.

### Installation

16 Inspect and clean all sealing surfaces of the timing chain cover and the block.

**Caution:** *Be very careful when scraping on aluminum engine parts. Aluminum is soft and gouges easily. Severely gouged parts may require replacement.*

17 If necessary, replace the crankshaft seal (see Section 9).

18 Apply RTV sealant to the cylinder block mating surfaces on the cover, the upper surface contact areas and to the oil pan mating surfaces. Also, apply a small amount of RTV

sealant to the inner thread holes.

19 Install a new timing chain cover O-ring.

20 Install the timing chain cover and fasteners. Make sure the fasteners are in their original locations. Tighten the fasteners by hand until the cover is contacting the block around its entire periphery.

21 Tighten the bolts to the torque listed in this Chapter's Specifications.

22 Install a new O-ring onto the oil cooler joint pipe and insert the pipe into the water pump. Tighten the bolt to the torque listed in this Chapter's Specifications.

23 Install the drivebelt tensioner, tightening the bolts to the torque listed in this Chapter's Specifications.

24 Install the crankshaft pulley (see Section 9).

25 Connect the wiring harness connectors. Secure the wiring harnesses with the clamps.

26 Reinstall the remaining parts in the reverse order of removal.

27 Fill the crankcase with the recommended oil (see Chapter 1).

28 Refill the cooling system (see Chapter 1).

29 Reconnect the battery (see Chapter 5).

30 Start the engine and check for leaks. Check all fluid levels.

## 8   Timing chain and sprockets - removal, inspection and installation

**Warning:** *Wait until the engine is completely cool before beginning this procedure.*

**Caution:** *The timing system is complex. Severe engine damage will occur if you make any mistakes. Do not attempt this procedure unless you are highly experienced with this type of repair. If you are at all unsure of your abilities, consult an expert. Double-check all your work and be sure everything is correct before you attempt to start the engine.*

### Removal

1 Disconnect the cable from the negative battery terminal (see Chapter 5).

2 Set the engine to TDC on the compres-

sion stroke for cylinder number 1 (see Section 3).

3 On 2015 and later CR-V models, remove the high-pressure fuel pump (see Chapter 4).

4 Remove the valve cover (see Section 4).

5 Remove the timing chain cover (see Section 7).

6 Rotate the crankshaft counterclockwise slightly to compress the chain tensioner. Install a 0.06 inch (1.5 mm) pin into the alignment holes (see illustration) and rotate the crankshaft slightly clockwise, returning it to TDC, to secure the pin.

7 Remove the mounting bolts and the timing chain tensioner.

8 Remove the upper timing chain guide from between the camshaft sprockets.

9 Remove the camshaft timing chain guide and the tensioner arm (chain guide).

10 Remove the timing chain.

### Inspection

11 Clean all parts with solvent. Dry with compressed air, if available.

12 Inspect the chain tensioner for excessive wear or other damage. Be sure to drain all the oil out of the chain tensioner if it is to be reused.

13 Inspect the timing chain guides for deep grooves, excessive wear, or other damage.

14 Inspect the timing chain for excessive wear or damage.

15 Inspect the crankshaft and camshaft sprockets for chipped or broken teeth, excessive wear, or damage. Replace any component that is in questionable condition.

### Installation

**Caution:** *Before starting the engine, carefully rotate the crankshaft by hand through at least two full revolutions (use a socket and breaker bar on the crankshaft pulley center bolt). If you feel any resistance, STOP! There is something wrong - most likely, valves are contacting the pistons. You must find the problem before proceeding. Check your work and see if any updated repair information is available.*

16 Make sure the timing mark (triangle) on the crankshaft sprocket is aligned with the pointer on the engine block.

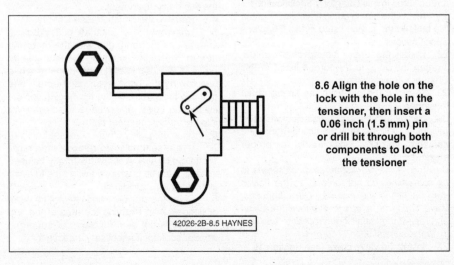

**8.6 Align the hole on the lock with the hole in the tensioner, then insert a 0.06 inch (1.5 mm) pin or drill bit through both components to lock the tensioner**

42026-2B-8.5 HAYNES

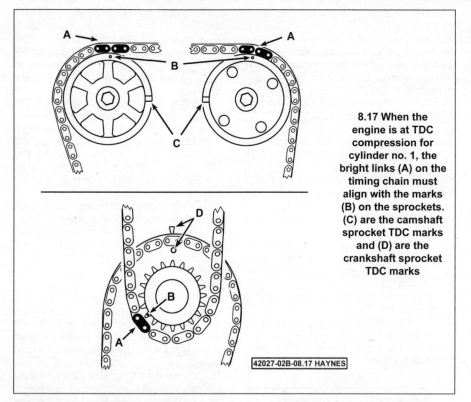

**8.17 When the engine is at TDC compression for cylinder no. 1, the bright links (A) on the timing chain must align with the marks (B) on the sprockets. (C) are the camshaft sprocket TDC marks and (D) are the crankshaft sprocket TDC marks**

17    Make sure the chain alignment dots (circular indentation) on the Variable valve Timing Control (VTC) actuator and the exhaust camshaft sprocket are approximately at the 12 o'clock position. The TDC alignment marks on the sprockets should be opposite each other at the 9 and 3 o'clock positions (see illustration).

18    Install the timing chain around the crankshaft sprocket with the colored link on the chain aligned with the dot (circular indentation) on the crankshaft sprocket (see illustration 8.17).

19    Install the timing chain over the exhaust camshaft sprocket and the VTC actuator (intake camshaft sprocket) with the marks aligned with each pair of colored chain links.

20    Install the camshaft timing chain guide and the tensioner arm. Tighten the bolts to the torque listed in this Chapter's Specifications.

21    Install the timing chain tensioner. Tighten the bolts to the torque listed in this Chapter's Specifications.

22    Install the upper timing chain guide. Tighten the bolts to the torque listed in this Chapter's Specifications.

23    Remove the pin from the timing chain tensioner.

24    Slowly turn the crankshaft clockwise two revolutions and recheck the timing marks and camshaft sprocket index marks for proper alignment.

**Caution:** *If the crankshaft binds or seems to hit something, do not force it, as the valves may be hitting the pistons. If this happens, valve timing is incorrect. Remove the chain and repeat the installation procedure and verify that the installation is correct.*

25    Install the valve cover (see Section 4).

26    Install the timing chain cover (see Section 7).

27    The remainder of installation is the reverse of the removal steps.

28    Reconnect the battery (see Chapter 5).

29    Run the engine and check for leaks.

## 9    Crankshaft pulley and front oil seal - removal and installation

### Removal

1    Disconnect the cable from the negative battery terminal (see Chapter 5). Loosen the right-front wheel lug nuts.

2    Raise the vehicle and support it securely on jackstands. Remove the right front wheel.

3    Remove the splash shield from below the engine compartment.

4    Remove the drivebelt (see Chapter 1).

5    Unscrew the crankshaft pulley bolt. A special tool that engages with the recessed hex in the pulley opening is available to prevent the crankshaft from turning while unscrewing the bolt. If you can't obtain one of these tools, remove the flywheel/driveplate inspection cover and wedge a screwdriver into the starter ring gear teeth.

6    Slide the pulley off the crankshaft.

7    Use a seal puller to remove the crankshaft front oil seal. A screwdriver may be used instead, if the tip is wrapped with tape to avoid scratching the crankshaft.

8    Clean the seal bore and check it for nicks or gouges. Also examine the area of the hub that rides in the seal for signs of abnormal wear or scoring. If necessary, replace it.

### Installation

9    Coat the lip of the new seal with clean engine oil and drive it into the bore with a seal driver or a socket slightly smaller in diameter than the seal. The open side of the seal faces into the engine.

10    Using clean engine oil, lubricate the sealing surface of the hub. Install the crankshaft pulley and tighten the bolt to the torque listed in this Chapter's Specifications.

11    The remainder of installation is the reverse of the removal procedure.

12    Reconnect the battery (see Chapter 5).

## 10    i-VTEC system - description and component checks

### General description

1    The i-VTEC system on the DOHC engines is similar to the VTEC system used on the SOHC engine, with the capability of being able to continuously change the intake cam timing. The intake camshaft has two different lobe profiles and is equipped with a Variable valve Timing Control (VTC) actuator, which alters the phasing of the camshaft to yield maximum potential power output for any given engine speed. For more information on the i-VTEC system, see Chapter 6.

### Component checks

**Note:** *The i-VTEC system will require specialized diagnostic equipment to access the onboard computer to test the electrical circuits, actuators and sensors. However, there are some mechanical tests of the i-VTEC system that the home mechanic can perform to check for obvious and simple problems within the system. Have the i-VTEC system diagnosed by a dealer service department or other qualified automotive repair facility. Also, some checks and inspections of the i-VTEC components require removal of the rocker arm assembly (see Section 11).*

#### i-VTEC solenoid valve

**Note:** *Most common problems in the i-VTEC system are associated with the solenoid valve and its filter. Regular engine oil and filter changes are necessary for trouble-free operation of the valve.*

2    The i-VTEC solenoid valve is located on the rear of the cylinder head, at the right end. The i-VTEC solenoid valve filter is mounted directly behind the i-VTEC solenoid valve (see Chapter 6).

3    Remove the i-VTEC solenoid valve (see Chapter 6) and check the filter for clogging. Clean and reinstall. A clogged filter screen is often the cause of system problems.

#### VTC oil control solenoid valve and strainer

**Note:** *Most common problems in the VTC system are associated with the oil control solenoid valve and its strainer. Regular engine oil and filter changes are necessary for trouble-free operation of the valve.*

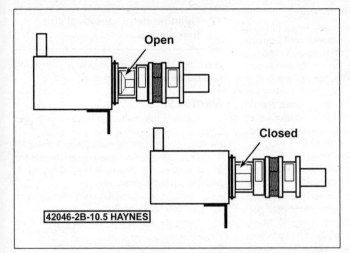

**10.5 Check the position of the VTC solenoid valve - if it's stuck open, replace the valve. Be sure to check the condition of the O-ring, too.**

**Note:** *Some models have three strainer screens, while others only have one*

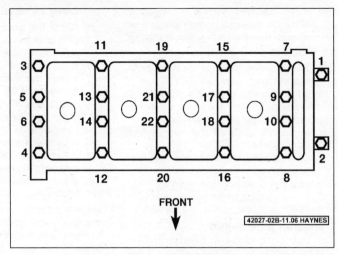

**11.6 Camshaft holder bolt loosening sequence**

4    The VTC oil control solenoid valve is located in the cylinder head on the timing chain end of the engine.

5    Remove the VTC oil control solenoid valve (see Chapter 6) and check the strainer for clogging, cleaning it as necessary (if it's too dirty to clean, replace the valve). Look at the position of the valve through the drain port (the port closest to the solenoid portion of the valve); it should be closed. If it's open (see illustration), the solenoid valve must be replaced.

### Rocker arms

6    Position the number one piston at Top Dead Center (see Section 3). Remove the valve cover (see Section 4).

7    Press on the primary intake rocker arm for cylinder number 1 to see that it moves independently of the secondary intake rockers. Check the rockers for the other cylinders at their own TDC positions.

### i-VTEC synchronizing assembly

8    Once the rocker arm assemblies have been removed and disassembled (see Section 11), separate the rocker arms and synchronizing components.

### i-VTEC components:

a) *Primary rocker arm*
b) *Secondary rocker arm*
c) *Synchronizing pistons*

9    Inspect the timing spring, making sure it's not broken or collapsed. Replace it if necessary.

10    Inspect all other parts (rocker arms and synchronizing pistons) for wear, galling, scoring or signs of overheating (bluish in color). Use your finger to push on the rocker arm pistons to check for smooth movement. Replace any parts, if necessary.

11    Reassemble each cylinder's components and wrap a rubber band around the rocker

arms before trying to assemble them on the rocker shaft (see Section 11).

---

### 11   Camshafts and rocker arms - removal, inspection and installation

**Note:** *The camshaft holders, the camshafts and the rocker arm assembly are bolted to the cylinder head as one complete assembly. After the assembly is removed from the cylinder head, the different components can be separated on the workbench.*

### *Removal*

1    Disconnect the cable from the negative battery terminal (see Chapter 5).

2    Position the number one piston at Top Dead Center on the compression stroke for no. 1 cylinder (see Section 3).

3    Remove the valve cover (see Section 4).

4    Remove the timing chain (see Section 8).

5    Loosen all of the rocker arm adjusting screws.

6    Remove the camshaft holder bolts. Follow the correct sequence (see illustration).

7    Remove the upper timing chain guide.

8    Lift the camshaft holders and camshafts off the rocker arm assembly. Remove the rocker arm assembly. Install each bolt into the original camshaft holder for correct reassembly.

**Caution:** *If the intake camshaft sprocket (VTC actuator) is removed from the camshaft and reused later, be sure to store the intake sprocket properly. First, seal the advance holes and the retard hole on the number 1 camshaft journal with tape. Next, punch a hole in the tape over one of the advance holes and blow compressed air through the opening to release the*

lock. Double-check that the sprocket moves freely in the advance and retard positions.

### *Inspection*

### Rocker arm assembly

9    If you wish to disassemble and inspect the rocker arm assembly (a good idea as long as you have them off), remove the retaining bolts and slip the rocker arms, springs, collars and bearing caps off the shafts. Mark the relationship of the shafts to the bearing caps and keep the components in order. They must be reassembled in the same positions they were removed from.

**Caution:** *It is a good idea to bundle the intake rocker arms together with rubber bands.*

10    Thoroughly clean the components and inspect them for wear and damage. Check the rocker arm faces that contact the camshaft and the rocker arm tips. Check the surfaces of the shafts that the rocker arms ride on, as well as the bearing surfaces inside the rocker arms, for scoring and excessive wear. Replace any parts that are damaged or excessively worn. Also, make sure the oil holes in the shafts are not plugged.

### Camshaft endplay and runout

11    To check camshaft endplay:

a) *Install the rocker shaft holders, the camshafts and the camshaft holders and follow the correct torque sequence (see Step 20).*

b) *Mount a dial indicator on the cylinder head with the pointer resting on the camshaft nose.*

c) *Using a large screwdriver as a lever at the opposite end, move the camshaft forward-and-backward and note the dial indicator reading.*

d) *Compare the reading with the endplay listed in this Chapter's Specifications.*

e) *If the indicated reading is excessive, either the camshaft or the cylinder head is worn. Replace parts as necessary.*

12  To check camshaft runout:

a) *With the camshafts on the workbench, support the camshaft with a pair of V-blocks and set up a dial indicator with the plunger resting against the center bearing journal on the camshaft.*

b) *Rotate the camshaft and note the indicated runout.*

c) *Compare the results to the camshaft runout listed in this Chapter's Specifications this Chapter's Specifications.*

d) *If the indicated runout exceeds the specified runout limit, replace the camshaft.*

### Camshaft lobe height

13  Check the camshaft bearing journals and caps for scoring and signs of wear. If they are worn, replace the camshaft holders and rocker arm assembly with a new or rebuilt assembly.

**11.14 Measure the camshaft lobe height with a micrometer**

14  Check the cam lobes for wear:

a) *Check the toe and ramp areas of each cam lobe for score marks and uneven wear. Also check for flaking and pitting.*

b) *If there's wear on the toe or the ramp, replace the camshaft, but first try to find the cause of the wear. Look for abrasive substances in the oil and inspect the oil pump and oil passages for blockage. Lobe wear is usually caused by inadequate lubrication or dirty oil.*

c) *Using a micrometer, measure the cam lobe height (see illustration), if lobe wear is indicated, replace the camshaft.*

15  If any of the conditions described above are noted, the cylinder head is probably getting insufficient lubrication or dirty oil. Make sure you track down the cause of this problem (low oil level, low oil pump capacity, clogged oil passage, etc.) before installing a new cylinder head, camshaft or rocker arm assembly.

### Installation

16  Lubricate all components with engine assembly lubricant or engine oil and reassemble rocker arms onto the shafts.

17  When installing the rocker arms, shafts and springs, note the markings and the difference between the left and right side components.

18  Coat the camshaft lobes and journals with camshaft installation lubricant (see illustration).

19  Make sure the camshaft sprocket timing marks face up and set the camshafts in the rocker shaft holders.

20  Tighten the camshaft holder bolts a little at a time, in the proper sequence (see illustration), to the torque listed in this Chapter's Specifications.

21  The remainder of installation is the reverse of removal. Adjust the valve clearances (see Chapter 1).

22  Run the engine and check for oil leaks and proper operation.

### 12  Cylinder head - removal and installation

**Warning:** *Wait until the engine is completely cool before beginning this procedure.*

### Removal

1  Relieve the fuel system pressure (see Chapter 4), then disconnect the cable from the negative battery terminal (see Chapter 5).

2  Drain the cooling system (see Chapter 1).

3  Remove the drivebelt (see Chapter 1) and the drivebelt tensioner.

4  Remove the catalytic converter/exhaust manifold (see Section 6).

5  Remove the intake manifold (see Section 5).

6  On 2015 and later CR-V models, remove the fuel rail, fuel injectors and the high-pressure fuel pump (see Chapter 4).

7  Remove the timing chain (see Section 8), camshafts and rocker arm assembly (see Section 11).

8  Label and disconnect the electrical connectors from the cylinder head that will interfere with removal. Use tape and mark each connector to insure correct reassembly. Also detach any coolant hoses that would interfere with removal.

9  Remove the cylinder head bolts, following the reverse of the tightening sequence (see illustration 12.17). Loosen the bolts in sequence 1/4-turn at a time. Discard the bolts; new ones should be used upon installation.

10  Lift the cylinder head off the engine. If resistance is felt, place a wood block against the end and strike the wood block with a hammer. If the cylinder head is still stuck, carefully pry on a casting protrusion to break the gasket seal.

**Caution:** *Do not pry between the cylinder head and block mating surfaces!*

11  Store the cylinder head on wood blocks to prevent damage to the gasket sealing surfaces.

12  Remove the old cylinder head gasket.

**11.18 Be sure to apply camshaft installation lubricant to the lobes and bearing journals before installing the camshaft**

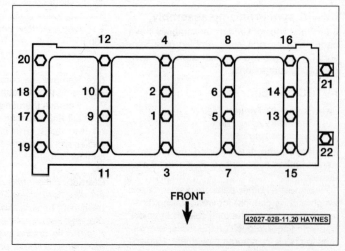

**11.20 Camshaft holder bolt tightening sequence**

## *Installation*

13   The mating surfaces of the cylinder head and block must be perfectly clean when the head is installed. Use a gasket scraper to remove all traces of carbon and old gasket material, then clean the mating surfaces with brake system cleaner. If there's oil on the mating surfaces when the cylinder head is installed, the gasket may not seal correctly and leaks may develop. When working on the engine block, cover the open areas of the engine with shop rags to keep debris out during repair and reassembly. Use a vacuum cleaner to remove any debris that falls into the cylinders.
14   Check the engine block and cylinder head mating surfaces for nicks, deep scratches and other damage. Have an automotive machine shop check the cylinder head for warpage.
15   Use a tap of the correct size to chase the threads in the cylinder head bolt holes. Dirt, corrosion, sealant and damaged threads will affect torque readings.
16   Make sure the new gasket is located on the dowels in the block.
17   Carefully position the cylinder head on the engine block without disturbing the gasket. Install new cylinder head bolts, and following the recommended sequence (see illustration), tighten the bolts to the torque listed in this Chapter's Specifications.
**Note:** *The method used for the head bolt tightening procedure is referred to as "torque-angle" or "torque-to-yield" method. A special torque angle gauge (available at most auto parts stores) is available to attach to a breaker bar and socket for better accuracy during the tightening procedure.*
18   Install the rocker arm assembly and camshafts (see Section 11).
19   Install the timing chain (see Section 8).
20   Install the exhaust manifold (see Section 6).
21   Install the intake manifold (see Section 5).

22   The remaining installation steps are the reverse of removal.
23   Reconnect the battery (see Chapter 5).
24   Change the engine oil and filter and refill the cooling system (see Chapter 1), then start the engine and check carefully for oil and coolant leaks.

### 13  Oil pan - removal and installation

## *Removal*

1   Drain the engine oil (see Chapter 1).
2   Remove the subframe (see Chapter 10).
3   On automatic transaxles, remove the torque converter cover bolts (see Chapter 7B).
4   On manual transaxles, remove the bell-housing brace from the transaxle and the engine block.
5   Remove the oil pan bolts, loosening them a little at a time in a criss-cross pattern.
6   Carefully remove the oil pan from the lower crankcase.
**Caution:** *If the oil pan is difficult to separate from the lower crankcase, use a rubber mallet or a block of wood and a hammer to jar it loose. If that doesn't work, an oil pan gasket cutter may be available from your local auto parts store.*

## *Installation*

7   Using a gasket scraper, thoroughly clean all old gasket material from the lower crankcase and oil pan. Remove residue and oil film with a solvent such as acetone or lacquer thinner.
8   Apply a 2 mm bead of RTV sealant to the perimeter of the oil pan, inboard of the bolt holes.
9   Install the oil pan and bolts. Tighten the bolts a little at a time, in a criss-cross pattern beginning with the center bolts and working outward, to the torque listed in this Chapter's Specifications.

10   The remaining installation is the reverse of removal.
11   Change the oil filter and fill the crankcase with the specified engine oil (see Chapter 1).

### 14  Oil pump - removal, inspection and installation

## *Removal*

**Note:** *The oil pump housing mounts directly to the front of the balance shaft housing.*
1   Set the engine to TDC no the compression stroke for cylinder number 1 (see Section 3).
2   Remove the oil pan (see Section 13).
3   Remove the balance shaft assembly (see Section 15).
4   Remove the oil pump housing mounting bolts. Loosen the oil pump mounting bolts one turn. Then, gradually and evenly, loosen each bolt in several steps.
5   When all bolts are loose, remove the bolts and oil pump.

## *Inspection*

6   Check the oil pump rotor-to-housing clearance, tooth tip clearance and rotor-to-body clearance (see illustrations). Compare your measurements to the figures listed in this Chapter's Specifications. Replace the pump if any of the measurements exceed the specified limits.
7   Remove the pressure relief valve plug and extract the spring and pressure relief valve plunger from the pump housing. Check the spring for distortion and the relief valve plunger for scoring. Replace parts as necessary.
8   Install the pump rotors. Pack the spaces between the rotors with petroleum jelly (this will prime the pump).
9   Apply clean engine oil to the pump housing bolts, install the housing and tighten the

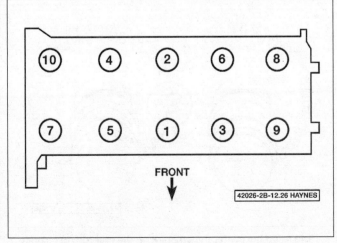

**12.17 Cylinder head bolt tightening sequence**

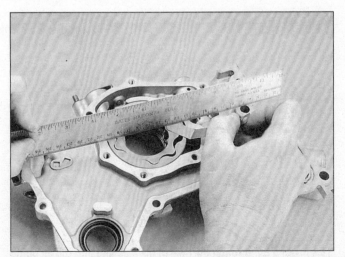

**14.6a Use a feeler gauge and straight-edge to check the clearance between the rotors and the housing (typical)**

bolts to the torque listed in this Chapter's Specifications. Install the oil pressure relief valve and spring assembly. Use a new sealing washer on the plug and tighten the plug to the torque listed in this Chapter's Specifications.

## Installation

10   Install the oil pump housing bolts and tighten by hand until snug. Tighten the bolts gradually and evenly to the torque listed in this Chapter's Specifications.
11   Make sure the engine is still set to TDC compression for cylinder number 1 (see Section 3).
12   Install the balance shaft assembly (see Section 15).
13   Refer to Chapter 1 and fill the engine with oil. Install a new oil filter.
14   Reconnect the battery (see Chapter 5).
15   Run the engine and make sure oil pressure comes up to normal quickly. If it doesn't, stop the engine and find out the cause. Severe engine damage can result from running an engine with insufficient oil pressure!

## 15   Balance shaft assembly and balance shafts - removal, inspection and installation

### Removal

**Note:** *The oil pump housing mounts directly to the front of the balance shaft housing.*
1   Remove the oil pan (see Section 13).
2   To prevent the sprocket from turning, insert a 6 mm guide pin into the maintenance hole of the balance shaft housing and through the rear balance shaft, directly behind the oil pump housing.
3   Rotate the crankshaft counterclockwise to compress the oil pump chain tensioner, then remove the crankshaft pulley (see Section 9).
4   Rotate the crankshaft slightly clockwise and insert a 7/64-inch (3 mm) pin into the holes of the oil pump chain tensioner (see illustration).
5   On Civic models, place a jack under the transaxle and raise the transmission approximately 1.18 to 1.57 inches (30 to 40 mm) then remove the oil pump chain tensioner.

6   Remove the oil pump sprocket bolt and sprocket.
7   Remove oil pump housing bolts then the balance shaft assembly mounting bolts and separate the assembly from the lower engine block.

### Inspection
8   Remove the balance shaft assembly mounting bolts and separate the upper and lower cases.
9   Clean all parts with clean solvent. Dry with compressed air.
10   Inspect the oil pump/balance shaft chain for excessive wear or damage.
11   Inspect the oil pump/balance shaft chain sprocket for chipped or broken teeth, excessive wear, or damage.
12   Inspect the balance shaft gears for chipping, scoring or missing teeth. Replace the assembly if necessary.

### Installation
13   Working on the two balance shafts, align the center punch mark on the rear (drive) balance shaft with the two marks on the front balance shaft (driven) (see illustration).

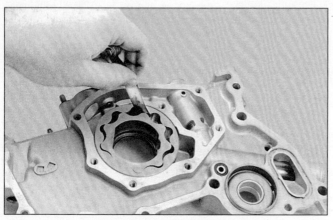

**14.6b Use a feeler gauge to check the tooth-tip clearance between the inner and outer rotors (typical)**

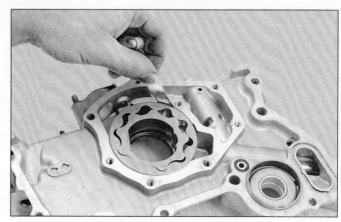

**14.6c Use a feeler gauge to check the outer rotor-to-pump body clearance (typical)**

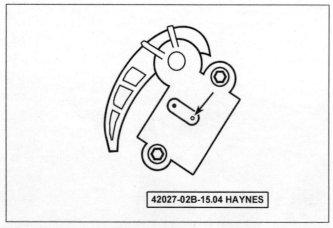

42027-02B-15.04 HAYNES

**15.4 Insert a pin through the hole in the lock and into the oil pump chain tensioner body**

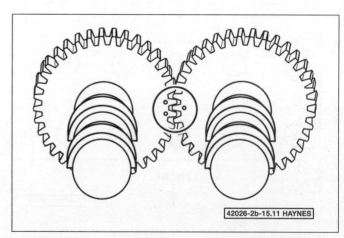

42026-2b-15.11 HAYNES

**15.13 Align the center punch mark on the rear (drive) balance shaft with the two marks on the front balance shaft (driven)**

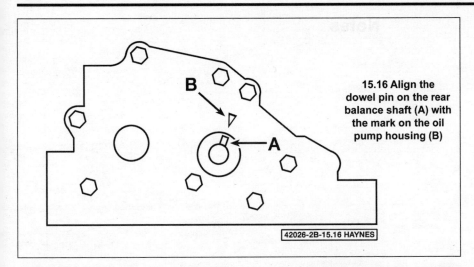

**15.16 Align the dowel pin on the rear balance shaft (A) with the mark on the oil pump housing (B)**

42026-2B-15.16 HAYNES

14   Apply engine oil to the threads and install the balance shaft case mounting bolts. Tighten the bolts to the torque listed in this Chapter's Specifications.
15   Install the oil pump housing (see Section 14).
16   Align the dowel pin on the rear balance shaft with the mark on the oil pump housing (see illustration).
17   Install the balance shaft assembly onto the lower engine block and install the bolts finger-tight.
18   Insert a 6 mm guide pin into the maintenance hole directly behind the oil pump housing (see Step 2).
19   Engage the oil pump sprocket with the chain, then with the balance shaft. Install the oil pump sprocket bolt. Tighten the bolt to the torque listed in this Chapter's Specifications.
20   Remove the guide pin.
21   Tighten the balancer assembly mounting bolts to the torque listed in this Chapter's Specifications.
22   Working with a new balance shaft chain tensioner, make sure the tensioner holder clip is installed onto the tensioner and install the tensioner onto the lower engine block.
23   Tighten the balance shaft chain tensioner bolts to the torque listed in this Chapter's Specifications.
24   Remove the holder clip from the tensioner to apply tension to the chain.

25   Install the oil pan (see Section 13).
26   Reconnect the battery (see Chapter 5).
27   Run the engine and make sure oil pressure comes up to normal quickly. If it doesn't, stop the engine and find out the cause. Severe engine damage can result from running an engine with insufficient oil pressure!

## 16   Flywheel/driveplate - removal and installation

1   This procedure is essentially the same as for the SOHC engine. Refer to Chapter 2A and follow the procedure outlined there. However, use the bolt torque listed in this Chapter's Specifications.

## 17   Rear main oil seal - replacement

1   This procedure is essentially the same as for the SOHC engine. Refer to Chapter 2A and follow the procedure outlined there.

## 18   Engine mounts - check and replacement

1   This procedure is essentially the same as for the SOHC engine. Refer to Chapter 2A and follow the procedure outlined there. However, use the bolt torque listed in this Chapter's Specifications.

# Notes

# Chapter 2 Part C
# General engine overhaul procedures

## Contents

## Specifications

### General
Displacement
    SOHC models ........................................................ 110 cubic inches (1.8 liters)
    DOHC models ....................................................... 144 cubic inches (2.4 liters)
Bore and stroke
    SOHC models ........................................................ 3.19 x 3.44 inches (81.0 x 87.3 mm)
    DOHC models
        2014 and earlier .............................................. 3.39 x 3.39 inches (86.0 x 86.0 mm)
        2015 and later ................................................. 3.42 x 3.90 inches (87.0 x 99.1 mm)
Cylinder compression
    SOHC models ........................................................
        Minimum ......................................................... 128 psi (930 kPa)
        Maximum variation between cylinders ............................ 28 psi (200 kPa)
    DOHC models
        Minimum ......................................................... 135 psi (930 kPa)
        Maximum variation between cylinders ............................ 28 psi (200 kPa)
Oil pressure (engine at operating temperature)
    SOHC models
        Idle speed ....................................................... 15.5 psi (107 kPa)
        2,000 rpm ....................................................... 54.5 psi (376 kPa)
    DOHC models ....................................................... 65.3 psi (450 kPa)
        Idle speed ....................................................... 10 psi (70 kPa)
        3,000 rpm ....................................................... 44 psi (300 kPa)

## Torque specifications                     Ft-lbs (unless otherwise indicated)     Nm

**Note:** *One foot-pound (ft-lb) of torque is equivalent to 12 inch-pounds (in-lbs) of torque. Torque values below approximately 15 foot-pounds are expressed in inch-pounds, because most foot-pound torque wrenches are not accurate at these smaller values.*

| | | |
|---|---|---|
| Subframe mounting bolts................................................................ | See Chapter 10 | |
| Connecting rod bearing cap bolts* | | |
|   SOHC models | | |
|     Step 1 ...................................................................... | 15 | 20 |
|     Step 2 ...................................................................... | Tighten an additional 90 degrees | |
|   DOHC models | | |
|     Step 1 ...................................................................... | 168 in-lbs | 19 |
|     Step 2 ...................................................................... | Tighten an additional 120 degrees | |
| Crankshaft Position Sensor (CKP) pulse plate bolts | | |
|   SOHC models................................................................... | 84 in-lbs | 9.0 |
|   DOHC models................................................................... | 16 | 22 |
| Main bearing bridge bolts | | |
|   SOHC models | | |
|   Main bridge bolts (inner bolts) (see illustration 10.19a) | | |
|     Step 1 ...................................................................... | 18 | 25 |
|     Step 2 ...................................................................... | Tighten an additional 57 degrees | |
|   Perimeter bolts (outer bolts) (see illustration 10.19b).................. | 17 | 24 |
|   DOHC models | | |
|   Main bridge bolts (inner bolts) (see illustration 10.19a) | | |
|   Step 1 | | |
|     2014 and earlier models................................................ | 18 | 25 |
|     2015 and later models.................................................. | 26 | 35 |
|   Step 2 | | |
|     2014 and earlier models................................................ | Tighten an additional 57 degrees | |
|     2015 and later models.................................................. | Tighten an additional 41 degrees | |
|   Perimeter bolts (outer bolts) (see illustration 10.19c).................. | 17 | 24 |

• *Replace with new bolts*

**1.10a An engine block being bored. An engine rebuilder will use special machinery to recondition the cylinder bores**

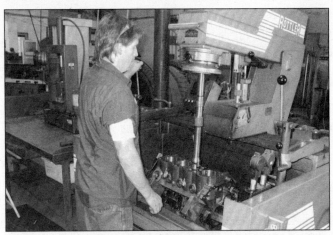

**1.10b If the cylinders are bored, the machine shop will normally hone the engine on a machine like this**

## 1   General information - engine overhaul

1   Included in this portion of Chapter 2 are general information and diagnostic testing procedures for determining the overall mechanical condition of your engine.

2   The information ranges from advice concerning preparation for an overhaul and the purchase of replacement parts and/or components to detailed, step-by-step procedures covering removal and installation.

3   The following Sections have been written to help you determine whether your engine needs to be overhauled and how to remove and install it once you've determined it needs to be rebuilt. For information concerning in-vehicle engine repair, see Chapter 2A or Chapter 2B.

4   The Specifications included in this Part are general in nature and include only those necessary for testing the oil pressure and checking the engine compression. Refer to Chapter 2A or Chapter 2B for additional engine Specifications.

5   It's not always easy to determine when, or if, an engine should be completely overhauled, because a number of factors must be considered.

6   High mileage is not necessarily an indication that an overhaul is needed, while low mileage doesn't preclude the need for an overhaul. Frequency of servicing is probably the most important consideration. An engine that's had regular and frequent oil and filter changes, as well as other required maintenance, will most likely give many thousands of miles of reliable service. Conversely, a neglected engine may require an overhaul very early in its service life.

7   Excessive oil consumption is an indication that piston rings, valve seals and/or valve guides are in need of attention. Make sure that oil leaks aren't responsible before deciding that the rings and/or guides are bad. Perform a cylinder compression check to determine the extent of the work required (see Section 3). Also check the vacuum readings under various conditions (see Section 4).

8   Check the oil pressure with a gauge installed in place of the oil pressure sending unit and compare it to this Chapter's Specifications (see Section 2). If it's extremely low, the bearings and/or oil pump are probably worn out.

9   Loss of power, rough running, knocking or metallic engine noises, excessive valve train noise and high fuel consumption rates may also point to the need for an overhaul, especially if they're all present at the same time. If a complete tune-up doesn't remedy the situation, major mechanical work is the only solution.

10   An engine overhaul involves restoring the internal parts to the specifications of a new engine. During an overhaul, the piston rings are replaced and the cylinder walls are reconditioned (rebored and/or honed) (see illustrations 1.10a and 1.10b). If a rebore is done by an automotive machine shop, new oversize pistons will also be installed. The main bearings, connecting rod bearings and camshaft bearings are generally replaced with new ones and, if necessary, the crankshaft may be reground to restore the journals (see illustration 1.10c). Generally, the valves are serviced as well, since they're usually in less-than-perfect condition at this point. While the engine is being overhauled, other components, such as the starter and alternator, can be rebuilt as well. The end result should be similar to a new engine that will give many trouble-free miles.

**Note:** *Critical cooling system components such as the hoses, drivebelts, thermostat and water pump should be replaced with new parts when an engine is overhauled. The radiator should be checked carefully to ensure that it isn't clogged or leaking (see Chapter 3). If you purchase a rebuilt engine or short block, some rebuilders will not warranty their engines unless the radiator has been professionally flushed. Also, we don't recommend overhauling the oil pump - always install a new one when an engine is rebuilt.*

11   Overhauling the internal components on today's engines is a difficult and time-consuming task which requires a significant amount of specialty tools and is best left to a professional engine rebuilder (see illustrations 1.11a, 1.11b and 1.11c). A competent engine rebuilder will handle the inspection of your old

**1.10c A crankshaft having a main bearing journal ground**

**1.11a A machinist checks for a bent connecting rod, using specialized equipment**

**1.11b A bore gauge being used to check the main bearing bore**

**1.11c Uneven piston wear like this indicates a bent connecting rod**

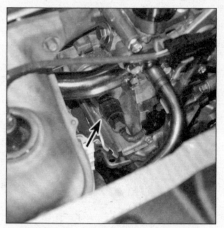

**2.3 Location of the oil pressure sending unit on 1.8L models. To check the pressure, remove the oil pressure sending unit and install an oil pressure gauge**

parts and offer advice concerning the reconditioning or replacement of the original engine; never purchase parts or have machine work done on other components until the block has been thoroughly inspected by a professional machine shop. As a general rule, time is the primary cost of an overhaul, especially since the vehicle may be tied up for a minimum of two weeks or more. Be aware that some engine builders only have the capability to rebuild the engine you bring them while other rebuilders have a large inventory of rebuilt exchange engines in stock. Also be aware that many machine shops could take as much as two weeks time to completely rebuild your engine depending on shop workload. Sometimes it makes more sense to simply exchange your engine for another engine that's already rebuilt to save time.

## 2    Oil pressure check

1    Low engine oil pressure can be a sign of an engine in need of rebuilding. A low oil pressure indicator (often called an "idiot light") is not a test of the oiling system. Such indicators only come on when the oil pressure is dangerously low. Even a factory oil pressure gauge in the instrument panel is only a relative indication, although much better for driver information than a warning light. A better test is with a mechanical (not electrical) oil pressure gauge.
2    Locate the oil pressure sending unit on the engine block:

a) *On 1.8L Single Overhead Camshaft (SOHC) engines, the oil pressure sending unit is located to the rear of the engine block on the side facing the radiator.*
b) *On 2.4L engines, the oil pressure sending unit is located to the front of the engine block, just below the cylinder head on the side facing the firewall.*

3    Unscrew and remove the oil pressure

sending unit and screw in the hose for your oil pressure gauge (see illustration). If necessary, install an adapter fitting. Use Teflon tape or thread sealant on the threads of the adapter and/or the fitting on the end of your gauge's hose.
4    Check the oil pressure with the engine idling (normal operating temperature) and at the specified engine speed, and compare it to this Chapter's Specifications. If it's extremely low, the bearings and/or oil pump are probably worn out.

## 3    Cylinder compression check

1    A compression check will tell you what mechanical condition the upper end of your engine (pistons, rings, valves, head gaskets) is in. Specifically, it can tell you if the compression is down due to leakage caused by worn piston rings, defective valves and seats or a blown head gasket.
**Note:** *The engine must be at normal operating temperature and the battery must be fully charged for this check.*
2    Begin by cleaning the area around the ignition coils and spark plugs before you remove them (compressed air should be used, if available). This is to prevent dirt from getting into the cylinders as the compression check is being done.
3    Remove all of the individual coils (see Chapter 5) and remove all of the spark plugs from the engine (see Chapter 1).
4    Disable the fuel system by removing the PGM-FI main relay number 2 (see Chapter 4, Section 3).
5    Install a compression gauge in the spark plug hole (see illustration).
6    Have an assistant depress the accelerator pedal to the floor and crank the engine over at least seven compression strokes while you watch the gauge. The compression should build up quickly in a healthy engine. Low compression on the first stroke, followed by gradually increasing pressure on succes-

sive strokes, indicates worn piston rings. A low compression reading on the first stroke, which doesn't build up during successive strokes, indicates leaking valves or a blown head gasket (a cracked head could also be the cause). Deposits on the undersides of the valve heads can also cause low compression. Record the highest gauge reading obtained.
7    Repeat the procedure for the remaining cylinders and compare the results to this Chapter's Specifications.
8    Add some engine oil (about three squirts from a plunger-type oil can) to each cylinder, through the spark plug hole, and repeat the test.
9    If the compression increases after the oil is added, the piston rings are definitely worn. If the compression doesn't increase significantly, the leakage is occurring at the valves or head gasket. Leakage past the valves may be caused by burned valve seats and/or faces or warped, cracked or bent valves.
10    If two adjacent cylinders have equally low compression, there's a strong possibility that the head gasket between them is blown.

**3.5 Use a compression gauge with a threaded fitting for the spark plug hole, not the type that requires hand pressure to maintain the seal**

The appearance of coolant in the combustion chambers or the crankcase would verify this condition.

11   If one cylinder is slightly lower than the others, and the engine has a slightly rough idle, a worn lobe on the camshaft could be the cause.

12   If the compression is unusually high, the combustion chambers are probably coated with carbon deposits. If that's the case, the cylinder head(s) should be removed and decarbonized.

13   If compression is way down or varies greatly between cylinders, it would be a good idea to have a leak-down test performed by an automotive repair shop. This test will pinpoint exactly where the leakage is occurring and how severe it is.

### 4   Vacuum gauge diagnostic checks

1   A vacuum gauge provides inexpensive but valuable information about what is going on in the engine. You can check for worn rings or cylinder walls, leaking head or intake manifold gaskets, restricted exhaust, stuck or burned valves, weak valve springs, improper ignition or valve timing and ignition problems.

2   Unfortunately, vacuum gauge readings are easy to misinterpret, so they should be used in conjunction with other tests to confirm the diagnosis.

3   Both the absolute readings and the rate of needle movement are important for accurate interpretation. Most gauges measure vacuum in inches of mercury (in-Hg). The following references to vacuum assume the diagnosis is being performed at sea level. As elevation increases (or atmospheric pressure decreases), the reading will decrease. For every 1,000 foot increase in elevation above approximately 2,000 feet, the gauge readings will decrease about one inch of mercury.

4   Connect the vacuum gauge directly to the intake manifold vacuum, not to ported (throttle body) vacuum (see illustration). Be sure no hoses are left disconnected during the test or false readings will result.

5   Before you begin the test, allow the engine to warm up completely. Block the wheels and set the parking brake. With the transaxle in Park, start the engine and allow it to run at normal idle speed.

**Warning:** *Keep your hands and the vacuum gauge clear of the fans.*

6   Read the vacuum gauge; an average, healthy engine should normally produce about 17 to 22 in-Hg with a fairly steady needle (see illustration). Refer to the following vacuum gauge readings and what they indicate about the engine's condition:

7   A low steady reading usually indicates a leaking gasket between the intake manifold and cylinder head(s) or throttle body, a leaky vacuum hose, late ignition timing or incorrect camshaft timing. Check ignition timing with a timing light and eliminate all other possible causes, utilizing the tests provided in this

Chapter before you remove the timing chain cover to check the timing marks.

8   If the reading is three to eight inches below normal and it fluctuates at that low reading, suspect an intake manifold gasket leak at an intake port or a faulty fuel injector.

9   If the needle has regular drops of about two-to-four inches at a steady rate, the valves are probably leaking. Perform a compression check or leak-down test to confirm this.

10   An irregular drop or down-flick of the needle can be caused by a sticking valve or

an ignition misfire. Perform a compression check or leak-down test and read the spark plugs.

11   A rapid vibration of about four in-Hg vibration at idle combined with exhaust smoke indicates worn valve guides. Perform a leak-down test to confirm this. If the rapid vibration occurs with an increase in engine speed, check for a leaking intake manifold gasket or head gasket, weak valve springs, burned valves or ignition misfire.

12   A slight fluctuation, say one inch up and

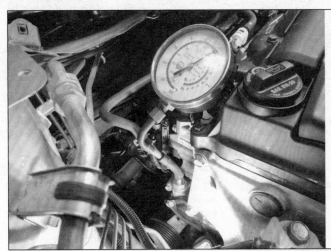

**4.4 A simple vacuum gauge can be handy in diagnosing engine condition and performance**

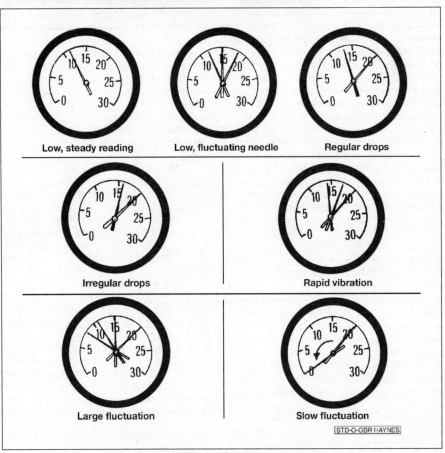

Low, steady reading   Low, fluctuating needle   Regular drops

Irregular drops   Rapid vibration

Large fluctuation   Slow fluctuation

STD-O-OBR HAYNES

**4.6 Typical vacuum gauge readings**

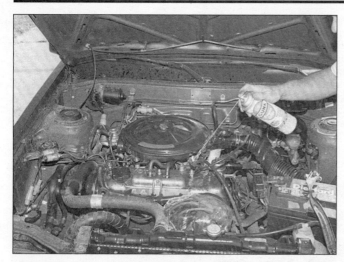

**6.3a After tightly wrapping water-vulnerable components, use a spray cleaner on everything, with particular concentration on the greasiest areas, usually around the valve cover and lower edges of the block. If one section dries out, apply more cleaner**

**6.3b Depending on how dirty the engine is, let the cleaner soak in according to the directions and hose off the grime and cleaner. Get the rinse water down into every area you can get at; then dry important components with a hair dryer or paper towels**

down, may mean ignition problems. Check all the usual tune-up items and, if necessary, run the engine on an ignition analyzer.

13   If there is a large fluctuation, perform a compression or leak-down test to look for a weak or dead cylinder or a blown head gasket.

14   If the needle moves slowly through a wide range, check for a clogged PCV system, incorrect idle fuel mixture, throttle body or intake manifold gasket leaks.

15   Check for a slow return after revving the engine by quickly snapping the throttle open until the engine reaches about 2,500 rpm and let it shut. Normally the reading should drop to near zero, rise above normal idle reading (about 5 in-Hg over) and return to the previous idle reading. If the vacuum returns slowly and doesn't peak when the throttle is snapped shut, the rings may be worn. If there is a long delay, look for a restricted exhaust system (often the muffler or catalytic converter). An easy way to check this is to temporarily disconnect the exhaust ahead of the suspected part and redo the test.

## 5   Engine rebuilding alternatives

1   The do-it-yourselfer is faced with a number of options when purchasing a rebuilt engine. The major considerations are cost, warranty, parts availability and the time required for the rebuilder to complete the project. The decision to replace the engine block, piston/connecting rod assemblies and crankshaft depends on the final inspection results of your engine. Only then can you make a cost effective decision whether to have your engine overhauled or simply purchase an exchange engine for your vehicle.

2   Some of the rebuilding alternatives include:

3   **Individual parts** - If the inspection procedures reveal that the engine block and most engine components are in reusable condition, purchasing individual parts and having a rebuilder rebuild your engine may be the most economical alternative. The block, crankshaft and piston/connecting rod assemblies should all be inspected carefully by a machine shop first.

4   **Short block** - A short block consists of an engine block with a crankshaft and piston/connecting rod assemblies already installed. All new bearings are incorporated and all clearances will be correct. The existing camshafts, valve train components, cylinder head and external parts can be bolted to the short block with little or no machine shop work necessary.

5   **Long block** - A long block consists of a short block plus an oil pump, oil pan, cylinder head, valve cover, camshaft and valve train components, timing sprockets and chain or gears and timing cover. All components are installed with new bearings, seals and gaskets incorporated throughout. The installation of manifolds and external parts is all that's necessary.

6   **Low mileage used engines** - Some companies now offer low mileage used engines which is a very cost effective way to get your vehicle up and running again. These engines often come from vehicles which have been in totaled in accidents or come from other countries which have a higher vehicle turnover rate. A low mileage used engine also usually has a similar warranty like the newly remanufactured engines.

7   Give careful thought to which alternative is best for you and discuss the situation with local automotive machine shops, auto parts dealers and experienced rebuilders before ordering or purchasing replacement parts.

## 6   Engine removal - methods and precautions

1   If you've decided that an engine must be removed for overhaul or major repair work, several preliminary steps should be taken. Read all removal and installation procedures carefully prior to committing to this job.

2   Locating a suitable place to work is extremely important. Adequate work space, along with storage space for the vehicle, will be needed. If a shop or garage isn't available, at the very least a flat, level, clean work surface made of concrete or asphalt is required.

3   Cleaning the engine compartment and engine before beginning the removal procedure will help keep tools clean and organized (see illustrations).

4   An engine hoist will also be necessary. Make sure the hoist is rated in excess of the combined weight of the engine and transaxle. Safety is of primary importance, considering the potential hazards involved in removing the engine from the vehicle.

5   A vehicle hoist will be necessary for engine removal, since on these models the subframe must be removed and the engine/transaxle assembly must be lowered from the engine compartment, then the vehicle is raised and the powertrain unit is removed from under the vehicle. If the necessary equipment is not available, the engine will have to be removed by a qualified automotive repair facility.

6   If you're a novice at engine removal, get at least one helper. One person cannot easily do all the things you need to do to remove a big heavy engine and transaxle assembly from the engine compartment. Also helpful is to seek advice and assistance from someone who's experienced in engine removal.

7   Plan the operation ahead of time. Arrange for or obtain all of the tools and

6.7a Get an engine stand sturdy enough to firmly support the engine while you're working on it. Stay away from three-wheeled models; they have a tendency to tip over more easily, so get a four-wheeled unit

6.7b A clutch alignment tool is necessary if you plan to install a rebuilt engine mated to a manual transaxle

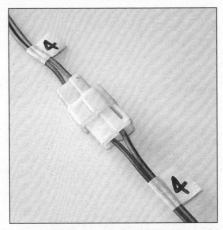

7.11 Label both ends of each wire and hose before disconnecting it

equipment you'll need prior to beginning the job (see illustrations). Some of the equipment necessary to perform engine removal and installation safely and with relative ease are (in addition to a vehicle hoist and an engine hoist) a heavy duty floor jack (preferably fitted with a transaxle jack head adapter), complete sets of wrenches and sockets as described in the front of this manual, wooden blocks, plenty of rags and cleaning solvent for mopping up spilled oil, coolant and gasoline.

8    Plan for the vehicle to be out of use for quite a while. A machine shop can do the work that is beyond the scope of the home mechanic. Machine shops often have a busy schedule, so before removing the engine, consult the shop for an estimate of how long it will take to rebuild or repair the components that may need work.

## 7    Engine - removal and installation

**Warning:** *Gasoline is extremely flammable, so take extra precautions when you work on any part of the fuel system. Don't smoke or allow open flames or bare light bulbs near the work area, and don't work in a garage where a gas-type appliance (such as a water heater or clothes dryer) is present. Since gasoline is carcinogenic, wear fuel-resistant gloves when there's a possibility of being exposed to fuel, and, if you spill any fuel on your skin, rinse it off immediately with soap and water. Mop up any spills immediately and do not store fuel-soaked rags where they could ignite. The fuel system is under constant pressure, so, if any fuel lines are to be disconnected, the fuel pressure in the system must be relieved first (see Chapter 4 for more information). When you perform any kind of work on the fuel system, wear safety glasses and have a Class B type fire extinguisher on hand.*

**Warning:** *The engine must be completely cool before beginning this procedure.*

**Note:** *Engine removal on these models is a difficult job, especially for the do-it-yourself mechanic working at home. Because of the vehicle's design, the manufacturer states that the engine and transaxle have to be removed as a unit from the bottom of the vehicle, not the top. With a floor jack and jackstands, the vehicle can't be raised high enough or supported safely enough for the engine/transaxle assembly to slide out from underneath. The manufacturer recommends that removal of the engine transaxle assembly only be performed with the use of a frame-contact type vehicle hoist.*

**Note:** *Read through the entire Section before beginning this procedure. The engine and transaxle are removed as a unit from below, then separated outside the vehicle.*

**Note:** *Keep in mind that during this procedure you'll have to adjust the height of the vehicle with the vehicle hoist to perform certain operations.*

### *Removal*

1    Park the vehicle on a frame-contact type vehicle hoist, then engage the arms of the hoist with the jacking points of the vehicle. Raise the hoist arms until they contact the vehicle, but not so much that the wheels come off the ground.

2    Relieve the fuel system pressure (see Chapter 4).

3    Disconnect the cable from the negative battery terminal (see Chapter 5).

4    Disconnect the fuel line from the fuel rail (see Chapter 4).

5    Remove the engine splash shields (see illustrations 14.3a and 14.3b in Chapter 2A), the inner fender splash shields and the hood (see Chapter 11). Cover the fenders and cowl using special pads. An old bedspread or blanket will also work.

6    Drain the cooling system (see Chapter 1).

7    Drain the engine oil (see Chapter 1).

8    Remove the accessory drivebelt(s) (see Chapter 1).

9    Remove the intake resonator and the air filter housing (see Chapter 4).

10    Remove the battery and the battery tray (see Chapter 5).

11    Clearly label and disconnect all vacuum lines, emissions hoses, wiring harness connectors and fuel lines. Masking tape and/or a touch up paint applicator work well for marking items (see illustration). Take photos or sketch the locations of components and brackets.

12    Remove the PCM (see Chapter 6). Detach the retaining clip on the engine compartment firewall and reposition the wiring harness.

13    Detach the positive cables and the electrical connectors from the engine compartment fuse/relay box (see Chapter 5).

14    Disconnect all ground straps/cables between the engine/transaxle and the chassis.

15    Detach any other electrical connectors between the engine and the vehicle.

16    Loosen the front wheel lug nuts, then raise the vehicle. Remove the front wheels.

17    Detach the heat shields, exhaust brackets and the exhaust pipes from the exhaust manifold(s) (see Chapter 4).

18    Remove the alternator (see Chapter 5).

19    Disconnect the electrical connector from the steering gear (see Chapter 10). Position the harness off to the side.

20    Remove the front portion of the exhaust system (see Chapter 6).

21    If equipped with a floor brace, remove the brace mounting bolts and brace from under the vehicle.

22    Detach the lower radiator hose from the engine (see Chapter 3).

23    Lower the vehicle and detach the heater hoses at the firewall (see Chapter 3).

**7.37 Attach the chain to the cylinder head using the engine lifting bracket on the front of the cylinder head and the other end of the chain to a transaxle mounting bolt**

**7.42 Typically the engine/transaxle assembly can be lowered onto the floor using the engine hoist**

24   Remove the upper radiator hose (see Chapter 3).

25   Remove the cooling fan(s) and shroud(s) (see Chapter 3).

26   Remove the radiator (see Chapter 3).

27   On models with a manual transaxle, remove the clutch release cylinder and hydraulic line (see Chapter 8).

28   Remove the starter (see Chapter 5).

29   On CR-V AWD models, remove the driveshaft (see Chapter 8).

30   On automatic transaxle models, disconnect the shift control cable from the transaxle (see Chapter 7B).

31   Working under the vehicle, remove the front brace mounting bolts and brace from under the radiator.

32   Disconnect the stabilizer bar links (see Chapter 10).

33   Disconnect the balljoints from the lower control arms (see Chapter 10).

34   Remove the driveaxles (see Chapter 8).

35   Unplug the downstream oxygen sensor electrical connectors.

36   Remove the air conditioning compressor without disconnecting the hoses (see Chapter 3). Use wire to tie the compressor to a bracket or other components mounted on the unibody structure (not the subframe).

37   Attach a lifting sling or chain to the engine, using the lifting brackets provided. At the transaxle end there should be a lifting eye built into the plate sandwiched between the transaxle and the engine (or secured to the transaxle by two of the mounting bolts). At the drivebelt end of the engine there should be a lifting eye in a bracket attached to the cylinder head. If not, lifting hooks may be available from your local auto parts store (see illustration). Take up the slack until there is slight tension on the hoist. Remember that the transaxle end of the engine will be heavier, so position the chain on the hoist so it balances the engine and the transaxle level with the vehicle.

**Note:** *Depending on the design of the engine hoist, it may be helpful to position the hoist from the side of the vehicle, so that when the engine/transaxle assembly is lowered, it will fit between the legs of the hoist.*

**Note:** *The sling or chain must be long enough to allow the engine hoist to lower the engine/transaxle assembly to the ground, without letting the hoist arm contact the vehicle.*

38   Remove the front and rear engine/transaxle mount through-bolts (see Chapter 2A or 2B).

39   Remove the engine mount and the transaxle mount (see Chapter 2A or 2B).

40   Recheck to be sure nothing is still connecting the engine or transaxle to the vehicle. Disconnect and label anything still remaining.

41   Remove the subframe mounting bolts (see Chapter 10). Separate the subframe from the chassis and the engine/transaxle assembly.

42   Lower the engine/transaxle assembly (see illustration). Once the engine/transaxle assembly is on the floor, disconnect the engine lifting hoist and raise the vehicle until it clears the engine/transaxle assembly.

**Caution:** *As you lower the engine assembly, check that any vacuum hoses, fuel hoses, coolant hoses, and the electrical wiring are free from the assembly.*

43   Reconnect the chain or sling to support the engine and transaxle.

44   Raise the engine/transaxle assembly, then support the engine with blocks of wood or another floor jack, while leaving the sling or chain attached. Support the transaxle with another floor jack, preferably one with a transaxle jack head adapter. At this point the transaxle can be unbolted and removed from the engine. Be very careful to ensure that the components are supported securely so they won't topple off their supports during disconnection.

45   Reconnect the lifting chain to the engine, then raise the engine and attach it to an engine stand.

## Installation

46   Installation is the reverse of removal, noting the following points:

a)   *Check the engine/transaxle mounts. If they're worn or damaged, replace them.*

b)   *Attach the transaxle to the engine following the procedure described in Chapter 7A or 7B.*

c)   *When installing the subframe, tighten the subframe mounting bolts to the torque listed in Chapter 10 Specifications. Note the locations of the various size bolts.*

d)   *Add coolant, oil, power steering and transaxle fluids as needed (see Chapter 1).*

e)   *Reconnect the battery (see Chapter 5).*

f)   *Run the engine and check for proper operation and leaks. Shut off the engine and recheck fluid levels.*

## 8   Engine overhaul - disassembly sequence

1   It's much easier to remove the external components if the engine is mounted on a portable engine stand. A stand can often be rented quite cheaply from an equipment rental yard. Before the engine is mounted on a stand, the flywheel/driveplate should be removed from the engine.

2   If a stand isn't available, it's possible to remove the external engine components with it blocked up on the floor. Be extra careful not to tip or drop the engine when working without a stand.

3   If you're going to obtain a rebuilt engine, all external components must come off first, to be transferred to the replacement engine. These components include:

*Clutch and flywheel (models with manual transaxle)*

*Driveplate (models with automatic transaxle)*

9.1 Before you try to remove the pistons, use a ridge reamer to remove the raised material (ridge) from the top of the cylinders

9.3 Checking the connecting rod endplay (side clearance) (typical)

9.4 If the connecting rods and caps are not marked, use paint to mark the caps to the rods by cylinder number (for example, this would be the No. 4 connecting rod)

Emissions-related components
Engine mounts and mount brackets
Engine rear cover (spacer plate between flywheel/driveplate and engine block)
Intake/exhaust manifolds
Fuel injection components
Oil filter
Ignition coils and spark plugs
Thermostat and housing assembly
Water pump

**Note:** *When removing the external components from the engine, pay close attention to details that may be helpful or important during installation. Note the installed position of gaskets, seals, spacers, pins, brackets, washers, bolts and other small items.*

4    If you're going to obtain a short block (assembled engine block, crankshaft, pistons and connecting rods), then remove the timing chain or belt, cylinder head(s), oil pan, oil pump pick-up tube, oil pump, oil jets and water pump from your engine so that you can turn in your old short block to the rebuilder as a core. See *Engine rebuilding alternatives* for additional information regarding the different possibilities to be considered.

## 9    Pistons and connecting rods - removal and installation

### Removal

**Note:** *Prior to removing the piston/connecting rod assemblies, remove the cylinder head and oil pan (see Chapter 2A).*

1    Use your fingernail to feel if a ridge has formed at the upper limit of ring travel (about 1/4-inch down from the top of each cylinder). If carbon deposits or cylinder wear have produced ridges, they must be completely removed with a special tool (see illustration). Follow the manufacturer's instructions provided with the tool. Failure to remove the ridges before attempting to remove the piston/connecting rod assemblies may result in piston breakage.

2    After the cylinder ridges have been

removed, turn the engine so the crankshaft is facing up.

3    Before the connecting rods are removed, check the connecting rod endplay with feeler gauges. Slide them between the first connecting rod and the crankshaft throw until the play is removed (see illustration). Repeat this procedure for each connecting rod. The endplay is equal to the thickness of the feeler gauge(s). Check with an automotive machine shop for the endplay service limit (a typical endplay limit should measure between 0.004 to 0.014 inch [0.10 to 0.35 mm]). If the play exceeds the service limit, new connecting rods will be required. If new rods (or a new crankshaft) are installed, the endplay may fall under the minimum allowable. If it does, the rods will have to be machined to restore it. If necessary, consult an automotive machine shop for advice.

4    Check the connecting rods and caps for identification marks. If they aren't plainly marked, use paint or marker to clearly identify each rod and cap (1, 2, 3, etc., depending on the cylinder they're associated with) (see illustration).

5    Remove the connecting rod cap bolts from the number one connecting rod.

**Note:** *New connecting rod cap bolts must be used when reassembling the engine, but save the old bolts - they'll be required for the bearing oil clearance check during reassembly.*

**Note:** *It will be necessary to remove the main bearing bridge to access the connecting rod bearing caps on all models. Refer to Section 10 and remove the main bearing bridge.*

6    Remove the number one connecting rod cap and bearing insert. Don't drop the bearing insert out of the cap.

7    Remove the bearing insert and push the connecting rod/piston assembly out through the top of the engine. Use a wooden dowel to push on the connecting rod. If resistance is felt, double-check to make sure that all of the ridge was removed from the cylinder.

8    Repeat the procedure for the remaining cylinders.

9    After removal, reassemble the con-

9.13 Install the piston ring into the cylinder, then push it down into position using a piston so the ring will be square in the cylinder

necting rod caps and bearing inserts in their respective connecting rods and install the cap bolts finger-tight. Leaving the old bearing inserts in place until reassembly will help prevent the connecting rod bearing surfaces from being accidentally nicked or gouged.

10    The pistons and connecting rods are now ready for inspection and overhaul at an automotive machine shop.

### Piston ring installation

11    Before installing the new piston rings, the ring end gaps must be checked. It's assumed that the piston ring side clearance has been checked and verified correct.

12    Lay out the piston/connecting rod assemblies and the new ring sets so the ring sets will be matched with the same piston and cylinder during the end gap measurement and engine assembly.

13    Insert the top (number one) ring into the first cylinder and square it up with the cylinder walls by pushing it in with the top of the piston (see illustration). The ring should be near the bottom of the cylinder, at the lower limit of ring travel.

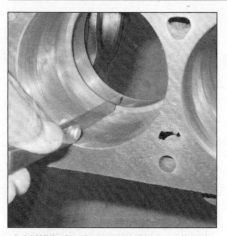

**9.14 With the ring square in the cylinder, measure the ring end gap with a feeler gauge**

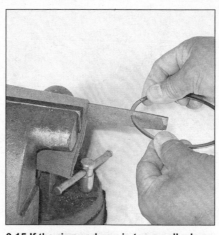

**9.15 If the ring end gap is too small, clamp a file in a vise as shown and file the piston ring ends - be sure to remove all raised material**

**9.19a Installing the spacer/expander in the oil ring groove**

14   To measure the end gap, slip feeler gauges between the ends of the ring until a gauge equal to the gap width is found (see illustration). The feeler gauge should slide between the ring ends with a slight amount of drag. A typical ring gap should fall between 0.008 and 0.020 inch (0.20 to 0.50 mm) for compression rings and up to 0.028 inch (0.70 mm) for the oil ring steel rails. If the gap is larger or smaller than specified, double-check to make sure you have the correct rings before proceeding.

15   If the gap is too small, it must be enlarged or the ring ends may come in contact with each other during engine operation, which can cause serious damage to the engine. If necessary, increase the end gaps by filing the ring ends very carefully with a fine file. Mount the file in a vise equipped with soft jaws, slip the ring over the file with the ends contacting the file face and slowly move the ring to remove material from the ends. When per-

forming this operation, file only by pushing the ring from the outside end of the file towards the vise (see illustration).

16   Excess end gap isn't critical unless it's greater than 0.031 inch (0.80 mm). Again, double-check to make sure you have the correct ring type.

17   Repeat the procedure for each ring that will be installed in the first cylinder and for each ring in the remaining cylinders. Remember to keep rings, pistons and cylinders matched up.

18   Once the ring end gaps have been checked/corrected, the rings can be installed on the pistons.

19   The oil control ring (lowest one on the piston) is usually installed first. It's composed of three separate components. Slip the spacer/expander into the groove (see illustration). If an anti-rotation tang is used, make sure it's inserted into the drilled hole in the ring groove. Next, install the upper side rail in

the same manner (see illustration). Don't use a piston ring installation tool on the oil ring side rails, as they may be damaged. Instead, place one end of the side rail into the groove between the spacer/expander and the ring land, hold it firmly in place and slide a finger around the piston while pushing the rail into the groove. Finally, install the lower side rail.

20   After the three oil ring components have been installed, check to make sure that both the upper and lower side rails can be rotated smoothly inside the ring grooves.

21   The number two (middle) ring is installed next. It's usually stamped with a mark which must face up, toward the top of the piston. Do not mix up the top and middle rings, as they have different cross-sections.

**Note:** *Always follow the instructions printed on the ring package or box - different manufacturers may require different approaches.*

22   Use a piston ring installation tool and make sure the identification mark is facing the top of the piston, then slip the ring into the middle groove on the piston (see illustration). Don't expand the ring any more than necessary to slide it over the piston.

23   Install the number one (top) ring in the same manner. Make sure the mark is facing up. Be careful not to confuse the number one and number two rings.

24   Repeat the procedure for the remaining pistons and rings.

### Installation

25   Before installing the piston/connecting rod assemblies, the cylinder walls must be perfectly clean, the top edge of each cylinder bore must be chamfered, and the oil jets and crankshaft must be in place.

26   Remove the cap from the end of the number one connecting rod (refer to the marks made during removal). Remove the original bearing inserts and wipe the bearing surfaces of the connecting rod and cap with a clean, lint-free cloth. They must be kept spotlessly clean.

**9.19b DO NOT use a piston ring installation tool when installing the oil control side rails**

**9.22 Use a piston ring installation tool to install the number 2 and the number 1 (top) rings - be sure the directional mark on the piston ring(s) is facing toward the top of the piston**

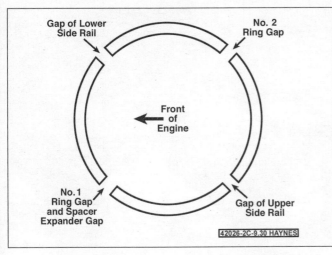

**9.30 Position the piston ring end gaps as shown**

**9.35 Use a plastic or wooden hammer handle to push the piston into the cylinder**

### Connecting rod bearing oil clearance check

27   Clean the back side of the new upper bearing insert, then lay it in place in the connecting rod.

28   Make sure the tab on the bearing fits into the recess in the rod. Don't hammer the bearing insert into place and be very careful not to nick or gouge the bearing face. Don't lubricate the bearing at this time.

29   Clean the back side of the other bearing insert and install it in the rod cap. Again, make sure the tab on the bearing fits into the recess in the cap, and don't apply any lubricant. It's critically important that the mating surfaces of the bearing and connecting rod are perfectly clean and oil free when they're assembled.

30   Position the piston ring gaps at the specified intervals around the piston as shown (see illustration).

31   Lubricate the piston and rings with clean engine oil and attach a piston ring compressor to the piston. Leave the skirt protruding about 1/4-inch to guide the piston into the cylinder. The rings must be compressed until they're flush with the piston.

32   Rotate the crankshaft until the number one connecting rod journal is at BDC (bottom dead center) and apply a liberal coat of engine oil to the cylinder walls.

33   With the arrow on top of the piston facing the front (timing belt end or timing chain) of the engine, gently insert the piston/connecting rod assembly into the number one cylinder bore and rest the bottom edge of the ring compressor on the engine block. Install the pistons with the cavity mark(s) or arrow facing toward the timing belt or timing chain end of the engine.

34   Tap the top edge of the ring compressor to make sure it's contacting the block around its entire circumference.

35   Gently tap on the top of the piston with the end of a wooden or plastic hammer handle (see illustration) while guiding the end of the connecting rod into place on the crankshaft journal (a pair of wooden dowels would

**9.37 Place Plastigage on each connecting rod bearing journal parallel to the crankshaft centerline**

be helpful for this). The piston rings may try to pop out of the ring compressor just before entering the cylinder bore, so keep some downward pressure on the ring compressor. Work slowly, and if any resistance is felt as the piston enters the cylinder, stop immediately. Find out what's hanging up and fix it before proceeding. Do not, for any reason, force the piston into the cylinder - you might break a ring and/or the piston.

36   Once the piston/connecting rod assembly is installed, the connecting rod bearing oil clearance must be checked before the rod cap is permanently installed.

37   Cut a piece of the appropriate size Plastigage slightly shorter than the width of the connecting rod bearing and lay it in place on the number one connecting rod journal, parallel with the journal axis (see illustration).

38   Clean the connecting rod cap bearing face and install the rod cap. Make sure the mating mark on the cap is on the same side as the mark on the connecting rod (see illustration 9.4).

**9.41 Use the scale on the Plastigage package to determine the bearing oil clearance - be sure to measure the widest part of the Plastigage and use the correct scale; it comes with both standard and metric scales**

39   Install the old rod bolts at this time, and tighten them to the torque listed in this Chapter's Specifications.

**Note:** *Use a thin-wall socket to avoid erroneous torque readings that can result if the socket is wedged between the rod cap and the bolt. If the socket tends to wedge itself between the fastener and the cap, lift up on it slightly until it no longer contacts the cap. DO NOT rotate the crankshaft at any time during this operation.*

40   Remove the fasteners and detach the rod cap, being very careful not to disturb the Plastigage. Install the cap bolts.

**Note:** *You MUST use new connecting rod bolts if the clearance is not as specified (see Step 5).*

41   Compare the width of the crushed Plastigage to the scale printed on the Plastigage envelope to obtain the oil clearance (see illustration). The connecting rod oil clearance is usually about 0.001 to 0.002 inch. Consult an automotive machine shop for the clearance specified for the rod bearings on your engine.

**10.1 Checking crankshaft endplay with a dial indicator**

**10.3 Checking the crankshaft endplay with feeler gauges at the thrust bearing journal**

42   If the clearance is not as specified, the bearing inserts may be the wrong size (which means different ones will be required). Before deciding that different inserts are needed, make sure that no dirt or oil was between the bearing inserts and the connecting rod or cap when the clearance was measured. Also, recheck the journal diameter. If the Plasti-gage was wider at one end than the other, the journal may be tapered. If the clearance still exceeds the limit specified, the bearing will have to be replaced with an undersize bear-ing.

**Caution:** *When installing a new crankshaft, always use a standard size bearing.*

### Final installation

43   Carefully scrape all traces of the Plasti-gage material off the rod journal and/or bear-ing face. Be very careful not to scratch the bearing - use your fingernail or the edge of a plastic card.

44   Make sure the bearing faces are per-fectly clean, then apply a uniform layer of clean moly-base grease or engine assembly lube to both of them. You'll have to push the piston into the cylinder to expose the face of the bearing insert in the connecting rod.

45   Slide the connecting rod back into place on the journal, install the rod cap, install the new bolts and tighten them to the torque listed in this Chapter's Specifications.

46   Repeat the entire procedure for the remaining pistons/connecting rods.

47   The important points to remember are:

a) *Keep the back sides of the bearing inserts and the insides of the connect-ing rods and caps perfectly clean when assembling them.*

b) *Make sure you have the correct piston/ rod assembly for each cylinder.*

c) *The arrow or mark on the piston must face the front (timing chain on four-cylin-der engines or timing belt on V6 engines) of the engine.*

d) *Lubricate the cylinder walls liberally with clean oil.*

e) *Lubricate the bearing faces when install-ing the rod caps after the oil clearance has been checked.*

48   After all the piston/connecting rod assemblies have been correctly installed, rotate the crankshaft a number of times by hand to check for any obvious binding.

49   As a final step, check the connecting rod endplay, as described in Step 3. If it was correct before disassembly and the original crankshaft and rods were reinstalled, it should still be correct. If new rods or a new crank-shaft were installed, the endplay may be inad-equate. If so, the rods will have to be removed and taken to an automotive machine shop for resizing.

---

## 10   Crankshaft - removal and installation

### Removal

**Note:** *The crankshaft can be removed only after the engine has been removed from the vehicle. It's assumed that the flywheel or driveplate, crankshaft pulley, timing chain, oil pan, baffle plate, oil screen, oil pump body, crankshaft position sensor, oil filter and piston/ connecting rod assemblies have already been removed.*

1   Before the crankshaft is removed, mea-sure the endplay. Mount a dial indicator with the indicator in line with the crankshaft and just touching the end of the crankshaft as shown (see illustration).

2   Pry the crankshaft all the way to the rear and zero the dial indicator. Next, pry the crank-shaft to the front as far as possible and check the reading on the dial indicator. The distance traveled is the endplay. A typical crankshaft endplay will fall between 0.004 to 0.014 inch (0.10 to 0.35 mm). If it is greater than that,

check the crankshaft thrust surfaces for wear after it's removed. If no wear is evident, new main bearings should correct the endplay.

3   If a dial indicator isn't available, feeler gauges can be used. Gently pry the crank-shaft all the way to the front of the engine. Slip feeler gauges between the crankshaft and the front face of the thrust bearing or washer to determine the clearance (see illustration).

4   Loosen the main bearing bridge perim-eter bolts, 1/4-turn at a time each, until they can be removed by hand. Follow the reverse of the tightening sequence (see illustrations 10.19a, 10.19b and 10.19c).

5   Remove the main bearing bridge, if equipped. Try not to drop the bearing inserts if they come out with the main bearing bridge assembly.

6   Carefully lift the crankshaft out of the engine. It may be a good idea to have an assistant available, since the crankshaft is quite heavy and awkward to handle. **Note:** *Remove the crankshaft position sensor (CKP) pulse plate mounting bolts and remove the plate from the rear of the crankshaft before servicing.* With the bearing inserts in place inside the engine block and main bearing bridge, or caps, reinstall the bridge or indi-vidual bearing caps onto the engine block and tighten the bolts finger-tight.

### Installation

7   Crankshaft installation is the first step in engine reassembly. It's assumed at this point that the engine block and crankshaft have been cleaned, inspected and repaired or reconditioned.

8   Position the engine block with the bottom facing up.

9   Remove the mounting bolts and lift off the lower crankcase or bearing bridge assem-bly.

10   If they're still in place, remove the origi-nal bearing inserts from the block and from the main bearing bridge. Wipe the bearing

**10.17 Place the Plastigage onto the crankshaft bearing journal as shown**

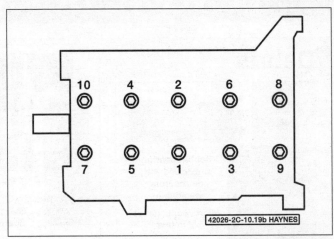

42026-2C-10.19b HAYNES

**10.19a Main bearing bridge bolt tightening sequence - inner bolts**

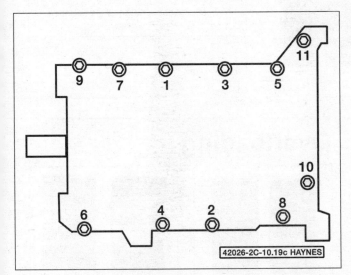

42026-2C-10.19c HAYNES

**10.19b Main bearing bridge bolt tightening sequence on 1.8L SOHC engines - outer bolts**

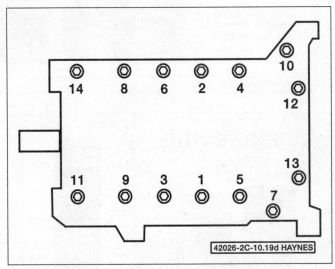

42026-2C-10.19d HAYNES

**10.19c Main bearing bridge bolt tightening sequence on 2.4L DOHC engines - outer bolts**

surfaces of the block and main bearing bridge saddle with a clean, lint-free cloth. They must be kept spotlessly clean. This is critical for determining the correct bearing oil clearance.

### Main bearing oil clearance check

11   Without mixing them up, clean the back sides of the new upper main bearing inserts (with grooves and oil holes) and lay one in each main bearing saddle in the engine block. Each upper bearing (engine block) has an oil groove and oil hole in it. Caution: The oil holes in the block must line up with the oil holes in the engine block inserts. The thrust washer or thrust bearing inserts must be installed in the engine block number 4 journal. Clean the back sides of the lower main bearing inserts and lay them in the corresponding location in the main bearing bridge. Make sure the tab on the bearing insert fits into the recess in the

block or main bearing caps.
**Caution:** *Do not hammer the bearing insert into place and don't nick or gouge the bearing faces. DO NOT apply any lubrication at this time.*
12   Clean the faces of the bearing inserts in the block and the crankshaft main bearing journals with a clean, lint-free cloth.
13   Check or clean the oil holes in the crankshaft, as any dirt here can go only one way - straight through the new bearings.
14   Once you're certain the crankshaft is clean, carefully lay it in position in the cylinder block.
15   Before the crankshaft can be permanently installed, the main bearing oil clearance must be checked.
16   Cut several strips of the appropriate size of Plastigage. They must be slightly shorter than the width of the main bearing journal.
17   Place one piece on each crankshaft main bearing journal, parallel with the journal

axis as shown (see illustration).
18   Clean the faces of the bearing inserts in the lower crankcase or main bearing caps. Hold the bearing inserts in place and install the lower crankcase or caps onto the crankshaft and cylinder block. DO NOT disturb the Plastigage.
19   Apply clean engine oil to all bolt threads prior to installation, then install all bolts finger-tight. Tighten the main bearing bridge bolts in the sequence shown (see illustrations) progressing in steps, to the torque listed in this Chapter's Specifications. DO NOT rotate the crankshaft at any time during this operation.
**Note:** *Be sure to torque the main bearing bridge inner bolts first, followed by the perimeter bolts.*
20   Remove the bolts in the reverse order of the tightening sequence and carefully lift the main bearing bridge straight up and off the block. Do not disturb the Plastigage or rotate the crankshaft.

# ENGINE BEARING ANALYSIS

## Debris

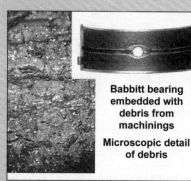

**Babbitt bearing embedded with debris from machinings**

**Microscopic detail of debris**

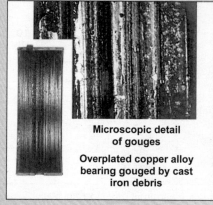

**Microscopic detail of gouges**

**Overplated copper alloy bearing gouged by cast iron debris**

**Aluminum bearing embedded with glass beads**

**Microscopic detail of glass beads**

**Damaged lining caused by dirt left on the bearing back**

## Misassembly

**Result of a lower half assembled as an upper - blocking the oil flow**

**Excessive oil clearance is indicated by a short contact arc**

**Polished and oil-stained backs are a result of a poor fit in the housing bore**

**Result of a wrong, reversed, or shifted cap**

## Overloading

**Damage from excessive idling which resulted in an oil film unable to support the load imposed**

**Damaged upper connecting rod bearings caused by engine lugging; the lower main bearings (not shown) were similarly affected**

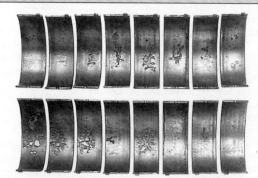

**The damage shown in these upper and lower connecting rod bearings was caused by engine operation at a higher-than-rated speed under load**

# Misalignment

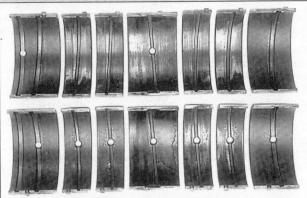

A warped crankshaft caused this pattern of severe wear in the center, diminishing toward the ends

A poorly finished crankshaft caused the equally spaced scoring shown

A tapered housing bore caused the damage along one edge of this pair

A bent connecting rod led to the damage in the "V" pattern

# Lubrication

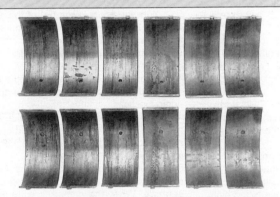

Result of dry start: The bearings on the left, farthest from the oil pump, show more damage

Result of a low oil supply or oil starvation

Severe wear as a result of inadequate oil clearance

# Corrosion

**Microscopic detail of corrosion**

Corrosion is an acid attack on the bearing lining generally caused by inadequate maintenance, extremely hot or cold operation, or inferior oils or fuels

**Microscopic detail of cavitation**

Example of cavitation - a surface erosion caused by pressure changes in the oil film

Damage from excessive thrust or insufficient axial clearance

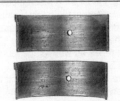

Bearing affected by oil dilution caused by excessive blow-by or a rich mixture

**10.21 Use the scale on the Plastigage package to determine the bearing oil clearance - be sure to measure the widest part of the Plastigage and use the correct scale; it comes with both standard and metric scales**

21   Compare the width of the crushed Plastigage on each journal to the scale printed on the Plastigage envelope to determine the main bearing oil clearance (see illustration). Check with an automotive machine shop for the oil clearance for your engine.

22   If the clearance is not as specified, the bearing inserts may be the wrong size (which means different ones will be required). Before deciding if different inserts are needed, make sure that no dirt or oil was between the bearing inserts and the caps or block when the clearance was measured. If the Plastigage was wider at one end than the other, the crankshaft journal may be tapered. If the clearance still exceeds the limit specified, the bearing insert(s) will have to be replaced with an undersize bearing insert(s).
**Caution:** *When installing a new crankshaft always install a standard bearing insert set.*

23   Carefully scrape all traces of the Plastigage material off the main bearing journals and/or the bearing insert faces. Be sure to remove all residue from the oil holes. Use your fingernail or the edge of a plastic card - don't nick or scratch the bearing faces.

### Final installation

24   Carefully lift the crankshaft out of the cylinder block. Install the crankshaft position sensor (CKP) pulse plate mounting bolts and tighten the bolts to the torque listed in this Chapter's Specifications.

25   Clean the bearing insert faces in the cylinder block, then apply a thin, uniform layer of moly-base grease or engine assembly lube to each of the bearing surfaces. Be sure to coat the thrust faces as well as the journal face of the thrust bearing.

26   Make sure the crankshaft journals are clean, then lay the crankshaft back in place in the cylinder block.

27   Clean the bearing insert faces and apply the same lubricant to them. Clean the engine block and the mating surface of the lower crankcase or the bearing caps thoroughly. The surfaces must be free of oil residue.

28   Apply liquid gasket or equivalent to the

lower main bearing bridge and inside edge of the threaded bolt holes. Install the lower main bearing bridge.
**Note:** *Once the liquid gasket has been applied, the bearing bridge must be installed within a few minutes or the gasket must be removed and the parts cleaned and applied again.*

29   Prior to installation, apply clean engine oil to all bolt threads, wiping off any excess, then install all bolts finger-tight.

30   Tighten the bolts to the torque listed in this Chapter's Specifications following the correct torque sequence (see illustrations 10.19a, 10.19b and 10.19c).

31   Recheck the crankshaft endplay with a feeler gauge or a dial indicator. The endplay should be correct if the crankshaft thrust faces aren't worn or damaged and if new bearings have been installed.

32   Rotate the crankshaft a number of times by hand to check for any obvious binding. It should rotate with a running torque of 50 in-lbs or less. If the running torque is too high, correct the problem at this time.

33   Install the new rear main oil seal (see Chapter 2A).
**Caution:** *You must wait at least 30 minutes before filling the engine with oil and at least 3 hours before starting the engine after installing the lower main bearing bridge to the cylinder block.*

### 11   Engine overhaul - reassembly sequence

1   Before beginning engine reassembly, make sure you have all the necessary new parts, gaskets and seals as well as the following items on hand:
*Common hand tools*
*A 1/2-inch drive torque wrench*
*New engine oil*
*Gasket sealant*
*Thread locking compound*

2   If you obtained a short block it will be necessary to install the cylinder head, the oil

pump and pick-up tube, the oil pan, the water pump, the timing chain and timing cover, and the valve cover (see Chapter 2A or Chapter 2B). In order to save time and avoid problems, the external components must be installed in the following general order:
*Thermostat and housing cover*
*Water pump*
*Intake and exhaust manifolds*
*Fuel injection components*
*Emission control components*
*Spark plug wires and spark plugs*
*Ignition coils or coil packs*
*Oil filter*
*Engine mounts and mount brackets*
*Clutch and flywheel (manual transaxle)*
*Driveplate (automatic transaxle)*

### 12   Initial start-up and break-in after overhaul

**Warning:** *Have a fire extinguisher handy when starting the engine for the first time.*

1   Once the engine has been installed in the vehicle, double-check the engine oil and coolant levels.

2   With the spark plugs out of the engine and the ignition system and fuel pump disabled (see Chapter 4, Section 3), crank the engine until oil pressure registers on the gauge or the light goes out.

3   Install the spark plugs, hook up the plug wires and restore the ignition system and fuel pump functions.

4   Start the engine. It may take a few moments for the fuel system to build up pressure, but the engine should start without a great deal of effort.

5   After the engine starts, it should be allowed to warm up to normal operating temperature. While the engine is warming up, make a thorough check for fuel, oil and coolant leaks.

6   Shut the engine off and recheck the engine oil and coolant levels.

7   Drive the vehicle to an area with minimum traffic, accelerate from 30 to 50 mph, then allow the vehicle to slow to 30 mph with the throttle closed. Repeat the procedure 10 or 12 times. This will load the piston rings and cause them to seat properly against the cylinder walls. Check again for oil and coolant leaks.

8   Drive the vehicle gently for the first 500 miles (no sustained high speeds) and keep a constant check on the oil level. It is not unusual for an engine to use oil during the break-in period.

9   At approximately 500 to 600 miles, change the oil and filter.

10   For the next few hundred miles, drive the vehicle normally. Do not pamper it or abuse it.

11   After 2,000 miles, change the oil and filter again and consider the engine broken in.

# COMMON ENGINE OVERHAUL TERMS

## B

**Backlash** - The amount of play between two parts. Usually refers to how much one gear can be moved back and forth without moving the gear with which it's meshed.

**Bearing Caps** - The caps held in place by nuts or bolts which, in turn, hold the bearing surface. This space is for lubricating oil to enter.

**Bearing clearance** - The amount of space left between shaft and bearing surface. This space is for lubricating oil to enter.

**Bearing crush** - The additional height which is purposely manufactured into each bearing half to ensure complete contact of the bearing back with the housing bore when the engine is assembled.

**Bearing knock** - The noise created by movement of a part in a loose or worn bearing.

**Blueprinting** - Dismantling an engine and reassembling it to EXACT specifications.

**Bore** - An engine cylinder, or any cylindrical hole; also used to describe the process of enlarging or accurately refinishing a hole with a cutting tool, as to bore an engine cylinder. The bore size is the diameter of the hole.

**Boring** - Renewing the cylinders by cutting them out to a specified size. A boring bar is used to make the cut.

**Bottom end** - A term which refers collectively to the engine block, crankshaft, main bearings and the big ends of the connecting rods.

**Break-in** - The period of operation between installation of new or rebuilt parts and time in which parts are worn to the correct fit. Driving at reduced and varying speed for a specified mileage to permit parts to wear to the correct fit.

**Bushing** - A one-piece sleeve placed in a bore to serve as a bearing surface for shaft, piston pin, etc. Usually replaceable.

## C

**Camshaft** - The shaft in the engine, on which a series of lobes are located for operating the valve mechanisms. The camshaft is driven by gears or sprockets and a timing chain. Usually referred to simply as the cam.

**Carbon** - Hard, or soft, black deposits found in combustion chamber, on plugs, under rings, on and under valve heads.

**Cast iron** - An alloy of iron and more than two percent carbon, used for engine blocks and heads because it's relatively inexpensive and easy to mold into complex shapes.

**Chamfer** - To bevel across (or a bevel on) the sharp edge of an object.

**Chase** - To repair damaged threads with a tap or die.

**Combustion chamber** - The space between the piston and the cylinder head, with the piston at top dead center, in which air-fuel mixture is burned.

**Compression ratio** - The relationship between cylinder volume (clearance volume) when the piston is at top dead center and cylinder volume when the piston is at bottom dead center.

**Connecting rod** - The rod that connects the crank on the crankshaft with the piston. Sometimes called a con rod.

**Connecting rod cap** - The part of the connecting rod assembly that attaches the rod to the crankpin.

**Core plug** - Soft metal plug used to plug the casting holes for the coolant passages in the block.

**Crankcase** - The lower part of the engine in which the crankshaft rotates; includes the lower section of the cylinder block and the oil pan.

**Crank kit** - A reground or reconditioned crankshaft and new main and connecting rod bearings.

**Crankpin** - The part of a crankshaft to which a connecting rod is attached.

**Crankshaft** - The main rotating member, or shaft, running the length of the crankcase, with offset throws to which the connecting rods are attached; changes the reciprocating motion of the pistons into rotating motion.

**Cylinder sleeve** - A replaceable sleeve, or liner, pressed into the cylinder block to form the cylinder bore.

## D

**Deburring** - Removing the burrs (rough edges or areas) from a bearing.

**Deglazer** - A tool, rotated by an electric motor, used to remove glaze from cylinder walls so a new set of rings will seat.

## E

**Endplay** - The amount of lengthwise movement between two parts. As applied to a crankshaft, the distance that the crankshaft can move forward and back in the cylinder block.

## F

**Face** - A machinist's term that refers to removing metal from the end of a shaft or the face of a larger part, such as a flywheel.

**Fatigue** - A breakdown of material through a large number of loading and unloading cycles. The first signs are cracks followed shortly by breaks.

**Feeler gauge** - A thin strip of hardened steel, ground to an exact thickness, used to check clearances between parts.

**Free height** - The unloaded length or height of a spring.

**Freeplay** - The looseness in a linkage, or an assembly of parts, between the initial application of force and actual movement. Usually perceived as slop or slight delay.

**Freeze plug** - See Core plug.

## G

**Gallery** - A large passage in the block that forms a reservoir for engine oil pressure.

**Glaze** - The very smooth, glassy finish that develops on cylinder walls while an engine is in service.

## H

**Heli-Coil** - A rethreading device used when threads are worn or damaged. The device is installed in a retapped hole to reduce the thread size to the original size.

## I

**Installed height** - The spring's measured length or height, as installed on the cylinder head. Installed height is measured from the spring seat to the underside of the spring retainer.

## J

**Journal** - The surface of a rotating shaft which turns in a bearing.

## K

**Keeper** - The split lock that holds the valve spring retainer in position on the valve stem.

**Key** - A small piece of metal inserted into matching grooves machined into two parts fitted together - such as a gear pressed onto a shaft - which prevents slippage between the two parts.

**Knock** - The heavy metallic engine sound, produced in the combustion chamber as a result of abnormal combustion - usually detonation. Knock is usually caused by a loose or worn bearing. Also referred to as detonation, pinging and spark knock. Connecting rod or main bearing knocks are created by too much oil clearance or insufficient lubrication.

## L

**Lands** - The portions of metal between the piston ring grooves.

**Lapping the valves** - Grinding a valve face and its seat together with lapping compound.

**Lash** - The amount of free motion in a gear train, between gears, or in a mechanical assembly, that occurs before movement can begin. Usually refers to the lash in a valve train.

**Lifter** - The part that rides against the cam to transfer motion to the rest of the valve train.

# M

**Machining** - The process of using a machine to remove metal from a metal part.

**Main bearings** - The plain, or babbit, bearings that support the crankshaft.

**Main bearing caps** - The cast iron caps, bolted to the bottom of the block, that support the main bearings.

# O

**O.D.** - Outside diameter.

**Oil gallery** - A pipe or drilled passageway in the engine used to carry engine oil from one area to another.

**Oil ring** - The lower ring, or rings, of a piston; designed to prevent excessive amounts of oil from working up the cylinder walls and into the combustion chamber. Also called an oil-control ring.

**Oil seal** - A seal which keeps oil from leaking out of a compartment. Usually refers to a dynamic seal around a rotating shaft or other moving part.

**O-ring** - A type of sealing ring made of a special rubberlike material; in use, the O-ring is compressed into a groove to provide the sealing action.

**Overhaul** - To completely disassemble a unit, clean and inspect all parts, reassemble it with the original or new parts and make all adjustments necessary for proper operation.

# P

**Pilot bearing** - A small bearing installed in the center of the flywheel (or the rear end of the crankshaft) to support the front end of the input shaft of the transmission.

**Pip mark** - A little dot or indentation which indicates the top side of a compression ring.

**Piston** - The cylindrical part, attached to the connecting rod, that moves up and down in the cylinder as the crankshaft rotates. When the fuel charge is fired, the piston transfers the force of the explosion to the connecting rod, then to the crankshaft.

**Piston pin (or wrist pin)** - The cylindrical and usually hollow steel pin that passes through the piston. The piston pin fastens the piston to the upper end of the connecting rod.

**Piston ring** - The split ring fitted to the groove in a piston. The ring contacts the sides of the ring groove and also rubs against the cylinder wall, thus sealing space between piston and wall. There are two types of rings: Compression rings seal the compression pressure in the combustion chamber; oil rings scrape excessive oil off the cylinder wall.

**Piston ring groove** - The slots or grooves cut in piston heads to hold piston rings in position.

**Piston skirt** - The portion of the piston below the rings and the piston pin hole.

**Plastigage** - A thin strip of plastic thread, available in different sizes, used for measuring clearances. For example, a strip of plastigage is laid across a bearing journal and mashed as parts are assembled. Then parts are disassembled and the width of the strip is measured to determine clearance between journal and bearing. Commonly used to measure crankshaft main-bearing and connecting rod bearing clearances.

**Press-fit** - A tight fit between two parts that requires pressure to force the parts together. Also referred to as drive, or force, fit.

**Prussian blue** - A blue pigment; in solution, useful in determining the area of contact between two surfaces. Prussian blue is commonly used to determine the width and location of the contact area between the valve face and the valve seat.

# R

**Race (bearing)** - The inner or outer ring that provides a contact surface for balls or rollers in bearing.

**Ream** - To size, enlarge or smooth a hole by using a round cutting tool with fluted edges.

**Ring job** - The process of reconditioning the cylinders and installing new rings.

**Runout** - Wobble. The amount a shaft rotates out-of-true.

# S

**Saddle** - The upper main bearing seat.

**Scored** - Scratched or grooved, as a cylinder wall may be scored by abrasive particles moved up and down by the piston rings.

**Scuffing** - A type of wear in which there's a transfer of material between parts moving against each other; shows up as pits or grooves in the mating surfaces.

**Seat** - The surface upon which another part rests or seats. For example, the valve seat is the matched surface upon which the valve face rests. Also used to refer to wearing into a good fit; for example, piston rings seat after a few miles of driving.

**Short block** - An engine block complete with crankshaft and piston and, usually, camshaft assemblies.

**Static balance** - The balance of an object while it's stationary.

**Step** - The wear on the lower portion of a ring land caused by excessive side and back-clearance. The height of the step indicates the ring's extra side clearance and the length of the step projecting from the back wall of the groove represents the ring's back clearance.

**Stroke** - The distance the piston moves when traveling from top dead center to bottom dead center, or from bottom dead center to top dead center.

**Stud** - A metal rod with threads on both ends.

# T

**Tang** - A lip on the end of a plain bearing used to align the bearing during assembly.

**Tap** - To cut threads in a hole. Also refers to the fluted tool used to cut threads.

**Taper** - A gradual reduction in the width of a shaft or hole; in an engine cylinder, taper usually takes the form of uneven wear, more pronounced at the top than at the bottom.

**Throws** - The offset portions of the crankshaft to which the connecting rods are affixed.

**Thrust bearing** - The main bearing that has thrust faces to prevent excessive endplay, or forward and backward movement of the crankshaft.

**Thrust washer** - A bronze or hardened steel washer placed between two moving parts. The washer prevents longitudinal movement and provides a bearing surface for thrust surfaces of parts.

**Tolerance** - The amount of variation permitted from an exact size of measurement. Actual amount from smallest acceptable dimension to largest acceptable dimension.

# U

**Umbrella** - An oil deflector placed near the valve tip to throw oil from the valve stem area.

**Undercut** - A machined groove below the normal surface.

**Undersize bearings** - Smaller diameter bearings used with re-ground crankshaft journals.

# V

**Valve grinding** - Refacing a valve in a valve-refacing machine.

**Valve train** - The valve-operating mechanism of an engine; includes all components from the camshaft to the valve.

**Vibration damper** - A cylindrical weight attached to the front of the crankshaft to minimize torsional vibration (the twist-untwist actions of the crankshaft caused by the cylinder firing impulses). Also called a harmonic balancer.

# W

**Water jacket** - The spaces around the cylinders, between the inner and outer shells of the cylinder block or head, through which coolant circulates.

**Web** - A supporting structure across a cavity.

**Woodruff key** - A key with a radiused backside (viewed from the side).

# Chapter 3
# Cooling, heating and air conditioning systems

## Contents

## Specifications

### General

| | |
|---|---|
| Radiator cap pressure rating .................................................. | 14 to 18 psi (93 to 123 kPa) |
| Thermostat rating (opening to fully open temperature range) ................ | 176 to 203 degrees F (80 to 95 degrees C) |
| Cooling system capacity.......................................................... | See Chapter 1 |
| Refrigerant type...................................................................... | R-134a |
| Refrigerant capacity................................................................ | Refer to HVAC specification tag |

### Torque specifications

**Ft-lbs** (unless otherwise indicated)     **Nm**

**Note:** *One foot-pound (ft-lb) of torque is equivalent to 12 inch-pounds (in-lbs) of torque. Torque values below approximately 15 ft-lbs are expressed in inch-pounds, because most foot-pound torque wrenches are not accurate at these smaller values.*

| | Ft-lbs | Nm |
|---|---|---|
| Compressor mounting bolts | 16 | 22 Nm |
| Compressor inlet and outlet bolt/nut................................................. | 86 in-lbs | 9.8 Nm |
| Condenser inlet and outlet nuts........................................................ | 86 in-lbs | 9.8 Nm |
| Receiver-drier | | |
| 2-door Civic and all CR-V models (dessicant bag cap)..................... | 25 in-lbs | 2.9 Nm |
| 4-door Civic models (bolts) ............................................................. | 25 in-lbs | 2.9 Nm |
| Thermostat housing cover bolts | | |
| 1.8L models ..................................................................................... | 89 in-lbs | 10 Nm |
| 2.4 models ....................................................................................... | 108 in-lbs | 12 Nm |
| Water pump bolts ............................................................................. | 108 in-lbs | 12 Nm |
| Water pump pulley bolts (1.8L engines) .......................................... | 120 in-lbs | 13.5 Nm |

## 1   General Information

**Warning:** *Do not allow antifreeze to come in contact with your skin or painted surfaces of the vehicle. Rinse off spills immediately with plenty of water. Antifreeze is highly toxic if ingested. Never leave antifreeze lying around in an open container or in puddles on the floor; children and pets are attracted by its sweet smell and may drink it. Check with local authorities about disposing of used antifreeze. Many communities have collection centers which will see that antifreeze is disposed of safely. Never dump used antifreeze on the ground or pour it into drains.*

### Engine cooling system

1   All modern vehicles employ a pressurized engine cooling system with thermostatically controlled coolant circulation. The cooling system consists of a radiator, a coolant reservoir, a pressure cap (located on the radi-

ator), a thermostat, a cooling fan, and a water pump.

2   The water pump circulates coolant through the engine. The coolant flows around each cylinder and around the intake and exhaust ports, near the spark plug areas and in close proximity to the exhaust valve guides.

3   A thermostat controls engine coolant temperature. During warm up, the closed thermostat prevents coolant from circulating through the radiator. As the engine nears normal operating temperature, the thermostat opens and allows hot coolant to travel through the radiator, where it's cooled before returning to the engine.

### Heating system

4   The heating system consists of a blower fan and heater core located in a housing under the dash, the hoses connecting the heater core to the engine cooling system and the heater/air conditioning control head on the

dashboard. Hot engine coolant is circulated through the heater core. When the heater mode is activated, a flap door in the housing opens to expose the heater core to the passenger compartment through air ducts. A fan switch on the control head activates the blower motor, which forces air through the core, heating the air.

### Air conditioning system

5   The air conditioning system consists of a condenser mounted in front of the radiator, an evaporator mounted adjacent to the heater core, a compressor mounted on the engine, a receiver-drier or accumulator and the plumbing connecting all of the above components.

6   A blower fan forces the warmer air of the passenger compartment through the evaporator core (sort of a radiator-in-reverse), transferring the heat from the air to the refrigerant. The liquid refrigerant boils off into low pressure vapor, taking the heat with it when it leaves the evaporator.

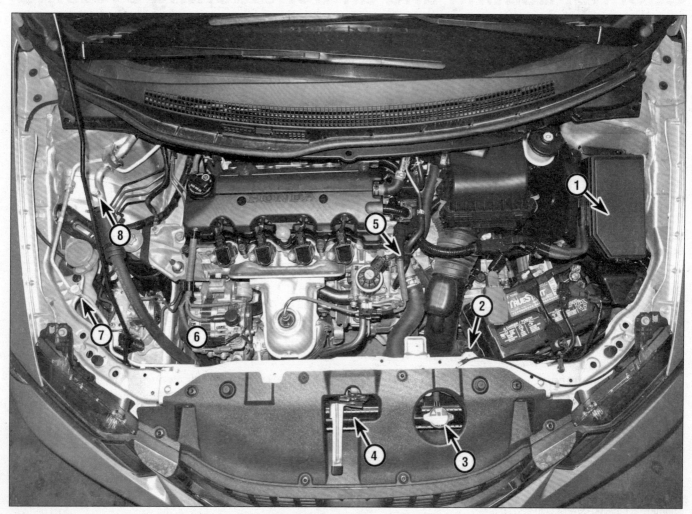

**1.0 Cooling, heating and air conditioning components - 2014 Civic with a 1.8L engine shown**

| | | | | | |
|---|---|---|---|---|---|
| 1 | Fuse and relay box | 4 | Radiator (below radiator support cover) | 7 | Air conditioning service port (high side) |
| 2 | Coolant reservoir | 5 | Thermostat housing | 8 | Air conditioning service port (low side) |
| 3 | Radiator cap | 6 | Water pump (right end of engine, not visible here) | | |

## 2   Troubleshooting

### *Coolant leaks*

1    A coolant leak can develop anywhere in the cooling system, but the most common causes are:

a)  *A loose or weak hose clamp*
b)  *A defective hose*
c)  *A faulty pressure cap*
d)  *A damaged radiator*
e)  *A bad heater core*
f)  *A faulty water pump*
g)  *A leaking gasket at any joint that carries coolant*

2    Coolant leaks aren't always easy to find. Sometimes they can only be detected when the cooling system is under pressure. Here's where a cooling system pressure tester comes in handy. After the engine has cooled completely, the tester is attached in place of the pressure cap, then pumped up to the pressure value equal to that of the pressure cap rating (see illustration). Now, leaks that only exist when the engine is fully warmed up will become apparent. The tester can be left connected to locate a nagging slow leak.

### *Coolant level drops, but no external leaks*

3    If you find it necessary to keep adding coolant, but there are no external leaks, the probable causes include:

a)  *A blown head gasket*
b)  *A leaking intake manifold gasket (only on engines that have coolant passages in the manifold)*
c)  *A cracked cylinder head or cylinder block*

4    Any of the above problems will also usually result in contamination of the engine oil, which will cause it to take on a milkshake-like appearance. A bad head gasket or cracked head or block can also result in engine oil contaminating the cooling system.

5    Combustion leak detectors (also known as block testers) are available at most auto parts stores. These work by detecting exhaust gases in the cooling system, which indicates a compression leak from a cylinder into the coolant. The tester consists of a large bulb-type syringe and bottle of test fluid (see illustration). A measured amount of the fluid is added to the syringe. The syringe is placed over the cooling system filler neck and, with the engine running, the bulb is squeezed and a sample of the gases present in the cooling system are drawn up through the test fluid (see illustration). If any combustion gases are present in the sample taken, the test fluid will change color.

6    If the test indicates combustion gas is present in the cooling system, you can be sure that the engine has a blown head gasket or a crack in the cylinder head or block, and will require disassembly to repair.

### *Pressure cap*

**Warning:** *Wait until the engine is completely cool before beginning this check.*

7    The cooling system is sealed by a spring-loaded cap, which raises the boiling point of the coolant. If the cap's seal or spring are worn out, the coolant can boil and escape past the cap. With the engine completely cool, remove the cap and check the seal; if it's cracked, hardened or deteriorated in any way, replace it with a new one.

8    Even if the seal is good, the spring might not be; this can be checked with a cooling system pressure tester (see illustration). If the cap can't hold a pressure within approximately 1-1/2 lbs of its rated pressure (which is marked on the cap), replace it with a new one.

9    The cap is also equipped with a vacuum relief spring. When the engine cools off, a vacuum is created in the cooling system. The vacuum relief spring allows air back into the system, which will equalize the pressure and prevent damage to the radiator (the radiator tanks could collapse if the vacuum is great enough). If, after turning the engine off and allowing it to cool down you notice any of the cooling system hoses collapsing, replace the pressure cap with a new one.

**2.2 The cooling system pressure tester is connected in place of the pressure cap, then pumped up to pressurize the system**

**2.5a The combustion leak detector consists of a bulb, syringe and test fluid**

**2.5b Place the tester over the cooling system filler neck and use the bulb to draw a sample into the tester**

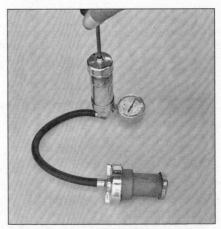

**2.8 Checking the cooling system pressure cap with a cooling system pressure tester**

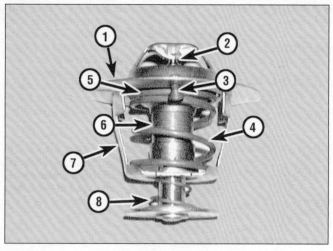

**2.10 Typical thermostat:**

| | | | |
|---|---|---|---|
| 1 | Flange | 5 | Valve seat |
| 2 | Piston | 6 | Valve |
| 3 | Jiggle valve | 7 | Frame |
| 4 | Main coil spring | 8 | Secondary coil spring |

**2.28 The water pump weep hole is generally located on the underside of the pump**

## Thermostat

10   Before assuming the thermostat (see illustration) is responsible for a cooling system problem, check the coolant level (see Chapter 1), drivebelt tension (see Chapter 1) and temperature gauge (or light) operation.

11   If the engine takes a long time to warm up (as indicated by the temperature gauge or heater operation), the thermostat is probably stuck open. Replace the thermostat with a new one.

12   If the engine runs hot or overheats, a thorough test of the thermostat should be performed.

13   Definitive testing of the thermostat can only be made when it is removed from the vehicle. If the thermostat is stuck in the open position at room temperature, it is faulty and must be replaced.

**Caution:** *Do not drive the vehicle without a thermostat. The computer may stay in open loop and emissions and fuel economy will suffer.*

14   To test a thermostat, suspend the (closed) thermostat on a length of string or wire in a pot of cold water.

15   Heat the water on a stove while observing thermostat. The thermostat should fully open before the water boils.

16   If the thermostat doesn't open and close as specified, or sticks in any position, replace it.

## Cooling fan

### Electric cooling fan

17   If the engine is overheating and the cooling fan is not coming on when the engine temperature rises to an excessive level, unplug the fan motor electrical connector(s) and connect the motor directly to the battery with fused jumper wires. If the fan motor doesn't come on, replace the motor.

18   If the radiator fan motor is okay, but it isn't coming on when the engine gets hot, the fan relay might be defective. A relay is used to control a circuit by turning it on and off in response to a control decision by the Powertrain Control Module (PCM). These control circuits are fairly complex, and checking them should be left to a qualified automotive technician. Sometimes, the control system can be fixed by simply identifying and replacing a bad relay.

19   Locate the fan relays in the engine compartment fuse/relay box.

20   Test the relay (see Chapter 12).

21   If the relay is okay, check all wiring and connections to the fan motor. Refer to the wiring diagrams at the end of Chapter 12. If no obvious problems are found, the problem could be the Engine Coolant Temperature (ECT) sensor or the Powertrain Control Module (PCM). Have the cooling fan system and circuit diagnosed by a dealer service department or repair shop with the proper diagnostic equipment.

**Note:** *These models are equipped with a cooling fan motor resistor. Have the resistor checked if the fan motor does not respond to the speed variations signaled by the PCM.*

### Belt-driven cooling fan

22   Disconnect the cable from the negative terminal of the battery and rock the fan back and forth by hand to check for excessive bearing play.

23   With the engine cold (and not running), turn the fan blades by hand. The fan should turn freely.

24   Visually inspect for substantial fluid leakage from the clutch assembly. If problems are noted, replace the clutch assembly.

25   With the engine completely warmed up, turn off the ignition switch and disconnect the negative battery cable from the battery. Turn the fan by hand. Some drag should be evident. If the fan turns easily, replace the fan clutch.

## Water pump

26   A failure in the water pump can cause serious engine damage due to overheating.

### Drivebelt-driven water pump

27   There are two ways to check the operation of the water pump while it's installed on the engine. If the pump is found to be defective, it should be replaced with a new or rebuilt unit.

28   Water pumps are equipped with weep (or vent) holes (see illustration). If a failure occurs in the pump seal, coolant will leak from the hole.

29   If the water pump shaft bearings fail, there may be a howling sound at the pump while it's running. Shaft wear can be felt with the drivebelt removed if the water pump pulley is rocked up and down (with the engine off). Don't mistake drivebelt slippage, which causes a squealing sound, for water pump bearing failure.

### Timing chain or timing belt-driven water pump

30   Water pumps driven by the timing chain or timing belt are located underneath the timing chain or timing belt cover.

31   Checking the water pump is limited because of where it is located. However, some

basic checks can be made before deciding to remove the water pump. If the pump is found to be defective, it should be replaced with a new or rebuilt unit.

32 One sign that the water pump may be failing is that the heater (climate control) may not work well. Warm the engine to normal operating temperature, confirm that the coolant level is correct, then run the heater and check for hot air coming from the ducts.

33 Check for noises coming from the water pump area. If the water pump impeller shaft or bearings are failing, there may be a howling sound at the pump while the engine is running.

**Note:** *Be careful not to mistake drivebelt noise (squealing) for water pump bearing or shaft failure.*

34 It you suspect water pump failure due to noise, wear can be confirmed by feeling for play at the pump shaft. This can be done by rocking the drive sprocket on the pump shaft up and down. To do this you will need to remove the tension on the timing chain or belt as well as access the water pump.

### All water pumps

35 In rare cases or on high-mileage vehicles, another sign of water pump failure may be the presence of coolant in the engine oil. This condition will adversely affect the engine in varying degrees.

**Note:** *Finding coolant in the engine oil could indicate other serious issues besides a failed water pump, such as a blown head gasket or a cracked cylinder head or block.*

36 Even a pump that exhibits no outward signs of a problem, such as noise or leakage, can still be due for replacement. Removal for close examination is the only sure way to tell. Sometimes the fins on the back of the impeller can corrode to the point that cooling efficiency is diminished significantly.

### Heater system

37 Little can go wrong with a heater. If the fan motor will run at all speeds, the electrical part of the system is okay. The three basic heater problems fall into the following general categories:

a) *Not enough heat*
b) *Heat all the time*
c) *No heat*

38 If there's not enough heat, the control valve or door is stuck in a partially open position, the coolant coming from the engine isn't hot enough, or the heater core is restricted. If the coolant isn't hot enough, the thermostat in the engine cooling system is stuck open, allowing coolant to pass through the engine so rapidly that it doesn't heat up quickly enough. If the vehicle is equipped with a temperature gauge instead of a warning light, watch to see if the engine temperature rises to the normal operating range after driving for a reasonable distance.

39 If there's heat all the time, the control valve or the door is stuck wide open.

40 If there's no heat, coolant is probably not reaching the heater core, or the heater core is plugged. The likely cause is a collapsed or plugged hose, core, or a frozen heater control valve. If the heater is the type that flows coolant all the time, the cause is a stuck door or a broken or kinked control cable.

## Air conditioning system

41 If the cool air output is inadequate:

a) *Inspect the condenser coils and fins to make sure they're clear*
b) *Check the compressor clutch for slippage.*
c) *Check the blower motor for proper operation.*
d) *Inspect the blower discharge passage for obstructions.*
e) *Check the system air intake filter for clogging.*

42 If the system provides intermittent cooling air:

a) *Check the circuit breaker, blower switch and blower motor for a malfunction.*
b) *Make sure the compressor clutch isn't slipping.*
c) *Inspect the plenum door to make sure it's operating properly.*
d) *Inspect the evaporator to make sure it isn't clogged.*
e) *If the unit is icing up, it may be caused by excessive moisture in the system, incorrect super heat switch adjustment or low thermostat adjustment.*

43 If the system provides no cooling air:

a) *Inspect the compressor drivebelt. Make sure it's not loose or broken.*
b) *Make sure the compressor clutch engages. If it doesn't, check for a blown fuse.*
c) *Inspect the wire harness for broken or disconnected wires.*
d) *If the compressor clutch doesn't engage, bridge the terminals of the A/C pressure switch(es) with a jumper wire; if the clutch now engages, and the system is properly charged, the pressure switch is bad.*
e) *Make sure the blower motor is not disconnected or burned out.*
f) *Make sure the compressor isn't partially or completely seized.*
g) *Inspect the refrigerant lines for leaks.*
h) *Check the components for leaks.*
i) *Inspect the receiver-drier/accumulator or expansion valve/tube for clogged screens.*

44 If the system is noisy:

a) *Look for loose panels in the passenger compartment.*
b) *Inspect the compressor drivebelt. It may be loose or worn.*
c) *Check the compressor mounting bolts. They should be tight.*
d) *Listen carefully to the compressor. It may be worn out.*
e) *Listen to the idler pulley and bearing and the clutch. Either may be defective.*
f) *The winding in the compressor clutch coil or solenoid may be defective.*
g) *The compressor oil level may be low.*
h) *The blower motor fan bushing or the motor itself may be worn out.*
i) *If there is an excessive charge in the system, you'll hear a rumbling noise in the high pressure line, a thumping noise in the compressor, or see bubbles or cloudiness in the sight glass.*
j) *If there's a low charge in the system, you might hear hissing in the evaporator case at the expansion valve, or see bubbles or cloudiness in the sight glass.*

---

## 3  Air conditioning and heating system - check and maintenance

### Air conditioning system

**Warning:** *The air conditioning system is under high pressure. Do not loosen any hose fittings or remove any components until after the system has been discharged. Air conditioning refrigerant should be properly discharged into an EPA-approved recovery/recycling unit at a dealer service department or an automotive air conditioning repair facility. Always wear eye protection when disconnecting air conditioning system fittings.*

**Caution:** *All models covered by this manual use environmentally friendly R-134a. This refrigerant (and its appropriate refrigerant oils) are not compatible with R-12 refrigerant system components and must never be mixed or the components will be damaged.*

**Caution:** *When replacing entire components, additional refrigerant oil should be added equal to the amount that is removed with the component being replaced. Be sure to read the can before adding any oil to the system, to make sure it is compatible with the R-134a system.*

1 The following maintenance checks should be performed on a regular basis to ensure that the air conditioning continues to operate at peak efficiency.

a) *Inspect the condition of the compressor drivebelt. If it is worn or deteriorated, replace it (see Chapter 1).*
b) *Check the drivebelt tension (see Chapter 1).*
c) *Inspect the system hoses. Look for cracks, bubbles, hardening and deterioration. Inspect the hoses and all fittings for oil bubbles or seepage. If there is any evidence of wear, damage or leakage, replace the hose(s).*
d) *Inspect the condenser fins for leaves, bugs and any other foreign material that may have embedded itself in the fins. Use a fin comb or compressed air to remove debris from the condenser.*
e) *Make sure the system has the correct refrigerant charge.*

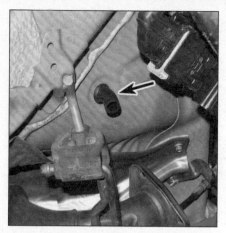

**3.1 Evaporator drain hose**

**3.9 Insert a thermometer in the center vent, turn on the air conditioning system and wait for it to cool down; depending on the humidity, the output air should be 30 to 40 degrees cooler than the ambient air temperature**

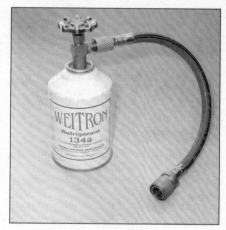

**3.11 R-134a automotive air conditioning charging kit**

*f) If you hear water sloshing around in the dash area or have water dripping on the carpet, check the evaporator housing drain tube (see illustration) and insert a piece of wire into the opening to check for blockage.*

2    It's a good idea to operate the system for about ten minutes at least once a month. This is particularly important during the winter months because long term non-use can cause hardening, and subsequent failure, of the seals. Note that using the Defrost function operates the compressor.

3    If the air conditioning system is not working properly, proceed to Step 6 and perform the general checks outlined below.

4    Because of the complexity of the air conditioning system and the special equipment necessary to service it, in-depth troubleshooting and repairs beyond checking the refrigerant charge and the compressor clutch operation are not included in this manual. However,

**3.13 When adding refrigerant, connect the charging kit hose to the low-side port only. The location of the port varies by model and year**

simple checks and component replacement procedures are provided in this Chapter. For more complete information on the air conditioning system, refer to the Haynes Automotive Heating and Air Conditioning Manual.

5    The most common cause of poor cooling is simply a low system refrigerant charge. If a noticeable drop in system cooling ability occurs, one of the following quick checks will help you determine if the refrigerant level is low.

### Checking the refrigerant charge

6    Warm the engine up to normal operating temperature.

7    Place the air conditioning temperature selector at the coldest setting and put the blower at the highest setting.

8    After the system reaches operating temperature, feel the larger pipe exiting the evaporator at the firewall. The outlet pipe should be cold (the tubing that leads back to the compressor). If the evaporator outlet pipe is warm, the system probably needs a charge.

9    Insert a thermometer in the center air distribution duct (see illustration) while operating the air conditioning system at its maximum setting - the temperature of the output air should be 35 to 40 degrees F below the ambient air temperature (down to approximately 40 degrees F). If the ambient (outside) air temperature is very high, say 110 degrees F, the duct air temperature may be as high as 60 degrees F, but generally the air conditioning is 35 to 40 degrees F cooler than the ambient air.

10    Further inspection or testing of the system requires special tools and techniques and is beyond the scope of the home mechanic.

### Adding refrigerant

**Caution:** *Make sure any refrigerant, refrigerant oil or replacement component you purchase is designated as compatible with R-134a systems.*

11    Purchase an R-134a automotive charging kit at an auto parts store (see illustration). A charging kit includes a can of refrigerant, a tap valve and a short section of hose that can be attached between the tap valve and the system low side service valve.

**Caution:** *Never add more than one can of refrigerant to the system. If more refrigerant than that is required, the system should be evacuated and leak tested.*

12    Back off the valve handle on the charging kit and screw the kit onto the refrigerant can, making sure first that the O-ring or rubber seal inside the threaded portion of the kit is in place.

**Warning:** *Wear protective eyewear when dealing with pressurized refrigerant cans.*

13    Remove the dust cap from the low-side charging port and attach the hose's quick-connect fitting to the port (see illustration). Warning: DO NOT hook the charging kit hose to the system high side! The fittings on the charging kit are designed to fit only on the low side of the system.

14    Warm up the engine and turn on the air conditioning. Keep the charging kit hose away from the fan and other moving parts.

**Note:** *The charging process requires the compressor to be running. If the clutch cycles off, you can put the air conditioning switch on High and leave the car doors open to keep the clutch on and compressor working. The compressor can be kept on during the charging by removing the connector from the pressure switch and bridging it with a paper clip or jumper wire during the procedure.*

15    Turn the valve handle on the kit until the stem pierces the can, then back the handle out to release the refrigerant. You should be able to hear the rush of gas. Keep the can upright at all times, but shake it occasionally. Allow stabilization time between each addition.

**Note:** *The charging process will go faster if you wrap the can with a hot-water-soaked rag to keep the can from freezing up.*

**3.24 Insert the nozzle of the disinfectant can into the evaporator housing**

**4.5 On 1.8L models remove the upper hose clamp and hose**

16   If you have an accurate thermometer, you can place it in the center air conditioning duct inside the vehicle and keep track of the output air temperature. A charged system that is working properly should cool down to approximately 40 degrees F. If the ambient (outside) air temperature is very high, say 110 degrees F, the duct air temperature may be as high as 60 degrees F, but generally the air conditioning is 35 to 40 degrees F cooler than the ambient air.

17   When the can is empty, turn the valve handle to the closed position and release the connection from the low-side port. Reinstall the dust cap.

18   Remove the charging kit from the can and store the kit for future use with the piercing valve in the up position, to prevent inadvertently piercing the can on the next use.

## Heating systems

19   If the carpet under the heater core is damp, or if antifreeze vapor or steam is coming through the vents, the heater core is leaking. Remove it (see Section 11) and install a new unit (most radiator shops will not repair a leaking heater core).

20   If the air coming out of the heater vents isn't hot, the problem could stem from any of the following causes:

a)  *The thermostat is stuck open, preventing the engine coolant from warming up enough to carry heat to the heater core. Replace the thermostat (see Section 4).*

b)  *There is a blockage in the system, preventing the flow of coolant through the heater core. Feel both heater hoses at the firewall. They should be hot. If one of them is cold, there is an obstruction in one of the hoses or in the heater core, or the heater control valve is shut. Detach the hoses and back flush the heater core with a water hose. If the heater core is clear but circulation is impeded, remove the two hoses and flush them out with a water hose.*

c)  *If flushing fails to remove the blockage from the heater core, the core must be replaced (see Section 12).*

## Eliminating air conditioning odors

21   Unpleasant odors that often develop in air conditioning systems are caused by the growth of a fungus, usually on the surface of the evaporator core. The warm, humid environment there is a perfect breeding ground for mildew to develop.

22   The evaporator core on most vehicles is difficult to access, and factory dealerships have a lengthy, expensive process for eliminating the fungus by opening up the evaporator case and using a powerful disinfectant and rinse on the core until the fungus is gone. You can service your own system at home, but it takes something much stronger than basic household germ-killers or deodorizers.

23   Aerosol disinfectants for automotive air conditioning systems are available in most auto parts stores, but remember when shopping for them that the most effective treatments are also the most expensive. The basic procedure for using these sprays is to start by running the system in the RECIRC mode for ten minutes with the blower on its highest speed. Use the highest heat mode to dry out the system and keep the compressor from engaging by disconnecting the wiring connector at the compressor.

24   The disinfectant can usually comes with a long spray hose. Insert the nozzle into an intake port inside the cabin, and spray according to the manufacturer's recommendations (see illustration). Follow the manufacturer's recommendations for the length of spray and waiting time between applications.

25   Once the evaporator has been cleaned, the best way to prevent the mildew from coming back again is to make sure your evaporator housing drain tube is clear (see illustration 3.1).

## Automatic heating and air conditioning systems

26   Some vehicles are equipped with an optional automatic climate control system. This system has its own computer that receives inputs from various sensors in the heating and air conditioning system. This computer, like the PCM, has self-diagnostic capabilities to help pinpoint problems or faults within the system. Vehicles equipped with automatic heating and air conditioning systems are very complex and considered beyond the scope of the home mechanic. Vehicles equipped with automatic heating and air conditioning systems should be taken to dealer service department or other qualified facility for repair.

## 4   Thermostat - replacement

**Warning:** *Do not remove the radiator cap, drain the coolant or replace the thermostat until the engine has cooled completely.*

1   Disconnect the cable from the negative battery terminal (see Chapter 5).

2   Drain the cooling system (see Chapter 1). If the coolant is relatively new or in good condition, save it and reuse it. Read the Warning in Section 1.

3   If you're working on a Civic with a 2.4L engine or a 2014 and earlier CR-V, access to the thermostat is from the underside of the engine compartment. Raise the front of the vehicle and support it securely on jackstands, then remove the under-vehicle splash shield (see Chapter 2A, illustrations 14.3a and 14.3b).

4   If you're working on a 1.8L Civic or a 2015 and later CR-V, access to the thermostat is from the top of the engine compartment. On CR-V models remove the PCM and bracket (see Chapter 6).

5   On 1.8L models, use a pair of pliers to squeeze the upper radiator hose clamp (see illustration), slide the hose clamp up the hose,

**4.7 Use pliers to squeeze the coolant hose clamp and slide the clamp away from the thermostat housing**

**4.10 Location of the thermostat housing cover bolts - 1.8L engine shown, 2.4L models have three bolts**

1    *Harness bracket bolts - 1.8L models*
2    *Thermostat housing bolts*

**4.11 Note the location of the jiggle valve (it should be at the top) - 1.8L engine shown, others similar**

**4.13 Install a new rubber seal over the thermostat**

then remove the hose. If it's stuck, grasp it near the end with a pair of adjustable pliers and twist it to break the seal, then pull it off. If the hose is old or deteriorated, cut it off and install a new one.

6    Follow the lower radiator hose to the engine to locate the thermostat housing cover.

7    Loosen the hose clamp, then detach the hose from the fitting (see illustration). If it's stuck, grasp it near the end with a pair of adjustable pliers and twist it to break the seal, then pull it off. If the hose is old or deteriorated, cut it off and install a new one.

8    If the outer surface of the large fitting that mates with the hose is deteriorated (corroded, pitted, etc.), it may be damaged further by hose removal. If it is, the thermostat housing cover will have to be replaced.

9    On 1.8L models, remove the harness bracket bolts (see illustration 4.14) and move the bracket out of the way.

10    Remove the thermostat cover bolts (see illustration) and detach the housing cover. If the cover is stuck, tap it with a soft-face hammer to jar it loose. Be prepared for some coolant to spill as the gasket seal is broken.

11    On 1.8L engines, note how it's installed - with the jiggle pin up - then remove the thermostat (see illustration).

**Note:** *The thermostat on 2.4L engine is an integral component of the thermostat cover. Replace the cover and thermostat as one complete assembly.*

12    Remove all traces of old gasket material and/or sealant from the housing and cover.

13    On 1.8L engines, install a new rubber seal over the thermostat (see illustration). Make sure the cutout is aligned correctly with the jiggle valve.

**Note:** *On 2.4L engines, install a new O-ring into the housing before installation.*

14    On 1.8L engines, install the new thermostat in the housing without using sealant.

Make sure the jiggle pin is at the top and the spring end is directed into the engine.

**Note:** *On 2.4L engines, the thermostat is positioned correctly by the manufacturer. Make sure the mating surfaces on the thermostat housing are perfectly clean to insure a tight seal before installing the thermostat assembly.*

15    Install the thermostat housing cover (1.8L) or the thermostat assembly (2.4L) and bolts. Tighten the bolts to the torque listed in this Chapter's Specifications.

16    Reattach the hose and tighten the hose clamp securely. Install all components that were removed for access.

17    Refill the cooling system (see Chapter 1).

18    Reconnect the battery (see Chapter 5).

19    Start the engine and allow it to reach normal operating temperature, then check for leaks and proper thermostat operation (as described in Steps 2 through 4).

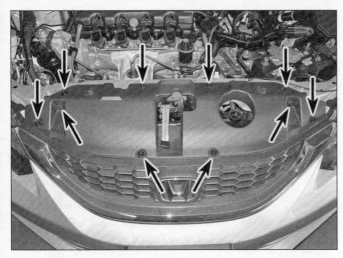

5.5 Radiator cover mounting fasteners - Civic models

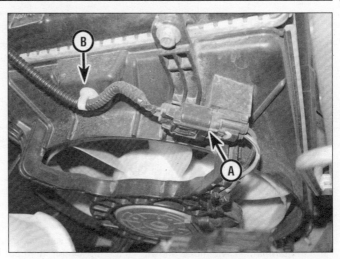

5.6 Disconnect the radiator fan electrical connector (A) then the harness retainer (B) and remove the fan shroud - condenser fan similar

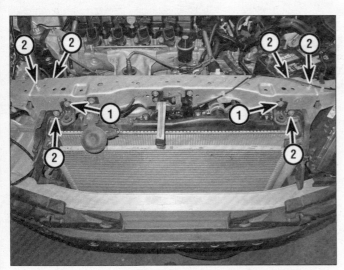

5.10 Radiator mount bolt (1) and crossmember mounting bolt (2) locations

5.12 Location of the radiator fan mounting bolts (condenser fan similar)

## 5  Engine cooling fans - replacement

**Warning:** *To avoid possible injury or damage, DO NOT operate the engine with a damaged fan. Do not attempt to repair fan blades - replace a damaged fan with a new one.*

**Note:** *All air-conditioned models have two complete fan circuits - one for the condenser fan and one for the radiator fan. The following procedures apply to both.*

**Warning:** *Wait until the engine is completely cool before beginning this procedure.*

1    Disconnect the cable from the negative battery terminal (see Chapter 5).

2    On 2.4L Civic models, remove the PCM from the mounting bracket, without discon-

necting the electrical connectors and secure the assembly out of the way.

3    On 2.4L models, remove the intake air duct and air filter housing (see Chapter 4).

4    On CR-V models, remove the grille pushpins and carefully disengage the lower clips, then separate the grille from the bumper cover, if necessary(see Chapter 11, Section 9 ). Once the grille is removed, remove the duct pushpins and duct assembly from the bumper cover.

5    On Civic models, remove the radiator support cover push pins and remove the cover (see illustration).

6    Remove the wiring harness clamp and position the harness off to the side (see illustration).

7    On Civic models, remove the battery and

the battery tray, and position the wiring harness off to the side (see Chapter 5).

8    On CR-V models, disconnect the electrical connector to the horn, then remove the horn and bracket as an assembly (see Chapter 12). Remove the hood latch (see Chapter 11).

9    Remove the radiator mount upper bracket bolts and brackets (see illustration 5.10).

10    On Civic models, remove the coolant reservoir (see Section 6), then remove the radiator crossmember (see illustration).

11    Disconnect the fan wiring connectors located near the top of the cooling fan shroud.

12    Unbolt the engine cooling fan(s) from the radiator at the top (see illustration).

5.13 Lift the radiator fan from the engine compartment - Civic model shown

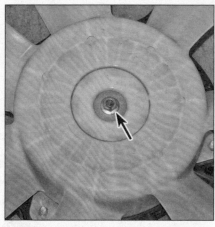

5.14 To remove the fan, unscrew the nut in the center, then pull the fan blade from the motor shaft

5.15 Engine cooling fan motor mounting screws

6.3 Disconnect the reservoir hose from the radiator filler neck (1), then remove the coolant reservoir mounting fastener (2) - 1.8L engine shown, other engines similar

7.5a Location of the transaxle cooling hose on the right side of the radiator . . .

7.5b . . . and the left side of the radiator

13   Carefully lift the condenser fan out first, then lift the radiator fan up slightly, sliding it to the right and pull it out of the engine compartment (see illustration).
14   To detach the fan from the motor, remove the motor shaft nut (see illustration).
15   To detach the fan motor from the shroud, remove the mounting screws (see illustration).
16   Installation is the reverse of removal.
17   Refill the cooling system (see Chapter 1).
18   Reconnect the battery (see Chapter 5).

## 6   Coolant reservoir - removal and installation

**Warning:** *Wait until the engine is completely cool before beginning this procedure.*
1   Disconnect the reservoir hose from the radiator filler neck. Plug the hose to

prevent leakage.
2   On some models it is necessary to remove the air filter housing (see Chapter 4) and the battery and battery tray (see Chapter 5) for access to the reservoir.
3   Remove the mounting fastener (see illustration).
4   Lift the reservoir out of the engine compartment.
5   Clean out the tank with soapy water and a brush to remove any deposits inside. Inspect the reservoir carefully for cracks. If you find a crack, replace the reservoir.
6   Installation is the reverse of removal.

## 7   Radiator - removal and installation

**Warning:** *Wait until the engine is completely cool before beginning this procedure.*

## *Removal*

1   Disconnect the cable from the negative battery terminal (see Chapter 5).
2   Raise the front of the vehicle and support it securely on jackstands, then remove the under-vehicle splash shield (see Chapter 2A, illustrations 14.3a and 14.3b).
3   Drain the cooling system (see Chapter 1). If the coolant is relatively new or in good condition, save it and reuse it. Read the Warning in Section 1.
4   Remove the engine cooling fans (see Section 5).
5   On automatic transaxle models, disconnect the transaxle fluid cooler lines from the bottom of the radiator (see illustrations).
6   Remove the radiator brackets (see illustration 5.10).
7   Disconnect the electrical connector to the #2 ECT sensor (see illustration).
8   Carefully lift out the radiator. Don't spill coolant on the vehicle or scratch the paint.

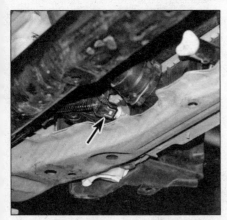

7.7 Number 2 ECT sensor location - 1.8L shown, 2.4L similar

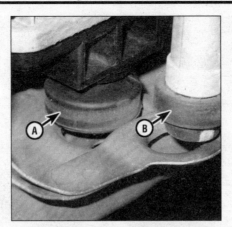

7.11 Location of the radiator (A) and the condenser (B) rubber mounts

8.6 On 1.8L models, hold the water pump pulley and remove the three mounting bolts

8.7 Drivebelt tensioner mounting bolt locations - 1.8L models

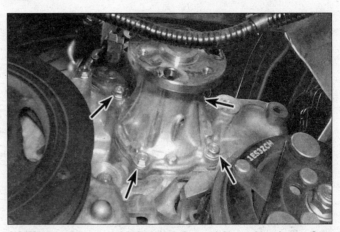

8.9 Water pump mounting bolt locations - 1.8L engine shown, four of five bolts shown

9    Inspect the radiator for leaks and damage. If it needs repair, have a radiator shop or dealer service department perform the work as special techniques are required.

10   Bugs and dirt can be removed from the radiator by spraying with a garden hose nozzle from the back side. The radiator should be flushed out with a garden hose before reinstallation.

11   Check the radiator mounts (see illustration) for deterioration and replace if necessary.

## Installation

12   Installation is the reverse of the removal procedure. Guide the radiator into the mounts until they seat properly.

13   After installation, fill the cooling system with the proper mixture of antifreeze and water (see Chapter 1).

14   Reconnect the battery (see Chapter 5).

15   Start the engine and check for leaks. Allow the engine to reach normal operating temperature, indicated by the upper radiator hose becoming hot. Recheck the coolant level and add more if required.

16   Check and add transaxle fluid as needed.

## 8   Water pump - replacement

**Warning:** *Wait until the engine is completely cool before beginning this procedure.*

1    Disconnect the cable from the negative battery terminal (see Chapter 5).

2    Drain the cooling system (see Chapter 1). If the coolant is relatively new or in good condition, save it and reuse it. Read the Warning in Section 1.

3    Remove the drivebelts (see Chapter 1).

4    On 2.4L engines, remove the drivebelt tensioner and idler pulley with bracket (see Chapter 1).

5    Remove the alternator (see Chapter 5).

6    On 1.8L engines, remove the water pump pulley bolts and pulley (see illustration).

7    Remove the drivebelt tensioner (see illustration).

8    On 2.4L enignes, remove the crankshaft pulley (see Chapter 2B).

9    Remove the bolts and detach the water pump from the engine (see illustration). Check the impeller on the backside for evidence of corrosion or missing fins.

10   Clean the bolt threads and the threaded holes in the engine to remove corrosion and sealant.

11   Compare the new pump to the old one to make sure they're identical.

12   Remove all traces of old gasket sealant and O-ring from the engine.

13   Clean the engine and new water pump mating surfaces with brake system cleaner.

14   Apply a thin layer of RTV sealant to the O-ring groove of the new pump, then carefully set a new O-ring in the groove.

15   Carefully attach the pump to the engine and thread the bolts into the holes finger-tight. Use a small amount of RTV sealant on the bolt threads, and make sure that the dowel pins are in their original locations.

16   Tighten the bolts, a little at a time, to the torque listed in this Chapter's Specifications. Don't overtighten the bolts or the pump may be distorted.

17   Reinstall all parts removed for access to the pump.

18   Refill the cooling system and check the drivebelt tension (see Chapter 1).

19   Reconnect the battery (see Chapter 5). Run the engine and check for leaks.

**9.4 Remove the passenger's side heater duct mounting screws**

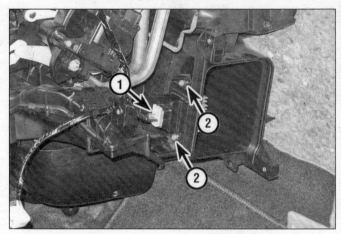

**9.5 Disconnect the power transistor electrical connector (1) and remove the transistor mounting screws (2) - Civic model shown**

**9.10 Disconnect the electrical connector to the blower motor (1) and remove the mounting screws (2) - Civic model shown**

**10.5 Disconnect the electrical connectors from the blower motor and mode control switches**

## 9    Blower motor power transistor and blower motor - replacement

**Warning:** *The models covered by this manual are equipped with a Supplemental Restraint System (SRS), more commonly known as airbags. Always disable the airbag system before working in the vicinity of any airbag system component to avoid the possibility of accidental deployment of the airbag, which could cause personal injury (see Chapter 12).*

### *Blower motor power transistor*

1    Disconnect the cable from the negative battery terminal (see Chapter 5).
2    Working in the passenger compartment under the glove box, remove the lower dash panel (see Chapter 11).
3    Remove the glove box (see Chapter 11).
4    Remove the mounting screws (see illustration) for the passenger's side heater duct and remove the duct.
5    Disconnect the electrical connector from the blower motor power transistor (see illustration).

6    Unscrew the mounting screws and remoev the blower motor power transistor from the blower housing.
7    Installation is the reverse of removal.
8    Reconnect the battery (see Chapter 5).

### *Blower motor*

9    Perform Steps 1 through 3 of this Section.
10   Disconnect the electrical connector from the blower motor (see illustration).
11   Remove the blower motor mounting screws and then remove the blower motor assembly.
12   Remove the blower motor circlip and remove the blower fan from the motor.
13   Installation is the reverse of removal.
14   Reconnect the battery (see Chapter 5).

## 10   Heater/air conditioning control assembly - removal and installation

**Warning:** *The models covered by this manual*

*are equipped with a Supplemental Restraint System (SRS), more commonly known as airbags. Always disable the airbag system before working in the vicinity of any airbag system component to avoid the possibility of accidental deployment of the airbag, which could cause personal injury (see Chapter 12).*
1    Disconnect the cable from the negative battery terminal (see Chapter 5).

### *Civic*
2    Remove the radio assembly and disconnect the electrical connectors (see Chapter 12).

### 2012 models
3    Remove the dashboard hood and center lower trim panel (see Chapter 11).
4    Unclip the control panel unit from the instrument panel, then disconnect the electrical connector from the back of the unit.

### 2013 and later models
5    Disconnect the electrical connector from the heater/air conditioning control module (see illustration).

10.6 Location of the air conditioning switch mounting screws

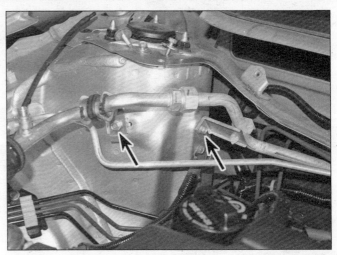

11.4 Evaporator side air conditioning line mounting bolt locations

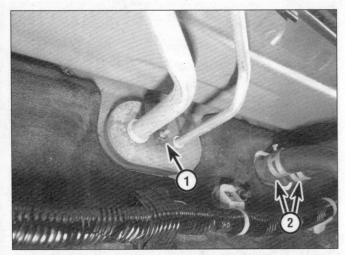

11.5 Disconnect air conditioning evaporator lines from the thermal expansion valve (1) and the heater hoses (2) from the heater core inside the engine compartment

11.6 Working on the inside of the engine compartment, remove the heater control unit mounting nut

6   Remove the heater/air conditioner control assembly retaining screws (see illustration) and remove the module from the radio assembly.

7   Installation is the reverse of removal.

8   Reconnect the battery (see Chapter 5).

## CR-V

9   Remove the shift lever top panel and the dashboard center trim panels (see Chapter 11).

10   Remove the screws and detach the control unit from the instrument panel, then disconnect the electrical connector.

11   Pull the knobs off of the control unit then remove the unit mounting screws and separate the control unit from the trim panel.

12   Installation is the reverse of removal.

13   Reconnect the battery (see Chapter 5).

## 11   Heater core - replacement

**Warning:** *The models covered by this manual are equipped with a Supplemental Restraint System (SRS), more commonly known as airbags. Always disable the airbag system before working in the vicinity of any airbag system component to avoid the possibility of accidental deployment of the airbag, which could cause personal injury (see Chapter 12).*

**Warning:** *The air conditioning system is under high pressure. DO NOT loosen any fittings or remove any components until after the system has been discharged. Air conditioning refrigerant must be properly discharged into an EPA-approved container at a dealer service department or an automotive air conditioning repair facility. Always wear eye protection when disconnecting air conditioning system fittings.*

**Warning:** *Wait until the engine is completely*

*cool before beginning this procedure.*

**Note:** *The following procedure covers the typical heater core removal for Civics. However, the heater core removal on CR-Vs is similar.*

1   If so equipped, have the air conditioning system discharged by a dealer service department or an automotive air conditioning shop before proceeding (see Warning above).

2   Disconnect the cable from the negative battery terminal (see Chapter 5).

3   Drain the cooling system (see Chapter 1).

4   Remove the evaporator side air conditioning line mounting bolts inside the engine compartment (see illustration).

5   Disconnect the air conditioning evaporator lines at the dash inside the engine compartment from the TXV, then disconnect the heater hoses from the heater core (see illustration).

6   Remove the heater control unit mounting nut on the inside of the engine compartment (see illustration), taking care not to damage

11.8a Remove the blower unit mounting
nut/bolts from the left side . . .

11.8b . . . and right side of the housing

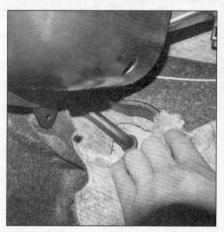

11.9 Pull the carpet back and pull the drain
hose out from the firewall

11.12 Remove the heater cover screws from the expansion
valve cover

11.13a Remove the expansion valve cover fasteners . . .

11.13b . . . then lift the cover from the
heater/air conditioning unit

11.14 Heater pipe bracket screw location

the fuel or brake lines.

7    Remove the instrument panel (see
Chapter 11).

8    Disconnect the blower motor and power
transistor electrical connectors. Remove the
heater/air conditioning assembly mounting
bolts (see illustrations), disconnect the electrical connectors and remove the assembly
from the vehicle.

9    Remove the evaporator drain (see illustration).

10   Remove the blower unit to heater/air
conditioning housing bolts and separate the
housings.

11   Remove the passenger's heater duct
screws and duct.

12   Remove the heater core cover (see illustration).

13   If equipped with air conditioning, remove
the expansion valve cover fasteners and the
seal (see illustrations).

14   Remove the heater pipe bracket screw
and bracket (see illustration).

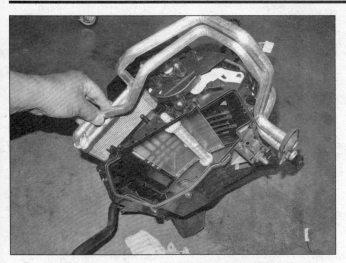

11.15 Lift the heater core from the heater/AC unit

12.7 Air conditioning compressor mounting details

| | | | |
|---|---|---|---|
| 1 | Suction line (Low side) | 3 | Compressor mounting |
| 2 | Discharge line (High side) | | bolts |

15  Lift the heater cover from the heater/air conditioning unit (see illustration).

16  Installation is the reverse of removal. Don't forget to reconnect the heater core inlet and outlet hoses at the firewall.

17  Reconnect the battery (see Chapter 5).

18  Refill the cooling system (see Chapter 1).

19  If equipped, have the air conditioning system evacuated, leak tested and recharged by the shop that discharged it.

## 12  Air conditioning compressor - removal and installation

**Warning:** *The air conditioning system is under high pressure. Do not loosen any hose fittings or remove any components until after the system has been discharged. Air conditioning refrigerant must be properly discharged into an EPA-approved recovery/recycling unit at a dealer service department or an automotive air conditioning repair facility. Always wear eye protection when disconnecting air conditioning system fittings.*

**Caution:** *When replacing entire components, additional refrigerant oil should be added equal to the amount that is removed with the component being replaced. Be sure to read the can before adding any oil to the system, to make sure it is compatible with the R-134a system.*

**Note:** *The receiver-drier should be replaced whenever the compressor is replaced.*

## Removal

1  Have the air conditioning system refrigerant discharged and recovered by an air conditioning technician.

2  Disconnect the cable from the negative battery terminal (see Chapter 5).

3  Set the parking brake, block the rear wheels and raise the front of the vehicle, supporting it securely on jackstands, then

remove the under-vehicle splash shield (see Chapter 2A, illustrations 14.3a and 14.3b).

4  Remove the engine cooling fans (see Section 5).

5  On 1.8L models and 2015 and later CR-V models, remove the alternator (see Chapter 5).

6  Disconnect the compressor clutch wiring harness.

7  Disconnect the refrigerant lines from the compressor. Plug the open fittings to prevent entry of dirt and moisture (see illustration).

8  Remove the compressor mounting bolts.

9  On all models except 2015 and later CR-V models, carefully guide the compressor through the opening below the engine compartment. On 2015 and later CR-V models, remove the compressor from the top.

## Installation

10  The clutch may have to be transferred from the old compressor to the new unit.

**Note:** *Since the oil separator is equipped inside the A/C compressor on these models, oil drainage is unnecessary at the time of compressor replacement when installing a new*

13.5 Remove the cap from the condenser

compressor. This applies to compressors supplied by Honda. Be sure to follow any specific instructions that come with a replacement compressor.

11  Installation is the reverse of removal, using new O-rings where the line fittings attach to the compressor.

12  Have the system evacuated, recharged and leak tested by an air conditioning technician.

13  Reconnect the battery (see Chapter 5).

## 13  Air conditioning receiver-drier - removal and installation

**Warning:** *The air conditioning system is under high pressure. Do not loosen any hose fittings or remove any components until after the system has been discharged. Air conditioning refrigerant must be properly discharged into an EPA-approved recovery/recycling unit at a dealer service department or an automotive air conditioning repair facility. Always wear eye protection when disconnecting air conditioning system fittings.*

**Caution:** *When replacing entire components, additional refrigerant oil should be added equal to the amount that is removed with the component being replaced. Be sure to read the can before adding any oil to the system, to make sure it is compatible with the R-134a system.*

1  Have the refrigerant discharged and recovered by an air conditioning technician.

2  Disconnect the cable from the negative battery terminal (see Chapter 5).

3  Remove the front bumper cover (see Chapter 11).

4  Remove the condenser (see Section 14).

5  On 2-door Civic and all CR-V models, remove the cap from the condenser (see illustration).

13.6 On 4-door Civic models, remove the two mounting bolts

13.7a Remove the filter from the condenser

13.7b Use pliers to remove the desiccant from the condenser

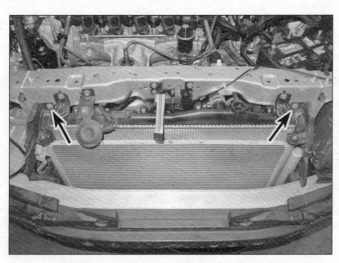

14.4 Condenser brackets and mounting bolts

14.5 Remove the discharge line-to-condenser mounting bolt

6    On 4-door Civic models, remove the two bolts (see illustration) and O-rings, then separate the receiver-drier from the condenser. The receiver-drier is replaced as a unit.

7    On 2-door Civic and all CR-V models, remove the filter from the condenser and remove the receiver-drier desiccant (see illustrations).

8    Installation is the reverse of removal. Be sure to install new O-rings onto the receiver-drier cap or mounting bolts. Apply a thin film of refrigerant oil to the desiccant before installing it. Also lubricate the O-rings with refrigerant oil. If the receiver-drier was replaced, add 1/3-fluid ounces (10 mL) of refrigerant oil to the condenser (see Section 14).

9    Reconnect the battery (see Chapter 5).

10   Have the system evacuated, charged and leak tested by an air conditioning technician.

## 14   Air conditioning condenser - removal and installation

**Warning:** *The air conditioning system is under high pressure. Do not loosen any hose fittings or remove any components until after the system has been discharged. Air conditioning refrigerant must be properly discharged into an EPA-approved recovery/recycling unit at a dealer service department or an automotive air conditioning repair facility. Always wear eye protection when disconnecting air conditioning system fittings.*

**Caution:** *When replacing entire components, additional refrigerant oil should be added equal to the amount that is removed with the component being replaced. Be sure to read the can before adding any oil to the system, to make sure it is compatible with the R-134a system.*

### Removal

1    Have the refrigerant discharged and recovered by an air conditioning technician.

2    Disconnect the cable from the negative battery terminal (see Chapter 5).

3    Remove the front bumper (see Chapter 11).

4    Remove the condenser brackets (see illustration) and on CR-V models, remove the upper radiator mount brackets.

5    Disconnect the condenser line and discharge line (see illustration) from the condenser. Cap the fittings on the condenser and lines to prevent entry of dirt or moisture.

6    Remove the condenser by lifting it from its lower mounts.

### Installation

7    Installation is the reverse of removal. Assemble all connections with new O-rings, lightly lubricated with R-134a refrigerant oil.

15.3 The air conditioning pressure sensor location - front bumper cover removed for clarity

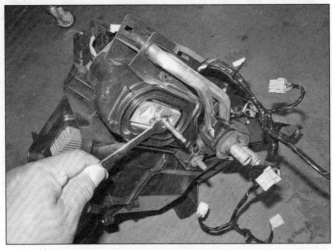

16.3a Remove the TXV stud from the valve

If a new condenser was installed, add the proper amount of fresh refrigerant oil to it.

   a)  *2-door Civic and all CR-V models (including receiver-drier): 1 2/3-ounce (50 mL)*
   b)  *4-door Civic models (including receiver-drier): 1 2/3-ounce (50 mL)*

8    Reconnect the battery (see Chapter 5).
9    Have the system evacuated, charged and leak tested by an air conditioning technician.

## 15  Air conditioning pressure sensor - replacement

**Warning:** *The air conditioning system is under high pressure. Do not loosen any hose fittings or remove any components until after the system has been discharged. Air conditioning refrigerant must be properly discharged into an EPA-approved recovery/recycling unit at a dealer service department or an automotive air conditioning repair facility. Always wear eye protection when disconnecting air conditioning system fittings.*

**Note:** *The A/C pressure sensor is mounted in the refrigerant line going from the condenser to the evaporator.*

**Note:** *The air conditioning pressure sensor detects low (28 psi) and high (455 psi) refrigerant line pressure and shuts the system off if the pressure drops below or exceeds these values.*

1    Have the refrigerant discharged and recovered by an air conditioning technician.
2    Set the parking brake, block the rear wheels and raise the front of the vehicle, supporting it securely on jackstands, then remove the under-vehicle splash shield (see Chapter 2A, illustrations 14.3a and 14.3b).

3    Locate the sensor on the right side of the vehicle and unplug the electrical connector from the air conditioning pressure switch (see illustration).
4    Unscrew the pressure sensor from the line, be sure to hold the stationary fitting on the line with an open-end wrench to prevent damaging the line.
5    Lubricate the sensor O-ring with clean refrigerant oil of the correct type.
6    Screw the new sensor onto the refrigerant line, then tighten it securely.
7    Reconnect the electrical connector.
8    Have the system evacuated, charged and leak tested by an air conditioning technician.

## 16  Air conditioning thermostatic expansion valve (TXV) - general information

**Warning:** *The air conditioning system is under high pressure. DO NOT loosen any hose fittings or remove any components until the system has been discharged. Air conditioning refrigerant must be properly discharged into an EPA-approved recovery/recycling unit by a dealer service department or an automotive air conditioning repair facility. Always wear eye protection when disconnecting air conditioning system fittings.*

1    There are several ways that air conditioning systems convert the high-pressure liquid refrigerant from the compressor to lower-pressure vapor. The conversion takes place at the air conditioning evaporator; the evaporator is chilled as the refrigerant passes through, cooling the airflow through the evaporator for delivery to the vents. The conversion is usu-

16.3b The Thermostatic Expansion Valve is located on the firewall

ally accomplished by a sudden change in the tubing size. Many vehicles have a removable controlled orifice in one of the refrigerant lines at the firewall.
2    The models covered by this manual use a Thermostatic Expansion Valve (TXV) that accomplishes the same thing as a controlled orifice. To remove the TXV, have the air conditioning system discharged by a licensed air conditioning technician, then disconnect the refrigerant lines from the TXV at the firewall, and remove the heater core housing (see Section 11).
3    Remove the TXV stud (see illustration), then remove the two bolts securing the valve (see illustration). Remove the valve and replace the four O-rings. Installation is the reverse of removal.

# Notes

# Chapter 4
# Fuel and exhaust systems

## Contents

## Specifications

**Fuel system pressure**

| | | |
|---|---|---|
| 1.8L engine | 55 to 63 psi | 380 to 430 kPa |
| 2.4L engine * | 48 to 55 psi | 330 to 380 kPa |

**Warning:** * For 2015 and later CR-V models with direct injection, fuel pressure specifications are for the in-tank fuel pump only (do not attempt to measure fuel pressure on the high-pressure side of the system.

## Torque specifications

**Note:** One foot-pound (ft-lb) of torque is equivalent to 12 inch-pounds (in-lbs) of torque. Torque values below approximately 15 ft-lbs are expressed in inch-pounds, since most foot-pound torque wrenches are not accurate at these smaller values.

| | Ft-lbs (unless otherwise indicated) | Nm |
|---|---|---|
| Accelerator pedal module fasteners | 5 | 7 |
| Throttle body mounting bolts | | |
| Civic | 16 | 22 |
| CR-V | | |
| 2014 and earlier | 16 | 22 |
| 2015 and later | 18 | 24 |
| Fuel pulsation damper | 16 | 22 |
| Fuel rail mounting nuts | | |
| Civic | 7.2 | 9.8 |
| CR-V | | |
| 2014 and earlier | 7.2 | 9.8 |
| 2015 and later | 9 | 12 |
| High-pressure fuel pump | | |
| Mounting bolts | 18 | 25 |
| Fuel pipe fittings | 27 | 36 |
| Fuel feed pipe banjo bolt | 30 | 40 |
| Fuel tank bolts | | |
| Civic | | |
| Strap bolts | 28 | 38 |
| Rear floor underbar bolts | 28 | 38 |
| CR-V | 28 | 38 |

## 1   General Information

### *Fuel system warnings*

1   Gasoline is extremely flammable and repairing fuel system components can be dangerous. Consider your automotive repair knowledge and experience before attempting repairs which may be better suited for a professional mechanic.

   a) *Don't smoke or allow open flames or bare light bulbs near the work area*
   b) *Don't work in a garage with a gas-type appliance (water heater, clothes dryer)*
   c) *Use fuel-resistant gloves. If any fuel spills on your skin, wash it off immediately with soap and water*
   d) *Clean up spills immediately*
   e) *Do not store fuel-soaked rags where they could ignite*
   f) *Prior to disconnecting any fuel line, you must relieve the fuel pressure (see Section 3)*
   g) *Wear safety glasses*
   h) *Have a proper fire extinguisher on hand*

### *Fuel system*

2   The fuel system consists of the fuel tank, electric fuel pump/fuel level sending unit (located in the fuel tank), fuel rail and fuel injectors. The fuel injection system is a multi-port system; multi-port fuel injection uses timed impulses to inject the fuel directly into the intake port of each cylinder. The Powertrain Control Module (PCM) controls the injectors. The PCM monitors various engine parameters and delivers the exact amount of fuel required into the intake ports.

3   Fuel is circulated from the in-tank fuel pump to the fuel rail through fuel lines running along the underside of the vehicle. Various sections of the fuel line are either rigid metal or nylon, or flexible fuel hose. The various sections of the fuel hose are connected either by quick-connect fittings or threaded metal fittings.

4   2015 and later CR-V models are equipped with direct injection utilizing a mechanical high-pressure fuel pump, located on the engine. The in-tank fuel pump supplies fuel to the high-pressure fuel pump. The high-pressure fuel pump supplies the fuel pressure for the direct injection fuel injectors. The direct injection injects fuel directly into the cylinders and requires high pressure to overcome the cylinder pressure.

### *Electronic throttle control system*

5   The Civic and CR-V use an electronically actuated throttle body; there is no direct cable link between the accelerator pedal and the throttle body. Instead, an electric actuator within the throttle body operates the throttle based on a signal it receives from the Powertrain Control Module (PCM). The accelerator pedal module provides input to the PCM of the actual position of the accelerator pedal.

### *Exhaust system*

6   The exhaust system consists of the exhaust manifold, catalytic converter(s), muffler(s), tailpipe and all connecting pipes, flanges and clamps. The catalytic converters are an emission control device added to the exhaust system to reduce pollutants. On some models, the exhaust manifold is incorporated into the cylinder head, and the primary catalytic converter bolts directly to it.

## 2   Troubleshooting

### *Fuel pump*

1   The fuel pump is located inside the fuel tank. Sit inside the vehicle with the windows closed, turn the ignition key to On (not Start) and listen for the sound of the fuel pump as it's briefly activated. You will only hear the sound for a second or two, but that sound tells you that the pump is working. Alternatively, have an assistant listen at the fuel filler cap.

2   If the pump does not come on, check the fuel pump fuse (fuse no. 4 (15A) in the interior fuse/relay box) and the PGM-FI relay no. 2. The PGM-FI no. 2 relay is located on the lower part of the interior fuse/relay box (see illustration) and the PGM-FI no. 1 relay is located at the top of the interior fuse/relay box. If the fuse and relay are okay, check the wiring back to the fuel pump. If the fuse, relay and wiring are okay, the fuel pump is probably defective. If the pump runs continuously with the ignition key in the On position, the Powertrain Control Module (PCM) is probably defective. Have the PCM checked by a professional mechanic.

### *Fuel injection system*

**Note:** *The following procedure is based on the assumption that the fuel pump is working and the fuel pressure is adequate (see Section 4).*

3   Check all electrical connectors that are related to the system. Check the ground wire connections for tightness.

4   Verify that the battery is fully charged (see Chapter 5).

5   Inspect the air filter element (see Chapter 1).

6   Check all fuses related to the fuel system (see Chapter 12).

7   Check the air induction system between the throttle body and the intake manifold for air leaks. Also inspect the condition of all vacuum hoses connected to the intake manifold and to the throttle body.

8   Remove the air intake duct from the throttle body and look for dirt, carbon, varnish, or other residue in the throttle body, particularly around the throttle plate. If it's dirty, clean it with carb cleaner, a toothbrush and a clean shop towel.

9   With the engine running, place an automotive stethoscope against each injector, one

**2.2 The PGM-FI no. 1 and 2 relays are located in the interior fuse/relay box (2015 Civic shown)**

**2.9 An automotive stethoscope is used to listen to the fuel injectors in operation**

at a time, and listen for a clicking sound that indicates operation (see illustration).
**Warning:** *Stay clear of the drivebelt and any rotating or hot components.*

10  If you can hear the injectors operating, but the engine is misfiring, the electrical circuits are functioning correctly, but the injectors might be dirty or clogged. Try a commercial injector cleaning product (available at auto parts stores). If cleaning the injectors doesn't help, replace the injectors.

11  If an injector is not operating (it makes no sound), disconnect the injector electrical connector and measure the resistance across the injector terminals with an ohmmeter. Compare this measurement to the other injectors. If the resistance of the non-operational injector is quite different from the other injectors, replace it.

12  If the injector is not operating, but the resistance reading is within the range of resistance of the other injectors, the PCM or the circuit between the PCM and the injector might be faulty.

## 3  Fuel pressure relief procedure

**Warning:** *The fuel delivery system on 2015 and later CR-V models is made up of a low-pressure system and a high-pressure system. This procedure relieves the pressure in both the low and high-pressure systems; however, wait at least two hours after relieving the pressure before disconnecting any fitting in the low- or high-pressure systems.*

1  Remove the gas cap to relieve the pressure inside the fuel tank.

2  Locate the PGM-FI main relay No. 2, then remove/unplug it (see the under-dash fuse/relay block illustration at the end of the wiring diagrams in Chapter).

3  Start the engine and allow it to die. The fuel pressure is now relieved, but there is still fuel in the lines, so be sure to have shop rags handy to mop up any spilled fuel when disconnecting fuel lines.
**Note:** *If the Malfunction Indicator Light (Check Engine light) on the instrument cluster comes on while you're cranking the engine, ignore it. If the light remains on after reconnecting the battery, erase the code as described in Chapter 6, Section 3.*

4  Disconnect the cable from the negative terminal of the battery (see Chapter 5). It's now safe to work on the fuel system.

5  After enabling the fuel system after repairs, clear any Diagnostic Trouble Codes (DTCs) that may set.

## 4  Fuel pressure - check

**Warning:** *Gasoline is extremely flammable. See* Fuel system warnings *in Section 1.*
**Note:** *The following procedure assumes that the fuel pump is receiving voltage and runs.*

1  Relieve the fuel system pressure (see Section 3), then disconnect the fuel line quick-connect fitting at the fuel rail. Using the proper adapters, tee-in a fuel pressure gauge between the fuel line and the fuel rail (see illustrations).
**Note:** *2015 and later CR-V models are direction injected and have a low and hi pressure fuel system. This procedure only tests the low pressure fuel supplied by the in-tank pump. Connect the fuel pressure gauge at the fuel line fitting below the wiper cowl.*

2  Start the engine and allow it to idle. Note the gauge reading as soon as the pressure stabilizes, and compare it with the pressure listed in this Chapter's Specifications.

3  If the fuel pressure is not within specifications, check the following:

a) *If the pressure is lower than specified, check for a restriction in the fuel system (kinked fuel line, plugged fuel pump inlet strainer or clogged fuel filter). If no restrictions are found, replace the fuel pressure regulator and fuel filter (see Sections 8 and 9).*

b) *Recheck the fuel pressure. If it is still lower than specified, replace the fuel pump (see Section 9).*

c) *If the fuel pressure is higher than specified, replace the fuel pressure regulator (see Section 8).*

4  Turn off the engine. Fuel pressure should not fall more than 8 psi over five minutes. If it does, the problem could be a leaky fuel injector, fuel line leak, or faulty fuel pump module.

5  Relieve the fuel pressure (see Section 3), then disconnect the fuel pressure gauge. Wipe up any spilled gasoline.

## 5  Fuel lines and fittings - general information and disconnection

**Warning:** *Gasoline is extremely flammable. See* Fuel system warnings *in Section 1.*

1  Relieve the fuel pressure before servicing fuel lines or fittings (see Section 3), then disconnect the cable from the negative battery terminal (see Chapter 5) before proceeding.

2  The fuel supply line connects the fuel pump in the fuel tank to the fuel rail on the engine. The Evaporative Emission (EVAP) system lines connect the fuel tank to the EVAP canister and connect the canister to the intake manifold.

3  Whenever you're working under the vehicle, be sure to inspect all fuel and evaporative emission lines for leaks, kinks, dents and other damage. Always replace a damaged fuel or EVAP line immediately.

4  If you find signs of dirt in the lines during disassembly, disconnect all lines and blow them out with compressed air. Inspect the fuel strainer on the fuel pump pick-up unit for damage and deterioration.

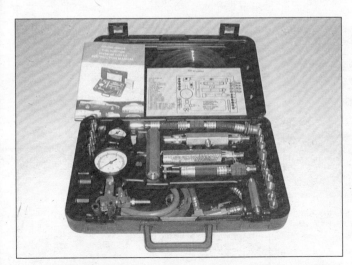

**4.1a This fuel pressure testing kit contains all the necessary fittings and adapters, along with the fuel pressure gauge, to test most automotive systems**

**4.1b Disconnect the fuel supply hose quick-connect fitting (arrow) from the fuel rail pipe, then attach the fuel pressure gauge set up to the fuel line and fuel rail fitting (2014 Civic 1.8L shown)**

# Disconnecting Fuel Line Fittings

Two-tab type fitting; depress both tabs with your fingers, then pull the fuel line and the fitting apart

On this type of fitting, depress the two buttons on opposite sides of the fitting, then pull it off the fuel line

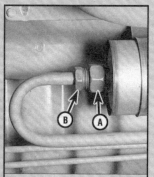

Threaded fuel line fitting; hold the stationary portion of the line or component (A) while loosening the tube nut (B) with a flare-nut wrench

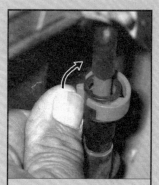

Plastic collar-type fitting; rotate the outer part of the fitting

Metal collar quick-connect fitting; pull the end of the retainer off the fuel line and disengage the other end from the female side of the fitting . . .

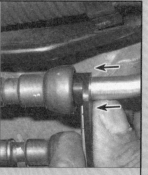

. . . insert a fuel line separator tool into the female side of the fitting, push it into the fitting and pull the fuel line off the pipe

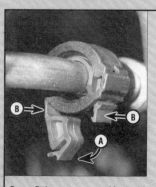

Some fittings are secured by lock tabs. Release the lock tab (A) and rotate it to the fully-opened position, squeeze the two smaller lock tabs (B) . . .

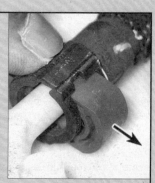

. . . then push the retainer out and pull the fuel line off the pipe

Spring-lock coupling; remove the safety cover, install a coupling release tool and close the tool around the coupling . . .

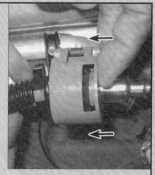

. . . push the tool into the fitting, then pull the two lines apart

Hairpin clip type fitting: push the legs of the retainer clip together, then push the clip down all the way until it stops and pull the fuel line off the pipe

**6.1 A typical exhaust system hanger. Inspect regularly and replace at the first sign of damage or deterioration**

**7.4 If equipped, remove the crossmember**

**7.5 Remove these screws to remove the fuel pump access cover (2014 Civic shown)**

## Steel tubing

5    It is critical that the fuel lines be replaced with lines of equivalent type and specification.
6    Some steel fuel lines have threaded fittings. When loosening these fittings, hold the stationary fitting with a wrench while turning the tube nut.

## Plastic tubing

7    When replacing fuel system plastic tubing, use only original equipment replacement plastic tubing.
**Caution:** *When removing or installing plastic fuel line tubing, be careful not to bend or twist it too much, which can damage it. Also, plastic fuel tubing is NOT heat resistant, so keep it away from excessive heat.*

## Flexible hoses

8    When replacing fuel system flexible hoses, use only original equipment replacements.
9    Don't route fuel hoses (or metal lines) within four inches of the exhaust system or within ten inches of the catalytic converter. Make sure that no rubber hoses are installed directly against the vehicle, particularly in places where there is any vibration. If allowed to touch some vibrating part of the vehicle, a hose can easily become chafed and it might start leaking. A good rule of thumb is to maintain a minimum of 1/4-inch clearance around a hose (or metal line) to prevent contact with the vehicle underbody.

## 6    Exhaust system servicing - general information

**Warning:** *Allow exhaust system components to cool before inspection or repair. Also, when working under the vehicle, make sure it is securely supported on jackstands.*
1    The exhaust system consists of the exhaust manifolds, catalytic converter, muffler, tailpipe and all connecting pipes, flanges and clamps. The exhaust system is isolated from the vehicle body and from chassis com-

ponents by a series of rubber hangers (see illustration). Periodically inspect these hangers for cracks or other signs of deterioration, replacing them as necessary.
2    Conduct regular inspections of the exhaust system to keep it safe and quiet. Look for any damaged or bent parts, open seams, holes, loose connections, excessive corrosion or other defects which could allow exhaust fumes to enter the vehicle. Do not repair deteriorated exhaust system components; replace them with new parts.
3    If the exhaust system components are extremely corroded, or rusted together, a cutting torch is the most convenient tool for removal. Consult a properly-equipped repair shop. If a cutting torch is not available, you can use a hacksaw, or if you have compressed air, there are special pneumatic cutting chisels that can also be used. Wear safety goggles to protect your eyes from metal chips and wear work gloves to protect your hands.
4    Here are some simple guidelines to follow when repairing the exhaust system:
   a)  *Work from the back to the front when removing exhaust system components.*

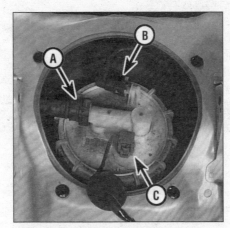

**7.6 Disconnect the fuel supply line (A), EVAP line (B) and the electrical connector from the fuel pump/fuel gauge sending unit (C) (2014 Civic shown)**

   b)  *Apply penetrating oil to the exhaust system component fasteners to make them easier to remove.*
   c)  *Use new gaskets, hangers and clamps.*
   d)  *Apply anti-seize compound to the threads of all exhaust system fasteners during reassembly.*
   e)  *Be sure to allow sufficient clearance between newly installed parts and all points on the underbody to avoid overheating the floor pan and possibly damaging the interior carpet and insulation. Pay particularly close attention to the catalytic converter and heat shield.*

## 7    Fuel pump/fuel gauge sending unit module - removal and installation

**Warning:** *Gasoline is extremely flammable, so take extra precautions when you work on any part of the fuel system. See the* Fuel system warnings *in Section 1.*

## In-tank pump

1    Relieve the fuel system pressure (see Section 3), then remove the fuel filler cap to relieve any pressure inside the fuel tank.
2    Disconnect the cable from the negative battery terminal (see Chapter 5).
3    On Civic models, remove the trunk carpet, rear seat cushion and rear seat backs (see Chapter 11). On CR-Vs, fold the rear seats forward and pull back the carpet to expose the fuel pump access cover.
4    If equipped, remove the crossmember over the fuel pump access cover (see illustration).
5    Remove the fuel pump access cover screws (see illustration) and remove the fuel pump access cover.
6    Disconnect the quick-connect fitting for the fuel supply and EVAP lines and set them aside (see Section 5) and disconnect the fuel pump/fuel gauge sending unit electrical connector (see illustration).

**7.7 This special tool for loosening and tightening the fuel pump/fuel gauge sending unit locknut is available at most auto parts stores (2014 Civic shown)**

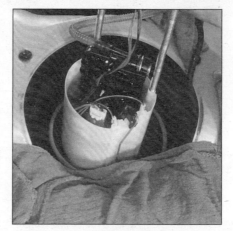

**7.8 Angle the fuel pump module when removing to prevent damage to the fuel level sending unit**

7   Remove the fuel pump/fuel gauge sending unit locknut (see illustration).

8   Remove the fuel pump/fuel gauge sending unit module from the tank. When removing the pump/sending unit from the tank, carefully angle the module to protect the float arm and float from damage (see illustration). After removing the pump/sending unit module, inspect the seal for cracks, tears and deterioration. If it's damaged, replace it.

9   Disconnect the fuel gauge sending unit connector from the module. Depress the tabs and remove the fuel gauge sending unit from the fuel pump module housing (see illustration).

10   Before installing the fuel pump/fuel gauge sending unit module in the fuel tank, install the seal in the hole first. Don't try to install it with the module, which might cause

it to become pinched or distorted (see illustration).

11   When installing the fuel pump/fuel gauge sending unit module, be sure to align the index mark on top of the module between the two marks on the edge of the hole.

12   Installation is otherwise the reverse of removal. Be sure to tighten the module locknut securely.

13   Installation is otherwise the reverse of removal, but before installing the fuel pump access cover, be sure to connect the cable to the negative battery terminal (see Chapter 5), start the engine and check for fuel leaks at the pump fuel line connection. If there are no leaks, install the access cover, the carpet and the rear seat (CR-V) or the seat cushion (coupe, sedan and hatchback).

## High-pressure pump

**Note:** *Only 2015 and later CR-V models equipped with direct injection have a high-pressure fuel pump.*

**Warning:** *The fuel delivery system on 2015 and later CR-V models is made up of a low-pressure system and a high-pressure system. This procedure relieves the pressure in both the low and high-pressure systems; however, wait at least two hours after relieving the pressure before disconnecting any fitting in the low or high-pressure systems.*

14   Relieve the fuel system pressure (see Section 3), then remove the fuel filler cap to relieve any pressure inside the fuel tank.

15   Set the engine to Top Dead Center (TDC) (see Chapter 2A or 2B). Once at TDC, rotate the engine counterclockwise 105 degrees.

16   On 2015 and later CR-V models, remove the PCM bracket bolts from the vehicle and position the PCM out of the way (see Chapter 6, Section 16).

17   Remove the cover from the high-pressure fuel pump located at the end of the cylinder head, above the transaxle. Remove the bracket and EVAP canister purge valve (see Chapter 6, Section 19).

18   Remove the intake manifold (see Chapter 2B, Section 5).

19   Disconnect the quick-connect fitting for the fuel feed hose. Remove the fuel pipe connecting the high-pressure fuel pump to the fuel rail (discard this pipe as it is not to be reused).

20   Disconnect the high-pressure fuel pump electrical connector. Alternately loosen the two high-pressure fuel pump bolts until they can be removed.

21   Carefully remove the high-pressure fuel pump, O-ring, and roller.

22   If the high-pressure fuel pump is to be replaced, remove the fuel feed pipe from the

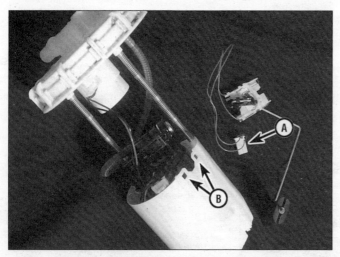

**7.9 Being careful not to damage the fuel gauge sending unit float arm and float, remove the fuel pump/fuel gauge sending unit module from the tank by disconnecting the connector (A) and disengaging the tabs (B). After removing the pump/sending unit, inspect the condition of the seal around the top of the module; if the seal is cracked, torn or deteriorated, replace it**

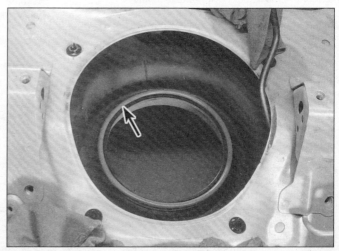

**7.10 Replace the O-ring with a new one.**

9.6 Remove the driver's rear wheel well liner (2014 Civic shown)

9.7 Disconnect the fuel filler neck hose and the fuel tank vapor hose quick connect fittings (2014 Civic shown)

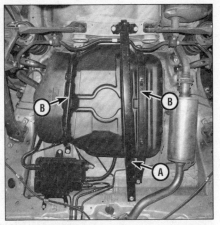

9.12 To remove the fuel tank from the underside of the vehicle, remove the underfloor bar (A) and fuel tank straps (B)

pump and discard the washers, as they are not to be reused.

23  Installation is the reverse of removal, noting the following points:
a) *Before installing the high-pressure fuel pump, ensure the engine is at 105 degrees counterclockwise from TDC.*
b) *Use NEW washers when installing the fuel feed pipe to the pump.*
c) *Use a NEW O-ring when installing the pump.*
d) *Coat the roller with clean engine oil before installation.*
e) *Use a new fuel pipe between the pump and fuel rail.*

24  Remainder of installation is reverse of removal. Tighten all fasteners and fuel pipe fittings to the proper torque found in this Chapter's Specifications. Start the engine and check for fuel leaks at the pump fuel line connections.

## 8   Fuel pressure regulator - replacement

**Warning:** *Gasoline is extremely flammable, so take extra precautions when you work on any part of the fuel system. See the* Fuel system warnings *in Section 1.*

1  Relieve the system fuel pressure (see Section 3), then remove the fuel filler neck cap to relieve any pressure inside the fuel tank.
2  Disconnect the cable from the negative battery terminal (see Chapter 5).
3  Remove the fuel pump/fuel gauge sending unit module from the fuel tank (see Section 7) and place it on a clean workbench.
4  The fuel pressure regulator is located under the fuel pump/fuel gauge sending unit assemblyreservoir. Place the fuel pump/fuel gauge sending unit assembly upside-down on a suitable working surface and carefully remove the reservoir by disconnecting the fuel level sending unit connector and remov-

ing the two fasteners attaching the reservoir to the upper part of the fuel pump/fuel gauge sending unit assembly.
5  Unsnap the bracket holding the fuel pressure regulator to the fuel pump/fuel gauge sending unit assembly.
6  Remove the fuel pressure regulator and ring.
7  Remove the old pressure regulator O-rings and discard them. Be sure to use new O-rings when you install the pressure regulator (regardless of whether you're installing the old regulator or a new unit).
8  Installation is the reverse of removal.

## 9   Fuel tank - removal and installation

**Warning:** *Gasoline is extremely flammable, so take extra precautions when you work on any part of the fuel system. See the* Fuel system warnings *in Section 1.*
**Note:** *The following procedure is much easier to perform if the fuel tank is empty. The tank has no drain plug, so the fuel must be siphoned from the tank with a siphoning kit, which is available at most auto parts stores. NEVER try to start the siphoning action with your mouth!*

1  Relieve the fuel system pressure (see Section 3).
2  Disconnect the cable from the negative battery terminal (see Chapter 5).
3  Access the fuel pump/fuel gauge sending unit and disconnect the fuel lines and/or the electrical connector (see Section 7).
4  Raise the vehicle and support it securely on jackstands.
5  If the fuel tank is empty or nearly empty, it's not necessary to siphon the remaining fuel from the tank. But if there is a lot of fuel in the tank, drain the fuel by removing the fuel pump/fuel gauge sending unit (see Section 7) and siphoning it out through the hole for the

pump/sending unit.
**Warning:** *Always siphon fuel into an approved gasoline container. Also, never start the siphoning action by mouth - use a siphoning pump (available at most auto parts stores).*

### Civic models

6  Remove the driver's rear wheel and wheel well liner (see illustration).
7  Disconnect and remove the fuel filler neck hose and the fuel tank vapor hose (see illustration). Inspect these two hoses for cracks, tears and other deterioration. If either hose is damaged or worn, replace it.
8  Remove the lower rear cover mounting fasteners and pull the back of the cover down, if equipped.
9  Disconnect the fuel line quick-connect fittings located at the front of the tank.
10  Remove the fuel tank shield.
11  Support the fuel tank with a transmission jack. If you don't have a transmission jack, use a floor jack. If you're going to use a floor jack, put a piece of plywood between the jack head and the fuel tank to protect the tank.
12  Remove the rear underfloor bar and unbolt the fuel tank retaining straps (see illustration) and remove them.
13  If equipped, remove the fuel tank baffle plates.
14  Carefully lower the fuel tank.
15  If you need to remove the fuel pump/fuel gauge sending unit module, but haven't yet done so, see Section 7.
16  Installation is the reverse of removal.

### CR-V models

17  Remove the driver's rear wheel.
18  Remove the left and right vehicle undercover panels.
19  Remove the exhaust pipe mounting bolts and pipe.
20  On 4WD models remove the driveshaft (see Chapter 8).
21  Remove the fuel tank guard fasteners and guard at the front of the tank.

**10.1 Disconnect the duct hose clamps (A) and any PCV hoses (B) (2014 1.8L Civic shown)**

**10.6 Disconnect the MAF/IAT sensor (A), loosen the intake duct hose clamp (B) and remove the housing fasteners (C) (2014 1.8L Civic shown)**

**10.8 Remove the air filter housing as an assembly**

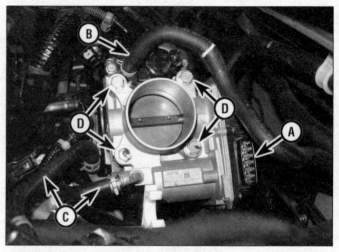

**11.2 Typical throttle body mounting details - Civic 1.8L shown, others similar**

| A | Throttle body actuator connector | C | Water bypass hoses |
|---|---|---|---|
| B | Vacuum hose | D | Throttle body mounting bolts |

22   Clean the area around the fuel filler neck hose and the fuel tank vapor hose at the fuel tank. Disconnect the fuel filler neck hose and the fuel tank vapor hose quick-disconnect fittings.

23   Disconnect the fuel tank vapor hose quick-disconnect fitting from the front of the fuel tank.

24   Support the fuel tank with a transmission jack. If you don't have a transmission jack, use a floor jack. If you're going to use a floor jack, put a piece of plywood between the jack head and the fuel tank to protect the tank.

25   Unbolt the fuel tank retaining straps and remove them.

26   Carefully lower the fuel tank.

27   If you need to remove the fuel pump/fuel gauge sending unit module, but haven't yet done so, refer to Section 5.

28   Installation is the reverse of removal.

## 10   Air filter housing - removal and installation

### Air intake duct

1   Loosen the hose clamp at the air filter housing-end of the duct (see illustration).

2   Loosen the hose clamp at the throttle body-end of the duct (see illustration).

3   Disconnect any crankcase vent hoses or pipes from the duct as necessary (see illustration).

4   Remove the air intake duct.

5   Installation is the reverse of removal.

### Air filter housing

6   Disconnect the MAF/IAT sensor electrical connector (see illustration).

7   Loosen the air intake duct clamp and separate the hose from the air filter housing (see illustration).

8   Remove the air filter housing fasteners and lift the housing out (see illustration).

**Note:** *You may need to pull firmly to disengage the rubber mounting points.*

9   Installation is the reverse of removal.

## 11   Throttle body - removal and installation

**Warning:** *Wait until the engine is completely cool before beginning this procedure.*

1   Remove the air intake duct (see Section 10).

**Note:** *On some models it may be necessary to remove the air filter housing (see Section 10).*

2   Disconnect all electrical connectors from the throttle body (see illustration).

3   Clamp off the two coolant bypass hoses

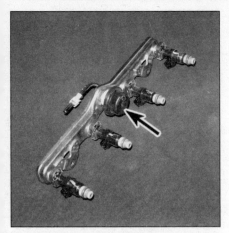

**12.1 Locate the pulsation damper on the underside of the fuel rail**

**12.2 Unscrew the pulsation damper (A) with one wrench while holding the hex on the fuel rail (B) with another**

**13.4 Remove the quick-connect fitting at the fuel rail**

to the throttle body, then disconnect them. Be prepared for a little coolant spillage. Plug the ends of the hoses.

4    If equipped, disconnect the vacuum hose and remove the harness clip from the throttle body.

5    Remove the throttle body mounting bolts and/or nuts and remove the throttle body.

6    Remove the old throttle body gasket o-ring from the intake manifold and discard it.

7    Installation is the reverse of removal. Be sure to use a new gasket and tighten the throttle body mounting bolts and nuts to torque listed in this Chapter's Specifications.

8    Check the coolant level and top it up if necessary (see Chapter 1).

9    Perform the PCM idle learn procedure (see Chapter 5).

10    Start the engine and check for vacuum and coolant leaks.

## 12   Fuel pulsation damper - removal and installation

**Note:** *Not all models are equipped with a fuel pulsation damper. Look under the fuel rail to determine if your model is equipped with one.*

1    The fuel pulsation damper is located on the fuel rail. To replace the fuel pulsation damper, you must remove the fuel rail (see Section 13) (see illustration).

2    Use one wrench to hold the fuel rail nut and a second wrench to remove the fuel pulsation damper (see illustration).

3    Installation is reverse of removal. Use a NEW washer when installing the fuel pulsation damper. Torque the damper to this Chapter's Specifications.

## 13   Fuel rail and injectors - removal and installation

**Warning:** *Gasoline is extremely flammable, so take extra precautions when you work on*

any part of the fuel system. See the Fuel system warnings in Section 1.

### Fuel rail

1    Relieve the system fuel pressure (see Section 3), then disconnect the cable from the negative battery terminal (see Chapter 5).

2    Remove the engine covers as necessary.

#### Except 2015 and later CR-V models

3    Disconnect the fuel injector electrical connectors and position the fuel injection harness to the side.

4    Remove the fuel line quick-connect fitting from the fuel rail (see illustration).

5    Remove the fuel rail fasteners and remove the fuel rail from the engine with the fuel injectors attached (see illustration). If any of the injectors are difficult to extract from their bores, carefully pry them loose by wiggling them from side to side and pulling up at the same time.

6    Remove the fuel injectors from the fuel rail as described later in this Section.

7    Installation is reverse of removal. Coat the lower O-rings with clean engine oil, then

**13.5 Remove the fuel rail from the engine with the injectors attached**

guide the fuel rail and injectors into place. Ensure the injectors are fully seated into the intake manifold.

8    Tighten all fasteners to the torque listed in this Chapter's Specifications. Start the engine and check for fuel leaks at the pump fuel line connections. Turn the ignition switch to On to activate the fuel pump and build up fuel pressure in the fuel lines and the fuel rail, but DON'T operate the starter yet. Repeat this step two or three times, then check the fuel lines, fuel rails and injectors for fuel leaks.

#### 2015 and later CR-V models

9    Remove the intake manifold (see Chapter 2A, Section 5 or Chapter 2B, Section 5).

10    Remove the fuel pipe from between the high-pressure fuel pump and fuel rail. Discard the pipe as it is recommended to not be reused.

11    Remove the fuel rail mounting bolts and carefully pull the injectors out of the the cylinder head.

12    Remove the fuel rail from the engine with the injectors attached. Pull the injectors straight out of the cylinder head.

13    Remove the fuel injectors as necessary.

**13.16a Remove the injector retaining clip . . .**

**13.16b . . . and remove the injector from the fuel rail (2015 Civic 1.8L shown)**

**13.22 Note that the upper O-ring (1) is installed above the back-up ring (2)**

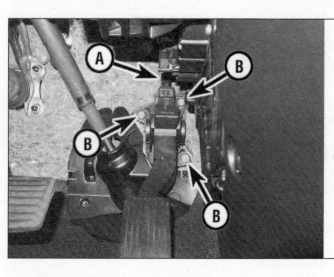

**14.2 Disconnect the accelerator pedal module electrical connector (A) and remove the mounting fasteners (B)**

bon from the injector using a paper towel. A special installation tool is required to install the new Teflon seal to the injector. Ensure the seal is not deformed after installation. Another tool is used to size (compress) the Teflon seal into its recess.

21    Remove the O-rings and back-up rings from the upper ends of the injectors.

22    Coat each new O-ring with clean engine oil, then install the back-up ring and O-ring (see illustration). Repeat this procedure for each injector.

23    Insert each injector into its corresponding bore in the fuel rail and use a new clip to secure the injector to the fuel rail.

24    Lightly lubricate the injector bores in the cylinder head with clean engine oil.

25    Install the fuel rail to the engine as described previously in this Section.

## 14   Accelerator pedal module - replacement

**Note:** *Civic and CR-V use an electronically actuated throttle body; there is no direct cable link between the accelerator pedal and the throttle body. Instead, an electric actuator within the throttle body operates the throttle based on a signal it receives from the Powertrain Control Module (PCM). The accelerator pedal module provides input to the PCM of the actual position of the accelerator pedal.*

1    Disconnect the accelerator pedal module electrical connector (see illustration).

2    Remove the fasteners securing the accelerator pedal module to the vehicle and remove the pedal module (see illustration).

3    Installation is the reverse of removal.

14    Installation is reverse of removal. Coat the lower seals with clean engine oil, then guide the fuel rail and injectors into place. Ensure the injectors are fully seated into the cylinder head.

15    Tighten all fasteners and fuel pipe fittings to the proper torque found in this Chapter's Specifications. Turn the ignition switch to On to activate the fuel pump and build up fuel pressure in the fuel lines and the fuel rail, but DON'T operate the starter yet. Repeat this step two or three times, then check the fuel lines, fuel rails and injectors for fuel leaks.

## Fuel injectors

### Except 2015 and later CR-V models

**Note:** *If you only removed the fuel rail assembly to replace a single injector or a leaking O-ring, it's a good idea to remove all of the injectors from the fuel rail and replace all the O-rings, cushion rings and seal rings at the same time.*

16    To remove each injector from the fuel rail, remove the retainer clip, then pull the injector out of its bore in the fuel rail (see illustrations).

17    Remove and discard the upper and lower O-rings from each injector, then install new O-rings. Lubricate the O-rings with a film of clean engine oil.

18    Insert each injector into the fuel rail and secure with the retaining clips.

19    Install the fuel rail and injectors and tighten the fasteners to the torque listed in this Chapter's Specifications.

### 2015 and later CR-V models

20    Use a pick tool to remove the Teflon seal at the lower end of the injector. Clean any car-

# Chapter 5
# Engine electrical systems

## Contents

## Specifications

### Torque specifications

**Ft-lbs (unless otherwise specified)    Nm**

**Note:** *One foot-pound (ft-lb) of torque is equivalent to 12 inch-pounds (in-lbs) of torque. Torque values below approximately 15 ft-lbs are expressed in inch-pounds, since most foot-pound torque wrenches are not accurate at these smaller values.*

| | Ft-lbs | Nm |
|---|---|---|
| Alternator bolts | | |
|   Civic 1.8L | 17 | 24 |
|   Civic 2.4L and 2014 and earlier CR-V models | 16 | 22 |
|   2015 and later CR-V models | 33 | 45 |
| Starter bolts | | |
|   Civic 2.4L | | |
|     Upper bolt | 33 | 45 |
|     Lower bolt | 47 | 64 |
|   Civic 1.8L and CR-V | 33 | 45 |

## 1   General information and precautions

### *General information*

#### Ignition system

1    The electronic ignition system consists of the Crankshaft Position (CKP) sensor, the Camshaft Position (CMP) sensor, the Knock Sensor (KS), the Powertrain Control Module (PCM), the ignition switch, the battery, the individual ignition coils or a coil pack, and the spark plugs. For more information on the CKP, CMP and KS sensors, as well as the PCM, refer to Chapter 6.

#### Charging system

2    The charging system includes the alternator (with an integral voltage regulator), the Powertrain Control Module (PCM), the Body Control Module (BCM), a charge indicator light on the dash, the battery, a fuse or fusible link and the wiring connecting all of these components. The charging system supplies electrical power for the ignition system, the lights, the radio, etc. The alternator is driven by a drivebelt.

#### Starting system

3    The starting system consists of the battery, the ignition switch, the starter relay, the Powertrain Control Module (PCM), the Transmission Range (TR) switch, the starter motor and solenoid assembly, and the wiring connecting all of the components.

### *Precautions*

4    Always observe the following precautions when working on the electrical system:

a)  *Be extremely careful when servicing engine electrical components. They are easily damaged if checked, connected or handled improperly.*

b)  *Never leave the ignition switched on for long periods of time when the engine is not running.*

c)  *Never disconnect the battery cables while the engine is running.*

d)  *Maintain correct polarity when connecting battery cables from another vehicle during jump starting - see the "Booster battery (jump) starting" Section at the front of this manual.*

e)  *Always disconnect the cable from the negative battery terminal before working on the electrical system, but read the battery disconnection procedure first (see Section 3).*

5    It's also a good idea to review the safety-related information regarding the engine electrical systems located in the Safety first! Section at the front of this manual before beginning any operation included in this Chapter.

## 2   Troubleshooting

### *Ignition system*

1    If a malfunction occurs in the ignition system, do not immediately assume that any particular part is causing the problem. First, check the following items:

a)  *Make sure that the cable clamps at the battery terminals are clean and tight.*

b)  *Test the condition of the battery (see Steps 21 through 24). If it doesn't pass all the tests, replace it.*

c)  *Check the ignition coil or coil pack connections.*

d)  *Check any relevant fuses in the engine compartment fuse and relay box (see Chapter 12). If they're burned, determine the cause and repair the circuit.*

#### Check

**Warning:** *Because of the high voltage generated by the ignition system, use extreme care when performing a procedure involving ignition components.*

**Note:** *The ignition system components on these vehicles are difficult to diagnose. In the event of ignition system failure that you can't diagnose, have the vehicle tested at a dealer service department or other qualified auto repair facility.*

**Note:** *You'll need a spark tester for the following test. Spark testers are available at most auto supply stores.*

2    If the engine turns over but won't start, verify that there is sufficient ignition voltage to fire the spark plugs as follows.

3    Remove an ignition coil and install the tester between the boot at the lower end of the coil and the spark plug (see illustration).

4    Crank the engine and note whether or not the tester flashes.

**Caution:** *Do NOT crank the engine or allow it to run for more than five seconds; running the engine for more than five seconds may set a Diagnostic Trouble Code (DTC) for a cylinder misfire.*

5    If the tester flashes during cranking, the coil is delivering sufficient voltage to the spark plug to fire it. Repeat this test for each cylinder to verify that the other coils are OK.

6    If the tester doesn't flash, remove a coil from another cylinder and swap it for the one being tested. If the tester now flashes, you know that the original coil is bad. If the tester still doesn't flash, the PCM or wiring harness is probably defective. Have the PCM checked out by a dealer service department or other qualified repair shop (testing the PCM is beyond the scope of the do-it-yourselfer because it requires expensive special tools).

7    If the tester flashes during cranking but a misfire code (related to the cylinder being tested) has been stored, the spark plug could be fouled or defective.

### *Charging system*

8    If a malfunction occurs in the charging system, do not automatically assume the alternator is causing the problem. First check the following items:

a)  *Check the drivebelt tension and condition, as described in Chapter 1. Replace it if it's worn or deteriorated.*

b)  *Make sure the alternator mounting bolts are tight.*

c)  *Inspect the alternator wiring harness and the connectors at the alternator and voltage regulator. They must be in good condition, tight and have no corrosion.*

d)  *Check the fusible link (if equipped) or main fuse in the underhood fuse/relay box. If it is burned, determine the cause, repair the circuit and replace the link or fuse (the vehicle will not start and/or the accessories will not work if the fusible link or main fuse is blown).*

e)  *Start the engine and check the alternator for abnormal noises (a shrieking or squealing sound indicates a bad bearing).*

f)  *Check the battery. Make sure it's fully charged and in good condition (one bad cell in a battery can cause overcharging by the alternator).*

g)  *Disconnect the battery cables (negative first, then positive). Inspect the battery posts and the cable clamps for corrosion. Clean them thoroughly if necessary (see Chapter 1). Reconnect the cables (positive first, negative last).*

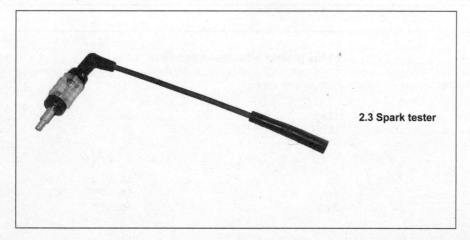

2.3 Spark tester

**2.15 To test the open circuit voltage of the battery, touch the black probe of the voltmeter to the negative terminal and the red probe to the positive terminal of the battery; a fully charged battery should be at least 12.6 volts**

**2.17 Connect a battery load tester to the battery and check the battery condition under load following the tool manufacturer's instructions**

## Alternator - check

9    Use a voltmeter to check the battery voltage with the engine off. It should be at least 12.6 volts (see illustration 2.15).

10    Start the engine and check the battery voltage again. It should now be approximately 13.5 to 15 volts.

11    If the voltage reading is more or less than the specified charging voltage, the voltage regulator is probably defective, which will require replacement of the alternator (the voltage regulator is not replaceable separately). Remove the alternator and have it bench tested (most auto parts stores will do this for you).

12    The charging system (battery) light on the instrument cluster lights up when the ignition key is turned to On, but it should go out when the engine starts.

13    If the charging system light stays on after the engine has been started, there is a problem with the charging system. Before replacing the alternator, check the battery condition, alternator belt tension and electrical cable connections.

14    If replacing the alternator doesn't restore voltage to the specified range, have the charging system tested by a dealer service department or other qualified repair shop.

## Battery - check

15    Check the battery state of charge. Visually inspect the indicator eye on the top of the battery (if equipped with one); if the indicator eye is black in color, charge the battery as described in Chapter 1. Next perform an open circuit voltage test using a digital voltmeter. With the engine and all accessories Off, touch the negative probe of the voltmeter to the negative terminal of the battery and the positive probe to the positive terminal of the battery (see illustration). The battery voltage should be 12.6 volts or slightly above. If the battery

is less than the specified voltage, charge the battery before proceeding to the next test. Do not proceed with the battery load test unless the battery charge is correct.

**Note:** *The battery's surface charge must be removed before accurate voltage measurements can be made. Turn on the high beams for ten seconds, then turn them off and let the vehicle stand for two minutes.*

16    Disconnect the negative battery cable, then the positive cable from the battery.

17    Perform a battery load test. An accurate check of the battery condition can only be performed with a load tester (see illustration). This test evaluates the ability of the battery to operate the starter and other accessories during periods of high current draw. Connect the load tester to the battery terminals. Load test the battery according to the tool manufacturer's instructions. This tool increases the load demand (current draw) on the battery.

18    Maintain the load on the battery for 15 seconds and observe that the battery voltage does not drop below 9.6 volts. If the battery condition is weak or defective, the tool will indicate this condition immediately.

**Note:** *Cold temperatures will cause the minimum voltage reading to drop slightly. Follow the chart given in the manufacturer's instructions to compensate for cold climates. Minimum load voltage for freezing temperatures (32 degrees F) should be approximately 9.1 volts.*

## Starting system

### The starter rotates, but the engine doesn't

19    Remove the starter (see Section 8). Check the overrunning clutch and bench test the starter to make sure the drive mechanism extends fully for proper engagement with the flywheel ring gear. If it doesn't, replace the starter.

20    Check the flywheel ring gear for missing teeth and other damage. With the ignition turned off, rotate the flywheel so you can check the entire ring gear.

### The starter is noisy

21    If the solenoid is making a chattering noise, first check the battery (see Steps 15 through 18). If the battery is okay, check the cables and connections.

22    If you hear a grinding, crashing metallic sound when you turn the key to Start, check for loose starter mounting bolts. If they're tight, remove the starter and inspect the teeth on the starter pinion gear and flywheel ring gear. Look for missing or damaged teeth.

23    If the starter sounds fine when you first turn the key to Start, but then stops rotating the engine and emits a zinging sound, the problem is probably a defective starter drive that's not staying engaged with the ring gear. Replace the starter.

### The starter rotates slowly

24    Check the battery (see Steps 15 through 18).

25    If the battery is okay, verify all connections (at the battery, the starter solenoid and motor) are clean, corrosion-free and tight. Make sure the cables aren't frayed or damaged.

26    Check that the starter mounting bolts are tight so it grounds properly. Also check the pinion gear and flywheel ring gear for evidence of a mechanical bind (galling, deformed gear teeth or other damage).

### The starter does not rotate at all

27    Check the battery (see Steps 15 through 18).

28    If the battery is okay, verify all connections (at the battery, the starter solenoid and motor) are clean, corrosion-free and tight. Make sure the cables aren't frayed or damaged.

29　Check all of the fuses in the underhood fuse/relay box.

30　Check that the starter mounting bolts are tight so it grounds properly.

31　Check for voltage at the starter solenoid "S" terminal when the ignition key is turned to the start position. If voltage is present, replace the starter/solenoid assembly. If no voltage is present, the problem could be the starter relay, the Transmission Range (TR) switch (see Chapter 6) or clutch start switch (see Chapter 8), or with an electrical connector somewhere in the circuit (see the wiring diagrams at the end of Chapter 12). Also, on many modern vehicles, the Powertrain Control Module (PCM) and the Body Control Module (BCM) control the voltage signal to the starter solenoid; on such vehicles a special scan tool is required for diagnosis.

### 3　Battery - disconnection and reconnection

**Warning:** *Always disconnect the cable from the negative battery terminal FIRST and hook it up LAST or the battery may be shorted by the tool being used to loosen the cable clamps.*

1　Some systems on the vehicle require battery power to be available at all times, either to maintain continuous operation (alarm system, power door locks, etc.), or to maintain control unit memory (radio station presets, Powertrain Control Module and other control units). When the battery is disconnected, the power that maintains these systems is cut. So, before you disconnect the battery, please note that on a vehicle with power door locks, it's a wise precaution to remove the key from the ignition and to keep it with you, so that it does not get locked inside if the power door locks should engage accidentally when the battery is reconnected!

2　Devices known as "memory-savers" can be used to avoid some of these problems. Precise details vary according to the device used. The typical memory saver is plugged into the cigarette lighter and is connected to a spare battery. Then the vehicle battery can be disconnected from the electrical system. The memory saver will provide sufficient current to maintain audio unit security codes, PCM memory, etc., and will provide power to always hot circuits such as the clock and radio memory circuits.

**Warning:** *Some memory savers deliver a considerable amount of current in order to keep vehicle systems operational after the main battery is disconnected. If you're using a memory saver, make sure that the circuit concerned is actually open before servicing it.*

**Warning:** *If you're going to work near any of the airbag system components, the battery MUST be disconnected and a memory saver must NOT be used. If a memory saver is used, power will be supplied to the airbag, which means that it could accidentally deploy and cause serious personal injury.*

### Disconnection

3　To disconnect the battery for service procedures requiring power to be cut from the vehicle, loosen the cable clamp nut and disconnect the cable from the negative battery terminal (see illustration 4.1). Isolate the cable end to prevent it from coming into accidental contact with the battery terminal. After disconnecting the negative battery terminal, it is OK to disconnect the positive terminal.

### Reconnection

4　If both terminals are disconnected, always reconnect the positive battery terminal first, then the negative battery cable. After reconnecting the battery, perform the Powertrain Control Module (PCM) idle learn procedure.

### Powertrain Control Module (PCM) idle learn procedure

5　Make sure that the PCM learns the engine idle characteristics after you perform any of the following procedures:

6　Disconnect the battery.

7　Replace (or reset) the PCM.

8　Replace the throttle body.

9　Replace the Idle Air Control (IAC) valve.

10　Remove the No. 6 (15 amp) PCM fuse

(in the engine compartment fuse and relay box).

11　Remove the No. 19 (120-amp) BATTERY fuse (in the engine compartment fuse and relay box).

12　Remove the PGM-FI main relay No. 1.

13　Remove any of the wires from the engine compartment fuse and relay box.

14　Disconnect any of the connectors from the engine compartment fuse and relay box.

15　Disconnect the electrical connector between the engine compartment wire harness and the PCM wire harness.

16　Disconnect the battery ground wire from the transmission housing.

17　Disconnect the ground wire from the body.

18　Disconnect the ground wire from the cylinder head.

### Relearn procedure

19　Make sure that all electrical components (air conditioning system, lights, rear window defogger, sound system, etc.) are turned OFF.

20　Start the engine, bring it up to 3000 rpm and hold it there, with no load (in Park or Neutral), until the radiator fan comes on or until the engine coolant temperature reaches 194-degrees F.

21　Allow the engine to idle for at least five minutes with no load on it and with the throttle fully closed.

**Note:** *If the radiator fan comes on during this five-minute period, don't include the time during which the fan runs as part of the five minutes.*

### 4　Battery - removal and installation

1　Disconnect the cable from the negative battery terminal first, then disconnect the cable from the positive battery terminal (see illustration).

2　Remove the battery hold-down clamp.

3　Lift out the battery. Be careful - it's heavy.

**Note:** *Battery straps and handlers are available at most auto parts stores for reasonable prices. They make it easier to remove and carry the battery.*

4　If you are replacing the battery, make sure you get one that's identical, with the same dimensions, amperage rating, cold cranking rating, etc.

5　Installation is the reverse of removal. Be sure to connect the positive cable first and the negative cable last.

### 5　Battery cables - replacement

1　When removing the cables, always disconnect the cable from the negative battery terminal first and hook it up last, or you might accidentally short out the battery with the tool you're using to loosen the cable clamps. Even if you're only replacing the cable for the posi-

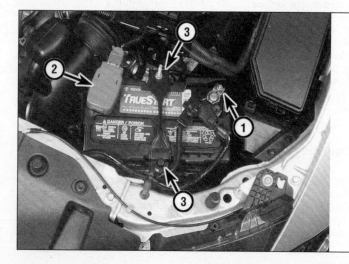

**4.1 Battery details:**

1　*Negative battery cable*

2　*Positive battery cable and terminal cover*

3　*Battery hold-down clamp fasteners*

tive terminal, be sure to disconnect the negative cable from the battery first.

2   Disconnect the old cables from the battery, then trace each of them to their opposite ends and disconnect them. Be sure to note the routing of each cable before disconnecting it to ensure correct installation.

3   If you are replacing any of the old cables, take them with you when buying new cables. It is vitally important that you replace the cables with identical parts.

4   Clean the threads of the solenoid or ground connection with a wire brush to remove rust and corrosion. Apply a light coat of battery terminal corrosion inhibitor or petroleum jelly to the threads to prevent future corrosion.

5   Attach the cable to the solenoid or ground connection and tighten the mounting nut/bolt securely.

6   Before connecting a new cable to the battery, make sure that it reaches the battery post without having to be stretched.

7   Connect the cable to the positive battery terminal first, then connect the ground cable to the negative battery terminal.

## 6   Ignition coils - replacement

1   On 2.4L Civic models, remove the wiper arms, cowl cover and cowl (see Chapter 11) to access the ignition coils.

2   Remove the ignition coil cover or engine cover.

3   Disconnect the electrical connector from the ignition coil (see illustration).

4   Remove the ignition coil mounting bolt.

5   Remove the ignition coil from the spark plug.

6   Installation is the reverse of removal. Be sure to tighten the ignition coil mounting bolt securely.

## 7   Alternator - removal and installation

1   Disconnect the cable from the negative terminal of the battery (see Section 3).

### Civic 1.8L models

2   Remove the drivebelt (see Chapter 1, Section 19).

3   Disconnect the electrical connectors and B+ terminal from the alternator (see illustration).

4   Remove the two bolts attaching the alternator to the engine.

5   Remove the alternator from the vehicle.

6   Installation is reverse of removal. Tighten the fasteners to the torque listed in this Chapter's Specifications.

### Civic 2.4L models and CR-V models

7   Remove the drivebelt and the tensioner and idler pulleys and brackets (see Chapter 1, Section 19). On 2014 and later CR-V models, only the tensioner assembly requires removal.

8   On Civic, remove the plastic cover above the grill that attaches to the grille and radiator support (see illustration 7.9).

9   On Civic, disconnect any electrical connectors or harness clips and remove the radiator support (see illustration).

10   On Civic models, remove the air conditioning condenser fan assembly from the passenger's side of the radiator (see Chapter 3).

11   On all models, remove the bolts attaching the alternator to the engine.

12   Disconnect the electrical connector(s) and B+ terminal from the alternator.

13   Remove the alternator from the vehicle.

14   Installation is the reverse of removal. Tighten the fasteners to the torque listed in this Chapter's Specifications.

## 8   Starter motor - removal and installation

1   Disconnect the cable from the negative terminal of the battery (see Section 3).

2   Raise and support the front of the vehicle on jackstands.

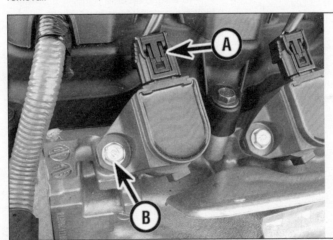

**6.3 Ignition coil details**

A   Ignition coil connector
B   Ignition coil mounting bolt

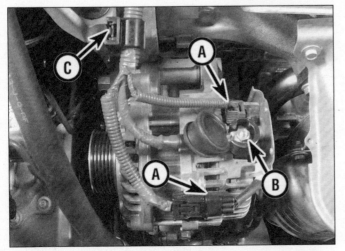

7.3 Disconnect the connectors (A), the B+ terminal (B) and the harness clip (C)

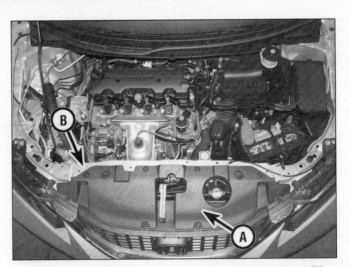

7.9 Remove the plastic cover (A) and the radiator support (B)

8.7 Starter mounting bolts (upper bolt not visible; location given)

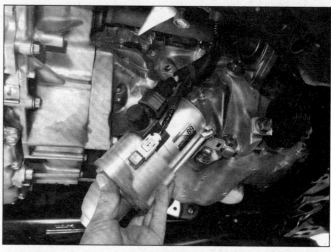

8.8 Remove the starter and disconnect the electrical connector and cable

## Civic 1.8L and 2015 and later CR-V models

3   On Civic models, remove the passenger front wheel.

4   On Civic, remove the engine under cover.

5   On CR-V, remove the exhaust pipe from under the engine.

6   On all models, remove the intake manifold bracket bolts and remove the bracket.

7   Remove the bolts attaching the starter to the transaxle (see illustration).

8   Disconnect the starter electrical connector and battery cable (see illustration).

9   To install, reverse removal procedure. Tighten the starter bolts to the torque listed in this Chapter's Specifications.

## Civic 2.4L and 2014 and earlier CR-V models

10   Remove the engine undercover.

11   Remove the bolts attaching the starter to the transaxle.

12   Disconnect the starter electrical connector and cable.

13   To install, reverse removal procedure. Tighten the starter bolts to the torque listed in this Chapter's Specifications.

# Chapter 6
# Emissions and engine control systems

## Contents

## Specifications

### Torque specifications

**Note:** *One foot-pound (ft-lb) of torque is equivalent to 12 inch-pounds (in-lbs) of torque. Torque values below approximately 15 ft-lbs are expressed in inch-pounds, since most foot-pound torque wrenches are not accurate at these smaller values.*

| | Ft-lbs (unless otherwise indicated) | Nm |
|---|---|---|
| EGR valve nuts | 16 | 22 |
| Knock sensor nut or bolt | 16 | 22 |
| IMT valve assembly cover bolts | 10 | 14 |

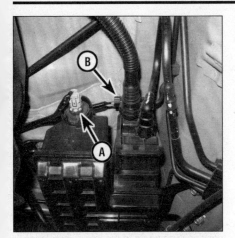

**19.10 EVAP canister vent shut valve (A) and the FTP sensor (B) (1.8L Civic shown)**

**20.3 EGR details (Civic 1.8L shown)**

*1    Electrical connector*
*2    Mounting nuts*

**21.1 Location of the oil pressure switch (1.8L Civic shown)**

EVAP canister and disconnect the electrical connector (see illustration 19.10).

16   Remove the FTP sensor retaining clip and remove the sensor.

17   Replace the O-ring on the sensor.

**Caution:** *Do not coat the O-rings with oil.*

18   Installation is the reverse of removal.

### EVAP canister

19   Raise the vehicle and place it securely on jackstands.

20   Remove the any covers necessary to access the EVAP canister for removal.

21   Disconnect the vapor hose and the electrical connector from the vent shut valve and FTP sensor and disconnect the two vapor hoses from the right end of the EVAP canister (see illustration 19.10).

22   Disengage any vapor hoses that are attached to the sides of the canister.

23   Remove the EVAP canister mounting bolts, then remove the canister.

24   If you're planning to replace the EVAP canister, be sure to remove the vent shut valve, and any other EVAP system components attached to the canister, and install them on the new canister.

25   Installation is the reverse of removal.

## 20   Exhaust Gas Recirculation (EGR) valve - replacement

1    Remove the engine cover (if equipped) and locate the EGR valve on the left end of the cylinder head.

2    Disconnect the electrical connector from the EGR valve.

3    Remove the EGR valve mounting nuts and remove the EGR valve from the coolant housing (see illustration).

**22.1 Location of the PCV valve on Civic 1.8L engines**

4    Remove and discard the old EGR valve gasket.

5    Installation is the reverse of removal. Be sure to use a new EGR valve gasket, and tighten the EGR valve mounting nuts securely.

## 21   Oil pressure switch - replacement

1    On Civic 1.8L engines, the oil pressure switch is located on the front of the engine, near the transaxle (see illustration). On CR-V and 2.4L Civic engines, the oil pressure switch is located on the lower rear of the engine, on the passenger side of the engine compartment.

2    Locate the switch and disconnect the electrical connector.

3    Unscrew the switch from the engine block

4    If reusing the original switch, clean the sealant from the threads.

5    Coat the threads with sealant or use teflon tape.

6    Install the switch into the engine block and tighten securely. Reconnect the electrical connector.

## 22   Positive Crankcase Ventilation (PCV) valve - replacement

1    On Civic 1.8L engines, the PCV valve is located on the right end of the engine, on the firewall side, accessible from above (see illustration). On CR-V and Civic 2.4L engines, the PCV valve is located near the alternator on the front of the engine block and also accessible from above.

2    Disconnect the crankcase ventilation hose from the PCV valve.

3    Unscrew and remove the PCV valve.

4    Installation is the reverse of removal. Be sure to tighten the PCV valve securely.

**23.12 Typical 1.8L rocker arm oil control valve details**

A   *Rocker arm oil control valve electrical connector*
B   *Rocker arm oil pressure sensor*

## 23   Variable Valve Timing and Lift Electronic Control (VTEC) system - description and component replacement

### *Description*

1   A low-lift, short-duration camshaft intake lobe produces good torque, quick response, good fuel economy and low emissions at lower engine speeds, but can't deliver sufficient air/fuel mixture to the combustion chamber at higher engine speeds. A high-lift, long-duration intake cam lobe produces good power at high engine speeds, but produces a lumpy idle and poor driveability, wastes fuel and produces unacceptable emissions at lower engine speeds. That's why camshaft intake lobe profiles are always a compromise between economy and performance. But Honda's Variable valve Timing and lift Electronic Control (VTEC) system allows an engine to operate economically and make good power at the same time.

2   The VTEC system is used on all engines. The principal differences between VTEC and non-VTEC engines are in the cylinder head, the camshaft(s) and the rocker arms. The block, the lubrication and cooling systems and most other components are identical on VTEC and non-VTEC engines. For more information about the cylinder head, the camshaft(s) and the rocker arms, refer to Chapter 2A. This Section is intended to familiarize you with how VTEC works and to show you how to replace the PCM-controlled components (the VTEC solenoid valve and the VTC oil control solenoid valve) in the VTEC system. If you don't know whether your vehicle is equipped with VTEC, look for the letters "VTEC" on top of the valve cover.

### VTEC system on SOHC models (coupes and sedans)

3   On 1.8L SOHC engines, there are five camshaft lobes, three for the intake rocker arm and two for the exhaust rocker arms. These "primary" and "secondary" lobe profiles

differ in lift and duration: the secondary lobe has lower lift and less duration (it opens later and closes sooner), while the primary lobe has higher lift and more duration (opens sooner and closes later). Each lobe operates its own rocker arm, which in turn pushes on its own valve. At low speeds, the secondary camshaft lobe operates one intake valve and the primary cam lobe operates the other valve. The low-lift, short-duration lobe produces good low-end torque and responsiveness.

4   When more power is needed at higher engine speeds, the PCM activates the VTEC solenoid valve, which allows higher oil pressure to a hydraulically-operated, spring-loaded pin inside the primary rocker arm. **Note:** *The VTEC solenoid is called the rocker arm oil control valve.* When hydraulic pressure overcomes spring pressure, the pin slides sideways and locks the secondary rocker arm to the primary rocker arm. The two rocker arms are both activated by the primary cam lobe; the secondary rocker arm no longer contacts its own camshaft lobe again until the system is disengaged. So both valves are now opened by the primary camshaft lobe with its higher lift and longer duration, increasing performance.

5   The PCM turns the VTEC solenoid on and off in accordance with engine rpm, vehicle speed, throttle opening angle, engine load and coolant temperature. Although diagnosis of the VTEC system is beyond the scope of the home mechanic, it's not difficult to replace the VTEC solenoid valve or to clean the filter for the system, both of which are outlined below.

### Intelligent Variable Valve Timing and Lift Electronic Control (i-VTEC) system on DOHC models (CR-V and Civic 2.4L engines)

6   The "intelligent" VTEC (i-VTEC) system used on the DOHC engines in these two models is similar in operation to the SOHC VTEC system, except that they also employ Variable Valve Timing Control (VTC).

### Variable Valve Timing Control (VTC)

7   The VTEC system changes the valve lift

and duration of the intake camshaft by using two different cam profiles. The VTC system, which is employed only on i-VTEC systems, changes the phase of the intake camshaft, which is another way of saying that it changes the cam timing, except that it does so continuously, not just when engine speed exceeds a certain threshold, as with the VTEC system. The VTC system, which is also operated by hydraulic (oil) pressure, improves fuel efficiency even more than VTEC alone, and it reduces exhaust emissions at all combinations of engine speed, vehicle speed and engine load.

8   When the engine is under a light load, the VTC control actuator (located inside the intake cam timing chain sprocket) is at its base position. The angle of the intake cam lobes is retarded to reduce the entry of exhaust gases into the intake ports and to achieve stable fuel consumption during lean burn.

9   When the engine is under a medium-to-high load, the VTC control actuator is at its advance control position. Cam angle is advanced slightly to reduce the effect of a diluted charge when the EGR system is operating by reducing the accompanying pumping loss. The intake valve is closed quickly to help reduce the entry of air/fuel mixture into the intake port and to improve the charging effect.

10   When the engine is operating at higher speeds, the VTC control actuator is at its advance-base position. The cam phase angle is controlled for maximum valve timing and maximum engine power.

### *Component replacement*
#### Civic 1.8L engines

#### Rocker arm oil control valve and oil pressure sensor

11   Remove the cowl cover.

12   Disconnect the electrical connector from the rocker arm oil control valve (see illustration).

13   Remove the rocker arm oil control valve mounting bolts and remove the valve from the cylinder head. Inspect the filter for clogging and, if necessary, clean it with fresh solvent. If the filter is too dirty to be cleaned, replace it, and replace the engine oil and the engine oil filter.

14   Remove the two control valve mounting bolts and separate the control valve from the housing.

15   Remove the old O-ring between the solenoid and the valve and discard it. Always install a new O-ring when you disassemble the solenoid and the valve.

16   Using a new O-ring, install the valve.

17   The oil pressure sensor screws into the side of the oil control valve housing. To replace the sensor, unscrew it and use a new copper washer when installing.

18   Installation is otherwise the reverse of removal. Be sure to tighten the solenoid-to-valve bolts and the rocker arm oil control valve mounting bolts securely.

## CR-V and Civic 2.4L engines

### VTEC solenoid valve and oil pressure sensor

19   Locate the VTEC solenoid valve at the right rear corner of the cylinder head and disconnect the electrical connector.

20   Remove the VTEC solenoid valve mounting bolts, remove the solenoid valve heat shield and remove the VTEC solenoid from the cylinder head.

21   Remove the VTEC solenoid valve filter. Inspect the filter for clogging and, if necessary, clean it with fresh solvent. If the filter is too dirty to be cleaned, replace it, and replace the engine oil and the engine oil filter (see Chapter 1).

22   Remove the solenoid-to-valve mounting bolts and separate the solenoid from the valve. Depress the plunger into the valve with your finger. It should move freely in its bore in the valve. If it doesn't, replace the VTEC sole-noid valve.

23   The oil pressure sensor screws into the top of the oil control valve housing. To replace the sensor, unscrew it and use a new copper washer when installing.

24   Installation is the reverse of removal. Be sure to tighten the VTEC solenoid valve mounting bolts securely.

### VTC oil control solenoid valve

25   Locate the VTC oil control solenoid valve on the right end of the cylinder head.

26   Disconnect the electrical connector from the VTC oil control solenoid valve.

**Note:** *If necessary, remove the ground cable from the motor mount for additional access.*

27   Remove the VTC oil control solenoid mounting bolt and remove the solenoid valve.

28   Remove and discard the old VTC oil control solenoid valve O-ring.

29   Inspect the VTC oil control solenoid valve for clogging. If the oil control solenoid valve is clogged, replace it and inspect the VTC oil strainer.

30   Using a new O-ring, install the VTC oil control solenoid valve, tighten the mounting bolt securely and plug in the electrical connector.

### VTC oil strainer

31   Locate the VTC oil control solenoid oil strainer on the right front corner of the cylinder head (the exhaust side).

32   Remove the VTC oil strainer cover bolts and remove the cover.

33   Remove the VTC oil strainer and inspect it for clogging. If the strainer is clogged, clean it in fresh solvent. If the strainer is too dirty to clean, replace it, then replace the engine oil and the oil filter (see Chapter 1).

34   Installation is the reverse of removal. Be sure to tighten the VTC oil strainer cover bolts securely.

# Notes

# Chapter 7 Part A
# Manual transaxle

---

## Contents

---

## Specifications

### General

Fluid type and capacity ........................................................... See Chapter 1

### Torque specifications

**Ft-lbs** (unless otherwise indicated)      **Nm**

**Note:** *One foot-pound (ft-lb) of torque is equivalent to 12 inch-pounds (in-lbs) of torque. Torque values below approximately 15 ft-lbs are expressed in inch-pounds, because most foot-pound torque wrenches are not accurate at these smaller values.*

| | Ft-lbs | Nm |
|---|---|---|
| Transaxle-to-engine mounting bolts | | |
|     10 mm bolts | 32 | 44 |
|     12 mm bolts | 47 | 64 |
| Transaxle mount and bracket | | |
|     Bolts | | |
|         Mount-to-chassis | 55 | 74 |
|         Bracket-to-transaxle | 61 | 83 |
|     Nuts | 61 | 83 |

## 1   General Information

1   Vehicles covered by this manual are equipped with either a five- or six-speed manual transaxle, a four- or five-speed automatic transaxle, or a Continuously Variable Transaxle (CVT).
2   All information on the manual transaxle is included in this Chapter. Service procedures for the four- and five-speed automatic transaxle, and Continuously Variable Transaxle (CVT) can be found in Chapter 7B. You'll also find certain procedures common to both transaxles - such as oil seal replacement - in this Chapter.
3   Depending on the expense involved in having a transaxle overhauled, it might be a better idea to consider replacing it with either a new or rebuilt unit. Your local dealer or transaxle shop should be able to supply information concerning cost, availability and exchange policy. Regardless of how you decide to remedy a transaxle problem, you can still save a lot of money by removing and installing the unit yourself.

## 2   Driveaxle oil seals - replacement

1   Oil leaks frequently occur due to wear of the driveaxle oil seals. Replacement of these seals is relatively easy, since the repair can usually be performed without removing the transaxle from the vehicle.
2   Driveaxle oil seals are located at the sides of the transaxle, where the driveaxles are attached. If leakage at the seal is suspected, raise the vehicle and support it securely on jackstands. If the seal is leaking, lubricant will be found on the sides of the transaxle, below the seals.
3   Refer to Chapter 8 and remove the driveaxles.
4   Use a screwdriver or prybar to carefully pry the oil seal out of the transaxle bore (see illustration).

5   If the oil seal cannot be removed with a screwdriver or prybar, a special oil seal removal tool (available at auto parts stores) will be required.
6   Using a large section of pipe or a large deep socket (slightly smaller than the outside diameter of the seal) as a drift, install the new oil seal (see illustration). Drive it into the bore squarely and make sure it's completely seated. Coat the seal lip with transaxle lubricant.
7   Install the driveaxle(s). Be careful not to damage the lip of the new seal.

## 3   Transaxle mount - check and replacement

1   Raise the front of the vehicle and place it securely on jackstands.
2   Insert a large screwdriver or prybar between the mount support arm and the frame and try to lever the support arm.
3   The transaxle support arm should not move up more than about 1/2 to 3/4-inch within the mount. If it does, replace the mount.
4   To replace the mount, support the transaxle with a jack, remove the nuts and bolts and remove the mount.
**Warning:** *Do not place any part of your body under the transaxle when it's supported only by a jack.*
5   Installation is the reverse of removal.

## 4   Shift lever/shift cables - removal and installation

1   Remove the center console (see Chapter 11).
2   Remove the cotter pins and detach the cable ends from the lock pins on the shift lever.
3   Remove the four bolts and remove the shift lever assembly.

4   Pry off the spring clips and detach the cables from the shift lever housing. Rotate the cables until the squared edge aligns with the slot in the shift lever housing cutout.
5   Remove the air filter housing and intake tube (see Chapter 4, Section 10).
6   Disconnect any harness clips or connectors to allow access to the shift cables at the transaxle.
7   Remove the clip(s) and washer(s) and detach the cable(s) from the shift lever(s) on the transaxle.
8   Pry off the spring clip(s) and detach the cable(s) from the bracket on the transaxle.
9   Raise the front of the vehicle and support it securely on jackstands.
10   Working under the vehicle, remove the heat shield attached to the vehicle's body. On Civic 2.4L engines, the catalytic converter and pipe must be removed before the heat shield can be removed.
11   Remove the cable bracket fasteners from under the vehicle.
12   Remove the rubber grommet where the cables pass through the vehicle body. Guide the cable(s) through the floorpan and remove from under the vehicle.
13   Installation is the reverse of removal

## 5   Back-up light switch - replacement

1   Remove the air filter housing (see Chapter 4, Section 10).
2   Unplug the back-up light switch electrical connector, located near the shift levers on the transaxle.
3   Unscrew the back-up light switch.
4   If equipped, discard the old washer. Using a new washer, install the new switch. On models without a washer, apply RTV sealant or Teflon tape to the threads of the new switch to prevent leakage.
5   Plug in the connector.

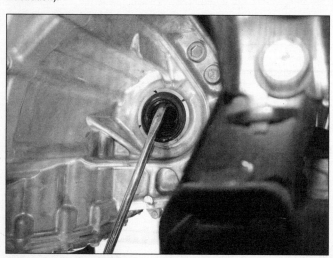

**2.4 Insert the tip of a large screwdriver or prybar behind the oil seal and very carefully pry it out**

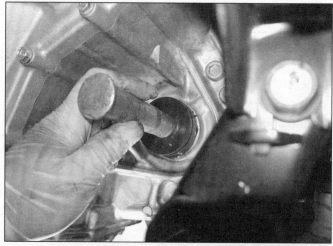

**2.6 Using a large socket or a section of pipe, drive the new seal squarely into the bore**

## 6   Manual transaxle - removal and installation

### *Removal*

1   Set the steering wheel straight ahead and lock the steering wheel in that position. Set the steering column tilt and telescoping to the center positions.

2   Working under the driver's side of the instrument panel, remove the steering column coupler cover at the base of the steering column.

3   Use a piece of wire and tie the upper and lower ends of the column shaft together at the U-joints. This is to prevent the lower part of the steering shaft from sliding out of the upper end after being disconnected from the rack and pinion.

4   Loosen the pinch bolt at the lower U-joint and disconnect from the rack and pinon splines.

5   Cover the fenders and cowl using special pads. An old bedspread or blanket will also work.

6   Remove the plastic fasteners and the upper cover above the grille.

7   Remove the wiper arms, the wiper cowl and both ends (see Chapter 1, Section 7). Remove the fasteners and the lower cowl panel from the vehicle.

8   Remove the air intake duct and the air filter housing (see Chapter 4, Section 10). Remove the air filter housing bolts and the bracket.

9   Remove the battery and the battery tray (see Chapter 5).

10   Remove the PCM from the engine compartment (see Chapter 6, Section 16).

11   Remove the clutch release cylinder and hydraulic line, without disconnecting any fittings. Support the cylinder out of the way with a length of wire or rope.

**Caution:** *Don't depress the clutch pedal while the release cylinder is removed.*

12   Disconnect the shift cables from the shift levers at the transaxle (see Section 4).

13   Clearly label and disconnect all vacuum lines, emissions hoses, electrical connectors and wiring harness clamps/brackets that may interfere with transaxle removal. Masking tape and/or a touch up paint applicator work well for marking items. Take instant photos or sketch the locations of components and brackets.

14   Support the engine with an engine support fixture or an engine hoist (an engine support fixture is recommended, as it doesn't have legs that extend under the vehicle that would get in the way). Connect the sling or chain to the lifting hook at the end of the engine near the transaxle, not to the lifting eye on the transaxle. If no lifting hook is provided, use the threaded hole(s) in the cylinder head to attach the sling or chain.

15   With the engine supported, remove the two upper transaxle mounting bolts.

16   Disconnect the ground strap from the transaxle mount. Remove the nuts and bolts attaching the transaxle mount and bracket and remove from the engine compartment.

17   Loosen the front wheel lug nuts, then raise the vehicle and support it securely on jackstands. Remove the wheels.

18   Remove the engine splash shield (see Chapter 2A, Section 5) and the inner fender splash shields (see Chapter 11).

19   Drain the transaxle fluid (see Chapter 1).

20   Remove the driveaxles (see Chapter 8) and the intermediate shaft.

21   Remove the subframe (see Chapter 10, Section 19).

22   Support the transaxle with a jack, preferably one made for this purpose. Secure the transaxle to the jack with straps or chains.

23   Remove the clutch inspection cover and the remaining transaxle-to-engine bolts.

24   Move the transaxle away from the engine to disengage the transaxle input shaft from the clutch disc, and far enough to clear the pressure plate. Lower the transaxle from the vehicle.

**Note:** *It may be necessary to slowly lower the engine a slight amount while the jack supporting the transaxle is being lowered. This will provide more clearance between the transaxle and the body.*

### *Installation*

25   If removed, install the clutch components (see Chapter 8).

26   Make sure the dowel pins are installed in the engine block. With the transaxle secured to the jack with a chain, raise it into position behind the engine, then carefully slide it forward, engaging the two dowel pins on the transaxle with the corresponding holes in the block and the input shaft with the clutch plate hub splines. Do not use excessive force to install the transaxle - if the input shaft does not slide into place, readjust the angle of the transaxle so it is level and/or turn the input shaft so the splines engage properly with the clutch plate hub.

27   Install the transaxle-to-engine bolts and tighten them to the torque listed in this Chapter's Specifications.

28   The remainder of installation is the reverse of removal, noting the following points:

a)  *Refill the transaxle with the specified type of lubricant (see Chapter 1, Section 27).*

b)  *Tighten the driveaxle/hub nuts to the torque listed in the Chapter 8 Specifications.*

c)  *Tighten the wheel lug nuts to the torque listed in the Chapter 1 Specifications.*

d)  *Road test the vehicle for proper operation and check for leaks.*

## 7   Manual transaxle overhaul - general information

1   Overhauling a manual transaxle is a difficult job for the do-it-yourselfer. It involves the disassembly and reassembly of many small parts. Numerous clearances must be precisely measured and, if necessary, changed with select fit spacers and snap-rings. As a result, if transaxle problems arise, it can be removed and installed by a competent do-it-yourselfer, but overhaul should be left to a transaxle repair shop. Rebuilt transaxles may be available - check with your dealer parts department and auto parts stores. At any rate, the time and money involved in an overhaul is almost sure to exceed the cost of a rebuilt unit.

2   Nevertheless, it's not impossible for an inexperienced mechanic to rebuild a transaxle if the special tools are available and the job is done in a deliberate step-by-step manner so nothing is overlooked.

3   The tools necessary for an overhaul include internal and external snap-ring pliers, a bearing puller, a slide hammer, a set of pin punches, a dial indicator and possibly a hydraulic press. In addition, a large, sturdy workbench and a vise or transaxle stand will be required.

4   During disassembly of the transaxle, make careful notes of how each piece comes off, where it fits in relation to other pieces and what holds it in place. Noting how the parts are installed when you remove them will make it much easier to get the transaxle back together.

5   Before taking the transaxle apart for repair, it will help if you have some idea what area of the transaxle is malfunctioning. Certain problems can be closely tied to specific areas in the transaxle, which can make component examination and replacement easier. Refer to the *Troubleshooting* section at the front of this manual for information regarding possible sources of trouble.

# Notes

# Chapter 7B
# Automatic transaxle

---

## Contents

---

## Specifications

## General

Fluid type and capacity ................................................................ See Chapter 1

## Torque specifications

**Ft-lbs (unless otherwise indicated)**    **Nm**

**Note:** *One foot-pound (ft-lb) of torque is equivalent to 12 inch-pounds (in-lbs) of torque. Torque values below approximately 15 ft-lbs are expressed in inch-pounds, since most foot-pound torque wrenches are not accurate at these smaller values.*

| | Ft-lbs (unless otherwise indicated) | Nm |
|---|---|---|
| ATF warmer | | |
|     Civic | 19 | 26 |
|     CR-V | | |
|         6 mm bolts | 108 in-lbs | 12 |
|         8 mm bolts | 20 | 27 |
| Driveplate-to-torque converter bolts | 108 in-lbs | 12 |
| Flywheel-to-driveplate bolts (Continuously Variable Transaxle) | 108 in-lbs | 12 |
| Transaxle mounting bolts | 47 | 64 |
| Catalytic converter pipe | | |
|     Bolts | 16 | 22 |
|     Nuts | 25 | 33 |

## 1   General Information

1    The vehicles covered by this manual are equipped with either a five- or six-speed manual transaxle, a four- or five-speed automatic transaxle, or a Continuously Variable Transaxle (CVT). All information on automatic transaxles and the Continuously Variable Transaxle is included in this Chapter. Information for the manual transaxle can be found in Chapter 7A. Information related to the transfer case on 4WD CR-V models can be found in Chapter 8.

2    Due to the complexity of the automatic transaxles and Continuously Variable Transaxles covered in this manual and the specialized equipment necessary to perform most service operations, this Chapter contains only those procedures related to general diagnosis, routine maintenance, adjustment and removal and installation.

3    If the transaxle requires major repair work, this should be left to a dealer service department or an automotive or transmission repair shop. You can, however, remove and install the transaxle yourself and save the expense, even if a transmission shop does the repair work (but be sure a proper diagnosis has been made before removing the transaxle).

## 2   Diagnosis - general

1    Automatic transaxle malfunctions may be caused by five general conditions:

a) *Poor engine performance*
b) *Improper adjustments*
c) *Hydraulic malfunctions*
d) *Mechanical malfunctions*
e) *Malfunctions in the computer or its signal network*

2    Diagnosis of these problems should always begin with a check of the easily repaired items: fluid level and condition (see Chapter 1), shift cable adjustment and shift lever installation. Next, perform a road test to determine if the problem has been corrected or if more diagnosis is necessary. If the prob-

**3.4 Insert a 6.0 mm (0.236 in) pin or drill bit into the positioning holes in the shifter assembly to lock the shift lever in Reverse**

lem persists after the preliminary tests and corrections are completed, additional diagnosis should be performed by a dealer service department or other qualified transmission repair shop. Refer to the Troubleshooting Section at the front of this manual for information on symptoms of transaxle problems.

## *Preliminary checks*

3    Drive the vehicle to warm the transaxle to normal operating temperature.
4    Check the fluid level as described in Chapter 1:

a) *If the fluid level is unusually low, add enough fluid to bring the level within the designated area of the dipstick, then check for external leaks (see* Fluid leak diagnosis *below).*
b) *If the fluid level is abnormally high, drain off the excess, then check the drained fluid for contamination by coolant. The presence of engine coolant in the automatic transmission fluid indicates that a failure has occurred in the internal radiator walls that separate the coolant from the transmission fluid (see Chapter 3).*
c) *If the fluid is foaming, drain it and refill the transaxle, then check for coolant in the fluid, or a high fluid level.*

5    Make sure the engine idle speed is correct. If the idle speed is incorrect, have it adjusted by a dealer service department or other qualified repair shop before proceeding.
6    Inspect the shift cable. Make sure that it's properly adjusted and operates smoothly (see Section 3).

## *Fluid leak diagnosis*

7    Most fluid leaks are easy to locate visually. Repair usually consists of replacing a seal or gasket. If a leak is difficult to find, the following procedure may help.
8    Identify the fluid. Make sure it's transmission fluid and not engine oil or brake fluid (automatic transmission fluid is a deep red color).
9    Try to pinpoint the source of the leak. Drive the vehicle several miles, then park it over a large sheet of cardboard. After a minute or two, you should be able to locate the leak by determining the source of the fluid dripping onto the cardboard.
10   Make a careful visual inspection of the suspected component and the area immediately around it. Pay particular attention to gasket mating surfaces. A mirror is often helpful for finding leaks in areas that are hard to see.
11   If the leak still cannot be found, clean the suspected area thoroughly with a degreaser or solvent, then dry it.
12   Drive the vehicle for several miles at normal operating temperature and varying speeds. After driving the vehicle, visually inspect the suspected component again.
13   Once the leak has been located, the cause must be determined before it can be properly repaired. If a gasket is replaced but the sealing flange is bent, the new gasket will not stop the leak. The bent flange must be straightened.

14   Before attempting to repair a leak, check to make sure that the following conditions are corrected or they may cause another leak.
**Note:** *Some of the following conditions cannot be fixed without highly specialized tools and expertise. Such problems must be referred to a transmission shop or a dealer service department.*

### Seal leaks

15   If a transaxle seal is leaking, the fluid level or pressure may be too high, the vent may be plugged, the seal bore may be damaged, the seal itself may be damaged or improperly installed, the surface of the shaft protruding through the seal may be damaged or a loose bearing may be causing excessive shaft movement.
16   Make sure the dipstick tube seal is in good condition and the tube is properly seated. Periodically check the area around the speedometer gear or sensor for leakage. If transmission fluid is evident, check the O-ring for damage.

### Case leaks

17   If the case itself appears to be leaking, the casting is porous and will have to be repaired or replaced.
18   Make sure the oil cooler hose fittings are tight and in good condition.

### Fluid comes out vent pipe or fill tube

19   If this condition occurs, the transaxle is overfilled, there is coolant in the fluid, the case is porous, the dipstick is incorrect, the vent is plugged or the drain-back holes are plugged.

## 3   Shift cable - replacement and adjustment

**Warning:** *These models are equipped with a Supplemental Restraint System (SRS), more commonly known as airbags. Always disable the airbag system before working in the vicinity of any airbag system component to avoid the possibility of accidental deployment of the airbag(s), which could cause personal injury (see Chapter 12).*
**Warning:** *Do not use a memory saving device to preserve the PCM or radio memory when working on or near airbag system components.*

1    Raise the vehicle and support it securely on jackstands.

## *Replacement*
### Civic

2    Set the parking brake.
3    Remove the center console (see Chapter 11).
4    Place the shift lever in the Reverse (R) position. Insert a 6.0 mm (0.236 in) alignment pin into the positioning holes in the shifter assembly base to lock the shift lever in Reverse (see illustration).
**Caution:** *If a drill bit is used, use the smooth end as a drill bit may damage the shifter assembly.*

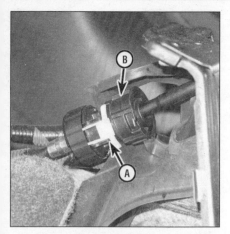

3.6 Pry the cable lock (A) up, then rotate the socket holder (B) counterclockwise and push the socket against the mounting bracket to remove

3.10 On CVT models, pull the clip and remove the the pin to disconnect the cable from the shift control lever

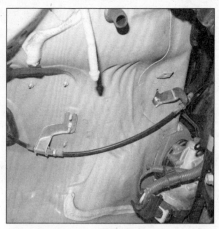

3.13 Remove the shift cable guide bracket bolts and the rubber grommet

3.18 CR-V shifter assembly access cover

3.20 Working through the access hole on CR-V, remove the shift cable nut

5    Remove the nut that secures the shift cable end.

6    Pry the lock up and rotate the socket holder counterclockwise, then push the socket in and slide the assembly out of the slotted recess (see illustration) to disconnect the cable from the shifter assembly.

7    Raise and support the vehicle.

8    Locate and remove the shift cable cover from the transaxle.

9    On non-CVT models, bend back the locking tab and remove the bolt attaching the shift cable to the shift control shaft.

10    On models with a CVT transaxle, remove the clip and pin to disconnect the shift cable from the shift control lever (see illustration).

11    On all models, remove the shift cable bracket from the transaxle with the cable attached.

12    Remove the under-car heat shield to expose the shift cable.

**Note:** *On models equipped with 2.4L engines, it may be necessary to remove the catalytic*

*converter and pipe to allow removal of the heat shield. You may be able to loosen the heat shield enough to remove the cable without removing the exhaust components.*

13    Remove the shift cable guide bracket mounting bolts (see illustration).

14    Pull the rubber grommet and shift cable out of the vehicle.

15    Installation is the reverse of the removal procedure, noting the following points:

a) *Install a new lock washer, then bend the locking tang against the bolt head.*

b) *Be sure to adjust the cable before reattaching it to the shift lever (see Adjustment).*

c) *When installing the cable to the shifter assembly, ensure the mounting stud is properly aligned with the cable end.*

### CR-V

16    Set the parking brake.

17    Remove the center console (see Chapter 11).

18    Remove the access panel from the left side of the shifter base (see illustration).

19    Place the shift lever in the Reverse (R) position. Insert a 6.0 mm (0.236 in) pin into the positioning holes in the shifter assembly to lock the shift lever in Reverse.

**Caution:** *Do not use a drill bit as it may damage the shifter assembly.*

20    Remove the nut securing the shift cable to the shifter assembly (see illustration).

21    Pry the lock retainer up and rotate the socket holder counterclockwise, then push the socket in and slide the assembly out of the slotted recess to disengage the shift cable housing from the bracket.

22    Raise and support the vehicle.

23    Remove the PCM and PCM bracket (see Chapter 6, Section 16).

24    Remove the shift cable cover.

25    On 2WD models, bend back the locking tab and remove the bolt attaching the shift cable to the shift control shaft.

26    On 4WD models, remove the clip and

**4.6 Identifying the O/D switch shift knob harness on CR-V**

**5.5 Disconnect these electrical connectors**

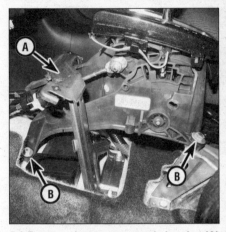

**5.6 Remove the center console bracket (A) then the shift lever assembly mounting bolts (B)**

pin to disconnect the shift cable from the shift control lever.

27   Remove the bolts attaching the shift cable bracket to the transaxle, and remove the bracket with the cable attached.

28   Remove the floor under cover from under the vehicle body to expose the shift cable and mounting brackets.

29   Remove the shift cable guide bracket and mounting bolts and separate it from the vehicle body.

30   Pull the rubber grommet and shift cable out of the vehicle.

31   Installation is the reverse of the removal procedure, noting the following points:

a) *Install a new lock tab on the shift cable end holder.*

b) *Be sure to adjust the cable before reattaching it to the shift lever (see Adjustment).*

## Adjustment

32   Set the parking brake. Remove the center console (see Chapter 11, Section 24).

33   Place the shift lever in the Reverse (R) position. Insert a 6.0 mm (0.236 in) pin into the positioning holes in the shifter assembly to lock the shift lever in Reverse.

34   With the shift cable disconnected from the shifter assembly and bracket. Push the shift cable until it stops and release your hand. Pull back one click until the cable stops (locks-in) in position. This is the Reverse (R) position. You can verify the correct position on the shift indicator with the ignition in run position.

35   Install the shift cable into the mounting bracket, then install the cable end to the shift lever mounting bolt and align the square surface with the alignment casting on the mounting bolt.

**Note:** *It may be necessary to rotate the shift cable mounting stud to align it with the slotted recess in the cable.*

36   Install the lock nut on the cable and tighten the cable in this position.

37   Remove the alignment pin from the shift lever bracket base.

38   Start the engine and check the shift lever in all gears. If any gear doesn't work properly, refer to Section 2.

---

## 4   Shift knob - replacement

### Civic

1   Pull downward on the lower half of the shift knob to release the clips, and expose the retaining screws.

2   Use a small, flat-tipped screwdriver and remove the bezel from around the shift knob itself.

3   Remove the two screws and remove the shift knob from the shift lever.

4   Installation is reverse of removal.

### CR-V

5   Remove the access panel from the left side of the shifter base.

6   Remove the shift knob harness straps and disconnect the shift knob (O/D switch) harness connector (see illustration).

7   Remove the two screws and remove the shift knob from the shift lever.

8   Installation is reverse of removal.

---

## 5   Shift lever - replacement

**Warning:** *These models are equipped with a Supplemental Restraint System (SRS), more commonly known as airbags. Always disable the airbag system before working in the vicinity of any airbag system component to avoid the possibility of accidental deployment of the airbag(s), which could cause personal injury (see Chapter 12).*

**Warning:** *Do not use a memory saving device to preserve the PCM or radio memory when working on or near airbag system components*

### Civic

1   Set the parking brake, then place the shift lever in the Neutral position.

2   Remove the center console panels. Remove the center console (see Chapter 11).

3   Remove the nut that secures the shift cable end (see Section 3).

4   Rotate the socket holder 1/4 turn until the flattened edge of the cable grommet guide aligns with the base and slide the assembly out of the slotted recess (see illustration 3.6).

5   Disconnect the shift lock solenoid electrical connector (see illustration) and park pin electrical connector.

6   Remove the center console bracket, then remove the four bolts and remove the shift lever assembly from the floor (see illustration).

7   Installation is the reverse of the removal procedure, but note the following points:

a) *Verify the indicator for the neutral position lights with the ignition switch on.*

b) *Adjust the shift cable, if necessary (see Section 3).*

### CR-V

8   Set the parking brake, then place the shift lever in the Reverse position.

9   Remove the center console (see Chapter 11, Section 24).

10   Remove the shifter trim panel from around the shift lever.

11   Remove the access panel from the left side of the shifter base.

12   Disconnect the shift knob (O/D switch) electrical connector (see Section 4).

13   Disconnect the shift cable from the shifter assembly (see Section 3).

14   Disconnect the shift lever connector from under the shifter assembly.

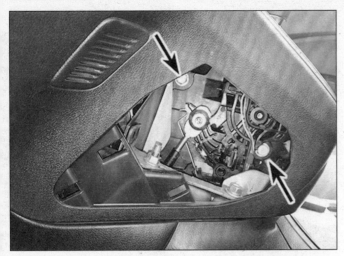

**5.15 Remove the shift lever assembly bolts through the access panel opening**

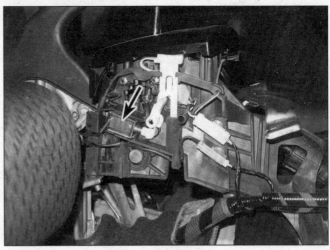

**6.7 Identifying the shift interlock solenoid on Civic models (type B shift lever shown)**

15  Working through the access panel opening and under the shifter assembly, remove the three bolts and remove the shift lever assembly (see illustration).

16  Installation is the reverse of the removal procedure, but note the following points:

a) *Verify the indicator for the neutral position lights with the ignition switch on.*

b) *Adjust the shift cable, if necessary (see Section 3).*

---

## 6    Interlock system - description and solenoid replacement

---

**Warning:** *These models are equipped with a Supplemental Restraint System (SRS), more commonly known as airbags. Always disable the airbag system before working in the vicinity of any airbag system component to avoid the possibility of accidental deployment of the airbag(s), which could cause personal injury (see Chapter 12).*

**Warning:** *Do not use a memory saving device to preserve the PCM or radio memory when working on or near airbag system components.*

### *Description*

1  Vehicles equipped with an automatic transaxle have an interlock system to prevent unintentional shifting. The interlock system consists of two subsystems: a shift lock system and a key interlock system.

### Key interlock system

2  The key interlock system prevents the ignition key from being removed from the ignition switch unless the shift lever is in the Park position.

### Shift lock system

3  The shift lock system prevents the shift lever from moving from the Park position

unless the brake pedal is depressed. Nor can the shift lever be shifted when the brake pedal and the accelerator pedal are depressed at the same time. In the event of a system malfunction, you can release the shift lever by inserting a screwdriver into the release slot near the shift lever (sedans/coupes) or into the slot in the upper steering column cover (CR-V).

### *Solenoid replacement*

**Note:** *The following procedure pertains only to the shift lock solenoid. For information on how to replace the key interlock solenoid, refer to the Ignition switch/key lock cylinder replacement Section in Chapter 12. The key interlock solenoid isn't available separately.*

### Civic

4  Remove the center console panels. Remove the center console (see Chapter 11).

5  Disconnect the shift lock solenoid electrical connector.

6  On type A shift levers, remove the shift knob (see Section 4) and the shifter trim panel. Depress the four locking tabs and remove the shift lock unit by pulling upward to remove and access the solenoid. Then pry the lock tabs to remove the solenoid.

7  On type B shift levers, pry the plastic lock tabs and slide the shift lock solenoid, clear the tabs and remove the solenoid (see illustration).

8  Installation is the reverse of removal. Install the plunger and plunger spring into the new shift lock solenoid.

9  Align the shift lock solenoid plunger with the tip of the shift lock stop.

10  Connect the shift lock solenoid electrical connector.

### CR-V

11  Remove the shift lever assembly (see Section 5).

12  Use a small, flat-tipped screwdriver to

release the lock tab under the solenoid.

13  Pull the solenoid straight up and off the shift lock stop lever pin, then disconnect the electrical connector.

14  Transfer the plunger and plunger spring into the new shift lock solenoid.

15  Installation is the reverse of removal. Slide the lock tab in the opposite direction of removal to lock the solenoid in place.

16  Verify operation.

---

## 7    Automatic transaxle and Continuously Variable Transaxle (CVT) - removal and installation

---

**Warning:** *These models are equipped with a Supplemental Restraint System (SRS), more commonly known as airbags. Always disable the airbag system before working in the vicinity of any airbag system component to avoid the possibility of accidental deployment of the airbag(s), which could cause personal injury (see Chapter 12).*

**Warning:** *Do not use a memory saving device to preserve the PCM or radio memory when working on or near airbag system components*

**Note:** *Read through the entire Section before beginning this procedure. The engine and transaxle are removed as a unit from below, then separated outside the vehicle.*

### *Removal*

1  Set the steering wheel straight ahead and lock the steering wheel in that position. Set the steering column tilt and telescoping to the center positions.

2  Working under the driver's side of the instrument panel, remove the steering column coupler cover at the base of the steering column.

3  Use a piece of wire and tie the upper and lower ends of the column shaft together at the

**7.24 Mark the relationship of the torque converter to the driveplate - Civic CVT model shown**

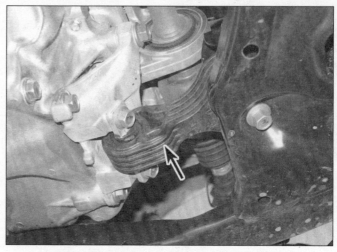

**7.28 If equipped, remove the engine torque bracket (Civic CVT model shown)**

U-joints. This is to prevent the lower part of the steering shaft from sliding out of the upper end after being disconnected from the rack and pinion.

4    Loosen the pinch bolt at the lower U-joint and disconnect from the rack and pinon splines.

5    Open the hood and cover the fenders and cowl using special pads. An old bedspread or blanket will also work. Remove the air intake duct and the air filter housing (see Chapter 4).

6    On Civic models, remove the plastic fasteners and the upper cover above the grille.

7    On Civic models, remove the wiper arms, the wiper cowl and both ends (see Chapter 11). Remove the fasteners and the lower cowl panel from the vehicle.

8    On all models, remove the air intake duct and the air filter housing (see Chapter 4, Section 10). Remove the air filter housing bolts and the bracket.

9    Remove the battery, battery tray and, if equipped, the battery bracket (see Chapter 5).

10    Remove the PCM and bracket from the engine compartment (see Chapter 6, Section 16).

11    On CR-V and Civic CVT models, disconnect the shift cable from the transaxle (see Section 3).

12    Clearly label and disconnect all vacuum lines, emissions hoses, electrical connectors and wiring harness clamps/brackets that may interfere with transaxle removal. Masking tape and/or a touch up paint applicator work well for marking items. Take instant photos or sketch the locations of components and brackets.

13    Disconnect the automatic transaxle fluid cooler lines from the transaxle. Be sure to position a pan to catch excess fluid. Plug the lines to prevent leakage.

14    On 2015 and later CR-V models, unbolt the ATF warmer from the transaxle. Be pre-

pared to catch any fluid that leaks. Replace the O-rings. Remove the high pressure fuel pump cover and the fuel pump bracket.

15    On all models, support the engine with an engine support fixture or an engine hoist (an engine support fixture is recommended, as it doesn't have legs that extend under the vehicle that would get in the way). Connect the sling or chain to the lifting hook at the end of the engine near the transaxle, not to the lifting eye on the transaxle. If no lifting hook is provided, use the threaded hole(s) in the cylinder head to attach the sling or chain.

16    Remove the upper transaxle-to-engine bolts.

17    Disconnect the ground cable and remove the transaxle mount and bracket.

18    Loosen the front wheel lug nuts, then raise the vehicle and support it securely on jackstands. Remove the wheels.

19    Remove the engine splash shield (see Chapter 2A, Section 5) and the inner fender splash shields (see Chapter 11, Section 12).

20    Drain the transaxle fluid (see Chapter 1). Be sure to use a new sealing washer when you reinstall the drain plug.

21    Remove the subframe (see Chapter 10, Section 19).

22    On Civic and 2014 and earlier CR-V models, unbolt the ATF warmer from the transaxle. Be prepared to catch any fluid that leaks. Replace the O-rings.

23    On all models, remove the torque converter cover.

24    Mark the relationship of the torque converter (conventional transaxle) or the flywheel (CVT) to the driveplate so that they can be reinstalled in the same relationship to one another (see illustration).

25    Remove the torque converter-to-driveplate bolts one at a time by rotating the crankshaft pulley for access to each bolt.

26    Remove the driveaxles, intermediate shaft and on AWD/4WD CR-V models, the driveshaft (see Chapter 8).

27    On CR-V models, remove the catalytic converter and pipe. If AWD/4WD, remove the transfer case (see Chapter 8, Section 14).

28    On all models, remove the engine torque rod and bracket (if equipped) (see illustration).

29    On Civic non-CVT models, disconnect the shift cable from the transaxle (see Section 3).

30    On all models, support the transaxle with a jack, preferably one made for this purpose. Secure the transaxle to the jack with straps or chains.

31    Remove the remaining transaxle-to-engine bolts.

32    Move the transaxle back to disengage it from the engine block dowel pins and make sure the torque converter is detached from the driveplate. Secure the torque converter to the transaxle so it will not fall out during removal. Lower the transaxle from the vehicle.

**Note:** *It may be necessary to slowly lower the engine a slight amount while the jack supporting the transaxle is being lowered. This will provide more clearance between the transaxle and the body.*

### Installation

33    Honda recommends flushing the transaxle cooler and the cooler hoses and lines with solvent whenever the transaxle is removed from the vehicle. Flush the lines and fluid cooler thoroughly and make sure no solvent remains in the lines or cooler after flushing. It's a good idea to repeat the flushing procedure with clean automatic transaxle fluid to ensure that no solvent remains in the lines or cooler.

34    Prior to installation, make sure that the torque converter hub is securely engaged in the transaxle pump. With the transaxle secured to the jack, raise it into position. Be sure to keep it level so the torque converter does not slide out.

35    Line-up the marks you made on the

torque converter and driveplate.

36   Make sure the dowel pins are still installed, then move the transaxle forward carefully until the dowel pins are engaged with the holes in the engine block.

37   Install the transaxle-to-engine bolts and tighten them to the torque listed in this Chapter's Specifications.

**Caution:** *Don't use the bolts to force the transaxle and engine together. If the transaxle doesn't slide easily up against the engine, find out why before you tighten the bolts.*

38   The remainder of installation is the reverse of the removal procedure, noting the following points:

a)   *Tighten subframe mounting bolts to the torque listed in the Chapter 10 Specifications.*

b)   *Install all of the driveplate bolts before tightening any of them. Tighten the driveplate bolts to the torque listed in this Chapter's Specifications.*

c)   *Tighten the driveaxle/hub nuts to the torque listed in the Chapter 8 Specifications.*

d)   *Use new O-rings on the ATF warmer.*

e)   *Tighten the wheel lug nuts to the torque listed in the Chapter 1 Specifications.*

f)   *Refill the transaxle with the specified type and amount of lubricant (see Chapter 1). Note that the transaxle may require more fluid than in a normal fluid and filter change, since the torque converter may be empty (the converter is not drained during a fluid change).*

g)   *Start the engine, set the parking brake and shift the transaxle through all gears three times. Make sure the shift cable is adjusted properly (see Section 3).*

h)   *Allow the engine to reach its proper operating temperature with the transaxle in Park or Neutral, then turn it off and check the fluid level again.*

i)   *Road test the vehicle and check for fluid leaks.*

## 8   Automatic transaxle overhaul - general information

1    In the event of a problem occurring, it will be necessary to establish whether the fault is electrical, mechanical or hydraulic in nature, before repair work can be contemplated. Diagnosis requires detailed knowledge of the transmission's operation and construction, as well as access to specialized test equipment, and so is deemed to be beyond the scope of this manual. It is therefore essential that problems with the automatic transmission are referred to a dealer service department or other qualified repair facility for assessment.

2    Note that a faulty transmission should not be removed before the vehicle has been diagnosed by a knowledgeable technician equipped with the proper tools, as troubleshooting must be performed with the transmission installed in the vehicle.

# Notes

# Chapter 8
# Clutch and driveline

## Contents

## Specifications

| | |
|---|---|
| Clutch fluid type | See Chapter 1 |
| Driveshaft runout (CR-V AWD and 4WD models) | 0.06 inch (1.5 mm) |
| Clutch pedal | |
| Pedal height | |
| With pedal pad cover | 6.1 inches (156 mm) |
| Without pedal pad cover | 5.9 inches (151 mm) |
| Pedal freeplay | 0.28 to 0.71 inch (7 to 18 mm) |

## Torque specifications

**Note:** *One foot-pound (ft-lb) of torque is equivalent to 12 inch-pounds (in-lbs) of torque. Torque values below approximately 15 ft-lbs are expressed in inch-pounds, since most foot-pound torque wrenches are not accurate at these smaller values.*

| | Ft-lbs (unless otherwise indicated) | Nm |
|---|---|---|
| Clutch master cylinder mounting nuts | 108 in-lbs | 13 |
| Clutch pressure plate-to-flywheel bolts | | |
| 1.8L models | 18 | 25 |
| 2.4L models | 19 | 26 |
| Clutch release cylinder mounting fasteners | 16 | 22 |
| Differential mounting bolts (AWD CR-V models) | | |
| Upper bracket to differential housing | 44 | 59 |
| Upper bracket to floorpan | 32 | 44 |
| Left and right brackets | | |
| Brackets to differential housing bolts | 44 | 59 |
| Brackets to frame bushing bolt and nut | 47 | 64 |
| Differential pinion flange locknut (AWD CR-V models) | | |
| AWD models | 80 | 108 |
| 2015 and later 4WD models | 108 | 147 |

## Torque specifications (continued)

| | Ft-lbs (unless otherwise indicated) | Nm |
|---|---|---|
| Driveshaft center support bearing mounting bolts (AWD CR-V models) | 29 | 39 |
| Driveshaft-to-differential pinion flange bolts (AWD CR-V models) ......... | 24 | 32 |
| Driveshaft-to-transfer case pinion flange bolts (AWD and 4WD CR-V models) ....................................................... | 24 | 32 |
| Driveaxle hub/nut | | |
| 1.8L models............................................................................... | 133 | 181 |
| 2.4L Civic models...................................................................... | 181 | 245 |
| CR-V models | | |
| Front ...................................................................................... | 242 | 328 |
| Rear (AWD models) | | |
| 2014 and earlier models ......................................................... | 133 | 181 |
| 2015 and later models............................................................. | 181 | 245 |
| Intermediate shaft bearing support mounting bolts ............................. | 29 | 39 |
| Transfer case mounting bolts (AWD CR-V models) ............................. | 32 | 44 |
| Wheel lug nuts........................................................................................ | See Chapter 1 | |

## 1  General Information

1    The information in this Chapter deals with the components from the rear of the engine to the drive wheels, except for the transaxle, which is dealt with in the previous Chapter.

2    Since nearly all the procedures covered in this Chapter involve working under the vehicle, make sure it's securely supported on sturdy jackstands or on a hoist where the vehicle can be easily raised and lowered.

## 2  Clutch - description and check

1    All vehicles with a manual transaxle use a single dry-plate, diaphragm-spring type clutch. The clutch disc has a splined hub which allows it to slide along the splines of the transaxle input shaft. The clutch and pressure plate are held in contact by spring pressure exerted by the diaphragm in the pressure plate.

2    The clutch release system is operated by hydraulic pressure. The hydraulic release system consists of the clutch pedal, a master cylinder and fluid reservoir, the hydraulic line, a release (or slave) cylinder which actuates the clutch release lever and the clutch release (or throwout) bearing.

3    When pressure is applied to the clutch pedal to release the clutch, hydraulic pressure is exerted against the outer end of the clutch release lever. As the lever pivots the shaft fingers push against the release bearing. The bearing pushes against the fingers of the diaphragm spring of the pressure plate assembly, which in turn releases the clutch plate.

4    Terminology can be a problem when discussing the clutch components because common names are in some cases different from those used by the manufacturer. For example, the driven plate is also called the clutch plate or disc, the clutch release bearing is sometimes called a throwout bearing, the release cylinder is sometimes called the operating or slave cylinder.

5    Other than to replace components with obvious damage, some preliminary checks should be performed to diagnose clutch problems. These checks assume that the transaxle is in good working condition.

a) *The first check should be of the fluid level in the clutch master cylinder (see Chapter 1). If the fluid level is low, add fluid as necessary and inspect the hydraulic system for leaks. If the master cylinder reservoir has run dry, bleed the system as described in Section 5 and retest the clutch operation.*

b) *To check clutch spin-down time, run the engine at normal idle speed with the transaxle in Neutral (clutch pedal up - engaged). Disengage the clutch (pedal down), wait several seconds and shift the transaxle into Reverse. No grinding noise should be heard. A grinding noise*

would most likely indicate a problem in the pressure plate or the clutch disc.

c) *To check for complete clutch release, run the engine (with the parking brake applied to prevent movement) and hold the clutch pedal approximately 1/2-inch from the floor. Shift the transaxle between 1st gear and Reverse several times. If the shift is rough, component failure is indicated. Check the release cylinder pushrod travel. With the clutch pedal depressed completely, the release cylinder pushrod should extend substantially. If it doesn't, check the fluid level in the clutch master cylinder.*

d) *Visually inspect the pivot bushing at the top of the clutch pedal to make sure there is no binding or excessive play.*

e) *Crawl under the vehicle and make sure the clutch release lever is solidly mounted on the ball stud.*

## 3  Clutch master cylinder - removal and installation

### *Removal*

1    Remove the center cowl cover and the under cowl panel (see Chapter 11).

2    Working under the dashboard, remove the cotter pin or spring clip from the master cylinder pushrod clevis. Pull out the clevis pin to disconnect the pushrod from the pedal. Unscrew the two clutch master cylinder retaining nuts.

3    Use a syringe or other suitable method, to remove and properly dispose of the hydraulic fluid from the clutch master cylinder reservoir.

**Caution:** *Don't allow brake fluid to come into contact with the paint as it will damage the finish.*

4    Remove the air filter housing and air cleaner bracket (see Chapter 4). Release the clutch hydraulic line from the retaining clamp that secures it to the coolant line. On 1.8L models, remove the battery and battery tray (see Chapter 5), the brake fluid reservoir (see Chapter 9) and ECM/PCM harness. The ECM/PCM connectors are labeled with symbols to identify their locations.

5    Disconnect the steel clutch line from the fitting where it joins the flexible clutch hose. Have rags handy as some fluid will be lost as the line is removed. Cap or plug the ends of the line (and/or hose) to prevent fluid leakage and the entry of contaminants. Clamp a pair of locking pliers onto the clutch fluid feed hose, a couple of inches downstream of the reservoir. The pliers should be just tight enough to prevent fluid flow when the hose is disconnected.

6    Remove the clutch master cylinder from the firewall with the hydraulic fluid reservoir and hydraulic lines still attached, then disconnect the clutch fluid feed hose and the hydraulic line at the cylinder. Again, have rags handy and cap or plug the ends of the lines (and/or hose) to prevent fluid leakage.

**Caution:** *Don't allow brake fluid to come into contact with the paint as it will damage the finish.*

### *Installation*

7    Installation is the reverse of removal, noting the following points:

a) *Use new gasket between the master cylinder and the firewall. Tighten the master cylinder mounting nuts to the torque listed in this Chapter's Specifications.*

b) *Install a new O-ring seal and retainer clip on the hydraulic line fitting at the master cylinder.*

c) *Fill the clutch master cylinder reservoir with brake fluid conforming to DOT 3 specifications and bleed the clutch system as outlined in Section 5.*

## 4  Clutch release cylinder - removal and installation

### *Removal*

1    Remove the intake air ducts and air filter housing (see Chapter 4).

2    On models so equipped, remove the hydraulic line bracket mounting bolt and bracket.

3    Use a flare nut wrench to disconnect the hydraulic line from the release cylinder. Have a small can and rags handy - some fluid will be spilled as the line is removed. Plug the line to prevent excessive fluid loss.

4    Remove the cylinder mounting bolts and remove the cylinder.

### *Installation*

5    Install the hydraulic line to the release cylinder. Use a second wrench to hold the connection fitting and tighten the flare nut.

6    Lightly lubricate the release cylinder pushrod and the release fork pocket with high temperature grease. Install but do not tighten the release cylinder onto the clutch housing. Make sure the pushrod is seated in the release fork pocket, then tighten the mounting bolts to the torque listed in this Chapter's Specifications.

7    The remainder of installation is the reverse of removal, noting the following points:

a) *Fill the clutch master cylinder with brake fluid conforming to DOT 3 specifications.*

b) *Bleed the system as described in Section 5.*

## 5  Clutch hydraulic system - bleeding

1    Bleed the hydraulic system whenever any part of the system has been removed or the fluid level has fallen so low that air has been drawn into the master cylinder. The bleeding procedure is very similar to bleeding a brake system.

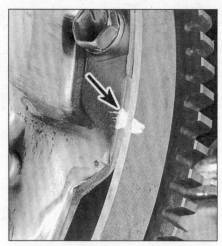

6.5 Mark the relationship of the pressure plate to the flywheel (if you're planning to re-use the old pressureplate)

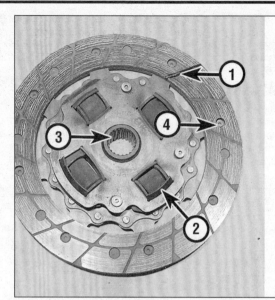

6.9 The clutch disc

1   **Lining** - *this will wear down in use*
2   **Springs or dampers** - *check for cracking and deformation*
3   **Splined hub** - *the splines must not be worn and should slide smoothly on the transmission input shaft splines*
4   **Rivets** - *these secure the lining and will damage the flywheel or pressure plate if allowed to contact the surfaces*

2    Fill the master cylinder with new brake fluid conforming to DOT 3 specifications.
**Caution:** *Do not re-use any of the fluid coming from the system during the bleeding operation or use fluid which has been inside an open container for an extended period of time.*
3    Remove the air filter housing and intake duct (see Chapter 4).
4    Remove the dust cap from the bleeder valve and push a length of plastic hose over the valve. Place the other end of the hose into a clear container with about two inches of brake fluid. The hose end must be in the fluid at the bottom of the container.
5    Have an assistant depress the clutch pedal and hold it. Open the bleeder valve on the release cylinder, allowing fluid to flow through the hose. Close the bleeder valve when the flow of fluid (and bubbles) ceases. Once closed, have your assistant release the pedal.
6    Continue this process until all air is evacuated from the system, indicated by a solid stream of fluid being ejected from the bleeder valve each time with no air bubbles in the hose or container. Keep a close watch on the fluid level inside the clutch master cylinder reservoir - if the level drops too far, air will get into the system and you'll have to start all over again.
7    Check carefully for proper operation before placing the vehicle into normal service.
8    If you're working on a CR-V or hatchback model, before reconnecting the battery, refer to Chapter 5.

## 6   Clutch components - removal, inspection and installation

**Warning:** *Dust produced by clutch wear is hazardous to your health. DO NOT blow it out with compressed air and DO NOT inhale it. DO NOT use gasoline or petroleum-based*

solvents to remove the dust. Brake system cleaner should be used to flush the dust into a drain pan. After the clutch components are wiped clean with a rag, dispose of the contaminated rags and cleaner in a covered, marked container.

### Removal
1    Access to the clutch components is normally accomplished by removing the transaxle, leaving the engine in the vehicle. If the engine is being removed for major overhaul, check the clutch for wear and replace worn components as necessary. However, the relatively low cost of the clutch components compared to the time and trouble spent gaining access to them warrants their replacement anytime the engine or transaxle is removed, unless they are new or in near-perfect condition. The following procedures are based on the assumption the engine will stay in place.
2    Remove the transaxle from the vehicle (see Chapter 7A). Support the engine while the transaxle is out. Preferably, an engine support fixture or a hoist should be used to support it from above.
3    The clutch fork and release bearing can remain attached to the transaxle housing for the time being.
4    To support the clutch disc during removal, install a clutch alignment tool through the clutch disc hub.
5    Carefully inspect the flywheel and pressure plate for indexing marks. The marks are usually an X, an O or a white letter. If they cannot be found, scribe or paint marks yourself so the pressure plate and the flywheel will be in the same alignment during installation (see illustration).
6    Turning each bolt a little at a time, loosen the pressure plate-to-flywheel bolts. Work in a criss-cross pattern until all spring pressure is relieved. Then hold the pressure plate securely and completely remove the bolts, followed by the pressure plate and clutch disc.

### Inspection
7    Ordinarily, when a problem occurs in the clutch, it can be attributed to wear of the clutch driven plate assembly (clutch disc). However, all components should be inspected at this time.
8    Inspect the flywheel for cracks, heat checking, grooves and other obvious defects. If the imperfections are slight, a machine shop can machine the surface flat and smooth, which is highly recommended regardless of the surface appearance. Refer to Chapter 2A for the flywheel removal and installation procedure.
9    Inspect the lining on the clutch disc. There should be at least 1/16-inch of lining above the rivet heads. Check for loose rivets, distortion, cracks, broken springs and other obvious damage (see illustration). As mentioned earlier in this Section, ordinarily the clutch disc is routinely replaced, so if in doubt about the condition, replace it with a new one.
10   The release bearing should also be replaced along with the clutch disc (see Section 7).
11   Check the machined surfaces and the diaphragm spring fingers of the pressure plate (see illustrations). If the surface is grooved or otherwise damaged, replace the pressure plate. Also check for obvious damage, distortion, cracking, etc. Light glazing can be removed with emery cloth or sandpaper. If a new pressure plate is required, new and re-manufactured units are available.

### Pilot bushing replacement
12   Remove the pilot bushing using a slide hammer and puller attachment (see illustration), which are available at most auto parts stores or tool rental yards.
13   To install a new pilot bushing, lightly lubricate the outside surface with grease, then drive it into the recess with a bearing driver or a socket (see illustration).

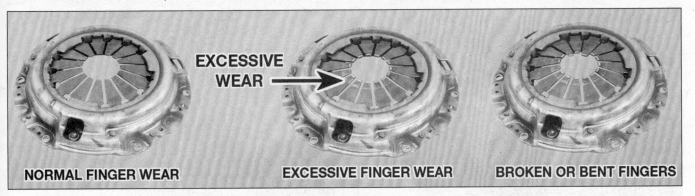

6.11a Replace the pressure plate if excessive wear or damage is noted

6.11b Inspect the pressure plate surface for excessive score marks, cracks and signs of overheating

6.12 A small slide hammer is handy for removing a pilot bushing

6.13 Tap the bushing into place with a bearing driver or a socket that is slightly smaller than the outside diameter of the bearing

## Installation

14   Before installation, clean the flywheel and pressure plate machined surfaces with brake cleaner. It's important that no oil or grease is on these surfaces or on the lining of the clutch disc. Handle the parts only with clean hands.

15   Position the clutch disc and pressure plate against the flywheel. Use a clutch alignment tool to hold the clutch in place (see illustration). Make sure the disc is installed properly (most replacement clutch discs will be marked "flywheel side" or something similar - if not marked, install the clutch disc with the damper springs toward the transaxle).

16   Align the indexing marks on the pressure plate and flywheel then insert the pressure plate-to-flywheel bolts but only finger tight, working around the pressure plate.

17   Center the clutch disc by ensuring the alignment tool extends through the splined hub and into the pilot bearing in the crankshaft. Wiggle the tool up, down or side-to-side as needed to center the disc. Tighten the pressure plate-to-flywheel bolts a little at a time, working in a criss-cross pattern to prevent distorting the cover. After all of the bolts are snug, tighten them to the torque listed in

this Chapter's Specifications. Remove the alignment tool.

18   Using high-temperature grease, lubricate the inner groove of the release bearing (see Section 7). Also place a small amount of grease on the release lever contact areas and the transaxle input shaft bearing retainer.

19   Install the clutch release bearing (see Section 7).

20   Install the transaxle and all components removed previously.

## 7   Clutch release bearing and lever - removal, inspection and installation

**Warning:** *Dust produced by clutch wear is hazardous to your health. DO NOT blow it out with compressed air and DO NOT inhale it. DO NOT use gasoline or petroleum-based solvents to remove the dust. Brake system cleaner should be used to flush the dust into a drain pan. After the clutch components are wiped clean with a rag, dispose of the contaminated rags and cleaner in a covered, marked container.*

6.15 Center the clutch disc in the pressure plate with a clutch alignment tool

## Removal

1   Remove the transaxle (see Chapter 7A).

2   Remove the rubber boot from the clutch release fork. Use a pair of pliers to squeeze the spring clip and pull the clutch release fork off the ballstud.

3   Slide the release bearing off the input shaft along with the release fork.

7.5 Hold the bearing by the outer race and rotate the inner race while applying pressure - if the bearing doesn't turn smoothly or if it's noisy, replace the bearing

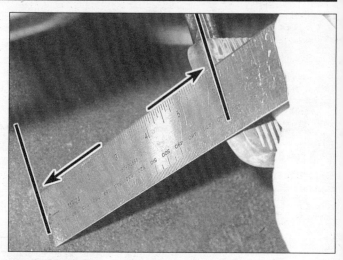

8.1 Pedal height is the distance between the pedal and the floor

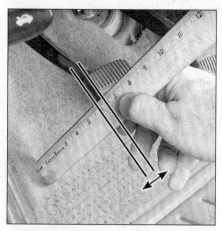

8.5 Pedal freeplay is the distance the pedal travels before resistance is felt

10.2 Use a punch or chisel and unstake the driveaxle/hub nut

## Inspection

4    Wipe off the bearing with a clean rag and inspect it for damage, wear and cracks. Don't immerse the bearing in solvent - it's sealed for life and immersion in solvent will ruin it.

5    Hold the center of the bearing and rotate the outer portion while applying pressure (see illustration). If the bearing doesn't turn smoothly or if it's noisy or rough, replace it.

**Note:** *Considering the difficulty involved with replacing the release bearing, we recommend replacing the release bearing whenever the clutch components are replaced.*

## Installation

6    Lightly lubricate the friction surfaces of the release bearing, ballstud and the input shaft bearing retainer with high-temperature grease.

7    Install the release lever and bearing onto the input shaft.

8    The remainder of installation is the reverse of removal.

## 8    Clutch pedal adjustment

### Pedal height

1    The height of the clutch pedal is the distance the pedal sits off the floor with the carpet pulled back (see illustration). If the pedal height is not within the specified range, it must be adjusted.

2    To adjust the clutch pedal, loosen the locknut on the clutch start switch or adjusting bolt and back the switch out until it no longer touches the pedal, then loosen the locknut on the clutch pushrod. Turn the pushrod to adjust the pedal height, then tighten the locknut.

3    Turn the switch or bolt clockwise until it just contacts the pedal arm, then turn it in an additional 3/4 to 1 turn. Tighten the locknut.

4    Adjust the clutch start switch as described in Section 9.

### Pedal freeplay

5    The freeplay is the pedal slack, or the distance the pedal can be depressed before it begins to have any effect on the clutch system (see illustration). If the pedal freeplay is not within the specified range, it must be adjusted.

6    To adjust the pedal freeplay, loosen the locknut on the clutch pushrod. Then back off the pushrod to adjust the pedal freeplay to the specified range and retighten the locknut.

7    Check and, if necessary, adjust the clutch start switch (see Section 9).

## 9    Clutch start switch - replacement

1    Unplug the switch electrical connector.

2    Loosen the locknut and unscrew the switch from the clutch pedal bracket.

3    Installation is the reverse of removal. To adjust the switch, loosen the locknut and turn the switch in or out, as necessary, to provide continuity through the switch when the clutch pedal is depressed.

## 10    Driveaxles - removal and installation

### Front
#### Removal

1    Loosen the front wheel lug nuts, raise the vehicle and support it securely on jackstands. Remove the wheel.

2    Unstake the driveaxle/hub nut with a punch or chisel (see illustration).

**10.3 To prevent the hub from turning while you're loosening the driveaxle/hub nut, wedge a prybar or punch into the slots in the brake disc**

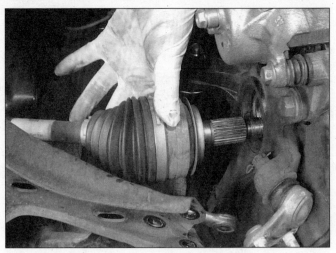

**10.5 Swing the steering knuckle out to free the outer end of the driveaxle**

**10.7 Use a large screwdriver or a prybar to pop the inner end of the driveaxle from the transaxle or intermediate shaft**

**10.9a Pry the old spring clip from the inner end of the driveaxle with a small screwdriver or awl**

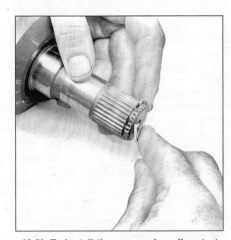

**10.9b To install the new spring clip, start one end in the groove and work the clip over the shaft end, into the groove**

3    Loosen the driveaxle/hub nut with a large socket and breaker bar (see illustration), then remove the driveaxle/hub nut from the axle and discard it.

4    Separate the balljoint from the control arm (see Chapter 10).

5    Swing the knuckle/hub assembly out (away from the vehicle) until the end of the driveaxle is free of the hub. Support the outer end of the driveaxle with a piece of wire to avoid unnecessary strain on the inner CV joint (see illustration).

**Note:** *If the driveaxle splines stick in the hub, tap on the end of the driveaxle with a plastic hammer.*

6    Remove the engine lower splash shield (see Chapter 2A, illustrations 14.3a and 14.3b)

7    Place a drain pan under the transaxle where you are working to catch any oil that may run out. Pry the inner CV joint out of the transaxle (or, on models so equipped, the intermediate shaft) using a large screwdriver or prybar (see illustration).

**Caution:** *Avoid pulling on the driveaxle to remove it or the inner CV joint could come apart. Pry the inner CV joint straight out to prevent damage to the seal.*

8    Support the CV joints and carefully remove the driveaxle from the vehicle.

### Installation

9    Pry the old spring clip from the inner end of the driveaxle (or, on models so equipped, the outer end of the intermediate shaft) and install a new one (see illustrations).

10    Installation is the reverse of removal, noting the following:

a)  *Apply a film of multi-purpose grease around the splines of the joints.*

b)  *When installing the driveaxle, hold the driveaxle straight out, then push it in sharply to seat the driveaxle spring clip.*

c)  *Clean all foreign matter from the driveaxle outer CV joint threads and coat the splines with multi-purpose grease. Guide the driveaxle into the hub splines and*

*install the new driveaxle/hub nut. Tighten the nut securely but not to the specified torque at this time.*

d)  *Reconnect the balljoint to the control arm, then tighten the fasteners to the torque listed in the Chapter 10 Specifications.*

e)  *Tighten the driveaxle/hub nut to the torque listed in this Chapter's Specifications.*

f)  *Install the wheel and lug nuts, then lower the vehicle.*

g)  *Tighten the wheel lug nuts to the torque listed in the Chapter 1 Specifications.*

h)  *Add transaxle lubricant if it was drained or if any fluid spilled out (see Chapter 1).*

### *Intermediate shaft*

#### Removal

11    Loosen the right front wheel lug nuts, raise the vehicle and support it securely on jackstands. Remove the wheel.

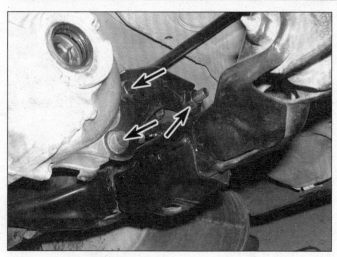

10.29 Differential mounting bracket bolts

10.30 Upper differential bracket-to-floorpan bolts

12   Remove the engine lower splash shield (see Chapter 2A, illustrations 14.3a and 14.3b).
13   Separate the lower control arm from the steering knuckle (see Chapter 10).
14   Pry the driveaxle inner CV joint from the intermediate shaft (see Step 7). Remove the set-ring from the end of the intermediate shaft.
15   Use a jack to support the engine, then remove the lower torque rod bolts and lower torque rod bracket (see Chapter 2A or 2B).
16   Remove the cover from the crankshaft position sensor.
17   Remove the bearing support mounting bolts and slide the intermediate shaft out of the transaxle. Be careful not to damage the transaxle seal when pulling the shaft out.
18   Check the support bearing for smooth operation by turning the shaft while holding the bearing. If you feel any roughness, take the intermediate shaft to an automotive machine shop or other qualified repair facility to have a new bearing installed.

### Installation
19   Install a new spring clip on the end of the intermediate shaft.
20   Lubricate the lips of the transaxle seal with multi-purpose grease. Carefully guide the intermediate shaft into the transaxle side gear then install the mounting bolts for the bearing support. Tighten the bolts to the torque listed in this Chapter's Specifications.
21   The remainder of installation is the reverse of removal.

## Rear (4WD CR-V models)
### Removal
22   Remove the wheel cover or hub cap. Loosen the wheel lug nuts. Unstake the driveaxle/hub nut with a punch or chisel (see illustration 10.2), then break the hub nut loose with a socket and large breaker bar.
23   Raise the rear of the vehicle and sup-

port it securely on jackstands. Block the front wheels to prevent the vehicle from rolling. Remove the wheel.
24   Remove the driveaxle/hub nut from the axle and discard it.
**Note:** *The rear driveaxles can be removed without draining the differential fluid but some may leak out during the process. Have some rags and a drain pan ready as well as some new oil to replace what was lost.*
25   Make reference marks where the rear driveshaft connects to the pinion flange so you can install the driveshaft in the same position to keep it in proper balance.
26   Remove the four bolts and separate the rear driveshaft from the rear pinion flange. Do not allow the driveshaft to hang by the center support bearing, use a loop of wire to suspend the driveshaft out of the way.
27   Disconnect the electrical connectors and the multiple breather hoses from the rear differential housing.
28   Use a transmission jack or floor jack to support the rear differential housing.
29   Remove and discard the fasteners from the left and right differential mounting brackets (see illustration).
30   Remove the two bolts and their circular plates that fasten the upper differential mounting bracket to the floorpan (see illustration).
31   Slowly lower the jack while insuring that all wire and hose connections are disconnected. As the differential lowers out of the vehicle, pry the left and right inner CV joints from the differential housing, being careful not to damage the CV joints or the differential housing.
32   Pull on the outer CV joint to remove it from the rear hub, being careful not to damage the wheelspeed sensor. If the splines are stuck in the rear hub, use a plastic hammer to tap the driveaxle out. Do not pull on the driveaxle or the outer joint may come apart.

### Installation
33   Pry the old set-ring from the inner end of the driveaxle and install a new one (see illustrations 10.8a and 10.8b).
34   Apply a light film of grease to the outer CV joint splines and insert the outer end of the driveaxle into the hub.
35   Apply a light film of grease to the area on the inner CV joint stub shaft where the seal rides. Raise the differential and insert the splined end of both inner CV joints into the differential. Make sure the spring clips lock into place.
36   The remainder of installation is the reverse of removal, noting the following:
37   When installing the upper differential bracket to the floorpan, rotate the circular plates to align with the tabs on the rubber bushings. Note that the heat insulator, if equipped, is installed on the right side.
38   Use all new fasteners when installing the left and right differential mounting brackets. Install the brackets on the differential housing first and tighten to the specified torque. Then install but do not tighten the bolts securing the brackets to the frame. Lower the jack then tighten the bolts to the specified torque.
39   Install a new driveaxle/hub nut. Tighten the hub nut securely, but don't try to tighten it to the actual torque specification until you've lowered the vehicle to the ground.
40   Install the wheel and lug nuts, then lower the vehicle. Tighten the lug nuts to the torque listed in the Chapter 1 Specifications.
41   Tighten the driveaxle/hub nut to the torque listed in this Chapter's Specifications, then use a hammer and a punch to stake the collar of the nut into the slot in the driveaxle. Install the wheel cover or hub cap.
42   Check the differential lubricant, adding as necessary to bring it to the appropriate level (see Chapter 1). Use a new sealing washer on the fill plug.

11.3 Mark the relationship of the driveshaft to the differential pinion flange and the transfer case flange

11.4 Immobilize the driveshaft by placing a screwdriver into the universal joint while loosening the bolts

11.5 Remove the driveshaft safety loops

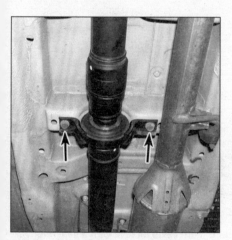

11.6 The driveshaft center support bearing is retained by two bolts

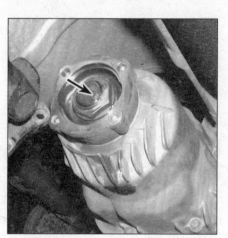

12.3 Insert a punch into the slot and unstake the pinion flange nut before unscrewing it

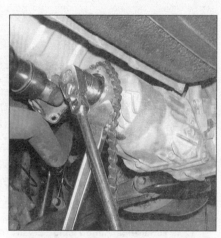

12.4 A chain wrench can be used to prevent the pinion flange from turning when loosening the nut

## 11  Driveshaft (4WD CR-V models) - removal and installation

1    Raise the rear of the vehicle and support it securely on jackstands. Block the front wheels to prevent the vehicle from rolling. Place the transaxle in Neutral with the parking brake off.

2    Remove the bolts and clips from the front underfloor splash shield and remove the shield. Do the same for the left middle underfloor splash shield.

3    Make reference marks on the driveshaft flanges, the differential pinion flange and the transfer case pinion flange in line with each other (see illustration). This is to make sure the driveshaft is installed in the same position to preserve the balance.

4    Remove the rear universal joint bolts. Turn the driveshaft (or wheels) as necessary to bring the bolts into the most accessible position. Insert a screwdriver into the joint while loosening the bolts to prevent the shaft from turning (see illustration).

5    Unbolt the driveshaft safety loops from the floorpan (see illustration).

6    Unbolt the center support bearing from the floorpan (see illustration).

7    Unbolt the front of the driveshaft from the transfer case flange and remove the driveshaft assembly.

8    Installation is the reverse of the removal procedure. Be sure to align the marks on the flanges and tighten all fasteners to the torque values listed in this Chapter's Specifications.

## 12  Differential oil seals (4WD CR-V models) - replacement

### Pinion oil seal

1    Raise the rear of the vehicle and support it securely on jackstands. Place the transaxle in Neutral with the parking brake off. Block the

front wheels to prevent the vehicle from rolling.

**Note:** *The pinion seal can be replaced without draining the differential fluid, but some may leak out during the process. Have some rags and a drain pan ready as well as some new oil to replace what was lost.*

2    Mark the relationship of the driveshaft to the pinion flange, then unbolt the driveshaft from the flange (see Section 11). Suspend the driveshaft with a piece of wire (don't let it hang by the center support bearing).

3    Using a hammer and a punch, unstake the pinion flange nut (see illustration).

4    A flange holding tool will be required to keep the companion flange from moving while the self-locking pinion nut is loosened. A chain wrench will also work (see illustration).

5    Loosen the locking nut slightly then tighten again to align it with the groove the on the shaft. Carefully clean any dirt from the groove.

6    Remove the locking nut, spring washer,

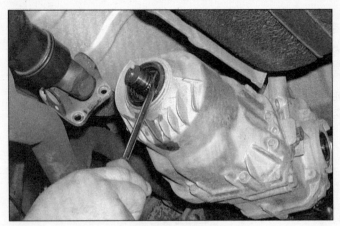

**12.8 Carefully pry out the old seal . . .**

**12.9 . . . and drive the new one in with a seal installation tool or a socket with an outside diameter slightly smaller than that of the seal**

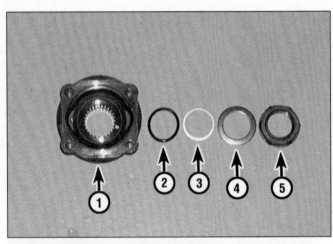

**12.12 Differential pinion flange details (4WD CR-V models)**

| | | | |
|---|---|---|---|
| 1 | Pinion flange | 4 | Spring washer |
| 2 | O-ring | 5 | Nut |
| 3 | Back-up ring | | |

**12.21 Carefully pry out the driveaxle oil seal with a seal removal tool or a large screwdriver; make sure you don't scratch the seal bore**

back-up ring and O-ring. Discard the O-ring and the back-up ring. You will need a new locking nut as well but keep the old one for now to use in the installation steps.

7    Withdraw the flange. It may be necessary to use a two-jaw puller engaged behind the flange to draw it off. Do not attempt to pry or hammer behind the flange or hammer on the end of the pinion shaft.

8    Pry out the old seal and discard it (see illustration).

9    Lubricate the lips of the new seal and fill the space between the seal lips with wheel bearing grease, then tap it evenly into position with a seal installation tool or a large socket (see illustration). Make sure it enters the housing squarely and is driven in until its flush with the end of the housing.

10    Install the pinion flange onto the shaft. Use a seal installation tool or large socket to evenly drive on the flange until two or three threads appear.

**Note:** *Do not hammer directly on the pinion flange. Doing so will result in a damaged*

*flange and could ruin the new seal.*

11    Apply a thin film of oil to the old pinion flange nut and install it on the shaft. Tighten the nut (you will need the flange holding tool or chain wrench again) until the flange is fully seated. Remove and discard the old pinion flange nut.

12    Install a new O-ring, (lubricated with clean differential lubricant), new back-up ring, spring washer (with the concave side facing the flange), and a new nut (see illustration).

13    Tighten the new nut to the torque listed in this Chapter's Specifications, then stake the collar of the nut into the slot in the pinion shaft.

14    Reconnect the driveshaft to the pinion flange (see Section 11).

15    Check the differential lubricant level and add some, if necessary, to bring it to the appropriate level (see Chapter 1).

### Driveaxle oil seals

16    Raise the rear of the vehicle and support it securely on jackstands. Place the transaxle

in Neutral with the parking brake off. Block the front wheels to prevent the vehicle from rolling.

17    Remove the drain plug and drain the fluid from the rear differential housing.

18    Remove both driveaxles from the rear differential housing (see Section 10). There is no need to remove the outer driveaxle nuts, the outer ends of the driveaxles can stay in the hubs. Do not allow the driveaxles to hang unsupported on the outer CV joints. Use wire to hold the inner ends of the driveaxles.

19    Remove and discard the set-ring from the inner ends of both driveaxles.

20    With the differential housing lowered, remove and discard the bolts that secure the upper mounting bracket to the differential housing, remove the bracket from the housing. It may be easier to do this with the differential housing pulled out from under the vehicle.

21    Use a seal removal tool to pry the seal(s) from the case (see illustration).

22    Using a seal installer or a large deep

socket as a drift, install the new oil seal. Drive it into the bore squarely until the outer face of the seal is flush with the machined outer surface of the seal bore (see illustration).

23   Installation is the reverse of removal. See Section 10 and note the following:

24   Use new bolts when installing the upper bracket to the differential housing.

25   Install new set-rings to the inner ends of both driveaxles.

26   Lubricate the lip of the driveaxle seals with multi-purpose grease before installing the driveaxles. Be careful not to damage the lip of the seals.

27   Use new sealing washers on the fluid drain and fill plugs. Refill the differential lubricant to bring it to the appropriate level (see Chapter 1).

**12.22 Use a seal installer or a large socket to install the new seal - whatever type of tool you use, make sure it doesn't contact the raised seal lip**

### 13   Differential (4WD CR-V models) - removal and installation

1   Raise the rear of the vehicle and support it securely on jackstands. Place the transaxle in Neutral with the parking brake off. Block the front wheels to prevent the vehicle from rolling.

2   Drain the differential lubricant (see Chapter 1).

3   Mark the relationship of the driveshaft to the pinion flange, then unbolt the driveshaft from the flange (see Section 11). Suspend the driveshaft with a piece of wire (don't let it hang by the center support bearing).

4   Remove both driveaxles from the rear differential housing (see Section 10). There is no need to remove the outer driveaxle nuts, the outer ends of the driveaxles can stay in the rear hubs. Do not allow the driveaxles to hang unsupported on the outer CV joints. Use a piece of wire to hold up the inner ends of the driveaxles.

5   With the differential housing lowered, remove and discard the bolts that secure the upper mounting bracket to the differential housing, remove the bracket from the hous-

ing. It may be easier to do this with the differential housing pulled out from under the vehicle.

6   Installation is the reverse of the removal procedure. See Section 10 and note the following: Tighten all fasteners to the torque values listed in this Chapter's Specifications. Fill the differential with the proper lubricant (see Chapter 1).

7   Use new bolts to install the upper mounting bracket to the differential housing.

8   Install new set-rings on the inner ends of the driveaxles.

9   Lubricate the lip of the driveaxle seals with multi-purpose grease before installing the driveaxles. Be careful not to damage the lip of the seals.

10   Fill the differential with the proper lubricant (see Chapter 1).

### 14   Transfer case (4WD CR-V models) - removal and installation

1   Raise the front of the vehicle and support it securely on jackstands.

2   Remove the bolts and fasteners that

secure the splash shield to the front bumper, front inner fender liner and body. Remove the shield.

3   Remove the bolts and fasteners from the front underfloor splash shield and remove this shield.

4   Mark the relationship of the driveshaft to the transfer case flange, then unbolt the driveshaft from the flange (see Section 11). Suspend the driveshaft with a piece of wire (don't let it hang by the center support bearing).

5   Drain the transaxle lubricant (see Chapter 1).

6   Remove the under-vehicle catalytic converter (see Chapter 6).

7   Remove the bolts securing the transfer case to the transaxle, note the locations of the short and long bolts and carefully remove the transfer case from the transaxle. There is one dowel pin that goes on the frontmost bolt.

8   Installation is the reverse of removal, noting the following points:

a) Install a new O-ring to the case.
b) Tighten the mounting bolts to the torque listed in this Chapter's Specifications.
c) Refill the transaxle with the proper type and amount of lubricant (see Chapter 1).

# Notes

# Chapter 9
# Brakes

## Contents

## Specifications

### General

| | |
|---|---|
| Brake fluid type | See Chapter 1 |
| Power brake booster pushrod-to-master cylinder piston clearance (with 20 in-Hg of vacuum applied to the booster) | 0.0 to 0.020 inch (0.0 to 0.5 mm) |
| Brake pedal height | |
| Civic | |
| Manual transaxle | |
| Except Si models | 5.87 - 6.26 inch (149 - 159 mm) |
| Si models | 5.94 - 6.34 inch (151 - 161 mm) |
| Automatic transaxle | 5.79 - 6.18 inch (147 - 157 mm) |
| CR-V models | 8.5 +/-.28 inch (216 +/- 7 mm) |
| Brake pedal freeplay | 3/64 to 13/64 inch (1 to 5 mm) |
| Parking brake adjustment | |
| Civic (rear disc brakes) | |
| Except Si | 8 to 10 clicks |
| Si models | 8 to 9 clicks |
| Civic (rear drum brakes) | 7 to 9 clicks |
| CR-V models | 5 to 6 clicks |

### Disc brakes

| | |
|---|---|
| Brake pad minimum thickness | See Chapter 1 |
| Disc lateral runout limit | 0016 inch (.04 mm) |
| Disc minimum thickness | Cast into disc |
| Parallelism (thickness variation) limit | 0.00059 inch (0.015 mm) |

### Drum brakes

| | |
|---|---|
| Maximum drum diameter | Cast into drum |
| Shoe lining minimum thickness | See Chapter 1 |

## Torque specifications

| | Ft-lbs (unless otherwise indicated) | Nm |
|---|---|---|

**Note:** *One foot-pound (ft-lb) of torque is equivalent to 12 inch-pounds (in-lbs) of torque. Torque values below approximately 15 ft-lbs are expressed in inch-pounds, since most foot-pound torque wrenches are not accurate at these smaller values.*

| | Ft-lbs (unless otherwise indicated) | Nm |
|---|---|---|
| Caliper mounting bracket bolts | | |
|   Civic | | |
|     Front | 80 | 108 |
|     Rear | 55 | 75 |
|   CR-V | | |
|     Front | 101 | 137 |
|     Rear | 80 | 108 |
| Caliper mounting bolts | | |
|   Civic | | |
|     Front | 25 | 34 |
|     Rear | 17 | 23 |
|   CR-V | | |
|     Front | | |
|       2WD (8 mm bolts) | 25 | 34 |
|       AWD (10 mm bolts) | 37 | 50 |
|     Rear | 17 | 23 |
| Master cylinder mounting nuts | 132 in-lbs | 15 |
| Power brake booster mounting bolts | 108 in-lbs | 12 |
| Brake reservoir bolt | 84 in-lbs | 9.5 |
| Wheel cylinder mounting bolts | 80 in-lbs | 9 |
| Wheel lug nuts | See Chapter 1 | |

## 1   General Information

### General

1   The vehicles covered by this manual are equipped with hydraulically operated front and rear brake systems. The front brakes are disc-type and the rear brakes are either disc or drum type brakes.

### Hydraulic system

2   The hydraulic system consists of two separate circuits. The master cylinder has separate reservoirs for the two circuits, and, in the event of a leak or failure in one hydraulic circuit, the other circuit will remain operative and a warning indicator will light up on the instrument panel when a substantial amount of brake fluid is lost, showing that a failure has occurred.

### Power brake booster

3   The power brake booster uses engine manifold vacuum to provide assistance to the brakes. It is mounted on the firewall in the engine compartment, directly behind the master cylinder.

### Parking brake

4   On models with rear disc brakes, control cables are routed to the rear axle, where they operate small drum brake shoes that apply pressure to the inner diameter of the rear brake discs. On models with drum brakes, the cables pull on levers that actuate the rear brake shoes.

### Service

5   After completing any operation involving disassembly of any part of the brake system, always test drive the vehicle to check for proper braking performance before resuming normal driving. When testing the brakes, perform the tests on a clean, dry, flat surface. Conditions other than these can lead to inaccurate test results.

6   Test the brakes at various speeds with both light and heavy pedal pressure. The vehicle should stop evenly without pulling to one side or the other. Under hard braking, the ABS system may engage, resulting in brake pedal pulsation. This is considered normal operation.

7   Tires, vehicle load and wheel alignment are factors which also affect braking performance.

### Precautions

8   There are some general cautions and warnings involving the brake system on this vehicle:

a)   *Use only brake fluid conforming to DOT 3 specifications.*

b)   *The brake pads and linings contain fibers which are hazardous to your health if inhaled. Whenever you work on brake system components, clean all parts with brake system cleaner. Do not allow the fine dust to become airborne. Also, wear an approved filtering mask.*

c)   *Safety should be paramount whenever any servicing of the brake components is performed. Do not use parts or fasteners which are not in perfect condition, and be sure that all clearances and torque specifications are adhered to. If you are at all unsure about a certain procedure, seek professional advice. Upon completion of any brake system work, test the brakes carefully in a controlled area before putting the vehicle into normal service. If a problem is suspected in the brake system, don't drive the vehicle until it's fixed.*

d)   *Used brake fluid is considered a hazardous waste and it must be disposed of in accordance with federal, state and local laws.*

e)   *DO NOT pour it down the sink, into septic tanks or storm drains, or on the ground.*

f)   *Clean up any spilled brake fluid immediately and then wash the area with large amounts of water. This is especially true for any finished or painted surfaces.*

## 2   Troubleshooting

| PROBABLE CAUSE | CORRECTIVE ACTION |
|---|---|

### No brakes - pedal travels to floor

| PROBABLE CAUSE | CORRECTIVE ACTION |
|---|---|
| 1 Low fluid level<br>2 Air in system | 1 and 2 Low fluid level and air in the system are symptoms of another problem a leak somewhere in the hydraulic system. Locate and repair the leak |
| 3 Defective seals in master cylinder | 3 Replace master cylinder |
| 4 Fluid overheated and vaporized due to heavy braking | 4 Bleed hydraulic system (temporary fix). Replace brake fluid (proper fix) |

### Brake pedal slowly travels to floor under braking or at a stop

| PROBABLE CAUSE | CORRECTIVE ACTION |
|---|---|
| 1 Defective seals in master cylinder | 1 Replace master cylinder |
| 2 Leak in a hose, line, caliper or wheel cylinder | 2 Locate and repair leak |
| 3 Air in hydraulic system | 3 Bleed the system, inspect system for a leak |

### Brake pedal feels spongy when depressed

| PROBABLE CAUSE | CORRECTIVE ACTION |
|---|---|
| 1 Air in hydraulic system | 1 Bleed the system, inspect system for a leak |
| 2 Master cylinder or power booster loose | 2 Tighten fasteners |
| 3 Brake fluid overheated (beginning to boil) | 3 Bleed the system (temporary fix). Replace the brake fluid (proper fix) |
| 4 Deteriorated brake hoses (ballooning under pressure) | 4 Inspect hoses, replace as necessary (it's a good idea to replace all of them if one hose shows signs of deterioration) |

**Troubleshooting (continued)**

| PROBABLE CAUSE | CORRECTIVE ACTION |
|---|---|

### Brake pedal feels hard when depressed and/or excessive effort required to stop vehicle

| | |
|---|---|
| 1 Power booster faulty | 1 Replace booster |
| 2 Engine not producing sufficient vacuum, or hose to booster clogged, collapsed or cracked | 2 Check vacuum to booster with a vacuum gauge. Replace hose if cracked or clogged, repair engine if vacuum is extremely low |
| 3 Brake linings contaminated by grease or brake fluid | 3 Locate and repair source of contamination, replace brake pads or shoes |
| 4 Brake linings glazed | 4 Replace brake pads or shoes, check discs and drums for glazing, service as necessary |
| 5 Caliper piston(s) or wheel cylinder(s) binding or frozen | 5 Replace calipers or wheel cylinders |
| 6 Brakes wet | 6 Apply pedal to boil-off water (this should only be a momentary problem) |
| 7 Kinked, clogged or internally split brake hose or line | 7 Inspect lines and hoses, replace as necessary |

### Excessive brake pedal travel (but will pump up)

| | |
|---|---|
| 1 Drum brakes out of adjustment | 1 Adjust brakes |
| 2 Air in hydraulic system | 2 Bleed system, inspect system for a leak |

### Excessive brake pedal travel (but will not pump up)

| | |
|---|---|
| 1 Master cylinder pushrod misadjusted | 1 Adjust pushrod |
| 2 Master cylinder seals defective | 2 Replace master cylinder |
| 3 Brake linings worn out | 3 Inspect brakes, replace pads and/or shoes |
| 4 Hydraulic system leak | 4 Locate and repair leak |

### Brake pedal doesn't return

| | |
|---|---|
| 1 Brake pedal binding | 1 Inspect pivot bushing and pushrod, repair or lubricate |
| 2 Defective master cylinder | 2 Replace master cylinder |

### Brake pedal pulsates during brake application

| | |
|---|---|
| 1 Brake drums out-of-round | 1 Have drums machined by an automotive machine shop |
| 2 Excessive brake disc runout or disc surfaces out-of-parallel | 2 Have discs machined by an automotive machine shop |
| 3 Loose or worn wheel bearings | 3 Adjust or replace wheel bearings |
| 4 Loose lug nuts | 4 Tighten lug nuts |

### Brakes slow to release

| | |
|---|---|
| 1 Malfunctioning power booster | 1 Replace booster |
| 2 Pedal linkage binding | 2 Inspect pedal pivot bushing and pushrod, repair/lubricate |
| 3 Malfunctioning proportioning valve | 3 Replace proportioning valve |
| 4 Sticking caliper or wheel cylinder | 4 Repair or replace calipers or wheel cylinders |
| 5 Kinked or internally split brake hose | 5 Locate and replace faulty brake hose |

### Brakes grab (one or more wheels)

| | |
|---|---|
| 1 Grease or brake fluid on brake lining | 1 Locate and repair cause of contamination, replace lining |
| 2 Brake lining glazed | 2 Replace lining, deglaze disc or drum |

**PROBABLE CAUSE**

**CORRECTIVE ACTION**

### Vehicle pulls to one side during braking

| PROBABLE CAUSE | CORRECTIVE ACTION |
|---|---|
| 1 Grease or brake fluid on brake lining | 1 Locate and repair cause of contamination, replace lining |
| 2 Brake lining glazed | 2 Deglaze or replace lining, deglaze disc or drum |
| 3 Restricted brake line or hose | 3 Repair line or replace hose |
| 4 Tire pressures incorrect | 4 Adjust tire pressures |
| 5 Caliper or wheel cylinder sticking | 5 Repair or replace calipers or wheel cylinders |
| 6 Wheels out of alignment | 6 Have wheels aligned |
| 7 Weak suspension spring | 7 Replace springs |
| 8 Weak or broken shock absorber | 8 Replace shock absorbers |

### Brakes drag (indicated by sluggish engine performance or wheels being very hot after driving)

| PROBABLE CAUSE | CORRECTIVE ACTION |
|---|---|
| 1 Brake pedal pushrod incorrectly adjusted | 1 Adjust pushrod |
| 2 Master cylinder pushrod (between booster and master cylinder) | 2 Adjust pushrod incorrectly adjusted |
| 3 Obstructed compensating port in master cylinder | 3 Replace master cylinder |
| 4 Master cylinder piston seized in bore | 4 Replace master cylinder |
| 5 Contaminated fluid causing swollen seals throughout system | 5 Flush system, replace all hydraulic components |
| 6 Clogged brake lines or internally split brake hose(s) | 6 Flush hydraulic system, replace defective hose(s) |
| 7 Sticking caliper(s) or wheel cylinder(s) | 7 Replace calipers or wheel cylinders |
| 8 Parking brake not releasing | 8 Inspect parking brake linkage and parking brake mechanism, repair as required |
| 9 Improper shoe-to-drum clearance | 9 Adjust brake shoes |
| 10 Faulty proportioning valve | 10 Replace proportioning valve |

### Brakes fade (due to excessive heat)

| PROBABLE CAUSE | CORRECTIVE ACTION |
|---|---|
| 1 Brake linings excessively worn or glazed | 1 Deglaze or replace brake pads and/or shoes |
| 2 Excessive use of brakes | 2 Downshift into a lower gear, maintain a constant slower speed (going down hills) |
| 3 Vehicle overloaded | 3 Reduce load |
| 4 Brake drums or discs worn too thin | 4 Measure drum diameter and disc thickness, replace drums or discs as required |
| 5 Contaminated brake fluid | 5 Flush system, replace fluid |
| 6 Brakes drag | 6 Repair cause of dragging brakes |
| 7 Driver resting left foot on brake pedal | 7 Don't ride the brakes |

### Brakes noisy (high-pitched squeal)

| PROBABLE CAUSE | CORRECTIVE ACTION |
|---|---|
| 1 Glazed lining | 1 Deglaze or replace lining |
| 2 Contaminated lining (brake fluid, grease, etc.) | 2 Repair source of contamination, replace linings |
| 3 Weak or broken brake shoe hold-down or return spring | 3 Replace springs |
| 4 Rivets securing lining to shoe or backing plate loose | 4 Replace shoes or pads |
| 5 Excessive dust buildup on brake linings | 5 Wash brakes off with brake system cleaner |
| 6 Brake drums worn too thin | 6 Measure diameter of drums, replace if necessary |
| 7 Wear indicator on disc brake pads contacting disc | 7 Replace brake pads |
| 8 Anti-squeal shims missing or installed improperly | 8 Install shims correctly |

**Troubleshooting (continued)**

| PROBABLE CAUSE | CORRECTIVE ACTION |
|---|---|

### Brakes noisy (scraping sound)

| | |
|---|---|
| 1 Brake pads or shoes worn out; rivets, backing plate or brake | 1 Replace linings, have discs and/or drums machined (or replace) shoe metal contacting disc or drum |

### Brakes chatter

| | |
|---|---|
| 1 Worn brake lining | 1 Inspect brakes, replace shoes or pads as necessary |
| 2 Glazed or scored discs or drums | 2 Deglaze discs or drums with sandpaper (if glazing is severe, machining will be required) |
| 3 Drums or discs heat checked | 3 Check discs and/or drums for hard spots, heat checking, etc. Have discs/drums machined or replace them |
| 4 Disc runout or drum out-of-round excessive | 4 Measure disc runout and/or drum out-of-round, have discs or drums machined or replace them |
| 5 Loose or worn wheel bearings | 5 Adjust or replace wheel bearings |
| 6 Loose or bent brake backing plate (drum brakes) | 6 Tighten or replace backing plate |
| 7 Grooves worn in discs or drums | 7 Have discs or drums machined, if within limits (if not, replace them) |
| 8 Brake linings contaminated (brake fluid, grease, etc.) | 8 Locate and repair source of contamination, replace pads or shoes |
| 9 Excessive dust buildup on linings | 9 Wash brakes with brake system cleaner |
| 10 Surface finish on discs or drums too rough after machining | 10 Have discs or drums properly machined (especially on vehicles with sliding calipers) |
| 11 Brake pads or shoes glazed | 11 Deglaze or replace brake pads or shoes |

### Brake pads or shoes click

| | |
|---|---|
| 1 Shoe support pads on brake backing plate grooved or | 1 Replace brake backing plate excessively worn |
| 2 Brake pads loose in caliper | 2 Loose pad retainers or anti-rattle clips |
| 3 Also see items listed under Brakes chatter | |

### Brakes make groaning noise at end of stop

| | |
|---|---|
| 1 Brake pads and/or shoes worn out | 1 Replace pads and/or shoes |
| 2 Brake linings contaminated (brake fluid, grease, etc.) | 2 Locate and repair cause of contamination, replace brake pads or shoes |
| 3 Brake linings glazed | 3 Deglaze or replace brake pads or shoes |
| 4 Excessive dust buildup on linings | 4 Wash brakes with brake system cleaner |
| 5 Scored or heat-checked discs or drums | 5 Inspect discs/drums, have machined if within limits (if not, replace discs or drums) |
| 6 Broken or missing brake shoe attaching hardware | 6 Inspect drum brakes, replace missing hardware |

### Rear brakes lock up under light brake application

| | |
|---|---|
| 1 Tire pressures too high | 1 Adjust tire pressures |
| 2 Tires excessively worn | 2 Replace tires |
| 3 Defective proportioning valve | 3 Replace proportioning valve |

### Brake warning light on instrument panel comes on (or stays on)

| | |
|---|---|
| 1 Low fluid level in master cylinder reservoir (reservoirs with fluid level sensor) | 1 Add fluid, inspect system for leak, check the thickness of the brake pads and shoes |
| 2 Failure in one half of the hydraulic system | 2 Inspect hydraulic system for a leak |
| 3 Piston in pressure differential warning valve not centered | 3 Center piston by bleeding one circuit or the other (close bleeder valve as soon as the light goes out) |

PROBABLE CAUSE          CORRECTIVE ACTION

## *Brake warning light on instrument panel comes on (or stays on) (continued)*

| | |
|---|---|
| 4 Defective pressure differential valve or warning switch | 4 Replace valve or switch |
| 5 Air in the hydraulic system | 5 Bleed the system, check for leaks |
| 6 Brake pads worn out (vehicles with electric wear sensors - small | 6 Replace brake pads (and sensors) probes that fit into the brake pads and ground out on the disc when the pads get thin) |

## *Disc brakes do not self adjust*

| | |
|---|---|
| 1 Defective caliper piston seals | 1 Replace calipers. Also, possible contaminated fluid causing soft or swollen seals (flush system and fill with new fluid if in doubt) |
| 2 Corroded caliper piston(s) | 2 Same as above |

## *Drum brakes do not self adjust*

| | |
|---|---|
| 1 Adjuster screw frozen | 1 Remove adjuster, disassemble, clean and lubricate with high-temperature grease |
| 2 Adjuster lever does not contact star wheel or is binding | 2 Inspect drum brakes, assemble correctly or clean or replace parts as required |
| 3 Adjusters mixed up (installed on wrong wheels after brake job) | 3 Reassemble correctly |
| 4 Adjuster cable broken or installed incorrectly (cable-type adjusters) | 4 Install new cable or assemble correctly |

## *Rapid brake lining wear*

| | |
|---|---|
| 1 Driver resting left foot on brake pedal | 1 Don't ride the brakes |
| 2 Surface finish on discs or drums too rough | 2 Have discs or drums properly machined |
| 3 Also see Brakes drag | |

---

### 3    Disc brake pads - replacement

**Warning:** *Disc brake pads must be replaced on both front or rear wheels at the same time - never replace the pads on one side. Also, the dust created by the brake system is harmful to your health. Never blow it out with compressed air and don't inhale any of it. An approved filtering mask should be worn when working on the brakes. Do not, under any circumstances, use petroleum-based solvents to clean brake parts. Use brake system cleaner only!*
**Note:** *This procedure applies to front and rear disc brakes.*
1     Remove the cap from the brake fluid reservoir.
2     Loosen the wheel lug nuts, raise the front, or rear, of the vehicle and support it securely on jackstands.
3     Remove the front, or rear, wheels. Work on one brake assembly at a time, using the assembled brake for reference if necessary.
4     Inspect the brake disc carefully as out-

lined in Section 5. If machining is necessary, follow the information in that section to remove the disc, at which time the calipers and pads can be removed as well.

### Front pads
5     Push the piston back into the bore to provide room for the new brake pads. A C-clamp can be used to accomplish this (see illustration). As the piston is depressed to the bottom of the caliper bore, the fluid in the master cylinder will rise. Make sure it doesn't overflow. If necessary, siphon off some of the fluid.
**Note:** *There are a variety of caliper press clamps available. Some require removing the caliper and using the old brake pad as a backing plate in order to squeeze the caliper piston back in, while others have two plates that spread apart to squeeze the piston. The method shown was used because it is the most common type of tool that most home garages would have on hand that will sufficiently perform the task.*

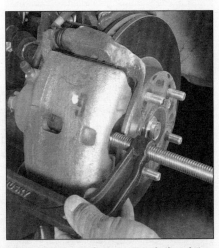

**3.5 Using a large C-clamp, push the piston back into the caliper - note that one end of the clamp is on the back side of the caliper and the other end (screw end) is pressing on the outer brake pad (front caliper shown, rear calipers similar). DO NOT press the rear calipers in with a C-clamp on the Civic models**

3.6a Before removing anything, spray the assembly with brake system cleaner to remove the dust produced by brake pad wear - DO NOT blow the dust off with compressed air!

3.6b Remove the caliper lower mounting bolt . . .

3.6c . . . then swing the caliper up and secure it to the strut with a piece of wire

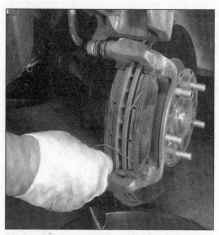

3.6d Remove the return springs

3.6e Remove the inner brake pad and shim(s)

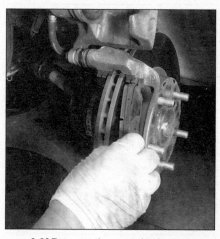

3.6f Remove the outer brake pad and shim(s)

3.6g The pad retainer clips should fit snugly into their respective grooves in the caliper mounting bracket; if they don't, replace them

Note: *Take note of which retainer is the upper and which is the lower (on some caliper types they are different).*

6    Follow the accompanying illustrations, beginning with 3.6a, for the actual pad replacement procedure. Be sure to stay in order and read the caption under each illustration.

7    Proceed to Step 22.

## Rear pads

8    Disconnect the brake line from its mounting bracket.

9    If you're working on a CR-V model, push the piston back into the bore to provide room for the new brake pads (see illustration 3.5). A C-clamp can be used to accomplish this.

Warning: *DO NOT push the rear caliper in with a C-clamp on the Civic models. These models use a different type of rear caliper. The caliper piston must be turned clockwise to retract it. Read all directions carefully before proceeding.*

3.6h Before replacing the retainer clips, clean the grooves with a wire brush

3.6i Check the caliper slide pins for wear. Slide them in and out making sure they don't stick along the way, then clean them off and lubricate them with a film of high-temperature brake grease

3.6j Install the retainer clips, making sure they are fully seated into the grooves

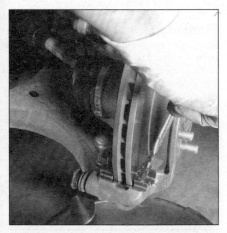

3.6k Using high-temperature brake grease, lightly lubricate the retainer clips where the pads will touch them

3.6l Install the new inner pad and shim(s)

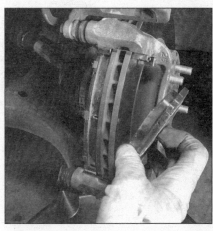

3.6m Install the new outer pad and shim(s)

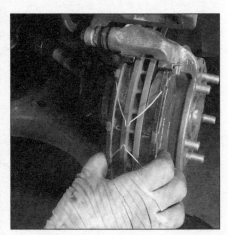

3.6n Install the return springs

3.6o While holding the pads in place, lower the caliper over the pads

3.6p Install the caliper lower mounting bolt and tighten it to the torque listed in this Chapter's Specifications

**3.11 Remove the outer pad and shim . . .**

**3.12 . . . and the inner pad and shim**

**3.19a To provide clearance for the new pads, back the piston into the bore by turning it clockwise**

**3.19b This is a typical caliper piston retracting tool which can be purchased at most parts stores. Use a 3/8-inch drive ratchet and extension to turn the caliper piston**

21    Read the instructions in the Final inspection procedures in Section 3.

*Final inspection procedures*

22    Install the wheel and lug nuts, lower the vehicle and tighten the lug nuts to the torque listed in the Chapter 1 Specifications.
23    Apply and release the brake pedal several times to bring the pads or shoes into contact with the brake discs/drums. Check the brake fluid level and add fluid, if necessary (see Chapter 1).
24    Check the operation of the brakes in an isolated area before driving the vehicle in traffic.

**4    Disc brake caliper - removal and installation**

**Warning:** *The dust created by the brake system is harmful to your health. Never blow it out with compressed air and don't inhale any of it. An approved filtering mask should be worn when working on the brakes. Do not, under any circumstances, use petroleum-based solvents to clean brake parts. Use brake system cleaner only!*
**Note:** *Always replace the calipers in pairs - never replace just one of them.*

*Front*
**Removal**

1    Loosen - but don't remove - the lug nuts on the front wheels. Raise the front of the vehicle and suport it securely on jackstands. Remove the front wheels.
2    Disconnect the brake line from the caliper and plug it to keep contaminants out of the brake system and to prevent losing any more brake fluid than is necessary.
**Note:** *If you're simply removing the caliper for access to other components, don't disconnect the hose.*
3    Remove the caliper mounting bolts.

10    Remove the caliper mounting bolts while holding the caliper pins with a second wrench, then remove the caliper from its mounting bracket and hang it out of the way with a piece of wire. Don't let the caliper hang by the brake hose.
11    Remove the outer and inner brake pads and shims (see illustration).
12    Remove the inner brake pad and shim (see illustration).
13    Remove and inspect the upper and lower pad retainer clips.
**Note:** *Take note of which retainer is the upper and which is the lower (on some caliper types they are different).*
14    Install the pad retainer clips. They should fit snugly in the caliper mounting bracket; if they don't, replace them. Apply a thin film of high-temperature grease to the retainer.
15    Apply a small amount of high-temperature grease to both sides of the shims.
16    Install the new inner pad and shim(s). Make sure the ears on the upper and lower ends of the pad are fully engaged with their respective grooves and the pad retainer clips.

17    Install the new outer pad and shim.
18    Before installing the caliper, remove the caliper pin dust boots and inspect them for tears and cracks; if they're damaged, replace them.
19    On Civic models, retract the piston by using a caliper piston tool or engaging the tips of a pair of needle-nose pliers with two of the grooves in the face of the piston and turning it clockwise until it bottoms in the bore (see illustrations). Now, rotate the piston out until one of its grooves is aligned with the tab on the inner brake pad when you install the caliper. You may have to adjust the piston position by turning it back and forth to fit the tab in the groove. If the piston dust boot becomes distorted when the piston is turned, turn the piston in the opposite direction to restore the shape of the boot, but make sure the groove is aligned properly.
20    Install the caliper mounting bolts while holding the caliper pins with a second wrench. Tighten them to the torque listed in this Chapter's Specifications. If the brake line was disconnected from its mounting bracket, reconnect the line and tighten the bolt securely.

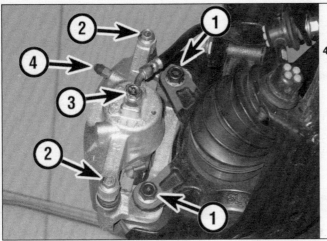

**4.4 Brake caliper details**

1  Caliper mounting bracket-to-steering knuckle bolts
2  Caliper mounting bolts
3  Brake hose banjo fitting bolt
4  Caliper bleeder screw

5.3 The brake pads on this vehicle were obviously neglected, as they wore down completely and cut deep grooves into the disc - wear this severe means the disc must be replaced

4  Detach the caliper from its mounting bracket (see illustration).

## Installation
5  Install the caliper by reversing the removal procedure. Remember to replace the sealing washers on either side of the brake line fitting with new ones. Tighten the caliper mounting bolts and the banjo bolt to the torque listed in this Chapter's Specifications.
6  Bleed the brake system (see Section 10).
7  Install the wheels and lug nuts and lower the vehicle. Tighten the lug nuts to the torque listed in the Chapter 1 Specifications.

## Rear
### Removal
8  Loosen - but don't remove - the lug nuts on the rear wheels. Raise the rear of the vehicle and place it securely on jackstands. Remove the rear wheels.
9  On Civic models, remove the clip securing the parking brake cable to the caliper parking brake lever, then separate the cable from the caliper.
10  Unscrew the banjo bolt and detach the brake line from the caliper. Plug the fitting to prevent fluid loss and contamination.
**Note:** If you're simply removing the caliper for access to other components, don't disconnect the hose.
11  Remove the caliper mounting bolts while holding the caliper pins with a second wrench.
12  Detach the caliper from its mounting bracket.

### Installation
13  Install the caliper by reversing the removal procedure. Remember to replace the sealing washers on either side of the brake line fitting with new ones. Tighten the caliper mounting bolts and the banjo bolt to the torque listed in this Chapter's Specifications.
14  Bleed the brake system (see Section 10).
15  Install the wheels and lug nuts. Lower the vehicle and tighten the lug nuts to the torque listed in the Chapter 1 Specifications.

## 5  Brake disc - inspection, removal and installation

**Warning:** The dust created by the brake system is harmful to your health. Never blow it out with compressed air and don't inhale any of it. An approved filtering mask should be worn when working on the brakes. Do not, under any circumstances, use petroleum-based solvents to clean brake parts. Use brake system cleaner only!

### Inspection
1  Loosen the wheel lug nuts, raise the vehicle and support it securely on jackstands. Remove the wheel and install the lug nuts to hold the disc in place against the hub flange.
**Note:** If the lug nuts don't contact the disc when screwed on all the way, install washers under them. If you're checking the rear disc, release the parking brake.
2  Remove the brake caliper as outlined in Section 4. It isn't necessary to disconnect the brake hose. After removing the caliper bolts, suspend the caliper out of the way with a piece of wire. Remove the two caliper mounting bracket-to-steering knuckle bolts (see illustration 4.4) or, on rear calipers, the bracket-to-knuckle bolts and remove the mounting bracket.

5.4a To check disc runout, mount a dial indicator as shown and rotate the disc

3  Visually inspect the disc surface for score marks and other damage. Light scratches and shallow grooves are normal after use and may not always be detrimental to brake operation, but deep scoring requires disc removal and refinishing by an automotive machine shop. Be sure to check both sides of the disc (see illustration). If pulsating has been noticed during application of the brakes, suspect disc runout.
4  To check disc runout, place a dial indicator at a point about 1/2-inch from the outer edge of the disc (see illustration). Set the indicator to zero and turn the disc. The indicator reading should not exceed the specified allowable runout limit. If it does, the disc should be refinished by an automotive machine shop.
**Note:** The discs should be resurfaced regardless of the dial indicator reading, as this will impart a smooth finish and ensure a perfectly flat surface, eliminating any brake pedal pulsation or other undesirable symptoms related to questionable discs. At the very least, if you elect not to have the discs resurfaced, remove the glaze from the surface with emery cloth or sandpaper, using a swirling motion (see illustration).

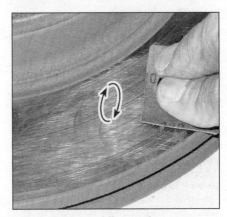

5.4b Using a swirling motion, remove the glaze from the disc surface with sandpaper or emery cloth

5.5 Use a micrometer to measure disc thickness

5.6a If the disc retaining screws are stuck, use an impact screwdriver to loosen them

5.6b If the disc is stuck, thread two bolts into the disc and tighten them to force the disc off the hub

6.4 Insert an 8 X 1.25 mm bolt in these holes to draw the drum off

6.6 Before removing anything, clean the brake assembly with brake cleaner and allow it to dry - position a drain pan under the brake to catch the residue - DO NOT USE COMPRESSED AIR TO BLOW BRAKE DUST OFF THE PARTS!

5    It's absolutely critical that the disc not be machined to a thickness under the specified minimum thickness. The minimum (or discard) thickness is cast or stamped into the disc. The disc thickness can be checked with a micrometer (see illustration).

### Removal
6    Remove the lug nuts which were installed to hold the disc in place, or remove the two disc retaining screws (see illustration) and remove the disc from the hub. If the disc is stuck to the hub and won't come off, thread two bolts into the holes provided (see illustration) and tighten them. Alternate between the bolts, turning them a couple of turns at a time, until the disc is free. Remove the disc from the hub.

### Installation
7    Place the disc in position over the threaded studs. Install the disc retaining screws and tighten them securely.
8    Install the caliper mounting bracket and caliper, tightening the bolts to the torque values listed in this Chapter's Specifications.
9    Install the wheel, then lower the vehicle to the ground. Tighten the lug nuts to the torque listed in the Chapter 1 Specifications. Depress the brake pedal a few times to bring the brake pads into contact with the disc. Bleeding won't be necessary unless the brake hose was disconnected from the caliper. Check the operation of the brakes carefully before driving the vehicle.

### 6    Drum brake shoes/parking brake shoes - replacement

**Warning:** *Drum brake shoes must be replaced on both wheels at the same time - never replace the shoes on only one wheel. Also, the dust created by the brake system is harmful to your health. Never blow it out with compressed air and don't inhale any of it. An approved fil-*

*tering mask should be worn when working on the brakes. Do not, under any circumstances, use petroleum-based solvents to clean brake parts. Use brake system cleaner only!*
**Caution:** *Whenever the brake shoes are replaced, the return and hold-down springs should also be replaced. Due to the continuous heating/cooling cycle the springs are subjected to, they can lose tension over a period of time and may allow the shoes to drag on the drum and wear at a much faster rate than normal.*
1    Loosen the wheel lug nuts, raise the rear of the vehicle and support it securely on jackstands. Block the front wheels to keep the vehicle from rolling.
**Note:** *All four rear brake shoes must be replaced at the same time, but to avoid mixing up parts, work on only one brake assembly at a time.*
2    Release the parking brake.
3    Remove the wheel.
4    Using two 8 X 1.25 mm bolts, thread the bolts in the two holes on the face of the drum. As you alternate from one screw to the other the drum will slowly separate from the hub (see illustration).
5    Remove the brake drum.
**Note:** *If the brake drum cannot be easily pulled off the axle and shoe assembly, make sure the parking brake is completely released. If the drum still cannot be pulled off, the brake shoes will have to be retracted. This is done by first removing the plug from the backing plate. With the plug removed, push the lever off the adjuster star wheel with a screwdriver while turning the adjuster wheel with another screwdriver, moving the shoes away from the drum. The drum should now come off.*
**Note:** *Inspect the drum for any coarse marks or heavy grooves left by the shoes or brake hardware. Have the drum machined or if severe enough, replace the drum.*

### Drum brake shoes
6    Clean the brake shoe assembly with brake system cleaner before beginning work (see illustration).

6.7a Remove the upper return spring

6.7b Remove the adjuster lever spring

6.7c Remove the adjuster lever

6.7d Push down on the hold-down spring and twist the pin 1/4-turn to free the spring

6.7e Remove the leading shoe from the backing plate

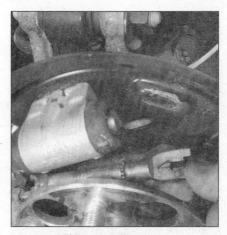

6.7f Remove the adjuster

7    Follow the accompanying illustrations for the brake shoe replacement procedure (see illustrations 6.7a through 6.7u). Be sure to stay in order and read the caption under each illustration.

8    Before reinstalling the drum, it should be checked for cracks, score marks, deep scratches and hard spots, which will appear as small discolored areas. If the hard spots cannot be removed with fine emery cloth or if any of the other conditions listed above exist, the drum must be taken to an automotive machine shop to have it resurfaced.

**Note:** *Professionals recommend resurfacing the drums each time a brake job is done. Resurfacing will eliminate the possibility of out-of-round drums. If the drums are worn so much that they can't be resurfaced without exceeding the maximum allowable diameter, then new ones will be required. At the very least, if you elect not to have the drums resurfaced, remove the glaze from the surface with emery cloth using a swirling motion.*

9    Install the brake drum on the hub flange.

Using a screwdriver inserted through the adjusting hole in the brake backing plate, turn the adjuster star wheel until the brake shoes drag on the drum as the drum is rotated, then back off the star wheel until the shoes don't drag. Reinstall the plug in the backing plate.

10    Mount the wheel and install the lug nuts. Lower the vehicle and tighten the lug nuts to the torque listed in the Chapter 1 Specifications.

11    Make a number of forward and reverse stops and operate the parking brake to adjust the brakes until satisfactory pedal action is obtained.

12    Check the operation of the brakes carefully before driving the vehicle.

### Parking brake shoes (CR-V models)

**Warning:** *The dust created by the brake system is harmful to your health. Never blow it out with compressed air and don't inhale any of it. An approved filtering mask should be worn*

*when working on the brakes. Do not, under any circumstances, use petroleum-based solvents to clean brake parts. Use brake system cleaner only!*

### Removal

13    Loosen the rear wheel lug nuts, raise the rear of the vehicle and support it securely on jackstands. Block the front wheels and remove the rear wheels. Release the parking brake.

**Warning:** *Replace the emergency brake shoes as a complete set. DO NOT change only one side. Do both sides or the emergency brake will only work on one wheel.*

14    Remove the rear calipers (see Section 4). Support the caliper assemblies with a coat hanger or heavy wire and don't disconnect the brake line from the caliper.

15    Remove the rear discs (see Section 5).

16    Clean the parking brake assembly with brake system cleaner.

17    Remove the two upper return springs.

18    Push the hold-down clips on the shoes

6.7g Remove the hold-down spring from the trailing shoe

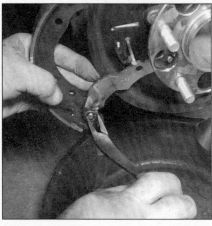

6.7h Spread open, then push off the C-clip retaining the parking brake lever pin . . .

6.7i . . . then remove the washer . . .

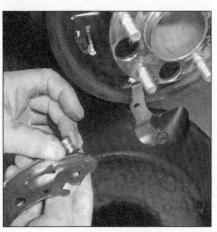

6.7j . . . and pin

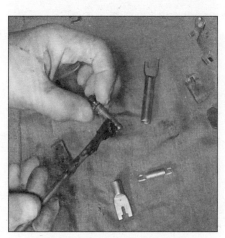

6.7k Disassemble and clean the components of the adjuster, then lubricate the moving parts with a film of high-temperature brake grease

6.7l Clean the backing plate, then lubricate the shoe contact areas with a light film of high-temperature brake grease

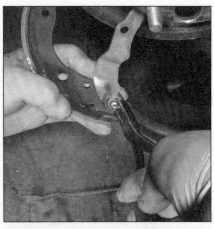

6.7m Connect the parking brake lever to the trailing shoe and install the pin, washer and C-clip. Squeeze the clip tight with a pair of pliers

6.7n Install the trailing shoe and hold-down spring

6.7o Install the adjuster, making sure the adjuster wheel is nearest the front of the vehicle

**6.7p Connect the lower return spring to the bottom of each shoe . . .**

**6.7q . . . then place the leading shoe against the backing plate and install the hold-down spring**

**6.7r Install the adjuster lever**

**6.7s Install the upper return spring**

**6.7t Install the adjuster lever spring**

**6.7u Turn the adjuster wheel so the brake drum just slides over the shoes**

and turn the pins 90-degrees, then remove the clips.

19   Remove the connecting rod and rod spring.

20   Remove the lower return spring, then pull the leading shoe back and remove the adjuster screw.

21   On the backing plate side of the trailing shoe, use diagonal cutters to pry the U-clip and washer from the top of the shoe.

22   Remove the parking brake lever from the trailing shoe and remove the shoe.

### Installation

23   With the backing plate cleaned, apply light dabs of high-temperature grease to the shoe contact areas.

24   Lubricate the parking brake lever pin, then assemble the parking brake lever to the new trailing shoe.

25   Position the trailing shoe against the stationary stop at the top of the backing plate, then insert the hold-down pin through the backing plate and install the hold-down clip.

26   Clean the adjuster bolt and clevis, then

lubricate the threads and ends with high-temperature grease.

27   Install the adjuster and lower return spring on each shoe, then position the leading shoe and insert the hold-down pin through the backing plate and install the hold-down clip.

28   Place the rod spring on the connecting rod, then separate the shoes and install the connecting rod.

29   Connect the two upper return springs to the top of each shoe.

30   Install the disc and caliper. Tighten the caliper mounting bolts to the torque listed in this Chapter's Specifications.

31   Using a screwdriver inserted through the adjusting hole in the disc, turn the adjuster star wheel until the brake shoes drag on the drum as the drum is rotated, then back off the star wheel until the shoes don't drag.

32   Mount the wheel and install the lug nuts. Lower the vehicle and tighten the lug nuts to the torque listed in the Chapter 1 Specifications.

33   Make a number of forward and reverse stops and operate the parking brake to adjust

the brakes until satisfactory pedal action is obtained.

34   Check the operation of the brakes carefully before driving the vehicle.

### 7   Wheel cylinder - removal and installation

**Warning:** *The dust created by the brake system is harmful to your health. Never blow it out with compressed air and don't inhale any of it. An approved filtering mask should be worn when working on the brakes. Do not, under any circumstances, use petroleum-based solvents to clean brake parts. Use brake system cleaner only!*

**Note:** *If replacement is indicated (usually because of fluid leakage or sticky operation), it is recommended that the wheel cylinders be replaced, not overhauled. Always replace the wheel cylinders in pairs - never replace just one of them.*

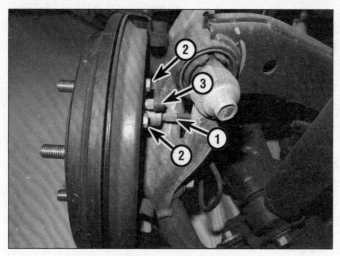

**7.4 Wheel cylinder details**

| 1 | Brake line fitting | 3 | Bleeder screw |
|---|---|---|---|
| 2 | Mounting bolts | | |

**8.6 Master cylinder mounting details**

| 1 | Mounting nuts | 3 | Remote fluid reservoir |
|---|---|---|---|
| 2 | Brake line fittings | | |

**8.10 The best way to bleed air from the master cylinder before installing it on the vehicle is with a pair of bleeder tubes that direct brake fluid into the reservoir during bleeding**

## Removal

1   Raise the rear of the vehicle and support it securely on jackstands. Block the front wheels to keep the vehicle from rolling.
2   Remove the brake shoe assembly (see Section 6).
3   Remove all dirt and foreign material from around the wheel cylinder.
4   Disconnect the brake line. Don't pull the brake line away from the wheel cylinder or you may find it much harder to get the line started back onto the wheel cylinder because of a slight bend in the line (see illustraton).
5   Remove the wheel cylinder mounting bolts.
6   Detach the wheel cylinder from the brake backing plate and immediately plug the brake line to prevent fluid loss and contamination.

## Installation

7   Apply a small amount of RTV sealant between the backing plate and wheel cylinder, then place the wheel cylinder in position and install the bolts finger-tight. Connect the

brake line to the cylinder, being careful not to cross thread the fitting. Tighten the wheel cylinder mounting bolts to the torque listed in this Chapter's Specifications. Now tighten the brake line fitting securely.
8   Install the brake shoe assembly (see Section 6).
9   Bleed the brakes (see Section 10).
10   Check the operation of the brakes carefully before driving the vehicle.

## 8   Master cylinder - removal and installation

## Removal

1   The master cylinder is located in the engine compartment, mounted to the power brake booster.
2   Remove the air filter housing (see Chapter 4).
3   Disconnect the electrical connector from the fluid level warning switch.

4   Using a syringe or equivalent, remove the brake fluid from the master cylinder reservoir and dispose of it properly.
**Caution:** *Brake fluid will damage paint. Cover all painted surfaces and avoid spilling fluid during this procedure. If you do spill fluid, wash it off with water immediately.*
5   Disconnect the electrical connector from the fluid level sensor on the remote reservoir, then remove the remote fluid reservoir mounting bolt (the reservoir will be removed along with the master cylinder).
6   Place rags under the fluid fittings and prepare caps or plastic bags to cover the ends of the lines once they are disconnected. Loosen the fittings at the ends of the brake lines where they enter the master cylinder (see illustration). To prevent rounding off the corners on these nuts, the use of a flare-nut wrench, which wraps around the nut, is preferred. Pull the brake lines slightly away from the master cylinder and plug the ends to prevent contamination.
7   Remove the mounting nuts from the master cylinder to separate it from the power booster. Pull the master cylinder off the studs and out of the engine compartment. Again, be careful not to spill the fluid as this is done.
8   If a new master cylinder is being installed, remove the reservoir from the master cylinder and transfer it to the new master cylinder.

## Installation

9   Bench bleed the new master cylinder before installing it. Mount the master cylinder in a vise, with the jaws of the vise clamping on the mounting flange.
10   Attach a pair of master cylinder bleeder tubes to the outlet ports of the master cylinder (see illustration).
11   Fill the reservoir with brake fluid of the recommended type (see Chapter 1).
12   Slowly push the pistons into the master cylinder (a large Phillips screwdriver can be

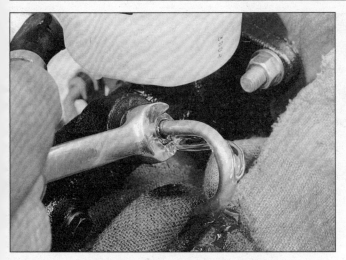

**8.18 Have an assistant depress the brake pedal and hold it down, then loosen the fitting nut, allowing the air and fluid to escape; repeat this procedure on both fittings until the fluid is clear of air bubbles**

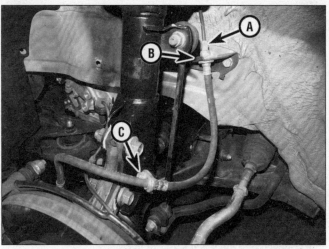

**9.3 Unscrew the brake line threaded fitting with a flare-nut wrench to protect the fitting corners from being rounded off (A), then pull off the U-clip (B) with a pair of pliers and remove the brake line mounting bolt (C)**

used for this) - air will be expelled from the pressure chambers and into the reservoir. Because the tubes are submerged in fluid, air can't be drawn back into the master cylinder when you release the pistons.

13    Repeat the procedure until no more air bubbles are present.

14    Remove the bleed tubes, one at a time, and install plugs in the open ports to prevent fluid leakage and air from entering. Install the reservoir cap.

15    Install a new O-ring on the master cylinder, then install the master cylinder over the studs on the power brake booster and tighten the attaching nuts only finger-tight at this time.

16    Thread the brake line fittings into the master cylinder. Since the master cylinder is still a bit loose, it can be moved slightly in order for the fittings to thread in easily. Do not strip the threads as the fittings are tightened.

17    Fully tighten the mounting nuts, then the brake line fittings. Tighten the nuts to the torque listed in this Chapter's Specifications.

18    Fill the master cylinder reservoir with fluid, then bleed the master cylinder. Have an assistant depress the brake pedal and hold the pedal to the floor. Loosen the front fluid line fitting at the master cylinder to allow air and fluid to escape (see illustration). Repeat this procedure on both fittings until the fluid is clear of air bubbles.

**Note:** *Have plenty of rags on hand to catch the fluid - brake fluid will ruin painted surfaces. After the bleeding procedure is completed, rinse the area under the master cylinder with clean water.*

19    Attach the remote fluid reservoir to its bracket and install the bolt, tightening it securely. Reconnect the electrical connector to the fluid level sensor.

20    The remainder of installation is the reverse of removal.

21    Bleed the rest of the brake hydraulic system (see Section 10).

22    Test the operation of the brake system carefully before placing the vehicle into normal service.

**Warning:** *Do not operate the vehicle if you are in doubt about the effectiveness of the brake system. On models equipped with ABS, it is possible for air to become trapped in the anti-lock brake system hydraulic control unit. If the pedal continues to feel spongy after repeated bleedings or the BRAKE or ANTI-LOCK light stays on, have the vehicle towed to a dealer service department or other qualified shop to be bled with the aid of a scan tool.*

## 9    Brake hoses and lines - inspection and replacement

1    About every six months, with the vehicle raised and placed securely on jackstands, the flexible hoses which connect the steel brake lines with the front and rear brake assemblies should be inspected for cracks, chafing of the outer cover, leaks, blisters and other damage. These are important and vulnerable parts of the brake system and inspection should be complete. A light and mirror will be needed for a thorough check. If a hose exhibits any of the above defects, replace it with a new one.

### Flexible hoses

2    Clean all dirt away from the ends of the hose.

3    To disconnect a brake hose from the brake line, unscrew the metal tube nut with a flare nut wrench, then remove the U-clip from

the female fitting at the bracket and remove the hose from the bracket (see illustration).

4    Disconnect the hose from the caliper, discarding the sealing washers on either side of the fitting.

5    Using new sealing washers, attach the new brake hose to the caliper.

6    To reattach a brake hose to the metal line, insert the end of the hose through the frame bracket, make sure the hose isn't twisted, then attach the metal line by tightening the tube nut fitting securely. Install the U-clip at the frame bracket.

7    Carefully check to make sure the suspension or steering components don't make contact with the hose. Have an assistant push down on the vehicle and also turn the steering wheel lock-to-lock during inspection.

8    Bleed the brake system (see Section 10).

### Metal brake lines

9    When replacing brake lines, be sure to use the correct parts. Don't use copper tubing for any brake system components. Purchase steel brake lines from a dealer parts department or auto parts store.

10    Prefabricated brake line, with the tube ends already flared and fittings installed, is available at auto parts stores and dealer parts departments. These lines can be bent to the proper shapes using a tubing bender.

11    When installing the new line make sure it's well supported in the brackets and has plenty of clearance between moving or hot components.

12    After installation, check the master cylinder fluid level and add fluid as necessary. Bleed the brake system as outlined in Section 10 and test the brakes carefully before placing the vehicle into normal operation.

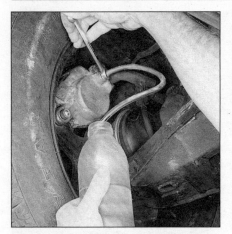

**10.8 When bleeding the brakes, a hose is connected to the bleed screw at the caliper and submerged in brake fluid - air will be seen as bubbles in the tube and container (all air must be expelled before moving to the next wheel)**

**11.9 Remove the clevis pin retaining clip (A) and clevis pin, then disconnect the pushrod clevis from the pedal. (B) is the pushrod and (C) is the pushrod locknut**

## 10   Brake hydraulic system - bleeding

**Warning:** *If air has found its way into the hydraulic control unit on models with ABS, the system must be bled with the use of a scan tool. If the brake pedal feels spongy even after bleeding the brakes, or the ABS light on the instrument panel does not go off, or if you have any doubts whatsoever about the effectiveness of the brake system, have the vehicle towed to a dealer service department or other repair shop equipped with the necessary tools for bleeding the system.*

**Warning:** *Wear eye protection when bleeding the brake system. If the fluid comes in contact with your eyes, immediately rinse them with water and seek medical attention.*

**Note:** *Bleeding the brake system is necessary to remove any air that's trapped in the system when it's opened during removal and installation of a hose, line, caliper, wheel cylinder or master cylinder.*

1    It will probably be necessary to bleed the system at all four brakes if air has entered the system due to low fluid level, or if the brake lines have been disconnected at the master cylinder.

2    If a brake line was disconnected only at a wheel, then only that caliper or wheel cylinder must be bled.

3    If a brake line is disconnected at a fitting located between the master cylinder and any of the brakes, that part of the system served by the disconnected line must be bled.

4    Remove any residual vacuum (or hydraulic pressure) from the brake power booster by applying the brake several times with the engine off.

5    Remove the master cylinder reservoir cap and fill the reservoir with brake fluid. Reinstall the cap.

**Note:** *Check the fluid level often during the bleeding operation and add fluid as necessary to prevent the fluid level from falling low*

enough to allow air bubbles into the master cylinder.

6    Have an assistant on hand, as well as a supply of new brake fluid, an empty clear plastic container, a length of plastic, rubber or vinyl tubing to fit over the bleeder valve and a wrench to open and close the bleeder valve.

7    Beginning at the front left wheel, loosen the bleeder screw slightly, then tighten it to a point where it's snug but can still be loosened quickly and easily.

8    Place one end of the tubing over the bleeder screw fitting and submerge the other end in brake fluid in the container (see illustration).

9    Have the assistant slowly depress the brake pedal and hold it in the depressed position.

10    While the pedal is held depressed, open the bleeder screw just enough to allow a flow of fluid to leave the valve. Watch for air bubbles to exit the submerged end of the tube. When the fluid flow slows after a couple of seconds, tighten the screw and have your assistant release the pedal.

11    Repeat Steps 9 and 10 until no more air is seen leaving the tube, then tighten the bleeder screw and proceed to the right front wheel, the right rear wheel and the left rear wheel, in that order, and perform the same procedure. Be sure to check the fluid in the master cylinder reservoir frequently.

12    Never use old brake fluid. It contains moisture which can boil, rendering the brake system inoperative.

13    Refill the master cylinder with fluid at the end of the operation.

14    Check the operation of the brakes. The pedal should feel solid when depressed, with no sponginess. If necessary, repeat the entire process.

**Warning:** *Do not operate the vehicle if you are in doubt about the effectiveness of the brake system. On models equipped with ABS, it's possible for air to become trapped in the anti-lock brake system hydraulic control unit, so, if the pedal continues to feel spongy after repeated bleedings or the BRAKE or ANTI-LOCK light stays on, have the vehicle towed to a dealer service department or other qualified shop to be bled with the aid of a scan tool.*

## 11   Power brake booster - removal and installation

### *Operating check*

1    Depress the brake pedal several times with the engine off and make sure there is no change in the pedal reserve distance.

2    Depress the pedal and start the engine. If the pedal goes down slightly, operation is normal.

### *Airtightness check*

3    Start the engine and turn it off after one or two minutes. Depress the brake pedal several times slowly. If the pedal goes down farther the first time but gradually rises after the second or third depression, the booster is airtight.

4    Depress the brake pedal while the engine is running, then stop the engine with the pedal depressed. If there is no change in the pedal reserve travel after holding the pedal for 30 seconds, the booster is airtight.

### *Removal*

5    Power brake booster units should not be disassembled. They require special tools not normally found in most automotive repair shops. They are fairly complex and because of their critical relationship to brake performance it is best to replace a defective booster unit with a new or rebuilt one.

6    Remove the brake master cylinder (see Section 8).

7    Disconnect the hose leading from the engine to the booster. Be careful not to damage the hose when removing it from the booster fitting.

8    Detach the brake lines from the clamp on the cowl. On CR-V models, remove the engine wiring harness clamp bolts and reposition the harness.

9    Locate the pushrod clevis pin connecting the booster to the brake pedal (see illustration). Remove the clevis pin retaining clip with pliers and pull out the pin.

**11.10 Remove the four booster mounting nuts**

**12.3 Parking brake adjusting nut (center console removed for clarity)**

10    Remove the four nuts (see illustration) holding the brake booster to the firewall.
11    Slide the booster straight out from the firewall until the studs clear the holes and pull the booster, brackets and gaskets from the engine compartment area.

## Installation

12    Installation procedures are the reverse of those for removal. Tighten the booster mounting nuts to the torque listed in this Chapter's Specifications. Also, be sure to use a new cotter pin on the clevis pin.
13    Install the master cylinder and bleed it (see Section 8), followed by the rest of the brake system (see Section 10).
14    Check and, if necessary adjust, the brake pedal height and freeplay (see Section 14).

## 12   Parking brake - adjustment

### Civic models

1    Remove the center console rear cover (see Chapter 11).
2    Block the front wheels, raise the rear of the vehicle and support it securely on jackstands. Apply the parking brake lever until you hear one click.
3    Tighten the adjusting nut on the equalizer while rotating the rear wheels (see illustration). Stop turning the nut when the brakes just start to drag on the rear wheels.
4    Release the parking brake lever and check to see that the brakes don't drag when the rear wheels are turned. The travel on the parking brake lever should be as listed in the Chapter 1 Specifications when properly adjusted.
5    Lower the vehicle and reinstall the center console rear cover.

**13.1 The brake light switch is mounted to a bracket near the top of the brake pedal**

### CR-V models

6    Block the front wheels, raise the rear of the vehicle and support it securely on jackstands.
7    Working inside the vehicle, pull the driver's seat all the way forward and pull back the carpet under the seat.
8    Remove the fasteners securing the parking brake equalizer cover, then remove the cover.
9    With the parking brake lever fully released, remove the return spring from the parking brake equalizer.
10    Apply the parking brake pedal until you hear one click.
11    Tighten the adjusting nut on the equalizer while rotating the rear wheels. Stop turning the nut when the brakes just start to drag on the rear wheels.
12    Release the parking brake and check to see that the brakes don't drag when the rear wheels are turned. The travel on the parking

brake pedal should be as listed in this Chapter's Specifications when properly adjusted.
13    Lower the vehicle and reinstall the equalizer return spring and cover.

## 13   Brake light switch - replacement

1    Disconnect the electrical connector from the brake light switch (see illustration).
2    Rotate the switch counterclockwise slightly, so it unlocks from its holder, then pull it out of the holder.
3    To install the switch, insert it into its holder (canted slightly counterclockwise as during removal) and push it in until the switch body contacts the bracket on the brake pedal. Rotate the switch 45-degrees clockwise to lock it into place.
4    Plug the electrical connector into the switch.

**14.2a With the brake pedal fully released, measure the distance from the top of the pedal pad to the floor**

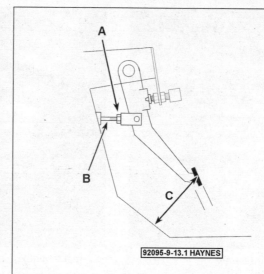

**14.2b Brake pedal details**

A   *Pushrod/clevis locknut*
B   *Power brake booster pushrod (turn this to raise or lower the pedal)*
C   *Pedal height measurement points*

92095-9-13.1 HAYNES

## 14   Brake pedal - adjustment

### Brake pedal height

1   Disconnect the brake light switch electrical connector, then remove the brake light switch (see Section 13).
2   Pull the carpet back and find the insulator cutout, then with the brake pedal fully released, measure the distance from the top of the pad to the floor (see illustrations).
3   If the height is not as listed in this Chapter's Specifications, it must be adjusted.
4   Loosen the locknut just in front of the clevis on the power brake booster pushrod.
5   Turn the booster pushrod until the pedal height is correct.
6   Tighten the locknut.
7   After adjusting the pedal height, check the freeplay, then install the brake light switch (see Section 13).

### Brake pedal freeplay

8   Press down lightly on the brake pedal and measure the distance that it moves freely before resistance is felt (see illustration). The freeplay should be within the specified limits. If it isn't, check the clevis, clevis pin and the hole in the brake pedal arm for excessive wear.

## 15   Anti-lock Brake System (ABS) and Vehicle Stability Assist (VSA) system - general information

### General information

1   All models are equipped with an Anti-lock Brake System (ABS)/Vehicle Stability Assist (VSA) system. These systems are designed to maintain vehicle steerability, directional stability and optimum deceleration under severe braking and handling conditions. It does so by

**14.8 To measure brake pedal freeplay, press down lightly on the pedal and measure the distance that it moves freely before resistance is felt**

monitoring the rotational speed of each wheel and controlling the brake line pressure to each wheel during braking. This prevents the wheels from locking up.
2   If a problem develops within the system, an "ABS" or "VSA" warning light will glow on the dashboard. Sometimes, a visual inspection of the ABS or VSA can help you locate the problem. Carefully inspect the ABS or VSA wiring harness. Pay particularly close attention to the harness and connections near each wheel. Look for signs of chafing and other damage caused by incorrectly routed wires. If a wheel sensor harness is damaged, the sensor must be replaced.
**Warning:** *Do NOT try to repair an ABS/VSA wiring harness. The ABS/VSA system is sensitive to even the smallest changes in resistance. Repairing the harness could alter resistance values and cause the system to malfunction. If the ABS/VSA wiring harness is damaged in any way, it must be replaced.*
**Caution:** *Make sure the ignition is turned off before unplugging or reattaching any electrical connections.*

### Diagnosis and repair

3   If the dashboard warning light comes on and stays on while the vehicle is in operation, the system requires attention. Although special electronic diagnostic testing tools are necessary to properly diagnose the system, you can perform a few preliminary checks before taking the vehicle to a dealer service department.
a) *Check the brake fluid level in the reservoir.*
b) *Verify that the computer electrical connectors are securely connected.*
c) *Check the electrical connectors at the hydraulic control unit.*
d) *Check the fuses.*
e) *Follow the wiring harness to each wheel and verify that all connections are secure and that the wiring is undamaged.*

4   If the above preliminary checks do not rectify the problem, the vehicle should be diagnosed by a dealer service department or other qualified repair shop. Due to the complex nature of this system, all actual repair work must be done by a qualified automotive technician.

## *Wheel speed sensor - removal and installation*

5    Loosen the wheel lug nuts, raise the vehicle and support it securely on jackstands. Remove the wheel.

6    Make sure the ignition key is turned to the Off position.

7    Trace the wiring back from the sensor, detaching all brackets and clips while noting its correct routing, then disconnect the electrical connector.

8    Remove the mounting bolt and carefully pull the sensor out from the knuckle or brake backing plate (see illustration).

9    Installation is the reverse of the removal procedure. Tighten the mounting bolt securely.

10   Install the wheel and lug nuts, tightening them securely. Lower the vehicle and tighten the lug nuts to the torque listed in the Chapter 1 Specifications.

**15.8 Rear wheel speed sensor mounting bolt (front similar)**

# Notes

# Chapter 10
# Suspension and steering

## Contents

## Specifications

### General

| | |
|---|---|
| Power steering fluid type | See Chapter 1 |

### Torque specifications

**Note:** One foot-pound (ft-lb) of torque is equivalent to 12 inch-pounds (in-lbs) of torque. Torque values below approximately 15 ft-lbs are expressed in inch-pounds, since most foot-pound torque wrenches are not accurate at these smaller values.

| | Ft-lbs (unless otherwise indicated) | Nm |
|---|---|---|
| **Front suspension** | | |
| Strut damper rod nut | | |
|     4 door models (except SI and GX models) | 40 | 54 |
|     2 door and 4 door Si and GX models | 32 | 44 |
| Strut upper mounting nuts* | 33 | 44 |
| Strut-to-steering knuckle bolts/nuts* | | |
|     With 14 mm bolts | 85 | 115 |
|     With 16 mm bolts | 116 | 157 |
|     18 inch wheel models | 125 | 169 |
| Stabilizer bar | | |
|     Civic | | |
|         Stabilizer bar link nuts* | | |
|             Upper | 28 | 38 |
|             Lower | 25 | 34 |
|         Stabilizer bar bracket bolts* | 29 | 39 |
|     CR-V | | |
|         Stabilizer bar link nuts* | 58 | 78 |
|         Stabilizer bar bracket bolts* | 58 | 78 |

*The manufacturer recommends that these fasteners(s) be replaced with new fasteners whenever they are loosened or removed.

## Torque specifications (continued)

| | Ft-lbs (unless otherwise indicated) | Nm |
|---|---|---|
| Control arm | | |
|   Arm-to-subframe* | | |
|     Civic (except 18 inch wheel models) | | |
|       12 mm bolts | 47 | 64 |
|       14 mm bolts | 61 | 83 |
|     Civic (18 inch wheel models) | | |
|       12 mm bolts | 47 | 64 |
|       16 mm bolts | 83 | 103 |
|     CR-V | | |
|       12 mm bolts | 44 | 59 |
|       14 mm bolts | 83 | 113 |
|   Balljoint-to-control arm mounting nuts and bolts* | | |
|     Civic | 44 | 59 |
|     CR-V | 38 | 52 |
| Subframe bolts* | | |
|   Main bolts | 77 | 104 |
|   Mid-bracket bolts (2) | 47 | 64 |
| Balljoint-to-steering knuckle nut | 44 to 51 | 59 to 69 |
| Driveaxle/hub nut | See Chapter 8 | |

*The manufacturer recommends that these fasteners(s) be replaced with new fasteners whenever they are loosened or removed.*

## Rear suspension

| | Ft-lbs | Nm |
|---|---|---|
| Rear hub mounting bolts | 47 | 64 |
| Shock absorber mounting fasteners* | | |
|   Civic | | |
|     Upper | 22 | 29 |
|     Lower | 44 | 59 |
|   CR-V | | |
|     Upper | 54 | 74 |
|     Lower | 69 | 93 |
| Damper rod nut* | 22 | 29 |
| Stabilizer bar clamp bolts | | |
|   8 mm bolts | 16 | 22 |
|   10 mm bolts | 36 | 49 |
| Link-to-trailing arm nuts* | 29 | 39 |
| Link-to-stabilizer bar nuts* | | |
|   Coupe, Sedan and Hatchback models | 28 | 38 |
|   CR-V models | 22 | 29 |
| Trailing arm-to-chassis mounting bracket bolts* | | |
|   Coupe and Sedan models | 80 | 108 |
|   CR-V models | 85 | 115 |
| Trailing arm-to-mounting bracket pivot bolt* | 43 | 59 |
| Trailing arm-to-knuckle bolts* | 43 | 59 |
| Upper arm-to-knuckle pivot bolt* | 43 | 59 |
| Upper arm-to-chassis mounting bolts (Coupe and Sedan models)* | 80 | 108 |
| Upper arm-to-chassis pivot bolt (CR-V models)* | 69 | 93 |

*The manufacturer recommends that these fasteners(s) be replaced with new fasteners whenever they are loosened or removed.*

## Steering system

| | Ft-lbs | Nm |
|---|---|---|
| Airbag module-to-steering wheel fasteners | 86 in-lbs | 9.5 |
| Electronic Power Steering (EPS) motor fasteners | 14 | 20 |
| Power steering pump-to-engine bracket mounting fasteners | 14 | 20 |
|   Coupe and Sedan models | 17 | 24 |
|   CR-V models | 16 | 22 |
| Power steering motor bolts (Hatchback models) | 14 | 20 |
| Steering gear mounting bolts/nuts | | |
|   Civic models | 40 | 54 |
|   CR-V models | 52 | 71 |
| Tie-rod end-to-steering knuckle nut | 40 | 54 |
| Intermediate shaft-to-universal joint pinch-bolt | 21 to 22 | 28 to 29 |
| Steering gear input shaft-to-universal joint pinch-bolt | 21 to 22 | 28 to 29 |
| Steering column mounting fasteners | 132 in-lbs | 16 |
| Steering wheel mounting bolt/nut | 29 | 39 |

**1.1 Front suspension and steering components (Civic model shown)**

| | | | | | |
|---|---|---|---|---|---|
| 1 | Strut/coil spring assembly | 4 | Balljoint | 7 | Stabilizer bar |
| 2 | Steering knuckle | 5 | Control arm | 8 | Subframe |
| 3 | Tie-rod end | 6 | Stabilizer bar link | 9 | Steering gear boot |

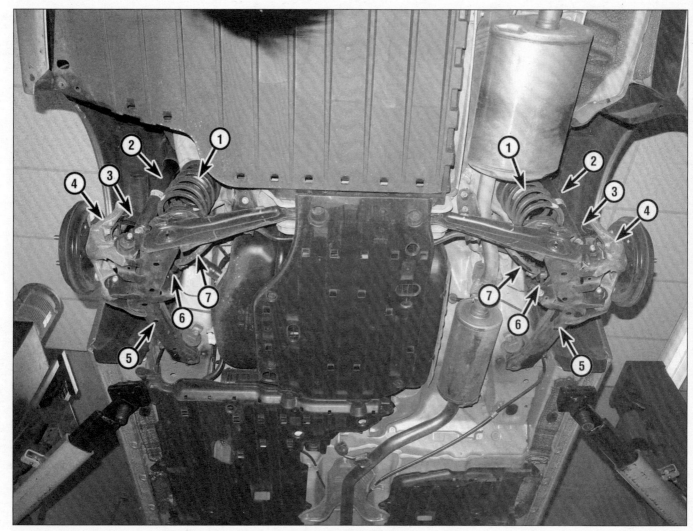

**1.2 Rear suspension components (Civic models)**

| | | | | | |
|---|---|---|---|---|---|
| 1 | Coil spring | 4 | Rear knuckle | 6 | Stabilizer bar link |
| 2 | Shock absorber | 5 | Trailing arm | 7 | Stabilizer bar |
| 3 | Upper control arm | | | | |

## 1   General Information

1   The front suspension is a MacPherson strut design. The upper end of each strut is attached to the vehicle's body strut support. The lower end of the strut is connected to the upper end of the steering knuckle. The steering knuckle is attached by a balljoint mounted to the outer end of the suspension control arm. A stabilizer bar connected to each control arm and mounted to the suspension crossmember reduces body roll during cornering (see illustrations).

2   The rear suspension employs trailing arms, upper control arms and either shock absorber/coil spring assemblies (CR-V models) or shock absorbers with independent coil springs (Civic models) (see illustrations). The stabilizer bar is clamped to a suspension support and connected to the trailing arms by two links.

3   The power-assisted rack-and-pinion steering gear is attached to the front suspension subframe. The assist comes from an electric motor mounted to the steering gear. The steering gear actuates the tie-rods, which are attached to the steering knuckles. The steering column is designed to collapse in the event of an accident.

4   Frequently, when working on the suspension or steering system components, you may come across fasteners that seem impossible to loosen. These fasteners on the underside of the vehicle are continually subjected to water, road grime, mud, etc., and can become rusted or frozen, making them extremely difficult to remove. In order to unscrew these stubborn fasteners without damaging them (or other components), be sure to use lots of penetrating oil and allow it to soak in for a while. Using a wire brush to clean exposed threads will also ease removal of the nut or bolt and prevent damage to the threads. Sometimes a sharp blow with a hammer and punch will break the bond between a nut and bolt threads, but care must be taken to prevent the punch from slipping off the fastener and ruining the threads. Heating the stuck fastener and surrounding area with a torch sometimes helps too, but isn't recommended because of the obvious dangers associated with fire.

5   Long breaker bars and extension, or cheater, pipes will increase leverage, but never use an extension pipe on a ratchet - the ratcheting mechanism could be damaged. Sometimes tightening the nut or bolt first will help to break it loose. Fasteners that require drastic measures to remove should always be replaced with new ones.

6   Since most of the procedures dealt with in this Chapter involve jacking up the vehicle and working underneath it, a good pair of jackstands will be needed. A hydraulic floor jack is the preferred type of jack to lift the vehicle, and it can also be used to support certain components during various operations.

**Warning:** *Never, under any circumstances, rely on a jack to support the vehicle while working on it. Whenever any of the suspension or steering fasteners are loosened or removed they must be inspected and, if necessary, replaced with new ones of the same part number or of original equipment quality and design. Torque specifications must be followed for proper reassembly and component retention. Never attempt to heat or straighten any suspension or steering components. Instead, replace any bent or damaged part with a new one.*

## 2   Stabilizer bar and bushings (front) - removal, inspection and installation

### *Removal*

1   Loosen the front wheel lug nuts, raise the front of the vehicle and support it securely on jackstands. Apply the parking brake and block the rear wheels to keep the vehicle from rolling off the stands. Remove the front wheels.

#### Stabilizer bar links

2   Remove the nuts securing the stabilizer bar links to the control arms and the stabilizer bar (see illustration).

3   Detach the link from the bar and control arm.

4   Installation is the reverse of removal. Tighten the nuts to the torque listed in this Chapter's Specifications.

#### Stabilizer bar and bushings

5   Working in the driver's footwell, remove the steering column joint cover, then detach the steering column shaft from the steering gear (see Section 18).

**Caution:** *Don't allow the steering wheel to turn after the shaft has been disconnected from the steering gear - the airbag clockspring could be damaged. To prevent this from happening, run the seat belt through the steering wheel and click it into its latch. Also, don't allow the slip joint of the shaft to become disengaged from the upper portion of the shaft; if necessary, restrain it with a length of wire.*

6   Detach the stabilizer bar links from the control arms as described previously in this Section.

7   Detach the balljoints from the steering knuckles (see Section 5).

8   Detach the tie-rod end from the steering knuckle (see Section 17).

9   Remove under-vehicle splash shields (see Chapter 2A, illustrations 14.3a and 14.3b).

10  Remove front section of the exhaust system (see Chapter 4).

#### CR-V models

11  If you're working on an AWD model, remove the driveshaft (see Chapter 8).

12  Support the rear of the subframe with a floor jack. Remove the rear subframe bolts and the mid (center) subframe bolts, and loosen the front subframe bolts approximately 1-3/16 inches (30 mm).

13  Remove the torque rod (roll restrictor)-to-engine bolts.

14  Lower the subframe approximately 5-18 inches (130 mm).

#### Civic models

15  Remove the steering gear fasteners (see Section 18).

16  Remove the steering gear stiffener brackets, if equipped (see Section 18).

#### All models

17  Remove the stabilizer bar brackets bolts and brackets (see illustration).

18  If you're working on a Civic model, lift up on the steering box a few inches and hold it in place while you slide the stabilizer bar out the driver's side of the vehicle.

**Note:** *When reinstalling the rubber bushings for the stabilizer bar be sure to have the slits in the bushing in the same direction as they previously were.*

### *Inspection*

19  Inspect for cracked, torn, or distorted stabilizer bar bushings, bushing retainers, and worn or damaged stabilizer bar links.

20  To replace damaged stabilizer bar bushings, remove the bracket (if not already done),

**2.2 Use an Allen wrench to prevent the stabilizer bar link ballstud from turning when removing the nut**

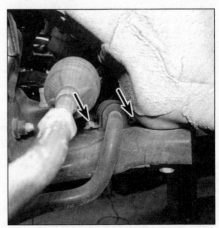

**2.17 Stabilizer bar bracket bolts**

**3.4 Mark the position of the strut to the steering knuckle, around the bolt heads and where the strut meets the knuckle**

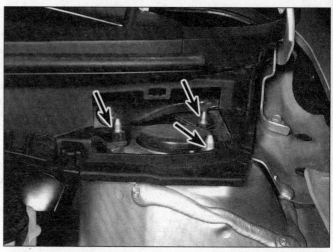

**3.5 Remove the access cover from the cowl panel to expose the upper strut mounting nuts. DO NOT remove the center nut (under the cover on top of the strut)**

open the bushing slit and peel the bushing from the stabilizer bar. On some models, it will be necessary to bend back the tabs holding the retainer together.
**Caution:** *Install the new bushings with the slits facing the same way that the original bushing slits faced.*

## Installation

21  Guide the stabilizer bar into position. Install the bushing bracket bolts, tightening them to the torque listed in this Chapter's Specifications.
22  On CR-V models, raise the subframe and install the bolts, tightening them to the torque listed in this Chapter's Specifications. Install the torque rod bolts, tightening them to the torque listed in the Chapter 2B Specifications.
23  Connect the stabilizer bar links to the lower control arms. Tighten the nuts to the torque listed in this Chapter's Specifications.
24  Connect the balljoints to the control arms, tightening the nuts to the torque listed in this Chapter's Specifications.
25  Install the wheels and lug nuts. Lower the vehicle and tighten the lug nuts to the torque listed in the Chapter 1 Specifications.
26  If you're working on a CR-V model, have the front end alignment checked and, if necessary, adjusted.

---

## 3   Strut assembly (front) - removal, inspection and installation

## Removal

**Note:** *If both strut assemblies are going to be removed, mark the assemblies Right and Left so they will be reinstalled on the correct side.*
1  Loosen the wheel lug nuts, raise the vehicle and support it securely on jackstands. Remove the wheels.
2  Unbolt the brake hose bracket from the strut. If the vehicle is equipped with ABS, detach the speed sensor wiring harness from

the strut by removing the clamp bracket bolt.
3  Remove the stabilizer bar link from the strut (see Section 2).
4  Mark the position of the strut to the steering knuckle, then remove the strut-to-knuckle nuts and bolts (see illustration).
**Note:** *This is only necessary if special camber adjusting bolts have been installed in place of the regular strut-to-knuckle bolts. Remove the strut-to-knuckle nuts, then knock the bolts out with a hammer and punch.*
5  Remove the access cover from the cowl panel, then remove the three upper nuts securing the strut assembly to the body (see illustration).
**Note:** *Support the strut assembly while removing the last nut.*
6  Separate the strut from the steering knuckle and remove it.
**Caution:** *Be careful not to overextend the inner CV joint. Also, don't let the steering knuckle fall outward and strain the brake hose.*
7  Installation is the reverse of removal.

## Inspection

8  Check the strut body for leaking fluid, dents, cracks and other obvious damage which would warrant repair or replacement.
9  Check the coil spring for chips or cracks in the spring coating (this will cause premature spring failure due to corrosion). Inspect the spring seat for cuts, hardness and general deterioration.
10  If any undesirable conditions exist, proceed to the strut disassembly procedure (see Section 4).

## Installation

11  Guide the strut assembly up into the fenderwell and insert the upper mounting studs through the holes in the body. Once the studs protrude, install the nuts so the strut won't fall back through. This is most easily accomplished with the help of an assistant, as the strut is quite heavy and awkward.
12  Slide the steering knuckle into the strut

flange and insert the two bolts. Install the nuts, align the previously made matchmarks and tighten them to the torque listed in this Chapter's Specifications.
13  The remainder of installation is the reverse of removal. Tighten all fasteners to the torque values listed in this Chapter's Specifications.
14  Install the wheel and lug nuts, then lower the vehicle and tighten the lug nuts to the torque listed in the Chapter 1 Specifications.
15  Tighten the upper mounting nuts to the torque listed in this Chapter's Specifications. Install the cowl panel cover.
16  Have the front end alignment checked and, if necessary, adjusted.

---

## 4   Strut/spring assembly - replacement

**Warning:** *Struts and/or coil springs must be replaced in pairs - never replace just one of them.*
1  If the struts or coil springs exhibit the telltale signs of wear (leaking fluid, loss of damping capability, chipped, sagging or cracked coil springs) explore all options before beginning any work. The strut/shock absorber assemblies are not serviceable and must be replaced if a problem develops. However, strut assemblies complete with springs may be available on an exchange basis, which eliminates much time and work. Whichever route you choose to take, check on the cost and availability of parts before disassembling your vehicle.
**Warning:** *Disassembling a strut is potentially dangerous and utmost attention must be directed to the job, or serious injury may result. Use only a high-quality spring compressor and carefully follow the manufacturer's instructions furnished with the tool. After removing the coil spring from the strut assembly, set it aside in a safe, isolated area.*

**4.3 Install the spring compressor following the tool manufacturer's instructions; compress the spring until all pressure is relieved from the upper spring seat (you can verify the spring is loose by wiggling it)**

**4.5 Lift the upper mount off the damper rod**

**4.6 Remove the upper spring seat and insulator from the damper rod**

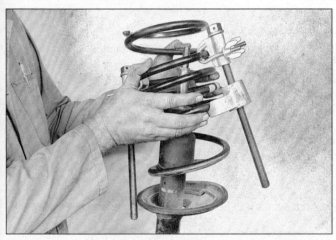

**4.7 Remove the compressed spring from the strut/shock absorber assembly - keep the ends of the spring pointed away from your body**

**4.11 When installing the spring, make sure the end fits into the recessed portion of the lower seat**

## Disassembly

2    Remove the strut and spring assembly (see Section 3). Mount the strut assembly in a vise. Line the vise jaws with wood or rags to prevent damage to the unit and don't tighten the vise excessively.

3    Following the tool manufacturer's instructions, install the spring compressor (which can be obtained at most auto parts stores or equipment yards on a daily rental basis) on the spring and compress it sufficiently to relieve all pressure from the upper spring seat (see illustration). This can be verified by wiggling the spring.

4    Hold the damper rod with an Allen wrench, and unscrew the damper rod nut with a box-end wrench.

5    Remove the nut and upper mount (see illustration). Lay the parts out in the exact order in which they are removed. Inspect the bearing in the suspension support for smooth operation. If it doesn't turn smoothly, replace

the upper mount. Check the rubber portion of the upper mount for cracking and general deterioration. If there is any separation of the rubber, replace it.

6    Remove the upper spring seat from the damper rod (see illustration). Check the spring seat for cracking and hardness; replace it if necessary. Remove the upper insulator from the damper shaft.

7    Carefully lift the compressed spring from the assembly (see illustration) and set it in a safe place.

**Warning:** *When removing the compressed spring, lift it off carefully and set it in a safe place. Keep the ends of the spring away from your body.*

**Note:** *If you are disassembling both struts, mark the springs LEFT and RIGHT so you don't mix them up (they're different).*

8    Remove the dust cover plate and dust cover.

9    Slide the rubber bump stop off the

damper rod. Check the bump stop for cracking and general deterioration. If there is any deterioration of the rubber, replace it.

## Reassembly

10    Extend the damper rod to its full length and install the rubber bump stop, dust cover and dust cover plate.

11    Carefully place the compressed coil spring onto the lower seat of the damper, with the end of the spring resting in the lowest part of the seat (see illustration).

12    Install the upper insulator and spring seat.

13    Install the bearing and suspension support.

14    Install the washer and damper rod nut and tighten it to the torque listed in this Chapter's Specifications. Remove the spring compressor tool.

15    Install the strut/spring assembly (see Section 3).

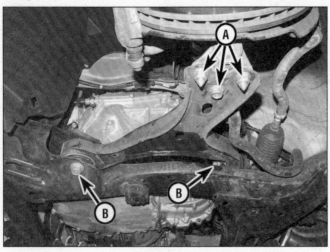

5.3 Balljoint-to-control arm bolt and nuts (A) and Control arm-to-subframe bolts (B)

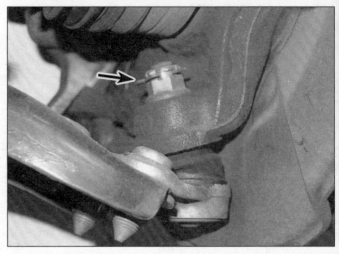

6.3 First note how it's installed, then remove the balljoint stud nut lock pin

## 5   Control arm (front) - removal and installation

1   Loosen the wheel lug nuts, raise the vehicle and support it securely on jackstands. Remove the wheel.
2   Detach the stabilizer bar link from the control arm (see Section 2).
3   Remove the fasteners securing the balljoint to the control arm (see illustration).
4   Remove the control arm-to-subframe mounting bolts.
5   Remove the control arm.
6   Installation is the reverse of removal.
7   Install the wheel and lug nuts, then lower the vehicle and tighten the lug nuts to the torque listed in the Chapter 1 Specifications.

## 6   Balljoints - replacement

1   Loosen the wheel lug nuts, raise the vehicle and support it securely on jackstands. Remove the wheel.
2   Remove the fasteners and separate the balljoint from the control arm (see Section 5).
3   Remove the lock pin and loosen the balljoint stud nut a few turns, but don't remove it (see illustration).
4   Use a balljoint separator to break the balljoint loose from the steering knuckle (see illustration).
5   Remove the nut and detach the balljoint from the steering knuckle.
6   Installation is the reverse of the removal procedure. Be sure to tighten the fasteners to the torque values listed in this Chapter's Specifications, then install the lock pin.
7   Install the wheel and lug nuts, then lower the vehicle and tighten the lug nuts to the torque listed in the Chapter 1 Specifications.

## 7   Steering knuckle and hub - removal and installation

**Warning:** *Dust created by the brake system is harmful to your health. Never blow it out with compressed air and don't inhale any of it. Do not, under any circumstances, use petroleum-based solvents to clean brake parts. Use brake system cleaner only.*

### Removal

1   Loosen the wheel lug nuts, raise the vehicle and support it securely on jackstands. Remove the wheel.
2   Remove the driveaxle/hub nut (see Chapter 8). Remove the brake caliper and support it with a piece of wire as described in Chapter 9. Remove the caliper mounting bracket, then remove the brake disc from the hub.

6.4 Use a balljoint separator like this (available at most auto parts stores) to pop the ballstud out of the steering knuckle

3   Remove the stabilizer end link nut.
4   Mark the strut to the steering knuckle, then remove the strut-to-steering knuckle nuts, but do not remove the bolts.
5   Detach the ABS wheel speed sensor from the steering knuckle (see Chapter 8).
6   Separate the control arm from the balljoint (see Section 5). Detach the tie-rod end from the steering knuckle (see Section 17).
7   Push the driveaxle from the hub as described in Chapter 8. Support the end of the driveaxle with a piece of wire.
8   Remove the bolts and separate the steering knuckle from the strut.
9   Installation is the reverse of removal.

### Installation

10   Guide the knuckle and hub assembly into position, inserting the driveaxle into the hub.
11   Push the knuckle into the strut flange and install the bolts and nuts, but don't tighten them yet.
12   Connect the balljoint to the control arm and tighten the fasteners to the torque listed in this Chapter's Specifications.
13   Tighten the strut bolt nuts and the tie-rod end nut to the torque values listed in this Chapter's Specifications.
14   Place the brake disc on the hub and install the caliper mounting bracket and caliper as outlined in Chapter 9.
15   Install the driveaxle/hub nut and tighten it to the torque listed in the Chapter 8 Specifications.
16   Install the wheel and lug nuts. Lower the vehicle and tighten the lug nuts to the torque listed in the Chapter 1 Specifications.
17   Have the front wheel alignment checked and, if necessary, adjusted.

## 8  Hub and bearing assembly (front) - replacement

**Warning:** *Dust created by the brake system is harmful to your health. Never blow it out with compressed air and don't inhale any of it. Do not, under any circumstances, use petroleum-based solvents to clean brake parts. Use brake system cleaner only.*
**Warning:** *Working with hydraulic presses or large gear pullers can be dangerous. If you are not confident in tackling this task we suggest you take this to a professional repair shop.*

1  Remove the steering knuckle (see Section 7).
2  Using the proper adapter and press plate, press the hub out of the knuckle/wheel bearing with a hydraulic, from the back side to the front.
3  Using a bearing splitter and the proper adapter, press the hub through the bearing inner race.
4  Remove the screws and detach the disc splash shield from the knuckle.
5  Remove the snap-ring from the back side of the knuckle.
6  Using the proper adapter and press plate, press the bearing out of the steering knuckle with a hydraulic press, from the back side to the front.
7  Clean the bore in the knuckle.
8  Reverse the removal procedure to install the new bearing.
**Caution:** *Install the bearing with the ABS wheel speed sensor encoder (the brown side of the bearing) facing the inside of the knuckle.*
**Note:** *Do not forget to reinstall the snap-ring before installing the hub. The hub and bearing must be fully seated back in the knuckle before installing the steering knuckle.*
9  Install the steering knuckle (see Section 7).

## 9  Shock absorber (rear, Civic models) - removal and installation

1  Loosen the rear wheel lug nuts. Raise the rear of the vehicle and support it securely on jackstands. Block the front wheels to prevent the vehicle from rolling. Remove the wheel.
2  Fold down the trim panel in the trunk for access to the shock absorber upper mount.
3  Support the lower arm with a floor jack placed under the trailing arm (where it meets the knuckle).
**Warning:** *Do not move the jack while it is supporting the lower arm and the coil spring tension.*
4  Remove the shock absorber upper mounting nut (see illustration).
**Note:** *Hold the damper shaft with a hex bit while loosening the nut to prevent the shaft from turning.*
5  Remove the shock absorber lower mounting bolt (see illustration), then remove

**9.4 Rear shock absorber upper mounting nut (Civic models)**

the shock absorber.
6  Check the shock body for leaking fluid, dents, cracks and other obvious damage which would warrant repair or replacement.
7  Guide the shock absorber up into the fenderwell and insert the damper through the hole in the body. Once the damper rod protrudes from the hole, install the bushing, washer and nut so the assembly won't fall back through.
**Note:** *Be sure to use new mounting bushings.*
8  Connect the shock to the trailing arm. Raise the trailing arm with the floor jack to simulate normal ride height, then tighten the shock absorber lower mounting bolt and damper mounting nut to the torque listed in this Chapter's Specifications.
9  Install the wheel and lug nuts, lower the vehicle and tighten the lug nuts to the torque listed in the Chapter 1 Specifications.

## 10  Shock absorber/coil spring assembly (rear, CR-V models) - removal, component replacement and installation

### Removal

1  Loosen the rear wheel lug nuts. Raise the rear of the vehicle and support it securely on jackstands. Block the front wheels to prevent the vehicle from rolling. Remove the wheel. Support the trailing arm with a floor jack (where it meets the knuckle).
2  Disconnect the stabilizer bar link from the trailing arm.
3  Unbolt the brake hose from the bracket on the trailing arm.
4  Unbolt the parking brake cable from the floorpan (near the trailing arm-to-floorpan mount).
5  Remove the bolts securing the front of the trailing arm to the floorpan.
6  Fold down the rear seat back and remove the side trim panel (shock absorber access cover) from the cargo area. Remove

**9.5 Rear shock absorber lower mounting bolt (Civic models)**

**10.6 Remove the nuts from the shock absorber mounting studs - DON'T remove the nut in the center (2005 and earlier Civic and all CR-V models)**

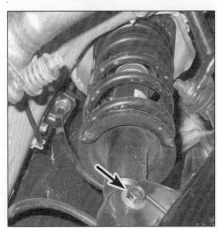

**10.7 Rear shock absorber lower mounting bolt (2005 and earlier Civic and all CR-V models)**

the shock absorber upper mounting nuts (see illustration).
7  Remove the shock absorber lower mounting bolt (see illustration), then remove the shock absorber/coil spring assembly.

**11.2 Raise the jack just enough to take the pressure off of the spring**

8    Check the shock body for leaking fluid, dents, cracks and other obvious damage which would warrant repair or replacement.

9    Check the coil spring for chips or cracks in the spring coating (this will cause premature spring failure due to corrosion). Inspect the spring seat for cuts, hardness and general deterioration.

10    If any undesirable conditions exist, proceed to the component replacement procedure.

### Component replacement

**Warning:** *Disassembling a shock/coil spring is potentially dangerous and utmost attention must be directed to the job, or serious injury may result. Use only a high-quality spring compressor and carefully follow the manufacturer's instructions furnished with the tool. After removing the coil spring from the shock absorber, set it aside in a safe, isolated area.*

**Note:** *If the shocks or coil springs exhibit the telltale signs of wear (leaking fluid, loss of damping capability, chipped, sagging or cracked coil springs), explore all options before beginning any work. The shock absorber/ coil spring assemblies are not serviceable and must be replaced if a problem develops. However, assemblies complete with springs may be available on an exchange basis, which eliminates much time and work. Whichever route you choose to take, check on the cost and availability of parts before disassembling your vehicle.*

11    Mount the shock/coil spring assembly in a vise. Line the vise jaws with wood or rags to prevent damage to the unit and don't tighten the vise excessively.

12    Following the tool manufacturer's instructions, install the spring compressor (which can be obtained at most auto parts stores or equipment yards on a daily rental basis) on the spring and compress it sufficiently to relieve all pressure from the upper spring seat. This can be verified by wiggling the spring.

**Note:** *Note the orientation of the upper mount in relation to the lower mounting eye (when reassembling the unit, the mount will have to be in the same position). Make a sketch or some matchmarks to help you get the mount positioned properly when reinstalling it.*

13    Hold the shock damper rod with an Allen wrench, and unscrew the retaining nut with a box-end wrench.

14    Disassemble the parts from the damper, taking care to lay the parts out in the exact order in which they are removed.

**Warning:** *When removing the compressed spring, lift it off carefully and set it in a safe place. Keep the ends of the spring away from your body.*

15    Reassembly is the reverse of removal, noting the following points:

a)  *Carefully place the spring onto the shock absorber body with the end of the spring resting in the lowest part of the seat.*

b)  *Use a new self-locking nut, then tighten the nut to the torque listed in this Chapter's Specifications.*

c)  *Before releasing the spring compressor, make sure the upper mount is oriented as it was before removal in Step 8.*

### Installation

16    Guide the shock absorber/coil spring assembly up into the fenderwell and insert the upper mounting studs through the holes in the body. Once the studs protrude from the holes, install the nuts so the assembly won't fall back through, but don't tighten the nuts completely yet. The shock absorber is heavy and awkward, so get an assistant to help you, if possible.

17    Connect the shock to the trailing arm. Install the trailing arm-to-floorpan bolts and tighten them to the torque listed in this Chapter's Specifications.

18    Raise the trailing arm with the floor jack to simulate normal ride height, Tighten the shock absorber lower mounting bolt to the torque listed in this Chapter's Specifications.

19    The remainder of installation is the reverse of removal.

20    Install the wheel and lug nuts, lower the vehicle and tighten the lug nuts to the torque listed in the Chapter 1 Specifications.

21    Tighten the upper mounting nuts to the torque listed in this Chapter's Specifcations 0.

22    Have the rear wheel alignment checked and, if necessary, adjusted.

### 11  Coil spring (rear, Civic models) - removal and installation

1    Loosen the rear wheel lug nuts. Raise the rear of the vehicle and support it securely on jackstands. Block the front wheels to prevent the vehicle from rolling. Remove the wheel.

2    Place a floor jack under the trailing arm (where it meets the rear knuckle). Slowly raise the jack until the spring begins to compress (see illustration).

3    Remove the ABS rear wheel speed sensor from the knuckle. Also unbolt the rear brake hose bracket from the knuckle (see Chapter 9).

4    Detach the stabilizer bar link from the trailing arm (see Section 14).

5    Remove the shock absorber lower mounting bolt (see Section 9).

6    Unbolt the upper arm from the rear knuckle (see Section 12).

7    Unbolt the forward end of the trailing arm from the floorpan (see Section 12).

8    Slowly lower the jack and remove the coil spring.

9    Check the coil spring for chips or cracks in the spring coating (this will cause premature spring failure due to corrosion). Inspect the spring seat for cuts, hardness and general deterioration, replacing it if necessary.

10    Installation is the reverse of removal, noting the following points:

a)  *Be sure to position the lower end of the coil spring in the depressed area of the trailing arm.*

b)  *Raise the outer end of the trailing arm with a floor jack to simulate normal ride height, then tighten the suspension fasteners to the torque listed in this Chapter's Specifications.*

c)  *Tighten the wheel and lug nuts to the torque listed in the Chapter 1 Specifications.*

d)  *Have the rear wheel alignment checked and, if necessary, adjusted.*

### 12  Suspension arms (rear) and rear knuckle - removal and installation

1    Loosen the rear wheel lug nuts. Raise the rear of the vehicle and support it securely on jackstands. Block the front wheels to prevent the vehicle from rolling. Remove the wheel.

### Upper arm

2    If you're working on a CR-V, detach the ABS wheel speed sensor harness bracket from the upper arm.

3    Support the trailing arm with a floor jack.

**Warning:** *The jack must remain in this position until the arm is reinstalled.*

4    Remove the upper arm-to-knuckle bolt,

**12.4 Upper arm-to-knuckle bolt and inner pivot shaft bolts (Civic model shown)**

**12.9 Mark the toe adjusting cam to the trailing arm**

then remove the bolt(s) from the inner end of the arm (see illustration).

5    Installation is the reverse of removal, noting the following points:

a) *Before fully tightening the fasteners, raise the trailing arm with the floor jack to simulate normal ride height.*

b) *Tighten all fasteners to the torque listed in this Chapter's Specifications.*

c) *Tighten the wheel lug nuts to the torque listed in the Chapter 1 Specifications.*

## Trailing arm

6    Support the trailing arm with a floor jack.

7    Unbolt the brake hose and ABS sensor mounting brackets.

8    Remove the rear undercarriage splash shield (if applicable).

9    Mark the relationship of the toe adjusting cam on the trailing arm-to-knuckle bolt (see illustration).

10    Remove the lower shock absorber bolt.

11    Remove the trailing arm-to-knuckle bolts, then disconnect the arm from the knuckle.

**Note:** *Suspend the knuckle with a bungee cord or piece of wire.*

12    Disconnect the stabilizer bar link from the trailing arm (see Section 14).

13    If you're working on a Civic model, remove the shock absorber lower mounting bolt, then remove the trailing arm-to-chassis front mounting bolts. Slowly lower the floor jack and remove the coil spring.

14    Remove the trailing arm-to-chassis front mounting bolts (CR-V models), then remove the trailing arm-to-chassis pivot bolt (see illustration).

15    Remove the trailing arm.

16    Installation is the reverse of removal, noting the following points:

a) *Align the mark you made on the adjuster cam with the mark on the trailing arm.*

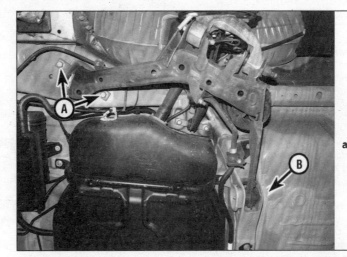

**12.14 Trailing arm-to-chassis front mounting bolts (A) and rear pivot bolt (B)**

b) *Before fully tightening the fasteners, raise the trailing arm with the floor jack to simulate normal ride height.*

c) *Tighten all fasteners to the proper torque specifications.*

d) *Tighten the wheel lug nuts to the torque listed in the Chapter 1 Specifications.*

e) *Have the rear wheel alignment checked and, if necessary, adjusted.*

## Rear knuckle

17    If you're working on an AWD CR-V model, remove the driveaxle/hub nut.

18    Remove the brake drum or brake caliper and disc (see Chapter 9).

19    Remove the parking brake shoes (if equipped), wheel speed sensor and parking brake cable (see Chapter 9).

20    Support the trailing arm with a floor jack, then disconnect the suspension arms from the knuckle.

21    Remove the rear wheel bearing hub assembly (see Section 13).

22    On drum brake models, remove the brake backing plate with the brake shoes attached.

23    Remove the upper and lower fasteners for the knuckle to the upper arm and trailing arm. Be sure to mark the cam bolt position before removing it.

24    Installation is the reverse of removal, noting the following points:

a) *Before fully tightening the suspension arm fasteners, raise the trailing arm with a floor jack to simulate normal ride height.*

b) *Align the matchmarks on the toe adjusting cam (see Section 13).*

c) *Tighten all fasteners to the proper torque specifications.*

d) *Tighten the caliper mounting bolts to the proper torque settings.*

e) *It won't be necessary to bleed the brakes unless a hydraulic fitting was loosened.*

f) *Have the rear wheel alignment checked and, if necessary.*

13.4 Hub assembly retaining bolts

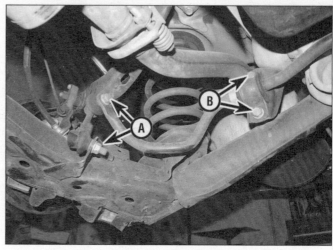

14.3 Stabilizer bar link nuts (A) and bracket bolts (B)

## 13   Hub and bearing assembly (rear) - removal and installation

**Warning:** *Dust created by the brake system is harmful to your health. Never blow it out with compressed air and don't inhale any of it. Do not, under any circumstances, use petroleum-based solvents to clean brake parts. Use brake system cleaner only.*

**Note:** *The rear hub and bearing are combined into a single assembly. The bearing is sealed for life and requires no lubrication or attention. If the bearing is worn or damaged, replace the entire hub and bearing assembly.*

1   Loosen the rear wheel lug nuts, raise the rear of the vehicle and support it securely on jackstands. Block the front wheels to prevent the vehicle from rolling. Remove the wheel.

2   If you're working on an AWD CR-V model, remove the driveaxle/hub nut.

3   Remove the brake drum or disc (see Chapter 9).

4   From the backside of the knuckle, remove the four retaining bolts securing the hub assembly to the knuckle (see illustration).

5   Remove the hub and bearing assembly from the spindle.

6   If equipped, remove the O-ring.

7   Installation is the reverse of removal, noting the following points:

a)   *Install a new O-ring (if applicable) and tighten the hub bolts to the torque listed in this Chapter's Specifications.*

b)   *On models with rear disc brakes, tighten the caliper mounting bracket bolts to the torque listed in the Chapter 9 Specifications.*

c)   *On AWD CR-V models, tighten the drive-axle/hub nut to the torque listed in the Chapter 8 Specifications.*

d)   *Install the wheel and lug nuts. Lower the vehicle and tighten the lug nuts to the torque listed in the Chapter 1 Specifications.*

## 14   Stabilizer bar and bushings (rear) - removal, inspection and installation

1   Loosen the rear wheel lug nuts. Raise the rear of the vehicle and support it securely on jackstands. Block the front wheels to prevent the vehicle from rolling. Remove the rear wheels.

2   If applicable, remove the undercarriage trim panel.

3   Remove the stabilizer bar link nuts and the stabilizer bar bracket bolts and remove the stabilizer bar (see illustration).

4   Pull the brackets off the stabilizer bar and inspect the bushings for cracks, hardness and other signs of deterioration. If the bushings are damaged, replace them.

5   Installation is the reverse of removal. Tighten the fasteners to the torque listed in this Chapter's Specifications.

15.2 Remove the panel from the underside of the steering wheel

## 15   Steering wheel - removal and installation

**Warning:** *These models are equipped with a Supplemental Restraint System (SRS), more commonly known as airbags. Always disable the airbag system before working in the vicinity of any airbag system component to avoid the possibility of accidental deployment of the airbag(s), which could cause personal injury (see Chapter 12).*

**Warning:** *Do not use a memory saving device to preserve the PCM or radio memory when working on or near airbag system components.*

### Removal

1   Make sure the front wheels are pointed straight ahead, then disconnect the cable from the negative terminal of the battery (see Chapter 5). Wait at least three minutes before proceeding.

2   Remove the airbag connector access panel from the bottom of the steering wheel (see illustration).

**15.3a Disconnect the electrical connector for the airbag module**

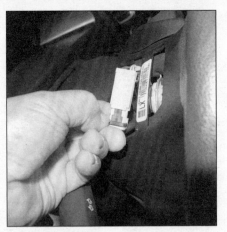

**15.3b Pull the connector off of the retaining clip, then disconnect the connector**

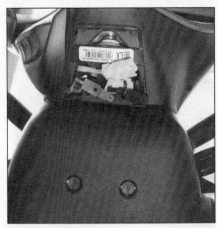

**15.3c Push the electrical connection back into the cavity but not back onto the retainer**

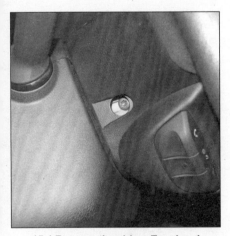

**15.4 Remove the airbag Torx-head fasteners on each side of the steering wheel**

**15.7 Steering wheel matchmarks**

**15.8 Use a steering wheel puller to remove the steering wheel**

3    Unplug the electrical connectors (see illustrations).

4    Remove the fasteners retaining the airbag module to the steering wheel (see illustration).

5    Pull off the airbag module, then carefully set it in a safe location.

**Caution:** *Carry the airbag module with the trim side facing away from you, and set the steering wheel/airbag module down with the trim side facing up. Don't place anything on top of the airbag module.*

6    Disconnect the connectors for the horn and the cruise control switch.

7    Check to see if there are matchmarks on the steering wheel and steering column shaft (see illustration). If there are none, make your own.

8    Remove the steering wheel using a steering wheel puller (see illustration). The puller screw must be contacting the steering wheel bolt or shaft.

**Caution:** *Don't thread the bolts of the puller*

into the steering wheel more than five turns, as they could contact the airbag clockspring and damage it.

**Caution:** *While the steering wheel is removed, DO NOT turn the steering shaft. If you do so, the airbag clockspring could be damaged. Once the steering wheel has been released from the shaft, remove the puller and retaining bolt. Make a mark indicating the relationship of the steering wheel hub to the steering shaft, then pull the steering wheel off the shaft.*

9    If it is necessary to remove the clockspring, remove the steering column covers (see Chapter 11). Tape the clockspring to prevent it from turning, then unplug the clockspring electrical connectors, release the retaining tabs and detach if from the steering column (see illustration).

## Installation

10   With the front wheels pointed straight ahead, make sure that the airbag clockspring is centered with the arrow on the clockspring

**15.9 Use a small screwdriver to release the clockspring retaining tabs**

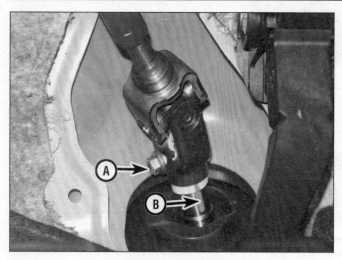

**16.8 Steering shaft U-joint**

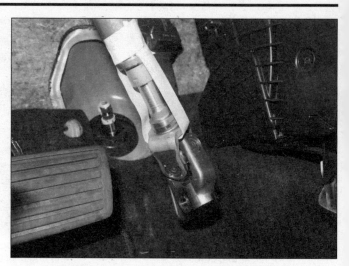

**16.9 Wire or tape the shaft so it doesn't slide apart**

A   Pinch bolt
B   Mark the U-joint to the steering gear input shaft

**16.10 Steering
column fasteners**

pointing up. This shouldn't be a problem as long as you have not turned the steering shaft while the wheel was removed. If for some reason the shaft was turned, center the clock-spring as follows:

a) *Rotate the clockspring clockwise until it stops.*
b) *Rotate the clockspring counterclockwise about 2-1/2 to 3 turns until the arrow on the clockspring points straight up.*

11    Be sure to align the index mark on the steering wheel hub with the mark on the shaft when you slip the wheel onto the shaft. Make sure the locating pins on the turn signal can-celing cam engage the holes in the backside of the steering wheel, and the notches in the steering wheel hub engage the tabs on the turn signal canceling cam. Install a NEW steering wheel bolt and tighten it to the torque listed in this Chapter's Specifications.
12    Connect the horn and the cruise control switch connectors.
13    Reattach the airbag module using NEW

fasteners and tighten them to the torque listed in this Chapter's Specifications.
14    Plug in the electrical connector for the airbag module and install the trim panel.
15    Reconnect the negative battery cable (see Chapter 5).

**16    Steering column - removal and installation**

**Warning:** *These models are equipped with a Supplemental Restraint System (SRS), more commonly known as airbags. Always disable the airbag system before working in the vicin-ity of any airbag system component to avoid the possibility of accidental deployment of the airbag(s), which could cause personal injury (see Chapter 12).*
**Warning:** *Do not use a memory saving device to preserve the PCM or radio memory when working on or near airbag system compo-nents.*

*Removal*

1    Park the vehicle with the wheels point-ing straight ahead. Disconnect the cable from the negative terminal of the battery (see Chapter 5).
2    Adjust the steering wheel tilt to the Neu-tral position, approximately 8 mm down from the uppermost position.
3    Remove the steering wheel (see Sec-tion 15).
4    Remove the steering column covers (see Chapter 11).
5    Remove the driver's knee bolster (see Chapter 11).
6    Remove the clockspring (see Sec-tion 15).
7    Remove the steering column switches (see Chapter 12).
8    Remove the steering column joint cover, mark the relationship of the steering shaft U-joint to the steering gear input shaft, then remove the pinch bolt (see illustration).
9    Collapse the intermediate shaft enough to free the splines. Then, using a piece of wire or tape, tie or tape the shaft so that it cannot slide apart (see illustration).
10    Remove the steering column mounting fasteners (see illustration), lower the column and pull it to the rear, making sure nothing is still connected, then remove the column.

*Installation*

11    Guide the steering column into position, then install the steering column mounting fas-teners and tighten them to the torque listed in this Chapter's Specifications.
12    Connect the U-joint to the intermediate shaft. Install the intermediate shaft pinch bolt and nut, tightening it to the torque listed in this Chapter's Specifications.
13    The remainder of installation is the reverse of removal. Reconnect the negative battery cable (see Chapter 5).

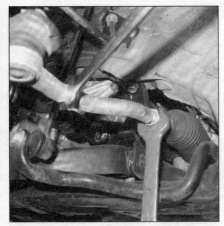

17.2a Use one wrench to hold the tie-rod, then loosen the jam nut

17.2b Mark the exposed threads for reinstalling the tie-rod end

17.3 Use a two-jaw puller or balljoint separator to push the tie-rod end out of the steering arm

18.5 EPS steering motor and electrical connector

A   EPS motor
B   EPS electrical connector

## 17  Tie-rod ends - removal and installation

### Removal

1   Loosen the wheel lug nuts, raise the front of the vehicle and support it securely on jackstands. Apply the parking brake and block the rear wheels to keep the vehicle from rolling off the jackstands. Remove the wheel.
2   Using a back-up wrench, loosen the tie-rod end jam nut. Mark the relationship of the tie-rod end to the threaded portion of the tie-rod. This will ensure the toe-in setting is restored when reassembled (see illustrations).
3   Remove the cotter pin and loosen the nut from the tie-rod end ballstud a few turns. Disconnect the tie-rod end ballstud from the steering arm with a puller (see illustration).
4   Remove the nut from the ballstud, separate the tie-rod end from the steering knuckle, then unscrew the tie-rod end from the tie-rod.

### Installation

5   Thread the tie-rod end onto the tie-rod to the marked position and connect the tie-rod end to the steering arm. Install the nut on the ballstud and tighten it to the torque listed in this Chapter's Specifications. Install a new cotter pin.
**Note:** *If necessary, tighten the nut a little more to allow insertion of the cotter pin. Never loosen the nut to align the cotter pin holes.*
6   Tighten the jam nut securely and install the wheel. Lower the vehicle and tighten the lug nuts to the torque listed in the Chapter 1 Specifications.
7   Have the front end alignment checked and, if necessary, adjusted.

## 18  Steering gear - removal and installation

**Warning:** *Make sure the steering shaft is not turned while the steering gear is removed or you could damage the clockspring for the airbag system. To prevent the shaft from turning, place the ignition key in the lock position or thread the seat belt through the steering wheel and clip it into place.*

### Removal

1   Park the vehicle with the front wheels pointing straight ahead. Loosen the front wheel lug nuts, raise the front of the vehicle and support it securely on jackstands. Apply the parking brake and remove the wheels.
2   Disconnect the cable from the negative terminal of the battery (see Chapter 5).
3   Mark the relationship of the universal joint to the steering gear input shaft and the intermediate shaft. Remove the universal joint pinch bolts and separate the shafts from the joint.
4   Remove the undercarriage trim panels.
5   Working at the steering gear, remove the bracket securing the power steering motor

18.10 Steering gear bracket location (passenger's side not shown)

electrical connector, then disconnect the connector (see illustration).
6   Remove the fasteners securing the power steering motor, then remove the motor.
7   Separate the tie-rod ends from the steering knuckles (see Section 17).
8   Disconnect the electrical connector for the steering gear, then separate the connector mounting bracket. Remove the ground connection at the steering gear.
9   Working in the engine compartment, separate the engine wire harness from the mounting brackets securing it to the firewall.
10   Remove the steering gear brackets (see illustration) (same on both sides).
11   Remove the steering gear mounting nuts and bolts, then pull on the steering gear to release it from the right-side mounting stud.
12   Lower the steering gearbox, then rotate the steering gear so that the input shaft is pointing upward. Carefully guide the steering gear assembly through the right wheel opening, then raise the left side of the steering gear up through the engine compartment and remove it from the vehicle.

**19.11a Subframe bolts (A, except middle bolts) and torque rod bolt (B) (Coupe and Sedan models shown, CR-V similar)**

**19.11b Subframe middle bolt (right side shown, left side identical)**

## Installation

13    Installation is the reverse of removal, noting the following points:

   a) *Raise the steering gear into position and connect the U-joint, aligning the marks.*

   b) *Install the mounting bolts and nuts and tighten them to the torque listed in this Chapter's Specifications.*

   c) *Install the U-joint pinch bolts and tighten them to the torque listed in this Chapter's Specifications.*

   d) *Be sure to use a new O-ring when installing the power steering motor.*

   e) *Install the wheels and lug nuts. Lower the vehicle, then tighten the lug nuts to the torque listed in the Chapter 1 Specifications.*

   f) *Have the front wheel alignment checked and, if necessary, adjusted.*

## 19   Subframe - removal and installation

**Warning:** *The manufacturer recommends replacing the subframe bolts with new ones whenever they are removed.*

## Removal

1    Disconnect the cable from the negative battery terminal (see Chapter 5).

2    Loosen the front wheel lug nuts, raise the front of the vehicle and support it securely on jackstands. Remove both front wheels.

**Note:** *The jackstands must be behind the front suspension subframe, not supporting the vehicle by the subframe.*

3    Remove the under-vehicle splash shields (see Chapter 2A, illustrations 14.3a and 14.3b).

4    Remove the front section of the exhaust system (see Chapter 6).

5    Disconnect the stabilizer bar links from the control arms (see Section 2).

6    Disconnect the control arms from the steering knuckles (see Section 5).

7    On automatic transaxle models, disconnect the shift control cable from the transaxle (see Chapter 7B).

8    Using two floor jacks, support the subframe. Position one jack on each side of the subframe, midway between the front and rear mounting points.

9    Attach an engine support fixture or a hoist to the engine with a length of heavy-duty chain. If the engine is equipped with lifting brackets, use them. If not, you'll have to fasten the chain to some substantial part of the engine - one that is strong enough to take the weight, but in a location that will provide good balance. If you're attaching the chain to a stud on the engine, or are using a bolt passing through the chain and into a threaded hole, place a washer between the nut or bolt head and the chain, and tighten the nut or bolt securely. Take up the slack in the chain, but don't lift the engine.

**Warning:** *DO NOT place any part of your body under the engine when it's supported only by a hoist or other lifting device.*

10    Remove the torque rod-to-subframe bolt.

11    Make alignment marks from each corner of the subframe to the vehicle body. With the jacks sufficiently supporting the subframe, remove the subframe-to-chassis mounting bolts (see illustrations).

12    Slowly lower the jacks, making sure nothing is still attached to the subframe.

## Installation

13    Installation is the reverse of removal, noting the following points:

   a) *Replace the subframe bolts with new ones. Align the reference marks on the subframe, then tighten the subframe*

     *mounting bolts to the torque listed in this Chapter's Specifications.*

   b) *Tighten the torque rod bolt to the torque listed in the Chapter 2A Specifications.*

   c) *Reconnect the negative battery cable (see Chapter 5).*

   d) *Have the front end alignment checked and, if necessary, adjusted.*

## 20   Wheels and tires - general information

1    All vehicles covered by this manual are equipped with metric-sized fiberglass or steel belted radial tires (see illustration). Use of other size or type of tires may affect the ride and handling of the vehicle. Don't mix different types of tires, such as radials and bias belted, on the same vehicle as handling may be seriously affected. It's recommended that tires be replaced in pairs on the same axle, but if only one tire is being replaced, be sure it's the same size, structure and tread design as the other.

2    Because tire pressure has a substantial effect on handling and wear, the pressure on all tires should be checked at least once a month or before any extended trips (see Chapter 1).

3    Wheels must be replaced if they are bent, dented, leak air, have elongated bolt holes, are heavily rusted, out of vertical symmetry or if the lug nuts won't stay tight. Wheel repairs that use welding or peening are not recommended.

4    Tire and wheel balance is important in the overall handling, braking and performance of the vehicle. Unbalanced wheels can adversely affect handling and ride characteristics as well as tire life. Whenever a tire is installed on a wheel, the tire and wheel should be balanced by a shop with the proper equipment.

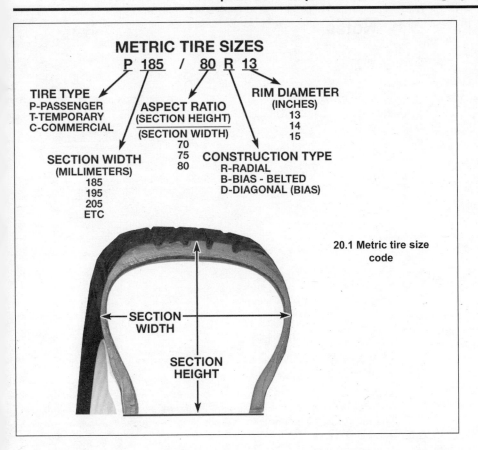

20.1 Metric tire size code

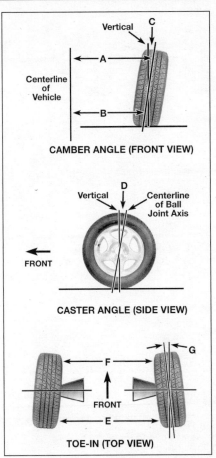

**21.1 Camber, caster and toe-in angles**

*A minus B = C (degrees camber)*
*D = degrees caster*
*E minus F = toe-in (measured in inches)*
*G = toe-in (expressed in degrees)*

## 21 Wheel alignment - general information

1    A wheel alignment refers to the adjustments made to the wheels so they are in proper angular relationship to the suspension and the ground. Wheels that are out of proper alignment not only affect vehicle control, but also increase tire wear. The front end angles normally measured are camber, caster and toe-in (see illustration). Toe-in is the only routine adjustment made; camber on the front end is adjustable, but only after installing special strut-to-knuckle bolts. If the caster is not correct, check for bent components.

2    Getting the proper wheel alignment is a very exacting process, one in which complicated and expensive machines are necessary to perform the job properly. Because of this, you should have a technician with the proper equipment perform these tasks. We will, however, use this space to give you a basic idea of what is involved with a wheel alignment so you can better understand the process and deal intelligently with the shop that does the work.

3    Toe-in is the turning in of the wheels. The purpose of a toe specification is to ensure parallel rolling of the wheels. In a vehicle with zero toe-in, the distance between the front edges of the wheels will be the same as the distance between the rear edges of the wheels. The actual amount of toe-in is normally only a fraction of an inch. At the front end, toe-in is controlled by the tie-rod end position on the tie-rod. At the rear, it's adjusted by a cam bolt at the inner end of the rear trailing arm bolt. Incorrect toe-in will cause the tires to wear improperly by making them scrub against the road surface.

4    Camber is the tilting of the wheels from vertical when viewed from one end of the vehicle. When the wheels tilt out at the top, the camber is said to be positive (+). When the wheels tilt in at the top the camber is negative (-). The amount of tilt is measured in degrees from vertical and this measure-ment is called the camber angle. This angle affects the amount of tire tread which contacts the road and compensates for changes in the suspension geometry when the vehicle is cornering or traveling over an undulating surface. On the front end it is adjusted using special camber adjusting bolts, which alter the relationship between the strut and the steering knuckle. At the rear end camber is not adjustable.

5    Caster is the tilting of the front steering axis from vertical. A tilt toward the rear is positive caster and a tilt toward the front is negative caster.

# Notes

# Chapter 11
# Body

---

## Contents

---

## 1  General Information

**Warning:** *The models covered by this manual are equipped with a Supplemental Restraint System (SRS), more commonly known as airbags. Always disable the airbag system before working in the vicinity of any airbag system components to avoid the possibility of accidental deployment of the airbags, which could cause personal injury (see Chapter 12).*

1   Certain body components are particularly vulnerable to accident damage and can be unbolted and repaired or replaced. Among these parts are the hood, doors, tailgate, liftgate, bumpers and front fenders.

2   Only general body maintenance practices, body panel repair, and component/trim removal and installation procedures within the scope of the do-it-yourselfer are included in this Chapter.

Make sure the damaged area is perfectly clean and rust free. If the touch-up kit has a wire brush, use it to clean the scratch or chip. Or use fine steel wool wrapped around the end of a pencil. Clean the scratched or chipped surface only, not the good paint surrounding it. Rinse the area with water and allow it to dry thoroughly

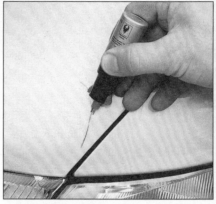

Thoroughly mix the paint, then apply a small amount with the touch-up kit brush or a very fine artist's brush. Brush in one direction as you fill the scratch area. Do not build up the paint higher than the surrounding paint

## 2   Repair of minor paint scratches

1    No matter how hard you try to keep your vehicle looking like new, it will inevitably be scratched, chipped or dented at some point. If the metal is actually dented, seek the advice of a professional. But you can fix minor scratches and chips yourself. Buy a touch-up paint kit from a dealer service department or an auto parts store. To ensure that you get the right color, you'll need to have the specific make, model and year of your vehicle and, ideally, the paint code, which is located on a special metal plate under the hood or in the door jamb.

## 3   Body repair - minor damage

### *Plastic body panels*

1    The following repair procedures are for minor scratches and gouges. Repair of more serious damage should be left to a dealer service department or qualified auto body shop. Below is a list of the equipment and materials necessary to perform the following repair procedures on plastic body panels.

*Wax, grease and silicone removing solvent*
*Cloth-backed body tape*
*Sanding discs*
*Drill motor with three-inch disc holder*
*Hand sanding block*
*Rubber squeegees*
*Sandpaper*
*Non-porous mixing palette*
*Wood paddle or putty knife*
*Curved-tooth body file*
*Flexible parts repair material*

### *Flexible panels (bumper trim)*

2    Remove the damaged panel, if necessary or desirable. In most cases, repairs can be carried out with the panel installed.

If the vehicle has a two-coat finish, apply the clear coat after the color coat has dried

3    Clean the area(s) to be repaired with a wax, grease and silicone removing solvent applied with a water-dampened cloth.
4    If the damage is structural, that is, if it extends through the panel, clean the backside of the panel area to be repaired as well. Wipe dry.
5    Sand the rear surface about 1-1/2 inches beyond the break.
6    Cut two pieces of fiberglass cloth large enough to overlap the break by about 1-1/2 inches. Cut only to the required length.
7    Mix the adhesive from the repair kit according to the instructions included with the kit, and apply a layer of the mixture approximately 1/8-inch thick on the backside of the panel. Overlap the break by at least 1-1/2 inches.
8    Apply one piece of fiberglass cloth to the adhesive and cover the cloth with additional adhesive. Apply a second piece of fiberglass cloth to the adhesive and immediately cover the cloth with additional adhesive in sufficient quantity to fill the weave.
9    Allow the repair to cure for 20 to 30 minutes at 60-degrees to 80-degrees F.

Wait a few days for the paint to dry thoroughly, then rub out the repainted area with a polishing compound to blend the new paint with the surrounding area. When you're happy with your work, wash and polish the area

10   If necessary, trim the excess repair material at the edge.
11   Remove all of the paint film over and around the area(s) to be repaired. The repair material should not overlap the painted surface.
12   With a drill motor and a sanding disc (or a rotary file), cut a "V" along the break line approximately 1/2-inch wide. Remove all dust and loose particles from the repair area.
13   Mix and apply the repair material. Apply a light coat first over the damaged area; then continue applying material until it reaches a level slightly higher than the surrounding finish.
14   Cure the mixture for 20 to 30 minutes at 60-degrees to 80-degrees F.
15   Roughly establish the contour of the area being repaired with a body file. If low areas or pits remain, mix and apply additional adhesive.
16   Block sand the damaged area with sandpaper to establish the actual contour of the surrounding surface.

17 If desired, the repaired area can be temporarily protected with several light coats of primer. Because of the special paints and techniques required for flexible body panels, it is recommended that the vehicle be taken to a paint shop for completion of the body repair.

## Steel body panels

### Repairing simple dents

**Note:** *These photos illustrate a method of repairing simple dents. They are intended to supplement Body repair - minor damage in this chapter and should not be used as the sole instructions for body repair on these vehicles.*

18 When repairing dents, the first job is to pull the dent out until the affected area is as close as possible to its original shape. There is no point in trying to restore the original shape completely as the metal in the damaged area will have stretched on impact and cannot be restored to its original contours. It is better to bring the level of the dent up to a point that is about 1/8-inch below the level of the surrounding metal. In cases where the dent is very shallow, it is not worth trying to pull it out at all.

19 If the backside of the dent is accessible, it can be hammered out gently from behind using a soft-face hammer. While doing this, hold a block of wood firmly against the opposite side of the metal to absorb the hammer blows and prevent the metal from being stretched.

20 If the dent is in a section of the body which has double layers, or some other factor makes it inaccessible from behind, a different technique is required. Drill several small holes through the metal inside the damaged area, particularly in the deeper sections. Screw long, self-tapping screws into the holes just enough for them to get a good grip in the metal. Now pulling on the protruding heads of the screws with locking pliers can pull out the dent.

21 The next stage of repair is the removal of paint from the damaged area and from an inch or so of the surrounding metal. This is easily done with a wire brush or sanding disk in a drill motor, although it can be done just as effectively by hand with sandpaper. To complete the preparation for filling, score the surface of the bare metal with a screwdriver or the tang of a file or drill small holes in the affected area. This will provide a good grip for the filler material. To complete the repair, see the section on filling and painting.

### Repair of rust holes or gashes

22 Remove all paint from the affected area and from an inch or so of the surrounding metal using a sanding disk or wire brush mounted in a drill motor. If these are not available, a few sheets of sandpaper will do the job just as effectively.

23 With the paint removed, you will be able to determine the severity of the corrosion and decide whether to replace the whole panel, if possible, or repair the affected area. New body panels are not as expensive as most

people think and it is often quicker to install a new panel than to repair large areas of rust.

24 Remove all trim pieces from the affected area except those which will act as a guide to the original shape of the damaged body, such as headlight shells, etc. Using metal snips or a hacksaw blade, remove all loose metal and any other metal that is badly affected by rust. Hammer the edges of the hole in to create a slight depression for the filler material.

25 Wire-brush the affected area to remove the powdery rust from the surface of the metal. If the back of the rusted area is accessible, treat it with rust inhibiting paint.

26 Before filling is done, block the hole in some way. This can be done with sheet metal riveted or screwed into place, or by stuffing the hole with wire mesh.

27 Once the hole is blocked off, the affected area can be filled and painted. See the following subsection on filling and painting.

### Filling and painting

28 Many types of body fillers are available, but generally speaking, body repair kits which contain filler paste and a tube of resin hardener are best for this type of repair work. A wide, flexible plastic or nylon applicator will be necessary for imparting a smooth and contoured finish to the surface of the filler material. Mix up a small amount of filler on a clean piece of wood or cardboard (use the hardener sparingly). Follow the manufacturer's instructions on the package, otherwise the filler will set incorrectly.

29 Using the applicator, apply the filler paste to the prepared area. Draw the applicator across the surface of the filler to achieve the desired contour and to level the filler surface. As soon as a contour that approximates the original one is achieved, stop working the paste. If you continue, the paste will begin to stick to the applicator. Continue to add thin layers of paste at 20-minute intervals until the level of the filler is just above the surrounding metal.

30 Once the filler has hardened, the excess can be removed with a body file. From then on, progressively finer grades of sandpaper should be used, starting with a 180-grit paper and finishing with 600-grit wet-or-dry paper. Always wrap the sandpaper around a flat rubber or wooden block, otherwise the surface of the filler will not be completely flat. During the sanding of the filler surface, the wet-or-dry paper should be periodically rinsed in water. This will ensure that a very smooth finish is produced in the final stage.

31 At this point, the repair area should be surrounded by a ring of bare metal, which in turn should be encircled by the finely feathered edge of good paint. Rinse the repair area with clean water until all of the dust produced by the sanding operation is gone.

32 Spray the entire area with a light coat of primer. This will reveal any imperfections in the surface of the filler. Repair the imperfections with fresh filler paste or glaze filler and once more smooth the surface with sandpaper. Repeat this spray-and-repair procedure

until you are satisfied that the surface of the filler and the feathered edge of the paint are perfect. Rinse the area with clean water and allow it to dry completely.

33 The repair area is now ready for painting. Spray painting must be carried out in a warm, dry, windless and dust free atmosphere. These conditions can be created if you have access to a large indoor work area, but if you are forced to work in the open, you will have to pick the day very carefully. If you are working indoors, dousing the floor in the work area with water will help settle the dust that would otherwise be in the air. If the repair area is confined to one body panel, mask off the surrounding panels. This will help minimize the effects of a slight mismatch in paint color. Trim pieces such as chrome strips, door handles, etc., will also need to be masked off or removed. Use masking tape and several thickness of newspaper for the masking operations.

34 Before spraying, shake the paint can thoroughly, then spray a test area until the spray painting technique is mastered. Cover the repair area with a thick coat of primer. The thickness should be built up using several thin layers of primer rather than one thick one. Using 600-grit wet-or-dry sandpaper, rub down the surface of the primer until it is very smooth. While doing this, the work area should be thoroughly rinsed with water and the wet-or-dry sandpaper periodically rinsed as well. Allow the primer to dry before spraying additional coats.

35 Spray on the top coat, again building up the thickness by using several thin layers of paint. Begin spraying in the center of the repair area and then, using a circular motion, work out until the whole repair area and about two inches of the surrounding original paint is covered. Remove all masking material 10 to 15 minutes after spraying on the final coat of paint. Allow the new paint at least two weeks to harden, then use a very fine rubbing compound to blend the edges of the new paint into the existing paint. Finally, apply a coat of wax

## 4   Body repair - major damage

1 Major damage must be repaired by an auto body shop specifically equipped to perform body and frame repairs. These shops have the specialized equipment required to do the job properly.

2 If the damage is extensive, the frame must be checked for proper alignment or the vehicle's handling characteristics may be adversely affected and other components may wear at an accelerated rate.

3 Due to the fact that all of the major body components (hood, fenders, etc.) are separate and replaceable units, any seriously damaged components should be replaced rather than repaired. Sometimes the components can be found in a wrecking yard that specializes in used vehicle components, often at considerable savings over the cost of new parts.

These photos illustrate a method of repairing simple dents. They are intended to supplement *Body repair - minor damage* in this Chapter and should not be used as the sole instructions for body repair on these vehicles.

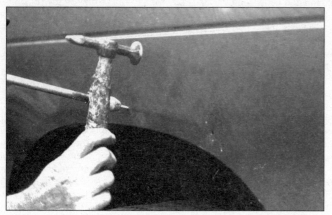

1  If you can't access the backside of the body panel to hammer out the dent, pull it out with a slide-hammer-type dent puller. Tap with a hammer near the edge of the dent to help 'pop' the metal back to its original shape, about 1/8-inch below the surface of the surrounding metal

2  Using coarse-grit sandpaper, remove the paint down to the bare metal. Clean the repair area with wax/silicone remover.

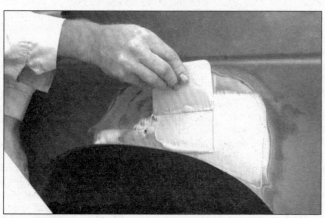

3  Following label instructions, mix up a batch of plastic filler and hardener, then quickly press it into the metal with a plastic applicator. Work the filler until it matches the original contour and is slightly above the surrounding metal

4  Let the filler harden until you can just dent it with your fingernail. File, then sand the filler down until it's smooth and even. Work down to finer grits of sandpaper - always using a board or block - ending up with 360 or 400 grit

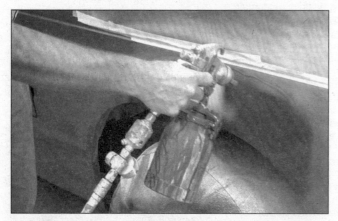

5  When the area is smooth to the touch, clean the area and mask around it. Apply several layers of primer to the area. A professional-type spray gun is being used here, but aerosol spray primer works fine

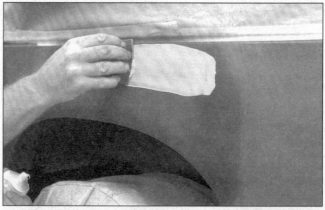

6  Fill imperfections or scratches with glazing compound. Sand with 360 or 400-grit and re-spray. Finish sand the primer with 600 grit, clean thoroughly, then apply the finish coat. Don't attempt to rub out or wax the repair area until the paint has dried completely (at least two weeks)

## 5  Upholstery, carpets and vinyl trim - maintenance

### Upholstery and carpets

1    Every three months remove the floormats and clean the interior of the vehicle (more frequently if necessary). Use a stiff whiskbroom to brush the carpeting and loosen dirt and dust, then vacuum the upholstery and carpets thoroughly, especially along seams and crevices.

2    Dirt and stains can be removed from carpeting with basic household or automotive carpet shampoos available in spray cans. Follow the directions and vacuum again, then use a stiff brush to bring back the "nap" of the carpet.

3    Most interiors have cloth or vinyl upholstery, either of which can be cleaned and maintained with a number of material-specific cleaners or shampoos available in auto supply stores. Follow the directions on the product for usage, and always spot-test any upholstery cleaner on an inconspicuous area (bottom edge of a backseat cushion) to ensure that it doesn't cause a color shift in the material.

4    After cleaning, vinyl upholstery should be treated with a protectant.

**Caution:** *Do not use protectant on vinyl-covered steering wheels.*

**Note:** *Make sure the protectant container indicates the product can be used on seats - some products may make a seat too slippery.*

5    Leather upholstery requires special care. It should be cleaned regularly with saddle-soap or leather cleaner. Never use alcohol, gasoline, nail polish remover or thinner to clean leather upholstery.

6    After cleaning, regularly treat leather upholstery with a leather conditioner, rubbed in with a soft cotton cloth. Never use car wax on leather upholstery.

7    In areas where the interior of the vehicle is subject to bright sunlight, cover leather seating areas of the seats with a sheet if the vehicle is to be left out for any length of time.

### Vinyl trim

8    Don't clean vinyl trim with detergents, caustic soap or petroleum-based cleaners. Plain soap and water works just fine, with a soft brush to clean dirt that may be ingrained. Wash the vinyl as frequently as the rest of the vehicle.

9    After cleaning, application of a high-quality rubber and vinyl protectant will help prevent oxidation and cracks. The protectant can also be applied to weather-stripping, vacuum lines and rubber hoses, which often fail as a result of chemical degradation, and to the tires.

## 6  Fastener and trim removal

1    There is a variety of plastic fasteners used to hold trim panels, splash shields and other parts in place in addition to typical screws, nuts and bolts. Once you are familiar with them, they can usually be removed without too much difficulty.

2    The proper tools and approach can pre-

# Fasteners

This tool is designed to remove special fasteners. A small pry tool used for removing nails will also work well in place of this tool

A Phillips head screwdriver can be used to release the center portion, but light pressure must be used because the plastic is easily damaged. Once the center is up, the fastener can easily be pried from its hole

Here is a view with the center portion fully released. Install the fastener as shown, then press the center in to set it

This fastener is used for exterior panels and shields. The center portion must be pried up to release the fastener. Install the fastener with the center up, then press the center in to set it

This type of fastener is used commonly for interior panels. Use a small blunt tool to press the small pin at the center in to release it . . .

. . . the pin will stay with the fastener in the released position

Reset the fastener for installation by moving the pin out. Install the fastener, then press the pin flush with the fastener to set it

This fastener is used for exterior and interior panels. It has no moving parts. Simply pry the fastener from its hole like the claw of a hammer removes a nail. Without a tool that can get under the top of the fastener, it can be very difficult to remove

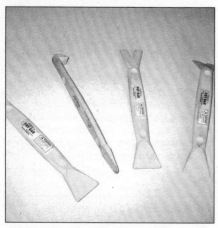

**6.4 These small plastic pry tools are ideal for prying off trim panels**

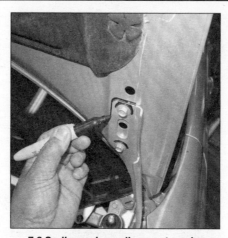

**7.2 Scribe or draw alignment marks around the bolt heads and the hood hinges to ensure proper alignment of the hood when it's reinstalled**

**7.4 Support the hood with your shoulder while removing the hood bolts**

**7.10 Scribe a line around the hood latch or as we have done, use a white paint marker to mark the original location so you can judge the movement. Then loosen the bolts and adjust the latch position**

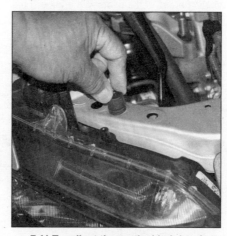

**7.11 To adjust the vertical height of the leading edge of the hood so it's flush with the fenders, turn each edge cushion clockwise (to lower the hood) or counterclockwise (to raise the hood)**

vent added time and expense to a project by minimizing the number of broken fasteners and/or parts.

3     The illustration on page 11-5 shows various types of fasteners that are typically used on most vehicles and how to remove and install them (see illustration). Replacement fasteners are commonly found at most auto parts stores, if necessary.

4     Trim panels are typically made of plastic and their flexibility can help during removal. The key to their removal is to use a tool to pry the panel near its retainers to release it without damaging surrounding areas or breaking-off any retainers. The retainers will usually snap out of their designated slot or hole after force is applied to them. Stiff plastic tools designed for prying on trim panels are available at most auto parts stores (see illustration). Tools that are tapered and wrapped in protective tape, such as a screwdriver or small pry tool, are also very effective when used with care.

## 7    Hood - removal, installation and adjustment

### Removal and installation

**Note:** *The hood is heavy and somewhat awkward to remove and install - at least two people should perform this procedure.*

1     Use blankets or pads to cover the fenders and cowl areas. This will protect the body and paint as the hood is lifted off.

2     Scribe or draw alignment marks around the bolt heads to ensure proper alignment during installation (see illustration).

3     Disconnect any cables or wire harnesses, which will interfere with removal.

4     Have an assistant support one side of the hood. Take turns removing the hinge-to-hood bolts and lift off the hood (see illustration).

5     Installation is the reverse of removal. If you position the hood so that the hinges fit within the scribe marks you made before loosening the bolts, in the same location they were in prior to removal, then the hood should still be aligned. Of course, if you're installing a new hood, or forgot to scribe the hinge positions, then you'll need to readjust the hood position.

### Adjustment

6     You can adjust the hood fore-and-aft and right-and-left by means of the elongated holes in the hinges.

7     Mark a line between the hood itself and the hinge plate so you can judge the amount of movement.

8     Loosen the bolts just enough to allow the hood to move. Close the hood and check alignment.

**Note:** *It's a good idea to remove the hood latch before closing the hood to check the alignment, just in case there is a severe bind when it closes which will make the hood harder to open.*

9     Carefully jiggle the hood around until the seams are all equal. Then, gently open the hood and snug the bolts.

**Note:** *You may have to do this step several times before the alignment is perfect.*

**Note:** *The hood should rest on the stops without any great amount of downward pressure.*

10    If necessary after installation, the entire hood latch assembly can be adjusted up-and-down as well as from side-to-side on the upper radiator support so the hood closes securely and is flush with the fenders (see illustration). To do this, scribe a line around the hood latch mounting bolts to provide a reference point. Then loosen the bolts and reposition the latch assembly as necessary. Following adjustment, retighten the mounting bolts.

11    Adjust the vertical height of the leading edge of the hood by screwing the edge cushions in or out so that the hood, when closed, is flush with the fenders (see illustration).

**Note:** *The hood latch assembly, as well as the hinges, should be periodically lubricated with white lithium-base grease to prevent sticking and wear.*

**8.1 Bolt locations for the hood latch**

**8.2 Detach the cable (A) then unhook the end from the latch (B)**

**8.6 Remove the release lever bolts and detach the cable and lever**

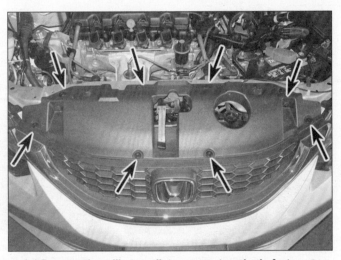

**9.1 Remove the grille-to-radiator support push-pin fasteners**

## 8 Hood latch and cable - removal and installation

### Latch

1 Remove the radiator grille opening cover (if equipped), then scribe a line around the latch (see illustration 7.10) to aid alignment when installing. Detach the latch retaining bolts (see illustration) from the radiator support and remove the latch.
2 Disconnect the hood release cable by disengaging the cable from the latch assembly (see illustration).
3 Installation is the reverse of removal.
**Note:** *Adjust the latch so the hood engages securely when closed and the hood bumpers are slightly compressed.*

### Cable

4 Disconnect the hood release cable from the latch assembly (see illustrations 8.1 and 8.2),

then detach the cable from any retaining clips securing it to the radiator support.
5 Attach a piece of wire or string to the latch end of the cable.
6 Working in the passenger's compartment, remove the driver's side kick panel (see Section 32). Then remove the release lever mounting bolts and detach the hood release lever (see illustration).
7 Remove the left side inner fender splash shield (see Section 11). Detach the cable from the retaining clip.
8 Push the grommet through the body and pull the cable into the passenger compartment. Ensure that the new cable has a grommet attached, then remove the old cable from the wire or string and replace it with the new cable.
9 Carefully guide the wire or string (with the new cable attached) back through the firewall and along the same route back to the latch.
10 Reconnect the retaining clips inside the fender and complete the procedure by refit-

ting the fender liner and hood latch to the new cable. The remainder of the installation is the reverse of removal.

## 9 Radiator grille - removal and installation

1 Remove the fasteners securing the upper grille close out panel (see illustration).
**Note:** *You can read up on how these fasteners are removed in Section 6 of this chapter.*
2 There are four lower clips and one clip hidden in each upper corner that need to be detached. Use a flat bladed screwdriver and lift or twist the plastic lever to disengage the clip as you slightly pull out on the grille. (If you don't apply any outward pressure the clip will just snap back into place.)
3 Pull the grille forward to disengage it from the bumper.
4 Installation is the reverse of removal.

10.2 Bumper cover lower retaining fasteners are located around the edges of the panel as well as in the center area. If the fasteners are in good condition after removal, save them. If not, replace them with new ones.

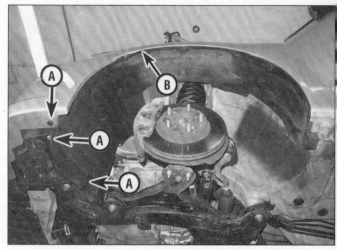

10.3 Remove the lower fasteners (A) then any inner fender fasteners between the lower fasteners and the arrow (B).

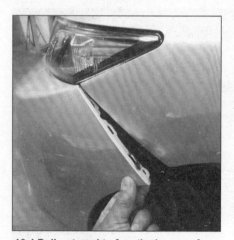

10.4 Pull outward to free the bumper from the fender edge

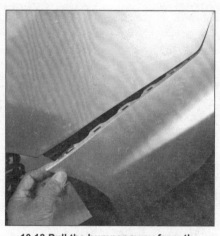

10.13 Pull the bumper away from the quarter panel to free up the pressure fastener clips

10.14 Remove these fasteners to remove the bumper

## 10   Bumper covers - removal and installation

### Front

1   Raise the vehicle and support it securely on jackstands.

2   Working under the vehicle, detach the push pins, bolts or screws securing the lower edges of the bumper cover (see illustration).

**Note:** *There are six lower fasteners and one fastener on each outside edge of the bumper. The outside edge fasteners are near the junction between the bumper fascia and the fender. It is not necessary to remove the entire lower trim panel, but it can get in the way when reinstalling the bumper.*

3   Working in the front wheel opening, remove the retaining screw securing the bumper cover to the fenderwell (see illustration).

**Note:** *If your car is equipped with wheel arch protector trim pieces, they will need to be removed as well. Plastic push pins hold them in place. See Section 6 for details on how to remove these pins.*

4   Detach the bumper to fender by pulling outward on the bumper to free it from the pressure fastener clips (see illustration).

5   Remove the front grille cover (see Section 9). Once the grille has been removed you'll find a plastic tab on either side (near the lower section of the headlamp assembly) that you will need to release with a screwdriver as you apply outward pressure to the bumper.

6   Now, while holding onto the bumper near the headlamp assembly and the outer edge of the bumper, pull outward to detach the pressure fittings that secure the bumper to the lower part of the headlamp assembly.

7   Disconnect the fog lamps (if applicable) and remove the bumper.

8   Installation is the reverse of removal.

### Rear

9   Raise the vehicle and support it securely on jackstands.

10   Working under the vehicle, detach the plastic clips and screws securing the splash guards and the lower edge of the bumper cover.

11   If your vehicle is equipped with wheel arch protector trim these will need to be removed as well. They are secured onto the wheel well arch with plastic fasteners. See Section 6 for details on the proper removal of these fasteners.

12   Remove the screws securing the bumper cover in the rear wheel openings.

13   Separate the bumper to quarter panel fasteners by pulling the bumper outward until it's free (see illustration).

14   Open the trunk or rear liftgate and remove the screws and clips securing the upper edge of the bumper cover (see illustration). Pull the bumper cover out and away from the vehicle.

15   Installation is the reverse of removal.

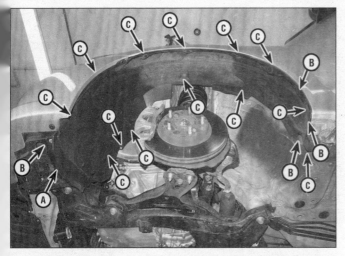

**11.5 Remove the fasteners retaining the inner fender liner**

A    Bolt                    B    Screw                    C    Plastic fastener

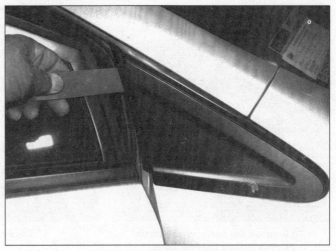

**11.6a Pry the trim off with a trim tool**

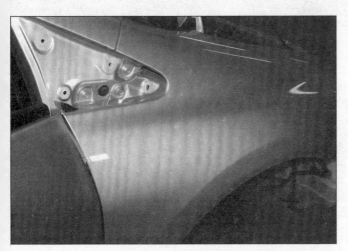

**11.6b Upper rear fender bolts**

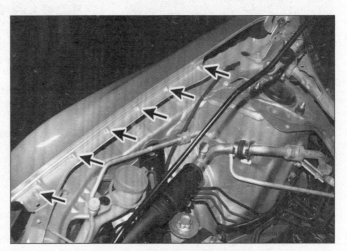

**11.7a Upper fender bolt locations**

## 11   Front fender - removal and installation

1    Loosen the wheel lug nuts, raise the front of the vehicle and support it securely on jackstands. Remove the wheel.

2    Remove the front bumper cover (see Section 10).

3    Remove the headlamp assembly (see Chapter 12).

4    If applicable, remove the wheel arch protector trim. The trim is held on by plastic fasteners. See Section 6 for details on how to properly remove this type of fastener.

5    Remove the inner fender liner (see illustration).

6    If applicable, remove the trim panel on the top rear edge of the fender and A pillar section, then remove the upper rear fender bolt (see illustrations).

7    Remove the remaining fender mounting bolts and the fender fairing clips (see illustrations).

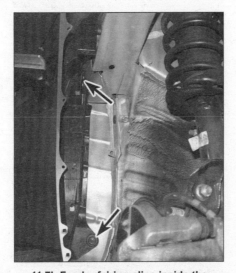

**11.7b Fender fairing clips inside the fender well**

**11.7c Lower rear fender bolt**

**11.7d Remove the bolt and detach the bracket behind the headlight**

**12.3 Hood to cowl seal**

**12.5 Center section (with hood to cowl seal in place)**

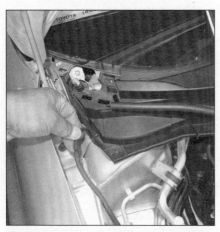

**12.6 Windshield washer hose connection**

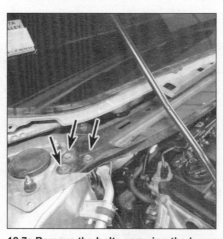

**12.7a Remove the bolts securing the lower cowl cover to the strut tower (repeat on the other side)**

**12.7b Lift the lower cowl cover out of the vehicle**

8    Lift the fender about an inch to free the locating tabs in the inner fender fairing. Remove the fender fairing from the vehicle, then remove the fender.

**Note:** *It's a good idea to have an assistant support the fender while it's being detached or moved away from the vehicle to prevent damage to the surrounding body panels.*

9    Installation is the reverse of removal.

---

**12    Cowl cover - removal and installation**

---

1    The cowl cover has four sections: left trim, right trim, center trim and lower cowl cover.

2    Remove the windshield wiper arms (see Chapter 12, Section 19).

3    Pull off the rubber hood to cowl seal (see illustration).

4    Remove the left and right cowl cover sections by removing the plastic fasteners, then releasing the tab that secures each one to the top of the fender. Then, lift up to unhook

them from the center cowl section.

5    Remove the center cowl section (see illustration).

6    Disconnect the windshield washer hose from the right side of the cowl cover (see illustration).

7    Remove the lower cowl cover (see illustrations).

8    Installation is the reverse of removal.

---

**13    Liftgate handle, latch and lock cylinder (hatchback models) - removal and installation**

---

1    Open the liftgate.

2    On the inside of the liftgate, remove the liftgate lower trim cover.

### Handle

3    Remove the fasteners securing the hatch lock cylinder and rear license trim panel.

4    Remove the clips securing the license trim panel, then remove the trim panel.

5    Remove the rear window wiper motor

(see Chapter 12).

6    Detach the liftgate release cable from the liftgate handle.

7    Remove the liftgate handle retaining nuts and remove the handle.

8    Installation is the reverse of removal.

### Latch

9    Disconnect the liftgate release cable and lock cylinder rod from the latch.

10    Disconnect the liftgate latch electrical connectors.

11    Remove the bolts securing the liftgate latch and remove the latch.

12    Installation is the reverse of removal.

### Lock cylinder

13    Remove the rear license trim panel.

14    Disconnect the lock cylinder rod from the cylinder.

15    Working outside of the liftgate, remove the bolt securing the lock cylinder.

16    Working inside the liftgate, remove the lock cylinder from inside of the liftgate.

17    Installation is the reverse of removal.

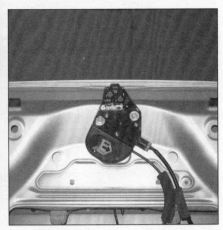

15.2a Two bolts secure the latch to the trunk lid

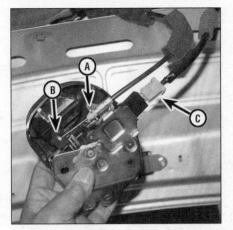

15.2b Turn the latch over to remove the release cable

A   Release cable end - pull off of the latch to remove
B   Release cable housing end - rotate the cable to align the tab to remove it
C   Electrical connector (if applicable)

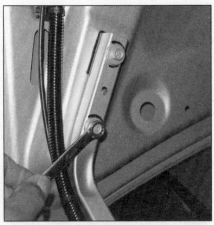

16.3 Draw around the hinge and the bolts with a marking pen before loosening the bolts to ensure proper alignment of the trunk lid when it's reinstalled

## 14   Liftgate (CR-V models) - removal, installation and adjustment

**Note:** *The liftgate is heavy and somewhat awkward to hold - at least two people should perform this procedure.*

### Removal and installation

1    Open the liftgate and support it securely.
2    Remove the upper trim molding from the liftgate opening and disconnect all wiring harness connectors leading to the liftgate.
3    While an assistant supports the liftgate, detach both ends of the support struts.
4    Remove the C-pillar trim panels, then carefully pull down the rear portion of the headliner.
5    Detach the liftgate hinge-to-body bolts and remove the liftgate from the vehicle.
6    Installation is the reverse of removal.

### Adjustment

7    Adjustments are made by loosening the liftgate hinge-to-body bolts and moving the liftgate. Proper alignment is achieved when the edges of the liftgate are parallel with the rear quarter panels and the roof panel.
8    Remove the rear trim panel and adjust the latch striker assembly as necessary to provide positive engagement with the latch mechanism.
9    Finally, adjust the height of the liftgate in relation to the body by screwing the rubber bumpers in-or-out.

## 15   Trunk lid latch and lock cylinder (coupe and sedan models) - removal and installation

### Trunk lid latch

1    Open the trunk and scribe a line around the trunk lid latch assembly for a reference

point to aid the installation procedure.
2    Unbolt the latch from the trunk lid (two bolts) (see illustration). Disconnect the release cable and electrical connector (if applicable) and remove the latch (see illustration).
3    Installation is the reverse of removal.

### Trunk lock cylinder

4    Open the trunk. Look upward through the trunk lid access hole and detach the rod from the lock cylinder.
5    Remove the mounting bolts and remove it from the trunk lid.
6    Installation is the reverse of removal.

## 16   Trunk lid (coupe and sedan models) - removal, installation and adjustment

**Note:** *The trunk lid is heavy and somewhat awkward to remove and install - at least two people should perform this procedure.*

### Removal and installation

1    Open the trunk lid and cover the edges of the trunk compartment with pads or cloths to protect the painted surfaces when the lid is removed.
2    Disconnect any cables or wire harness connectors attached to the trunk lid that would interfere with removal.
3    Remove the hinge trim cover (if equipped) and make alignment marks around the hinge (see illustration).
4    While an assistant supports the trunk lid, remove the lid-to-hinge bolts on both sides and lift it off.
5    Installation is the reverse of removal.
**Note:** *When reinstalling the trunk lid, align the lid-to-hinge bolts with the marks made during removal.*

16.9 Loosen these two bolts to reposition the striker. Be sure to mark the location of the striker for a reference as to how far you have moved it

### Adjustment

6    Fore-and-aft and side-to-side adjustment of the trunk lid is accomplished by moving the lid in relation to the hinge after loosening the bolts or nuts.
7    Scribe a line around the hinge plate as described earlier in this section so you can determine the amount of movement.
8    Loosen the bolts and move the trunk lid into correct alignment. Move it only a little at a time. Tighten the hinge bolts or nuts and carefully lower the trunk lid to check the alignment.
9    If necessary after installation, the entire trunk lid striker assembly can be adjusted up and down as well as from side to side (see illustration) so the lid closes securely and is flush with the rear quarter panels. To do this, scribe a line around the trunk lid striker assembly to provide a reference point, then loosen the bolts and reposition the striker as necessary. Following adjustment, retighten the mounting bolts.

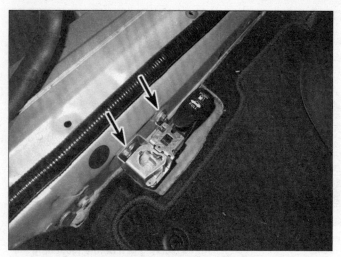

**17.2 Release lever bolt locations**

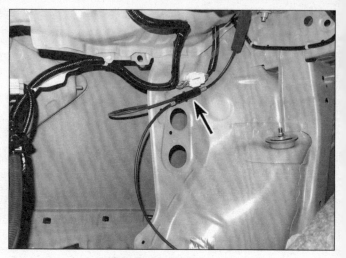

**17.5a Typical retaining clip**

**17.5b Trunk release cable location at the rear wall. Push out the grommet and remove the cable**

10   The trunk lid latch assembly, as well as the hinges, should be periodically lubricated with white lithium-base grease to prevent sticking and wear.

11   Finally, adjust the height of the trunk lid in relation to the body by screwing the rubber bumpers in-or-out.

## 17   Trunk and fuel door release lever, cables and latches - removal and installation

### Release lever

1   Remove the driver's side sill plate trim (see Section 32).

2   Unbolt the trunk release lever handle from the sill (see illustration).

3   Disconnect the cable from the handle by rotating the cable 90 degrees or until the cable end aligns with the open tab. Now, remove the cable from the handle.

4   Installation is the reverse of removal.

### Cables

5   Working in the trunk or rear compartment, remove the plastic clips securing the driver's side and rear inside finishing panels to allow access to the fuel door assembly.

**Note:** *For the trunk release cable, mark the location of the trunk latch bolts and latch assembly before removing the latch. Now, unbolt the latch. Twist the cable ball end and cable 90 degrees so that the cable aligns with the open slot. Then remove the cable retaining clips and follow the cable to the left side of the trunk, removing any retaining clips along the way until you get to the rear wall of the trunk (see illustrations).*

**Note:** *To detach the fuel door release cable, unbolt the fuel door latch assembly from the vehicle. Twist the cable ball end and cable 90 degrees so that the cable aligns with the open slot, then remove the cable.*

6   Remove the left door sill plate (see Section 32), the rear seat (see Section 28), The B pillar lower trim panel (see Section 32), and the left rear quarter trim panel (see Section 32).

Pull the carpet back and detach all the cable retaining clips.

7   From the lever end of the cable, attach a string or thin wire to the end of the cable.

**Note:** *Make sure the string or wire is long enough that you still can grab a hold of it from inside the car after you have pulled the old cable through.*

8   Working from inside the trunk or rear compartment, pull the old cable assembly toward the rear of the vehicle.

9   Remove the old cable and attach the string (or thin wire) to the replacement cable.

10   Guide the replacement cable through the body by pulling on the string or wire. Reattach any retaining clips that were removed, then reattach the cable to the latch and release lever.

11   The remainder of the installation is the reverse of removal.

### Electric trunk and fuel door release latch - removal and installation

#### Trunk release latch

12   Remove the inner trunk lid trim panels (if applicable).

13   Mark the location of the bolts and latch assembly before removing.

14   Disconnect the electrical connector and remove the bolts securing the latch to the trunk lid.

15   Remove the latch.

16   Installation is the reverse of removal.

#### Fuel door release latch

17   Remove the trunk liner trim on the fuel door side of the vehicle.

18   Disconnect the electrical connection or cable.

19   Unbolt the fuel door latch assembly and remove it.

20   Installation is the reverse of removal.

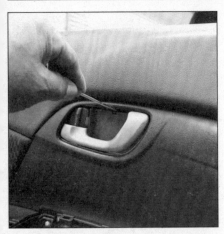

18.2a Remove the inside door handle trim cover . . .

18.2b . . . then remove the screw from the inside pull handle

18.3a Pry the window switch assembly off with a flat trim tool

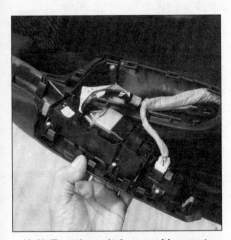

18.3b Turn the switch assembly over to disconnect the electrical connectors

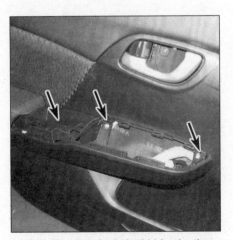

18.3c Remove the bolts hidden by the switch assembly and the single screw in the hand grab cup

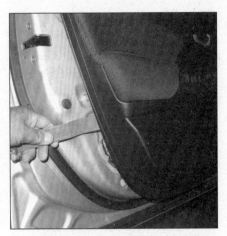

18.6 Carefully pry the clips free so the door trim panel can be removed

## 18   Door trim panels - removal and installation

1    On manual window regulator equipped models, remove the window crank.
**Note:** *If a tool is not available for removing the clip, use a shop rag instead. Hold the shop rag by two corners and slide the edge of the rag under the handle (handle arm facing downward). By tugging on either corner of the shop rag work the shop rag up against the clip. The clip will come off as you work the rag back and forth.*
2    Remove the inside door handle trim cover. Remove the mounting screw (see illustrations).
3    On models without inside grab handles but with electric windows, remove the window switch assembly (see illustrations). Remove the retaining bolts hidden by the window switch assembly.
4    On models with inside grab handles, remove the pull handle trim cover by pulling straight away from the door panel. (It's some-

times easier to get it started by using a small flat bladed screwdriver at a corner to release the plastic retaining clips.) Remove the retaining screws hidden by the grab handle trim.
5    If applicable, remove the mirror trim cover (sail trim cover) by pulling it straight away from the door. Disconnect the outside mirror cable (if applicable) by unscrewing the retaining nut.
6    Remove the door trim panel using a door panel removal tool (see illustration). Start from the bottom corner of the trim panel and work around the perimeter until all the fasteners have been released from the door.
7    Lift the trim panel up to disengage the panel from the upper door ridge, unplug any electrical connectors, and remove the panel.
**Note:** *For those stubborn door panels that just don't seem to want to lift off the door, try applying upward pressure by holding onto the bottom of the door panel and then use your other hand to firmly smack the top of the door panel where it meets the door. This usually will get it off.*
8    Installation is the reverse of removal.

### Trunk liner trim panels

9    The trunk liner trim panels are held on with pressure clips. Follow the steps in Section 6 for the proper procedures to remove the different types of clips.
10    Each trim panel will have several clips that need to be removed. Keep track of which clips go to which area of the panels. Some locations will have different size clips. Replace any clips that are damaged or not reusable. (Most parts stores carry a variety of replacement fasteners.)

### Tailgate trim panel

#### Upper trim

11    Carefully pry the notch on the outside edges of the upper trim where it meets with the side trim out away from the door. Then, pull the trim to release the pressure clips.
12    Installation is the reverse of removal.

#### Side trim

13    Remove the upper trim. Then pull the side trim panels off of the pressure clips.
14    Installation is the reverse of removal.

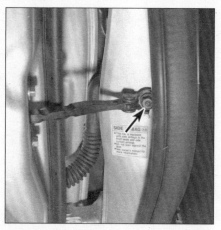

19.5 Remove the door strut retaining bolt

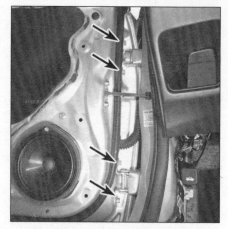

19.7 Remove the door hinge bolts

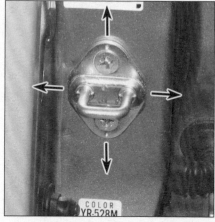

19.12 Adjust the door lock striker by loosening the mounting screws and gently tapping the striker in the desired direction

### Lower trim panel

15   Remove the screw to the hand hold pocket on the bottom edge of the door trim. Remove the hand hold pocket.
16   Remove the panel pressure clips. See Section 6 for details on the proper procedures for the various pressure clip removal.
17   Installation is the reverse of removal.

### *Installation*

18   Prior to installation of the door trim panels and/or the tailgate trim panel, be sure to reinstall any clips in the panel which may have come out when you removed the panel.
19   Align several of the clips to their appropriate holes in the door. Then, press firmly to seat the clips back into place.
20   The remainder of the installation is the reverse of removal.

---

### 19  Door - removal, installation and adjustment

**Caution:** *The door is heavy and somewhat awkward to remove and install. For your personal safety, at least two people should perform this procedure if a door dolly that is specifically made for this procedure is not available.*

### *Removal and installation*

1   Lower the window completely in the door, then disconnect the cable from the negative battery terminal (see Chapter 5).
2   Open the door all the way and support it on jacks or blocks covered with rags to prevent damaging the paint.
3   Remove the kick panel Section 32 and disconnect the electrical leads running to the door.
4   Detach the rubber conduit between the body and the door. Then pull the wiring harness from the body side into the door jamb area.

5   Remove the door stop strut (see illustration).
6   Mark around the door hinges with a pen or a scribe to facilitate realignment during reassembly.
7   With an assistant supporting the door, remove the hinge-to-door bolts (see illustration) and remove the door.
8   Installation is the reverse of removal.

### *Adjustment*

9   Having proper door-to-body alignment is a critical part of a well functioning door assembly. First check the door hinge pins for excessive play. Fully open the door and lift up and down on the door without lifting the body. If a door has 1/16-inch or more excessive play, the hinges should be replaced.
10   Door-to-body alignment adjustments are made by loosening the hinge-to-body bolts (see illustration) or hinge-to-door bolts and moving the door. Proper body alignment is achieved when the top of the doors are parallel with the roof section, the front door is flush with the fender, the rear door is flush with

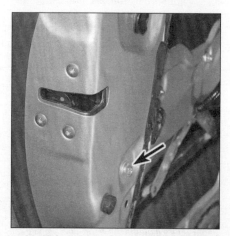

20.2 Rear window track retaining bolt

the rear quarter panel and the bottom of the doors are aligned with the lower rocker panel. If these goals can't be reached by adjusting the hinge-to-body or hinge-to-door bolts, body alignment shims may have to be purchased and inserted behind the hinges to achieve correct alignment.
11   To adjust the door closed position, scribe a line or mark around the striker plate to provide a reference point, then check that the door latch is contacting the center of the latch striker. If not, adjust the up-and-down position first.
12   Finally adjust the latch striker sideways position, so that the door panel is flush with the center pillar or rear quarter panel and provides positive engagement with the latch mechanism (see illustration).

---

### 20  Door latch, lock cylinder and handles - removal and installation

---

**Caution:** *Wear gloves when working inside the door openings to protect against cuts from sharp metal edges.*
**Note:** *All door lock rods are attached by plastic clips. The plastic clips can be removed by unsnapping the portion that clips around the connecting rod, then pulling the rod out of its locating hole. On models with power door locks, disconnect the electrical connectors at the latch.*

### *Door latch*

1   Raise the window, then remove the door trim panel and watershield (see Section 18).
2   Pry the rear window guide track lining out of the rear guide track. Then, remove the single bolt securing the rear window guide track (see illustration). Remove the guide track from the door.
3   Remove the release cables from the door

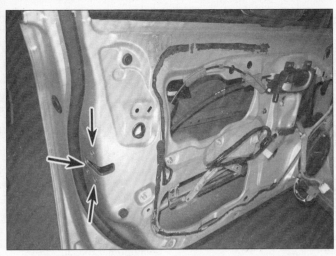

20.3 Remove the latch screws from the end of the door

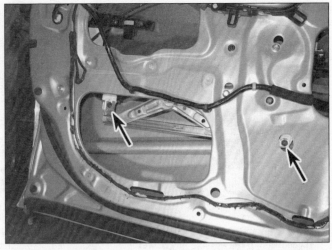

21.2 Raise the window just enough to access the glass retaining bolts through the holes in the door frame - remove the bolts securing the glass to the equalizer arm

cable clips. Then remove the three screws securing the door latch to the door (see illustration).

4    Slide the latch downward to release the outside latch handle actuator rod.

5    On the actual latch, open up the latch protector door. Disconnect the cables from the latch assembly.

6    Remove the latch.

7    Installation is the reverse of removal.

### Outside handle and door lock cylinder

8    To remove the outside handle and lock cylinder assembly, raise the window and remove the door trim panel and watershield (see Section 18).

9    Working from the rear edge of the door remove the plastic protector cap that hides the lock cylinder bolt.

10    Remove the door lock cylinder by pulling straight away from the door handle.

11    Working from inside the door release the clip securing the door latch actuator rod to the outside door handle.

12    From the inside of the door, remove the outside handle retaining fastener.

13    Now pull the rear section of the door handle back to release the rear section, then pivot the rear section away from the door to free the front section. Remove the handle.

14    Installation is the reverse of removal.

### Inside handle

15    Remove the door panel trim (see Section 18).

16    Pull the inside door handle to the rear to release the retaining hooks. (The retaining screw should already have been removed when you removed the door trim panel.)

17    Remove the cable from the inside door handle and remove the handle.

18    Installation is the reverse of removal.

### 21  Door window glass - removal and installation

**Caution:** *Wear gloves when working inside the door openings to protect against cuts from sharp metal edges.*

1    Remove the door trim panel and the plastic watershield (see Section 18).

2    Raise the window glass just enough to access the window retaining bolts through the holes in the door frame (see illustration).

3    Place a rag over the glass to help prevent scratching the glass and remove the two glass mounting bolts.

4    Remove the glass by tilting it slightly, pulling it up and out.

5    Installation is the reverse of removal.

### 22  Door window regulator - removal and installation

**Caution:** *Wear gloves when working inside the door openings to protect against cuts from sharp metal edges.*

1    Remove the door trim panel and the plastic watershield (see Section 18).

2    Remove the window glass assembly or support the glass in the closed position with good adhesive tape in three places (see Section 21).

3    On power operated windows, disconnect the electrical connector from the window regulator motor.

4    Remove the regulator mounting bolts (see illustration), then slide the regulator assembly out of the service hole in the door frame to remove it.

5    Installation is the reverse of removal. Lubricate the track guides where the roller wheels glide back and forth.

**Note:** *Applying a small amount of liquid dish soap to the felt tracks periodically will not only keep the track free from dirt build up but can also make the window motor last longer due to less drag from the window sliding up and down on a dirty track.*

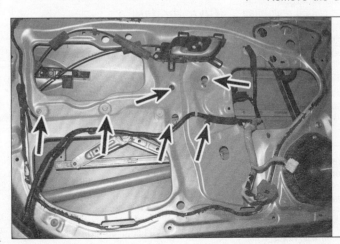

22.4 Door window glass regulator fastener locations

**23.4 To remove the mirror, remove these three nuts - if the vehicle has power mirrors, also unplug the electrical connector**

**23.7 Slide the mirror assembly off of the base**

**24.2 Using a trim tool, carefully pry the top shifter trim cover off**

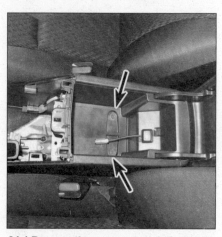

**24.4 Remove the center console fasteners under the arm rest**

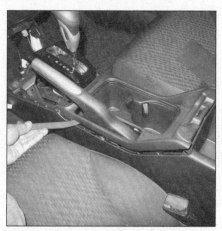

**24.5 Pry the cup holder assembly out to remove the fasteners below the cup holder assembly**

**24.6 Save these fasteners for reinstalling**

## 23   Mirrors - removal and installation

### *Outside door mirrors*

1   Pry off the mirror trim cover (see Section 18).
2   Remove the mirror retaining screws.
3   On some of the electric mirror models, remove the door trim panel to gain access to the retaining bolts and the electrical connector (see Section 18).
4   Remove the three mirror retaining nuts and detach the mirror from the vehicle (see illustration).
5   Installation is the reverse of removal.

### *Inside mirror*

6   Remove the trim cover from the mirror base.
7   Loosen the set screw and slide the mirror up and off of the base mount (see illustration).

8   Disconnect the electrical connector (if equipped) and remove the mirror.
9   Installation is the reverse of removal.
**Note:** *If the mounting bracket for the mirror has come off the windshield, it can be reattached with a special mirror adhesive kit available at auto parts stores. Clean the glass and support base thoroughly and follow the directions on the adhesive package, allowing the base to bond overnight before attaching the mirror.*

## 24   Center console - removal and installation

**Warning:** *Models covered by this manual are equipped with a Supplemental Restraint System (SRS), more commonly known as airbags. Always disable the airbag system before working in the vicinity of any airbag system component to avoid the possibility of accidental deployment of the airbag, which could*

*cause personal injury (see Chapter 12).*
1   Disconnect the cable from the negative terminal of the battery (see Chapter 5).

### *Civic models*

2   If you're working on an automatic transmission model, pry off the gear selector trim bezel and center console trim (see illustration). On manual transmission models, unscrew the shift lever knob.
3   Disconnect the electrical connections (if applicable) and remove the gear selector trim panel.
4   Open the center console arm rest, remove the mat and retaining screws (see illustration).
5   Remove the cup holder assembly to gain access to the bolts (see illustration).
6   Remove the fasteners in the front edges of the console (see illustration). There's one on each side.
7   Disconnect any electrical connections and remove the console from the vehicle.

25.2 Grasp the edges and pull the trim panel off. Disconnect any electrical connectors

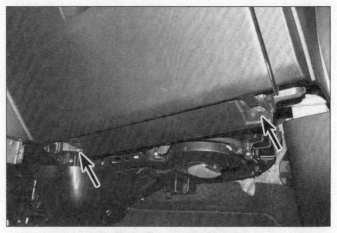

25.5a Glove box screw locations

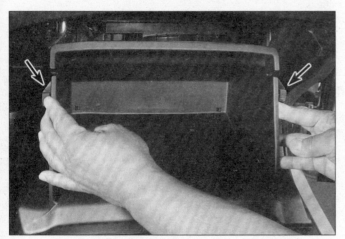

25.5b Press in on the tabs to lower the glove box

25.7 Removing the cluster bezel

8    There are several locking slots that secure the console. Slide the console back just a bit and lift the console off of these locking slots. Then, remove the console.

9    Installation is the reverse of removal.

## CR-V models

10    Remove the forward side trim covers by pulling them away from the center console. (There are no screws, only pressure snap connectors.)

11    Pull the rear trim cover off of the console. (There are no screws, only pressure snap connectors.)

12    Pry the lower center dash trim panel off. (It's just above the center console.)

13    Remove the bolts securing the rear portion of the console to the body. (They're located under the rear trim you previously removed.)

14    Remove the mat from the center console and then remove the retaining bolts.

15    Remove the pressure snap connectors on either side of the console that secure the console to the dash. (They're behind the forward side trims previously removed.)

16    Slide the front seats all the way to the front and lift the rear portion of the console up, then pull the console rearward to remove it from the vehicle.

17    Installation is the reverse of removal.

## 25  Dashboard trim panels - removal and installation

**Warning:** *Models covered by this manual are equipped with a Supplemental Restraint System (SRS), more commonly known as airbags. Always disable the airbag system before working in the vicinity of any airbag system component to avoid the possibility of accidental deployment of the airbag, which could cause personal injury (see Chapter 12).*

1    Disconnect the cable from the negative battery terminal (see Chapter 5).

### Driver's instrument panel lower cover

2    Using a flat bladed trim tool pry the edges up far enough to get your fingers around the trim panel. Then, pull the panel straight off (see illustration). (It is only held on with pressure connectors.)

3    Installation is the reverse of removal.

### Glove box

4    Open the glove box door and remove the glove box stops, then lower the glove box from the instrument panel. Disconnect the glove box damper hooks from the top corner of the glove box (if applicable).

5    At the bottom of the glovebox, remove the screws from the hinges and press in on the tabs to lower the glove box (see illustrations).

6    Installation is the reverse of removal.

### Instrument cluster bezel

#### Civic

7    Grasp the bezel securely and pull back to detach the clips from the instrument panel (see illustration).

8    Installation is the reverse of removal.

25.27 Remove the upper instrument panel

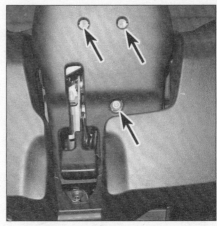

26.4 Steering column cover retaining screws (sedan model shown, other models similar)

## CR-V

9    Lower the steering column using the tilt steering release.

10   Remove the driver's instrument panel lower cover just above the steering wheel upper cover by prying it out with a flat bladed trim tool.

11   Grasp the instrument cluster bezel and pull it away from the instrument cluster.

12   Unplug any electrical connectors, then remove the panel.

13   Installation is the reverse of removal.

### *Center trim panel*

#### CR-V center display visor

14   Remove the center HVAC vents by prying the edge loose and pulling them away from the dash.

15   Remove the radio/navigation assembly (see Chapter 12).

16   Remove the center display visor mounting bolts (on the bottom edges) then release the trim panel clips.

17   Carefully remove the trim panel out far enough to unplug any electrical connectors, then remove the trim panel from the dashboard.

18   Installation is the reverse of removal.

#### Civic lower center trim panel

19   Remove the screws securing the lower edge of the center trim panel.

20   Lift the lower edge of the panel and work your way upward along the edges to detach the clips. Unplug any electrical connectors, then remove the panel.

21   Installation is the reverse of removal.

### *Driver's instrument panel upper cover (instrument cluster visor)*

#### Civic models

22   Remove the driver's side lower trim panel.

23   Remove the driver's side A pillar.

24   Remove the instrument cluster bezel.

25   Using a trim tool, carefully pry up and remove the instrument panel side trim.

26   Remove the fasteners securing the instrument upper cover to the dash.

27   Pry the outer edges of the instrument cluster visor off with flat bladed trim tool. Once the clips are free lift the upper cover off (see illustration).

28   Installation is the reverse of removal.

### CR-V upper dash trim pad - removal and installation

29   Disconnect the negative battery terminal (see Chapter 5) and wait at least three minutes before proceeding.

30   Tilt the steering wheel as far down as possible. On automatic transmissions, set parking brake and shift to the lowest gear. On manual transmissions, set parking brake and place the shift lever in second gear.

31   Remove the instrument cluster trim bezel.

32   Remove the right and left dash end trim panels.

33   Remove the passenger side HVAC vent outlets. (Pry them out with a flat bladed trim tool.)

34   Remove the passenger side assist handle. Reach into the HVAC vent openings, depress the release tabs and remove the handle.

35   Remove the right and left side A pillar trim (see Section 32).

36   Remove the screw securing the upper instrument cluster trim panel.

37   Installation is the reverse of removal. Tighten all the screws to 18 ft-lbs.

## 26   Steering column covers - removal and installation

**Warning:** *Models covered by this manual are equipped with a Supplemental Restraint System (SRS), more commonly known as airbags. Always disable the airbag system before working in the vicinity of any airbag system component to avoid the possibility of accidental deployment of the airbag, which could cause personal injury (see Chapter 12).*

1    Disconnect the cable from the negative

battery terminal (see Chapter 5).

2    Remove the driver's side instrument panel lower cover (see Section 25).

3    On tilt steering columns, move the column to the lowest position.

4    Remove the retaining screws, then separate the halves and remove the covers (see illustration).

5    Installation is the reverse of the removal procedure.

## 27   Instrument panel - removal and installation

**Warning:** *Models covered by this manual are equipped with a Supplemental Restraint System (SRS), more commonly known as airbags. Always disable the airbag system before working in the vicinity of any airbag system component to avoid the possibility of accidental deployment of the airbag, which could cause personal injury (see Chapter 12).*

**Note:** *This is a difficult procedure for the home mechanic. There are many hidden fasteners, difficult angles to work in and many electrical connectors to tag and disconnect/connect. We recommend that this procedure be done only by an experienced do-it-yourselfer.*

**Note:** *During removal of the instrument panel, make careful notes of how each piece comes off, where it fits in relation to other pieces and what holds it in place. If you note how each part is installed before removing it, getting the instrument panel back together again will be much easier.*

**Note:** *It is not necessary, but it is suggested to remove both front seats to allow additional working space and lessen the chance of damage to the seats during this procedure.*

1    Disconnect the cable from the negative battery terminal (see Chapter 5).

2    Remove the instrument cluster bezel (see Section 25).

3    Remove the instrument cluster (see Chapter 12).

4    Remove the nuts and lower the steering column (see Chapter 10).

27.6 Use a plastic trim tool to pry the vents out

27.7 Pry the side covers from the dash

27.15 Instrument panel support center bolts

27.16a Pull off the covers in the door jambs and remove the lower bolts from each end of the dash . . .

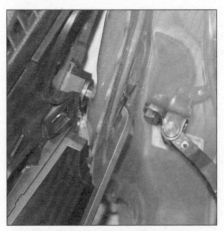

27.16b Then, using an Allen wrench, thread the screw insert into the instrument panel (when installing the instrument panel, be sure to back out these inserts before installing the bolts)

27.16c Pry off the covers at the upper rear corner of each fender . . .

5    Remove the side kick panels (see Section 32).
6    Remove the center, driver and passenger vents (see illustration).
7    Remove the dashboard side covers (see illustration).
8    Remove the A pillar trim (see Section 32).
9    Remove the steering column (see Chapter 10).
10   Remove the glovebox (see Section 25).
11   Remove the radio (see Chapter 12) and the heater control assembly (see Chapter 3).
12   Remove the center console (see Section 24), (if applicable).
13   Remove the rear vent duct.
14   Disconnect the instrument panel electrical connectors including the passenger's side airbag (see Chapter 12).
15   Remove the fasteners securing the lower center part of the instrument panel (see illustration).
16   Remove the fasteners from each end of the instrument panel (see illustrations).

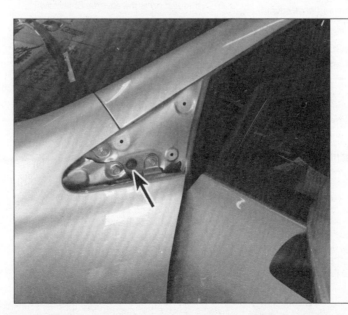

27.16d . . . and remove the upper dash bolts

**27.17a Right side instrument panel support beam nuts**

**27.17b Brake pedal bracket-to-support beam bolt and left side support bracket bolt**

**27.18 Depress the tab, swing open the lock and unplug the electrical connectors from the fuse/relay box**

17   Remove the instrument panel support beam fasteners (see illustrations).
18   Unplug the electrical connectors from the interior fuse/relay box (see illustration).
19   Pull the instrument panel toward the rear of the vehicle and detach any electrical connectors interfering with removal.
**Note:** *A number of electrical connectors must be disconnected in order to remove the instrument panel. Most are designed so that they will only fit on the matching connector (male or female), but if there is any doubt, mark the connectors with masking tape and a marking pen before disconnecting them.*
**Caution:** *Double check for any brackets or electrical connections you might have missed before proceeding any farther.*
20   Once all the electrical connectors are detached, with the aid of an assistant, lift the instrument panel, then pull it away from the windshield and take it out through the passenger's door opening.
21   Installation is the reverse of removal.
22   Reconnect the battery. Refer to Chapter 5.

---

**28   Seats - removal and installation**

---

**Warning:** *The front seat belts on some models are equipped with pre-tensioners, which are pyrotechnic (explosive) devices designed to retract the seat belts in the event of a collision. On models equipped with pre-tensioners, do not remove the front seat belt retractor assemblies, and do not disconnect the electrical connectors leading to the assemblies. Problems with the pre-tensioners will turn on the SRS (airbag) warning light on the dash. If any pre-tensioner problems are suspected, take the vehicle to a dealer service department.*
**Warning:** *On models with side-impact airbags, be sure to disarm the airbag system before beginning this procedure (see Chapter 12).*

## Front seat

1   Disconnect the cable from the negative battery terminal (see Chapter 5).
2   Position the seat all the way forward, then all the way to the rear to access the seat retaining bolts.
3   Detach any bolt trim covers and remove the retaining bolts.
4   Tilt the seat upward to access the underside, then disconnect any electrical connectors and lift the seat from the vehicle.
5   Installation is the reverse of removal.

## Rear seat

6   Remove the seat cushion bolt and remove the cushion. Pull back the seat back trim cover, then remove the fasteners securing the seat hinge and remove the seat backs.
7   On CR-V models, tilt the seat forward and remove the retaining bolts at the front of the seat. Remove the seat from the vehicle.
8   Installation is the reverse of removal.

---

**29   Tailgate latch, lock cylinder and handle (CR-V models) - removal and installation**

---

**Caution:** *Wear gloves when working inside the door openings to protect against cuts from sharp metal edges.*
1   Open the tailgate and remove the tailgate trim panel (see Section 18).

## Latch

2   Reaching through the access hole, detach the tailgate rod and cylinder rod, then disconnect the actuator connector from the latch.
3   On 2006 and later models, remove the actuator connector and latch switch connector.
4   Remove the latch mounting screws and remove the latch from the tailgate.
5   Installation is the reverse of removal.

## Lock cylinder

6   Reaching through the access hole, detach the actuating rod from the rear of the lock cylinder.
7   Remove the lock cylinder retaining clip and pull it outward to remove it from the tailgate handle.
8   Installation is the reverse of removal.

## Handle

9   Reaching through the access hole, remove the lock cylinder (see Steps 6 and 7).
10   Remove the bolt securing the lock cylinder protector and handle to the tailgate. Release the clip and remove the protector.
11   Remove the bolt securing the handle and spacer handle to the tailgate.
12   Carefully remove the handle from the tailgate.
13   Installation is the reverse of removal.

---

**30   Tailgate replacement, alignment and support struts - removal and installation**

---

## Tailgate replacement

**Note:** *The tailgate is heavy and somewhat awkward to hold - at least two people should perform this procedure.*
1   Raise and support the tailgate.
2   Remove the trim panels to gain access to the hinge bolts.
3   Disconnect the electrical connections and the rear wiper washer hose.
4   With the aid of an assistant remove the strut shocks.
5   Now, remove the hinge bolts.
**Caution:** *The tailgate is surprisingly heavy so be prepared as you remove the last bolt.*
6   Installation is the reverse of removal. Align the tailgate after installing.

## Tailgate alignment

7   Remove the striker trim cap from the rear trim panel.
8   Loosen the striker plate and tailgate hinges just far enough to allow the tailgate to be shifted.
9   Gently close the tailgate and check the body lines.
10   Shift the tailgate using a plastic wedge or flat bladed trim tool to gently persuade the door into alignment.
11   Open the tailgate and tighten the striker and tailgate hinge bolts.
12   Close and recheck the alignment.
13   Adjust the door stops (rubber adjusters) so that the door rests on the stops but is not putting any pressure on the door when it is latched properly.
14   Recheck alignment and if necessary readjust the tailgate.

## Tailgate trim

15   All the tailgate trim is held in place with pressure clips except for the hand grab pocket. One screw holds it in place. To remove any of the trim, grasp the edges firmly and pull outward away from the door.
16   Installation is the reverse of removal.

## Strut replacement

17   Using a small pocket screwdriver, gently pry the retaining clip off of the strut socket.
18   Pull the the strut from the ball socket while supporting the tailgate.
**Note:** *Some replacement struts will come with the ball socket already installed onto the strut. On these, unscrew the ball socket from the body and the door to replace the strut. Tighten to 16 ft-lbs.*
19   Install the replacement struts and snap the retaining clip into place.
20   Check that the door closes and opens correctly.

---

**31   License plate trim panel**

---

## Civic and CR-V sedan and coupe models

1   On models with the trunk liner trim package, remove the trunk lid inner trim panel. It is held on with pressure clips. Pull the center of the grommet up, then remove the grommet. Pull the panel straight off while applying pressure to the edges.
2   From inside the trunk, remove the single bolt securing the trim to the trunk lid.
3   From the outside, using a flat bladed trim tool and something to protect the paint finish, pry the pressure clips loose.
**Note:** *If the clips appear to be damaged, replace them.*
4   Remove the license plate trim.
5   Installation is the reverse of removal.

## CR-V hatchback models

6   Remove the tailgate inner trim panels (see Section 30).
7   Remove the two bolts securing the license plate trim to the tailgate. The bolts are located on the far edge of the license plate trim.
8   Working from the outside of the tailgate, spray a solution of soapy water along the bottom edge of the license plate trim.
9   Using a utility knife and something to protect the paint finish, slide the utility knife along the lower edge of the license plate trim to separate the double sided tape.
10   On the upper edge of the license plate trim, remove the grommet clips. Pull the center section up, then pry the remaining grommet out of the license plate trim.
11   Remove the license plate trim.
12   To reinstall, clean off the old double sided tape and replace with new tape. Check the condition of all the grommet clips. If any are damaged replace them.
13   The remainder of the installation is the reverse of removal.

---

**32   Interior trim components - removal and installation**

## Sun visor

1   Use a small flat bladed screwdriver to push in the tab on the swivel base of the visor. Then, rotate the visor base 45 degrees to align the tab with the slot in the roof. Pull down while turning to release the sun visor from the roof.
2   If the tab is not completely lined up the sun visor will not come down. Rotate the sun visor back and forth to find the exact location of the tab. The actual tab location is hidden by the sun visor mounting trim and you won't be able to see it until the sun visor is actually removed.
3   Disconnect the electrical connector and remove the sun visor.
4   To install, reattach the electrical connector and align the notch in the slot to the tab of the visor, then push up firmly and rotate 45 degrees.

## Sun visor hook

5   Remove the visor from the hook.
6   Grasp the hook and rotate it counterclockwise 45 degrees to remove it.
7   To install, align the tab to the slot, then push up firmly and rotate it clockwise 45 degrees.

## Rear parcel shelf

8   Remove the rear seat cushion and seat back (see Section 28).
9   Open the trunk and disconnect the high mounted brake light.
10   Detach the quarter panel trim pieces on both sides and detach the shelf trim panel.

11   Installation is the reverse of the removal procedure.

## A pillar

12   Pull the rubber door seal down far enough to expose the entire A pillar trim.
13   Remove the headliner upper door trim panel.
14   Apply outward pressure to free the pressure clips while applying upward pressure to remove the A pillar trim.
15   Installation requires removing the upper clip from the body. Press in on the top and bottom clips. Reattach the upper clip to the A pillar trim. Then install the A pillar trim back into place.

## B pillar

16   Start by removing the lower B pillar trim first.
**Note:** *2013 models have two different shaped lower B pillar trim panels, depending on the interior configuration for the four-door or two-door models. Both come off in relatively the same way.*
17   Remove the door sill trim panels (see Section 32).
18   Pull the rubber door seals down far enough to expose the entire upper and lower B pillar trim.
19   Remove the coat hanger hooks and the headliner upper door trim panel.
20   Slide the front seats as far forward as possible.
21   Grasp the edges of the lower B pillar trim and pull it off of the retaining clips.
22   Remove the trim cap from the shoulder seat belt mount.
23   Remove the bolt securing the shoulder seat belt to the B pillar.
24   Grasp the upper B pillar trim and pull the bottom section away from the body. Then pivot the upper B pillar trim upward to disengage the upper hook.
25   Remove the upper B pillar trim.
26   Installation is the reverse of removal.

## C pillar

27   Grasp the C pillar trim by the lower (or upper) edges and pull straight off.
28   Before reinstalling, check for any of the pressure snap clips that have separated from the C pillar trim. Reattach them to the trim panel and press back into place.

## Quarter panel trim

29   Remove the rear seat (see Section 28).
30   Remove the rear seat shoulder seat belt mounting bolts.
31   Remove the coat hanger hooks.
32   Remove the headliner rear upper door trim panels.
33   Remove the square button and fastener mounted on the quarter trim panel.
34   Pull the quarter panel trim off by applying pressure along the edges to release the pressure snap connectors.
35   Installation is the reverse of removal.

**32.36 Pry up on the sill plate to remove it**

**32.37 Remove the lock trim cover, then remove the screw (A)**

**32.40 Pry the kick panel plate out to remove**

**32.44a Driver's side end trim panel removal**

**32.44b Passenger side end trim panel removal**

### Door sill plate trim

36   Remove the rubber door seal by pulling it off. Then, using a flat bladed trim tool, pry upward to disengage the plastic pressure snap clips (see illustration).

37   On models with a locking gas cap door, remove the trim over the lock cylinder and remove the lock cylinder by lifting it up (a slight twist may be needed). Then remove the screw securing the sill plate trim to the body (see illustration).

**Note:** *On four-door models, flip the seat bottom out of the way to gain full access to the door sill trim plate.*

38   Installation is the reverse of removal.

### Kick panel

39   Remove the sill plate trim panel (see Section 32).

40   Pull or pry the edge of the panel until the clips are disengaged and remove the panel (see illustration).

41   Installation is the reverse of removal.

### Grab handles

42   With the grab handle in the down position, look for two small holes on either side of the grab handle trim cap. Insert the appropriate fitting tool in each side and pull from both sides at the same time to remove the grab handle.

**Note:** *It may take some force to actually remove the grab handle. There are no screws securing the handle to the roof, only the pressure of the retaining clips.*

43   To remove the retaining clips, press inward on the top and bottom edges of the clips and pull the clip straight out.

### Dash end trim panels

44   Using a flat bladed trim tool pry the dash end trim panels off (see illustrations).

### Headliner

**Warning:** *All models covered by this manual are equipped with a Supplemental Restraint System (SRS), more commonly known as airbags. Always disable the airbag system before working in the vicinity of any airbag system component to avoid the possibility of accidental deployment of the airbag, which could cause personal injury (see Chapter 12).*

45   Disconnect the negative battery terminal (see Chapter 5).

46   Remove the dome light fixtures (see Chapter 12).

47   Remove the A pillar trim (see Section 32).

48   Remove the B pillar trim (see Section 32).

49   Remove the headliner trim above each door as well as the grab handles (see Section 32).

50   Remove the C pillar or quarter panel trim (depending on which model you're working on) (see Section 32).

**Note:** *On the four-door models remove the seat bolster trim. (This is the trim between the seat and the C pillar.) Pull the trim off by grasping the edges and pull straight off.*

51   Remove sun visors (see Section 32).

52   Slide the front seats as far back as possible and tilt the back as far as possible.

53   Lower the headliner far enough to gain access to the electrical connectors. Disconnect the electrical connectors.

**Note:** *According to the manufacturer's removal descriptions, on some models the electrical connectors to the overhead wiring harnesses are in the kick panel area. Most are behind the headliner. If applicable, remove the kick panels to disconnect the electrical leads to the headliner harness (see Section 32).*

54   Tilt the headliner down in the front and slide it out through the passenger front door.

55   Installation is the reverse of removal.

# Notes

# Chapter 12
# Chassis electrical system

## Contents

## 1  General Information

1    The electrical system is a 12-volt, negative ground type. Power for the lights and all electrical accessories is supplied by a lead/acid-type battery that is charged by the alternator.

2    This chapter covers repair and service procedures for the various electrical components not associated with the engine. Information on the battery, alternator, ignition system and starter motor can be found in Chapter 5.

3    It should be noted that when portions of the electrical system are serviced, the negative cable should be disconnected from the battery to prevent electrical shorts and/or fires.

## 2  Electrical troubleshooting - general information

1    A typical electrical circuit consists of an electrical component, any switches, relays, motors, fuses, fusible links or circuit breakers related to that component and the wiring and connectors that link the component to both the battery and the chassis. To help you pinpoint an electrical circuit problem, wiring diagrams are included at the end of this chapter.

2    Before tackling any troublesome electrical circuit, first study the appropriate wiring diagrams to get a complete understanding of what makes up that individual circuit. Trouble spots, for instance, can often be narrowed down by noting if other components related to the circuit are operating properly.

If several components or circuits fail at one time, chances are the problem is in a fuse or ground connection, because several circuits are often routed through the same fuse and ground connections.

3    Electrical problems usually stem from simple causes, such as loose or corroded connections, a blown fuse, a melted fusible link or a failed relay. Visually inspect the condition of all fuses, wires and connections in a problem circuit before troubleshooting the circuit.

4    If test equipment and instruments are going to be utilized, use the diagrams to plan ahead of time where you will make the necessary connections in order to accurately pinpoint the trouble spot.

5    The basic tools needed for electrical troubleshooting include a circuit tester or

voltmeter (a 12-volt bulb with a set of test leads can also be used), a continuity tester, which includes a bulb, battery and set of test leads, and a jumper wire, preferably with a circuit breaker incorporated, which can be used to bypass electrical components (see illustrations). Before attempting to locate a problem with test instruments, use the wiring diagram(s) to decide where to make the connections.

## Voltage checks

6     Voltage checks should be performed if a circuit is not functioning properly. Connect one lead of a circuit tester to either the negative battery terminal or a known good ground. Connect the other lead to a connector in the circuit being tested, preferably nearest to the battery or fuse (see illustrations). If the bulb of the tester lights, voltage is present, which means that the part of the circuit between the connector and the battery is problem free. Continue checking the rest of the circuit in the same fashion. When you reach a point at which no voltage is present, the problem lies between that point and the last test point with voltage. Most of the time the problem can be traced to a loose connection.
**Note:** *Keep in mind that some circuits receive voltage only when the ignition key is in the Accessory or Run position.*

## Finding a short

7     One method of finding shorts in a circuit is to remove the fuse and connect a test light or voltmeter in place of the fuse terminals. There should be no voltage present in the circuit. Move the wiring harness from side-to-side while watching the test light. If the bulb goes on, there is a short to ground somewhere in that area, probably where the insulation has rubbed through. The same test can be performed on each component in the circuit, even a switch.

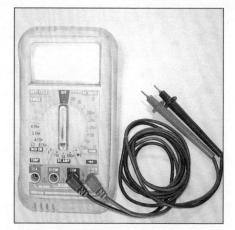

**2.5a The most useful tool for electrical troubleshooting is a digital multimeter that can check volts, amps, and test continuity**

**2.5b A test light is a very handy tool for checking voltage**

## Ground check

8     Perform a ground test to check whether a component is properly grounded. Disconnect the battery and connect one lead of a continuity tester or multimeter (set to the ohms scale), to a known good ground. Connect the other lead to the wire or ground connection being tested. If the resistance is low (less than 5 ohms), the ground is good. If the bulb on a self-powered test light does not go on, the ground is not good.

## Continuity check

9     A continuity check is done to determine if there are any breaks in a circuit - if it is passing electricity properly. With the circuit off (no power in the circuit), a self-powered continuity tester or multimeter can be used to check the circuit. Connect the test leads to both ends of the circuit (or to the power end and a good ground), and if the test light comes

on the circuit is passing current properly (see illustration). If the resistance is low (less than 5 ohms), there is continuity; if the reading is 10,000 ohms or higher, there is a break somewhere in the circuit. The same procedure can be used to test a switch, by connecting the continuity tester to the switch terminals. With the switch turned On, the test light should come on (or low resistance should be indicated on a meter).

## Finding an open circuit

10   When diagnosing for possible open circuits, it is often difficult to locate them by sight because the connectors hide oxidation or terminal misalignment. Merely wiggling a connector on a sensor or in the wiring harness may correct the open circuit condition. Remember this when an open circuit is indicated when troubleshooting a circuit. Intermittent problems may also be caused by oxidized or loose connections.

**2.6 In use, a basic test light's lead is clipped to a known good ground, then the pointed probe can test connectors, wires or electrical sockets - if the bulb lights, the part being tested has battery voltage**

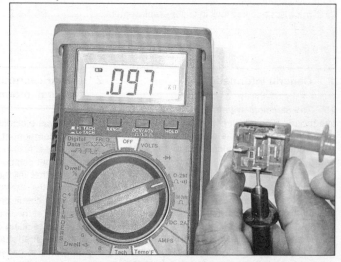

**2.9 With a multimeter set to the ohms scale, resistance can be checked across two terminals - when checking for continuity, a low reading indicates continuity, a high reading indicates lack of continuity**

3.1a Remove the driver's dashboard lower cover to expose the under-dash fuse and relay box (on CR-Vs, the under-dash fuse/relay box is located in the same spot but has an access door in the driver's dashboard lower cover, so you don't have to remove the cover)

3.1b On coupes and sedans, the engine compartment fuse/relay box is located on the right side of the engine compartment. The functions and locations of the various fuses and relays are listed on the fuse/relay box cover (on CR-Vs and hatchbacks, this fuse/relay box is located on the left side of the engine compartment)

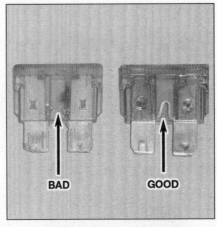

3.3 When a fuse blows, the element between the terminals melts

11   Electrical troubleshooting is simple if you keep in mind that all electrical circuits are basically electricity running from the battery, through the wires, switches, relays, fuses and fusible links to each electrical component (light bulb, motor, etc.) and to ground, from which it is passed back to the battery. Any electrical problem is an interruption in the flow of electricity to and from the battery.

## 3   Circuit breakers, fuses and fusible links - general information

### Fuses

1   The electrical circuits of the vehicle are protected by a combination of fuses, circuit breakers and fusible links. The main fuse/relay panel is in the engine compartment (see illustration), while the interior fuse/relay panel is located inside the passenger compartment (see illustration). Each of the fuses is designed to protect a specific circuit, and the various circuits are identified on the fuse panel itself.

2   Several sizes of fuses are employed in the fuse blocks. There are small, medium and large sizes of the same design, all with the same blade terminal design. The medium and large fuses can be removed with your fingers, but the small fuses require the use of pliers or the small plastic fuse-puller tool found in most fuse boxes.

3   If an electrical component fails, always check the fuse first. The best way to check the fuses is with a test light. Check for power at the exposed terminal tips of each fuse. If power is present at one side of the fuse but not the other, the fuse is blown. A blown fuse

can also be identified by visually inspecting it (see illustration).

4   Be sure to replace blown fuses with the correct type. Fuses (of the same physical size) of different ratings may be physically interchangeable, but only fuses of the proper rating should be used. Replacing a fuse with one of a higher or lower value than specified is not recommended. Each electrical circuit needs a specific amount of protection. The amperage value of each fuse is molded into the top of the fuse body.

5   If the replacement fuse immediately fails, don't replace it again until the cause of the problem is isolated and corrected. In most cases, this will be a short circuit in the wiring caused by a broken or deteriorated wire.

### Fusible links

6   Some circuits are protected by fusible links. The links are used in circuits which carry high current.

7   Cartridge-type fusible links are located in the engine compartment fuse/relay box and are similar to a large fuse. After disconnecting the negative battery cable, simply unplug the fusible link and replace it with a fusible link of the same amperage.

### Circuit breakers - general information

8   Circuit breakers protect certain circuits, such as the power windows or heated seats. Depending on the vehicle's accessories, there may be one or two circuit breakers, located in the fuse/relay box in the engine compartment.

9   Because the circuit breakers reset automatically, an electrical overload in a circuit breaker-protected system will cause the cir-

cuit to fail momentarily, then come back on. If the circuit does not come back on, check it immediately.

10   For a basic check, pull the circuit breaker up out of its socket on the fuse panel, but just far enough to probe with a voltmeter. The breaker should still contact the sockets. With the voltmeter negative lead on a good chassis ground, touch each end prong of the circuit breaker with the positive meter probe. There should be battery voltage at each end. If there is battery voltage only at one end, the circuit breaker must be replaced.

11   Some circuit breakers must be reset manually.

## 4   Relays - general information

1   Several electrical accessories in the vehicle, such as the fuel injection system, horns, starter, and fog lamps use relays to transmit the electrical signal to the component. Relays use a low-current circuit (the control circuit) to open and close a high-current circuit (the power circuit). If the relay is defective, that component will not operate properly. Most relays are mounted in the engine compartment and interior fuse/relay boxes (see illustrations 3.1a and 3.1b).

## 5   Electrical connectors - general information

1   Most electrical connections on these vehicles are made with multiwire plastic connectors. The mating halves of many connectors are secured with locking clips molded into the plastic connector shells. The mating

# Electrical connectors

Most electrical connectors have a single release tab that you depress to release the connector

Some electrical connectors have a retaining tab which must be pried up to free the connector

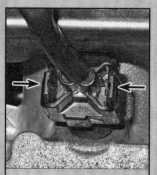

Some connectors have two release tabs that you must squeeze to release the connector

Some connectors use wire retainers that you squeeze to release the connector

Critical connectors often employ a sliding lock (1) that you must pull out before you can depress the release tab (2)

Here's another sliding-lock style connector, with the lock (1) and the release tab (2) on the side of the connector

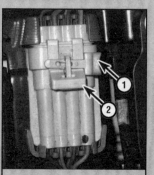

On some connectors the lock (1) must be pulled out to the side and removed before you can lift the release tab (2)

Some critical connectors, like the multi-pin connectors at the Powertrain Control Module employ pivoting locks that must be flipped open

halves of some large connectors, such as some of those under the instrument panel, are held together by a bolt through the center of the connector.

2    To separate a connector with locking clips, use a small screwdriver to pry the clips apart carefully, then separate the connector halves. Pull only on the shell, never pull on the wiring harness as you may damage the individual wires and terminals inside the connectors. Look at the connector closely before trying to separate the halves. Often the locking clips are engaged in a way that is not immediately clear. Additionally, many connectors have more than one set of clips.

3    Each pair of connector terminals has a male half and a female half. When you look at the end view of a connector in a diagram, be sure to understand whether the view shows the harness side or the component side of the connector. Connector halves are mirror images of each other, and a terminal shown on the right side end-view of one half will be on the left side end-view of the other half.

4    It is often necessary to take circuit voltage measurements with a connector connected. Whenever possible, carefully insert a small straight pin (not your meter probe) into the rear of the connector shell to contact the terminal inside, then clip your meter lead to the pin. This kind of connection is called "backprobing." When inserting a test probe into a terminal, be careful not to distort the terminal opening. Doing so can lead to a poor connection and corrosion at that terminal later. Using the small straight pin instead of a meter probe results in less chance of deforming the terminal connector.

## 6   Key fob - battery replacement

1    Replace the battery when the key fob transmitter doesn't operate the locks at a distance of 10 feet. Normal range should be about 30 feet.
**Note:** *Before replacing the key fob battery, insert the key into the ignition and start the vehicle. If the vehicle starts with the key, but the door locks are not working with the key fob, replace the battery in the key fob.*

6.2a Remove the screw . . .

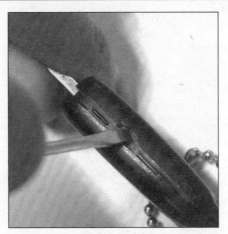

6.2b . . . and pry the case halves apart at the slot

6.3 Note which way the battery faces, then pry it out and install a new one

7.3a Ignition switch electrical connector

7.3b Pull the release tab to remove the connector

7.3c Leave the pull tab out until you reinstall the connector to the switch. Slide the connector into place and then push the tab in to secure the switch and connector together

**Note:** *If the immobilizer code is not recognized, the security light will flash once then blink until the key is turned back to the lock position. The immobilizer light will then flash 10 tens and go out. (This indicates the security system is back to the ready sequence awaiting the correct immobilizer code). If, after several attempts the immobilizer is not recognized it will need to be reprogrammed or replaced using the factory scan tool. Take the vehicle to a dealer service department or a qualified repair facility with a factory scanner and have it reprogrammed.*
**Note:** *If the door locks do not work from the remote or the door lock switch, diagnose the door lock system first.*

2    Remove the screw, pry the key fob apart at the seam and carefully separate the case halves (see illustrations).
**Note:** *Check for any water or moisture damage first. If any, discard the remote and replace it. The replacement key fob will need to be programmed.*

3    Remove the battery, noting which way it is facing before you remove it, then install the new one (see illustration). The replacement battery number is CR2032.

4    Snap the case halves together and install the screw.
5    Press the lock or unlock button and check its operation. If the doors lock or unlock the transmitter is programmed and set. If the doors do not lock or unlock, the immobilizer and transmitter must be reprogrammed using a factory scan tool. Take the vehicle to a dealer service department or other qualified repair facility and have it reprogrammed.
**Caution:** *Only use Honda authorized immobilizer key fobs for replacement.*

## Key fob strength testing

6    If for some reason your key fob fails to operate even after you've tried a replacement battery, take your key fob to a repair shop that has a tire monitor reset tool. Most of these tools have an RF strength indicator test as part of their diagnostics features. The technician can check whether or not your key fob is in working order or not. If there is no RF signal, the key fob is more than likely faulty. If the signal is weak, chances are the battery needs to be replaced.

## 7    Ignition switch and key lock cylinder - replacement

**Warning:** *All models covered by this manual are equipped with a Supplemental Restraint System (SRS), more commonly known as airbags. Always disable the airbag system before working in the vicinity of any airbag system component to avoid the possibility of accidental deployment of the airbag, which could cause personal injury (see Section 24).*
1    Disconnect the cable from the negative battery terminal (see Chapter 5), then wait at least three minutes before proceeding.
2    Remove the driver's dashboard panel assembly and the steering column covers (see Chapter 11).

## Ignition switch (key type)

3    Disconnect the electrical connector from the ignition switch (see illustrations).
4    Remove the ignition switch mounting screws and remove the switch.

**7.9a Disconnect the immobilizer connector**

**7.9b Carefully lift the top and bottom tab to remove the immobilizer from the ignition lock housing**

**7.10 To detach the key lock cylinder housing from the steering column, drill out the bolts with a 3/16-inch (5 mm) drill bit and remove the bolts with a screw extractor**

5    Installation is the reverse of removal. Reconnect the cable to the negative battery terminal and verify that the ignition switch operates correctly in the Lock, Acc, On and Start positions.

### Key lock cylinder (key type)

**Note:** *If the key lock cylinder is being replaced, the immobilizer and transmitter must be reprogrammed using the factory scan tool. Take the vehicle to a dealer service department or other qualified repair facility and have it reprogrammed.*

6    Disconnect the negative battery terminal and wait at least three minutes before continuing (see Chapter 5).
7    Remove the steering column covers and the dashboard panels (see Chapter 11).
8    Disconnect the ignition switch electrical connector and the connectors for the ignition key lock cylinder, the immobilizer control unit/ receiver and the ignition key lock cylinder/key light.

**8.3 To disconnect the electrical connector from the multi-function switch, depress this release tab**

9    Remove the ignition switch (electrical part) and remove the immobilizer unit (see illustrations).
10    Center-punch the shear-head bolts that secure the key lock cylinder housing to the steering column, then drill a hole in the center of each bolt with a 3/16-inch (5 mm) drill bit (see illustration) and unscrew them with a screw extractor.
11    Remove the key lock cylinder assembly from the steering column.
12    Before tightening the new shear-head bolts, insert the ignition key and verify that the steering wheel lock mechanism functions correctly and that the ignition key turns freely in the key lock cylinder. Then tighten the shear-head bolts until the heads break off.
13    Installation is otherwise the reverse of removal. Reconnect the cable to the negative battery terminal (see Chapter 5).

### Ignition switch (Push button start system)

14    Disconnect the negative battery terminal and wait at least three minutes before proceeding.
15    Remove the driver's side dash vent trim (see Chapter 11).
16    Remove the dash center pocket (see Chapter 11).
17    Remove the audio/navigation unit (see Section 11).
18    Remove the driver's side lower dash trim panels (see Chapter 11).
19    Remove the instrument cluster display trim panel (see Chapter 11). Disconnect the electrical connector to the ignition push button switch.
20    Turn the instrument cluster display trim cover and remove the screws securing the ignition push button switch to the trim cover.
21    Installation is the reverse of removal.

### 8    Steering column switches - replacement

**Warning:** *All models covered by this manual are equipped with a Supplemental Restraint System (SRS), more commonly known as airbags. Always disable the airbag system before working in the vicinity of any airbag system component to avoid the possibility of accidental deployment of the airbag, which could cause personal injury (see Section 24).*

1    Disconnect the cable from the negative battery terminal (see Chapter 5), then wait at least three minutes before proceeding.
2    Remove the driver's dashboard panel trim assembly and the steering column covers (see Chapter 11).

### Multi-function switch

3    Disconnect the electrical connector from the multi-function switch (see illustration).
4    Remove the multi-function switch by pressing in on the upper and lower tabs (see illustration).

**8.4 To detach the multi-function switch press in on the tabs and pull outward**

8.11 Press in on the upper and lower tabs and pull outward to remove the wiper switch

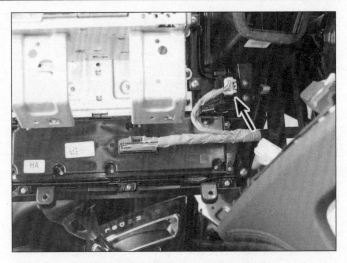

9.10a Disconnect the electrical connector

5   Remove the multi-function switch.

6   Installation is the reverse of removal.

7   Reconnect the cable to the negative battery terminal (see Chapter 5).

## Windshield wiper/washer switch

8   Disconnect the negative battery terminal and wait at least three minutes before proceeding.

9   Remove the driver's dashboard trim assembly and steering column covers (see Chapter 11).

10   Disconnect the electrical connector from the windshield wiper/washer switch.

11   Remove the windshield wiper/washer switch by pressing in on the upper and lower tabs (see illustration).

12   Installation is the reverse of removal.

13   Reconnect the cable to the negative battery terminal (see Chapter 5).

---

## 9   Instrument panel switches

**Warning:** *All models covered by this manual are equipped with a Supplemental Restraint System (SRS), more commonly known as airbags. Always disable the airbag system before working in the vicinity of any airbag system component to avoid the possibility of accidental deployment of the airbag, which could cause personal injury (see Section 24).*

## Cruise control switch installation and removal

1   Disconnect the cable from the negative battery terminal (see Chapter 5), then wait at least three minutes before proceeding.

2   Remove the steering wheel (see Chapter 10 ).

3   Remove the steering wheel rear cover.

9.10b To remove the hazard switch unscrew the fasteners and pull it out of the trim panel

4   Remove the screws retaining the cruise control switch to the steering wheel.

5   Installation is the reverse of removal. Reconnect the cable to the negative battery terminal (see Chapter 5).

## Hazard flasher switch - Civic

6   Disconnect the cable from the negative battery terminal (see Chapter 5), then wait at least three minutes before proceeding.

7   Remove the lower driver's side trim panel (knee bolster) (see Chapter 11).

8   Remove the instrument cluster assembly trim (see Chapter 11).

9   Pull the trim panel out far enough to disconnect the electrical connections.

10   Turn the instrument panel assembly trim over and remove the hazard flasher switch (see illustrations).

11   Installation is the reverse of removal. Reconnect the cable to the negative battery terminal (see Chapter 5).

## Hazard flasher switch - CR-V

12   Disconnect the negative battery terminal and wait at least three minutes before proceeding.

13   Remove the two inner HVAC vents (see Chapter 11).

14   Remove the audio system (see Section 11).

15   Remove the hazard flasher switch retaining screws.

16   Disconnect the electrical connection.

17   Installation is the reverse of removal. Reconnect the negative battery terminal (see Chapter 5).

## Rear window defogger switch

18   The rear window defogger switch is an integral part of the heater and air conditioning control assembly. To replace the rear window defogger switch, you must replace the heater and air conditioning control assembly (see Chapter 3).

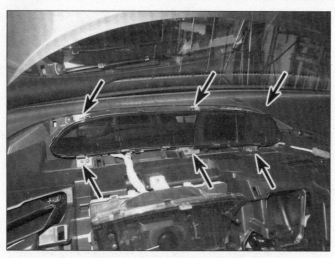

**10.4a On your model the configuration may be slightly different but the process for removal is the same**

**10.4b Side view of the instrument cluster**

## 10   Instrument cluster - removal and installation

**Warning:** *All models covered by this manual are equipped with a Supplemental Restraint System (SRS), more commonly known as airbags. Always disable the airbag system before working in the vicinity of any airbag system component to avoid the possibility of accidental deployment of the airbag, which could cause personal injury (see Section 24).*

1   Disconnect the cable from the negative battery terminal and wait at least three minutes before proceeding (see Chapter 5).

**Warning:** *Replacing the instrument cluster requires the use of the factory scanner to store the information retained in the old cluster and then download it into the replacement cluster.*

### Civic

2   Remove the driver's side lower trim (knee bolster) (see Chapter 11).

3   Remove the instrument cluster assembly trim panels (see Chapter 11).

4   Remove the screws retaining the instrument cluster to the dash (see illustrations).

5   Disconnect the electrical connectors and remove the cluster.

6   Installation is the reverse of removal.

7   Reconnect the cable to the negative battery terminal (see Chapter 5).

### CR-V

8   Disconnect the negative battery terminal and wait at least three minutes before proceeding.

9   Carefully pry the instrument cluster blind trim panel off (on top side of the steering wheel covers).

10   Using a flat bladed trim tool carefully pry the instrument cluster trim off.

11   Remove the three screws retaining the instrument cluster to the dash.

12   Disconnect the electrical connections and remove the cluster.

13   Installation is the reverse of removal. Reconnect the negative battery terminal (see Chapter 5).

## 11   Radio and speakers - removal and installation

**Warning:** *All models covered by this manual are equipped with a Supplemental Restraint System (SRS), more commonly known as airbags. Always disable the airbag system before working in the vicinity of any airbag system component to avoid the possibility of accidental deployment of the airbag, which could cause personal injury (see Section 24).*

**Note:** *Before beginning these procedures, make sure that you have the anti-theft code for the radio.*

To obtain the audio/navigation codes go to https://radio-navicode.honda.com/.

1   Disconnect the cable from the negative battery terminal and wait at least three minutes before proceeding (see Chapter 5).

### Civic with audio display system

2   Remove dash center pocket (see Chapter 11).

3   Remove the lower bolts securing the radio to the dash (see illustration).

4   Carefully pull the radio assembly out of the dash far enough to reach the connections (see illustration).

5   Disconnect the connectors and remove the assembly (see illustration).

6   Remove the brackets on the side of the radio assembly and unscrew the radio from the trim panel (see illustration).

7   Installation is the reverse of removal.

### Civic with premium sound system or navigation system

8   Remove the driver's side lower trim panels (knee bolster) (see Chapter 11).

9   Remove the instrument cluster assembly trim panel (see Chapter 11).

10   Remove the center lower trim panel (see Chapter 11).

**11.3 Removing the lower radio retaining screws**

**11.4 Gently pry the trim and radio assembly out of the dash**

**11.5 Disconnect the electrical connectors**

**11.6 Remove these brackets to remove the radio assembly**

**11.42 Remove the single screw, then tilt out and lift it out of the door. . .**

11  Remove the lower bolts securing the radio to the dash. (Look up into the cavity of the center lower trim panel to see the bolts.)
12  Carefully pull the radio assembly out of the dash far enough to reach the connections. Disconnect the connectors and remove the assembly.
13  Remove the brackets on the side of the radio assembly and unscrew the radio from the trim panel.
14  Installation is the reverse of removal.
15  Reconnect the cable to the negative battery terminal (see Chapter 5).

## CR-V with audio display system
16  Remove the center HVAC vents (see Chapter 11).
17  Remove the bolts securing the radio system to the dash supports.
18  Carefully pry the radio unit forward enough to disconnect the electrical connectors and remove the radio assembly from dash.
19  Remove the hazard switch from the trim panel.
20  Remove the radio bracket mounting bolts and separate the radio from the center panel.
21  Installation is the reverse of removal.
22  Reconnect the cable to the negative battery terminal (see Chapter 5).

## CR-V with premium sound or navigation system
23  Remove the center HVAC vents (see Chapter 11).
24  Remove the bolts securing the assembly to the dash supports.
25  Slide the assembly out far enough to disconnect the electrical connectors, then remove the assembly.
26  Disconnect the FM distributor assembly (mounted on the bottom of the assembly) and remove the FM distributor assembly.
27  Remove the assembly from the trim, and

**11.43 . . . then disconnect the electrical connector**

then remove the locating brackets on either side of the assembly.
28  Installation is the reverse of removal.

### Speakers

#### Tweeters - dashboard mounted
29  Tweeters on 2011 and earlier models are mounted to the underside of grilles located on top of the dashboard.
30  Carefully pry up the tweeter grille until it separates from the dashboard, taking care not to scratch or gouge the dashboard or grille.
31  Lift the grille away from the dashboard as far as you can with the wiring harness connected and turn it over.
32  Disconnect the tweeter two-pin wiring connector.
33  Check the capacitor, located next to the electrical connector on the tweeter, for damage. Replace the tweeter if any problems are visible.
34  With the tweeter electrical connector facing you, connect an ohmmeter between the right-hand terminal of the electrical connector

and the left-hand terminal of the capacitor.
35  With the ohmmeter set to ohms X 1, check the resistance. It should be about 4 ohms. If not, replace the tweeter.
36  Installation is the reverse of removal.

#### Tweeters - door mounted
37  Carefully pry the sail trim from the top corner of the door.
38  Disconnect the electrical connector to the tweeter.
39  Pry the retaining clips away from the speaker then remove it.
40  Installation is the reverse of removal.

#### Door speakers
41  Remove the front door trim panel (see Chapter 11).
42  Remove the upper mounting screw, then lift up on the speaker to release the lower tab (see illustration).
43  Disconnect the electrical connector (see illustration) and remove the speaker from the vehicle.
44  Installation is the reverse of removal.

**11.47 To detach a rear speaker from the rear shelf area, remove the screw, then tilt up and pull upward to remove**

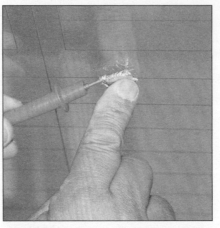

**13.4 When measuring the voltage at the rear window defogger grid, wrap a piece of aluminum foil around the positive probe of the voltmeter and press the foil against the wire with your finger**

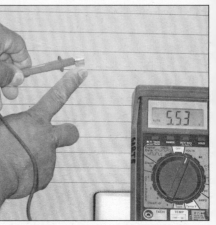

**13.5 To determine if a heating element has broken, check the voltage at the center of each element; if the voltage is 5- or 6-volts, the element is unbroken, but if the voltage is 10- or 12-volts, the element is broken between the center and the ground side. If there is no voltage, the element is broken between the center and the positive side**

### Rear speakers - 2 door models

45   Remove the rear shelf trim panel (see Chapter 11).
46   Open the trunk and disconnect the electrical connector from the speaker.
47   Remove the speaker mounting screw (see illustration) and pull the speaker out of its receptacle.
48   Installation is the reverse of removal.

### Sub-woofer removal and installation

49   Remove the rear shelf trim (see Chapter 11).
50   Unscrew the fasteners securing the sub-woofer to the rear shelf. Raise the speaker and disconnect the electrical connections. Then remove the speaker.
51   Installation is the reverse of removal.

**13.7 To find the break, place the voltmeter negative lead against the defogger ground terminal, place the voltmeter positive lead with the foil strip against the heating element at the positive terminal end and slide it toward the negative terminal end. The point at which the voltmeter reading changes abruptly is the point at which the element is broken**

## 12   Antenna - removal and installation

### Standard antenna

1   Coupes and sedans use a rear window-mounted antenna grid, which is similar to the defogger grid on the rear window. To replace the antenna, you have to replace the rear window. However, you can easily repair the antenna grid as long as the broken part is no more than one inch long. The procedure for repairing the antenna grid is identical to repairing the rear window defogger grid (see Section 13).
**Warning:** *The manufacturer recommends that any repair on the antenna grid should not exceed one inch long. If the break is longer than one inch, replace the rear window glass.*

### XM antenna

2   Remove the headliner (see Chapter 11).
3   Disconnect the electrical connector.
4   Remove the nut securing the antenna base to the roof.
5   Lift the antenna off of the roof.
6   To install, double check that the gasket is in place before securing the nut.
7   Tighten the nut to 3.2 ft-lbs.
8   Disconnect the electrical connector and pull the XM antenna off the roof.
9   The remainder of the installation is reverse of removal
Note: The XM receiver is mounted in the trunk on the passenger side behind the inner panel.

## 13   Rear window defogger - check and repair

1   The rear window defogger consists of a number of horizontal elements baked onto the glass surface.
2   Small breaks in the element can be repaired without removing the rear window.

### Check

3   Turn the ignition switch and defogger system switches to the On position. Using a voltmeter, place the positive probe against the defogger grid positive terminal and the negative probe against the ground terminal. If battery voltage is not indicated, check the fuse, defogger switch and related wiring. If voltage is indicated, but all or part of the defogger doesn't heat, proceed with the following tests.
4   When measuring voltage during the next two tests, wrap a piece of aluminum foil around the tip of the voltmeter positive probe and press the foil against the heating element with your finger (see illustration). Place the negative probe on the defogger grid ground terminal.
5   Check the voltage at the center of each heating element (see illustration). If the voltage is 5- or 6-volts, the element is okay (there is no break). If the voltage is zero, the element is broken between the center of the element and the positive end. If the voltage is 10- to 12-volts the element is broken between the center of the element and ground. Check each heating element.
6   Connect the negative lead to a good body ground. The reading should stay the same. If it doesn't, the ground connection is bad.
7   To find the break, place the voltmeter negative probe against the defogger ground terminal. Place the voltmeter positive probe with the foil strip against the heating element at the positive terminal end and slide it toward the negative terminal end. The point at which the voltmeter deflects from several volts to zero is the point at which the heating element is broken (see illustration).

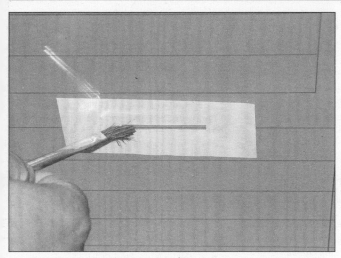

**13.13 To use a defogger repair kit, apply masking tape to the inside of the window at the damaged area, then brush on the special conductive coating**

**14.4 One screw on the top and two screws on the bottom**

## Repair

8    Repair the break in the element using a repair kit for this purpose (available at most auto parts stores). Make sure that the repair kit includes plastic conductive epoxy.

9    Prior to repairing a break, turn off the system and allow it to cool off for a few minutes.

10    Lightly buff the element area with fine steel wool, then clean it thoroughly with rubbing alcohol.

11    Use masking tape to mask off the area being repaired.

12    Thoroughly mix the epoxy, following the instructions provided with the repair kit.

13    Apply the epoxy material to the slit in the masking tape, overlapping the undamaged area about 3/4-inch on either end (see illustration).

14    Allow the repair to cure for 24 hours before removing the tape and using the system.

## 14    Headlight housing - replacement

1    Make sure that the headlight switch and the ignition switch are turned off.

2    Remove the front bumper cover for both the Civic and the CR-V. See Chapter 11 for the removal procedures.

## Civic

3    Disconnect the electrical connections and harness clips.

4    Remove the headlight housing mounting bolts (see illustration).

5    Remove the assembly.

6    If you're replacing the headlight housing, detach the corner bumper beam (the small black metal piece that's attached to the underside of the headlight housing) and install it on the new headlight housing unit (see illustration).

7    Installation is the reverse of removal.

**14.6 Detach the corner bumper beam if you are replacing the headlamp housing**

## CR-V

8    Disconnect the electrical connections and harness clips.

9    Remove the four screws and the release pin securing the headlamp assembly to the core support.

10    Release the clips holding the corner upper beam assembly to the headlamp assembly and remove it.

11    Reinstall the corner upper beam assembly to the replacement headlamp assembly.

12    The remainder of the installation is the reverse of removal.

## 15    Headlight bulb - replacement

**Warning:** *Halogen gas filled bulbs are under pressure and can shatter if the surface is scratched or the bulb is dropped. Wear eye protection and handle the bulbs carefully, grasping only the base whenever possible.*

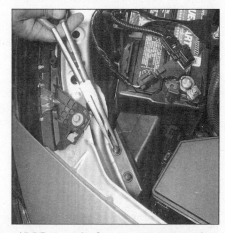

**15.5 Pry out the fasteners to remove the air intake duct cover**

*Do not touch the surface of the bulb with your fingers because the oil from your skin could cause it to overheat and fail prematurely. If you do touch the bulb surface, clean it with rubbing alcohol.*

1    Make sure that the headlight switch and the ignition switch are both turned off, then open the hood.

## Civic

### Right-side low beam bulb

2    Working from under the hood, reach behind the right headlamp assembly and turn the bulb socket 45 degrees to remove it. Disconnect the electrical connector.

3    Installation is the reverse of removal.

### Left-side low beam bulb

4    Remove the upper left hand side fender trim panel.

5    Remove the air intake duct cover and air intake duct (see illustration).

**15.6 With the air intake duct removed, the bulb can easily be removed**

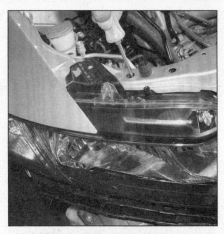

**16.1a The vertical adjuster is located on the upper backside of each headlight housing**

6    Rotate the bulb socket 45 degrees and remove the electrical connection (see illustration).
7    Installation is the reverse of removal.

### High beam bulb

8    Rotate the bulb socket 45 degrees and remove the bulb. Disconnect the electrical connector.
9    Installation is the reverse of removal.

## CR-V

10   Disconnect the electrical connector to the headlamp.
11   Remove the rubber dust boot.
12   Lift the retaining bail off of the bulb fixture.

13   Remove the bulb.
14   Installation is the reverse of removal.

---

## 16   Headlights - adjustment

**Caution:** *The headlights must be aimed correctly. If adjusted incorrectly they could blind the driver of an oncoming vehicle and cause a serious accident or seriously reduce your ability to see the road. The headlights should be checked for correct aim every 12 months and any time a new headlight is installed or front end body work is performed. It should be emphasized that the following procedure is only an interim step that will provide temporary ad-*

*justment until a properly equipped shop can adjust the headlights.*

1    The vertical adjuster (see illustration) is located on the upper backside of each headlight housing. Use a Phillips screwdriver to turn the adjusters (see illustration). There are no horizontal adjustment screws.
2    There are several methods for adjusting the headlights. The simplest method requires masking tape, a blank wall and a level floor.
3    Position masking tape vertically on the wall in relation to the vehicle centerline and in relation to the centerlines of both headlights (see illustration).
4    Position a horizontal tape line in reference to the centerline of all the headlights.
**Note:** *It might be easier to position the tape on the wall with the vehicle parked only a few inches away.*
5    Adjustment should be made with the vehicle parked 25 feet from the wall, sitting level, the gas tank half-full and no heavy load in the vehicle.
6    With the low beams turned on, position the high intensity zone so it is two inches below the horizontal line.
7    With the high beams on, the high intensity zone should be vertically centered with the exact center just below the horizontal line. Note:It might not be possible to position the headlight aim exactly for both high and low beams. If a compromise must be made, keep in mind that the low beams are the most used and have the greatest effect on safety.
8    If you have any difficulty adjusting the headlights, have them adjusted by a dealer service department as soon as possible.

**16.1b Using a Phillips screwdriver, adjust the headlight by turning the adjuster clockwise for Up and counterclockwise for Down**

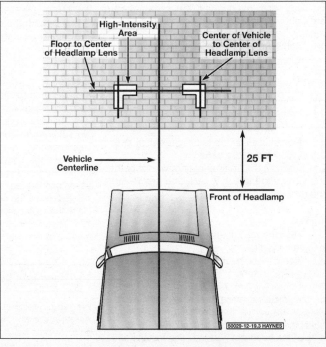

**16.3 Headlight adjustment details**

## 17  Bulb replacement

### *Civic*
### Exterior light bulbs

#### Front turn signal/side marker and parking light bulb(s)

1    If you're changing a bulb on the left side, turn the wheels all the way to the right. If you're replacing a bulb on the right side, turn the wheels all the way to the left.

2    Remove the front part of the left or right inner fender liner (see Chapter 11). On the two-door models, pull the intake duct tube out of the way (left side only).

3    Locate the front turn signal bulb holder and the front parking light bulb holder (see illustration). Disconnect the electrical connector from the front turn signal bulb holder (see illustration) or from the front parking light bulb holder. To remove the bulb holder, turn it counterclockwise (see illustration) and pull it out of the housing.

**17.3a After removing the front part of the inner fender liner, locate the electrical connector for the front turn signal light bulb and disconnect the electrical connector**

**17.3b To remove the bulb holder from the headlight housing, turn it counterclockwise and pull it out of the housing**

# Bulb removal

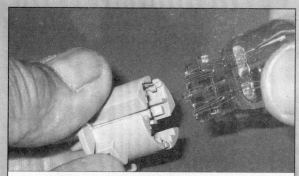

To remove many modern exterior bulbs from their holders, simply pull them out

On bulbs with a cylindrical base ("bayonet" bulbs), the socket is spring-loaded; a pair of small posts on the side of the base hold the bulb in place against spring pressure. To remove this type of bulb, push it into the holder, rotate it 1/4-turn counterclockwise, then pull it out

If a bayonet bulb has dual filaments, the posts are staggered, so the bulb can only be installed one way

To remove most overhead interior light bulbs, simply unclip them

**17.4 To remove the front turn signal/side marker bulb or the front parking light bulb from its holder, grasp the holder firmly and pull the bulb straight out**

**17.10 Disconnect the electrical connector from the high-mount brake light bulb holder, then turn the bulb holder counterclockwise to remove it from the high-mount brake light housing**

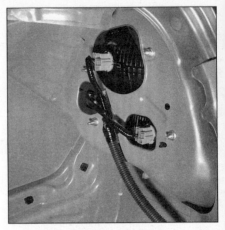

**17.21 Bulb locations**

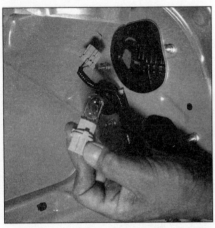

**17.22a Twist the bulb fixture to remove**

**17.22b Pull bulb straight out from the bulb fixture**

**17.25 Rotate the bulb socket counterclockwise to remove**

4    Remove the turn signal bulb from the bulb holder. Pull the bulb straight out of its holder (see illustration). To install a new bulb, push it straight into the bulb holder, then give it a clockwise turn to lock it into place in the holder.

5    Installation is the reverse of removal.

**High-mount brake light with spoiler**

6    Remove the two caps that cover the screws to the lens.

7    Unscrew the lens.

8    Remove the bulb connection, then remove the bulb.

9    Installation is the reverse of removal.

**High-mounted brake light without spoiler**

10    Open the trunk and look for the electrical connector for the high-mount brake light, which is located in the underside of the rear shelf area, just ahead of the trunk light (see illustration).

11    Disconnect the electrical connector from the bulb holder.

12    To remove the bulb holder from the high-mount brake light assembly, rotate the bulb holder counterclockwise and pull it out.

13    To remove the old bulb from the bulb holder, pull it straight out of the holder. To install a new bulb, push it straight into the bulb holder.

14    Installation is the reverse of removal.

**License plate light**

15    Open the trunk and locate the electrical connector for the license plate bulb you wish to replace.

16    To remove the bulb holder, depress the release tabs on the sides of the holder (see illustration 17.10) and pull it out. It's not necessary to disconnect the electrical connector from the bulb holder in order to remove the holder.

17    To remove the bulb from the socket, pull it straight out.

18    To install a new bulb in the holder, push it straight into the holder.

19    Installation is the reverse of removal.

**Taillight bulbs (in rear fender)**

20    To access the outer taillight bulbs (in the vehicle's rear fender) with trunk carpeting, detach and peel back the carpeting.

21    After peeling back the carpeting, you'll see the bulb holders (see illustration). The upper bulb holder is for the brake/tail/rear side marker light bulb; the lower bulb holder is for the turn signal light bulb. To remove a bulb holder from an inner taillight, rotate the holder counterclockwise and pull it out.

22    To remove a taillight bulb from its holder, pull it straight out (see illustrations).

23    To install a bulb in its socket, push it straight into the socket.

24    Installation is the reverse of removal.

**Taillight bulbs (in trunk lid)**

25    Open the trunk lid and locate the bulb holders for the taillight and back-up light bulbs (see illustration).

26    To remove either bulb holder, turn it counterclockwise and pull it out.

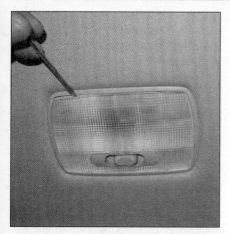

**17.29 To remove the lens from the ceiling light, pry it off with a small screwdriver. Be careful not to damage the plastic trim around the edge of the lens**

**17.30 To remove the old bulb from the ceiling light, pull it straight out of the two metal clips**

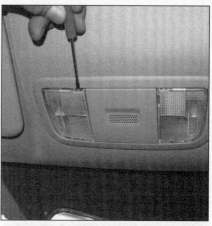

**17.33 To remove the lens for the spotlight or the lens for the ceiling light/spotlight, carefully pry it loose with a small screwdriver**

27   To remove either bulb from its bulb holder, pull it straight out of the holder.
28   To install either bulb in its bulb holder, push it straight into the holder.

## Interior lights

### Ceiling light (dome light)
29   Using a small flat bladed screwdriver, pry off the lens (see illustration). Be careful not to damage the plastic trim around the edge of the lens.
30   Remove the old bulb from the two metal clips (see illustration).
31   Install the new bulb. Make sure that it's fully seated between the two metal clips.
32   Install the lens. Make sure that it snaps back into place.
**Note:** *To remove the actual fixture, remove the lens and then remove the retaining screws. Pull it down and disconnect the electrical connector. Installation is the reverse of removal.*

### Spotlight or ceiling light/spotlight
33   Carefully pry off the lens with a small flat bladed screwdriver (see illustration).
34   Remove the old bulb. On models without a sunroof, pull the bulb out from the two metal retaining clips (see illustration). On models with a sunroof, pull the bulb straight down from its receptacle.
35   Install a new bulb. On models without a sunroof, make sure that the bulb is fully seated in the two metal clips. If the vehicle is equipped with a sunroof, insert the bulb into its receptacle and push it straight up until it stops.
36   Install the lens. Make sure that it snaps into place.

### Hazard flasher switch light bulb
37   Remove the hazard flasher switch (see Section 9 ).
38   Unscrew and remove the light bulb from the hazard flasher switch.
39   Installation is the reverse of removal.

### Trunk light bulb
40   Open the trunk. Remove the trunk light lens.

41   To remove the old bulb, pull it straight out.
42   To install a new bulb, push it straight in until it stops.
43   Install the trunk light lens. Make sure that it snaps into place.

## CR-V models

### Exterior lights

#### Front side marker/turn signal light bulb
44   The electrical connector for the front side marker/turn signal light bulb is located near the headlight bulb connector. The procedure for replacing the bulb is similar to the procedure for Civic.

#### Front parking light bulbs
45   Remove the radiator cover.
46   The electrical connector for the front side marker/turn signal light bulb is located near the outer edge of the grille. The procedure for replacing the bulb is similar to the procedure for the Civic.

#### High-mount brake light bulb
47   Open the tailgate. To remove the high-mount brake light housing, push in on the tabs on the ends of the housing and pull off the housing.
48   To remove the bulb holder, turn it counterclockwise and pull it out.
49   To remove the bulb from the holder, pull it straight out.
50   To install the new bulb in the holder, push it straight in.
51   To install the housing, place it in position and push on it until it snaps into place.

#### License plate light bulb
52   License plate light removal is identical to the Civic. Follow the procedure for the Civic license plate bulb removal.

#### Taillight bulbs
53   Open the tailgate. Each of the two mounting screws for each taillight assembly is hidden by a trim cover. To remove the two

**17.34 To remove a bulb from a spotlight assembly, pull it out of the two metal clips**

trim covers, carefully pry off each of them with a small flat-tipped screwdriver. Put a piece of tape or a clean shop rag over the tip to protect the finish on the trim covers, then use the slot provided in each cover to pry it off.
54   Remove the two taillight assembly mounting screws and remove the taillight assembly.
55   There are four bulbs in the taillight assembly. They are, from top to bottom, the turn signal light bulb, the brake light bulb, the side marker/running light bulb and the back-up light bulb. To remove any of the bulb sockets, turn it counterclockwise and pull it out.
56   To remove a bulb from its socket, pull it straight out of the socket.
57   To install a new bulb in its socket, push it straight into the socket.
58   To install a bulb socket into the taillight assembly, insert the socket into its receptacle and give it a quarter-turn clockwise.
59   When installing the taillight assembly, make sure the locator pins on the taillight assembly are aligned with their respective holes in the pillar.
60   Installation is otherwise the reverse of removal.

## Interior lights

### Ceiling light and cargo area light bulbs

61   If you're replacing a ceiling light (dome light) bulb, carefully pry on the rear edge of the lens with a small flat-tipped screwdriver and remove the lens. Don't pry on the housing around the lens. If you're replacing a cargo area light bulb, pry on the front edge of the lens.
62   The ceiling light and cargo area light bulbs are identical. To remove an old bulb, pull it straight down.
63   To install a new bulb, push it straight up until it's fully seated in the two metal tabs.
64   Install the lens. Make sure that it snaps into place.
**Note:** *To remove the actual fixture, remove the lens and then remove the retaining screws. Pull it down and disconnect the electrical connector. Installation is the reverse of removal.*

### Spotlight bulbs

65   Pry on the front edge of the lens with a small flat-tipped screwdriver (just in front of the two spotlight bulbs).
66   Pull the spotlight bulb straight down to remove it.
67   Push the new spotlight bulb straight up until it's fully seated.
68   Install the lens. Make sure that it snaps into place.

### Hazard switch light bulb

69   Remove the hazard flasher switch (see Section 9).
70   Remove the illumination bulb from the hazard flasher switch. (Turn the bulb socket 90 degrees, then remove the bulb socket.)
71   Install a new illumination bulb in the switch.
72   Install the hazard flasher switch (see Section 9).

### Glove box light bulb

73   Open the glovebox and locate the glovebox light in the upper front part of the glovebox ceiling.
74   Remove the bulb by pulling it straight out of the two metal mounting tabs.
75   To install the new bulb, push it into the two metal tabs until it's fully seated.

## Hatchback models

### Exterior lights

### Front turn signal bulbs

76   Using a flat-tipped screwdriver, remove the holding clip from the inner fender cover (see Chapter 11 if necessary).
77   Pull back the inner fender cover.
78   To remove the bulb socket from the headlight housing, turn it counterclockwise and pull it out.
79   To remove the old bulb from the socket, push it in and turn it counterclockwise until it unlocks, then pull it out.
80   To install the new bulb in the socket, push it in and turn it clockwise until it stops.

### Front parking light bulbs

81   Open the hood and locate the electrical connector for the front parking light bulb, which is next to the headlight bulb connector.
82   To remove the bulb socket from the housing, turn it counterclockwise and pull it out of the housing.
83   To remove the old bulb from the socket, pull it straight out of the socket.
84   To install a new bulb in the socket, push it straight into the socket until it stops.
85   Insert the bulb socket into the parking light housing and turn it clockwise to lock it into place.

### Front side marker bulbs

86   Push the front edge of the side marker lens toward the rear of the vehicle until the front edge of the lens pops out of the bumper cover.
87   To remove the bulb socket from the lens, turn the bulb socket counterclockwise and pull it out.
88   To remove the old bulb from the socket, pull it straight out of the socket.
89   To install a new bulb in the socket, push it straight into the socket until it stops.
90   Insert the bulb socket into the lens assembly and turn it clockwise until it stops.
91   Insert the tabbed end of the side marker assembly into the hole first, then the looped end, then press on the looped end until the assembly snaps into place.

### High-mount brake light bulbs

92   Open the hatch. To remove the trim covering the high-mount brake light assembly, put your fingers between the trim and the hatch glass, then carefully pull down on the trim to unsnap the trim retaining clips from the hatch.
93   To remove the bulb holder from the high-mount brake light assembly, push the tabs on both sides and pull down the bulb holder.
94   To remove an old bulb from the holder, pull it straight out of the holder.
95   To install a new bulb in the holder, push it straight into the holder until it stops.
96   Push the bulb holder into the high-mount brake light assembly until it locks into place.
97   Align the clips on the trim with their corresponding holes in the hatch, then push the trim until the clips snap into place.

### License plate light bulbs

98   To remove the license plate light assembly, slide the lens to the right until the left end pops out of the body, then pull out the license plate light assembly.
99   To remove the lens from the bulb socket, pull on the lens and squeeze the tabs on both sides of the socket at the same time.
100  To remove the old bulb from the bulb socket, pull the bulb straight out of the socket.
101  To install a new bulb in the socket, push it straight into the socket until it stops.
102  To install the lens on the bulb socket, push it into place until it latches.
103  To install the license plate light assembly, slide the right end of the assembly into the

hole and push on the left end until the assembly snaps into place.

### Side turn signal bulbs

104  Push the front of the side turn signal assembly toward the rear of the vehicle until it pops out of the body.
105  To remove the bulb socket from the lens, turn the socket counterclockwise.
106  To remove the old bulb from the bulb socket, pull it straight out.
107  To install a new bulb in the socket, push it straight into the socket until it stops.
108  To install the bulb socket into the lens, insert it into the hole in the lens and turn it clockwise until it stops.
109  To install the side turn signal assembly in the body, insert it into the hole rear end first, then push on the front end until it snaps into place.

### Taillight bulbs

110  Open the hatch. Locate the trim cover in the corner of the cargo area. To remove the trim cover, carefully pry on the upper front edge with a small flat-tipped screwdriver.
111  You'll see three bulb sockets. The upper socket is for the turn signal light bulb, the middle socket is for the back-up light bulb and the lower one is for the brake light/taillight bulb. All three sockets are removed the same way.
112  To remove a bulb socket, turn it counterclockwise and pull it out.
113  To remove an old bulb from its socket, push it in and turn it counterclockwise until it unlocks.
114  To install a new bulb into a socket, push it in and turn it clockwise until it stops.
115  Insert the bulb socket into the taillight assembly and turn it clockwise until it locks into place.
116  Install the trim cover.

## Interior lights

### Front ceiling light/spotlight bulbs

117  To remove the lens for the front ceiling light/spotlight, pry on the middle of the front edge of the lens.
118  To remove one of the old bulbs, pull it straight down.
119  To install a new bulb, push it straight up until it stops.
120  To install the lens, place the side with the tabs in position, then push the other side into place until it snaps into position.
**Note:** *To remove the actual fixture, remove the lens and then remove the retaining screws. Pull it down and disconnect the electrical connector. Installation is the reverse of removal.*

### Center ceiling light bulb

121  To remove the lens for the center ceiling light, pry on the middle of the side edge of the lens.
122  To remove the old bulb, pull it straight down from the two metal tabs.
123  To install a new bulb, insert it into the metal tabs until it snaps into place.
124  To install the lens, place the edge with

the tabs in position, then push the other edge into place until it snaps into position.
**Note:** *To remove the actual fixture, remove the lens and then remove the retaining screws. Pull it down and disconnect the electrical connector. Installation is the reverse of removal.*

### Cargo area light bulb

125  Open the hatch. To remove the lens for the cargo area light, carefully pry on the front edge of the lens with a small screwdriver. Put a shop towel or a piece of tape on the tip of the screwdriver to protect the trim.
126  To remove the old bulb pull it straight out of the bulb holder.
127  To install a new bulb, push it straight into the holder until it's fully seated.
128  To install the lens, insert it into the mounting hole rear side first, then push on the front side until it snaps into place.
Note:To remove the actual fixture, remove the lens and then remove the retaining screws. Pull it down and disconnect the electrical connector. Installation is the reverse of removal.

---

## 18  Horn - replacement

### Civic

1  Raise the front of the vehicle and place it securely on jackstands.
2  Remove the front bumper cover (see Chapter 11).
3  The high tone horn is on the driver's side, and the low tone horn is mounted on the passenger's side (see illustration).
4  Disconnect the electrical connector from the horn.
5  Remove the horn mounting bracket bolt and remove the horn.
6  Installation is the reverse of removal.

**18.3 Horn location passenger's side - driver's side is mounted the same way**

A - Electrical connection
B - Bracket bolt for the horn

### CR-V

7  Raise the front of the vehicle and place it securely on jackstands.
8  Remove the lower radiator splash shield.
9  Reach up and disconnect the horn mounting bolt.
10  Remove the horn and bracket as an assembly.
11  Disconnect the electrical connectors.
12  Installation is the reverse of removal.

---

## 19  Wiper motor - check and replacement

### Wiper motor circuit check

1  If the wipers work slowly, make sure the battery is fully charged and in good condition

(see Chapter 5). Check for binding linkage and pivots. Lubricate or repair the linkage or pivots as necessary. If the wipers are still operating slowly, replace the motor.

### Wiper motor replacement

#### Windshield wiper motor

2  Remove the windshield wiper arm retaining nut covers, then remove the nuts. Be sure to mark the position of each wiper arm in relation to its splined shaft (see illustration), then remove the wiper arms.
3  Remove the hood seal and cowl covers (see Chapter 11).
4  Remove the windshield wiper linkage/motor assembly mounting bolts (see illustration), then disconnect the electrical connector from the windshield wiper motor.
5  Mark the relationship of the linkage arm to the wiper motor shaft and base plate. Sep-

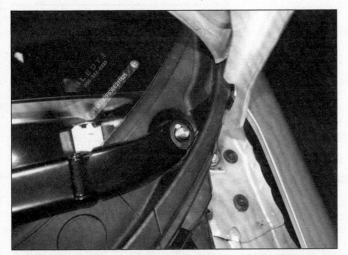

**19.2 Pry off the trim caps and remove the windshield wiper arm retaining nuts, then mark the relationship of each wiper arm to its splined shaft before removing the arm**

**19.4 To detach the windshield wiper linkage/motor assembly from the cowl area, remove the two bolts on each end and the one bolt in the middle (driver's side bolts not shown)**

**19.5a Mark the relationship of the linkage arm and the motor mounting bracket to ensure that the arm is correctly realigned during reassembly**

**19.5b To separate the windshield wiper linkage from the linkage arm, pry the two halves of the spherical bearing apart**

**19.5c Using an adjustable wrench (shown) or a pair of large adjustable pliers to immobilize the linkage arm, loosen the arm retaining nut and remove the arm from the motor shaft**

**19.5d Mark the relationship of the linkage arm to the motor shaft, then remove the arm from the shaft**

**19.6 To detach the windshield wiper motor from its mounting bracket, remove these three bolts**

arate the windshield wiper linkage from the wiper motor (see illustrations).

6    Remove the windshield wiper motor mounting bolts (see illustration) and separate the motor from its mounting bracket.

7    Before installing the windshield wiper linkage (especially if you're installing the old linkage), be sure to grease the moving parts.

8    Installation is otherwise the reverse of removal. Be sure to align the marks you made between the linkage arm and the motor mounting bracket and between the windshield wiper arm and the motor shaft.

9    Turn on the windshield wipers and verify that the wiper motor operates correctly in all modes.

### Rear window wiper motor

10    Open the hatch. Remove the hatch trim panel (see Chapter 11).

11    Remove the windshield wiper arm retaining nut cover, then remove the nut. Be sure to mark the position of the wiper arm in relation to its splined shaft, then remove the wiper arm.

12    Disconnect the electrical connector from the rear window wiper motor.

13    Remove the three wiper motor mounting bolts.

14    Remove the rear window wiper motor.

15    Installation is the reverse of removal.

## 20    Cruise control system - general information

1    The cruise control system maintains vehicle speed with an electrically operated motor located in the engine compartment, which is connected to the throttle body by a cable. The system consists of the Powertrain Control Module, the speed control actuator, the speed control cable, the speed control indicator light, the speed control actuator switches, the Brake Pedal Position (BPP) switch and the transmission range switch. The cruise control system requires diagnostic procedures that are beyond the scope of this

manual, but there are some general procedures that will help you identify common problems.

2    Check the fuses (see Section 3).

3    Have an assistant operate the brake lights while you check their operation (voltage from the brake light switch deactivates the cruise control).

4    If the brake lights don't come on or stay on all the time, correct the problem and retest the cruise control system.

5    Visually inspect the control cable between the cruise control motor and the throttle linkage for free movement. Replace it if necessary.

6    Test drive the vehicle to determine if the cruise control is now working. If it isn't, take it to a dealer service department or an automotive electrical specialist for further diagnosis.

## 21    Power window system - general information

1    The power window system operates electric motors, mounted on the doors, which lower and raise the windows. The system consists of the control switches, the motors, regulators, glass mechanisms and associated wiring.

2    The power windows can be lowered and raised from the master control switch by the driver or by the switch located at the passenger window. Each window has a separate motor that is reversible. The position of the control switch determines the polarity and therefore the direction of operation.

3    The circuit is protected by fuses and a circuit breaker. Check the fuses in the fuse panel at the left end of the instrument panel. Each motor is equipped with an internal circuit breaker; this prevents one stuck window from disabling the whole system. Refer to the wiring diagrams at the end of this chapter. Problems within this system can only be diagnosed with

a factory scan tool. If you have eliminated the obvious causes of a problem, have the vehicle checked at a dealership service department or other properly equipped repair shop.

## 22  Power door lock system - general information

1   A power door lock system operates the door lock actuators mounted in each door. The system consists of the switches, actuators, a control unit and associated wiring. On some models, the power door lock system is part of the security alarm system. On these models, the power door lock system is more complex, and more difficult to diagnose. Therefore, home troubleshooting is limited to simple checks of the wiring connections and actuators for minor faults that can be easily repaired.

2   Power door lock systems are operated by bi-directional solenoids located in the doors. The lock switches have two operating positions: Lock and Unlock. When activated, the switch sends a ground signal to the door lock control unit to lock or unlock the doors. Depending on which way the switch is activated, the control unit reverses polarity to the solenoids, allowing the two sides of the circuit to be used alternately as the feed (positive) and ground side.

3   The following general guidelines should help you quickly identify and repair typical problems. If you're unable to locate the trouble using these guidelines, consult a dealer service department.

4   Always check the fuses first (see Section 3 and your owner's manual).

5   Operate the door lock switches in both directions (Lock and Unlock) with the engine off. Listen for the click of the solenoids operating.

6   Test the switches for continuity. Remove the switches and have them checked by a dealer service department.

7   Check the wiring between the switches, control unit and solenoids for continuity. Repair the wiring if there's no continuity.

8   Check for a bad ground at the switches and at the control unit.

9   If only one lock solenoid doesn't operate, remove the trim panel from the door with the bad solenoid (see Chapter 11) and check for voltage at the solenoid while the lock switch is operated. One of the wires should have voltage in the Lock position; the other should have voltage in the Unlock position.

10   If the inoperative solenoid is receiving voltage, replace the solenoid.

11   If the inoperative solenoid isn't receiving voltage, check for an open or short in the wire between the lock solenoid and the control unit.

## 23  Sun roof - removal and installation

**Note:** *The sun roof utilizes a motor and CPU assembly that drives the cables to operate the*

*sun roof. To diagnose the sun roof requires a factory equivalent scanner.*

### Removal
1   Remove the headliner (see Chapter 11).
2   Remove the sun roof trim.
3   Pull off the front and rear drain tubes.
4   Disconnect the electrical connection to the motor and CPU.
5   Loosen the fasteners to the sun roof assembly.
6   With the aid of an assistant on each side of the sun roof, remove the fasteners and lower the sun roof.
7   Carefully guide the sun roof out of the vehicle.

### Installation
8   Following the same path you used to remove the sun roof, reattach the fasteners but not entirely tightened down.
9   Reattach the electrical connectors and drain tubes.
10   With the headliner still out, check the operation of the sun roof.
11   With the sun roof in its fully closed position, check for proper alignment between the seal and the roof lines. Once you're satisfied with the alignment, tighten the fasteners.
**Note:** *The glass can be removed separately and adjusted separately from the sun roof track. The four bolts that secure the glass to the track are elongated for the purpose of making small adjustments to the final fit.*
12   Reinstall the sun roof trim and the headliner.

## 24  Airbag system - general information

1   These models are equipped with a Supplemental Restraint System (SRS), more commonly known as airbags, designed to protect the driver and the passenger from serious injury in the event of a head-on or side collision. The system consists of various air bag modules, impact sensors, a control unit (SRS module) and the seat belts. The system operates electrically by a signal from the front impact sensors when a high enough velocity and impact has occurred. (Very low speed bumps like in a parking lot, generally do not carry enough force to deploy the air bags.) The system also is aware of the weight in the passenger seat (called the Passenger Presence System). This allows the SRS module to determine if the passenger air bag needs to be deployed during a collision.
**Warning:** *The SRS system must be properly diagnosed and if needed, programmed by a dealer or a qualified independent repair shop any time the module is replaced or if any other fault is indicated in the system.*
**Warning:** *Do not use a used SRS module. The module must be a new one and must be programmed to the individual vehicle. A salvaged component cannot be "un-programmed" or re-flashed.*

**Warning:** *If your vehicle is ever involved in a flood, or the interior carpeting is soaked for any reason, disconnect the battery and do not start the vehicle until the airbag system can be checked by your dealer or qualified independent repair facility. If the SRS module is subjected to flooding, the airbags could go off upon starting the vehicle, even without an accident taking place.*

### Airbag modules
2   The airbag modules consist of a housing incorporating the cushion (airbag) and inflator unit. The inflator assembly is mounted on the back of the housing over a hole through which gas is expelled, inflating the bag almost instantaneously when an electrical signal is sent from the system. The specially-wound wire on the driver's side that carries this signal to the driver's module is called a spiral cable or more commonly called the "clockspring." The spiral cable is a flat, ribbon-like electrically conductive tape that is wound many times so that it can transmit an electrical signal regardless of steering wheel position. Airbag modules are located in the steering wheel, on the passenger's side above the glovebox, on the upper side of each front seat (side-impact airbags) and head-level airbags located along the roof rails (side curtain airbags).

### Control unit and sensors
3   The sensing/diagnostic control unit contains an on-board microprocessor which monitors the operation of the system, and the crash sensors. The crash sensors are located in the front of the vehicle. It checks this system every time the vehicle is started, causing the "Airbag" light to illuminate for five seconds, then go off, if the system is operating properly. If there is a fault in the system, the airbag light will stay on, and the unit will store fault codes indicating the nature of the fault. See your dealer or qualified independent repair facility for any service work.

### Operation
4   For the airbag(s) to deploy, the impact sensor(s) must be activated. When this condition occurs, the circuit to the airbag inflator is closed and the airbag inflates.

### Self-diagnosis system
5   A self-diagnosis circuit in the SRS unit displays a light on the instrument panel when the ignition switch is turned to the On position. If the system is operating normally, the light should go out after about five seconds. If the light doesn't come on, or doesn't go out after a short time, or if it comes on while you're driving the vehicle, or if it blinks at any time, there's a malfunction in the SRS system. Have it inspected and repaired as soon as possible. Do not attempt to troubleshoot or service the SRS system yourself. Even a small mistake could cause the SRS system to malfunction when you need it.

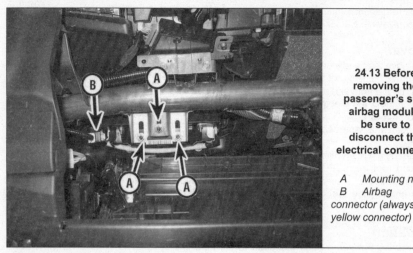

**24.13 Before removing the passenger's side airbag module, be sure to disconnect the electrical connector**

A   Mounting nuts
B   Airbag connector (always a yellow connector)

## Servicing components near the SRS system

6   There are times when you need to remove the steering wheel, radio or service other components on or near the dashboard. At these times, you'll be working around components and wire harnesses for the SRS system. The airbag wiring is always bright yellow with double locked connectors on all the components. Do not pierce or cut into these wires.

**Warning:** *Do not use electrical test equipment such as an ohmmeter on airbag system wires; it could cause the airbag(s) to deploy. ALWAYS DISABLE THE SRS SYSTEM BEFORE WORKING NEAR THE SRS SYSTEM COMPONENTS OR RELATED WIRING.*

## Disabling the SRS system

**Warning:** *Any time you are working in the vicinity of airbag wiring or components, DISABLE THE SRS SYSTEM.*

**Warning:** *An auxiliary voltage input device (memory saver) must not be used when working near airbag system components.*

**Caution:** *Disconnecting the battery can cause driveability problems that require a scan tool to rectify. Additionally, disconnecting the battery may cause one or more warning lights on the instrument panel to illuminate, which will also require the use of a scan tool to turn off. Most scan tools available to the public do not have the capability to perform either of these tasks, which will necessitate taking the vehicle to a dealer service department or other properly equipped repair facility after service work has been performed. See Chapter 5 for other precautions related to battery disconnection.*

**Caution:** *These models are equipped with an anti-theft radio. Before performing a procedure that requires disconnecting the battery, make sure you have the proper activation code.*

7   To disable the airbag system, perform the following steps:

a)   *Turn the steering wheel to the straight-ahead position and turn the ignition switch to the Lock position, then remove the key.*

b)   *Disconnect the negative battery cable. Refer to the Cautions in Chapter 5.*

c)   *Before touching any airbag system component, ground yourself to a metal part of the vehicle to discharge any static electricity built up in your body.*

## Enabling the system

8   To enable the airbag system, perform the following steps:

**Caution:** *If you have any concerns that the airbags might deploy after reinstalling the driver's airbag or the passenger's airbag, do not reconnect the battery. Have the vehicle towed to the dealer service center or a qualified independent repair facility and have the airbag system checked.*

a)   *Turn the ignition switch to the On position.*

b)   *Watch the airbag indicator in the instrument cluster. The light should go out after the initial self check. If the light does not go out, take the vehicle to a dealer service department or a qualified independent repair facility and have the airbag system diagnosed.*

**Warning:** *If the airbag indicator light is "On" the airbag system is "Off."*

## Airbag module removal and installation

### Driver's side airbag module and clockspring

9   Refer to Chapter 10, Steering wheel - removal and installation, for the driver's side airbag module and clockspring removal and installation procedures.

### Passenger's side airbag module (Civic and Hatchback models)

10   Disarm the airbag system as described previously in this section.

11   Remove the passenger's side A pillar (see Chapter 11).

12   Remove the glovebox (see Chapter 11).

13   Disconnect the passenger's side airbag module electrical connector (see illustration).

14   Remove the mounting nuts from the airbag.

15   Gently lift the passenger's airbag out through the top.

16   Installation is the reverse of removal.

### Passenger's side airbag module CR-V models

17   Remove the upper instrument panel trim pad (see Chapter 11).

18   Disconnect the airbag electrical connector.

19   Remove the airbag module mounting nuts.

20   Installation is the reverse of removal. Tighten the airbag module mounting nuts to 80 ft-lbs.

21   Reconnect the cable to the negative battery terminal (see Chapter 5).

### Side-impact modules

22   Under normal circumstances, there would never be any reason to remove the side-impact airbags (modules). However, if it has been determined that there is a problem with a side-impact airbag module, the work must be left to a dealer service department or a qualified independent repair shop.

## Impact seat belt retractors

23   All models are equipped with pyrotechnic (explosive) units in the front seat belt retracting mechanisms for both the lap and shoulder belts. During an impact that would trigger the airbag system, the airbag control unit also triggers the seat belt retractors. When the pyrotechnic charges go off, they accelerate the retractors to instantly take up any slack in the seat belt system to more fully prepare the driver and front seat passenger for impact.

**Caution:** *The airbag system should be disabled any time you are working on the seats.*

---

### 25   Wiring diagrams - general information

---

1   Since it isn't possible to include all wiring diagrams for every year and model covered by this manual, the following diagrams are those that are typical and most commonly needed.

2   Prior to troubleshooting any circuits, check the fuses and circuit breakers (if equipped) to make sure they're in good condition. Make sure the battery is properly charged and check the cable connections (see Chapter 1).

3   When checking a circuit, make sure that all connectors are clean, with no broken or loose terminals. When disconnecting a connector, do not pull on the wires. Pull only on the connector housings themselves.

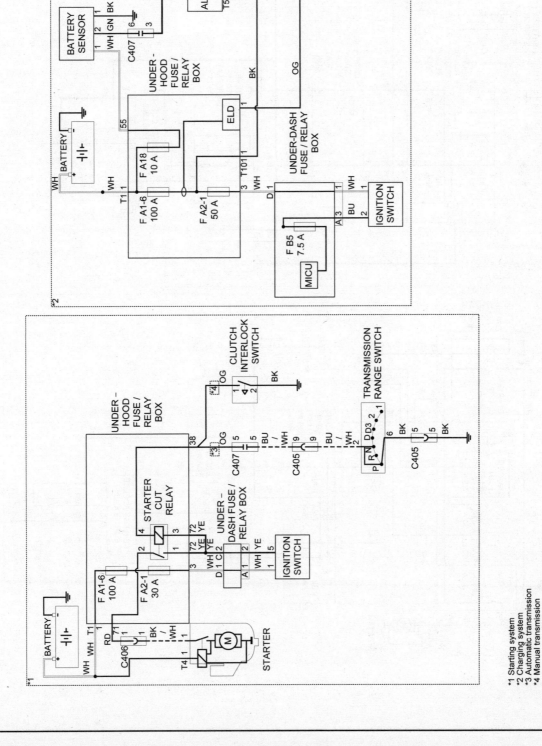

**Starting and charging systems - 2012 and 2013 Civic models**

*1 Starting system
*2 Charging system
*3 Automatic transmission
*4 Manual transmission

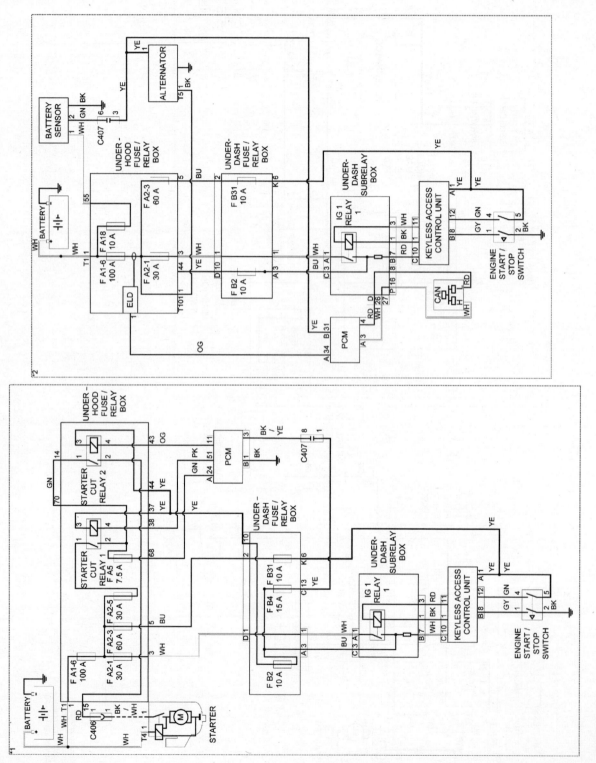

**Starting and charging systems - 2014 and 2015 Civic models**

*1 Starting system
*2 Charging system

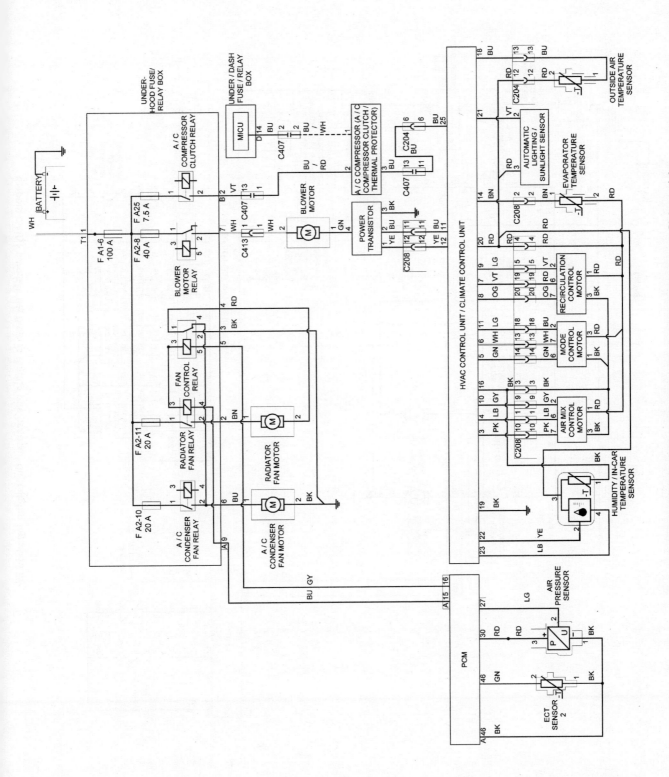

**Air conditioning/heating (automatic) and engine cooling fan systems - Civic models**

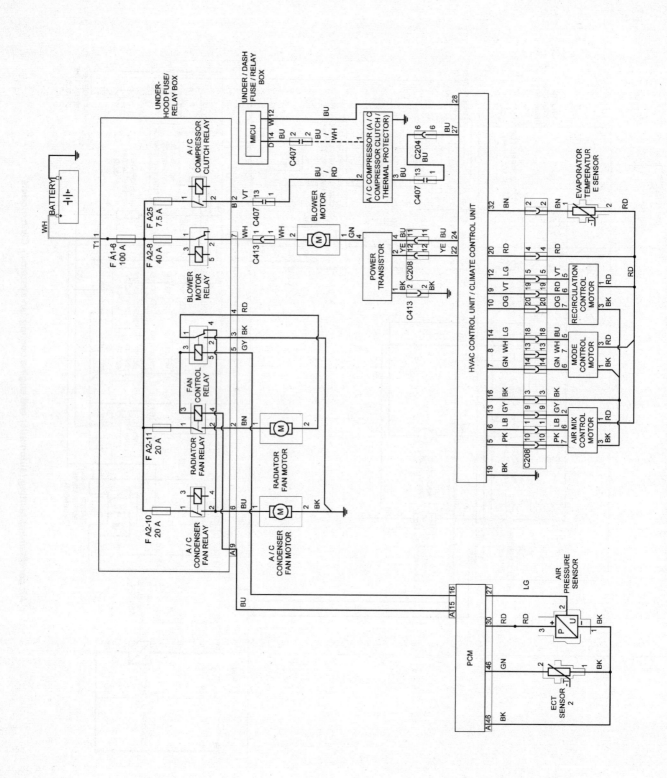

**Air conditioning/heating (manual) and engine cooling fan systems - Civic models**

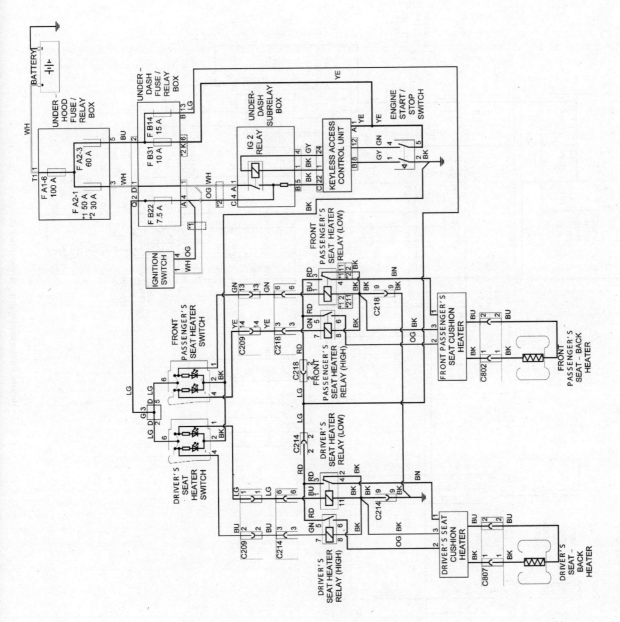

**Seat heater system - Civic models**

*1 From 2012 to 2013
*2 From 2014 to 2015

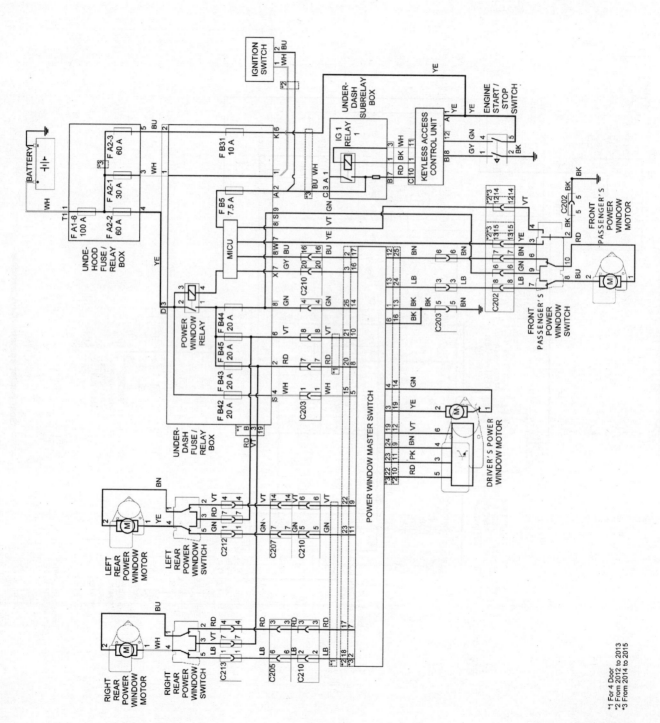

**Power window system - Civic models**

*1 For 4 Door
*2 From 2012 to 2013
*3 From 2014 to 2015

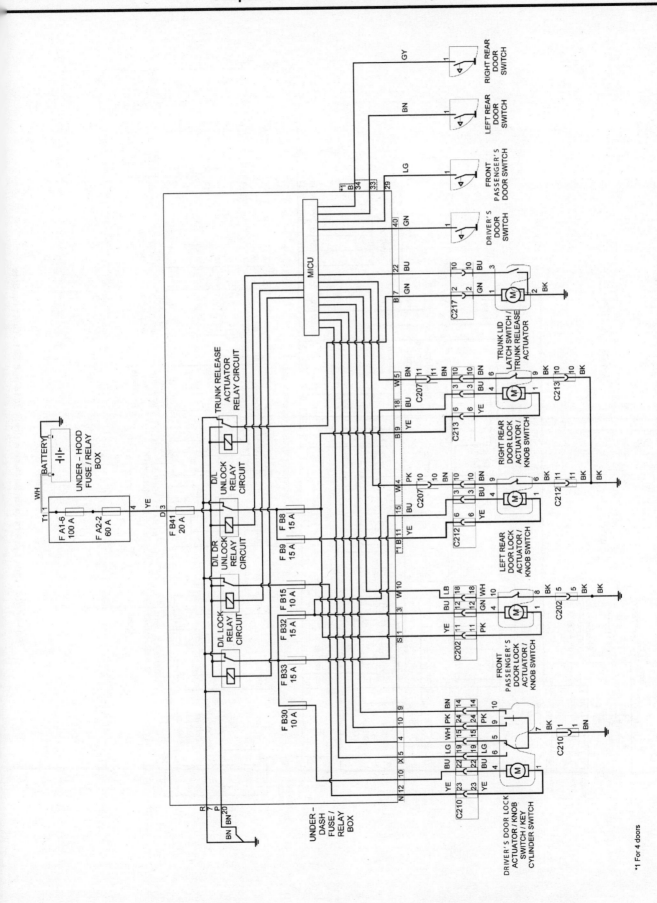

**Power door lock system - 2012 and 2013 Civic models**

*1 For 4 doors

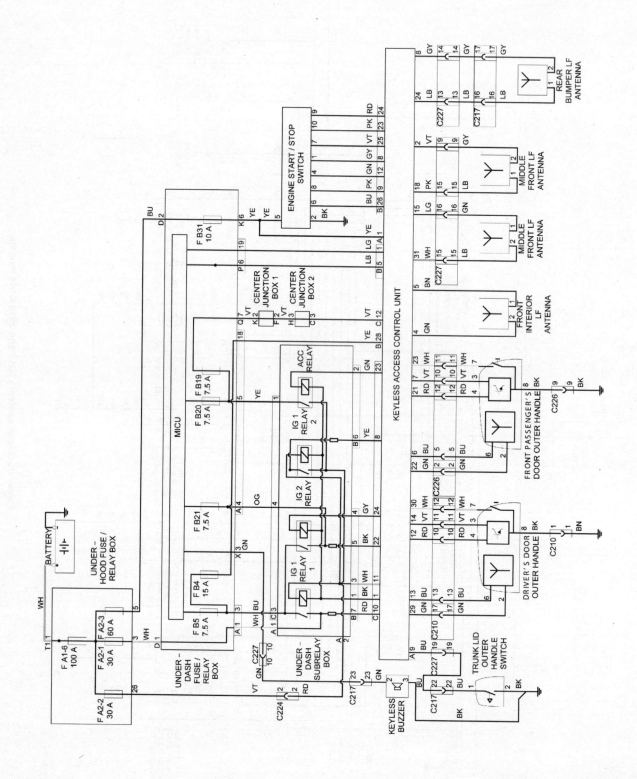

**Power door lock system (with keyless entry) - 2014 and 2015 Civic models**

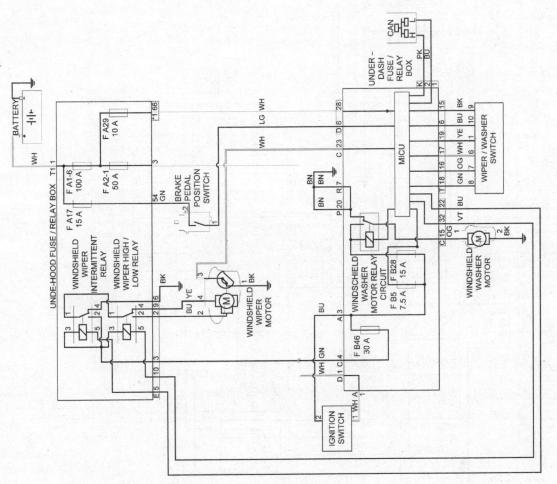

Windshield wiper and washer system - 2012 and 2013 Civic models

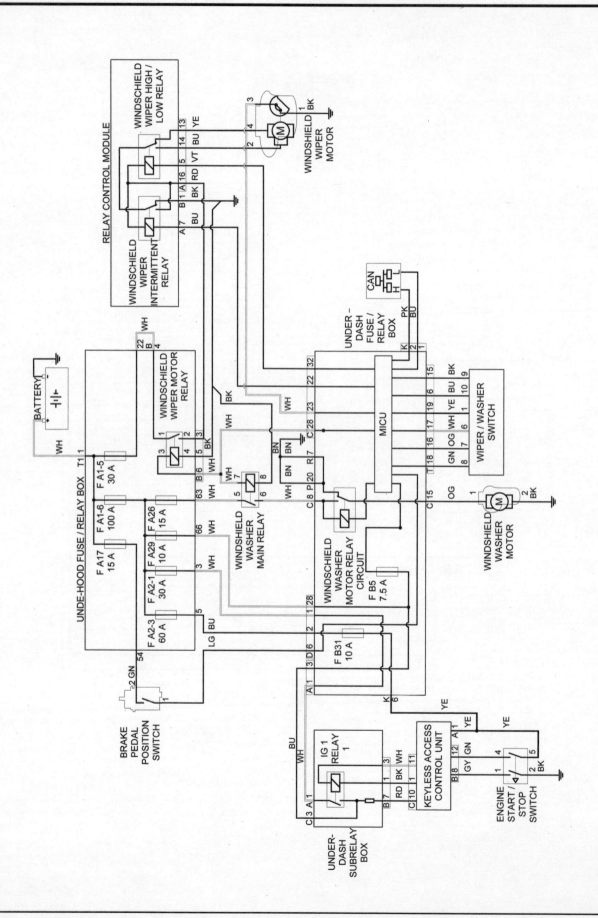

**Windshield wiper and washer system - 2014 and 2015 Civic models**

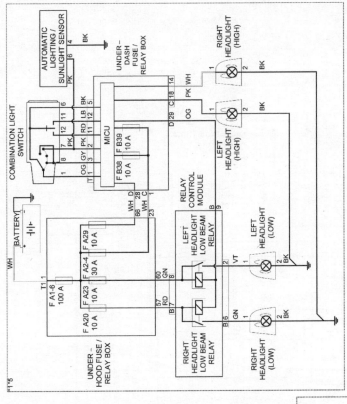

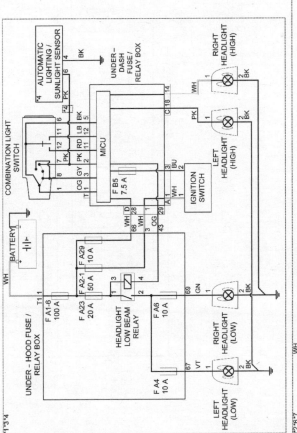

Headlights/fog lights and back-up lights - Civic models

*1 Headlights
*2 Front fog lights and back-up lights
*3 Manual transmission From 2012 to 2015
*4 Automatic transmission From 2012 to 2013

*5 Automatic transmission From 2014 to 2015
*6 Manual transmission
*7 Automatic transmission

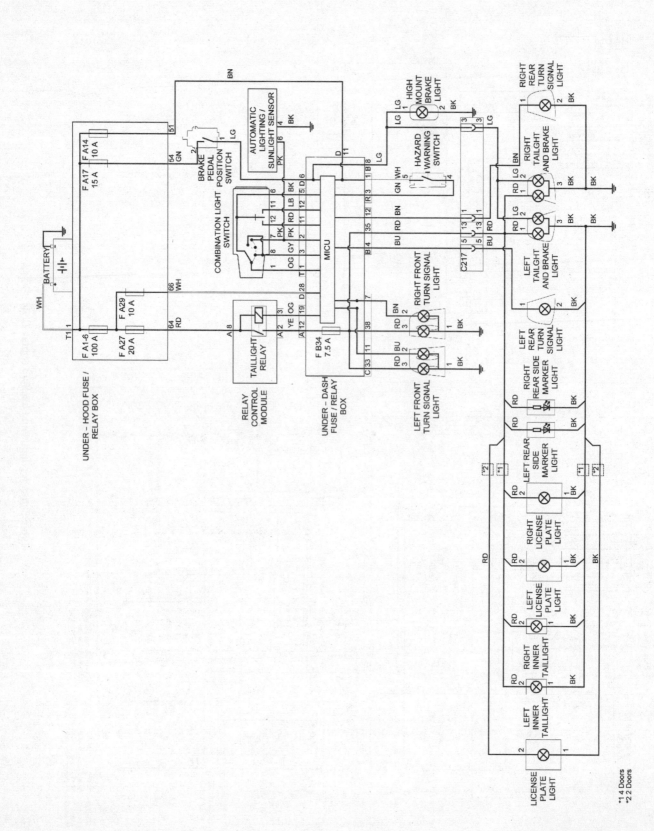

**Exterior lighting system (except headlights/fog lights/back-up lights) - Civic models**

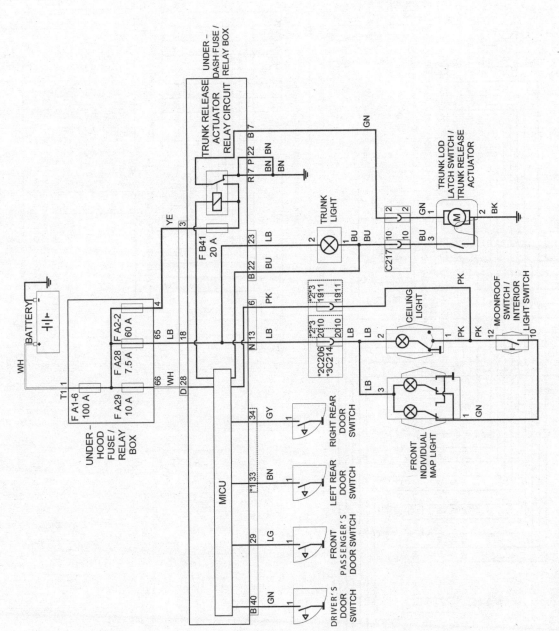

Interior lighting system - Civic models

*1 4 Doors
*2 From 2012 to 2013
*3 From 2014 to 2015

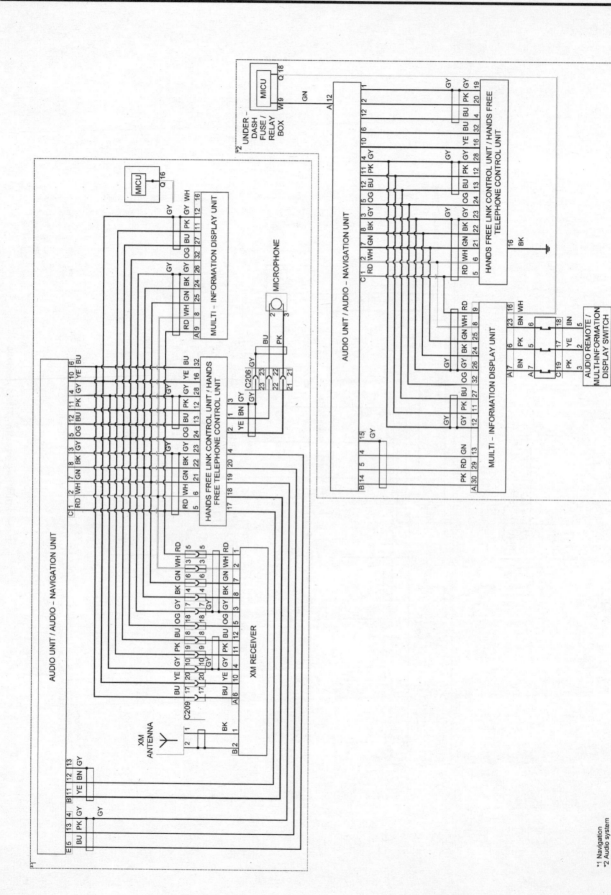

**Audio system - 2012 and 2013 Civic models**

*1 Navigation
*2 Audio system

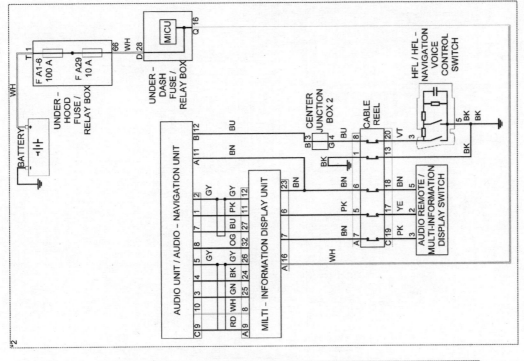

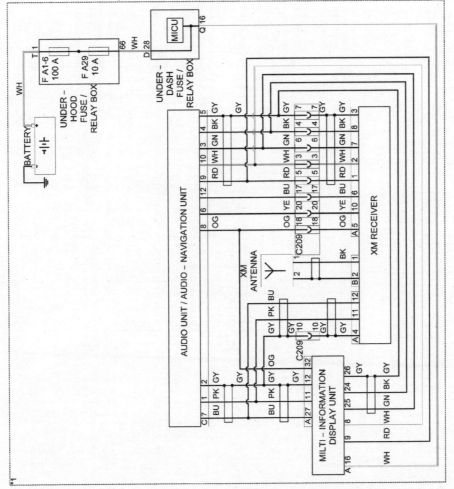

Audio system - 2014 and 2015 Civic models

*1 Navigation
*2 Audio system

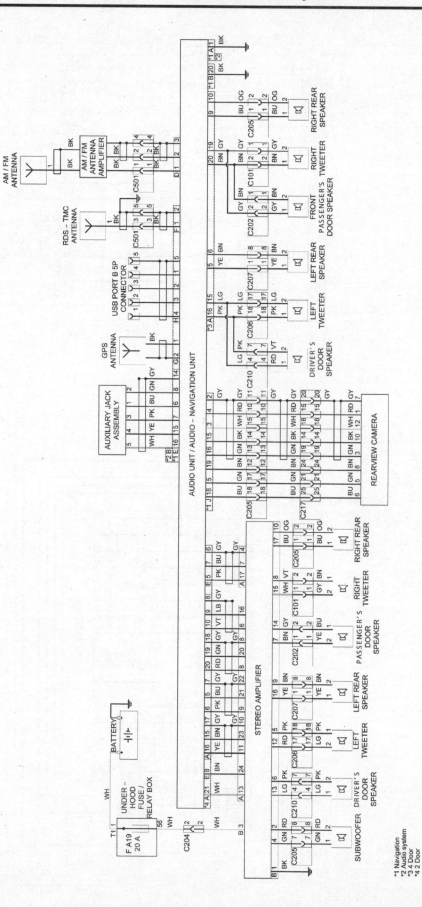

Audio system (speakers) - 2012 and 2013 Civic models

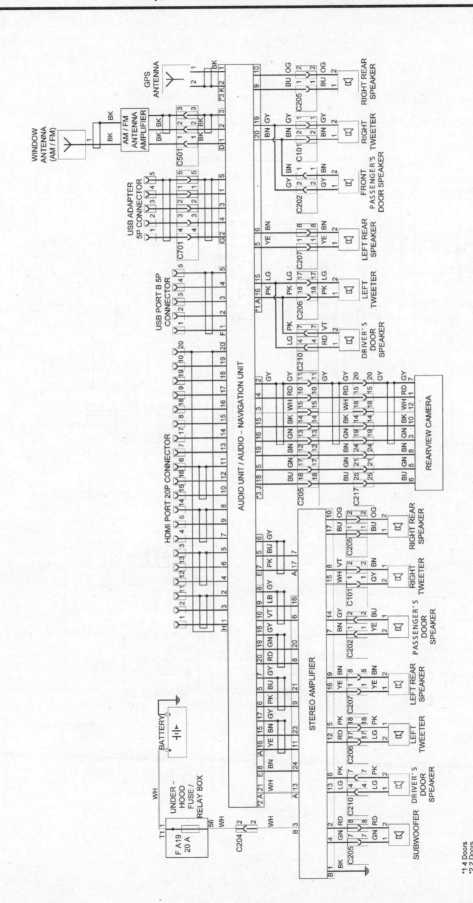

Audio system (speakers) - 2014 and 2015 Civic models

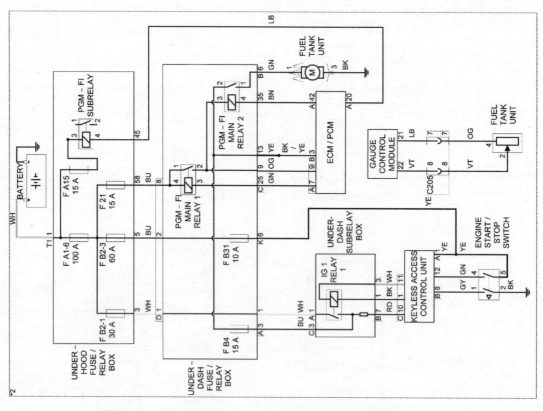

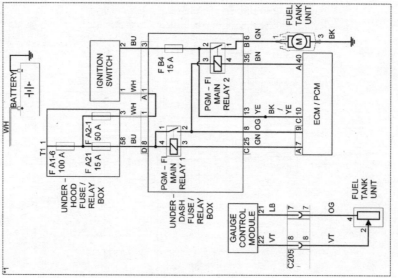

**Fuel pump circuit - Civic models**

*1 From 2012 to 2013
*2 From 2014 to 2015

**PASSENGER COMPARTMENT**

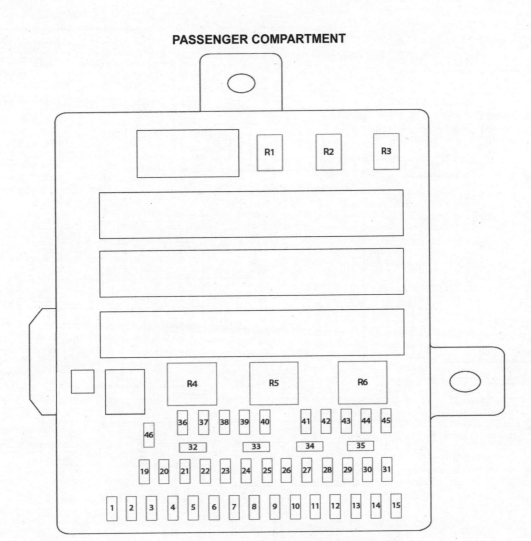

| FUSE/RELAY | VALUE | DESCRIPTION |
|---|---|---|
| F1 | 20 A | Keyless Access System , Under-Dash Fuse/Relay Box  or not used |
| F2 | 10 A | A/T Gear Position Indicator, Charging System, Cruise Control, Cvt Control System, ECM/PCM (All) , EVAP System , PGM-FI, System , Power Supply , Starting System , Under-Dash Fuse/Relay Box |
| F3 | 10 A | Power Supply, SRS , Under-Dash Fuse/Relay Box |
| F4 | 15 A | CVT Control System, ECM/PCM (All) , ECM/PCM Power and Ground , ETCS (Electronic Throttle Control System) , Fuel Supply System , Ignition System , Keyless Access System , Keyless/Power Door, Locks/Security System , PGM-FI System , Power Supply , Starting System , Under-Dash Fuse/Relay Box |

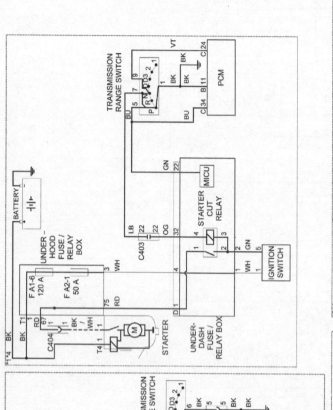

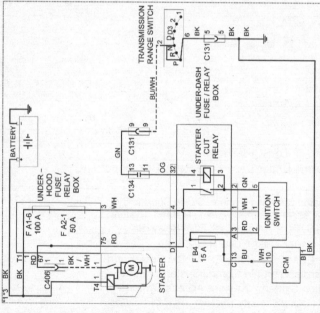

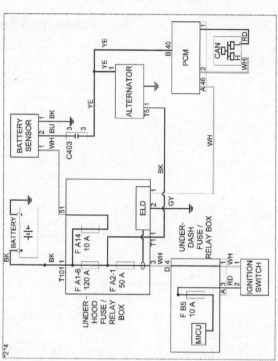

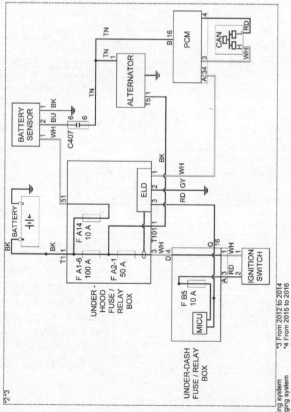

**Starting and charging systems - CR-V models**

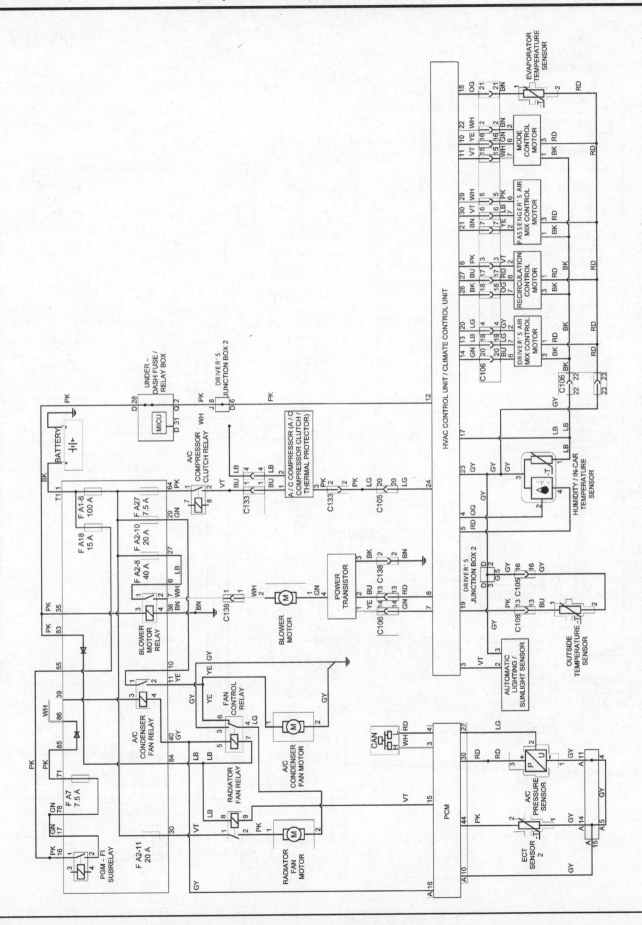

**Air conditioning, heating and engine cooling fan systems - 2014 and earlier CR-V models**

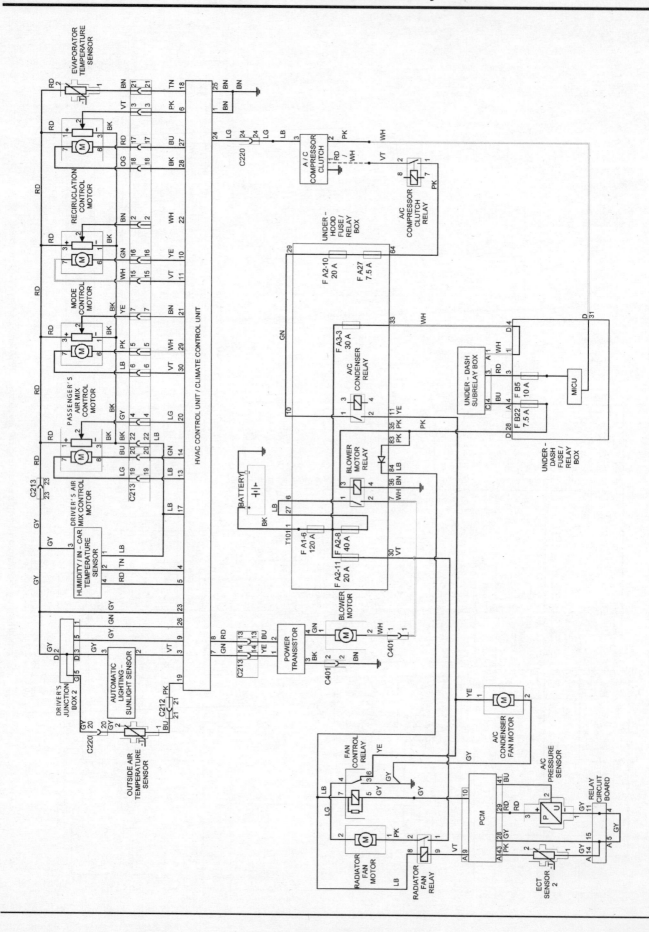

**Air conditioning, heating and engine cooling fan systems – 2015 and later CR-V models**

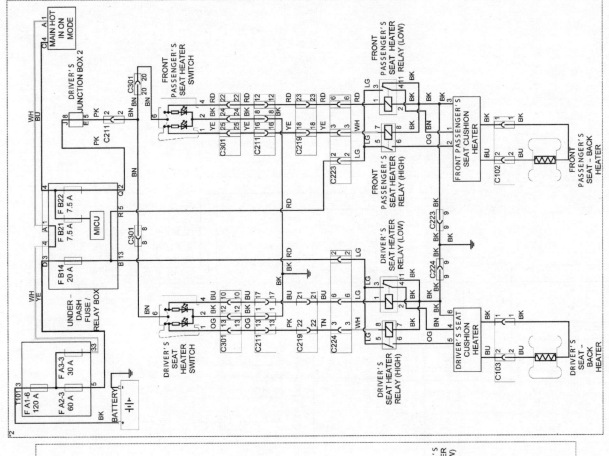

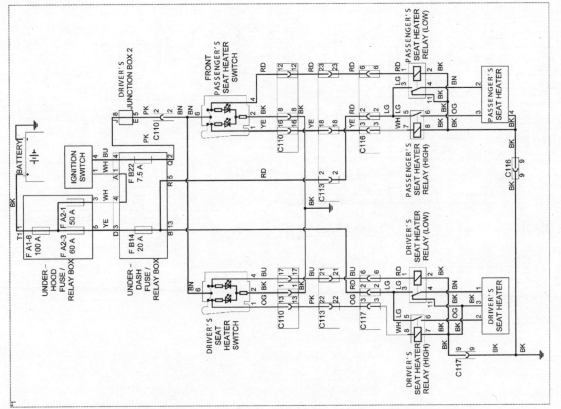

Seat heater system - CR-V models

*1 From 2012 to 2014
*2 From 2015 to 2016

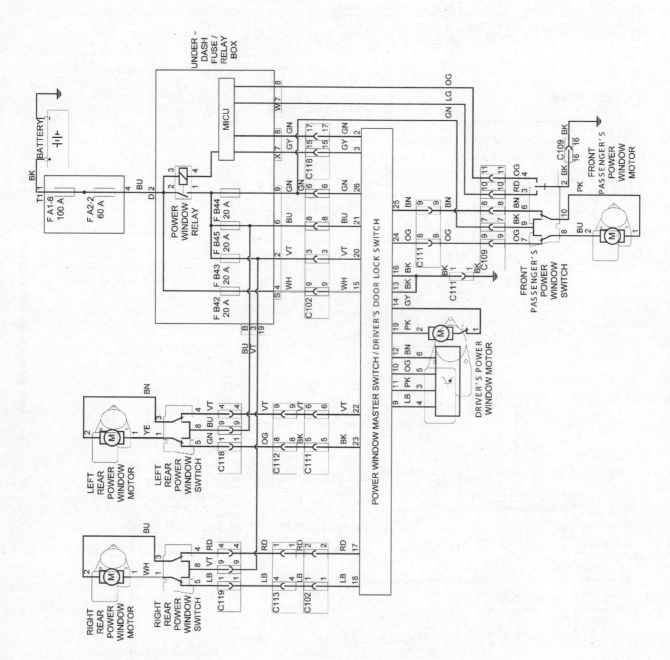

**Power window system - 2014 and earlier CR-V models**

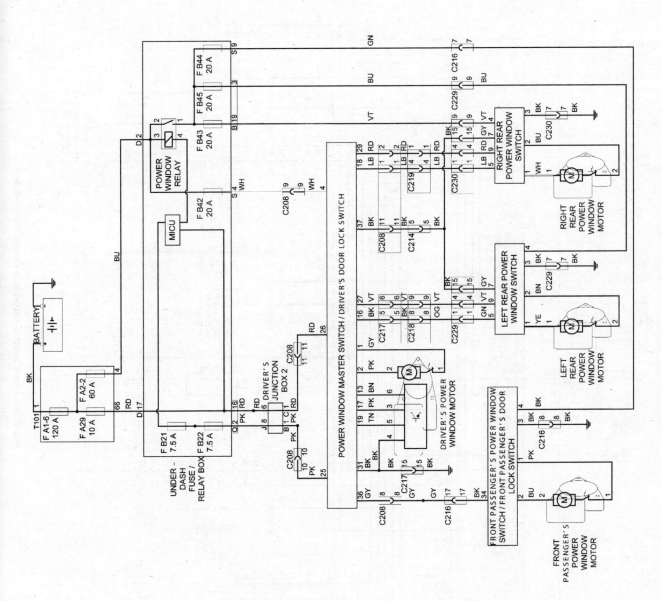

**Power window system - 2015 and later CR-V models**

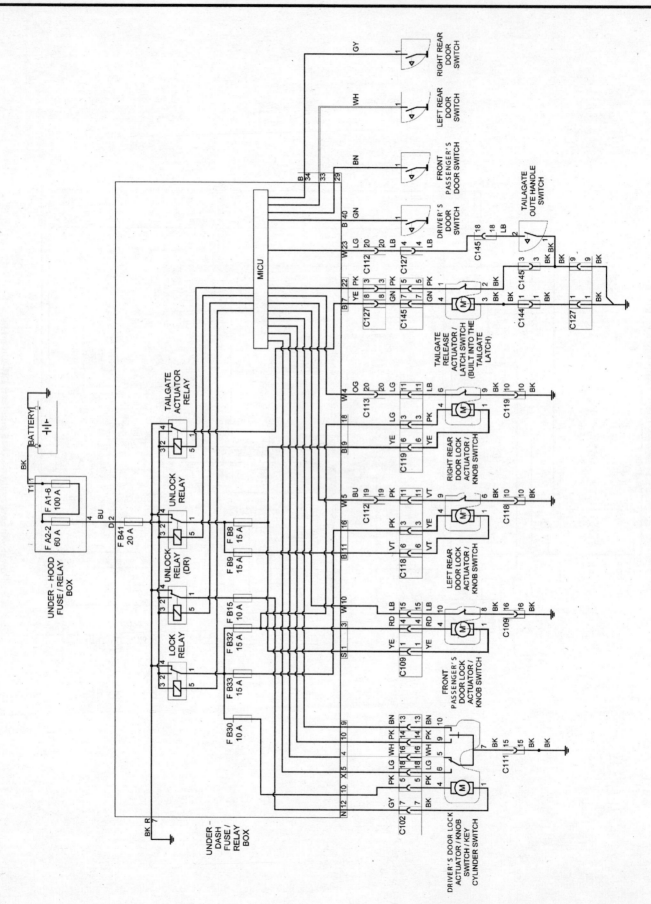

Power door lock system - 2014 and earlier CR-V models

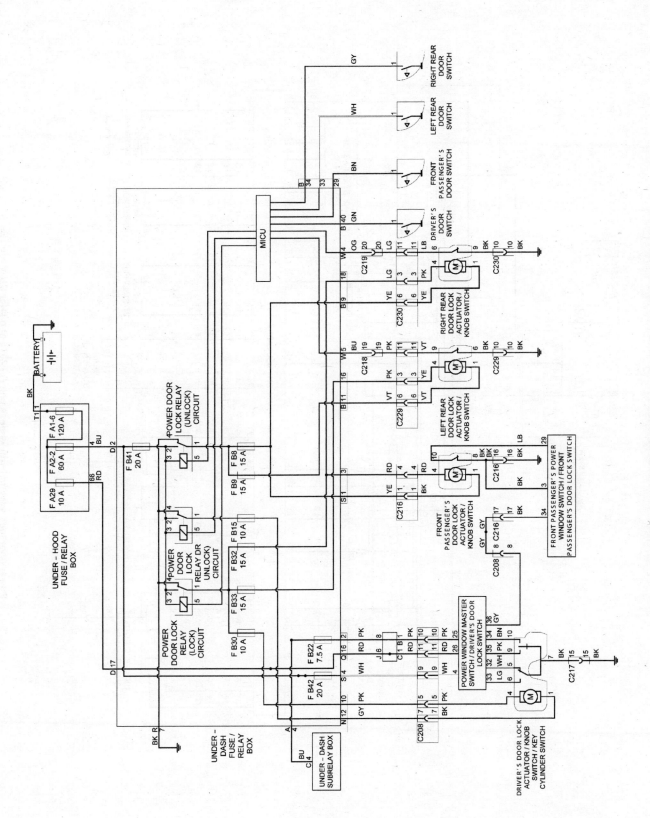

**Power door lock system (without keyless entry) - 2015 and later CR-V models**

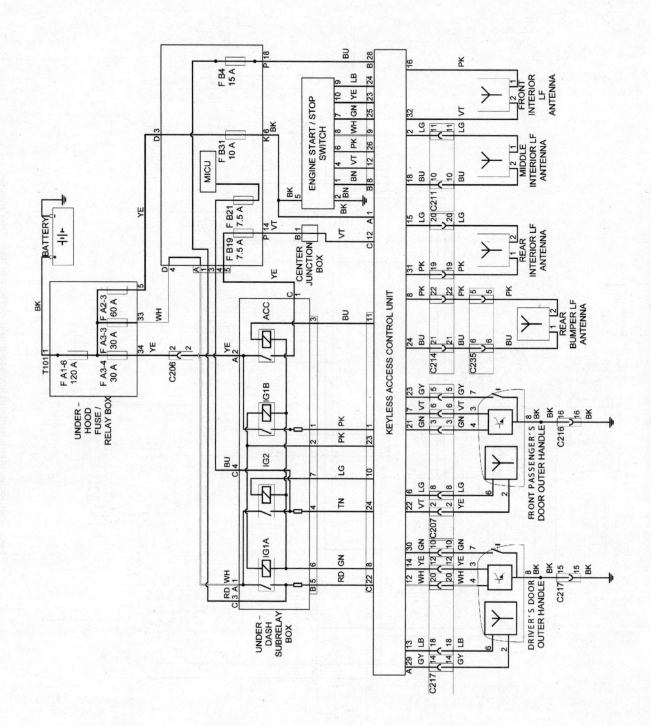

Power door lock system (with keyless entry) - 2015 and later CR-V models

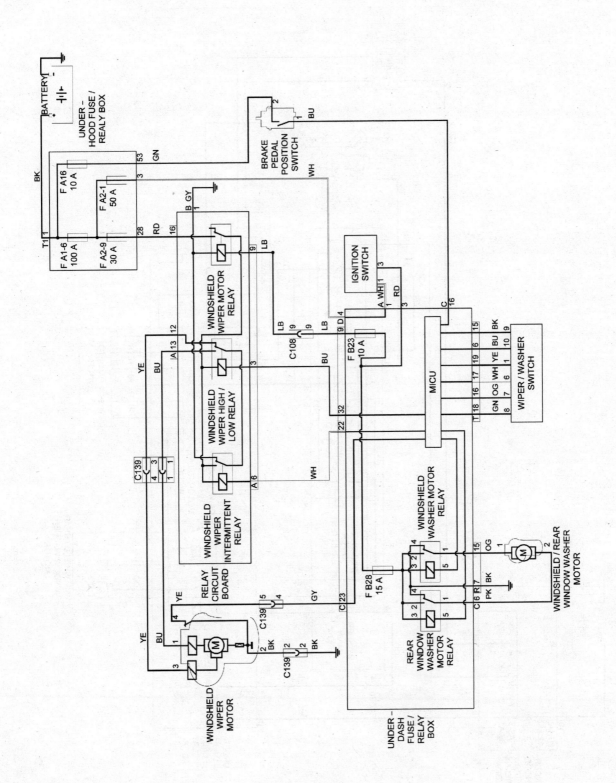

Windshield wiper/washer system - 2014 and earlier CR-V models

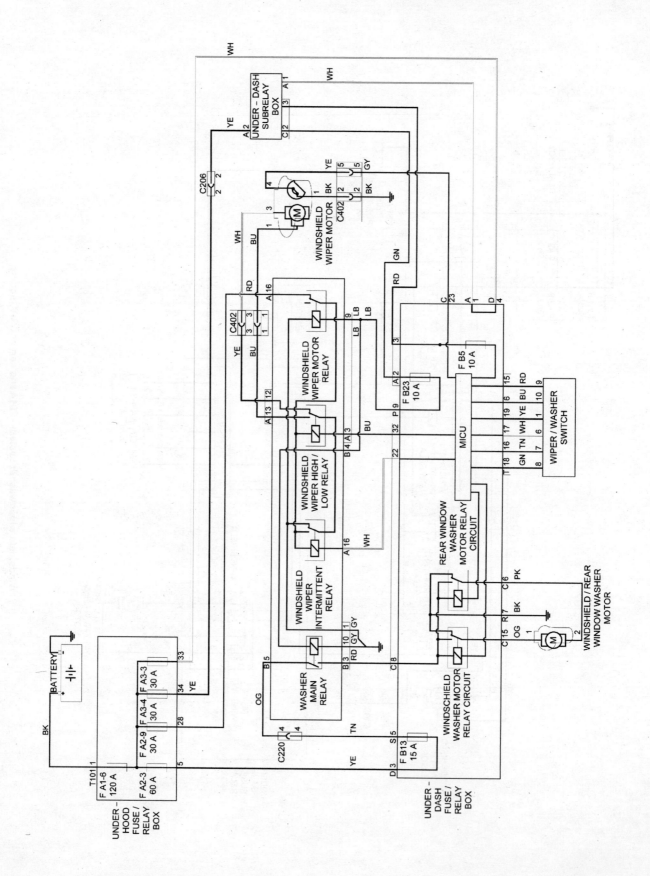

Windshield wiper/washer system - 2015 and later CR-V models

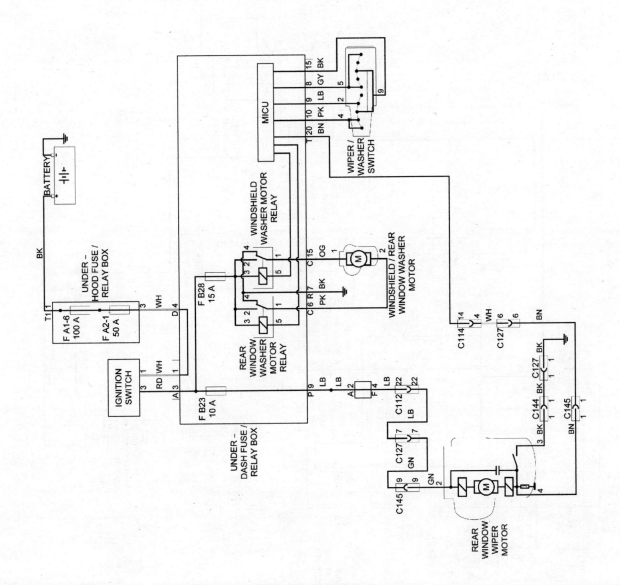

Rear window wiper/washer system - 2014 and earlier CR-V models

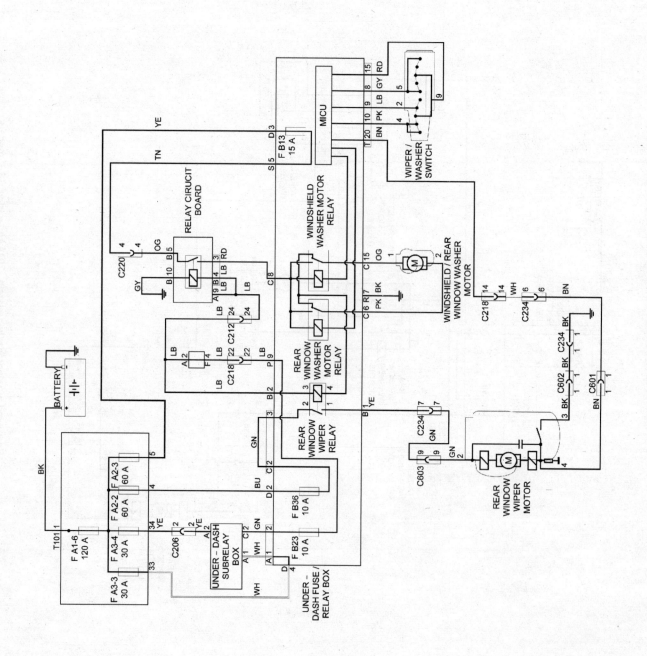

**Rear window wiper/washer system - 2015 and later CR-V models**

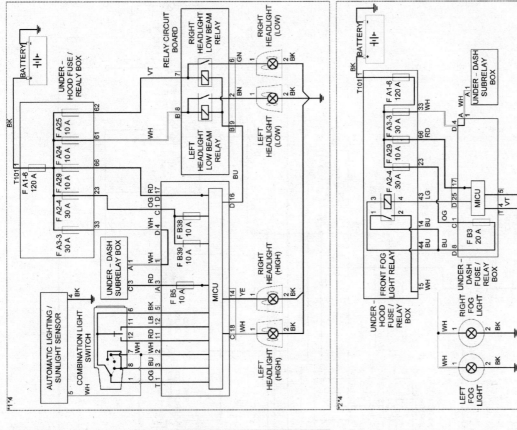

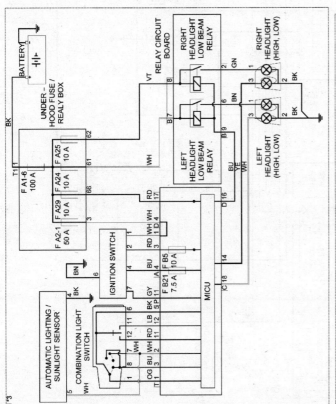

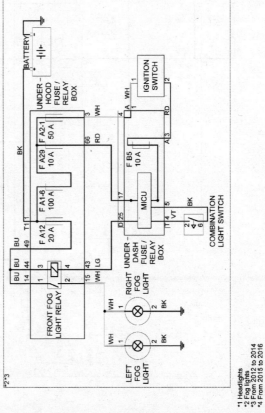

Headlight system - CR-V models

*1 Headlights
*2 Fog lights
*3 From 2012 to 2014
*4 From 2015 to 2016

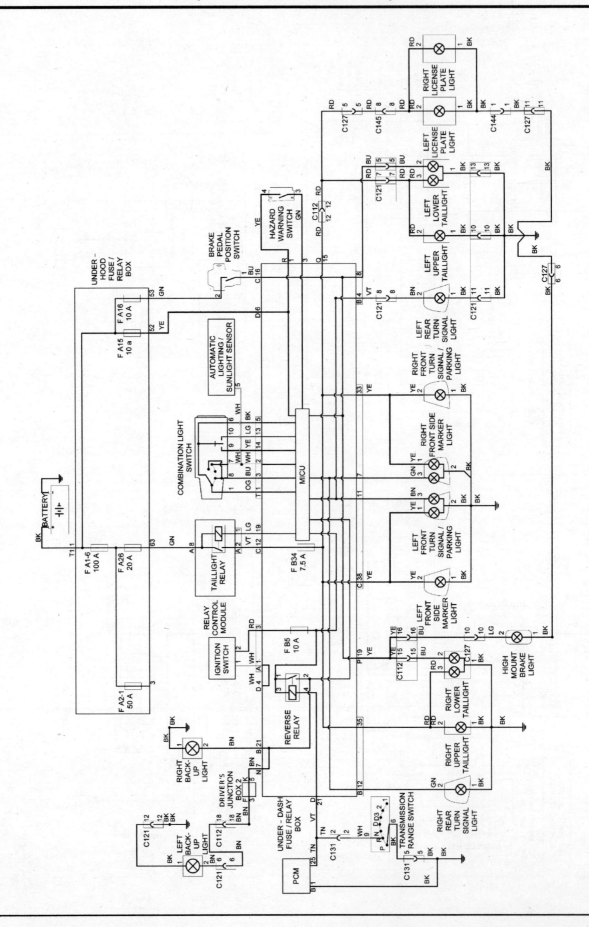

**Exterior lighting system (except headlights) - 2014 and earlier CR-V models**

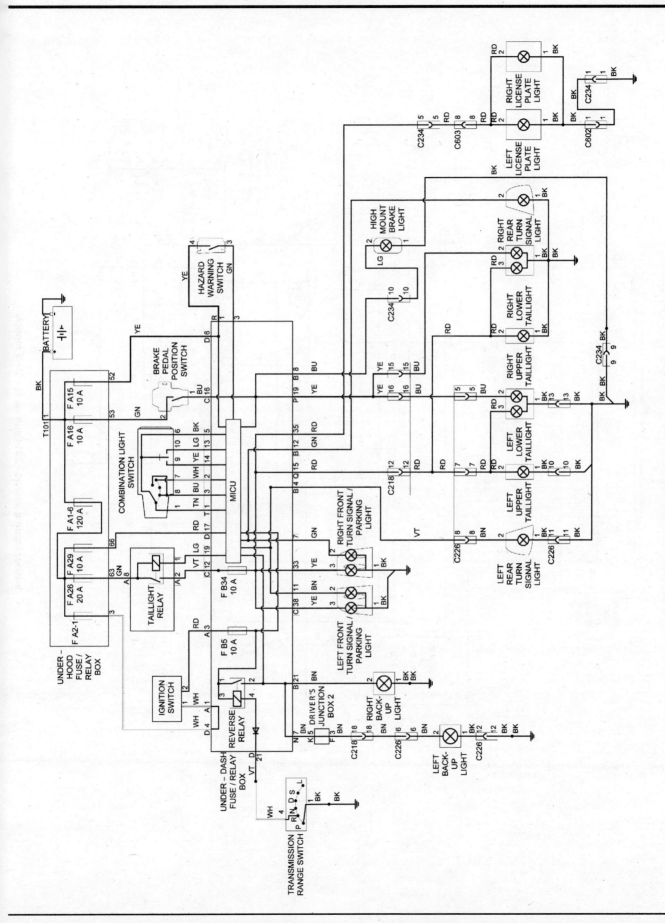

**Exterior lighting system (except headlights) - 2015 and later CR-V models**

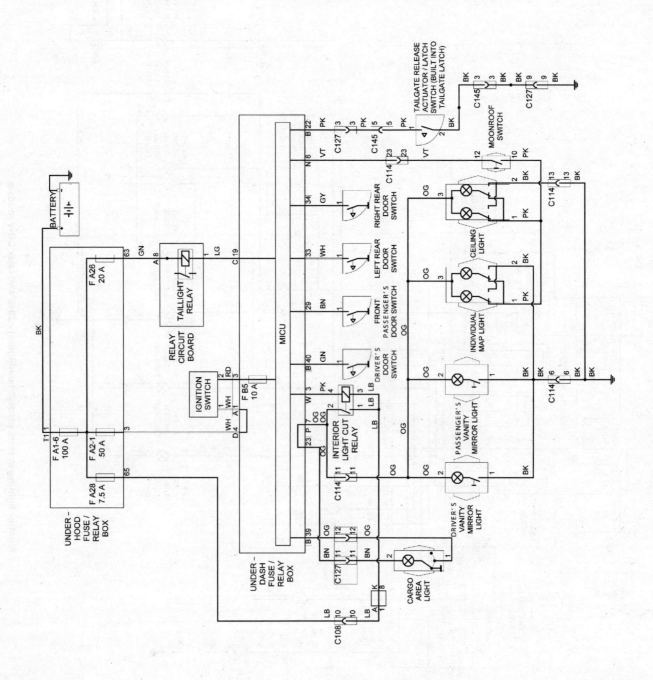

Interior lighting system - 2014 and earlier CR-V models

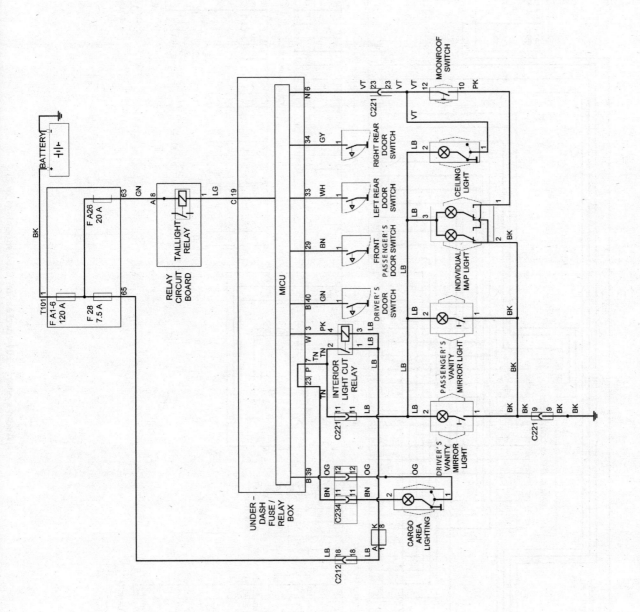

Interior lighting system - 2015 and later CR-V models

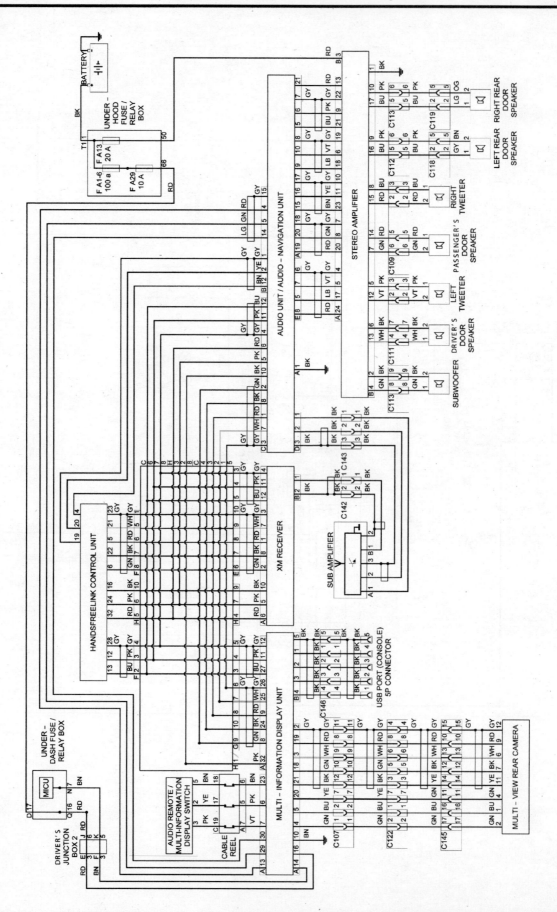

**Audio system - 2014 and earlier CR-V models (1 of 2)**

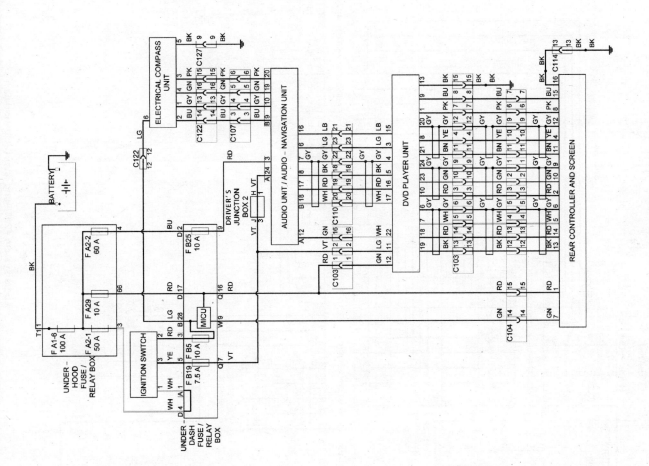

**Audio system - 2014 and earlier CR-V models (2 of 2)**

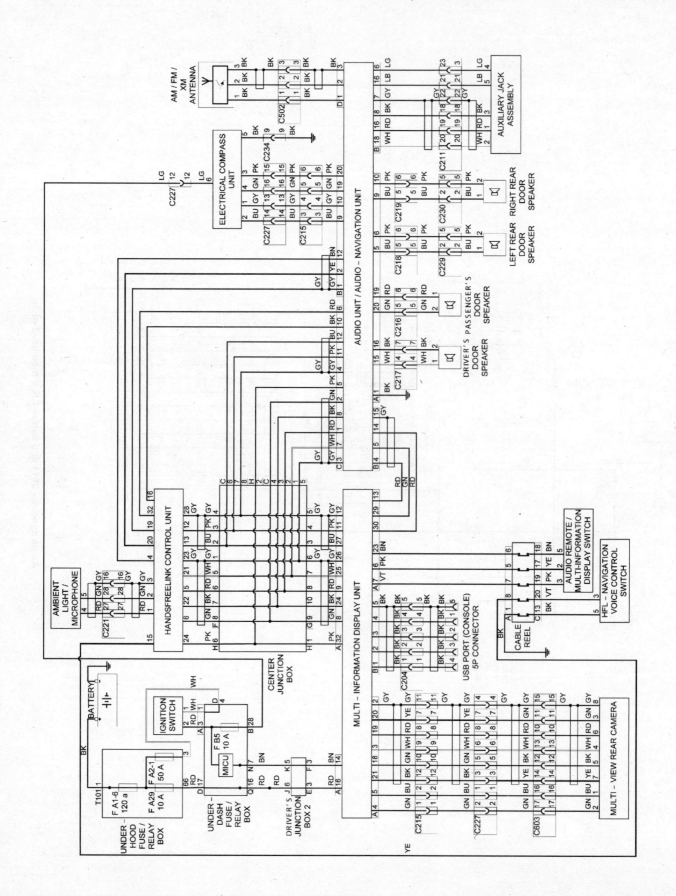

**Audio system - 2015 and later CR-V models**

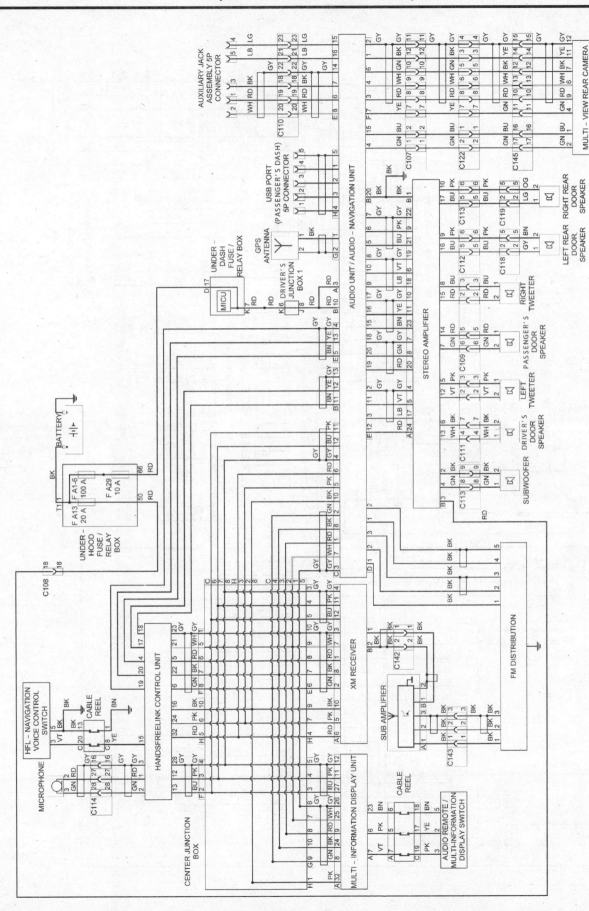

**Audio system (with navigation) – 2014 and earlier CR-V models**

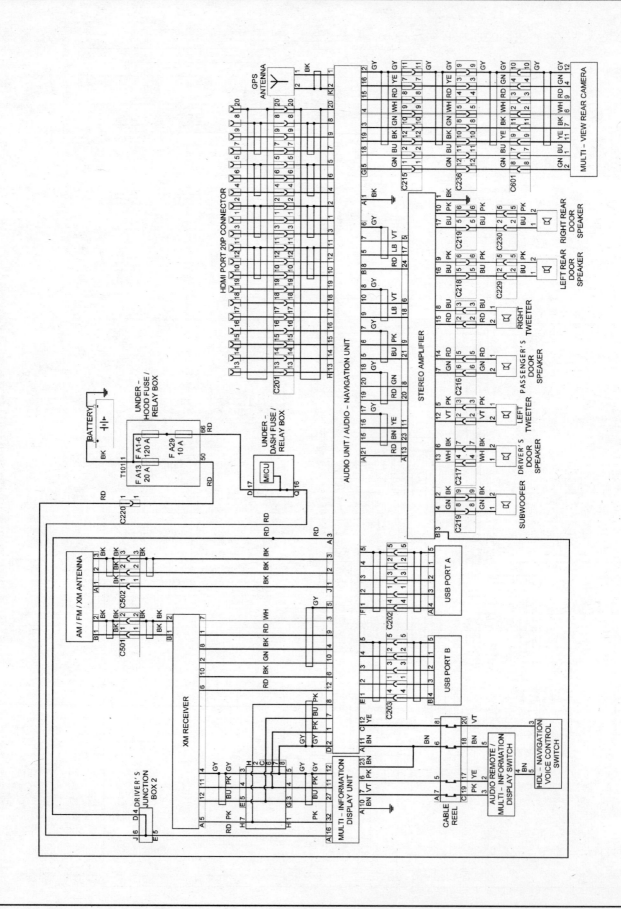

**Audio system (with navigation) - 2015 and later CR-V models**

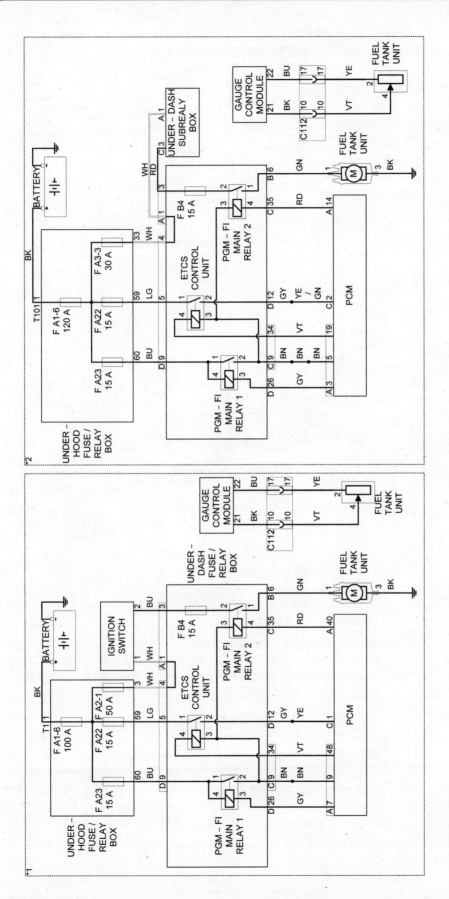

Fuel pump circuit - CR-V models

*1 From 2012 to 2014
*2 From 2015 to 2016

## PASSENGER COMPARTMENT

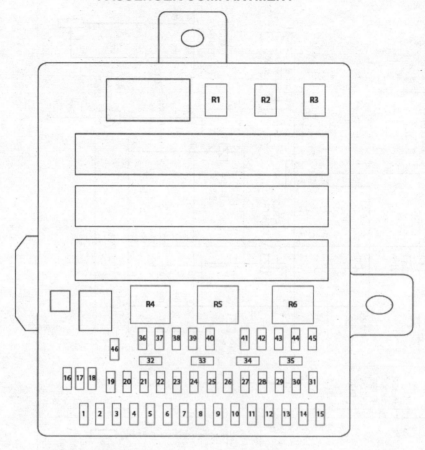

| FUSE/RELAY | VALUE | DESCRIPTION |
|---|---|---|
| F1 | - | Not used |
| F2 | 10 A | Adaptive Cruise Control, Charging System , Collision Mitigation Brake System (CMBS) , Cruise Control , EVAP System , Idle Control System , Lane Keeping Assist, System (LKAS) , PCM (All) , PGM-FI System , Power Supply , Starting System , Under-Dash Fuse/Relay Box |
| F3 | 10 A | Power Supply, SRS , Under-Dash Fuse/Relay Box |
| F4 | 15 A | A/T Gear Position Indicator, A/T Interlock System , CVT Control System , ETCS (Electronic Throttle Control System) , EVAP System , Fuel Supply System , Ignition, System , Keyless Access System , PCM (All) , PCM Power and Ground , PGM-FI System , Power Supply , Under-Dash Fuse/Relay Box , Wiper/Washer (Rear Window) |

# Index

# Haynes Automotive Manuals

*NOTE: If you do not see a listing for your vehicle, please visit* ***haynes.com*** *for the latest product information and check out our* ***Online Manuals!***

## ACURA

12020 **Integra** '86 thru '89 **& Legend** '86 thru '90
12021 **Integra** '90 thru '93 **& Legend** '91 thru '95
**Integra** '94 thru '00 *- see HONDA Civic (42025)*
**MDX** '01 thru '07 *- see HONDA Pilot (42037)*
12050 **Acura TL** all models '99 thru '08

## AMC

14020 **Mid-size models** '70 thru '83
14025 **(Renault) Alliance & Encore** '83 thru '87

## AUDI

15020 **4000** all models '80 thru '87
15025 **5000** all models '77 thru '83
15026 **5000** all models '84 thru '88
**Audi A4** '96 thru '01 *- see VW Passat (96023)*
15030 **Audi A4** '02 thru '08

## AUSTIN-HEALEY

**Sprite** *- see MG Midget (66015)*

## BMW

18020 **3/5 Series** '82 thru '92
18021 **3-Series** incl. Z3 models '92 thru '98
18022 **3-Series** incl. Z4 models '99 thru '05
18023 **3-Series** '06 thru '14
18025 **320i all 4-cylinder models** '75 thru '83
18050 **1500 thru 2002** except Turbo '59 thru '77

## BUICK

19010 **Buick Century** '97 thru '05
**Century (front-wheel drive)** *- see GM (38005)*
19020 **Buick, Oldsmobile & Pontiac Full-size (Front-wheel drive)** '85 thru '05
**Buick** Electra, LeSabre and Park Avenue; **Oldsmobile** Delta 88 Royale, Ninety Eight and Regency; **Pontiac** Bonneville
19025 **Buick, Oldsmobile & Pontiac Full-size (Rear wheel drive)** '70 thru '90
**Buick** Estate, Electra, LeSabre, Limited, **Oldsmobile** Custom Cruiser, Delta 88, Ninety-eight, **Pontiac** Bonneville, Catalina, Grandville, Parisienne
19027 **Buick LaCrosse** '05 thru '13
**Enclave** *- see GENERAL MOTORS (38001)*
**Rainier** *- see CHEVROLET (24072)*
**Regal** *- see GENERAL MOTORS (38010)*
**Riviera** *- see GENERAL MOTORS (38030, 38031)*
**Roadmaster** *- see CHEVROLET (24046)*
**Skyhawk** *- see GENERAL MOTORS (38015)*
**Skylark** *- see GENERAL MOTORS (38020, 38025)*
**Somerset** *- see GENERAL MOTORS (38025)*

## CADILLAC

21015 **CTS & CTS-V** '03 thru '14
21030 **Cadillac Rear Wheel Drive** '70 thru '93
**Cimarron** *- see GENERAL MOTORS (38015)*
**DeVille** *- see GENERAL MOTORS (38031 & 38032)*
**Eldorado** *- see GENERAL MOTORS (38030)*
**Fleetwood** *- see GENERAL MOTORS (38031)*
**Seville** *- see GM (38030, 38031 & 38032)*

## CHEVROLET

10305 **Chevrolet Engine Overhaul Manual**
24010 **Astro & GMC Safari Mini-vans** '85 thru '05
24013 **Aveo** '04 thru '11
24015 **Camaro V8** all models '70 thru '81
24016 **Camaro** all models '82 thru '92
24017 **Camaro & Firebird** '93 thru '02
**Cavalier** *- see GENERAL MOTORS (38016)*
**Celebrity** *- see GENERAL MOTORS (38005)*
24018 **Camaro** '10 thru '15
24020 **Chevelle, Malibu & El Camino** '69 thru '87
**Cobalt** *- see GENERAL MOTORS (38017)*
24024 **Chevette & Pontiac T1000** '76 thru '87
**Citation** *- see GENERAL MOTORS (38020)*
24027 **Colorado & GMC Canyon** '04 thru '12
24032 **Corsica & Beretta** all models '87 thru '96
24040 **Corvette** all V8 models '68 thru '82
24041 **Corvette** all models '84 thru '96
24042 **Corvette** all models '97 thru '13
24044 **Cruze** '11 thru '19
24045 **Full-size Sedans** Caprice, Impala, Biscayne, Bel Air & Wagons '69 thru '90
24046 **Impala SS & Caprice and Buick Roadmaster** '91 thru '96
**Impala** '00 thru '05 *- see LUMINA (24048)*
24047 **Impala & Monte Carlo** all models '06 thru '11
**Lumina** '90 thru '94 *- see GM (38010)*
24048 **Lumina & Monte Carlo** '95 thru '05
**Lumina APV** *- see GM (38035)*
24050 **Luv Pick-up** all 2WD & 4WD '72 thru '82
24051 **Malibu** '13 thru '19
24055 **Monte Carlo** all models '70 thru '88
**Monte Carlo** '95 thru '01 *- see LUMINA (24048)*
24059 **Nova** all V8 models '69 thru '79
24060 **Nova and Geo Prizm** '85 thru '92
24064 **Pick-ups** '67 thru '87 - Chevrolet & GMC
24065 **Pick-ups** '88 thru '98 - Chevrolet & GMC
24066 **Pick-ups** '99 thru '06 - Chevrolet & GMC
24067 **Chevrolet Silverado & GMC Sierra** '07 thru '14
24068 **Chevrolet Silverado & GMC Sierra** '14 thru '19
24070 **S-10 & S-15 Pick-ups** '82 thru '93, **Blazer & Jimmy** '83 thru '94,
24071 **S-10 & Sonoma Pick-ups** '94 thru '04, including **Blazer, Jimmy & Hombre**
24072 **Chevrolet TrailBlazer, GMC Envoy & Oldsmobile Bravada** '02 thru '09
24075 **Sprint** '85 thru '88 **& Geo Metro** '89 thru '01
24080 **Vans - Chevrolet & GMC** '68 thru '96
24081 **Chevrolet Express & GMC Savana** Full-size Vans '96 thru '19

## CHRYSLER

10310 **Chrysler Engine Overhaul Manual**
25015 **Chrysler Cirrus, Dodge Stratus, Plymouth Breeze** '95 thru '00
25020 **Full-size Front-Wheel Drive** '88 thru '93
**K-Cars** *- see DODGE Aries (30008)*
**Laser** *- see DODGE Daytona (30030)*
25025 **Chrysler LHS, Concorde, New Yorker, Dodge** Intrepid, **Eagle** Vision, '93 thru '97
25026 **Chrysler LHS, Concorde, 300M, Dodge** Intrepid, '98 thru '04
25027 **Chrysler 300** '05 thru '18, **Dodge Charger** '06 thru '18, **Magnum** '05 thru '08 **& Challenger** '08 thru '18
25030 **Chrysler & Plymouth Mid-size** front wheel drive '82 thru '95
**Rear-wheel Drive** *- see Dodge (30050)*
25035 **PT Cruiser** all models '01 thru '10
25040 **Chrysler Sebring** '95 thru '06, **Dodge Stratus** '01 thru '06 **& Dodge Avenger** '95 thru '00
25041 **Chrysler Sebring** '07 thru '10, **200** '11 thru '17 **Dodge Avenger** '08 thru '14

## DATSUN

28005 **200SX** all models '80 thru '83
28012 **240Z, 260Z & 280Z** Coupe '70 thru '78
28014 **280ZX** Coupe & 2+2 '79 thru '83
**300ZX** *- see NISSAN (72010)*
28018 **510 & PL521 Pick-up** '68 thru '73
28020 **510** all models '78 thru '81
28022 **620 Series Pick-up** all models '73 thru '79
**720 Series Pick-up** *- see NISSAN (72030)*

## DODGE

**400 & 600** *- see CHRYSLER (25030)*
30008 **Aries & Plymouth Reliant** '81 thru '89
30010 **Caravan & Plymouth Voyager** '84 thru '95
30011 **Caravan & Plymouth Voyager** '96 thru '02
30012 **Challenger & Plymouth Sapporro** '78 thru '83
30013 **Caravan, Chrysler Voyager & Town & Country** '03 thru '07
30014 **Grand Caravan & Chrysler Town & Country** '08 thru '18
30016 **Colt & Plymouth Champ** '78 thru '87
30020 **Dakota Pick-ups** all models '87 thru '96
30021 **Durango** '98 & '99 **& Dakota** '97 thru '99
30022 **Durango** '00 thru '03 **& Dakota** '00 thru '04
30023 **Durango** '04 thru '09 **& Dakota** '05 thru '11
30025 **Dart, Demon, Plymouth Barracuda, Duster & Valiant** 6-cylinder models '67 thru '76
30030 **Daytona & Chrysler Laser** '84 thru '89
**Intrepid** *- see CHRYSLER (25025, 25026)*
30034 **Neon** all models '95 thru '99
30035 **Omni & Plymouth Horizon** '78 thru '90
30036 **Dodge & Plymouth Neon** '00 thru '05
30040 **Pick-ups** full-size models '74 thru '93
30042 **Pick-ups** full-size models '94 thru '08
30043 **Pick-ups** full-size models '09 thru '18
30045 **Ram 50/D50 Pick-ups & Raider and Plymouth Arrow Pick-ups** '79 thru '93
30050 **Dodge/Plymouth/Chrysler** RWD '71 thru '89
30055 **Shadow & Plymouth Sundance** '87 thru '94
30060 **Spirit & Plymouth Acclaim** '89 thru '95
30065 **Vans - Dodge & Plymouth** '71 thru '03

## EAGLE

**Talon** *- see MITSUBISHI (68030, 68031)*
**Vision** *- see CHRYSLER (25025)*

## FIAT

34010 **124 Sport Coupe & Spider** '68 thru '78
34025 **X1/9** all models '74 thru '80

## FORD

10320 **Ford Engine Overhaul Manual**
10355 **Ford Automatic Transmission Overhaul**
11500 **Mustang '64-1/2 thru '70 Restoration Guide**
36004 **Aerostar Mini-vans** all models '86 thru '97
36006 **Contour & Mercury Mystique** '95 thru '00
36008 **Courier Pick-up** all models '72 thru '82
36012 **Crown Victoria & Mercury Grand Marquis** '88 thru '11
36014 **Edge** '07 thru '19 **& Lincoln MKX** '07 thru '18
36016 **Escort & Mercury Lynx** all models '81 thru '90
36020 **Escort & Mercury Tracer** '91 thru '02
36022 **Escape** '01 thru '17, **Mazda Tribute** '01 thru '11, **& Mercury Mariner** '05 thru '11
36024 **Explorer & Mazda Navajo** '91 thru '01
36025 **Explorer & Mercury Mountaineer** '02 thru '10
36026 **Explorer** '11 thru '17
36028 **Fairmont & Mercury Zephyr** '78 thru '83
36030 **Festiva & Aspire** '88 thru '97
36032 **Fiesta** all models '77 thru '80
36034 **Focus** all models '00 thru '11
36035 **Focus** '12 thru '14
36045 **Fusion** '06 thru '14 **& Mercury Milan** '06 thru '11
36048 **Mustang V8** all models '64-1/2 thru '73
36049 **Mustang II** 4-cylinder, V6 & V8 models '74 thru '78
36050 **Mustang & Mercury Capri** '79 thru '93
36051 **Mustang** all models '94 thru '04
36052 **Mustang** '05 thru '14
36054 **Pick-ups & Bronco** '73 thru '79
36058 **Pick-ups & Bronco** '80 thru '96
36059 **F-150** '97 thru '03, **Expedition** '97 thru '17, **F-250** '97 thru '99, **F-150 Heritage** '04 **& Lincoln Navigator** '98 thru '17
36060 **Super Duty Pick-ups & Excursion** '99 thru '10
36061 **F-150** full-size '04 thru '14
36062 **Pinto & Mercury Bobcat** '75 thru '80
36063 **F-150** full-size '15 thru '17
36064 **Super Duty Pick-ups** '11 thru '16
36066 **Probe** all models '89 thru '92
**Probe** '93 thru '97 *- see MAZDA 626 (61042)*
36070 **Ranger & Bronco II** gas models '83 thru '92
36071 **Ranger** '93 thru '11 **& Mazda Pick-ups** '94 thru '09
36074 **Taurus & Mercury Sable** '86 thru '95
36075 **Taurus & Mercury Sable** '96 thru '07
36076 **Taurus** '08 thru '14, **Five Hundred** '05 thru '07, **Mercury Montego** '05 thru '07 **& Sable** '08 thru '09
36078 **Tempo & Mercury Topaz** '84 thru '94
36082 **Thunderbird & Mercury Cougar** '83 thru '88
36086 **Thunderbird & Mercury Cougar** '89 thru '97
36090 **Vans** all V8 Econoline models '69 thru '91
36094 **Vans** full size '92 thru '14
36097 **Windstar** '95 thru '03, **Freestar & Mercury Monterey Mini-van** '04 thru '07

## GENERAL MOTORS

10360 **GM Automatic Transmission Overhaul**
38001 **GMC Acadia** '07 thru '16, **Buick Enclave** '08 thru '17, **Saturn Outlook** '07 thru '10 **& Chevrolet Traverse** '09 thru '17
38005 **Buick Century, Chevrolet Celebrity, Oldsmobile Cutlass Ciera & Pontiac 6000** all models '82 thru '96
38010 **Buick Regal** '88 thru '04, **Chevrolet Lumina** '88 thru '04, **Oldsmobile Cutlass Supreme** '88 thru '97 **& Pontiac Grand Prix** '88 thru '07
38015 **Buick Skyhawk, Cadillac Cimarron, Chevrolet Cavalier, Oldsmobile Firenza, Pontiac J-2000 & Sunbird** '82 thru '94
38016 **Chevrolet Cavalier & Pontiac Sunfire** '95 thru '05
38017 **Chevrolet Cobalt** '05 thru '10, **HHR** '06 thru '11, **Pontiac G5** '07 thru '09, **Pursuit** '05 thru '06 **& Saturn ION** '03 thru '07
38020 **Buick Skylark, Chevrolet Citation, Oldsmobile Omega, Pontiac Phoenix** '80 thru '85
38025 **Buick Skylark** '86 thru '98, **Somerset** '85 thru '87, **Oldsmobile Achieva** '92 thru '98, **Calais** '85 thru '91, **& Pontiac Grand Am** all models '85 thru '98
38026 **Chevrolet Malibu** '97 thru '03, **Classic** '04 thru '05, **Oldsmobile Alero** '99 thru '03, **Cutlass** '97 thru '00, **& Pontiac Grand Am** '99 thru '03
38027 **Chevrolet Malibu** '04 thru '12, **Pontiac G6** '05 thru '10 **& Saturn Aura** '07 thru '10
38030 **Cadillac Eldorado, Seville, Oldsmobile Toronado & Buick Riviera** '71 thru '85
38031 **Cadillac Eldorado, Seville, DeVille, Fleetwood, Oldsmobile Toronado & Buick Riviera** '86 thru '93
38032 **Cadillac DeVille** '94 thru '05, **Seville** '92 thru '04 **& Cadillac DTS** '06 thru '10
38035 **Chevrolet Lumina APV, Oldsmobile Silhouette & Pontiac Trans Sport** all models '90 thru '96
38036 **Chevrolet Venture** '97 thru '05, **Oldsmobile Silhouette** '97 thru '04, **Pontiac Trans Sport** '97 thru '98 **& Montana** '99 thru '05
38040 **Chevrolet Equinox** '05 thru '17, **GMC Terrain** '10 thru '17 **& Pontiac Torrent** '06 thru '09

## GEO

**Metro** *- see CHEVROLET Sprint (24075)*
**Prizm** *- '85 thru '92 see CHEVY (24060), '93 thru '02 see TOYOTA Corolla (92036)*
40030 **Storm** all models '90 thru '93
**Tracker** *- see SUZUKI Samurai (90010)*

***(Continued on other side)***

# Haynes Automotive Manuals (continued)

NOTE: If you do not see a listing for your vehicle, please visit *haynes.com* for the latest product information and check out our **Online Manuals!**

## GMC
**Acadia** - *see GENERAL MOTORS (38001)*
**Pick-ups** - *see CHEVROLET (24027, 24068)*
**Vans** - *see CHEVROLET (24081)*

## HONDA
42010 **Accord CVCC** all models '76 thru '83
42011 **Accord** all models '84 thru '89
42012 **Accord** all models '90 thru '93
42013 **Accord** all models '94 thru '97
42014 **Accord** all models '98 thru '02
42015 **Accord** '03 thru '12 & **Crosstour** '10 thru '14
42016 **Accord** '13 thru '17
42020 **Civic 1200** all models '73 thru '79
42021 **Civic 1300 & 1500 CVCC** '80 thru '83
42022 **Civic 1500 CVCC** all models '75 thru '79
42023 **Civic** all models '84 thru '91
42024 **Civic & del Sol** '92 thru '95
42025 **Civic** '96 thru '00, **CR-V** '97 thru '01 & **Acura Integra** '94 thru '00
42026 **Civic** '01 thru '11 & **CR-V** '02 thru '11
42027 **Civic** '12 thru '15 & **CR-V** '12 thru '16
42030 **Fit** '07 thru '13
42035 **Odyssey** all models '99 thru '10
**Passport** - *see ISUZU Rodeo (47017)*
42037 **Honda Pilot** '03 thru '08, **Ridgeline** '06 thru '14 & **Acura MDX** '01 thru '07
42040 **Prelude CVCC** all models '79 thru '89

## HYUNDAI
43010 **Elantra** all models '96 thru '19
43015 **Excel & Accent** all models '86 thru '13
43050 **Santa Fe** all models '01 thru '12
43055 **Sonata** all models '99 thru '14

## INFINITI
**G35** '03 thru '08 - *see NISSAN 350Z (72011)*

## ISUZU
**Hombre** - *see CHEVROLET S-10 (24071)*
47017 **Rodeo** '91 thru '02, **Amigo** '89 thru '94 & '98 thru '02 & **Honda Passport** '95 thru '02
47020 **Trooper** '84 thru '91 & **Pick-up** '81 thru '93

## JAGUAR
49010 **XJ6** all 6-cylinder models '68 thru '86
49011 **XJ6** all models '88 thru '94
49015 **XJ12 & XJS** all 12-cylinder models '72 thru '85

## JEEP
50010 **Cherokee, Comanche & Wagoneer Limited** all models '84 thru '01
50011 **Cherokee** '14 thru '19
50020 **CJ** all models '49 thru '86
50025 **Grand Cherokee** all models '93 thru '04
50026 **Grand Cherokee** '05 thru '19 & **Dodge Durango** '11 thru '19
50029 **Grand Wagoneer & Pick-up** '72 thru '91 Grand Wagoneer '84 thru '91, Cherokee & Wagoneer '72 thru '83, Pick-up '72 thru '88
50030 **Wrangler** all models '87 thru '17
50035 **Liberty** '02 thru '12 & **Dodge Nitro** '07 thru '11
50050 **Patriot & Compass** '07 thru '17

## KIA
54050 **Optima** '01 thru '10
54060 **Sedona** '02 thru '14
54070 **Sephia** '94 thru '01, **Spectra** '00 thru '09, **Sportage** '05 thru '20
54077 **Sorento** '03 thru '13

## LEXUS
**ES 300/330** - *see TOYOTA Camry (92007, 92008)*
**ES 350** - *see TOYOTA Camry (92009)*
**RX 300/330/350** - *see TOYOTA Highlander (92095)*

## LINCOLN
**MKX** - *see FORD (36014)*
**Navigator** - *see FORD Pick-up (36059)*
59010 **Rear-Wheel Drive Continental** '70 thru '87, **Mark Series** '70 thru '92 & **Town Car** '81 thru '10

## MAZDA
61010 **GLC** (rear-wheel drive) '77 thru '83
61011 **GLC** (front-wheel drive) '81 thru '85
61012 **Mazda3** '04 thru '11
61015 **323 & Protegé** '90 thru '03
61016 **MX-5 Miata** '90 thru '14
61020 **MPV** all models '89 thru '98
**Navajo** - *see Ford Explorer (36024)*
61030 **Pick-ups** '72 thru '93
**Pick-ups** '94 thru '09 - *see Ford Ranger (36071)*
61035 **RX-7** all models '79 thru '85
61036 **RX-7** all models '86 thru '91
61040 **626** (rear-wheel drive) all models '79 thru '82
61041 **626 & MX-6** (front-wheel drive) '83 thru '92
61042 **626** '93 thru '01 & **MX-6/Ford Probe** '93 thru '02
61043 **Mazda6** '03 thru '13

## MERCEDES-BENZ
63012 **123 Series Diesel** '76 thru '85
63015 **190 Series** 4-cylinder gas models '84 thru '88
63020 **230/250/280** 6-cylinder SOHC models '68 thru '72
63025 **280 123 Series** gas models '77 thru '81
63030 **350 & 450** all models '71 thru '80
63040 **C-Class:** C230/C240/C280/C320/C350 '01 thru '07

## MERCURY
64200 **Villager & Nissan Quest** '93 thru '01
*All other titles, see FORD Listing.*

## MG
66010 **MGB** Roadster & GT Coupe '62 thru '80
66015 **MG Midget, Austin Healey Sprite** '58 thru '80

## MINI
67020 **Mini** '02 thru '13

## MITSUBISHI
68020 **Cordia, Tredia, Galant, Precis & Mirage** '83 thru '93
68030 **Eclipse, Eagle Talon & Plymouth Laser** '90 thru '94
68031 **Eclipse** '95 thru '05 & **Eagle Talon** '95 thru '98
68035 **Galant** '94 thru '12
68040 **Pick-up** '83 thru '96 & **Montero** '83 thru '93

## NISSAN
72010 **300ZX** all models including Turbo '84 thru '89
72011 **350Z & Infiniti G35** all models '03 thru '08
72015 **Altima** all models '93 thru '06
72016 **Altima** '07 thru '12
72020 **Maxima** all models '85 thru '92
72021 **Maxima** all models '93 thru '08
72025 **Murano** '03 thru '14
72030 **Pick-ups** '80 thru '97 & **Pathfinder** '87 thru '95
72031 **Frontier** '98 thru '04, **Xterra** '00 thru '04, & **Pathfinder** '96 thru '04
72032 **Frontier & Xterra** '05 thru '14
72037 **Pathfinder** '05 thru '14
72040 **Pulsar** all models '83 thru '86
72042 **Roque** all models '08 thru '20
72050 **Sentra** all models '82 thru '94
72051 **Sentra & 200SX** all models '95 thru '06
72060 **Stanza** all models '82 thru '90
72070 **Titan pick-ups** '04 thru '10, **Armada** '05 thru '10 & **Pathfinder Armada** '04
72080 **Versa** all models '07 thru '19

## OLDSMOBILE
73015 **Cutlass** V6 & V8 gas models '74 thru '88
*For other OLDSMOBILE titles, see BUICK, CHEVROLET or GENERAL MOTORS listings.*

## PLYMOUTH
*For PLYMOUTH titles, see DODGE listing.*

## PONTIAC
79008 **Fiero** all models '84 thru '88
79018 **Firebird** V8 models except Turbo '70 thru '81
79019 **Firebird** all models '82 thru '92
79025 **G6** all models '05 thru '09
79040 **Mid-size Rear-wheel Drive** '70 thru '87
**Vibe** '03 thru '10 - *see TOYOTA Corolla (92037)*
*For other PONTIAC titles, see BUICK, CHEVROLET or GENERAL MOTORS listings.*

## PORSCHE
80020 **911** Coupe & Targa models '65 thru '89
80025 **914** all 4-cylinder models '69 thru '76
80030 **924** all models including Turbo '76 thru '82
80035 **944** all models including Turbo '83 thru '89

## RENAULT
**Alliance & Encore** - *see AMC (14025)*

## SAAB
84010 **900** all models including Turbo '79 thru '88

## SATURN
87010 **Saturn** all S-series models '91 thru '02
**Saturn Ion** '03 thru '07- *see GM (38017)*
**Saturn Outlook** - *see GM (38001)*
87020 **Saturn L-series** all models '00 thru '04
87040 **Saturn VUE** '02 thru '09

## SUBARU
89002 **1100, 1300, 1400 & 1600** '71 thru '79
89003 **1600 & 1800** 2WD & 4WD '80 thru '94
89080 **Impreza** '02 thru '11, **WRX** '02 thru '14, & **WRX STI** '04 thru '14
89100 **Legacy** all models '90 thru '99
89101 **Legacy & Forester** '00 thru '09
89102 **Legacy** '10 thru '16 & **Forester** '12 thru '16

## SUZUKI
90010 **Samurai/Sidekick & Geo Tracker** '86 thru '01

## TOYOTA
92005 **Camry** all models '83 thru '91
92006 **Camry** '92 thru '96 & **Avalon** '95 thru '96
92007 **Camry, Avalon, Solara, Lexus ES 300** '97 thru '01
92008 **Camry, Avalon, Lexus ES 300/330** '02 thru '06 & **Solara** '02 thru '08
92009 **Camry, Avalon & Lexus ES 350** '07 thru '17
92015 **Celica Rear-wheel Drive** '71 thru '85
92020 **Celica Front-wheel Drive** '86 thru '99
92025 **Celica Supra** all models '79 thru '92
92030 **Corolla** all models '75 thru '79
92032 **Corolla** all rear-wheel drive models '80 thru '87
92035 **Corolla** all front-wheel drive models '84 thru '92
92036 **Corolla & Geo/Chevrolet Prizm** '93 thru '02
92037 **Corolla** '03 thru '19, **Matrix** '03 thru '14, & **Pontiac Vibe** '03 thru '10
92040 **Corolla Tercel** all models '80 thru '82
92045 **Corona** all models '74 thru '82
92050 **Cressida** all models '78 thru '82
92055 **Land Cruiser FJ40, 43, 45, 55** '68 thru '82
92056 **Land Cruiser FJ60, 62, 80, FZJ80** '80 thru '96
92060 **Matrix** '03 thru '11 & **Pontiac Vibe** '03 thru '10
92065 **MR2** all models '85 thru '87
92070 **Pick-up** all models '69 thru '78
92075 **Pick-up** all models '79 thru '95
92076 **Tacoma** '95 thru '04, **4Runner** '96 thru '02 & **T100** '93 thru '08
92077 **Tacoma** all models '05 thru '18
92078 **Tundra** '00 thru '06 & **Sequoia** '01 thru '07
92079 **4Runner** all models '03 thru '09
92080 **Previa** all models '91 thru '95
92081 **Prius** all models '01 thru '12
92082 **RAV4** all models '96 thru '12
92085 **Tercel** all models '87 thru '94
92090 **Sienna** all models '98 thru '10
92095 **Highlander** '01 thru '19 & **Lexus RX330/330/350** '99 thru '19
92179 **Tundra** '07 thru '19 & **Sequoia** '08 thru '19

## TRIUMPH
94007 **Spitfire** all models '62 thru '81
94010 **TR7** all models '75 thru '81

## VW
96008 **Beetle & Karmann Ghia** '54 thru '79
96009 **New Beetle** '98 thru '10
96016 **Rabbit, Jetta, Scirocco & Pick-up** gas models '75 thru '92 & Convertible '80 thru '92
96017 **Golf, GTI & Jetta** '93 thru '98, **Cabrio** '95 thru '02
96018 **Golf, GTI, Jetta** '99 thru '05
96019 **Jetta, Rabbit, GLI, Golf** '05 thru '11
96020 **Rabbit, Jetta & Pick-up** diesel '77 thru '84
96021 **Jetta** '11 thru '18 & **Golf** '15 thru '19
96023 **Passat** '98 thru '05 & **Audi A4** '96 thru '01
96030 **Transporter 1600** all models '68 thru '79
96035 **Transporter 1700, 1800 & 2000** '72 thru '79
96040 **Type 3 1500 & 1600** all models '63 thru '73
96045 **Vanagon Air-Cooled** all models '80 thru '83

## VOLVO
97010 **120, 130 Series & 1800 Sports** '61 thru '73
97015 **140 Series** all models '66 thru '74
97020 **240 Series** all models '76 thru '93
97040 **740 & 760 Series** all models '82 thru '88
97050 **850 Series** all models '93 thru '97

## TECHBOOK MANUALS
10205 **Automotive Computer Codes**
10206 **OBD-II & Electronic Engine Management**
10210 **Automotive Emissions Control Manual**
10215 **Fuel Injection Manual** '78 thru '85
10225 **Holley Carburetor Manual**
10230 **Rochester Carburetor Manual**
10305 **Chevrolet Engine Overhaul Manual**
10320 **Ford Engine Overhaul Manual**
10330 **GM and Ford Diesel Engine Repair Manual**
10331 **Duramax Diesel Engines** '01 thru '19
10332 **Cummins Diesel Engine Performance Manual**
10333 **GM, Ford & Chrysler Engine Performance Manual**
10334 **GM Engine Performance Manual**
10340 **Small Engine Repair Manual**, 5 HP & Less
10341 **Small Engine Repair Manual**, 5.5 thru 20 HP
10345 **Suspension, Steering & Driveline Manual**
10355 **Ford Automatic Transmission Overhaul**
10360 **GM Automatic Transmission Overhaul**
10405 **Automotive Body Repair & Painting**
10410 **Automotive Brake Manual**
10411 **Automotive Anti-lock Brake (ABS) Systems**
10420 **Automotive Electrical Manual**
10425 **Automotive Heating & Air Conditioning**
10435 **Automotive Tools Manual**
10445 **Welding Manual**
10450 **ATV Basics**

**Over a 100 Haynes motorcycle manuals also available**

10/22

---

**Haynes North America, Inc. • (805) 498-6703 • www.haynes.com**